HEALTHCARE TECHNOLOGIES SERIES 44

Medical Information Processing and Security

Other volumes in this series:

Medical Information Processing and Security

Techniques and applications

Edited by
Amit Kumar Singh and Huiyu Zhou

The Institution of Engineering and Technology

Published by The Institution of Engineering and Technology, London, United Kingdom

The Institution of Engineering and Technology is registered as a Charity in England & Wales (no. 211014) and Scotland (no. SC038698).

The Institution of Engineering and Technology
Futures Place
Kings Way, Stevenage
Herts, SG1 2UA., United Kingdom

www.theiet.org

British Library Cataloguing in Publication Data
A catalogue record for this product is available from the British Library

ISBN 978-1-83953-525-3 (hardback)
ISBN 978-1-83953-526-0 (PDF)

Typeset in India by Exeter Premedia Services Private Limited
Printed in the UK by CPI Group (UK) Ltd, Croydon
Cover Image: janiecbros/ E+ via Getty Images

Contents

About the Editors

Amit Kumar Singh is an assistant professor in the Computer Science and Engineering Department at the National Institute of Technology Patna, India. Stanford University, USA recognized him as "World ranking of top 2% scientists" in the area of "Biomedical Research" in 2019 and "Artificial Intelligence & Image Processing" in 2020. He is the associate editor of several IEEE and ACM journals. His research interests include multimedia data hiding, image processing, biometrics, and cryptography.

Huiyu Zhou is a professor and head of The Biomedical Image Processing Lab at the University of Leicester, UK. He is editor-in-chief of *Recent Advances in Electrical & Electronic Engineering*, and associate editor of numerous reputed international journals. He is area chair of British Machine Vision Conference and the International Joint Conference on Artificial Intelligence. His research interests include machine learning, computer vision and signal processing.

Foreword

This book entitled "Medical Information Processing and Security: Techniques and Applications" has made a significant effort on the digital medical records, which focuses on the healthcare applications. This book intends to enhance the understanding of opportunities and challenges in medical data processing and security for healthcare as well as other real-world applications at the global level.

It is a challenge for researchers and scholars to identify the most popular topics on medical data processing and security in any instant due to rapid progress on research and development. This book summarizes the recent trends in medical data in terms of processing and security. The book focuses on identifying new directions to academic professionals, practicing engineers and scientists. Given this, summarizing the vast literature in healthcare applications and identifying the cutting edge technologies is a challenging task. I hope the readers will find this book of great value in its visionary words.

We look forward to seeing it in print soon.

Dr. Amit Kumar Singh, Editor
Assistant Professor
Department of Computer Science and Engineering
National Institute of Technology Patna, Bihar, India

Prof. Huiyu Zhou, Editor
Professor
School of Computing and Mathematical Sciences
University of Leicester, Leicester, UK United Kingdom

Preface

As smart healthcare systems are highly connected to advanced wearable devices, internet of things (IoT) and mobile internet, valuable patient information and other significant medical records are easily transmitted over public networks. Personal patient information and clinical records are also stored on existing databases and local servers of hospitals and healthcare centres. This information not only provides a reference for healthcare professionals to make correct decisions regarding patients, but also provides a basis for other professionals to schedule effective treatments and develop future plans for correct diagnosis. Furthermore, the related databases may be used by various research communities, so they need to ensure that there will be no privacy violations. However, the stealing of healthcare data is a growing crime that greatly impacts institutions and can lead to financial losses. The Coronavirus pandemic has been declared a global health emergency by the World Health Organization (WHO). The large amount of the collected data to combat COVID 19 pandemic raises certain security and privacy concerns. To guarantee the security of e-patient records in the transfer process, it is imperative to set up proper security and authentication measures and systems. Proper medical information and data security are therefore becoming essential in smart healthcare.

Outline of the book and chapter synopsis

This book covers cutting-edge research from both academia and industry with a particular emphasis on interdisciplinary approaches, novel techniques and solutions to provide medical information processing and security for smart healthcare applications. The book can be used as a reference book for practicing engineers, researchers and practitioners. It will also be useful for senior under- and post-graduate students, and practitioners from government and industry as well as healthcare technology professionals working on state-of-the-art security solutions for smart healthcare applications. Divided in two parts, the first seven chapters deal with the recent trends and state-of-the-art approaches in the field of medical information processing, and the next eight chapter showcase new concepts, state-of-the-art security approaches, theories and practices with a focus on information security and privacy solutions for smart healthcare applications. We will end up with a chapter on future perspectives and research directions. A brief summary of each chapter is introduced below.

Beginning with introduction of the detailed concepts of medical information processing and security, *Chapter 1* presents background information of Internet of Medical Things, interesting and utilized applications, and security requirement of smart healthcare. This is followed by detailed overview of important medical information processing and security techniques along with their merits and limitations. In Chapter 2, the authors used the American College of Surgeons National Surgical Quality Improvement Program (ACS-NSQIP) database to compare the performance of logistic regression to other machine learning algorithms for predicting complications during spine surgery. The current procedural terminology (CPT) code is used to identify patients that underwent spine surgery. Chapter 3 presents the recent developments in the automated histopathological analysis of cancer. The authors further summarise different publicly available datasets and also emphasize the key challenges along with limitations of emerging deep learning techniques for Computer Aided Diagnosis (CAD) of cancer. Afterwards, the chapter provides an insight into possible avenues for future research in this area. Chapter 4 mainly presents the research status and prospects of several terahertz medical imaging systems and applications for medical imaging in biological tissues. Furthermore, the latest developments of several terahertz time-domain spectroscopy-based imaging methods, including tomography imaging and near-field imaging are highlighted with its performance improvement. Chapter 5 describes, compares and discusses approaches related to interoperability such as e-health standards, terminologies and Internet of Things (IoT) ontology. The chapter further reviews and discusses summarization-based Electronic Health Record (HER) systems and visualization-based EHR systems in order to show how interoperability issues can enhance EHR analysis to build accurate summarization- and visualization-based EHR systems. Chapter 6 presents a robust energy based least squares projection twin support vector machine for the classification of EEG signals. The proposed model implements the structural risk which results in avoiding the overfitting issues. In Chapter 7, the medical image segmentation using fuzzy c-means, which is based on minimizing an objective function, is reviewed along with its variants proposed in the past. This survey comprises a decadal study on various effective methods which are suggested to segment the noisy medical images including various other artefacts. Chapter 8 presents recent state-of-the-art artificial intelligence methods for genomics on different prospects and scenario.

Chapter 9 presents a seminal summary and comparison of advanced anonymous communication techniques on wireless medical online systems firstly. On this basis, a trust-based secure directed diffusion routing protocol is elaborated to establish reliable routing and protect the transmission of health data. The chapter also expounds a lightweight anonymous communication model, which can provide identity authentication and data privacy transmission, thus safeguarding the user's personal information and the communication relationship in the communication flow, and realizing the user's anonymity and the confidentiality of health data. Chapter 10 presents a basic outline of information security paradigms and the need for securing medical data. After this, this chapter surveys various state-of-the-art medical data encryption techniques, discusses several evaluation metrics, and further presents comparative studies based on the applicability of the methods for data modalities and metric-based performance. The author emphasises the potential challenges of the existing methods and proposes a way forward by discussing promising research directions. Chapter 11 presents a dual watermarking for ECG signals to resolve the issues of copy protection and ownership conflicts, and offer a good relationship between invisibility, capacity, and robustness. Chapter 12 introduces in detail the methods and frameworks of traditional AutoEncoder models, as well as some applications in craniofacial reconstruction and face generation after the model has been improved. Furthermore, the chapter summarizes the development and research status of AutoEncoder models in recent years. In addition, this chapter compares and analyzes these AutoEncoder models from many aspects. The future direction of face generation is pointed out, which can promote the technology of craniofacial reconstruction to be applied in identification of unknown corpse in forensic medicine, medical plastic surgery and many other fields The most current research, suggested approaches, and existing smart healthcare system technologies are discussed in Chapter 13. Additionally, the chapter discusses the positive and negative aspects of various security techniques with IoT in health care industries. Chapter 14 provides a detailed overview of watermarking along with its characteristics, and current applications. The authors then provide a comparative survey of the different state-of-the-art approaches along with their merits and limitations. Furthermore, the chapter summarizes each of the state-of-the-art approaches in detail, including objectives, goals, dataset used, evaluation metrics, and weaknesses, and discusses the recent challenges and their possible solutions. In Chapter 15, the author introduces three kinds of secure authentication schemes for remote medical systems. Compared with other similar protocols, the proposed protocols have advantages in terms of efficiency, safety, dynamics, etc. In Chapter 16, the author presents an encryption method before the compression algorithm to resolve the security, high communication costs and storage space issues related to the medical images. The outcomes prove that the proposed algorithm is secure against different popular attacks, and reduces the bandwidth, high communication costs and storage space. Further, extensive experimental results on real-world datasets demonstrate that the proposed algorithm outperforms the state of-the-art approaches.

To conclude, we would like to sincerely thank all the authors for submitting their high quality chapters to this book, and the large number of potential reviewers who have participated in the review process, and provided helpful comments and suggestions to the authors to improve their chapters.

We especially thank the IET book series on E-health Series Editor, *Prof. Joel J. P. C. Rodrigues* for their continuous support and great guidance.

We would also like to thank publishers at IET, in particular *Val Moliere*, Senior Consultant Commissioning Book Editor for their helpful guidance and encouragement during the creation of this book.

We are sincerely thankful to all the authors, reviewers, editors and the publisher who have directly / indirectly contributed to this book.

The Editors believe that our book will be helpful to the senior undergraduate and graduate students, researchers, professionals, and providers working in the area demanding state-of-the-art solutions for healthcare applications.

Special Acknowledgements

The first editor gratefully acknowledges the authorities of National Institute of Technology Patna, India, for their kind support to come up with this book.

The second editor gratefully acknowledges the authorities of School of Computing and Mathematical Sciences, University of Leicester, Leicester, UK, for their kind support to come up with this book.

This work is supported by research project order no. IES\R2\212111 - International Exchanges 2021 Round 2, dt. 28 February, 2022, under Royal Society, UK

Patna, India   Dr. Amit Kumar Singh
Leicester, United Kingdom   Prof. Huiyu Zhou

IET Book Series on e-Health Technologies – Call for Authors

Book Series Editor: Professor Joel P.C. Rodrigues, the National Institute of Telecommunications (Inatel), Brazil and Instituto de Telecomunicações, Portugal

While the demographic shifts in populations display significant socio-economic challenges, they trigger opportunities for innovations in e-Health, m-Health, precision and personalized medicine, robotics, sensing, the Internet of things, cloud computing, Big Data, Software Defined Networks, and network function virtualization. Their integration is however associated with many technological, ethical, legal, social, and security issues. This new Book Series aims to disseminate recent advances for e-Health Technologies to improve healthcare and people's wellbeing.

Topics considered include Intelligent e-Health systems, electronic health records, ICT-enabled personal health systems, mobile and cloud computing for eHealth, health monitoring, precision and personalized health, robotics for e-Health, security and privacy in e-Health, ambient assisted living, telemedicine, Big Data and IoT for e-Health, and more.

Proposals for coherently integrated International multiauthored edited or coauthored handbooks and research monographs will be considered for this Book Series. Each proposal will be reviewed by the Book Series Editor with additional external reviews from independent reviewers. Please email your book proposal for the IET Book Series on e-Health Technologies to: Professor Joel Rodrigues at joeljr@ieee.org or joeljr@inatel.br

Chapter 1

Introduction to medical information processing and security: techniques and applications

Ashima Anand¹, Amit Kumar Singh², and Huiyu Zhou³

With continuous technological advances in cloud environments, wearable devices and the Internet of Medical Things (IoMT), the generation and distribution of medical multimedia has increased [1]. These records, often termed as Electronic Health Data (EHD), are highly sensitive and used by remote healthcare professionals to devise more appropriate diagnostic decisions. Figure 1.1 shows the framework of an IoMT-based smart healthcare system which has three major components, including participants, technologies and management [2, 3]. It uses advanced technologies involving sensors and wearable devices to collect medical information, fast internet services, Internet of Things (IoT) devices, big data, cloud computing and artificial intelligence to securely collect, transmit and manage a large number of medical records [4]. The connecting technologies such as Bluetooth, WiFi, internet, Zigbee, NFS and GPS play a key role in developing the applications for which the healthcare system is considered. Health system management under smart healthcare focuses on database, remote monitoring, networks and security management. The joint effort of these components helps in reducing the cost and risks of critical medical processes, enhances the efficiency of clinical resources and makes the healthcare system more intelligent and smart [2, 3].

These smart healthcare systems ensure secure and reliable transmission of EHR and hold responsibility for adaptive behaviour by offering real-time monitoring, high accuracy, low power consumption, on-time delivery and smart processing. Some of the major applications of smart healthcare are listed in Figure 1.2 [3].

Furthermore, during COVID pandemic, a lot of the patient's digital records were collected and uploaded to local servers, while these records are frequently circulated among several hospitals and medical staff. According to a report, a significant rise of up to 38 times in telehealth services was experienced when compared with pre-COVID times [5]. Moreover, it is expected to reach USD 232.02 billion by

¹Department of CSE, Thapar Institute of Engineering and Technology, Patiala, Punjab, India
²Department of Computer Science & Engineering, National Institute of Technology Patna, Patna, Bihar, India
³School of Computing and Mathematical Sciences, University of Leicester, Leicester, UK

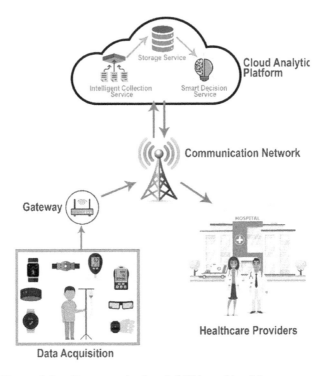

Figure 1.1   Framework of an IoMT-based healthcare system

the year 2027 [6]. Also, the use of cloud services in smart healthcare applications requires high security, integrity and confidentiality to provide an uninterrupted clinical diagnosis with mobility support and low latency [7]. However, the exchange of these records through untrusted communication networks has escalated the issues of illegal distribution, alteration, identity theft and threat to copyright. Therefore, proper medical information processing and its security are becoming essential in smart healthcare.

Security and privacy of medical information are mostly presented as major issues in telehealth services. Some of the important security requirements of the healthcare records are summarized in Figure 1.3.

Furthermore, patients' health is continuously monitored with several sensors and wearable devices. The generated digital health information is utilized by

Figure 1.2   Applications of smart healthcare systems

Figure 1.3   Security requirements of a smart healthcare system

healthcare workers to ensure accurate disease diagnosis and clinical care. Processing of these data involves computer processing and understanding of perceptual inputs from speech, text and images and reacting to it is much more complex and involves research from engineering, computer science and cognitive science. This is the newest area of research that has seen an upsurge over the last few years. Presently, soft computing, deep learning and artificial intelligence are emerging fields that consist of complementary elements of fuzzy logic, neural computing, evolutionary computation, machine learning, optimization algorithms and probabilistic reasoning, which have gained the attention of multimedia processing. Due to their strong learning, cognitive ability, good tolerance of uncertainty and imprecision, these techniques have found wide applications in healthcare and ensure a higher level of accuracy in the early diagnosis and detection of diseases. Also, medical image segmentation, classification and object identification have been inferred by virtue of medical image processing and deep learning. The management and analysis of large volumes of medical data require machine support and intelligent data analysis. Hence, we require a scalable technique using deep learning and multimedia processing which can provide more reconcilable solutions and effective decision-making strategies in the emerging IoMT.

Nowadays, medical data security is gaining engrossment and has become a proactive area of research which demands strong algorithms that can resolve the discussed threats to medical data. In Reference 3, the author suggested some potential solutions focusing on technology upgrades, proper certification and comprehensive guidelines for the secure design of medical devices, compatibility between platforms and advanced networks. Apart from that, many researchers have addressed the security and confidentiality issues of EHD using data hiding techniques, blockchain,

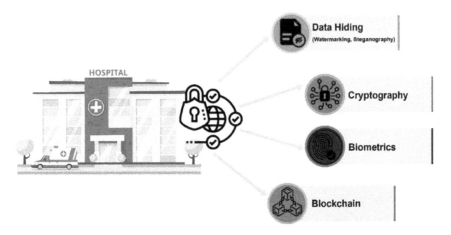

Figure 1.4   Techniques to protect the digital medical records

cryptography or a combination of these methods. Figure 1.4 summarizes some of the techniques to protect digital records [8]. These methods provide secure authentication to the medical records of patients while maintaining their confidentiality [9]. The blockchain-based techniques are recommended to ensure secure transmission of patients' information and their medical data. Their immutable property and decentralized structure help in maintaining the integrity and confidentiality of medical records. It also ensures the security and privacy of data, as only encrypted data are stored in the blockchain network. Furthermore, cryptographic techniques help in resolving the issues of illegal access by encoding the information values of the data into an unreadable secret code [10–13]. It also offers hashing and digital signature for owner verification and tamper detection [14]. However, the data are insecure once it is decrypted.

Biometrics is the science of establishing the identity of an individual based on the physical, chemical or behavioural characteristics of the person [15]. Currently, biometric-based security is being implemented in many applications including healthcare systems using biometric traits such as DNA, fingerprint, iris, palm print, face, keystroke, signature, retina, voice and hand vein [16, 17]. It allows for secure authentication of medical records of the patients, with easy implementation and scalability. However, fail to enrol rates and accuracy are the major drawbacks of a biometric-based system. The main goals for implementing data hiding in healthcare systems are tamper detection, user authentication and secure transmission of sensitive records [11, 18]. Inserting the medical records into images also saves the space and bandwidth required for the storage and transmission of medical records. However, a balance among the three major parameters including robustness, imperceptibility and capacity has to be maintained [19–21].

Furthermore, a combination of two or more security methods can be employed to ensure security measures such as copyright protection, integrity and non-repudiation [22]. They also help in enhancing the confidentiality of patient data [12]. However, managing the database, cost and time during the implementation of these security methods remains an open issue that needs to be resolved.

References

[1]   Anand A., Singh A.K. 'SDH: secure data hiding in fused medical image for smart healthcare'. *IEEE Transactions on Computational Social Systems*. 2019, pp. 1–9.

[2]   Sundaravadivel P., Kougianos E., Mohanty S.P., Ganapathiraju M.K. 'Everything you wanted to know about smart health care: evaluating the different technologies and components of the internet of things for better health'. *IEEE Consumer Electronics Magazine*. 2019, vol. 7(1), pp. 18–28.

[3]   Tian S., Yang W., Grange J.M.L., Wang P., Huang W., Ye Z. 'Smart healthcare: making medical care more intelligent'. *Global Health Journal*. 2019, vol. 3(3), pp. 62–65.

[4]   Alam M.M., Malik H., Khan M.I., Pardy T., Kuusik A., Le Moullec Y. 'A survey on the roles of communication technologies in IoT-based personalized healthcare applications'. *IEEE Access: Practical Innovations, Open Solutions*. 2020, vol. 6, pp. 36611–31.

[5]   Bestsennyy O., Gilbert G., Harris A., Rost J. *Telehealth: A Quarter-Trillion-Dollar Post-Covid-19 Reality*. McKinsey & Company. Available from https://www.mckinsey.com/industries/healthcare-systems-and-services/our-insights/telehealth-a-quarter-trillion-dollar-post-covid-19-reality

[6]   *At 24.8 % CAGR, telemedicine market size is projected to reach USD 49.21 billion by 2027, says bbrandessence market research [online]*. GlobeNewswire. Available from https://www.globenewswire.com/news-release/2021/10/19/2316300/0/en/At-24-8-CAGR-Telemedicine-Market-Size-is-Projected-to-Reach-USD-49-21-Billion-by-2027-Says-Brandessence-Market-Research.html

[7]   Salehi S., Abedi A., Balakrishnan S., Gholamrezanezhad A. 'Coronavirus disease 2019 (COVID-19): a systematic review of imaging findings in 919 patients'. *American Journal of Roentgenology*. 2021, vol. 215(1), pp. 87–93.

[8]   Singh A.K., Anand A., Lv Z., Ko H., Mohan A. 'A survey on healthcare data: a security perspective'. *ACM Transactions on Multimedia Computing, Communications, and Applications*. 2021, vol. 17(2s), pp. 1–26.

[9]   Silva H., Lourenço A., Fred A., Filipe J. 'Clinical data privacy and customization via biometrics based on ECG signals'. *Lecture Notes in Computer Science (Including Subser. Lect. Notes Artif. Intell. Lect. Notes Bioinformatics)*. 2011, vol. 7058 LNCS, pp. 121–32.

[10]   Anand A., Singh A.K., Lv Z., Bhatnagar G. 'Compression-then-encryption-based secure watermarking technique for smart healthcare system'. *IEEE MultiMedia*. 2021, vol. 27(4), pp. 133–43.

[11] Anand A., Singh A.K. 'Joint watermarking-encryption-ECC for patient record security in wavelet domain'. *IEEE MultiMedia*. 2015, vol. 27(3), pp. 66–75.

[12] Acharya U.R., Niranjan U.C., Iyengar S.S., Kannathal N., Min L.C. 'Simultaneous storage of patient information with medical images in the frequency domain'. *Computer Methods and Programs in Biomedicine*. 2004, vol. 76(1), pp. 13–19.

[13] Thakur S., Singh A.K., Ghrera S., Dave M. 'Watermarking techniques and its applications in tele-health: a technical survey'. *Cryptographic and Information Security*. 2019, pp. 467–508.

[14] Al-Haj A., Abandah G., Hussein N. 'Crypto-based algorithms for secured medical image transmission'. *IET Information Security*. 2015, vol. 9(6), pp. 365–73. Available from https://onlinelibrary.wiley.com/toc/17518717/9/6

[15] Jain A.K., Flynn P., Ross A.A. *Handbook of Biometrics*. Boston, MA: Springer Science; 2015. Available from http://link.springer.com/10.1007/978-0-387-71041-9

[16] Yang W., Wang S., Hu J., Zheng G., Valli C. 'Security and accuracy of fingerprint-based biometrics: a review'. *Symmetry*. 2004, vol. 11(2), 141.

[17] Jain A.K., Ross A., Prabhakar S. 'An introduction to biometric recognition'. *IEEE Transactions on Circuits and Systems for Video Technology*. 2004, vol. 14(1), pp. 4–20.

[18] Singh A.K., Kumar B., Singh G., Mohan A. Medical Image Watermarking. Cham: Springer International Publishing; 2004. Available from http://link.springer.com/10.1007/978-3-319-57699-2

[19] Anand A., Singh A.K. 'Watermarking techniques for medical data authentication: a survey'. *Multimedia Tools and Applications*. 2021, vol. 80(20), pp. 30165–97.

[20] Anand A., Singh A.K. 'An improved DWT-SVD domain watermarking for medical information security'. *Computer Communications*. 2004, vol. 152, pp. 72–80.

[21] Singh A.K. 'Data hiding: current trends, innovation and potential challenges'. *ACM Transactions on Multimedia Computing, Communications, and Applications*. 2020, pp. 1–16.

[22] Gupta B.B., Perez G.M., Agrawal D.P., Gupta D. Handbook of Computer Networks and Cyber Security. Cham; 2020. Available from http://link.springer.com/10.1007/978-3-030-22277-2

Chapter 2

Prediction of complications in spine surgery using machine learning: a Health 4.0 study on National Surgical Quality Improvement Program beyond logistic regression model

Mohammad Alja'afreh[1,2], Mohamad Hoda[1], Philippe Phan[3], Eugene Wai[3], and Abdulmotaleb Elsaddik[1,2]

With the advancement of the revolutionary artificial intelligence (AI) technologies, health-care services are rapidly moving toward an intelligent cyber physical system referred to as Health 4.0. In essence, the ability to predict surgical complications is all-important for both surgeons and patients. Recently, the use of machine learning (ML) algorithms for predicting complications has gained much attention. Even though many mature and reliable algorithms exist in the field of ML, the logistic regression (LR) algorithm has been the most widely used in complication prediction. In this study, we used the American College of Surgeons National Surgical Quality Improvement Program (ACS-NSQIP) database to compare the performance of LR to other ML algorithms for predicting complications during spine surgery. The database included 177 681 patients who underwent spine surgery. The occurrence of intraoperative morbidity was relatively low (9.4 per cent) in comparison to the total number of the dataset population, and hence, the dataset under study was considered imbalanced. To thoroughly evaluate and compare the proposed ML algorithms, the dataset was balanced and the algorithms were applied on both the balanced and imbalanced dataset. The results indicated that, in general, no significant difference was found between the performance of LR and random forest (RF), boosted tree (BT), and decision tree (DT).

[1]School of Electrical Engineering and Computer Sciences, University of Ottawa, Ottawa, ON, Canada
[2]Mohamed bin Zayed University of Artificial Intelligence, Masdar City, Abu Dhabi, UAE
[3]Ottawa Spine Collaborative Analytics Network, The Ottawa Hospital, Ottawa, ON, Canada

2.1   Introduction

AI in health care is getting a considerable amount of attention because of new challenges faced by caregivers, patients, and providers in the health-care field [1].

The ability to simulate, experience, and adjust the real-world environment, process or product based on learning from working on a digital replica of an equipment/product/process played a huge role in helping scientists and engineers improve the success rate, enhancing the understanding and predictability of positive outcome in various domains [2].

With the merits of ML engineering, the success experienced by stakeholders in other verticals is adding to the motivation from patient advocates, payers, clinician practicians, and researchers to improve the experience, monitor, and adhere to compliance and reduce cost. The potential of implementing Health 4.0 technology, via the incorporation of AI solutions, in health care to improve quality of service and understanding, monitoring, and reducing risks in many use-cases is tremendous [2, 3].

In the same context, spine surgery is associated with a high incidence of complications that range from minor to life-threatening. The incidence of adverse events in the literature is variable; however, 30-day readmission rates due to complications have been shown to range from 4.2 per cent to 7.4 per cent [4]. Knowing which patients are at increased risk for surgical complications helps patients and surgeons make informed treatment decisions. Recently, the use of ML algorithms for predicting complications has gained attention and popularity. ML models have been used in particular because of their objective, reproducible, and easily implementable nature. Of these models, LR models have often been used in medical research due to their ability to avoid overfitting and to produce good output probabilistic interpretation. For example, two studies applied LR on datasets obtained from patients who underwent lumbar and posterior cervical fusion to investigate the relationship between preoperative anemia and postoperative complications [4, 5]. Bekelis *et al.* [6] studied the potential use of LR as a complication prediction model for patients undergoing spine surgery. To better understand the relationship between the patient's individual characteristics and postoperative complications, the authors calculated the area under the curve (AUC). The result indicated well to excellent predictive ability of the proposed model. Later studies used other ML algorithms namely, support vector machines (SVM) [7–11], artificial neural networks (ANN) [12–15], RFs [8, 16–19], and DTs [20–23] to predict surgical risk. For example, Esbroeck *et al.*'s SVM model, trained using the word-frequency vectors in the current procedural terminology (CPT) code, was able to estimate the surgical risk of individual procedures [11]. Another example is Kim *et al.*'s study [14], which used ANN and LR to benchmark the American Society for Anesthesiology (ASA) scores and stratify the risk of developing complications following posterior lumbar spine fusion. This study found that ML produced more accurate results than benchmark ASA scores. Finally, Durand *et al.* [18] used both DT and RF algorithms to successfully predict the need for blood transfusion following adult spinal deformity surgery.

Although the results of the previous studies are encouraging, they are not conclusive as the populations studied were of relatively small size (not exceeding 3000 records); therefore, more studies are required to generalize their conclusions. Additionally, no studies that thoroughly investigate and compare different ML algorithms have been conducted. Before ML algorithms are implemented in a clinical setting, it is important that their differences and abilities are well understood. To the best of the authors' knowledge, the employment of ML engineering in the context of predicting the success percentage of spine surgeries has not been adequately in the literature.

Unlike our previous article [24], which addresses only the deployment of LR only in this domain, this study aims to determine and compare the performances of four ML algorithms at predicting complications associated with spine surgery. The algorithms will be tested on the National Surgical Quality Improvement Program (NSQIP) dataset which contains over 177 000 records of spine surgery patients between 2005 and 2016. LR, RFs, DTs, and BTs have been chosen as algorithms to be tested and compared since they are efficient and easily applicable. While these models have not been extensively studied in the literature, the goal is to find the model that is best applied to create an objective and reliable tool for physicians and patients to help with surgical decision- making.

2.2 Methods

Datasets: The data collected by the ACS NSQIP were used to build and train the ML models. It is worth noting that the ACS NSQIP incorporates up to date encryption techniques to enforce the security and privacy of the collected patient's data. The CPT codes were used to identify patients who underwent spine surgery. The NSQIP dataset contained 177 681 spine surgery cases submitted between 2005 and 2016 by 680 of participating hospitals. However, the dataset used was not cohesive in terms of number, format, and definitions of the variables from one year to another. For example, the NSQIP dataset contained 239 variables while the 2016 dataset contained 323 variables. Due to this and other reasons (e.g. participant fails to respond to all the questions and data entry errors), there were many incidences of missing and/or incomplete data. While some variables contained nearly 100 per cent of the data, others were almost undefined. For this reason, data preparation and noise-reduction steps had to be taken before the analysis. More information about the ACS-NSQIP dataset is available at http://www.acsnsqip.org.

2.2.1 Feature selection

In order to obtain high-accuracy ML prediction results, the most significant variables (features) were selected. The selection process involved three staff spine surgeons at our hospital, each with a fellowship in spine surgery. The participants were asked to rate the collected variables (features) based on the likelihood of influencing the rate of complications associated with surgery: (1) less likely to influence complication occurrence, (2) likely to influence complication occurrence, and (3) very

Table 2.1　Kappa agreement between surgeons 1 and 2, surgeons 1 and 3, and surgeons 2 and 3

Surgeons	1 and 2	1 and 3	2 and 3
Value Kappa	0.7	0.91	0.66
Level of agreement*	Substantial	Almost perfect	Substantial

*[0.6 – 0.79]: substantial; [0.8 – 0.9]: strong; above 0.9: almost perfect.

likely to influence complication occurrence. All variables missing more than 5 per cent of their data were excluded, leaving 93 variables to be rated by the surgeons. To assure the independence and objectivity of each surgeon, the rating process was done individually. Cohen's Kappa was then used to assess the agreement between the surgeons. The agreement between the three surgeons was substantial (Table 2.1).

The surgeons' rating of the variables is shown in Table 2.2. Out of the 93 variables, 26 variables were selected to be used in predicting the occurrence of complications during surgery (Table 2.3). Overall, 17 variables were rated by all surgeons as "very likely to influence complication occurrence," 9 variables were rated as "likely to influence complication occurrence," and 48 variables were rated as "less likely to influence complication occurrence". Considering the remaining 19 variables, the 3 surgeons were not in full agreement. In the analysis, all variables rated as "very likely to influence complication occurrence" or "likely to influence complication occurrence" were included (Table 2.3). It is worth noting that five features, namely sex, age, smoking, emergency, and ASA

Table 2.2　Agreement of features rating between (a) surgeons 1 and 2, (b) surgeons 1 and 3, and (c) surgeons 2 and 3

		Surgeon 1 Less likely	Likely	Very likely
	Less likely	49	1	0
Surgeon 1	Likely	2	9	8
	Very likely	0	7	17
	(a)			
		Surgeon 1 Less likely	Likely	Very likely
	Less likely	50	2	0
Surgeon 2	Likely	1	14	1
	Very likely	0	1	24
	(b)			
		Surgeon 2 Less likely	Likely	Very likely
	Less likely	48	2	2
Surgeon 3	Likely	1	9	6
	Very likely	1	7	17

Table 2.3 *Patient features statistics: values are shown in percentage or (mean)*

Dataset		Imbalanced data		Balanced data	
		Training (N = 123 435)		Train (N=23 527)	
Feature		% Feat	% Comp	% Feat	% Comp
Sex*	Male	52.19	53.24	50.181	46.76
Workrvu*		(19.63)	(21.266)	(20.36)	(21.27)
Age*		(57.36)	(62.214)	(59.50)	(62.21)
Body mass index		(31.04)	(31.431)	(31.17)	(31.43)
Diabetes	No	83.12	77.13	80.50	77.13
	Noninsulin	10.94	13.10	12.17	13.10
	Insulin	5.85	9.74	7.29	9.74
	Oral	0.07	0.03	0.05	0.03
Smoke*	Yes	77.65	19.576	21.11	19.58
Dyspnea	No	95.19	92.412	93.91	92.41
	Moderate exertion	4.52	6.76	5.53	6.76
	At rest	0.28	0.83	0.56	0.83
Fnstatus2	Independent	97.01	92.05	94.84	92.05
	Partially dependent	2.2	6.16	3.95	6.16
	Totally dependent	0.22	0.957	0.54	0.96
	Unknown	0.55	0.83	0.66	0.83
Ventilat	Yes	0.13	1.256	0.63	1.26
Hxcopd	Yes	4.35	6.53	5.36	6.53
Ascites	Yes	0.04	0.16	0.09	0.16
Hxchf	Yes	0.39	1.22	0.79	1.22
Hypermed	Yes	49.94	37.88	55.48	62.12

(Continues)

Table 2.3 Continued

Dataset		Imbalanced data	Balanced data
		Training (N = 123 435)	Train (N=23 527)
Renafail	Yes	0.08	0.24	0.45
Dialysis	Yes	0.34	0.73	1.29
Discancr	Yes	1.21	2.99	5.22
Wndinf	Yes	0.67	1.70	3.05
Steroid	Yes	4.16	5.41	7.12
Wtloss	Yes	0.41	0.90	1.53
Emergency*	Yes	2	3.96	6.51
Wndclas	Clean	98.29	95.66	92.22
	Dirty/infected	0.97	3.13	5.97
	Clean/contaminated	0.5	0.70	0.93
	Contaminated	0.23	0.51	0.87
Asaclas*†	Mild disturb	48.75	40.00	29.31
	Severe disturb	43.54	50.70	59.65
	No disturb	4.6	3.28	1.29
	Life threat	2.98	5.90	9.56
	None assigned	0.1	0.09	0.1
	Moribund	0.01	0.05	0.08
Optime†		(120)	(190.37)	(245.53)
Tothlos†		(2.9)	(5.21)	(8.04)
Htooday†		(0.33)	(0.69)	(1.15)
Returnor†	Yes	3	8.52	15.47
Complication	Yes	9.49	49.73	49.74

*Super important feature for complication prediction.
†Important features selected by the InfoGain algorithm.

classification, were considered as being of paramount importance in predicting complications by all three surgeons.

For each categorical variable (e.g. sex), the proportion of each observation (e.g. male) was calculated. The percentage of each observation with complications has been also calculated. In addition, for continuous variables, the mean of each variable was calculated. Moreover, the records have been filtered to only include the data of patients who experienced complications during surgery and the mean of each continuous variable of these patients has been calculated again (shown in Table 2.3 between brackets). The calculations were performed on the whole dataset (imbalanced dataset) and the balanced dataset. There was no statistically important difference between the distribution of variables of the imbalanced and balanced datasets (all p-values < 0.05).

2.2.2   Data preparation

Since missing data can reduce the model's prediction accuracy, the dataset was cleaned prior to running the ML algorithms. Five of the twenty-seven features selected by the surgeons contained missing or wrong data. In the NSQIP dataset, missing data are represented by -99 or Not a Number (NaN) depending on the variable's data type. We applied two noise-reduction techniques to the collected dataset: (1) deletion of missing data and (2) imputation of missing data. Deleting missing data is the simplest and most commonly used technique in statistics [25]. However, an obvious drawback of such a technique is that a significant number of rows that might contain useful data are lost. Therefore, the imputation technique overcomes the data loss problem by using a statistical model that operates with a maximum likelihood function.

2.2.2.1   Features preprocessing

Occurrences of superficial surgical site infection, occurrences of pneumonia, and 19 other complications reported in the NSQIP dataset were aggregated into a single Boolean variable (complication) whose value was true in case a patient experienced any surgical complication, and false otherwise. We also replaced the height and weight variables with a single variable, the body mass index. In the dataset, all ages above 90 years were labeled with the string 90+. Nonetheless, keeping this format would mix numbers (ages below or equal to 90 years) with strings (ages above 90 years). This would prevent the dataset from being parsed properly by the graphlab python framework. For this reason, ages of 90 and 90+ years were treated the same. Figure 2.1 presents the flowchart of our preliminary data preparation approach.

2.2.2.2   Data noise reduction

The data were cleaned using the deletion technique. In total, 1 773 rows were deleted: 315 rows whose complication value was true and 1 458 rows whose complication value was false. Even though the number of deleted rows was small compared to the total number of records in the dataset, in an imbalanced dataset with 90 per cent of

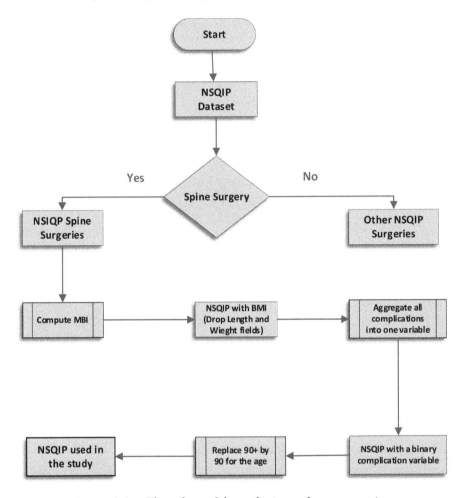

Figure 2.1   Flow chart of the preliminary data preparation

the complication values being false, every true complication value counts. This issue highlighted the possible need for an alternative data cleaning technique that would avoid the deletion of true complication values.

Thus, a maximum likelihood function was used instead of the deletion technique to impute the missing data. The data were then separated into two groups: (1) rows with no missing data and (2) rows with missing data. There were no data entries with a missing target value (occurrence of complications). For each missing value, the likelihood function iterated through all the rows with no missing data and calculated in each iteration the number of features the two rows (with and without missing data) had in common. The missing value was replaced by the value found in the row with the highest number of common features. If there was more than one row with the same number of common features as the row with missing data, the average value would be calculated to replace the missing value. Finally, it is worth noting that even though the likelihood function is computationally expensive, it is still possible to evaluate it within a reasonable period of time since the number of missing and complete rows is relatively small. A pseudocode of the process is shown in Algorithm 1 hereafter.

Algorithm 1 Data-cleaning(*CC*, *CM*)

Input: Set of clean and complete records of patients with a complication: *CC*

        Set of clean but not complete records of patients with complication: *CM*

Output: CM with missing data imputed
Initialize: *cc_features* = set of features of *CC*
cm_features = set of features of *CM*
while *cm_tuple* **IN** *CM* **do**
  while *cm_f* **IN** *cm_features* **do**
  cm_tuple_miss_f = missing features in cm_tuple
  cm_tuple_found_f = unmissing features in cm_tuple
  counter = 0
  max_counter = counter
  best_match_tuple = NULL
  while *cc_tuple* > *CC* **do**
   while *found_f* **IN** *cm_tuple_found_f* **do**
    while *cc_f* **IN** *cc_features* **do**
    if *cc_f* = *found_f* **then**
     counter = counter + 1
     break
    max_counter = MAX(counter, max_counter)
    best_match_tuple = TUPLE(max_counter)
   best_match_tuple_features = set of features for best_match_tuple
   while *missing_f* **IN** *cm_tuple_miss_f* **do**
    while *best_match_f* **IN** *best_match_tuple_features* **do**
    if *missing_f* = *best_match_f* **then**
     while *cm_f* **IN** *cm_features* **do**
     if *cm_f* = *missing_f* **then**
      cm_f = best_match_f

2.2.2.3   Statistical analysis

The primary objective of ML is to develop a model that has a high ability to generalize well beyond its training dataset. We wanted to measure the effectiveness of the proposed model and estimate its performance on a new dataset. For this reason, the data were split into two sets: a training set and a testing set. Seventy per cent of the records were

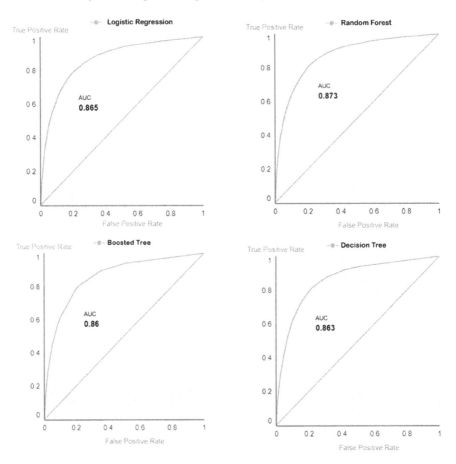

*Figure 2.2   Performance results of the prediction models (imbalanced dataset):
(a) LR, (b) RF, (c) BT, and (d) DT*

randomly selected to serve as the training dataset, while the remaining 30 per cent were
used to validate the output model.

Data cleaning, statistical tests, and model building were conducted with Python-
based libraries for ML. Area under the receiver operating characteristics curve
(ROC) values were obtained using the Graphlab create library. Matplotlib, Numpy,
Pandas, and other libraries were also used for data manipulation and finding results.

2.3   Results

Figure 2.2 shows the AUCs of the tested models using the imbalanced dataset. The
AUCs for LR, RF, BT, and DT were not significantly different. However, the RF
model tended to have a slightly higher predictive power (higher AUC) than any of
the other proposed models.

On the basis of the AUC alone, no general conclusions can be drawn. Hence, a more extensive analysis was needed to assess the performance of the obtained models. The true positives (TPs), true negatives (TNs), accuracies, precisions, recalls, and F1 scores were calculated and are presented in Table 2.4. The RF, BT, and DT models had very similar TP prediction values, which were much lower than the TP predictive value of the LR model. However, the LR model had a higher false-positive (FP) prediction rate. Therefore, the LR model was much less precise than the other models (precision = 0.32). On the other hand, false negatives (FNs) were lower with the LR model. Thus, the recall of this model was higher than the others (recall = 0.75).

Even though the accuracy of the LR model was not as high as the accuracy of the other models, its F1 score was higher. This result raises a performance metric problem: by what can one or should one measure the obtained ML model?

To answer the previous question, two data manipulation techniques were performed to better compare the ML algorithms.

First, an under-sampling technique was used to balance the dataset and re-evaluate the performance of the different models. This technique would give a better indication of the true accuracy of the ML algorithms. Records were deleted from the majority class (patients without complications). The TP and FP rates were used to plot the ROC curve (illustrated in Figure 2.3). Once again, the difference between the values of the AUCs was not significant. The results of a comparative analysis suggested that the number of the TP predictions obtained by RF, BT, and DT were higher than those obtained by LR (Table 2.5). However, LR had the best TN predictions of all the proposed ML algorithms. Concerning the accuracy, no significant difference was found between any of the models. Finally, a related point to consider is that the accuracy values were very close to those of the F1 score, the precision, and the recall.

Second, the prediction power of the features ranked as being of paramount importance by the surgeons and the ones selected by the InfoGain algorithm were compared. This allowed for the assessment of prediction capability in datasets with fewer features. The results of complication prediction are shown in Table 2.6a, 2.6b, 2.6c, and 2.6d.

Table 2.6a shows the prediction performance derived by applying the ML models to the imbalanced dataset with six features ranked by the InfoGain algorithm. The data were once again divided into a training set and a testing set.

Although the number of features dropped from 26 to 6, the Tukey test revealed that the F1 scores and the AUCs of the two datasets were not significantly different, as shown in Tables 2.4 and 2.6a. However, the F1 scores and AUCs of the two imbalanced datasets with features selected by the surgeons and those selected by the InfoGain algorithm were significantly different (Tables 2.6a and 2.6c). Moreover, a significant difference was found between the AUCs in the balanced and imbalanced datasets with features ranked by the InfoGain algorithm (Tables 2.6a and 2.6b). There is also a significant difference between the F1 score and the AUCs of the two imbalanced datasets (with 6 or 26 features). The difference between the F1 scores and AUCs was statistically significant in the imbalanced dataset ranked balanced dataset ranked by the InfoGain algorithm (Tables 2.6b and 2.6d). Moreover, there

Table 2.4   Performance of the four machine-learning algorithms on the unbalanced dataset

	TP	FP	TN	FN	Accuracy	Recall	Precision	F1	AUC
LR	3 773	7 979	39 798	1 237	0.83	0.75	0.32	0.45	0.86
RF	1 237	669	47 108	3 773	0.92	0.25	0.64	0.36	0.87
BT	1 328	908	46 869	3 682	0.91	0.27	0.60	0.37	0.86
DT	1 328	956	46 821	3 682	0.91	0.27	0.58	0.36	0.86

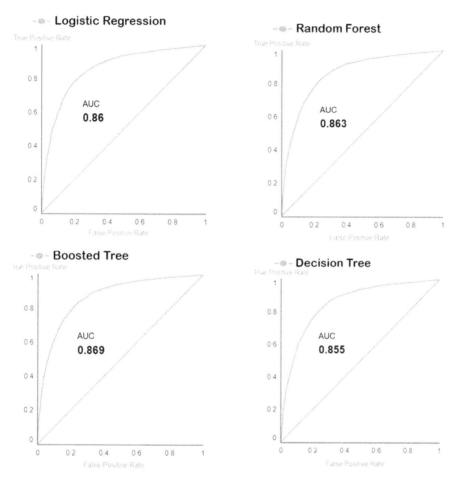

Figure 2.3   Performance results of the predictions models (balanced dataset):
(a) LR, (b) RF, (c) BT, and (d) DT

was a statistically significant difference between F1 scores and AUCs of the proposed machine models applied on the balanced dataset that included all the features
and the one that included the features ranked by the surgeons (Tables 2.5 and 2.6d),
by surgeons and the imbalanced dataset with all features (Tables 2.4 and 2.6d).

2.4   Discussion

In this study, we compared four different ML algorithms for the prediction of complications during spine surgery. The average accuracy (>90 per cent) and the average
AUC (>0.79) of the imbalanced datasets demonstrate a fairly high level of performance for predicting complications during surgery. However, the values of the
F1 scores of the same imbalanced datasets appear to be low (<45 per cent), which

Table 2.5 Performance of the four ML algorithms on the balanced dataset

	TP	FP	TN	FN	Accuracy	Recall	Precision	F1	AUC
LR	3 758	861	4 204	1 252	0.79	0.75	0.81	0.78	0.86
RF	3 993	1 084	3 981	1 017	0.79	0.79	0.78	0.79	0.86
BT	4 018	1 074	3 991	992	0.79	0.8	0.8	0.80	0.87
DT	3 768	972	4 093	1 242	0.78	0.75	0.79	0.77	0.85

Table 2.6a   *Performance of the four ML algorithms based on six features ranked by the InfoGain algorithm (imbalanced dataset)*

	TP	FP	TN	FN	Accuracy	Recall	Precision	AUC	F1
LR	1 047	669	47 108	3 963	0.91	0.21	0.61	0.85	0.31
RF	812	334	47 443	4 189	0.91	0.16	0.7	0.86	0.26
BT	1 232	812	46 965	3 778	0.91	0.25	0.60	0.86	0.35
DT	1 187	717	47 060	3 823	0.91	0.23	0.62	0.86	0.34

Table 2.6b   *Performance of the four ML algorithms based on six features ranked by the InfoGain algorithm (balanced dataset)*

	TP	FP	TN	FN	Accuracy	Recall	Precision	AUC	F1
LR	3 682	876	4 189	1 328	0.78	0.74	0.8	0.85	0.77
RF	4 028	1 094	3 971	982	0.79	0.8	0.79	0.86	0.8
BT	3 798	983	4 082	1 212	0.78	0.76	0.8	0.85	0.78
DT	3 803	983	4 082	1 207	0.78	0.76	0.8	0.85	0.78

Table 2.6c   *Performance of the four ML algorithms based on six features ranked by the surgeons as super important (imbalanced dataset)*

	TP	FP	TN	FN	Accuracy	Recall	Precision	AUC	F1
LR	90	48	47 729	4 920	0.9	0.02	0.65	0.68	0.04
RF	125	96	47 681	4 885	0.9	0.03	0.57	0.68	0.05
BT	130	96	47 681	4 880	0.9	0.03	0.58	0.67	0.05
DT	130	96	47 681	4 880	0.9	0.03	0.58	0.67	0.05

Table 2.6d   *Performance of the four ML algorithms based on six features ranked by the surgeons as super important (balanced dataset)*

	TP	FP	TN	FN	Accuracy	Recall	Precision	AUC	F1
LR	3 161	1 935	3 130	1 849	0.62	0.63	0.62	0.67	0.63
RF	3 452	2 198	2 867	1 558	0.63	0.67	0.61	0.68	0.65
BT	3 707	2 487	2 578	1 303	0.62	0.74	0.6	0.67	0.66
DT	2 936	1 727	3 338	2 074	0.62	0.59	0.63	0.67	0.6

indicates that the proposed ML models are likely considered poor predictors of complication rates. Such differences in the interpretation of the AUCs and the F1 scores imply that one of these metrics may be misleading when applied to imbalanced datasets.

Comparing the four models, the RF, BT, and DT models tend to miss patients with complications more than the LR model. This could be problematic because having an unexpected complication during surgery is life-threatening. On the other hand, the LR model has a higher rate of FPs. Hence, it is less precise than the RF, BT, and DT algorithms; however, it is better at identifying patients with complications (high TP rate). Thus, the recall of the LR model is significantly higher than the recall of the RF, BT, and DT models.

The examined ML models perform well on the balanced dataset. The results show that the performance of the LR, RF, BT, and DT models are almost identical (Table 2.5). Moreover, there is no statistical difference between the AUCs, F1 scores, precisions, recalls, and accuracies among the proposed models. Accordingly, the AUC scores are adequate to evaluate the performance of the models in a balanced dataset.

Our results are comparable to other studies that have used ML algorithms to predict the occurrence of complications after spinal fusion and the need for blood transfusion following spine surgery [14, 18]. However, our analysis of the data has identified an important issue: choosing which score (AUC, accuracy, or F1 score) should be used to evaluate the performance of the ML models is unclear. There exists a significant difference when comparing AUC and F1 score on the imbalanced data ($p < 0.05$), but this significance disappears when the data are balanced ($p > 0.05$). The TP, FP, and FN indicate that the F1 score is more informative than the AUC. Both, the AUC and the F1 score depend on the TP, FP, and FN. However, AUC depends also on the value of TN which is quite very high in the case of the imbalanced dataset. Remember, the formula to calculate: $F1 = 2TP/(2TP + FP + FN)$. The value of AUC depends on the sensitivity [$SE = TP/(TP + FN)$] and specificity [$SP = TN/(FP + TN)$] of the obtained model. Due to the imbalance toward negative classifications, the AUC was unable to provide an accurate assessment, even with more than double the number of FPs compared to TPs. Therefore, the F1 score seems to be a better indicator of the performance of binary ML algorithms when applied to imbalanced datasets.

We have conducted more studies and found four more cases that confirm our conclusion. In the first case, the value of AUC is significantly higher than the value of the F1 score. In this case, we could conclude that the performance of the current machine model is inadequate and should not be considered a good model for predictions of complications. In the second case, the value of the AUC is low, and there is no statistically significant difference between the value of the AUC and the value of F1. Again, in this case, the model is not considered to be a good predictor of complications. In the third case, the values of the AUC and the F1 are high, which suggests that the model is a good predictor of complication rates. In the last and fourth cases, the AUC value is significantly lower than that of the F1. In this case, the model is a good predictor of complication rates, but this will not hold true when the value of the threshold is changed.

Our study nonetheless has several limitations. First, the future use of our models in clinical settings would require a clear definition of "complications." A new study by [26] demonstrated that unrecorded adverse events could bring the rate of complications in spine surgery up to 87 per cent. This study included minor complications, such as medication effects, mild transient confusion, transient constipation, episodes of electrolyte imbalance, and hypoglycemia. To specify that our algorithm is built only for major life-threatening adverse events due to surgery is of great importance.

Automatic feature selection using the InfoGain algorithm showed that workrvu, optime, htooday, tothlos, returnor, and asaclas had powerful predictive capabilities of complications. Indeed, the performance of the models using the features ranked by the InfoGain algorithm overcame by far the performance of the models with features ranked by the surgeons. One reason for this finding could be that the algorithm has ranked the features depending on the existing data, while the surgeons have used their own experiences regardless of the current data. More on this will come in our future work.

2.5 Conclusion and future works

RF, BT, and DT are powerful algorithms for predicting complications during spine surgery. However, the previously mentioned algorithms do not provide a higher prediction of complications during spine surgery compared to LR. The algorithms under the study have been applied again on two specific sets of features; the first set was selected by InfoGain algorithm, while the second set was selected by the surgeons. The results have shown that features selected by the InfoGain algorithm are far exceeded those selected by surgeons. One more finding was that in the past the AUC has been the most commonly used metric for models' performance evaluation. However, our analysis has shown that F1 score is more robust and more accurate metric than AUC, especially in the case of imbalanced data.

In essence and since there is always room for improvement, we are aiming to increase the size of the data set (collecting more data) to utilize more powerful ML algorithms such as the superior deep learning functions to precisely forecast and predict complications during spine surgery.

References

[1] El Saddik A., Laamarti F., Alja'Afreh M. 'The potential of digital twins'. *IEEE Instrumentation & Measurement Magazine*. 2011, vol. 24(3), pp. 36–41.

[2] Ja'afreh M.A., Adhami H., Alchalabi A.E., Hoda M., El Saddik A. 'Toward integrating software defined networks with the internet of things: a review'. *Cluster Computing*. 2022, vol. 25(3), pp. 1619–36.

[3] Alja'Afreh M. 2021. 'A QoE Model for Digital Twin Systems in the Era of the Tactile Internet'. [Doctoral dissertation]. Université d'Ottawa/University of Ottawa

[4]   Kim B.D., Edelstein A.I., Patel A.A., Lovecchio F., Kim J.Y.S. 'Preoperative anemia does not predict complications after single-level lumbar fusion: a propensity score-matched multicenter study'. *Spine.* 2014, vol. 39(23), pp. 1981–89.

[5]   Phan K., Dunn A.E., Kim J.S, *et al.* 'Impact of preoperative anemia on outcomes in adults undergoing elective posterior cervical fusion'. *Global Spine Journal.* 2017, vol. 7(8), pp. 787–93.

[6]   Bekelis K., Desai A., Bakhoum S.F., Missios S. 'A predictive model of complications after spine surgery: the national surgical quality improvement program (NSQIP) 2005-2010'. *The Spine Journal.* 2014, vol. 14(7), pp. 1247–55.

[7]   Assi K.C., Labelle H., Cheriet F. 'Statistical model based 3D shape prediction of postoperative trunks for non-invasive scoliosis surgery planning'. *Computers in Biology and Medicine.* 2014, vol. 48, pp. 85–93.

[8]   Cooper J.N., Wei L., Fernandez S.A., Minneci P.C., Deans K.J. 'Preoperative prediction of surgical morbidity in children: comparison of five statistical models'. *Computers in Biology and Medicine.* 2015, vol. 57, pp. 54–65.

[9]   Vapnik V., Izmailov R. 'Learning using privileged information: similarity control and knowledge transfer'. *Journal of Machine Learning Research: JMLR.* 2015, vol. 16(1), pp. 2023–49.

[10]   Krishnamoorthy B., Bay B.K., Hart R.A. 'Bone mineral density and donor age are not predictive of femoral ring allograft bone mechanical strength'. *Journal of Orthopaedic Research.* 2014, vol. 32(10), pp. 1271–76.

[11]   Van Esbroeck A., Rubinfeld I., Hall B., Syed Z. 'Quantifying surgical complexity with machine learning: looking beyond patient factors to improve surgical models'. *Surgery.* 2014, vol. 156(5), pp. 1097–105.

[12]   Azimi P., Benzel E.C., Shahzadi S., Azhari S., Mohammadi H.R. 'Use of artificial neural networks to predict surgical satisfaction in patients with lumbar spinal canal stenosis: clinical article'. *Journal of Neurosurgery Spine.* 2014, vol. 20(3), pp. 300–05.

[13]   Burke H.B., Goodman P.H., Rosen D.B, *et al.* 'Artificial neural networks improve the accuracy of cancer survival prediction'. *Cancer.* 1997, vol. 79(4), pp. 857–62.

[14]   Kim J.S., Merrill R.K., Arvind V, *et al.* 'Examining the ability of artificial neural networks machine learning models to accurately predict complications following posterior lumbar spine fusion'. *Spine.* 2018, vol. 43(12), pp. 853–60.

[15]   Rughani A.I., Dumont T.M., Lu Z, *et al.* 'Use of an artificial neural network to predict head injury outcome'. *Journal of Neurosurgery.* 2010, vol. 113(3), pp. 585–90.

[16]   Dente C.J., Bradley M., Schobel S, *et al.* 'Towards precision medicine: accurate predictive modeling of infectious complications in combat casualties'. *The Journal of Trauma and Acute Care Surgery.* 2017, vol. 83(4), pp. 609–16.

[17]   Deo R.C. 'Machine learning in medicine'. *Circulation.* 2015, vol. 132(20), pp. 1920–30.

[18] Durand W.M., DePasse J.M., Daniels A.H. 'Predictive modeling for blood transfusion after adult spinal deformity surgery: a tree-based machine learning approach'. *Spine*. 2018, vol. 43(15), pp. 1058–66.

[19] Kerezoudis P., McCutcheon B., Murphy M.E, *et al.* 'Thirty-day postoperative morbidity and mortality after temporal lobectomy for medically refractory epilepsy'. *Journal of Neurosurgery*. 2018, vol. 128(4), pp. 1158–64.

[20] Forestier G., Petitjean F., Riffaud L., Jannin P. 'Automatic matching of surgeries to predict surgeons' next actions'. *Artificial Intelligence in Medicine*. 2017, vol. 81, pp. 3–11.

[21] McAnany S.J., Anwar M.A.F., Qureshi S.A. 'Decision analytic modeling in spinal surgery: a methodologic overview with review of current published literature'. *The Spine Journal*. 2015, vol. 15(10), pp. 2254–70.

[22] Menezes A.H. 'Craniovertebral junction database analysis: incidence, classification, presentation, and treatment algorithms'. *Child's Nervous System*. 2008, vol. 24(10), pp. 1101–08.

[23] Scheer J.K., Smith J.S., Schwab F, *et al.* 'Development of a preoperative predictive model for major complications following adult spinal deformity surgery'. *Journal of Neurosurgery. Spine*. 2017, vol. 26(6), pp. 736–43.

[24] DeVries Z., Locke E., Hoda M, *et al.* 'Using a national surgical database to predict complications following posterior lumbar surgery and comparing the area under the curve and F1-score for the assessment of prognostic capability'. *The Spine Journal*. 2021, vol. 21(7), pp. 1135–42.

[25] Nakagawa S., Freckleton R.P. 'Model averaging, missing data and multiple imputation: a case study for behavioural ecology'. *Behavioral Ecology and Sociobiology*. 2011, vol. 65(1), pp. 103–16.

Chapter 3

Recent trends in histopathological image analysis

Abhinav Kumar[1], Sanjay Kumar Singh[1], Sonal Saxena[2], Amit Kumar Singh[3], and Sameer Shrivastava[2]

Histopathological images provide a plethora of phenotypic information that forms the basis for proven to be the gold standard for cancer diagnosis and monitoring the progression of the disease in cancer patients. However, such images are challenging to analyse, even for experienced pathologists. Moreover, manual analysis is a tedious and costly task in terms of labour, time, etc. The manual analysis is also affected by intra- and inter-observer disagreement, as reported in several studies. Therefore, computer-aided diagnosis (CAD) systems are being explored to speed up the analysis process. Nowadays, artificial intelligence (AI)-based solutions are quite popular in the medical domain, and deep learning (DL) is becoming the most popular methodological choice for researchers to analyse histopathological images. Usually, feature extraction, image segmentation and histopathological image classification are the popular tasks for which several machine learning (ML) approaches and deep models have been developed. There are also few works that are designed for Internet-of-Things-based applications while also addressing security concerns. Therefore, this chapter briefly presents the recent developments in the automated histopathological analysis of cancer. We further summarise different publicly available datasets and also emphasise the key challenges along with limitations of emerging DL techniques for CAD of cancer. We also provide an insight into possible avenues for future research in this area. It helps the researchers working in this area to leverage the opportunities and challenges that direct towards innovative developments in the field.

[1]Department of Computer Science and Engineering, Indian Institute of Technology (BHU), Varanasi, Uttar Pradesh, India

[2]Division of Veterinary Biotechnology, ICAR-Indian Veterinary Research Institute, Izatnagar, Uttar Pradesh, India

[3]Department of Computer Science and Engineering, NIT Patna, Patna, Bihar, India

3.1   Introduction

AI is becoming more powerful, reliable and capable of outperforming humans in a wide range of tasks. Nowadays, AI is permeating numerous aspects of human life and assisting people in their everyday lives, such as autonomous transportation, virtual assistants, personalised healthcare, drones, smart devices, self-driving cars, smart devices, etc. AI is being developed at an increasing rate every day, becoming more intelligent and being applied in various fields, with the goal to improve human life. Image classification is an elementary problem in computer vision. Despite its simplicity, it has numerous practical applications and serves as the foundation for other computer vision applications. With the advent of ML and DL, combined with powerful hardware and graphical processing units, remarkable performance on image classification tasks is now possible. AI advancements have revolutionised the entire field of image recognition, object detection and image classification. Many recently designed algorithms outperform humans in terms of real-time object recognition and image classification. AI is used in the healthcare system to manage and record massive amounts of medical data, as well as to analyse data and assist doctors in making decisions. The machine outperforms humans when it comes to performing repetitive tasks quickly and consistently. In addition, the machine can pay closer attention to even the smallest information, such as a single pixel in an image. Digitization of histopathology images has opened up new avenues for CAD in the field of healthcare. As an emerging discipline, AI-based CAD systems have recently shown considerable potential in histopathological image classification. Figure 3.1 shows different steps in manual and digital pathology workflow.

The breakthroughs in AI over the last decade have revolutionised cancer detection and treatment. Cancer is a long-standing and severe disease that endangers both human and animal health. In 2020, cancer was the leading cause of death globally, accounting for over 10 million deaths [1]. According to the WHO most recent cancer data, 19.29 million new cancer cases were reported globally in 2020. Among these cancers, breast cancer is the most prevalent with 2.26 million cases, preceded by lung cancer with 2.21 million cases. Amongst all animals, pet animals are more susceptible to cancer [2]. Canine mammary tumours (CMT) are the most prevalent neoplasms in female canines, with poor prognoses and high death rates when compared to human breast cancer (HBC) [3]. Despite wider advancements in technology, approaches for cancer detection and analysis remain a hot research area. AI also seeks great attention not only from pathologists but also from researchers and scientists worldwide involved in animal healthcare due to the need for early detection of crucial disease for better treatment. Nevertheless, histopathological analysis for cancerous tissues is a gold standard for breast cancer detection. Thus, a CAD system is fast, readily available, reliable and affordable, which can be used by health centres in urban areas to enhance the health care system. From the last decade there is an enormous effort made in this area, which results in various CAD systems like cell classification [4], mitosis detection [5] and nuclei segmentation [6]. Yassin *et al.* [7] have made efforts to analyse the CAD systems applied for breast cancer

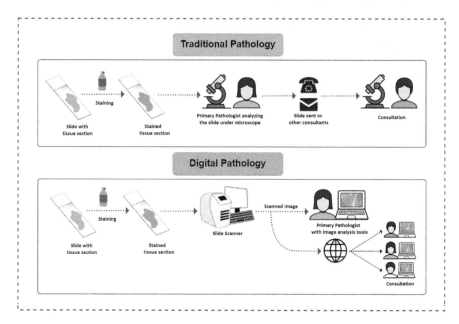

Figure 3.1   Comparison between the workflow of traditional and digital pathology

analysis by reviewing articles from 2012 to 2017. However, they have presented general information without any specifics like challenges, limitations and characteristics of the system developed. Therefore, our main objective is to provide any information related to the state-of-the-art method used for breast cancer histopathological analysis along with available datasets for cancer. Challenges, limitations and future opportunities are also listed in this chapter which will be helpful for readers and researchers in their future studies.

The remaining chapter is organised in the following sections: section 3.2 explains the need for CAD for cancer diagnosis, section 3.3 details the CAD and intelligent techniques used in breast cancer histopathology and section 3.4 lists the different challenges. Section 3.5 gives the detail of available datasets and their specifications. Section 3.6 describes different AI approaches, section 3.7 highlights the paradigm shift from automated classification to a secure classification model and finally, the chapter is concluded in section 1.8 with future directions.

3.2   Why computer-assisted diagnosis for cancer diagnosis?

Undoubtedly, manual analysis of H&E stained histopathological sections of tumour tissue can accurately diagnose breast cancer and its type [8]. However, manual examination of histopathology slides is a tedious and labour-intensive task that is heavily reliant on the availability of highly experienced oncopathologists. In manual

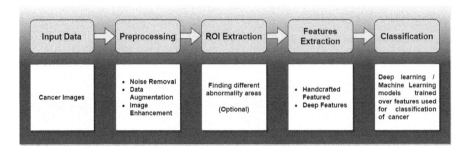

Figure 3.2   Generalized overview of CAD system for cancer classification

analysis, there is also the possibility of subjectivity and ambiguity owing to inter- and intra-observer variances with around 75% diagnostic concordance between specialists [9]. Furthermore, technological factors such as poor image quality and noise might increase the incidence of misclassification. All of these factors may unintentionally lead to biopsies being misinterpreted during cancer identification and classification. Thus, CAD is being studied in cancer pathology to produce faster and repeatable results. The adoption of CAD approaches reduces the likelihood of errors compared to those made by a single pathologist. As a result, CAD aids in classification accuracy and reduces variability in interpretations [10].

The trend towards digitization of pathology has opened new avenues for computer-based image analysis having the potential for a more objective and quantitative analysis [3]. Recent advances in high-throughput tissue banking and preservation of digital histology images have paved the path for the use of CAD to aid in cancer classification. To overcome these shortcomings in the early accurate detection and prognosis of breast cancer, CAD has emerged as a preferable alternative. CAD may also help pathologists reduce their workload by screening out evident benign regions, allowing them to focus on more difficult-to-diagnose cases. Thus, CAD has enormous potential for accurate cancer detection in classifying tumours as benign or malignant and subclassifying them into different classes. Furthermore, it saves a significant amount of time and energy for human experts. A generalised overview of the CAD system for the classification of cancer is depicted in Figure 3.2.

3.3   Breast cancer and CAD in cancer histopathology

As previously discussed, breast cancer is the most common disease in women and has a significant morbidity and fatality rate. Aside from that, the WHO anticipates a 70% increase in the number of new breast cancer patients over the next two decades. Moreover, breast cancer has a current late-stage survival rate of roughly 30%. Early diagnosis and treatment are critical in improving diagnosis and increasing the survival rate of patients with breast cancer from 30% to 50% [1]. In general, breast tumours are classified into two types: benign and malignant. Non-invasive tumours are benign, whereas invasive cancerous tumours are malignant. It is critical to first classify tumours as benign or malignant to select the best treatment plan. Mammography, computed tomography, histopathological image analysis, ultra-sound imaging or sonograms and magnetic resonance imaging are the techniques used to diagnose HBC [11, 12]. In histopathological image analysis, tumour tissues or biopsy samples from an abnormal breast region are collected and fixed on microscopic glass slides. A pathologist examines the sections under a microscope to detect cancerous changes in tissues after they have been stained with an H&E stain. In addition to breast cancer, histopathology imaging is the gold standard for various other forms of cancers, such as lung cancer, liver cancer and bladder cancer [13]. In cases where more than one pathologist is available, a final decision is made only after two pathologists reach an agreement; otherwise, only one pathologist is responsible for reporting findings.

A reliable breast cancer identification and classification is dependent on an expert pathologist's professional experience and domain knowledge. These issues may lead to a misdiagnosis, particularly in the early stages of breast cancer. However, as a second opinion, CAD systems can be used to address classification issues in breast cancer. A CAD system is a low-cost, rapid and dependable source of early diagnosis [14, 15]. As a result, such a system reduces human reliance, improves diagnostic rates and decreases total treatment costs by minimizing false-positive and false-negative predictions, resulting in reduced death rates [16]. Sadaf *et al*. [15] also demonstrated that employing a CAD system for breast cancer diagnosis enhances sensitivity by 10%. Therefore, scientists are continuously trying to develop CAD systems [17] for histological diagnosis of cancers to improve overall diagnostic performance. In the mid-1980s, researchers started exploring computer-aided detection approaches for providing prompt diagnosis [18]. Advances in computerized technologies and techniques such as ML and DL have played a critical role in improving diagnosis and assisting professionals in their workflow throughout the last decade. Figure 3.3 shows the generalised overview of the ML and DL approaches from histopathological image classification. The neural network has been extensively used in the development of research to explore intelligent ways to assist medical image diagnosis and has attained tremendous success in the field. Recently, convolutional neural networks (CNN), along with multiple-instance learning, have achieved remarkable progress in the histological classification of cancers. In fact, CNNs are now being looked upon as a method of choice for interpreting histopathology images [19]. A CNN is a feedforward neural network that combines **rectified linear activation unit (**ReLU) and pooling layers. It is typically made up of one or more convolutional layers as well as fully connected layers, as discussed in an earlier section. In a classical CNN for image processing, convolutional filter layers are combined with pooling or data reduction layers. A convolution filter transforms a small portion of an image and can detect highly relevant visual features in a manner similar to the low-level pixel processing of the human brain. CNNs generally eliminate the necessity for manual feature extraction, which is very time-consuming. Many studies have shown that the neural network-based CAD technique outperforms the old method on tasks such as tumour segmentation and classification, implying that the neural network-based method has a broader scope and potentially higher value for

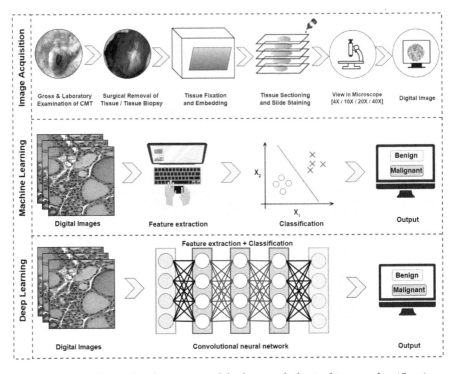

Figure 3.3   Generalized overview of the histopathological image classification

clinical applications [20]. Table 3.1 provides a historical tour of intelligent analysis for breast cancer histopathology.

While preliminary results in the field of HBC image classification are promising, this is a rapidly changing subject with new knowledge arising in both cancer biology and DL, allowing chances to improve upon existing algorithms.

3.4   Challenges

The development of classification techniques for histopathological image classification is difficult for several reasons, including:

1. **Complexity of cancer histopathology images:** histopathological image classification itself is a very difficult problem due to the biological heterogeneities and rich geometrical structures. Moreover, cancer is a complex disease and diverse histological subtypes are present. Thus, accurate interpretation of cancer histopathological images is a big challenge. Furthermore, enumeration, detection and classification of mitotic structures in histological images are tedious operations in many histopathological grading systems.

Table 3.1 *Overview of the intelligent analysis of breast cancer histopathology*

Authors	Year	Methodology	Conclusion
Stenkvist *et al.* [21]	1978	Authors developed a new approach for assessing variations in nuclear detail in chrome alum gallocyanin-stained nuclei of human breast cancer (HBC) cells and compared it to traditional subjective grading and classification methods.	According to the findings of this study, individual cells acquired from human tumours through fine-needle aspiration biopsy are suitable for high-resolution image analysis.
Elston and Ellis [22]	1991	Authors proposed modified Bloom–Richardson system.	The modified Bloom–Richardson technique that includes a semi-quantitative assessment of nuclear atypia, tubule formation and mitotic activity is frequently used to determine histological tumour grade.
Meijer *et al.* [23]	1997	Authors have provided a brief summary of image analysis s roots in pathology.	The goal of this study is to present an overview of the innovations that have led to image analysis as it is now used in routine diagnostic cytopathology and histopathology, as well as in research.
Yang *et al.* [24]	2005	Authors provided a robust colour-based segmentation technique for histological structures that dealt with stain variability by using image gradients computed in the LUV colour space.	They defined the colour gradient in LUV colour space in order to replace the grey level gradient of the original gradient vector flow (GVF) snake. Despite the fact that the original GVF snake has a vast capture range, it may fail to detect the edges of the object when given incorrect beginning coordinates.
Can *et al.* [25]	2008	Authors employed mutual information-based error metrics to register nucleus images from subsequent staining processes.	A two-step technique was used to remove the autofluorescence from fluorescent microscopy images. Rather than obtaining images of all the dyes at once, images of specific dyes are acquired in two stages using a set of optimal filter cubes.

(Continues)

Table 3.1 *Continued*

Authors	Year	Methodology	Conclusion
Alomari *et al.* [26]	2009	Authors proposed a systematic approach to solving the localization problem in pathology images.	This method utilizes a feedforward backpropagation Neural Network with pre- and post-processing and many features, including; colour, texture, appearance and location.
Irshad *et al.* [27]	2014	This survey covers major trends of various nuclei detection, segmentation, feature computation and classification techniques used in histopathology images, specifically in H&E staining.	It is shown that only a few supervised machine learning (ML) techniques are used for nuclei segmentation and feature extraction. So as future research work, more domain-specific feature extraction and efficient ML techniques can be explored.
Oquab *et al.* [28]	2014	Authors developed a technique for reusing ImageNet-trained layers to compute mid-level image representation for images.	In this paper, they show how image representations learned with convolutional neural networks (CNNs) on large-scale annotated datasets can be effectively transferred to other visual recognition tasks with a small number of training samples.
Spaniel *et al.* [29]	2016	Authors presented a collection of 7,909 breast histopathology images obtained from 82 patients. In the same study, the authors assessed six distinct textural descriptors and classifiers and reported a set of experiments with accuracy varying from 80% to 85%, depending on the magnification factor of images.	It is apparent that texture descriptors can provide a useful representation for training classifiers. Some researchers, however, argue that the major limitation of existing ML approaches lies in this feature engineering stage.
Spaniel and Caroline [30]	2016	Author has performed preliminary studies utilizing the deep learning technique to categorize breast cancer histopathology images from the publicly accessible dataset, BreakHis.	This technique aims to facilitate the use of high-resolution histopathology images from BreakHis as input to existing CNN in order to demonstrate that the CNN performance is superior to previously reported findings from other ML models trained with handwritten textural descriptors.

(Continues)

Table 3.1 *Continued*

Authors	Year	Methodology	Conclusion
Vahadane et al. [31]	2016	Authors suggested a unique structure-preserving colour normalization approach that alters the colour of one image (source) to match the colour of another (target) image while consistently retaining the source structural information.	Colour normalization is an important step in removing unwanted colour in histopathological imaging and it is beneficial for analysing disease and its progression on huge datasets from various pathology laboratories.
Bejnordi et al. [32]	2016	Author reported and tests a completely automated approach for detecting ductal carcinoma in situ in digitized H&E stained histopathology slides of breast tissue.	The results of the experiments show that the proposed method is efficacious and accurate, as well as has the potential to be used in routine pathological diagnostics.

2. **Availability of datasets:** limited datasets with a sufficient number of high-resolution correctly labelled histopathology images are available for HBC histopathology images. Benchmark datasets generally have hundreds or thousands of images for training. In histopathology slide analysis, we do not have that many images, so we have to figure out a way to train a generalized network without overfitting on the training set.

3. **Data imbalance:** the majority of publicly accessible datasets suffer from data imbalance at various levels. For example, the imbalance ratio between malignant/benign classifications in the BreakHis histopathological dataset is 0.41 at the patient-level and 0.45 at the image-level. At the image and patient levels, there is also an unequal distribution of distinct subcategories. This data imbalance issue may bias a CAD system's discriminative capabilities towards the majority class during classification tasks at the image as well as patient levels.

4. **Colour variations in histopathology images:** there can be differences in colour of the images owing to minor differences in the staining protocols, variations in the reactivity of chemical stains from different manufacturers and differences in the slide storage times. Variations in colour can also occur because of differences in the slide scanners or slide thickness, which leads to variability in the transmission of light. Despite these AI systems' impressive accuracy in binary cancer classification, colour fluctuations in histopathology pictures are an issue for automated analysis. These colour changes may not be a hindrance to a pathologist's analysis, but they can have a substantial impact on picture interpretation in automated image analysis. Stain normalization is required to resolve this issue and choosing an algorithm for stain normalization is a critical responsibility.

5. **Illumination:** illumination is another factor in visible light images since even minor variances in lighting can impact algorithmic outcomes. Many digital microscopy images have poor illumination at the edges, which is often caused by factors related to the light path between the camera and the microscope. Thus, developing an illumination invariant approach for feature extraction from histopathological images is also an area of concern.

6. **Designing efficient feature extraction models:** undoubtedly, CNNs have achieved remarkable success in the field of computer vision; yet, a key stumbling block for DL-based algorithms is the demand for huge volumes of labelled data. In the realm of medical imaging, large labelled datasets are limited. With few datasets, ML-based algorithms might be a viable alternative to DL for medical imaging. Traditional ML algorithms have a basic problem in that they require complicated processing to extract discriminatory characteristics. Efficient feature engineering simplifies the model by minimizing training and execution durations, lowering input requirements and computational costs. Furthermore, reducing unnecessary features from the dataset enhances model compactness and transparency while allowing for quick interpretation. As a result, extracting relevant characteristics poses a significant problem for automated cancer histopathology. Different feature extraction methodologies for cancer histopathology image analysis have been studied, but none have yet been shown to be

completely reliable. Thus, developing an effective feature extractor for such complicated tissue prediction remains an open and challenging problem.

7. **Data security and privacy:** the advancements in Internet of things (IoT) and cloud services have made smart e-healthcare services available in a remote and distributed scenario. Nevertheless, this has prompted serious questions about privacy and efficiency, which must be resolved. When exchanging healthcare data over the cloud, which frequently contains private patient-related information, security is a big concern. Increased public trust in medical research is aided by adequate patient data privacy protection. Aside from that, DL-based models are complicated and efficiently processing data in such models in a cloud-based manner is difficult. DL in healthcare may be used as a quick diagnostic tool to aid doctors in making critical decisions, but it must also be protected from malicious attacks. Developing a safe and private learning model for histopathology image categorization is a research challenge that has yet to be solved.

8. **Application of CAD models on resource-constrained devices:** edge computing is becoming more popular in the healthcare industry [33] and researchers are concentrating on developing models that can be readily deployed in edge devices without sacrificing performance. DL-based techniques, on the other hand, are computationally expensive and have a large number of parameters, making them unsuitable for edge devices. To make them inexpensive for edge devices, the categorization model as a whole must be reduced while preserving accuracy. In today's edge-computing era, providing a low-cost solution for histopathology diagnosis is crucial. The combination of AI, edge computing and IoTs has the potential to transform healthcare, notably in the field of cancer theranostics. Thus, developing a robust histopathological image classification model for resource-constrained devices with high accuracy is a challenging and priority research area to work upon.

3.5   Datasets

The availability of datasets linked to biomedical imaging encourages researchers in computer vision, ML and the medical community. There are several databases available for cancer histopathology images used by researchers for breast cancer classification such as BreakHis [29], Kaggle Invasive ductal carcinoma (IDC) [34], BACH [35], CMTHis [36], Camelyon [37] and so on, as shown in Figure 3.4.

3.6   AI approaches: a bridge between manual and automated intelligent histopathological image analysis

3.6.1   ML-based approaches

CAD systems first developed for the BreakHis dataset were based upon a dual-stage traditional approach, whereby handcrafted features were extracted from the images and

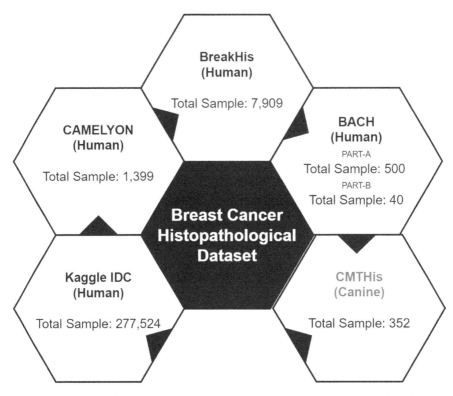

Figure 3.4   Popular histopathology datasets used for breast cancer classification

utilized to train a standalone classifier. In Reference [29], the researchers studied the efficacy of six cutting-edge handcrafted features descriptors namely: Local binary patterns (LBP) [38], its variant Compound LBP (CLBP) [39], **gray-level co-occurrence matrix** (GLCM) [40], Local Phase Quantization (LPQ) [41], Oriented FAST and rotated BRIEF (ORB) [42] and Parameter Free Threshold Statistics (PFTAS) [43]. The performance of these feature descriptors was evaluated along with four different classifiers: support vector machines (SVM) [44], 1-nearest neighbour [45], quadratic linear analysis [46] and random forests [47]. In Reference [48], researchers trained an SVM classifier with the fractal dimension [49] of each image and proved that utilizing fractal dimension as a distinct feature descriptor is more appropriate to classify lower magnification (40×) images, which are having a number of self-similarities; however, it is of little use for higher magnification images having fewer self-similarities.

Authors in [48] also attempted multicategory classification using 16 experiments, each classifying malignant and benign subclasses. In [50], authors experimented with various handcrafted feature descriptors in combination with a k-NN classifier, including LBP, GLCM, tree-structured wavelet transform (TWT) and pyramid-structured wavelet transforms (PWT). In [51], an L1-norm sparse SVM is proposed for the selection of the most relevant features from the BreakHis dataset of cancer histopathology images. They observed that the L1-norm is unreliable for precise feature selection and the SVM showed biasness towards large hyper-plane coefficients. For improving the quality of feature selection, a weight was assigned to each feature based on its Wilcoxon rank-sum [52]. Sanchez-Morillo *et al.* [53] tested the performance of KAZE features [54] using a bag-of-features approach.

Limitations: the traditional handcrafted features demonstrated relatively acceptable but highly unstable preliminary results. The main concern with these traditional approaches is that the model's quality is dependent on the feature extraction task, and obtaining representative features in a real sense is a very difficult task. A major difficulty is in choosing the appropriate descriptor. Even after combining different descriptors for enhancing their discriminative power, or their post-transformation for selecting the best ones, the results remain somewhat inferior and are sometimes not stable between different magnification levels. As a result, researchers are coming up with new innovative ideas to overcome ML limited ability to reveal the most sophisticated features in complex tissue images. Few studies have been conducted in the same vein, with the goal of providing solutions in the case of limited annotated medical data, which is an important aspect of healthcare applications. In Reference 55, a novel feature extractor CoMHisP is proposed for CMT classification. CoMHisP is designed using interdisciplinary concepts centre of mass for feature extraction from histopathological cancerous tissue images, and to enhance the robustness and fault tolerance of ML classifier, they utilized fuzzy theory and reported performance on binary classification. Furthermore, MetaMed [56] is another approach in which the lack of well-annotated medical data, which affects classification performance, is rigorously addressed. The authors proposed the MetaMed approach for low regime medical histopathological image classification using meta-learning and few-shot learning. Advanced augmentation techniques were used for regularisation and the performance for breast cancer histopathology image classification, as well as the classification of the other two medical datasets, was significantly improved.

3.6.2   DL-based approaches

Researchers in Reference 10 were the first to evaluate a DL-based system for this BreakHis dataset by a CNN model incorporating features extraction and classification tasks. First, they explored LeNet [57] and found that it gives a poor performance as compared to traditional methods in Reference 29. Then, researchers tried AlexNet [58] as a comparatively deeper network. Though CNN models use raw images as input, but in Reference 59 authors utilized texture and pixel distributions in handcrafted features obtained using LBP or histogram descriptors. Upon comparison of different combinations, they achieved the best results with the Model1-CNN-CH model. This model is based upon CNN architecture with residual blocks derived from ResNet [60] and involves contourlet transform and histogram information descriptors for concatenation of extracted local features [61]. Different popular schemes in DL utilized for histopathology breast cancer analysis are detailed below. Recently authors have proposed a framework based on VGGNet-16, where

VGGNet-16 is used as a feature extractor, and these extracted features from breast cancer and CMT are further classified by different classifiers, namely SVM and random forest and reported 97% and 93% accuracy on respective datasets [36].

3.6.2.1   Autoencoder

A method of unsupervised learning, "back-propagation," is used by the autoencoder, which adjusts the target values to match the inputs. It's a three-layer neural network containing the input layer, hidden layer and decoding layer. An autoencoder is a device for converting input data into a hidden layer, which is then reconstructed by the decoder. Denoising autoencoders, sparse autoencoders (SAE), variational autoencoders and contractive autoencoders are the four types of autoencoders. By lowering the data's dimensionality, auto-encoders provide us with an edge. They can do both linear and non-linear transformations. The training of an autoencoder requires considerable volumes of data, execution time, hyperparameter tweaking and model validation. For classification of nucleus patches on HBC histopathological images, a stacked sparse autoencoder (SSAE) framework is presented consisting of two SAE [62]. For nuclei patch classification, SSAE + softmax performed better than the traditional softmax classifiers, principal component analysis (PCA) + softmax and SAE + softmax. The breast cancer images, though, in this study were taken from only 17 patients. Following that, authors in Reference 63 suggested a method for detecting breast cancer nuclei using the SSAE framework on 537 H&E stained histological images. They did not; however, examine any pre-processing procedures. Kadam *et al.* [64] suggested feature ensemble learning with SSAE and showed that it outperforms the SSAE + softmax framework.

3.6.2.2   Transfer learning

It is a popular technique in computer vision since it allows us to quickly develop an accurate model. It is widely used for prediction modelling issues that employ image data as input. The aim of using transfer learning is to use what we have learnt in one task to boost generalization in another one. Collecting very big image datasets of a specific domain is challenging and time-consuming, and transfer learning is of great help in these situations. CNNs require a lot of data and processing power. Training of CNNs on image datasets, like the ImageNet database, which comprises around million annotated images, allows training rather big networks with more than a hundred layers with excellent precision. In cases where data are insufficient, one solution is to use transfer learning in CNNs models that are supervised and pre-trained on natural image datasets or in a separate health domain [65]. In one technique, an input image is fed into pre-trained CNNs, and the outputs are recovered from the network layers. If a medium-sized dataset is available for the task, fine-tuning is another option. It starts the network with pre-trained CNNs and then supervises to train some or every network layer using the new input/data for the task at hand [66]. Furthermore, fine-tuning deep CNNs architectures with millions of parameters have obtained state-of-the-art performance in numerous computer vision problems [67, 68]. However, training CNNs from scratch requires a massive volume of images in order to prevent the model from overfitting. Thus, researchers utilized the concept of transfer learning, VGG-19, as a base model to classify breast cancer histopathological images [69].

3.6.2.3 CNN-based approaches

CNN has given new life to computer vision, and its huge success in different application areas attracts the healthcare domain also for addressing complex tissue analysis along with critical disease diagnosis. With the same inspiration in 2015, CNNs were applied for breast cancer classification, including binary classification with an accuracy of 83.3% and multi-class classification task with 77.8% accuracy, using datasets released in bioimaging breast histology classification challenge [70]. As designing and training CNN from scratch in case of a complex problem is a tedious task hence pre-trained networks were introduced, which can be used for representation learning and also for fine-tuning. For fine-tuning pre-trained networks (CNN), various approaches are used. Some approaches promote fine-tuning of all layers in pre-trained CNNs, whereas others only use the last fully connected layer for pre-training. In Reference 71, a strategy of fine-tuning based on dual-stage tuning is proposed, where the first stage comprises retraining of dense layers only while the second stage involves entire network training. The authors also evaluated the two stages independently and discovered that the dual-stage model performs better.

Another way in which high-level representations of cancer tissues are expected to be extracted from a pre-trained CNN using ImageNet is also popular. Yet, the CNN utilized for feature extraction in BreakHis classification is unsupervised, leading to a gap between the obtained features-information and the desired domain-specific features-information [72]. To overcome such a knowledge gap, the authors of Reference 73 presented a hybrid approach based on transfer learning along with domain-specific knowledge for representation learning and classification.

Furthermore, in Reference 74 authors explored an approach based upon transfer learning using a pre-trained AlexNet and also in Reference 75 DeCAF-based features learning has been studied. Here, features were extracted from the last layers of pre-trained AlexNets and used to train a standalone classifier. Following that, the authors of Reference 76 evaluated PCA, correlation-based feature selection and Gaussian random projection, on features obtained from a pre-trained VGG network [77]. In Reference 78 authors introduced a sequential features extraction framework in combination with XGBoost classifier [79], for evaluating the learning capabilities of a pre-trained DenseNet169 layers [80]. The results showed that extracted features from the last convolutional layers are significantly more informative than the features from the final dense layers. It was also discovered that contribution from lower layers in the network is more significant in classifying low magnification (40×) images, mid-level features are useful for 100× and 200× magnifications, and higher-level layers effectively represent 400× magnification images.

For the 2015 Breast Cancer Classification Challenge, the work presented in Reference 81 proposed a methodology using residual network transfer learning frameworks, Inception v4 and a recurrent CNN architecture that solved classification tasks. They employed data-augmentation techniques to resolve the data imbalance problem. Experimental results demonstrated an accuracy of $97.57 \pm 0.89\%$ for multi-class and $97.95 \pm 1.07\%$ for binary classification of cancers using the BreakHis dataset. Another work [82], used BreakHis dataset with augmentation techniques such as cropping, rotation etc. and further single and multi-task CNN were applied for malignancy prediction at different image magnification. They achieved 82.13% accuracy using multi-task CNN architecture and 83.72% classification rate using a single job for the benign/malignant binary classification task.

For binary breast cancer classification, Kassani *et al.* [83] applied an ensemble learning approach where different transfer learning-based deep networks-MobileNet, VGG19 and DenseNet were ensembled and tested on 4 datasets, namely BreakHis, 2015 Bioimaging Challenge, PatchCamelyon and 2018 ICIAR datasets with accuracies of 98.13%, 94.64%, 95% and 83.1%, respectively. Data augmentation techniques (flipping, rotation, zooming and shear) were also performed to supplement the data.

On the BreakHis dataset, Khan *et al.* [84] employed a DL model integrating bi-LSTM and fully connected network architectures for binary classification and achieved 96.32% accuracy. In Reference 85, researchers utilized a Deep network to classify histopathological images into benign/malignant categories. BreakHis dataset has been used for experiments. They used belief theory for the experiments by merging DeepNets (AlexNet, ResNet-18 and ResNet-50) and reached 96.88% accuracy (image-wise). Another work [19] used BreakHis dataset histopathology images to develop a weakly supervised method for binary categorization (benign/ malignant) of tumours and achieved 92.1% accuracy at $40\times$ magnification-level. The method works well without the need for labelled images, which is a significant benefit of their method. Furthermore, in Reference 74 researchers presented a framework which consists of a CNN model that pre-trained on the histopathology data (BreakHis), achieving a subject level F1-score of 90.3. In Reference 86, a matrix power normalization approach is presented by the authors to include global covariance information into a simple CNN model. The framework produced successful representations from histology images on the BreakHis dataset with 97.92% accuracy at the subject level for the binary classification task by exploiting second-order statistical information. The authors also used standard augmentation methods (cropping and flipping) to artificially increase the dataset size.

Budak *et al.* [85] employed BreakHis and a custom dataset for binary classification (benign versus malignant) of tumour cells by applying several transfer learning architectures (GoogleNet, VGGNet and ResNet). They used data augmentation methods such as scaling, translation, colour augmentation and rotation to attain a classification accuracy of 97.67%. In another work [87], authors have presented a lightweight CNN framework-MobiHisNet for breast cancer histopathology image classification. Results are presented by deploying this model on edge devices.

Akbar *et al.* [88] presented "Transition module," a newer version of the GoogleNet inception module and its integration with AlexNet. The updated version was created to make the transition from the last convolution layer to the first completely connected layer less abrupt. This transition module, unlike the inception module, does not incorporate any prior dimensionality reduction. A new CNN archi-tecture comprised of 50 convolutions is evaluated in comparison to a variety of handcrafted feature-based models [89]. BiCNN, a new CNN based on the GoogleNet architecture, is proposed in Reference 90 and binary class label, as well as sub-class information of each image, is utilized for using it in the binary classification task. Taking into account both information might aid the presented model in learning feature distance between binary classes more efficiently.

3.6.2.4 Deep features versus traditional features learning

Researchers in Reference 91 compared features extracted with conventional hand-crafted feature descriptors to those obtained from a pre-trained CNN, AlexNet. The authors discovered that the performance of LBP handcrafted feature extraction is marginally better than that of AlexNet features. The comparison; however, was very limited with a somewhat shallow CNN, which was also found to outperform hand-crafted based models in Reference 10.

Limitations: the results obtained using various DL models are far better in com-parison to standard methods. DL models, on the other hand, are very data-hungry and demand a huge amount of data, whereas medical applications like breast cancer classification are typically data-short. To get rid of this, researchers are frequently required to use artificial data augmenters as a pre-processing step. Furthermore, there is no guiding principle for choosing the appropriate hyper-parameters for these types of models. Moreover, unlike manually constructed models, DL algorithms are unable to provide users with feedback on the discriminative features that are utilized to determine each individual's diagnosis. Aside from HBC, there are several DL opportunities and a variety of web-based medical applications, each with its own set of constraints [92].

3.7 Technical paradigm-shifting from automated healthcare services to secure automated healthcare services

Cloud computing facilitates the collaborative training of huge model and thus over-come the resource constraint issues for big data analysis as well as the DL model. However, despite several advantages, it also raised concerns related to data privacy and model security. It becomes more challenging when we deal with sensitive infor-mation or data like in healthcare for model training where we cannot compromise privacy because any changes in both data as well as a model leads to wrong inter-pretation and can be life-threatening to the patient. Adversarial attacks, security vio-lations, influence attacks, poisoning, specificity attack and model stealing are all potential security threats to AI systems [93, 94]. It can be further sub-grouped into a white-box attack in which the model's parameters are accessible to the adversaries, whereas, in a black-box, it is not. Among the various adversarial attacks, security violations attempt to compromise integrity by supplying malicious data, whereas influence attacks try to obtain ownership of valuable data. Furthermore, privacy violations attempt to reveal confidential data used for model training. DL models are mostly used in computer vision and they are a popular target for adversaries. To undermine the integrity of DL frameworks, adversaries carefully design (unnoticeable) perturbations to the original training samples and are successful in misinterpretation of confidential data, which can be life-threatening in the case of healthcare applications or self-driving cars. As a result, adversarial attacks have arisen as a serious security risk for ML/DL systems [94–98]. As security concerns about DL-based approaches have been raised, research communities associated with critical and sensitive application domains such as healthcare automated systems, where data privacy, model security and secure predictive analysis are prominent, begin looking for solutions. As a result, in the new era of smart Health-tech and cloud-based clinical diagnostic frameworks, secure modelling and data privacy have appeared as active research areas.

Considering the prevailing demand, researchers are still working to address privacy concerns by proposing various models under the umbrella of private ML or privacy-preserved DL methods [99]. Another approach, a cooperative learning framework, has been proposed for addressing data privacy, in which the data owner of each client shared the encrypted form of data with each other and then globally trained the learning model. It is a common paradigm used by most cloud-based applications because learning models like DL require huge amounts of data for training, and in the healthcare domain, this data is collected from distributed sources or clients. In addition, different ML approaches, such as K-means [100], the naive-Bayes model [101], neural networks [102] and random decision trees [103, 104], are being tested in the same spirit of privacy preserved learning models, but with additional communication and computational cost. On the other hand, researchers have also made significant efforts to find a solution for an untrusted environment in which multiple clients are involved in solving a specific problem with their own data. In such cases, secure multiparty computation (SMPC) is a popular approach in which multiple clients contribute to model training without disclosing their own data, and SMPC assists in the securing learning model's parameters (weights) by utilizing a new technique known as federated learning (FL). FL is now widely used in distributed settings to secure models. However, an attacker can circumvent this secure training process by conducting a reverse-engineering attack and obtaining sensitive information from learning methods. As a result, the differentially private (DP) concept was introduced, which aids in data protection and paves the way for SMPC in a new direction in which even mutually distrusting clients can perform overall training of publicly known learning models without revealing anything.

Furthermore, three decades ago, the multiparty computation was theoretically introduced [105]. It is currently being used to solve real-world problems in which multiple clients can obtain predictive information from their data in a secure manner in which the learning model and query are hidden from other participants [106]. Several multi-party computation-based ML approaches have been proposed, such as Secure ML [107], HyCC [108], Gazelle [109], MinioNN [110], Secure NN [111], CHET [112], ABY3 [113] and so on. Moreover, the aforementioned methods are difficult to implement, and their performance with small datasets on small deep networks has only been reported. Recent work [114] has been presented by authors where they provided the solution that addressed the privacy and security concern of patients' data and model for cancer classification problems in a cloud-based model by utilizing DP-SGD and MPC. While in another work [115], the authors addressed the security concern in medical dataset classification by utilizing federated learning and knowledge distillation.

3.8   Future directions

It is worth mentioning that the healthcare industry revolution has created a plethora of opportunities in histopathology cancer analysis. The following are promising future directions that can be explored.

1. We can explore other potential deep architectures with an attention mechanism. We can also integrate a deep framework with other private prediction techniques. Another option is to design an efficient model for multi-class classification.
2. Quality of features in classification model plays a crucial role. The whole feature extraction and classification problem can be reformulated as a "multi-modal multi-task learning" to get an efficient framework for CAD.
3. It will be quite interesting and challenging to use "multi-modality information fusion" for histopathological cancer diagnosis. In this case, we can also analyse the genomic data of the same patient along with the features of a histopathological image extracted by feature descriptors or deep features for classification. In such cases, it would be advantageous to explore multi-task learning as a multi-objective optimization problem.
4. Future research should concentrate on developing a framework that can efficiently solve the multi-class problem by designing a more robust classification model using computational intelligence concepts such as fuzzy theory, etc.
5. It would also be intriguing to develop a more effective and trustworthy approach for edge-based histopathology image classification for cancer diagnosis that takes component-wise computing costs as well as energy consumption into account.
6. Availability of labelled data is one of the major challenges in developing a classification model; thus, an unsupervised technique can be adopted at the first stage. Deep active learning is still unexplored in this area that will also help in the auto-annotation of data and reduce the burden on pathologists for manual data labelling.
7. The proposed approaches are generalized so they can be used for solving different medical image classifications as well. Knowledge distillation with federated learning can be explored for the secure classification of histopathological cancer images.

3.9   Conclusion

A transformation in pathology is being witnessed as a result of the widespread adoption of digital pathology, which presents new horizons in the application of AI for cancer histopathology. In the era of smart technology, the healthcare domain has also evolved into smart HealthTech. Advanced technology and AI assist in providing personalized services to patients at a low cost and with ease. Even in cancer diagnosis, there are several tasks that are labour intensive and require high precision, such as identifying and classifying benign and malignant tumour tissues with high precision and accuracy. Furthermore, data annotation is a complex and time-consuming task; therefore, by utilizing smart technology and AI, several complex procedures are automated, which subsequently improves the diagnosis process in terms of quality and time, reduces error due to human interventions, and significantly contributes to smart healthcare services. Since AI is a rapidly evolving field, the latest developments in the area have opened up new avenues for developing improved models with higher accuracy than state-of-the-art. Therefore, this chapter briefly discussed the recent development, challenges and also highlighted the future possibilities in histopathological image analysis.

References

[1]   *Breast cancer [online]*. Available from https://www.who.int/news-room/fact-sheets/detail/breast-cancer

[2]   Grüntzig K., Graf R., Hässig M, *et al*. 'The Swiss Canine Cancer registry: a retrospective study on the occurrence of tumours in dogs in Switzerland from 1955 to 2008'. *Journal of Comparative Pathology*. 2015, vol. 152(2–3), pp. 161–71.

[3]   Egenvall A., Bonnett B.N., Ohagen P., Olson P., Hedhammar A., von Euler H. 'Incidence of and survival after mammary tumors in a population of over 80,000 insured female dogs in Sweden from 1995 to 2002'. *Preventive Veterinary Medicine*. 2005, vol. 69(1–2), pp. 109–27.

[4]   Pan X., Yang D., Li L, *et al*. 'Cell detection in pathology and microscopy images with multi-scale fully convolutional neural networks'. *World Wide Web*. 2018, vol. 21(6), pp. 1721–43.

[5]   Wang H., Cruz-Roa A., Basavanhally A, *et al*. 'Mitosis detection in breast cancer pathology images by combining handcrafted and convolutional neural network features'. *Journal of Medical Imaging (Bellingham, Wash.)*. 2014, vol. 1(3), p. 034003.

[6]   Baker Q.B., Zaitoun T.A., Banat S., Eaydat E., Alsmirat M. 'Automated detection of benign and malignant in breast histopathology images'. *2018 IEEE/ACS 15th International Conference on Computer Systems and Applications (AICCSA)*; Aqaba, Jordan, IEEE, USA, 2018. pp. 1–5.

[7]   Yassin N.I.R., Omran S., El Houby E.M.F., Allam H. 'Machine learning techniques for breast cancer computer aided diagnosis using different

image modalities: a systematic review'. *Computer Methods and Programs in Biomedicine*. 2018, vol. 156, pp. 25–45.

[8] Zhang Y., Zhang B., Coenen F., Lu W. 'Breast cancer diagnosis from biopsy images with highly reliable random subspace classifier ensembles'. *Machine Vision and Applications*. 2013, vol. 24(7), pp. 1405–20.

[9] Elmore J.G., Longton G.M., Carney P.A., *et al*. 'Diagnostic concordance among pathologists interpreting breast biopsy specimens'. *JAMA*. 2015, vol. 313(11), pp. 1122–32.

[10] Spanhol F.A., Oliveira L.S., Petitjean C., Heutte L. 'Breast cancer histopathological image classification using convolutional neural networks'. *International Joint Conference on Neural Networks (IJCNN)*; Vancouver, BC, Canada, IEEE, 2013. pp. 2560–67.

[11] Goceri E. 'Advances in digital pathology'. *International Journal of Emerging Trends in Health Sciences*. 2017, vol. 1(2), pp. 33–39.

[12] Kasban H., El-Bendary M., Salama D. 'A comparative study of medical imaging techniques'. *International Journal of Information Science and Intelligent System*. 2015, vol. 4(2), pp. 37–58.

[13] Rubin R., Strayer D.S., Rubin E, *et al*. *Rubin's Pathology: Clinicopathologic Foundations Of Medicine*. Philadelphia, PA: Lippincott Williams & Wilkins; 2008.

[14] Doi K. 'Computer-aided diagnosis in medical imaging: historical review, current status and future potential'. *Computerized Medical Imaging and Graphics*. 2007, vol. 31(4–5), pp. 198–211.

[15] Sadaf A., Crystal P., Scaranelo A., Helbich T. 'Performance of computer-aided detection applied to full-field digital mammography in detection of breast cancers'. *European Journal of Radiology*. 2011, vol. 77(3), pp. 457–61.

[16] Schneider M., Yaffe M. 'Better detection: improving our chances'. *5th International workshop on digital mammography (IWDM)*; Toronto, Canada, Medical Physics Publishing, 2000. pp. 3–6.

[17] Tang J., Rangayyan R.M., Xu J., El Naqa I., Yang Y. 'Computer-aided detection and diagnosis of breast cancer with mammography: recent advances'. *IEEE Transactions on Information Technology in Biomedicine*. 2009, vol. 13(2), pp. 236–51.

[18] Erickson B.J., Bartholmai B. 'Computer-aided detection and diagnosis at the start of the third millennium'. *Journal of Digital Imaging*. 2002, vol. 15(2), pp. 59–68.

[19] Sudharshan P.J., Petitjean C., Spanhol F., Oliveira L.E., Heutte L., Honeine P. 'Multiple instance learning for histopathological breast cancer image classification'. *Expert Systems with Applications*. 2019, vol. 117, pp. 103–11.

[20] Yao X., Wang X., Wang S.-H., Zhang Y.-D. 'A comprehensive survey on convolutional neural network in medical image analysis'. *Multimedia Tools and Applications*. 2019, pp. 1–45.

[21] Stenkvist B., Westman-Naeser S., Holmquist J, *et al.* 'Computerized nuclear morphometry as an objective method for characterizing human cancer cell populations'. *Cancer Research.* 1978, vol. 38(12), pp. 4688–97.

[22] Elston C.W., Ellis I.O. 'Pathological prognostic factors in breast cancer. I. the value of histological grade in breast cancer: experience from a large study with long-term follow-up'. *Histopathology.* 1991, vol. 19(5), pp. 403–10.

[23] Meijer G.A., Beliën J.A., van Diest P.J., Baak J.P. 'Origins of... image analysis in clinical pathology'. *Journal of Clinical Pathology.* 1997, vol. 50(5), pp. 365–70.

[24] Yang L., Meer P., Foran D.J. 'Unsupervised segmentation based on robust estimation and color active contour models'. *IEEE Transactions on Information Technology in Biomedicine.* 2005, vol. 9(3), pp. 475–86.

[25] Can A., Bello M., Cline H.E, *et al.* 'Multi-modal imaging of histological tissue sections'. *5th IEEE International Symposium on Biomedical Imaging (ISBI 2008)*; Paris, France, 2008.

[26] Alomari R.S., Karssemeijer N., Giger M.L., Allen R., Sabata B., Chaudhary V. 'Localization of tissues in high-resolution digital anatomic pathology images'. *SPIE Medical Imaging*; Lake Buena Vista, Florida, United States, International Society for Optics and Photonics, SPIE, 2009. pp. 726016.

[27] Irshad H., Veillard A., Roux L., Racoceanu D. 'Methods for nuclei detection, segmentation, and classification in digital histopathology: a review-current status and future potential'. *IEEE Reviews in Biomedical Engineering.* 2014, vol. 7, pp. 97–114.

[28] Oquab M., Bottou L., Laptev I., Sivic J. *IEEE Conference on Computer Vision and Pattern Recognition (CVPR)*; Columbus, OH, IEEE USA, 2009. pp. 1717–24.

[29] Spanhol F.A., Oliveira L.S., Petitjean C., Heutte L. 'A dataset for breast cancer histopathological image classification'. *IEEE Transactions on Bio-Medical Engineering.* 2016, vol. 63(7), pp. 1455–62.

[30] Spanhol F.A., Oliveira L.S., Petitjean C., Heutte L. 'Breast cancer histopathological image classification using convolutional neural networks'. *2016 International Joint Conference on Neural Networks (IJCNN)*; Vancouver, BC, Canada, IEEE USA, 2016. pp. 2560–67.

[31] Vahadane A., Peng T., Sethi A, *et al.* 'Structure-preserving color normalization and sparse stain separation for histological images'. *IEEE Transactions on Medical Imaging.* 2016, vol. 35(8), pp. 1962–71.

[32] Ehteshami Bejnordi B., Balkenhol M., Litjens G, *et al.* 'Automated detection of DCIS in whole-slide H&E stained breast histopathology images'. *IEEE Transactions on Medical Imaging.* 2016, vol. 35(9), pp. 2141–50.

[33] Abbas N., Zhang Y., Taherkordi A., Skeie T. 'Mobile edge computing: A survey'. *IEEE Internet of Things Journal.* 2017, vol. 5(1), pp. 450–65.

[34] Mooney P. *Breast histopathology images [online].* 2017. Available from https://www.kaggle.com/datasets/paultimothymooney/breast-histopathology-images

[35] Aresta G., Araújo T., Kwok S, *et al.* 'BACH: grand challenge on breast cancer histology images'. *Medical Image Analysis*. 2019, vol. 56, pp. 122–39.

[36] Kumar A., Singh S.K., Saxena S, *et al.* 'Deep feature learning for histopathological image classification of canine mammary tumors and human breast cancer'. *Information Sciences*. 2020, vol. 508, pp. 405–21.

[37] Litjens G., Bandi P., Ehteshami Bejnordi B, *et al.* '1399 H&E-stained sentinel lymph node sections of breast cancer patients: the CAMELYON dataset'. *GigaScience*. 2018, vol. 7(6).

[38] Ojala T., Pietikäinen M., Harwood D. 'A comparative study of texture measures with classification based on featured distributions'. *Pattern Recognition*. 2020, vol. 29(1), pp. 51–59.

[39] Ojala T., Pietikainen M., Maenpaa T. 'Multiresolution gray-scale and rotation invariant texture classification with local binary patterns'. *IEEE Transactions on Pattern Analysis and Machine Intelligence*. 2020, vol. 24(7), pp. 971–87.

[40] Haralick R.M., Shanmugam K., Dinstein I.H. 'Textural features for image classification'. *IEEE Transactions on Systems, Man, and Cybernetics*. 2020, vol. SMC-3(6), pp. 610–21.

[41] Ojansivu V., Heikkilä J. 'Blur insensitive texture classification using local phase quantization'. *International Conference on Image and Signal Processing*; Cherbourg-Octeville, France, Berlin, Heidelberg: Springer, 2008. pp. 236–43.

[42] Rublee E., Rabaud V., Konolige K., Bradski G. 'Orb: an efficient alternative to SIFT or SURF'. *IEEE International Conference on Computer Vision (ICCV)*; Barcelona, Spain, 2011. pp. 2564.

[43] Coelho L.P., Ahmed A., Arnold A, *et al.* 'Structured literature image finder: extracting information from text and images in biomedical literature' in *Linking Literature, Information, and Knowledge For Biology*. Springer; 2010. pp. 23–32.

[44] Boser B.E., Guyon I.M., Vapnik V.N. 'A training algorithm for optimal margin classifiers'. *The Fifth Annual Workshop*; Pittsburgh, Pennsylvania, United States, New York, New York, USA, 1992. pp. 144–52. Available from http://portal.acm.org/citation.cfm?doid=130385

[45] Weinberger K.Q., Saul L.K. 'Distance metric learning for large margin nearest neighbor classification'. *Journal of Machine Learning Research*. 2009, vol. 10(2).

[46] Tharwat A. 'Linear vs. quadratic discriminant analysis classifier: a tutorial'. *International Journal of Applied Pattern Recognition*. 2016, vol. 3(2), p. 145.

[47] Lepetit V., Fua P. 'Keypoint recognition using randomized trees'. *IEEE Transactions on Pattern Analysis and Machine Intelligence*. 2006, vol. 28(9), pp. 1465–79.

[48] Chan A., Tuszynski J.A. 'Automatic prediction of tumour malignancy in breast cancer with fractal dimension'. *Royal Society Open Science*. 2016, vol. 3(12), p. 160558.

[49] Mandelbrot B.B., Mandelbrot B.B. *The fractal geometry of nature.* Vol. 1. WH Freeman New York; 1982.

[50] Samah A.A., Fauzi M.F.A., Mansor S. 'Classification of benign and malignant tumors in histopathology images'. *2017 IEEE International Conference on Signal and Image Processing Applications (ICSIPA)*; Kuching, Sarawak, Malaysia, IEEE, 2016. pp. 102–06.

[51] Kahya M.A., Al-Hayani W., Algamal Z.Y. 'Classification of breast cancer histopathology images based on adaptive sparse support vector machine'. *Journal of Applied Mathematics and Bioinformatics.* 2017, vol. 7(1), pp. 49–69.

[52] Liao C., Li S., Luo Z. 'Gene selection using Wilcoxon Rank sum test and support vector machine for cancer classification'. *International Conference on Computational and Information Science*; Berlin, Heidelberg: Springer, 2006. pp. 57–66.

[53] Sanchez-Morillo D., González J., García-Rojo M, *et al.* 'Classification of breast cancer histopathological images using KAZE features'. *International Conference on Bioinformatics and Biomedical Engineering*; Granada (Spain), Springer, Cham, 2018. pp. 276–86.

[54] Alcantarilla P.F., Bartoli A., Davison A.J. 'KAZE features'. *European Conference On Computer Vision*; Florence, Italy, Berlin, Heidelberg: Springer, 2012. pp. 214–27.

[55] Kumar A., Singh S.K., Saxena S, *et al.* 'CoMHisP: A novel feature extractor for histopathological image classification based on fuzzy SVM with within-class relative density'. *IEEE Transactions on Fuzzy Systems.* 2021, vol. 29(1), pp. 103–17.

[56] Singh R., Bharti V., Purohit V., Kumar A., Singh A.K., Singh S.K. 'MetaMed: few-shot medical image classification using gradient-based meta-learning'. *Pattern Recognition.* 2021, vol. 120, 108111.

[57] LeCun Y., Boser B., Denker J, *et al.* 'Handwritten digit recognition with a back-propagation network'. *Advances in Neural Information Processing Systems.* 1989, vol. 2.

[58] Krizhevsky A., Sutskever I., Hinton G.E. 'Imagenet classification with deep convolutional neural networks' in *Advances In Neural Information Processing Systems.* Vol. 25; 2012. pp. 1097–105.

[59] Nahid A.A., Kong Y. 'Histopathological breast-image classification using local and frequency domains by convolutional neural network'. *Information.* 2021, vol. 9(1), p. 19.

[60] He K., Zhang X., Ren S., Sun J. 'Deep residual learning for image recognition'. *IEEE Conference on Computer Vision and Pattern Recognition (CVPR)*; Las Vegas, NV, IEEE, 2021. pp. 770–78.

[61] Do M.N., Vetterli M. 'The contourlet transform: an efficient directional multiresolution image representation'. *IEEE Transactions on Image Processing.* 2005, vol. 14(12), pp. 2091–106.

[62] Xu J., Xiang L., Hang R., Wu J. 'Stacked sparse autoencoder (SSAE) based framework for nuclei patch classification on breast cancer histopathology'.

2014 IEEE 11th International Symposium on Biomedical Imaging (ISBI 2014); Beijing, China, IEEE, 2014. pp. 999–1002.

[63] Xu J., Xiang L., Liu Q, *et al*. 'Stacked sparse autoencoder (SSAE) for nuclei detection on breast cancer histopathology images'. *IEEE Transactions on Medical Imaging*. 2016, vol. 35(1), pp. 119–30.

[64] Kadam V.J., Jadhav S.M., Vijayakumar K. 'Breast cancer diagnosis using feature ensemble learning based on stacked sparse autoencoders and softmax regression'. *Journal of Medical Systems*. 2019, vol. 43(8), pp. 1–11.

[65] Greenspan H., van Ginneken B., Summers R.M. 'Guest editorial deep learning in medical imaging: overview and future promise of an exciting new technique'. *IEEE Transactions on Medical Imaging*. 2016, vol. 35(5), pp. 1153–59.

[66] Zhou S.K., Greenspan H., Shen D. *Deep learning for medical image analysis*. London, United Kingdom: Academic Press; 2017.

[67] Bar Y., Diamant I., Wolf L., Lieberman S., Konen E., Greenspan H. 'Chest pathology detection using deep learning with non-medical training'. *2015 IEEE 12th International Symposium on Biomedical Imaging (ISBI 2015)*; Brooklyn, NY: ISBI. Citeseer, 2015. pp. 294–97.

[68] Ciompi F., de Hoop B., van Riel S.J, *et al*. 'Automatic classification of pulmonary peri-fissural nodules in computed tomography using an ensemble of 2D views and a convolutional neural network out-of-the-box'. *Medical Image Analysis*. 2015, vol. 26(1), pp. 195–202.

[69] Singh R., Ahmed T., Kumar A., Singh A.K., Pandey A.K., Singh S.K. 'Imbalanced breast cancer classification using transfer learning'. *IEEE/ACM Transactions on Computational Biology and Bioinformatics*. 2021, vol. 18(1), pp. 83–93.

[70] Araújo T., Aresta G., Castro E, *et al*. 'Bioimaging challenge 2015 breast histology dataset'. *INESC TEC*. 2017. Available from https://rdm.inesctec.pt/dataset/nis-2017-003

[71] Zhi W., Yueng H.W.F., Chen Z, *et al*. 'Using transfer learning with convolutional neural networks to diagnose breast cancer from histopathological images'. *International Conference on Neural Information Processing (ICONIP 2017)*; Guangzhou, China, Springer, Cham, 2017. pp. 669–76.

[72] Lee S.-J., Chen T., Yu L., Lai C.-H. 'Image classification based on the boost convolutional neural network'. *IEEE Access: Practical Innovations, Open Solutions*. 2018, vol. 6, pp. 12755–68.

[73] Zhang G., Xiao M., Yh H. 'Histopathological image recognition with domain knowledge based deep features'. *International Conference on Intelligent Computing (ICIC 2018)*; Springer, Cham, 2018. pp. 349–59.

[74] Spanhol F.A., Oliveira L.S., Cavalin P.R, *et al*. 'Deep features for breast cancer histopathological image classification'. *2017 IEEE International Conference on systems, man, and cybernetics (SMC)*; Banff Canada, IEEE, 2017. pp. 1868–73.

[75] Donahue J., Jia Y., Vinyals O, *et al*. 'DECAF: A deep convolutional activation feature for generic visual recognition'. *International Conference on Machine Learning*; Beijing China, PMLR, 2014. pp. 647–55.

[76] Cascianelli S., Bello-Cerezo R., Bianconi F, *et al*. 'Dimensionality reduction strategies for CNN-based classification of histopathological images'. *International Conference on Intelligent Interactive Multimedia Systems and Services*; Gold Coast, Australia, Springer, Cham, 2018. pp. 21–30.

[77] Simonyan K., Zisserman A. 'Very deep convolutional networks for large-scale image recognition'. *ArXiv Preprint*. 2014, arXiv:14091556.

[78] Gupta V., Bhavsar A. 'Sequential modeling of deep features for breast cancer histopathological image classification'. *2018 IEEE/CVF Conference on Computer Vision and Pattern Recognition Workshops (CVPRW)*; Salt Lake City, UT, IEEE, 2018. pp. 2254–2261.

[79] Chen T., Guestrin C. 'Xgboost: A scalable tree boosting system'. *Proceedings of the 22nd ACM Sigkdd International Conference on Knowledge Discovery and Data Mining*; San Francisco California USA, NY, United States: Association for Computing Machinery, 2016. pp. 785–794.

[80] Huang G., Liu Z., Van Der Maaten L., Weinberger K.Q. 'Densely connected convolutional networks'. *2017 IEEE Conference on Computer Vision and Pattern Recognition (CVPR)*; Honolulu, HI, 2018. pp. 4700–08. Available from https://ieeexplore.ieee.org/xpl/mostRecentIssue.jsp?punumber=8097368

[81] Alom M.Z., Yakopcic C., Nasrin M.S., Taha T.M., Asari V.K. 'Breast cancer classification from histopathological images with inception recurrent residual convolutional neural network'. *Journal of Digital Imaging*. 2019, vol. 32(4), pp. 605–17.

[82] Bayramoglu N., Kannala J., Heikkila J. 'Deep learning for magnification independent breast cancer histopathology image classification'. *23rd International Conference on Pattern Recognition (ICPR)*; Cancún, Mexico, IEEE, 2016. pp. 2440–2445.

[83] Kassani S.H., Kassani P.H., Wesolowski M.J, *et al*. 'Classification of histopathological biopsy images using ensemble of deep learning networks'. *ArXiv Preprint*. 2019, arXiv:190911870.

[84] Budak Ü., Cömert Z., Rashid Z.N., Şengür A., Çıbuk M. 'Computer-aided diagnosis system combining FCN and bi-LSTM model for efficient breast cancer detection from histopathological images'. *Applied Soft Computing*. 2019, vol. 85, 105765.

[85] Khan S., Islam N., Jan Z., Ud Din I., Rodrigues J.J.P.C. 'A novel deep learning based framework for the detection and classification of breast cancer using transfer learning'. *Pattern Recognition Letters*. 2019, vol. 125, pp. 1–6.

[86] Li J., Zhang J., Sun Q, *et al*. 'Breast cancer histopathological image classification based on deep second-order pooling network'. *2020 International Joint Conference on Neural Networks (IJCNN)*; Glasgow, United Kingdom, IEEE, 2017. pp. 1–7. Available from https://ieeexplore.ieee.org/xpl/mostRecentIssue.jsp?punumber=9200848

[87] Kumar A., Sharma A., Bharti V., Singh A.K., Singh S.K., Saxena S. 'MobiHisNet: a lightweight CNN in mobile edge computing for histopathological image classification'. *IEEE Internet of Things Journal*. 2017, vol. 8(24), pp. 17778–89.

[88] Akbar S., Peikari M., Salama S, *et al.* 'Transitioning between convolutional and fully connected layers in neural networks' in *Deep learning in medical image analysis and multimodal learning for clinical decision support*. Québec City, Canada: Springer, Cham; 2017. pp. 143–150.

[89] Nejad E.M., Affendey L.S., Latip R.B., Bin Ishak I. 'Classification of histopathology images of breast into benign and malignant using a single-layer convolutional neural network'. *the International Conference*; Penang, Malaysia, New York, NY, 2017. pp. 50–53. Available from http://dl.acm.org/citation.cfm?doid=3132300

[90] Wei B., Han Z., He X. 'Deep learning model based breast cancer histopathological image classification'. *2017 IEEE 2nd International Conference on Cloud Computing and Big Data Analysis (ICCCBDA*; IEEE, 2017. pp. 348–53.

[91] Badejo J.A., Adetiba E., Akinrinmade A, *et al.* 'Medical image classification with hand-designed or machine-designed texture descriptors: a performance evaluation'. *International Conference on Bioinformatics and Biomedical Engineering*; Springer, Cham, 2018. pp. 266–275.

[92] Senaras C., Gurcan M.N. 'Deep learning for medical image analysis'. *Journal of Pathology Informatics*. 2018, vol. 9(1), 25.

[93] Fredrikson M., Jha S., Ristenpart T. 'Model inversion attacks that exploit confidence information and basic countermeasures'. *Proceedings of the 22nd ACM SIGSAC Conference on Computer and Communications Security*; New York, NY, 2015.

[94] Goodfellow I.J., Shlens J., Szegedy C. 'Explaining and harnessing adversarial examples'. *ArXiv Preprint*. 2014, arXiv:14126572.

[95] Szegedy C., Zaremba W., Sutskever I, *et al.* 'Intriguing properties of neural networks'. *ArXiv Preprint*. 2013, arXiv:13126199.

[96] Papernot N., McDaniel P., Jha S., Fredrikson M., Celik Z.B., Swami A. 'The limitations of deep learning in adversarial settings'. *2016 IEEE European Symposium on Security and Privacy (EuroS&P)*; Saarbrücken, Germany, IEEE, 2017. pp. 372–387.

[97] Papernot N., McDaniel P., Goodfellow I., Jha S., Celik Z.B., Swami A. 'Practical black-box attacks against machine learning'. *ASIA CCS '17*; Abu Dhabi, UAE, 2017. pp. 506–519. Available from https://dl.acm.org/doi/proceedings/10.1145/3052973

[98] Usama M., Qadir J., Al-Fuqaha A., Hamdi M. 'The adversarial machine learning conundrum: can the insecurity of ML become the Achilles' heel of cognitive networks?'. *IEEE Network*. 2019, vol. 34(1), pp. 196–203.

[99] Qayyum A., Qadir J., Bilal M., Al-Fuqaha A. 'Secure and robust machine learning for healthcare: A survey'. *IEEE Reviews in Biomedical Engineering*. 2021, vol. 14, pp. 156–180.

[100]   Jagannathan G., Wright R.N. 'Privacy-preserving distributed k-means clus-
        tering over arbitrarily partitioned data'. *Proceeding of the Eleventh ACM
        SIGKDD International Conference*; Chicago, IL, 2017. pp. 593–599.
        Available from http://portal.acm.org/citation.cfm?doid=1081870
[101]   Vaidya J., Shafiq B., Basu A., Hong Y. 'Differentially private naive bayes
        classification'. *IEEE/WIC/ACM International Joint Conferences on Web
        Intelligence (WI) and Intelligent Agent Technologies (IAT)*; Atlanta, Georgia,
        IEEE, 2013. pp. 571–576.
[102]   Shokri R., Shmatikov V. 'Privacy-preserving deep learning'. *CCS'15*; Denver,
        CO, 2015. Available from https://dl.acm.org/doi/proceedings/10.1145/2810103
[103]   Lindell Y., Pinkas B. 'Privacy preserving data mining' in *Advances in cryp-
        tology — CRYPTO 2000*. Lecture Notes in Computer Science. Berlin, hei-
        delberg: Springer; 2000. pp. 36–54.
[104]   Vaidya J., Shafiq B., Fan W., Mehmood D., Lorenzi D. 'A random decision
        tree framework for privacy-preserving data mining'. *IEEE Transactions on
        Dependable and Secure Computing*. 2013, vol. 11(5), pp. 399–411.
[105]   Yao A.C.C. 'How to generate and exchange secrets'. *27th Annual Symposium
        on Foundations of Computer Science (SFCS 1986)*; IEEE, USA, 1986. pp.
        162–167.
[106]   Goldreich O., Micali S., Wigderson A. 'How to play any mental game, or
        a completeness theorem for protocols with honest majority' in *Providing
        sound foundations for cryptography: on the work of Shafi Goldwasser and
        Silvio Micalishafi Goldwasser and Silvio Micali*. NY, USA: Association for
        Computing Machinery; 2019. pp. 307–28.
[107]   Mohassel P., Zhang Y. 'SecureML: A system for scalable privacy-preserving
        machine learning'. *2017 IEEE Symposium on Security and Privacy (SP)*;
        San Jose, CA, USA, IEEE, USA, 2019. pp. 19–38.
[108]   Büscher N., Demmler D., Katzenbeisser S, *et al*. 'HyCC: compilation of
        hybrid protocols for practical secure computation'. *Proceedings of the 2018
        ACM SIGSAC Conference on Computer and Communications Security*;
        2018. pp. 847–861.
[109]   Juvekar C., Vaikuntanathan V., Chandrakasan A. 'GAZELLE: A low la-
        tency framework for secure neural network inference'. *27th USENIX
        Security Symposium (USENIX Security 18)*; Baltimore, Maryland, USENIX
        Association, USA, 2018. pp. 1651–69.
[110]   Liu J., Juuti M., Lu Y., Asokan N. 'Oblivious neural network predictions via
        minion transformations'. *CCS '17*; Dallas, TX, 2019. pp. 619–631. Available
        from https://dl.acm.org/doi/proceedings/10.1145/3133956
[111]   Wagh S., Gupta D., Chandran N. 'SecureNN: 3-party secure computation for
        neural network training'. *Proceedings on Privacy Enhancing Technologies*.
        2019, vol. 2019(3), pp. 26–49.
[112]   Dathathri R., Saarikivi O., Chen H, *et al*. 'CHET: an optimizing compiler for
        fully-homomorphic neural-network inferencing'. *PLDI '19*; Phoenix, AZ,
        2019. pp. 142–156. Available from https://dl.acm.org/doi/proceedings/10.
        1145/3314221

[113] Mohassel P., Rindal P. 'ABY3: A mixed protocol framework for machine learning'. *2018 ACM SIGSAC Conference on Computer and Communications Security*; Toronto Canada, NY United States: Association for Computing Machinery, 2018. pp. 35–52.

[114] Kumar A., Singh S.K., Lakshmanan K., Saxena S., Shrivastava S. 'A novel cloud-assisted secure deep feature classification framework for cancer histopathology images'. *ACM Transactions on Internet Technology*. 2021, vol. 21(2), pp. 1–22.

[115] Kumar A., Purohit V., Bharti V., Singh R., Singh S.K. 'MediSecFed: private and secure medical image classification in the presence of malicious clients'. *IEEE Transactions on Industrial Informatics*. 2021, vol. 18(8), pp. 5648–5657.

Chapter 4
Terahertz imaging in healthcare
Isha Malhotra[1] and Ghanshyam Singh[2]

Terahertz (THz) is an electromagnetic spectrum with a frequency range from 0.1 to 10 THz, which is located in between the microwave and infrared regions. The unique features of THz waves make them eligible for use in various medical applications. The THz imaging is one of them, which is mainly based on the analysis and processing of the transmission and reflection spectrum information of the sample. This chapter mainly presents the research status and prospects of several THz medical imaging systems and their applications for medical imaging in biological tissues. As the demand for technology grows, high-performance THz imaging systems are becoming indispensable. The ability of the THz time-domain spectroscopy (THz-TDS) system to extract spectra from amplitude and phase information opens virtually unlimited possibilities for imaging applications. The performance achievements of THz-TDS-based imaging with potential research on its fast-imaging components for solving the existing limitations of imaging speed are also presented. Furthermore, the latest developments of several THz-TDS-based imaging methods, including tomography imaging and near-field imaging, are highlighted with their performance improvement. Additionally, the rapid development of THz-TDS as a highly versatile analytical tool for the characterisation of pharmaceutical materials has drawn considerable attention. One of the greatest biomedical potentials of THz imaging is the use of molecular spectroscopy for diagnostics, which is exponentially advanced and moving closer to progress. It is now evident that different types of biomolecules leave distinctive spectral fingerprints in the THz region, which considerably widens the coverage of its technology application including in-vitro and in-vivo measurements of small molecules of clinical importance in point of care and diagnostic systems. In-vivo molecular imaging is considered the next frontier in medical diagnostics, which would be ideally performed non-invasively. Recent achievements in the field of medical imaging have dramatically enhanced the early detection and treatment of many pathological conditions. THz imaging systems can help in

[1]Department of Electronics and Communication Engineering, Global Institute of Technology and Management, Gurugram, India
[2]Centre for Smart Information and Communication Systems, Department of Electrical and Electronic Engineering Science, University of Johannesburg, Johannesburg, South Africa

detecting early cancer before it is visible or sensitive to any other identification resources. The THz images can distinguish between healthy tissue and basal cell carcinoma and therefore help in mapping the exact margins of early-stage tumours. By obtaining both frequency and time-domain information, the THz imaging can ensure enhanced detection of cancer and provide sharper imaging and molecular fingerprinting. THz biomedical imaging has become a modality of interest due to its ability to simultaneously acquire both image and spectral information. Advanced digital image processing algorithms are greatly needed to assist in screening, diagnosis and treatment. Finally, we summarise the obstacles in the way of the application of THz biomedical imaging application technology in clinical detection, which need to be investigated and overcome in the future.

4.1   Introduction

Terahertz (THz) technology based on thermal radiation has exceptionally in use for several applications. The THz region of the electromagnetic spectrum (300 GHz to 10 THz) is found between electronic and optical signal generation schemes [1], i.e., a gap that lies between microwave and infrared. As reported in Reference [2], the global THz market had reached nearly \$318.6 million and is still progressive in growth, which is expected to exceed \$906.2 million by 2024. With the development of ultra-fast time-domain spectroscopy (TDS) systems using advanced THz sources and detectors, a growing number of research groups and companies are now getting involved to investigate more about THz technologies, especially in the range of sensing and imaging applications. The significant possessions of THz radiations in the field of sensing and imaging applications are the abilities of THz waves to penetrate materials such as paper, plastics and organic compounds, including human tissues and cloth but not metals. Moreover, in comparison with hazardous ionising radiation such as X-rays, THz radiations do not provide potential damage to human tissues nor trigger detrimental reactions in human tissues because of low photon energies. Furthermore, it provides a means of identifying specific materials by using their characteristic spectra. Since molecular rotations and vibrations occur in the THz range, it can be used to identify deoxyribonucleic acid (DNA) and for other medical diagnosis purposes.

Over recent years, the commercial availability of optically pumped THz lasers and laser-gated semiconductor sources (photosensitive semiconductors with a pair of antennas etched onto their surface) has advanced the usage of THz waves for several applications in multiple sectors, such as healthcare for the detection of tumour and its characterisation, detection of a decayed tooth, etc., pharmaceuticals for the purpose of characterisation of tablet coating and identifying packaging defects, aerospace and automotive industry for damage or defect detection in a space shuttle and painted vehicle panels, respectively, security applications to detect concealed weapons and explosives, material science and microelectronics for characterising and testing materials and inspecting silicon wafers and electronic components. THz

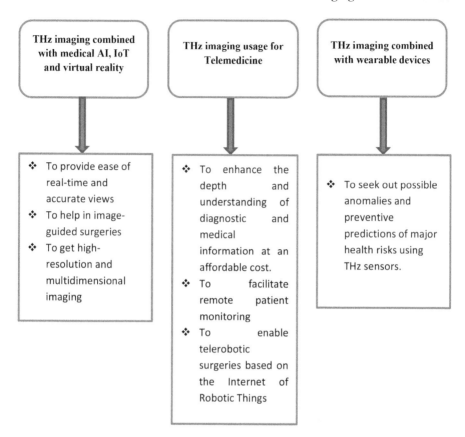

Figure 4.1   Promising fields of THz imaging for advanced medical THz healthcare technologies

wave yields can penetrate materials and provide high-resolution imaging, which are required promising features for biomedical and healthcare technologies.

Currently, most of the medical imaging in the healthcare sector is performed using X-rays, ultrasounds, computed tomography scans and magnetic resonance imaging (MRI) techniques; however, with the development of the effective use of electromagnetic imaging techniques such as THz imaging, infrared imaging and thermography, preferred choices are becoming diversified in the medical sector. Figure 4.1 shows the promising scope of amalgamation of high-end technology with electromagnetic imaging techniques under an effective area of research and development for deploying THz healthcare technologies. An artificial intelligence (AI)-integrated THz technology has the potential to enhance healthcare performance in terms of remote patient monitoring, medical information technology, medical data analysis and accurate diagnosis with proper decision-making technology. The THz technology contributes to supporting such sectors in terms of quality control, operation, preventive healthcare and non-destructive evaluation. In THz medical imaging, the obtained intrinsic properties and morphological information about the suspected area can be combined in an image-spectrum merging modality from which amplitude-phase information can be found synchronously [3].

Moreover, in comparison with MRI, THz medical imaging has a significant penetration depth of up to a few hundred micrometres which is useful for intraoperative imaging and identification of distinctive molecular fingerprints using miniaturised instruments. However, certain factors do affect crucially the THz medical imaging, such as (1) the higher interstitial water present around tumorous, unhealthy and diseased tissues due to abundant vascularity can alter the results obtained through THz absorption, (2) variation in THz image contrast due to morphology, deterioration and compositional alterations in the cellular structure of tissues and (3) enhancement

Table 4.1   THz wave features usable in biomedical and healthcare technology [3]

Feature	Biomedical application
Spectral fingerprint	The characteristic spectral signatures of biomolecules can be measured in the THz range. It happens because of the molecule-specific motion in terms of vibration, rotation and translation that can be observed when the photon energy of the THz wave gets to coincide with energy levels of low-frequency motion of the molecular skeleton.
Transparency of materials comprising non-polar molecules	To detect hazardous substances without opening packages, THz waves can be used as most of the packaging material either paper or plastic is transparent in the THz range. The THz wave can penetrate easily such common packing materials.
Strong absorption by water	At 1 THz, the absorption coefficient of water is nearly 220 cm^{-1} at room temperature. Therefore, THz radiations have the potential to determine the living state of bacteria on the basis of different hydration levels in it. Moreover, using the THz wave it is easier to differentiate normal tissue from cancer tissue as the water content is different in the two types.
Excellent time and spatial resolution	THz spectroscopy provides time-resolved investigations about the collective vibration modes of biomolecules in solution with exceptional sensing capability. It also reveals time-resolved dynamics of near-field spectroscopic modalities on the sub-picosecond to picosecond timescales having a spatial resolution of several micrometres.
Non-invasive and non-ionising properties	THz wave can be applied for in vivo real-time diagnosis without causing ionization damage. THz wave being longer in wavelength in comparison to infrared and visible light offers negligible scattering losses in biological tissues.

in sensitivity of THz molecular imaging due to absorption of water and higher temperature variations. However, with an advanced THz imaging system such challenges can be minimized as the THz spectrum has offered multiple usages with its salient features for biomedical and healthcare technology as listed in Table 4.1.

For THz medical imaging, either passive or active imaging systems are used. In 2002, StarTiger developed a 16-pixel passive THz imaging chip, which created the first THz image of a human hand. Later, in 2004, ThruVision developed T4000 and T5000 systems having the capability to create images from stationary or mobile targets through THz radiation exposure of an object hidden beneath a person's clothing or baggage screening. Such systems were effectively used and deployed at the Canary Wharf complex in London for the purpose of security, law enforcement and anti-terrorism checking systems to detect concealed weapons and solid/liquid explosives.

Another cost-effective passive THz imaging system TeraEye was developed under the European sixth framework programme in 2007. The THz passive detector had a hybrid structure of nano-fabricated semiconductor quantum dot with a coupled metal single electron transistor. The sensitivity of the system exceeds as it converts a single THz photon into 10 million electrons. Correspondingly, a passive 2D scanning imaging system operates at 0.85 THz, which was developed at the University of Massachusetts. The system comprises a hot electron bolometer as a superconducting device that measures THz radiation after mixing it with a stable internal THz signal and the resultant temperature difference seemed prominent to be used in the healthcare sector to identify the difference between tumours and healthy tissues. Some of the prominent THz passive imaging systems developed during early stage are shown in Figure 4.2.

Passively emitted THz signals are generally weak such that the system takes about 20 minutes to create a single 40×40 pixel image. Therefore, the researchers are also showing more inclination towards active THz imaging systems for faster scanning and better spatial resolution. In 2007, the AT&T research lab licensed Picometrix and launched the active THz imaging system T-Ray 4000, which operates in either reflection or transmission mode. T-Ray 4000 featured fibre-coupled

(a)

(b)

Figure 4.2 (a) The ThruVision THz camera and an image of a person created on a laptop; (b) the T5000 tripod mounted on a pan/tilt unit with 25 m imaging range (passive imaging systems) [4]

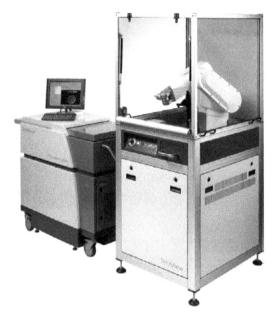

Figure 4.3   TPI imaga 2000 active imaging system enabled with robotic tablet handling system

sensor heads allow rapid creation of scanned images using picosecond duration THz pulses. Toshiba's European research centre at Cambridge had also developed flat-bed scanning system TeraView for material identification and analysis.

Other scanning systems, such as TPI imaga 1000 and TPI imaga 2000, have also been developed by the company, which are based on Ti:sapphire laser-gated photoconductive semiconductor emitter as a source in active THz imaging systems for healthcare, dentistry and pharmaceutical industry for material characterisation, tablet coating, core inspection, dislocations delamination in single and multilayer tablet cores. Figure 4.3 shows TPI imaga 2000 coupled to the robotic tablet handling system. The system has a spatial resolution of 160 μm at 2.58 THz at the surface and 320 μm at a depth of 1 mm with a penetration depth of 3 mm.

Moreover, it is likely predicted that THz imaging for the healthcare sector will complement existing imaging systems thereby offering greater power and sensitivity at a reduced cost. One such amalgamated system developed based on THz computed tomography (THz-CT) showed the potential to directly measure the transmitted amplitude and phase of broadband THz pulses at multiple projection angles to extract a large amount of information about the target including its 3D structure and frequency-dependent optical properties. Near-field interferometric, synthetic aperture THz imaging and laser THz emission microscopy are other promising systems that are proved to be very useful in the healthcare sector. This chapter focuses on current state-of-the-art medical imaging techniques and their performance comparison. A detailed review of THz antennas used in medical healthcare applications has also been discussed. Further sections of the chapter also include the description of the THz medical imaging system to observe biological tissues and the effective use of THz-TDS for the same. Most recently, the utilisation of machine learning (ML) techniques for analysing THz images has also been included in the discussion. The limitations of the THz imaging system, which need to be addressed for future work, are also mentioned, which will create interest of readers for the relevant research area considering the mentioned recommendations at the end of this chapter.

4.2 Comparative study of medical imaging techniques

The non-invasive medical imaging techniques are extensively in use for looking inside the body without performing surgery on the body. The techniques such as X-ray radiography [5, 6], computed tomography [7–10], positron emission tomography [11, 12], single-photon emission-computed tomography [13], optical imaging [14], MRI [15], ultrasonography [16], thermography [17] and THz imaging [18] are the prominent medical imaging techniques, and each of them has different salient features as well as risks of usage. With respect to spatial resolution, contrast, the effect of ionising radiation and the heating effect of radiation on the human body, it is important to understand the comparison of all these medical imaging techniques. Along with this, it is also important to locate the effectiveness of real-time information provided by these techniques including the cost involved with each of them. A basic medical imaging system as shown in Figure 4.4 consists of a source of energy that penetrates the human body. The energy gets passed through the body and is absorbed/attenuated at different levels. The signals are created from the extracted values of varying densities and the atomic numbers of different body tissues. These signals are then detected using special detectors that are compatible with the used energy source. Using mathematical algorithms, an image is created through the energy received from human tissue, which helps to determine classification based on applied energy to the body.

There are several techniques that can be used to look inside the body of the patient. Many of these techniques consider a signal travelling directly from the patient through absorption or attenuation. Table 4.2 highlights some of such medical imaging techniques that are prominent in use.

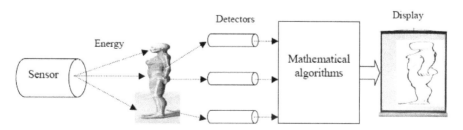

Figure 4.4   General concept of medical imaging system [19]

Table 4.2   Features, risks and applications of prominent medical imaging techniques.

Type of medical imaging	Features	Risks or limitations in its use	Applications
X-ray radiography	• Non-invasive, quick and painless. • Support medical and surgical treatment planning. • Guide medical personnel as the practitioner inserts catheters or stents inside the body to treat tumours or to remove blood clots.	• Exposure to ionising radiation that makes the body prone to development of cancer at later stage. • Tissues get affected such as cataracts, skin reddening and hair loss, which occur at high levels of radiation exposure.	• Used in chiropractic, dental surgeries. • Fluoroscopy radiographs are used for showing the movement of organs (stomach, intestine, colon, etc.). It can also be used for studding the blood vessels of the heart and the brain. • Projectional radiographs are used to determine the type and extent of a fracture and are also useful for detecting pathological changes in the lungs. • Mammography used for diagnosing and screening of the breast tissue. • Bone densitometry used for measuring bone mineral content and density. • Arthrography used to examine the inside view of joint.

(Continues)

Table 4.2   Continued

Type of medical imaging	Features	Risks or limitations in its use	Applications
X-Ray-computed tomography	• Non-invasive, quick and painless. • Good spatial resolution. • Global view of veins. • Distinguished by small differences in physical density. • Avoid invasive insertion of an arterial catheter and guidewire.	• No real-time information. • Exposure can cause later stage cancer. • Cannot detect intra-luminal abnormalities. • Cannot be performed without contrast (allergy or toxicity). • Less contrast resolution where soft tissue contrast is low.	• Examining several human body parts such as brain, facial bones, sinus, dental, spines, cervical, hands, wrist, elbow, shoulder, hip, knee, ankle, foot, etc. • Diagnosing disease, trauma and abnormality. • Planning and guiding the interventional or therapeutic procedures. • Monitoring the effectiveness of therapy of cancer treatment.
Magnetic resonance imaging (MRI)	• Non-invasive and painless. • Without ionising radiation. • High spatial resolution. • Operator independent. • Easy to blind and ability to measure flow and velocity with advanced technique. • Can be performed without contrast. • Good soft tissue contrast.	• Relatively low sensitivity. • Long scan and post processing time. • Mass quantity of the probe is required. • Cannot detect intra-luminal abnormalities. • Can make some people feel claustrophobic. • Sedation may be required for young children who cannot remain still. • Relatively expensive.	• Examining the abnormalities of the brain and spinal cord. • To examine tumours, cysts injuries and abnormalities of the joint. • Examining the disease of the liver and other abdominal organs. • Finding unhealthy tissue in the body. • Planning the surgery. • Providing a global view of collateral veins. • Providing a global view of intra and extra cranial.

(Continues)

Table 4.2   Continued

Type of medical imaging	Features	Risks or limitations in its use	Applications
Ultrasonography	• Non-invasive and painless • Without using ionising radiation. • High resolution. • Real-time information. • Sensitive to detect flow changes, intra- and extra-luminal abnormalities. • Ability to measure velocity. • Possible control of respiratory phases.	• No standardized guidelines. • Operator dependent. • Time consuming. • Blinding procedures are challenging. • Cannot perform global view of the veins. • Influenced by hydration status.	• Checking the development of the foetus during pregnancy. • Imaging most structures of the head, neck including thyroid and parathyroid glands, lymph nodes and salivary glands. • Imaging the solid organs of the abdomen such as pancreas, aorta, inferior vena cava, liver, gall bladder, bile ducts, kidney and spleen. • Guiding the injecting of needles when placing local anaesthetic solutions near nerves. • Echocardiography used for diagnosing the heart and function of heart ventricles and valves.
Elastography	• Non-invasive and non-ionising radiation. • Results are obtained immediately. • High precision 2D time shift-based strain estimation techniques. • High frame rate to obtain a detailed map of the transmural strain in normal.	• By increasing the applied pressure, the elastography is influenced by both elastography images and elasticity score, which lead to wrong diagnosis. • Suffering from medical conditions that cause stiffness in tissues affected by abnormal growths. • Low resolution.	• Detecting and evaluating liver disease, particularly cirrhosis. • Investigations of the soft tissues. • Measuring the mechanical response of the cardiac muscle at the various phases of the cardiac cycle. • Ultrasound elastography is used for determining the muscle material properties and stiffness of the plantar fascia.

(Continues)

Table 4.2 Continued

Type of medical imaging	Features	Risks or limitations in its use	Applications
Optical imaging	• Non-invasive. • Non-ionising radiation. • Longitudinal measurements can be made over a period of time. • Potential to differentiate between soft tissues due to their different absorption or scatter. • Specific absorption by natural chromophores allows functional information to be obtained.	• Low spatial resolution due to the diffusive nature of light propagation in breast tissue. • Sensitive to water blood concentration, blood oxygenation and lipid concentration in breast tissue.	• Probing hemodynamics. • Detecting tumours. • Providing functional imaging of the brain. • Scanning breast cancer. • Scanning the bone health. • Scanning the teeth, gums and jaws.
Radionuclide imaging	• Provides functional information that is often highly accurate and specific. • Provides a global view of the system of interest. • Good tissue-specific contrast. • Can check how far the cancer has spread and how well the treatment is working.	• Uses ionising radiation and makes the patient radioactive for a variable period of time. • Relatively low spatial resolution. • High cost involved in equipment and isotope production. • Extra care required in handling radioactive materials.	• Diagnosing the cancers (breast, cervical, colorectal, esophageal, head and neck, lung, pancreatic and thyroid). • Evaluating the potential effectiveness of therapy. • Diagnosing the cardiovascular disease. • Diagnosing the Alzheimer's disease, Parkinson's disease, dementia, epilepsy and other neurological diseases.

(Continues)

Table 4.2 Continued

Type of medical imaging	Features	Risks or limitations in its use	Applications
Infrared thermography	• Non-invasive. • Non-ionising radiation. • Low cost. • Uniquely suited to observing dynamic physiological changes in the body. • Able to identify connections and causes of pain and disease at a very early stage. • Low processing time as single image may contain several thousands of temperature points recorded in a fraction of a second.	• Limited as a primary (stand-alone) breast cancer diagnostic. • By increasing temperature, breast cancer cells produce nitric oxide, this oxide interferes with the nervous system control of breast tissue blood vessel flow by causing regional vasodilation in the early stages of cancerous cell growth and enhancing new blood vessel formation in later stages. • Poor spatial resolution. • Poor calibration systems.	• Determining the areas of the body that have inflammation. • Breast imaging thermography offers women information that no other procedure can provide, but breast thermography is not a replacement for or alternative to mammography or any other form of breast imaging.
Terahertz imaging	• Safe and non-ionising radiation. • Uniquely sensitive to the vibration modes of water. • THz radiation can penetrate many materials due to the long wavelength of the THz photons.	• THz detectors were characterized by poor signal-to-noise ratio and slow processing. • The emitters produce only incoherent and low-brightness THz radiation. • THz sources require cryogenic operating temperatures. • Low contrast between healthy and pathological tissues. • Poor source performance.	• Detecting the cancer (skin, breast and colon). • Imaging the tooth crown. • Used in medical imaging experiments on different in-vitro and some in-vivo biological tissues and has shown promising results in differentiating certain features in those tissues. • Detecting polar molecules due to molecules' fingerprints in the THz range of frequencies tissues.

The choice of adopting any medical imaging technique amongst all mentioned in Table 4.2 is categorised on the basis of the requirement of (1) image quality in terms of spatial resolution and contrast, (2) safety with respect to the effect of ionizing radiation, heating and the effect of radiation on the body and (3) system availability and the need for real-time information as well as cost.

4.3 THz antennas for healthcare

The THz antenna plays a significant role in the THz imaging system [20]. However, there are challenges involved to enable THz technologies in laboratories of non-specialists and effective management of THz wave through THz antenna both for the far-field and near-field [21–24]. The special broadband THz antennas are used for far-field enhancement; however, the near-field enhancement is the promising one to localise the study of biomolecules in medical imaging systems [25]. For the medical imaging system, there is a growing interest in developing high-power THz sources and sensitive detectors. Therefore, several research groups are working to design THz antennas keeping in mind the challenge of reduced size and increased gain of an antenna. For medical sensing and imaging purposes, there is a limitation on the size of the antenna as it is difficult to implant large-sized antennas on or under the skin of the patient [26]. Moreover, the size of an antenna depends on the material used for fabrication and the frequency of operation [27]. For the emission or detection of THz waves by diverse optical and electrical methods, a THz photoconductive antenna (PCA) is used. However, the THz PCA lacks in harnessing the modern technological advancement for the high-power THz emission [28]. Another approach for developing a THz antenna for medical imaging is based on the adaptation of ultra-wideband microwave imaging antennas at THz frequencies [29]. Figure 4.5 shows a basic set-up having a coaxial scanning probe electrode excited by a THz source with detection done in transmission through a cell membrane.

Although the long-range broadband THz propagation is limited by the atmosphere, close-in detection and near-field point detection are possible, wherein the

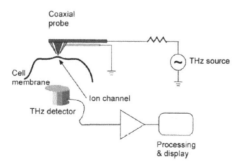

Figure 4.5   *Co-axial scanning probe set-up to enable imaging and diagnostics of ion channel of cell membrane of nervous system using THz source and detector [30]*

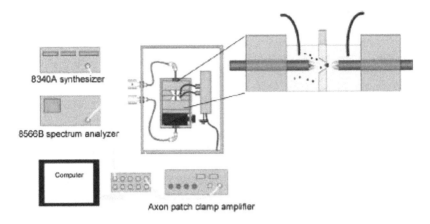

Figure 4.6   Instrumental set-up to record analogue video output [25]

THz spectrometer probes a localized phenomenon, providing a sensitive, label-free technique for detecting chemical or biological contrast. In Figure 4.6, the set-up is developed to understand the nervous system function in human health and disease. The central nervous system's integrative activity critically depends on the molecular activity of neuron's ion channels. In Hamill *et al.* [30], the authors have made a better presentation of understanding ion-channel functions using the development of the glass microelectrode and the invention of the patch-clamp technique. Along with the ion channel, a pore-forming protein (α-Hemolysin) is a useful prototype for exploring the interaction of high frequencies generated by THz antenna (non-ionised waves) and single membrane proteins similar to ion channels. To localise the high-frequency excitation and detection set-up as shown in Figure 4.6 is required to provide analogue signal video output to simultaneously record the conventional patch clamp amplifier and transmission mode through α-Hemolysin.

Therefore, with the use of advanced coherent generation and its amplification, antenna and efficient modulation scheme, it becomes possible to design an array of electronic sources and detectors in the medical imaging system to develop a novel spectroscopic imaging and screening technology. Several research groups have contributed to the prominent antenna designs for THz medical imaging system. Considering the vast development and tremendous growth in wireless body area network (WBAN) that provides freedom to the patient from the bedridden situation for regular monitoring, several THz antennas have been designed. Furthermore, the exposure of THz wave is safe on human tissue because the photo energy of the THz band is significantly low and has no severe effect on chemical bond breakage or even the change of examined material. Moreover, THz band-emitted power from THz antenna also does not lead to trivial heating so its deployment is very useful for health monitoring, medical diagnosis, imaging and biological identification applications. In Kumar *et al.* [31], the authors have presented a design of rectangular patch THz wearable antenna made up of gold placed on gallium arsenide (GaAs) substrate. Gold is a conductive material and is suitable to human body; however, GaAs is a toxic and non-biocompatible that can be replaced with some biocompatible material [32] in order to avoid any harm to human tissue. The THz antenna has been designed to detect different stages of lung cancer and using dumbbell-shaped defected ground structure below the substrate, the improvement in the gain of antenna has been reported by authors of Kumar *et al.* [31]. Another group working on WBAN has bring down their concerns on important metrics such as signal-to-noise ratio (SNR) and bit error rate (BER), which are determined by evaluating the path loss (PL) absorption coefficient of human model at THz range. Antenna is an integral part of the sensor node and the sensor node is the heart of WBAN. To ensure better link quality of a radiated signal in WBAN, high SNR and low BER are required. The equation to compute SNR and BER is determined using (4.1) and (4.2), which further depends on the PL occurred over the distance between transmitting antenna and receiving antenna [33]. The link quality further depends on the amount of power transmitted, bit rate, energy and gain.

$$SNR = \left(\frac{(E_{on}R_b - P_{total})\, G_t\, G_r}{PLM_lN_f\,(1 + \alpha)\, N_b} \right) \tag{4.1}$$

$$BER = \left(\frac{PLM_lN_f\,(1 + \alpha)\, N_0}{(E_{on}R_b - P_{total})\, G_tG_r} \right)^k \tag{4.2}$$

where k, PL, P_{total}, R_b, N_f, M_l and α are the specific subcarrier index, pathloss between transmitter and receiver, total transmitted power, bit rate, noise figure, constant threshold power and the absorption coefficient, respectively. The absorption coefficient is evaluated as $\alpha = \frac{4\pi K}{\lambda_0}$ and K is the extinction coefficient. It defines the attenuation of an electromagnetic field at a per unit distance from transmitter when propagating through the medium. The dielectric parameter of the material determines the refractive index and the excitation coefficient. In order to evaluate *PL* absorption coefficient of simplified human model within WBAN operating at THz, frequency range is specified in Elayan *et al.* [34].

$$PL\,[dB] = PL_{spread} + PL_{absorption}$$

where $PL_{spread} = -10\, log_{10} \left(\frac{\lambda_g}{4\pi d} \right)^?$ and $PL_{absorption} = -10\, log_{10}\, e^{-\alpha d}$ and λ_g is the wavelength of the medium $\left(\frac{\lambda_0}{n} \right)$ where λ_0 is the free-space wavelength and n is the refractive index of the material.

Considering the above relations for antenna design and functionality for THz WBAN application can provide good link quality of the compact medical imaging system. For one of the medical imaging applications for breast cancer detection, a THz patch antenna with a rectangular complementary split ring resonator has been designed and reported by Geetharamani and Aathmanesan [35]. Likewise, for the same medical imaging application, a THz patch antenna with a circular split ring resonator has been designed and compared with the performance of a rectangular patch antenna by Geetharamani and Aathmanesan [36]. The performance of a circular split ring resonator is better than a rectangular split ring resonator for detecting breast cancer tissue detection application in terms of size, efficiency and gain.

The resonant frequency of the circular split ring resonator-inspired THz antenna [36] can be calculated using the following equation:

$$f_{CSRR} = \frac{1}{2\pi \sqrt{L_{CSRR}C_{CSRR}}}$$

where $L_{CSRR} = 4 \mu_0 \left[L - (N-1)(S = W) \right] \left[\ln \left(\frac{0.98}{\rho} \right) + 1.84\rho \right]$

and

$$\rho = \frac{(N-1)(W+S)}{1-(N-1)(w+S)} ;$$

$$C_{CSRR} = \left[\frac{(N-1)}{2} \right] \left[2L - (2N-1)(W+S) \right] C_0$$

$$C_0 = \varepsilon_0 \left[\frac{k\left(\sqrt{(1-k^2)} \right)}{K(k)} \right]$$

and

$$k = \frac{\frac{S}{2}}{\left(w + \frac{S}{2} \right)}$$

The antenna array improves the gain as well as the directivity of the transmitting source. Therefore, it is always useful to enhance the medical imaging capabilities using the THz antenna array [37] to address considerations such as limited depth-of-field (which is the distance over which an object is considered in focus) and size-weight-and-power. For medical imaging applications, in Rabbani and Ghafouri-Shiraz [38], the authors have discussed liquid crystalline polymer substrate-based THz microstrip antenna arrays at 0.835 and 0.635 THz for cancer detection through THz spectroscopy techniques and vital sign detection using Doppler radar on-body techniques. Furthermore, in order to increase the imaging rate of the THz antenna array, a compressed sensing technique for image reconstruction with fewer sampling points has been considered by Hu *et al.* [39]. Using a linear sparse periodic array (SPA), the transmitting elements are allowed to switch on sequentially, and when each transmitting element is on, the echo data of each transmitting and receiving set are recorded. Then using the mechanical system, the array of antennas is mechanically moved to the next scanning position along the vertical direction and allowed to repeat the previous electronic scanning until finishing the planar scanning. Such implementation of the THz antenna array maintains high image quality with fewer array elements [40, 41]. The experimental THz-SPA imaging system is shown in Figures 4.7 and 4.8.

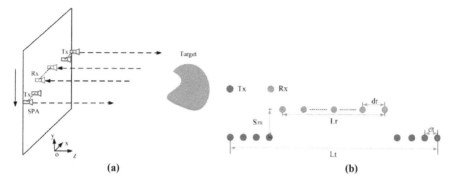

Figure 4.7 *THz scanning scheme with (a) separated SPA and (b) two scanning tracks [39]*

The plasmonic antennas also have the capability to enhance the detection sensitivity for bacterial layers. Moreover, fast diagnosis of bacterial infections is a challenging task in medical applications. Several unique methods such as the use of pre-functionalization to capture specific bacteria [42] and optical methods operating in the visible range especially based on evanescent waves, i.e., surface plasmon polaritons. Many bacteria show their mechanical stability on to their outer cell wall. Therefore, in order to distinguish two main types of bacteria , such as Gram-positive or Gram-negative, the nature and thickness of the bacteria are the prominent distinctive features required to extract through the imaging technique. The polymerase chain reaction is one of the most accurate techniques that is dependable on expensive equipment and took hours to provide the result [43]. On the other hand, semiconductor Plasmonic THz antennas [44] offer the possibility to actively control THz response within picoseconds of time. Doped silicon THz bowtie Plasmonic antennas as reported in References 45, 46 have been designed to interact optimally with the Gram type of the bacteria for its selective recognition. The resonant behaviour of the Plasmonic antennas depends on the material permittivity and the geometry of the antenna; therefore, by modifying the size as well as the shape of THz Plasmonic antennas, it is feasible to make THz antennas to resonate at different frequency ranges.

4.4 THz-TDS for medical imaging

The THz spectroscopy that reveals its existence for 0.1–10 THz has the ability to penetrate a broad range of non-conductive materials and is non-ionising. Initially, the THz spectroscopy was established for the purpose to measure transmission and dispersion characteristics of the structures of a few chemical compounds [47]. In medical imaging, the THz-TDS is the most frequently used technique as it enables the determination of complex permittivity of a sample above 0.23 THz [48]. Using THz-TDS, the sample's static properties, molecular spectroscopy, quality control and biological tissue strength can be determined. In 1989, the first THz-TDS was

(a)

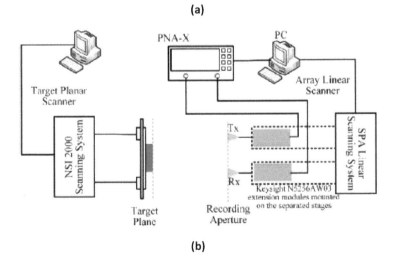

(b)

Figure 4.8   (a) Experimental set-up of THz-SPA imaging system; (b) block diagram representation of THz-SPA imaging system [39]

reported by authors in Exter *et al.* [49] for evaluating the water vapour and later in 1990 [50] for semiconductors and dielectrics. In medical imaging, the THz-TDS has its significant applications and is useful for protein analysis, crystalline study and determining the aging variation of medicine. Moreover, spectroscopy with high spectral resolution at frequencies in the THz regime of the electromagnetic spectrum is a powerful analytical tool for investigating the structure and the energy levels of molecules and atoms. Considering the progress of THz spectroscopy detection technology, several manufacturers of spectrometers have shown the development of handheld spectroscopy devices, such as the Terakit-DODS spectrometer produced by Rainbow Photonics Corporation in Switzerland has a spectral range from 0.1 to 20 THz, which has the widest spectral range at present and its average power is up to 180 mW, and Mini-Z Terahertz Time Domain spectrometer produced by Zomega Corporation of American, whose size is $10.5 \times 6.25 \times 2.75$ cm^3, is having the spectral range 0.1–4 THz, the dynamic range is more than 70 dB and the frequency resolution is less than 500 Hz. This spectrometer is very portable and suited for the on-site component analysis of chemicals and drug inspection [51]. The low-frequency end of the THz spectral region extends to frequencies that are easily achievable using high-precision electronic instruments and long temporal scans are required. To the high-frequency limit above about 10 THz, the Fourier transform spectroscopy (FTS) is used. The pulsed THz spectrometers are inherently broadband systems, a result of using ultrafast optical pulses to generate the THz radiation. The THz spectroscopy has determined the far-infrared optical properties of the material as a function of frequency, which yield insight into material characteristics for a wide range of applications. Moreover, the FTS is the most commonly used technique for studying molecular resonances that provide extremely wide bandwidth, enabling material characterization from the THz frequencies to the infrared band. The spectral measurements, which have much higher resolution, have been made using a narrowband system with a tunable THz source or detector. However, both FTS and narrowband spectroscopy are also widely used in passive systems for monitoring the thermal-emission lines of molecules, particularly, in astronomy applications. The THz-TDS measures the change in the time-resolved electric fields of THz pulses propagating through a sample and an equal length of free space. In a THz-TDS, both generation and detection occur in the same system. The system uses an ultrafast laser pulse, which gets divided into two optical beams in the system. One generates the THz pump beam, and the other detects the probe beam. The probe beam explores amplitude of the THz pulse over time. Thus, the THz waveform is time-dependent and is used as a reference. The THz radiation probes the sample to generate a sample waveform, and by comparing the two waveforms under Fourier transform, it gives the spectroscopic information. However, based on the sample geometry, the change in THz pulse shape allows the analytic or numeric calculations of the complex sample index, dielectric permittivity or conductivity when it is assumed that the linear interaction between the electric field and the sample. Although the spectral resolution of THz-TDS is much coarser than narrowband techniques and its spectral range much lesser than that of FTS and has several advantages that have given rise to some important recent applications. The transmitted THz electric field is measured coherently, which provides both high sensitivity and time-resolved phase information. Moreover, the delay line is a crucial part of every time-domain spectrometer, which needs to carry out the sampling of the electric field over the time. There are a number of uncertainties in TDS measurements, but the delay line uncertainty is significant in the sensing and imaging and thus it has been rigorously analysed by Oberto and Koch [52]. They have modelled the impact of a delay line uncertainty on the acquired THz-TDS data and have emphasized the effect of a small random deviation in delay-line position on the time axis and the measured electric field. The authors have also shown that in a single measurement, a high SNR is achieved by using a high precision delay line. Any small deviation in the positioning of the delay line introduces a small uncertainty in the measured THz transient and may directly lead to the error in the material property characterization [53]. In principle, also the delay lines with a lower precision can yield an overall acceptable SNR if either averaging or the over-sampling of the pulse signals can be performed.

In a THz-TDS system, there are main four components that include a femtosecond pulsed laser, a THz emitter (THz antenna), a delay mechanism to be deployed in between a pump and the probe beam and a time-gated detector [54]. Ouchi *et al.* [55] have shown the development of a fibre-based THz-TDS system and demonstrated 3D imaging of biological tissue using it. The set-up used is shown in Figure 4.9, using which they have observed the difference in physical properties between tumour tissues and normal tissues. Detecting the accurate location and spread of tumour is one of the important applications in its diagnosis and is challenge to develop a THz imaging system with that much accuracy. Ouchi *et al.* [55] have calculated the reflectance spectra using THz-TDS wherein the high reflectance of tumour tissue attributes to higher water content or high density of the cell nucleus. In their results, the tumour tissue can easily be discriminated due to its high reflectance.

Therefore, in conjunction with a hand-held THz transceiver/receiver module as an integral part of the THz spectroscopy system has the great potential for the development of an accurate, precise, low-cost and fast technique to detect and identify the affected area inside the human tissues may be some bacterial infection, formation of tumours, nervous system or any infectious agent presence in the point-of-care environment. Moreover, THz-TDS has the potential to be explored in medical or pharmaceutical prospects. It can be used for analysis for the analysis of proteins in the solution phase, to determine conformational changes in proteins, to understand the dynamics of proteins and their intermolecular interaction, etc.

4.5   ML techniques for THz image analysis

ML is a process that sets on a learning-based approach and can develop machines to perform a given task. A task is learned by using training data and not the explicit determination of task functions [56]. The THz-TDS system acquired the THz signal from test samples including 1D time-domain signal and 2D spatial-domain images either through transmission mode or reflection mode and contains information about the samples at specific frequencies. On analysing the acquired THz signal, significant

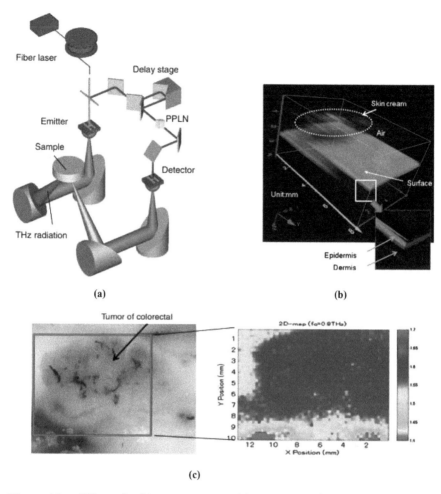

Figure 4.9   *THz medical imaging system: (a) experimental set-up, (b) 3D image*
            of porcine skin and (c) microscope image and refractive index image
            for sample of colorectal cancer [55]

and relevant embedded information can be extracted, which serves as a signature of
the feature of interest. Therefore, such a task that analyses a signal in order to extract
the embedded information can be considered as a potential application of artificial
intelligence either for speech recognition or image recognition [57–59]. With reference to THz medical imaging applications, ML approaches have been developed
for object detection and object classification using supervised, unsupervised and a
combination of the two approaches. Table 4.3 shows the summarised representation
of all three approaches to use of ML for THz medical imaging applications.

From the above, it is clearly understood that several ML approaches have
been developed to classify, segment and analyse the THz medical images. Support

Table 4.3   Machine learning algorithms and techniques explored for THz–TDS medical imaging applications

Machine learning approach	Technique	THz-TDS imaging application area	References
Supervised	Support vector machine (SVM)	• Used to differentiate between normal and cancerous tissues with the help of Kernel function. • Used for T-ray-pulsed classification for RNA samples and powder samples with Gaussian kernels for two class and polynomial kernels for multiclass classification.	Berryman *et al.* [60] and Yin *et al.* [61]
	K-nearest neighbour (KNN)	• Used to detect and classify breast cancer cells from THz images that are preprocessed with the help of texture features that include grey-level co-occurrence matrix GLCM and invariant moment algorithm.	Motlak *et al.* [62]
	Mahalanobis distance (MD)	• Used to perform biomaterial classification of paper, bacterial spores, soda, salt, flour and Chinese seasoning by measuring the distance from a given point to the mean value for a certain class normalised by the variance of the training vectors in the particular direction.	Te *et al.* [63]
	Deep neural network	• Used for screening method with the support of MLP model and Kohonen self-organising map (KSOM) to identify lethal agents in the reconstructed interferometric images.	Bandyopadhyay *et al.* [64]
	Extreme learning machine	• Used on THz pulse transient signals over RNA samples having binary class data sets to address complex value problems considering features both from the amplitude and the phase of the recorded spectra.	Yin *et al.* [65]

(Continues)

Table 4.3 *Continued*

Machine learning approach	Technique	THz-TDS imaging application area	References
Unsupervised	K-means clustering	• Used for the identification and classification of molecules from THz absorption spectrum of the molecules with enhanced accuracy using factor analysis (FA) along with K-means clustering.	Huang *et al.* [66]
	Agglomerative hierarchical	• Used to diagnose cancerous tissues with the extraction of cancer information systematically out of the huge amount of multidimensional spectra.	Nakajima *et al.* [67]
	Self-organising map	• Used to classify THz interferometric images being required less training in comparison to multilayer Perceptron (MLP).	Sinyukov *et al.* [68]
Combined supervised and unsupervised	KNN, SVM and random forest (RF)	• Used for recognising traumatic brain injury (TBI) from THz images by generating new feature vectors combining the transmittance distribution features in the spatial domain and statistical distribution features in the normalised grey histogram.	Shi *et al.* [69]
	Bayesian mixture model with Markov chain Monte Carlo scheme	• Used to classify formalin-fixed, paraffin-embedded and fresh murine breast tumour from THz images.	Bowman *et al.* [70]
	Multiplicative scatter correction, Savitzky–Golay smoothing and first derivative, principal component orthogonal signal correction and emphatic orthogonal signal correction for SVM.	• Used to classify THz images for rapid and accurate detection of cervical cancer.	Qi *et al.* [71]

vector machine in THz classification helps in the medical diagnosis of DNA samples, tumour tissues and breast cancer classification. Likewise, using unsupervised Iterative SelfOrganizing Data Analysis Technique yAy! (ISODATA) multispectral classification with K-means clustering has been used in histopathological examination in Berry *et al.* [72]. Therefore, developing a compact THz-TDS device and making it compatible with ML can not only enhance the accuracy of analysis but also support image reconstruction, image enhancement, image segmentation, image registration and automatic report generation.

4.6   Limitations to THz biomedical imaging application technology

The THz waves are sensitive to water molecules and hence help to probe the dynamics of biological samples; however, it also limits the penetration depth of THz radiation into water-abundant specimens [73]. Moreover, the spectral fingerprints of biomedical samples by the motion of biological molecules are not readily observed. It happens because of the relaxational absorption of THz radiation by water molecules and second due to the inhomogeneous broadening of resonances in macromolecules. However, using techniques such as paraffin-embedded [74], freezing [75] and penetration enhancing gels [76], these issues can be addressed.

Furthermore, in spite of enormous progress in the construction of sources and detectors of the THz-TDS system, it is always difficult to detect the THz signal at room temperature because of blackbody radiations. The atmospheric attenuation of the THz wave is also a major concern that limits the range of its use. Selecting appropriate optics in THz medical imaging application is also a huge constraint as lenses are not widely used due to a lack of convenient materials and anti-reflecting coating materials over the frequency of use. In diffraction-limited cases, the frequency determines the resolution because an absolute upper-performance limit is controlled by the law of physics, which is further optimised by the size of the sensor, its f-number and the wavelength of light that passes through the lens [77].

4.7   Future scope and recommendations

As evident from the literature available on the THz wave and its use for medical imaging purposes, a technological race has resulted in its enormous progress both in generation and detection techniques. However, for effective implementation of THz-TDS, the system requires a complete understanding of the inspection process, the complete physical properties of the object being diagnosed and the imaging technique in use. To improve SNR in the THz-TDS system for static objects, THz images can be created using mechanical scanning of an object pixel-by-pixel using a coherent source. The use of an imaging array and deploying the potential of ML approaches can bring out significant and accurate results of the diagnosis. In order to reduce the constraint of atmospheric attenuation on the THz wave, the imaging system should be short-range. The concept of hybrid imaging is also developing for structure health monitoring [78], which combines the simultaneous image analysis of two or more spectral bands, thus enhancing the efficiency of vision inspections. The use of a high-resolution VIS/VIS INR (visible/visible-infrared) camera along with backlighting set-ups can also facilitate high accuracy for external edge detection. Such a technique also demands the development of special algorithms for image fusion and sophisticated calibration methods.

References

[1] Malhotra I., Jha K.R., Singh G. 'Terahertz antenna technology for imaging applications: a technical review'. *International Journal of Microwave and Wireless Technologies*. 2018, vol. 10(3), pp. 271–90.

[2] Andy T. *Terahertz (THz) technology market increasing exigency with top key players: brainware terahertz information* [online]. Advantest Corporation, Hubner. 2019. Available from https://newsexterior.com/terahertz-technology-market-increasing-exigency-with-top-key-players-brainware-terahertz-information-advantest-corporation-hubner/17264/

[3] Yang X., Zhao X., Yang K., *et al.* 'Biomedical applications of terahertz spectroscopy and imaging'. *Trends in Biotechnology*. 2016, vol. 34(10), pp. 810–24.

[4] Bogue R. 'Terahertz imaging: a report on progress'. *Sensor Review*. 2009, vol. 29(1), pp. 6–12.

[5] Seibert J.A., Boone J.M. ' X-ray imaging physics for nuclear medicine technologists. Part 2: X-ray interactions and image formation '. *Journal of Nuclear Medicine Technology*. 2005, vol. 33(1), pp. 3–18.

[6] Ritman E.L. 'Medical X-ray imaging, current status and some future challenges'. *Advances in X-Ray Analysis*. 2006, vol. 49, pp. 1–12.

[7] Roobottom C.A., Mitchell G., Morgan-Hughes G. ' Radiation-reduction strategies in cardiac computed tomographic angiography '. *Clinical Radiology*. 2010, vol. 65(11), pp. 859–67.

[8] Claesson T. 2001. *A Medical Imaging Demonstrator of Computed Tomography and Bone Mineral Densitometry*. [Master Thesis]. Stockholm, Sweden, Department of Physics, Royal Institute of Technology.

[9] Hiriyannaiah H.P., Cupertino C.A. ' X-ray computed tomography for medical imaging '. *IEEE Signal Processing Magazine*. 1997, vol. 14(2), pp. 42–59.

[10] Xu J., Tsui B.M.W. 'Quantifying the importance of the statistical assumption in statistical X-ray CT image reconstruction'. *IEEE Transactions on Medical Imaging*. 2014, vol. 33(1), pp. 61–73.

[11] Lang C., Habs D., Parodi K., Thirolf P.G. 'Sub-millimeter nuclear medical imaging with high sensitivity in positron emission tomography using $\beta + \gamma$ coincidences'. *Journal of Instrumentation*. 2014, vol. 9(1), P01008/1-17.

[12]   Jones T., Townsend D. 'History and future technical innovation in positron emission tomography'. *Journal of Medical Imaging (Bellingham, Wash.)*. 2017, vol. 4(1), 011013/1-18.

[13]   Holly T.A., Abbott B.G., Al-Mallah M., *et al*. 'Single photon-emission computed tomography'. *Journal of Nuclear Cardiology*. 2010, vol. 17(5), pp. 941–73.

[14]   Orfanoudaki I.M., Kappou D., Sifakis S. 'Recent advances in optical imaging for cervical cancer detection'. *Archives of Gynecology and Obstetrics*. 2011, vol. 284(5), pp. 1197–208.

[15]   Nazarian S., Hansford R., Rahsepar A.A., *et al*. 'Safety of magnetic resonance imaging in patients with cardiac devices'. *The New England Journal of Medicine*. 2017, vol. 377(26), pp. 2555–64.

[16]   Whitson M.R., Mayo P.H. 'Ultrasonography in the emergency department'. *Critical Care (London, England)*. 2016, vol. 20(1), 227/1-18.

[17]   Li X., Zhang Y., Sun H, *et al*. 'Infrared thermography in the diagnosis of musculoskeletal injuries: a protocol for a systematic review and meta-analysis'. *Medicine*. 2020, vol. 99(49), E23529/1-5.

[18]   Yan Z., Zhu L.G., Meng K., Huang W., Shi Q. 'THz medical imaging: from in vitro to in vivo'. *Trends in Biotechnology*. 2022, vol. 40(7), pp. 816–30.

[19]   Kasban H. 'A comparative study of medical imaging techniques'. *International Journal of Information Science and Intelligent System*. 2015, vol. 4(2), pp. 37–58.

[20]   Malhotra I., Singh G. *Terahertz Antenna Technology for Imaging and Sensing Applications*. Cham, Switzerland: Springer Nature; 2021.

[21]   Deibel J.A., Escarra M.D., Mittleman D.M. 'Photoconductive terahertz antenna with radial symmetry'. *Electronics Letters*. 2005, vol. 41(5), 226.

[22]   Malhotra I., Singh G. 'Beam-steering characteristics of highly directive photoconductive dipole phased array antenna' in *Terahertz antenna technology for imaging and sensing applications*. Springer, Cham; 2021. pp. 203–15.

[23]   van der Weide D.W. 'The nanoscilloscope: combined topography and AC field probing with a micromachined tip'. *Journal of Vacuum Science & Technology B: Microelectronics and Nanometer Structures Processing, Measurement, and Phenomena*. 2005, vol. 14, pp. 4144–4147.

[24]   Wang K., Mittleman D.M., van der Valk N.C.J., Planken P.C.M. 'Antenna effects in terahertz apertureless near-field optical microscopy'. *Applied Physics Letters*. 2005, vol. 85(14), pp. 2715–2717.

[25]   Grade J., Haydon P., van der Weide D. 'Electronic terahertz antennas and probes for spectroscopic detection and diagnostics'. *Proceedings of the IEEE*. 2005, vol. 95(8), pp. 1583–91.

[26]   Kalra P., Sidhu E. 'Rectangular terahertz microstrip patch antenna design for riboflavin detection applications'. *Proceeding of the IEEE International Conference on Big Data Analytics and Computational Intelligence (ICBDAC)*; India, 2017. pp. 303–306.

[27] Malhotra I., Thakur P., Pandit S., Jha K.R., Singh G. 'Analytical framework of small-gap photoconductive dipole antenna using equivalent circuit model'. *Optical and Quantum Electronics*. 2017, vol. 49(10), pp. 1–23.

[28] Malhotra I., Ranjan Jha K., Singh G. 'Analysis of highly directive photoconductive dipole antenna at terahertz frequency for sensing and imaging applications'. *Optics Communications*. 2017, vol. 397, pp. 129–139.

[29] Li X., Hagness S.C., Choi M.K., van der Weide D.W. 'Numerical and experimental investigation of an ultrawideband ridged pyramidal horn antenna with curved launching plane for pulse radiation'. *IEEE Antennas and Wireless Propagation Letters*. 2003, vol. 2, pp. 259–262.

[30] Hamill O.P., Marty A., Neher E., Sakmann B., Sigworth F.J. 'Improved patch-clamp techniques for high-resolution current recording from cells and cell-free membrane patches'. *Pflugers Archiv*. 1981, vol. 391(2), pp. 85–100.

[31] Kumar M., Goel S., Rajawat A., Gupta S.H. 'Design of optical antenna operating at terahertz frequency for in-vivo cancer detection'. *Optik*. 2020, vol. 216, 164910.

[32] Mitra D., Das S., Paul S. 'SAR reduction for an implantable antenna using ferrite superstrate'. *Proceeding of the International Workshop on Antenna Technology (iWAT)*; Miami, FL, USA, 2019. pp. 1–4.

[33] Salayma M., Al-Dubai A., Romdhani I., Nasser Y. 'Reliability and energy efficiency enhancement for emergency-aware wireless body area networks (WBANS)'. *IEEE Transactions on Green Communications and Networking*. 2018, vol. 2(3), pp. 804–16.

[34] Elayan H., Shubair R.M., Jornet J.M., Johari P. 'Terahertz channel model and link budget analysis for intrabody nanoscale communication'. *IEEE Transactions on Nanobioscience*. 2017, vol. 16(6), pp. 491–503.

[35] Geetharamani G., Aathmanesan T. 'Metamaterial inspired thz antenna for breast cancer detection'. *SN Applied Sciences*. 2019, vol. 1(6), pp. 1–9.

[36] Geetharamani G., Aathmanesan T. 'Split ring resonator inspired thz antenna for breast cancer detection'. *Optics & Laser Technology*. 2020, vol. 126, p. 106111.

[37] Malhotra I., Jha K.R., Singh G. 'Design of highly directive terahertz photoconductive dipole antenna using frequency-selective surface for sensing and imaging applications'. *Journal of Computational Electronics*. 2020, vol. 17(4), pp. 1721–40.

[38] Rabbani M.S., Ghafouri-Shiraz H. 'Liquid crystalline polymer substrate-based thz microstrip antenna arrays for medical applications'. *IEEE Antennas and Wireless Propagation Letters*. 2020, vol. 16, pp. 1533–36.

[39] Hu S., Shu C., Alfadhl Y., Chen X. 'THz sparse periodic array imaging system using compressed sensing'. *IET Microwaves, Antennas & Propagation*. 2020, vol. 14(11), pp. 1157–61.

[40] Hu S.Q., Shu C., Alfadhl Y., Chan X. 'A thz imaging system using linear sparse periodic array'. *IEEE Sensors Journal*. 2019, vol. 20(6), pp. 3285–92.

[41] Lockwood G.R., Pai-ChiL., O'Donnell M., Foster F.S. 'Optimizing the radiation pattern of sparse periodic linear arrays'. *IEEE Transactions on*

Ultrasonics, Ferroelectrics and Frequency Control. 1996, vol. 43(1), pp. 7–14.

[42]   Su L., Jia W., Hou C., Lei Y. 'Microbial biosensors: a review'. *Biosensors & Bioelectronics*. 2011, vol. 26(5), pp. 1788–99.

[43]   Lazcka O., Del Campo F.J., Muñoz F.X. 'Pathogen detection: a perspective of traditional methods and biosensors'. *Biosensors & Bioelectronics*. 2007, vol. 22(7), pp. 1205–17.

[44]   Berrier A., Albella P., Poyli M.A, *et al.* 'Detection of deep-subwavelength dielectric layers at terahertz frequencies using semiconductor plasmonic resonators'. *Optics Express*. 2012, vol. 20(5), pp. 5052–60.

[45]   Berrier A., Ulbricht R., Bonn M., Rivas J.G. 'Ultrafast active control of localized surface plasmon resonances in silicon bowtie antennas'. *Optics Express*. 2010, vol. 18(22), pp. 23226–35.

[46]   Berrier A., Schaafsma M.C., Nonglaton G., Bergquist J., Rivas J.G. 'Selective detection of bacterial layers with terahertz plasmonic antennas'. *Biomedical Optics Express*. 2012, vol. 3(11), pp. 2937–49.

[47]   Ozbay E., Michel E., Tuttle G, *et al.* 'Terahertz spectroscopy of three-dimensional photonic band-gap crystals'. *Opt Lett*. 1994, vol. 19(15), pp. 1155–57.

[48]   Patil M.R., Ganorkar S.B., Patil A.S., Shirkhedkar A.A. 'Terahertz spectroscopy: encoding the discovery, instrumentation, and applications toward pharmaceutical prospectives'. *Critical Reviews in Analytical Chemistry*. 2022, vol. 52(2), pp. 343–55.

[49]   Exter M.V., Fattinger C., Grischkowsky D. 'Terahertz time-domain spectroscopy of water vapor'. *Opt Lett*. 1989, vol. 14(20), pp. 1128–30.

[50]   Grischkowsky D., Keiding S., van Exter M., Fattinger C. 'Far-infrared time-domain spectroscopy with terahertz beams of dielectrics and semiconductors'. *Journal of the Optical Society of America B*. 1990, vol. 7(10), p. 2006.

[51]   Dexheimer S.L. *THz spectroscopy: principles and applications*. Boca Raton, USA: CRC Press; 2008.

[52]   Jahn D., Lippert S., Bisi M., Oberto L., Balzer J.C., Koch M. 'On the influence of delay line uncertainty in thz time-domain spectroscopy'. *Journal of Infrared, Millimeter, and Terahertz Waves*. 2020, vol. 37(6), pp. 605–13.

[53]   Jepsen P.U., Fischer B.M. 'Dynamic range in terahertz time-domain transmission and reflection spectroscopy'. *Opt Lett*. 2005, vol. 30(1), pp. 29–31.

[54]   Bawuah P., Markl D., Farrell D, *et al.* 'Terahertz-based porosity measurement of pharmaceutical tablets: a tutorial'. *Journal of Infrared, Millimeter, and Terahertz Waves*. 2020, vol. 41(4), pp. 450–469.

[55]   Ouchi T., Kajiki K., Koizumi T, *et al.* 'Terahertz imaging system for medical applications and related high efficiency terahertz devices'. *Journal of Infrared, Millimeter, and Terahertz Waves*. 2020, vol. 35(1), pp. 118–130.

[56]   Park H., Son J.H. 'Machine learning techniques for thz imaging and time-domain spectroscopy'. *Sensors (Basel, Switzerland)*. 2021, vol. 21(4), p. 1186.

[57] Shin S.H., Yun H.W., Jang W.J., Park H. 'Extraction of acoustic features based on auditory spike code and its application to music genre classification'. *IET Signal Processing*. 2019, vol. 13(2), pp. 230–34.

[58] Zhang J., Xie Y., Wu Q., Xia Y. 'Medical image classification using synergic deep learning'. *Medical Image Analysis*. 2019, vol. 54, pp. 10–19.

[59] Wang W., Yang Y., Wang X., Wang W., Li J. 'Development of convolutional neural network and its application in image classification: a survey'. *Optical Engineering*. 2019, vol. 58(4), p. 040901.

[60] Berryman M.J., Rainsford T. 'Classification of terahertz data as a tool for the detection of cancer'. *Biomedical Applications of Micro- and Nanoengineering III*. 2006, vol. 6416.

[61] Yin X., Ng B.W.-H., Fischer B.M., Ferguson B., Abbott D. 'Support vector machine applications in terahertz pulsed signals feature sets'. *IEEE Sensors Journal*. 2015, vol. 7(12), pp. 1597–608.

[62] Motlak H.J., Hakeem S.I. 'Detection and classification of breast cancer based-on terahertz imaging technique using artificial neural network & K-nearest neighbour algorithm'. *International Journal of Applied Engineering Research*. 2017, vol. 12(21), pp. 10661–68.

[63] Te C.C., Ferguson B., Abbott D. 'Investigation of biomaterial classification using T-rays'. *Biomedical Applications of Micro- and Nanoengineering*. 2003, vol. 4937, pp. 294–306.

[64] Bandyopadhyay A. 'Artificial neural network analysis in interferometric thz imaging for detection of lethal agents'. *International Journal of Infrared and Millimeter Waves*. 2006, vol. 27(8), pp. 1145–58.

[65] Yin X.X., Hadjiloucas S., He J., Zhang Y., Wang Y., Zhang D. 'Application of complex extreme learning machine to multiclass classification problems with high dimensionality: a thz spectra classification problem'. *Digital Signal Processing*. 2015, vol. 40(1), pp. 40–52.

[66] Huang J., Liu J., Wang K., Yang Z., Liu X. 'Classification and identification of molecules through factor analysis method based on terahertz spectroscopy'. *Spectrochimica Acta. Part A, Molecular and Biomolecular Spectroscopy*. 2018, vol. 198, pp. 198–203.

[67] Nakajima S., Hoshina H., Yamashita M., Otani C., Miyoshi N. 'Terahertz imaging diagnostics of cancer tissues with a chemometrics technique'. *Applied Physics Letters*. 2007, vol. 90(4), 041102.

[68] Sinyukov A., Zorych I., Michalopoulou Z.H., Gary D., Barat R., Federici J.F. 'Detection of explosives by terahertz synthetic aperture imaging—focusing and spectral classification'. *Comptes Rendus Physique*. 2007, vol. 9(2), pp. 248–61.

[69] Shi J., Wang Y., Chen T, *et al.* 'Automatic evaluation of traumatic brain injury based on terahertz imaging with machine learning'. *Optics Express*. 2018, vol. 26(5), pp. 6371–81.

[70] Bowman T., Chavez T., Khan K, *et al.* 'Pulsed terahertz imaging of breast cancer in freshly excised murine tumors'. *Journal of Biomedical Optics*. 2018, vol. 23(2), pp. 1–13.

[71]   Qi N., Zhang Z., Xiang Y., Yang Y., Liang X., Harrington P. de B. 'Terahertz time-domain spectroscopy combined with support vector machines and partial least squares-discriminant analysis applied for the diagnosis of cervical carcinoma'. *Analytical Methods*. 2015, vol. 7(6), pp. 2333–38.

[72]   Berry E., Handley J.W., Fitzgerald A.J, *et al.* 'Multispectral classification techniques for terahertz pulsed imaging: an example in histopathology'. *Medical Engineering & Physics*. 2004, vol. 26(5), pp. 423–30.

[73]   Son J.H. 'Challenges and opportunities in terahertz biomedical imaging'. *2015 40th International Conference on Infrared, Millimeter, and Terahertz waves (IRMMW-THz)*; Hong Kong, China, August, 2004.

[74]   Oh S.J., Kim S.H., Ji Y.B, *et al.* 'Study of freshly excised brain tissues using terahertz imaging'. *Biomedical Optics Express*. 2014, vol. 5(8), pp. 2837–42.

[75]   Sim Y.C., Ahn K.M., Park J.Y., Park C.S., Son J.H. 'Temperature-dependent terahertz imaging of excised oral malignant melanoma'. *IEEE Journal of Biomedical and Health Informatics*. 2013, vol. 17(4), pp. 779–84.

[76]   Oh S.J., Kim S.H., Jeong K, *et al.* 'Measurement depth enhancement in terahertz imaging of biological tissues'. *Optics Express*. 2013, vol. 21(18), pp. 21299–305.

[77]   Lizarraga J., Rio C.D. 'Resolution capabilities of future thz cameras'. *Radio engineering*. 2011, vol. 20, pp. 373–79.

[78]   Cheng Y., Deng Y., Cao J., Xiong X., Bai L., Li Z. 'Multi-wave and hybrid imaging techniques: a new direction for nondestructive testing and structural health monitoring'. *Sensors (Basel, Switzerland)*. 2013, vol. 13(12), pp. 16146–90.

Chapter 5

The current state of summarization and visualization in Electronic Health Record (EHR) based on EHR interoperability

Amal Beldi[1], Salma Sassi[2], Richard Chbeir[3], and Abderrazek Jemai[4]

Recently, several health-care organizations store heterogeneous health information about patients aiming to improve the quality of health care. The Electronic Health Record (EHR) contains a huge amount of patients' information making it difficult and time-saving to find the most pertinent information. Accurate, concise, and automated summarization and visualization have the potential to save time by increasing patient safety, improving efficiency, helping clinical decision-making, and reducing medical error as well as costs. Although interoperability and standardization are considered keys to improve the quality of care services and to coordinate care and practice effective summarization, several studies have shown the difficulty of improving the quality of health care using the current summarization- and visualization-based systems since they lack interoperability and do not allow to easily express clinician needs. We found that there is no study that discusses the impact of semantic and syntactic interoperability on the EHR summarization approach, which motivated us to provide and discuss studies on the above topics. In this study, we will review health-care summarization and visualization approaches and systems and analyze the proposed studies according to interoperability and clinicians' needs and challenges. To construct our review, we adopted the Preferred Reporting Items for Systematic Reviews and Meta-Analyses (PRISMA) methodology and examined papers between 1980 and 2021. Selected studies focus on health-care sub-areas, EHR visualization, EHR summarization, interoperability, and standards. Based on the above papers, we provide a systematic view of development in this field and

[1]Tunis El Manar University, Faculty of Mathematical Physical and Natural Sciences of Tunis, SERCOM Laboratory, Tunis, Tunisia
[2]Jendouba University, Faculty of Law Economics and Management of Jendouba, VPNC Laboratory, Jendouba, Tunisia
[3]University Pau & Pays Adour, LIUPPA, Anglet,, France
[4]Carthage University, Polytechnic School of Tunisia, SERCOM Laboratory, INSAT, Tunis, Tunisia

possible future directions. We conclude that most research studies in summarizing systems lack semantic interoperability and do not rely on clinicians' needs. Besides, EHR visualization systems lack the ability to analyze efficiently health data and integrate expert knowledge domains in the decision-making process. This will promote new research to solve these issues.

5.1   Introduction

Information and Communication Technologies (ICT) are adopted to support health-care services. ICT enhance the quality of care, improve health-care service efficiencies, and enable efficient follow-up of care plan [1, 2]. E-health is very critical mainly for patients since it facilitates and provides high-quality and safe health-care services through accessing their relevant health information and ensures their well-being.

E-health is also important for the General Practitioner since it provides him with a decision-making system to let him be informed about patient health state and eventual complications based on accessing more accurate health and accessing to medical knowledge and better practices.

It has a great interest to digitize the EHR and all information and documents related to the patient's health. However, since the EHR system contains a mix of highly heterogeneous data, the most critical component in a health system is still the EHR database having different architectures that can be centralized, distributed, or hybrid solutions. In the beginning, health-care systems were isolated solutions in hospitals. After that, multiple specialized health-care system-oriented institutions or domains appeared thus contributing to interoperability and information sharing issues since it seems crucial to access and make available at any time, anywhere all relevant clinical data and to improve the quality and delivery of care services. Interoperable EHRs have an important role in ensuring more effective and efficient patient care and facilitating the retrieval and processing of health data from heterogeneous systems to provide coordinated care and practice effective communication, aid GP decision-making, reduce medical errors, and save time. Also, we are interested in automated summarization and visualization challenges. Many works have discussed the topic of how to summarize structured health record data in a more accessible way. Thus, interoperability and standardization are considered primordial issues to enhance and better coordinate care and practice effective summarization.

Several studies have used visualization interfaces [3–5]. Other works have been interested to generate descriptions of structured time series by using natural language [6–10], in order to generate an understandable summary of methods for summarizing health record data. These studies show the lacking of interoperability of current summarization- and visualization-based systems makes it difficult to improve the quality-of-care services and to easily express GP needs. Here, we conclude that most of the studies in summarizing and visualizing systems lack semantic and syntactic interoperability and the ability to efficiently analyze health data and integrate domain expert knowledge in the decision-making process which motivated us to construct a literature review on the above topics.

This chapter is organized as follows. Section 5.2 presents research questions and motivation. Section 5.3 explains our reviewing methodology. In section 5.4, we discuss e-health syntactic and semantic interoperability issues by presenting and discussing the background of knowledge about standards, terminologies, and ontologies in health-care domain and EHR-based systems. Section 5.5 describes a background knowledge on EHR, reviews, and discusses recent approaches to EHR summarization. In section 5.6, we review recent approaches to EHR visualization and discuss their techniques, data quality, and interoperability axes. Section 5.7 concludes and provides some discussions on future trends.

5.2   Research questions and motivation

5.2.1   Motivation

Figure 5.1 is a summing-up diagram that demonstrates the motivation for the study of our review through visualization of keywords in the reviewed papers. First, the importance of synthesis and visualization of the EHR to obtain brief and concise information that satisfies the user's need through beneficial results becomes the primordial challenge. So, we note the variety and diversity of synthesis techniques, extractive, abstractive, indicative, informative, and visualization tools: natural language processing, event sequence simplification (ESS), clustering, comparison,

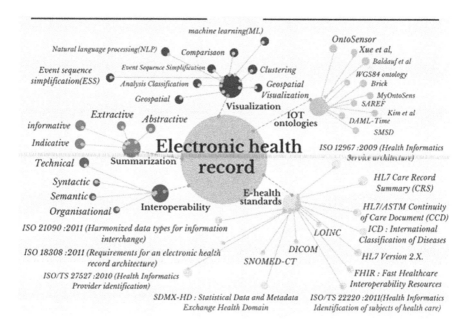

Figure 5.1   Visualization of high-frequency keywords of the reviewed papers

machine learning (ML), but no work has been done about the combination of summarization and visualization of the EHR. The above works [8, 11] are involved in each process separately. Second, interoperability aims at communicating and exchanging data accurately, effectively, and consistently between heterogeneous clinical systems. So, its four issues, functional interoperability, technical interoperability, semantic interoperability, and syntactic interoperability, remain the essential concept for enhancing the process of synthesis and process of visualization. Thirdly, various medical standards and IOT ontologies are important to frame and enhance the accessibility of the Electronic Health Record (EHR).

For these reasons, we conduce to combine our study to maintain these two processes of summarization and visualization for the EHR, to adopt the four interoperability techniques and challenges, to discuss different e-health standards and e-health ontologies, and to identify data types in the input, output processes, the objectives, and the techniques that should be used to maintain the process to orient users and the taken of different contexts from the user (patient) or the device (medical device) side.

5.2.2   Challenges

Our choice for the topic was motivated by the importance of data and systems' interoperability problems to provide efficient health-care services. E-health is a promising field to manage, predict health states and adapt care plans. So, summarization of patient information is an essential practice for effective communication in medicine. It has the potential to save time and doing so includes increasing patient safety, improving efficiency, aiding clinical decision-making, standardizing notes, and reducing medical errors and costs. The need for making EHR more interoperable provides more efficient care services for patients which was our main motivation to conduct this study. The purpose of this review is to provide an understanding and a review of EHR summarization and of syntactic and semantic interoperability in current EHR systems and to provide recommendations for summarization systems based on EHR. In this chapter, the following challenges are addressed:

- What are the main techniques and approaches to summarize and visualize the EHR?
- How, today, syntactic, and semantic interoperability are treated in EHR and EHR summary?
- How to better provide syntactic and semantic interoperability in EHR-based summarization and visualization?

5.3   Reviewing methodology

In this chapter, we adopted PRISMA [3] as a reviewing methodology. To assess the quality of the selected papers, we used the Checklist for Systematic Reviews and

Research Syntheses [12] of the Joanna Briggs Institute (JBI) and the qualitative research checklist [13] of the Critical Appraisal Skills Programme.

5.3.1   Input literature

Here, we provide details about the selection process of the chosen papers. Initially, we made a two-phase advanced keyword search on the Web of Science database. After that, we conducted a search in Google Scholar and PubMed for the period January 1, 2005 to December 31, 2021 in "all fields." The used keywords include "electronic Health record" summarization, EHR summary, data, medical data, interoperability, standard, semantic interoperability, syntactic interoperability, ontology IoT, user profile. They were used in different phases.

5.3.2   Methodology

To begin, we searched papers from the following conferences and journals:

- VIS: IEEE VIS conferences
- EuroVis: EuroVis conferences
- TVCG: We have carefully selected papers on EHR Vis from the IEEE Transactions on Visualization and Computer Graphics journal
- Summ: IEEE summarization conference
- VAHC: Literature published in the IEEE Workshop on Visual Analytics in Healthcare. After analyzing the references, we found more literature that we need to conduct our review.

Figures 5.2 and 5.3 summarize our methodology used for searching relevant papers. Indeed, in the first phase, thousands of papers were narrowed down. In the second phase, we found 5,384 on the Web of Science and PubMed. We are also conducted with the same keywords in Google Scholar search engines that resulted 700 articles. After that, we removed duplicate articles. Finally, after eliminating duplicate articles, 240 articles were retained for our overview. About 40 articles focus on EHR, 100 on EHR interoperability, 40 on EHR summarization, and 60 on EHR visualization. Based on the outcome of the review process and the output results, we elaborated the subsequent sections.

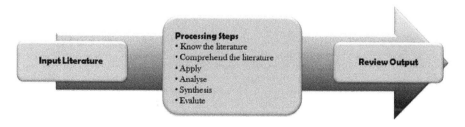

Figure 5.2   Literature review process [3]

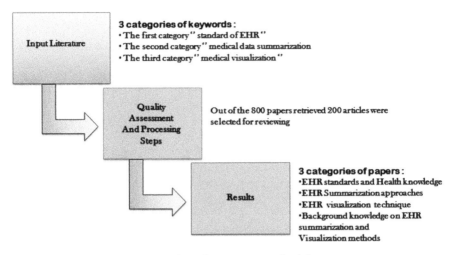

Figure 5.3   Our review methodology

5.4   E-health interoperability

E-health interoperability aims at communicating and exchanging data accurately, effectively, and consistently between heterogeneous clinical and Internet of Things (IoT) health systems [1]. Handling heterogeneous issues is critical in EHR-based systems to ensure better communication and cooperation between health applications in order to share information through EHR and other health applications [14–16]. On the other hand, there are many challenges that emerged to integrate health information systems, due to the following reasons:

i.   The existence of multiple suppliers of systems and technologies.
ii.   A lot of heterogeneous clinical and administrative applications share information between them within the same organization.
iii. Each application can ensure communication through multiple and heterogeneous interfaces. Thus, achieving interoperability between clinical applications is a challenging problem since it aims at reducing health costs and contributing to more effective care.

Ensuring the effectiveness of a clinical information system and its interoperability with other clinical applications consists of defining and using health standards and terminologies [1]. Using interoperable systems ensures instant access to clinical data whenever and wherever needed and avoids clinical data redundancy in every system [2, 17]. Several standards, terminologies, and IoT-based ontologies were identified to be related to syntactic interoperability [18, 19], semantic interoperability [20], or IoT-based ontologies [21, 22]. So, in the next sub-sections, we first provide and discuss the background of terminologies and standards. Second, we

Table 5.1   E-health interoperability levels

Interoperability levels	Human can understand Information	Machine can understand Information
Syntactic	No	No
Functional	Yes	No
Semantic	Yes	Yes
Organizational	Yes	Yes

describe and discuss existing ontologies that can be used for the IoT domain ensuring also the interoperability between connected health systems.

5.4.1   E-health standards

Several health systems took into account health information exchange to ensure more appropriate, efficient, and secure access to patient's medical information. There are different classifications of interoperability that include four levels: semantic level, structural level, syntactic level, and system level. ISO [23] defines two main levels: functional and semantic interoperability. In Table 5.1, we discuss the four levels of interoperability issues classified based on the way that the information can be understood by humans and machines.

- Functional interoperability: It includes the definition of the inter-connectivity ensuring safer communication of data for one application or system [24].
- Syntactic interoperability: It includes the definition of the format of data, its syntax, and how it can be organized for better interpretation [24].
- Semantic interoperability: It describes a unified semantic model including normalized data and definitions to provide a common understanding to the user [25].
- Organizational interoperability: It aims at simplifying a more secure and prompt communication and facilitates the use of data within and between clinical applications [26].

We note that interoperability standards and terminologies ensure syntactic and semantic interoperability [27]. In other words, we need to standardize health-care data to ensure interoperability and allow using it by different actors in different contexts. Health-care applications exchange clinical information about a patient through messages. Several terminologies and standards are proposed in order to address the e-health syntactic interoperability issue such as the Health Level 7 (HL7) [28], Fast Healthcare Interoperability Resources (FHIR) [29], Clinical Document Architecture (CDA) [30], CEN EN 13606 EHRcom [31], openEHR [32], Digital Imaging and Communications in Medicine (DICOM) [33], or Statistical Data and Metadata Exchange Health Domain (SDMX-HD) [32]. These standards focus on structuring and normalizing the health data for a more accurate exchange. For the same purpose, Integrating the Healthcare Enterprise (IHE) [34] is an industry initiative specifying the Cross-Enterprise Document Sharing (XDS) to facilitate the integration profile [35]. IHE XDS aims at storing health-care documents in anebXML registry/repository architecture and facilitating their sharing [36]. We also note the existence of many terminologies such as Systematized Nomenclature of Medicine -- Clinical Terms (SNOMED-CT) [37], Unified Medical Lexicon System (UMLS) [23], International Classification of Diseases (ICD)-11 [38], OpenEHR [39], and Logical Observation Identifiers Names & Codes (LOINC) [40].

5.4.1.1 ISO 12967:2009 (Health Informatics Service Architecture)

It allows the development of interoperable e-health applications and integration of existing ones and aims to share information within and across a health organization. This standard is composed of three parts. The first one aims to design middleware-based architecture integrating common data and business logic [32]. The second one defines the information model and its main components to be implemented by the middleware-based architecture defined in the first level [32]. The last one aims to facilitate the exchange of information within the organization by simplifying a comprehensive and integrated interface and supporting the business processes [32].

5.4.1.2 ISO/TS 22220:2011 (Health Informatics Identification of subjects of health care)

It specifies the structure and the main data of a patient as well as the communication of this information among e-health applications. In other words, it defines demographic and other relevant data to be captured, and how they have to be implemented based on an ICT-supported environment [32].

5.4.1.3 ISO/TS 27527:2010 (Health Informatics Provider Identification)

It allows for identifying and defining health-care practitioners and health-care organizations. It intends to model the required data used to identify a general practitioner and the organization in order to correctly model their authorization and authentication in accessing health records. It also defines user roles and delegation of authority [32].

5.4.1.4 HL7 Version 2.X

It is an industry-standard based on a messaging exchange for application. It aims at covering clinical and administrative information between heterogeneous health applications. It facilitates data exchange among heterogeneous health-care systems. The exchanged data can be information about admission, discharge, or transfer of orders, and results of laboratory tests and clinical observations. HL7 messages are used to exchange the above data. It can also be used to transmit administrative data, ranging from appointment schedules and billing information [34]. In 1988, the HL7 standard was published its first version HL7 Version 1 [41]. After that, the HL7 standard provided many other revisions [2]. The second one was HL7 Version 2 specifying the structure of the messages transmitted between applications. The HL7 message is a set of segments following pre-defined sequences. Segments are composed of fields that hold values for defined data types.

5.4.1.5   HL7 Version 3

It was developed to overcome one of the limits of HL7 Version 2 such as the lack of a flexible data model taking into account the optional existence of data elements and segments. HL7 Version 3 adopts an object-oriented approach, and it used the Reference Information Model (RIM), which is a static model and represents the domain of medical information. It models the grammar and semantics of HL7 Version 3 messages and uses generic classes to model health, which can be easily instantiated. To develop a health application based on HL7 v3, first, we define the rules used in the implementation and instantiate domain models from RIM. After that, we generate an XML diagram definition for each message type. Thus, HL7 RIM structure envelopes supporting exchanging messages between health systems and aiming at structuring and encoding information and separating content from formatting.

5.4.1.6   DICOM

It defines a clinical object, data structure, their semantics, and the protocols used for medical images exchanged between heterogeneous applications. It also defines the format to be used to store medical images [42].

5.4.1.7   SDMX-HD: Statistical Data and Metadata Exchange Health Domain

It defines the indicators, aggregates data, and metadata that have to be used in healthcare applications. SDMX-HD is implemented based on ISO/TS 17369:2005 SDMX standard. It aims at defining the structure and semantics of SDMX-HD messages based on XML mark-up [43].

5.4.1.8   ASTM E2369-12: Standard Specification for Continuity of Care Record

It aims at structuring the summary of data including administrative information, demographic information, and clinical information. Then, an XML coding diagram is used to transmit a summary between general practitioners and/or health services. We can visualize the constructed Continuity of Care Record document as a web browser, a CDA document, a PDF or word document, or in an e-mail message [34].

5.4.1.9   HL7 Clinical Document Architecture

It defines a universal model of centralized EHR [44]. It also specifies the structure and semantics of clinical documents to ensure documents' interpretation by both machines and users. CDA is based on HL7 Version 3 and is the most adopted [41]. The current version of CDA, Release 2, aims at enabling human readability while being machine processable at the same time [34] by specifying the structure of the header and the body of clinical documents.

5.4.1.10   HL7/ASTM Continuity of Care Document

It integrates HL7 CDA and American Society for Testing and Materials (ASTM) Continuity of Care Record. It uses HL7 CDA to ensure reusability and interoperability by exchanging a summary of clinical data and providing a common template for the whole parts of the summary [45].

5.4.1.11   HL7 Care Record Summary

It is an application of HL7 CDA. It models the summary of various cares provided to a patient and facilitates its exchange between heterogeneous applications through a standard format [45, 46].

5.4.1.12   SNOMED-CT

It is a medical terminology representing over 300,000 medical concepts. SNOMED-CT uses standardized and hierarchized medical concepts linked to other concepts through relationships in order to facilitate semantic interoperability [41]. It also aims at enabling the re-use of coded data for specific purposes by supporting cross-mapping to other coding schemes and clinical terminology [2].

5.4.1.13   LOINC

It is a clinical coding system that aims at exchanging laboratory results and using a set of universal codes, names, and clinical observations to facilitate the interoperability between health-care applications [2, 47].

5.4.1.14   ICD

It is an international coding system used to classify diseases, health conditions, and the causes of death. It aims at coding vital health statistics, including morbidity, mortality, and medical care reimbursement. It uses universal code disease conditions to support interoperability [2, 48].

5.4.1.15   ICPC-2: International Classification of Primary Care, Second edition

It is a medical classification developed by the World International Classification Committee. The World Health Organization (WHO) has adopted the International Classification of Primary Care (ICPC)-2 to classify patient's diagnosis, interventions, and model the care episode in a common structure. ICPC-2 can be used both in primary health care and general practice settings [49].

5.4.1.16   CPT: Current Procedural Terminology

It is a clinical terminology developed and maintained by the American Medical Association. It models medical and surgical procedures using a common coding scheme in order to simplify their exchange among health-care institutions and general practitioners [50, 51].

5.4.1.17   ISO 21090:2011 (harmonized data types for information interchange)

It enables the exchange of basic medical concepts by specifying their data types to facilitate their exchange between health-care systems. It uses and extends the terminologies, notations, and data types defined in ISO/IEC 11404 to define and model the basic medical concepts [31].

5.4.1.18   ISO 18308:2011 (requirements for an EHR architecture)

It models the required components for an EHR architecture. The above architecture has to ensure the following characteristics such as reliability and clinical validation, ethical sound, and compliance with the prevailing legal requirements. EHR-based architecture also aims at supporting good clinical practice and enabling data analysis [32].

5.4.1.19   HL7 EHR system functional model, release

It specifies a common list of user perspective functionalities provided in an EHR architecture in order to facilitate their reuse in a health-care system [47].

5.4.1.20   ISO/TS 22600 (privilege management and access control)

It allows the management of user privileges, ensures access control to clinical data, and supports their exchange among health-care institutions and general practitioners [32, 32, 38].

5.4.1.21   FHIR

It is developed to address the limits of HL7 v3 including specifically how HL7 messaging standards could be improved. FHIR provided a new approach for health-care information exchange initially called resources for Health [52]. FHIR used RESTful principles [29]. The FHIR is easier and more consumable than HL7 standard, but it is more robust. It also uses open Internet standard where possible.

5.4.2   Discussion

In Table 5.2, we provide an overview of the purposes of the EHR standards regarding the proposed content structure. We note that the four standards are similar in terms of content structure. All standards aim at storing persistent and structured documents, and they also support and reference unstructured data, especially multimedia content (images, signals, and videos). Clinical data are usually stored as structured and normalized databases. Data are transformed into a standardized document

Table 5.2   The interoperability of health standards and terminologies

Standard	Interoperability			
	Technical	Syntactic	Semantic	Organizational
Identifier				
ISO/TS2220:2011		*	*	
ISO/TS27527:2010		*	*	*
Messaging/information exchange				
HL7V2.X		*	*	
HL7V3		*	*	
DICOM		*	*	
FHIR		*	*	
SDMX HD		*		
Content and Structure				
ASTM E2369-12		*	*	
HL7 CDA		*	*	
HL7 ASTM Continuity of Care Document		*	*	
HL7 Care Record Summary		*	*	
ISO21090		*	*	
Health Terminology				
SNOMED		*	*	
LOINC		*	*	
ICD		*	*	
ICPC-2		*	*	
CPT		*	*	
EHR				
ISO18308:2011		*	*	*
System Function Model				
HL7,EHR_system Functional Model release 1.1	*	*	*	*
Security and Access Control				
ISO/TS22600				*

to be communicated between heterogeneous e-health organizations, for example, in the form of HL7 messages.

5.4.3   Semantic interoperability: IoT-based ontologies

The IoT health object aims at collecting a huge amount of health data. We highlight here that these data will be a multimodal structure containing multiple formats. Handing the heterogeneous data generated by various sources and processing them in real-time will be critical toward building a connected EHR system. Several sensor ontologies are described in the literature [2, 32, 32, 43, 43, 47, 48, 53–60] and aim to solve heterogeneity problems concerning the data management, the software, and the hardware aspects of sensors. There are several proposed ontologies based on generic IoT concepts such as Semantic Sensor Network (SSN) ontology [32, 53, 54], M3 ontology [55] OntoSensor [34], MyOntoSens [56, 57], SAREF [58], and Brick [43]. In addition, Reference [59] describes the places, the agents, and the events by defining the components of a new context. It provides four types of context classification such as external, internal, physical, and logical. In order to effectively label contextual data collected from various devices, several ontologies have been proposed for context-aware systems such as References [21, 22, 33, 47, 59, 61] worked on the location describing the spatial context of both user and devices and estimating the location of the device through a reasoner built upon sensor data and information from location sensors. Many IoT-based ontologies are defined in temporal context by reusing some existing ontologies DAML-Time (DARPA (Defense Advanced Research Projects Agency) Agent Markup Language project Time initiative) [2], DAML-S (DAML for Web Services), KSL-Time (Stanford Knowledge Systems Lab Time ontology [2]), and OWL-Time ontology. To provide a universal definition of time, DAML-Time and KSL-Time defined various types of time intervals and their granularity. Ontology provides concepts. Hobbs and Pan [62] propose OWL-Time ontology describing time-based information in Gregorian calendar format. Several ontological approaches extended and implemented OWL-Time. Another ontology was proposed by Xue *et al.* [63] aiming at annotating semantically data sensors using modular ontology Semantic Medical Sensor Data ontology, which is built by extending multiple relevant ontologies. In this study, the authors propose a new model describing sensors with semantic metadata aiming at understanding their context and making them machine-understandable, interoperable, as well as facilitating data integration.

5.4.4   Discussion of IoT-based ontologies

To summarize, in Table 5.3, all discussed IoT-based ontologies that are compared with regard to relevant aspects they manage. We propose a classification of the IoT ontologies. In order to achieve semantic consistency in different system modules, most systems propose proprietary ontologies. However, the majority of systems reuse existing ontologies to improve interoperability. Several studies combine and reuse existing ontologies to propose new ontologies for the IoT domain: IoT-Lite [64], OpenIoT ontology [65], IoT-O ontology [20], FIESTA-IoT ontology [66], oneM2M ontology [67], and Open-MultiNet (ONM) [13]. These new ontologies are designed for specific problems in order to collect and integrate IoT data. However, the above ontologies are still incomplete since they lack one or more concepts for the IoT domain. Thus, we note the absence of IoT-generic ontologies defining a common ontology including core concepts. Reusing existing ontologies and merging them into new ontologies seem crucial to reusing concepts and relationships from existing ones. In order to use sensor data effectively, we identified six criteria aiming at choosing the appropriate ontology. The first criterion is the data description that describes the collected data to make them machine-understandable, interoperable, and facilitate data integration. First, it seems important to describe the medical device and its capability to search specific medical contents or events. Second, it seems very important that the Medical Devices (MD) network is capable to facilitate new MD implementation

Table 5.3   Existing IoT ontologies

Ontology	Describing data	Discovering sensor	Capabilities of sensor	Accessing data and sharing	Extensibility	Context	
						Location	Time
Semantic Sensor Network	X		X				
Xue et al.			X	X			
Shi et al.				X			
M3	X						
OntoSensor			X				
MyOntoSens	X						
Hirmer et al.		X			X		
SAREF		X			X		
Brick		X					
Event ontology		X	X				
Baldauf et al.						X	
Chen et al.						X	
Kim et al.						X	
WGS84 ontology						X	X
Flury et al.							
DAML-Time							X
KSL-Time							X
OWL-Time							X
Semantic Medical Sensor Data	X		X	X	X	X	

for time and cost savings. Thus, it has to be extensible and capable to support various ways. Finally, it seems critical to propose new approaches to model the semantics of concepts and their relationships in a particular context. For example, to correctly model the relationships between clinical concepts, we have to capture the context of medical devices by detecting the patient's activities, his/her location, and temporal properties of the captured data and environment. In a conclusion, we provide some challenges to be addressed in order to build a semantic model taking into account the context of information and its devices. These are as follows:

- How to reuse existing concepts as much as possible?
- How to align them with equivalence relations?
- How to validate the constructed ontology using an ontology validator?
- How to annotate the evaluated ontology with relevant metadata?
- How to make the ontology accessible anytime and anywhere?
- How to ensure a modular approach to be sure that the ontology is reusable?
- How to document the ontology with samples to demonstrate its usage?

The majority of the existing works in health care do not reuse defined IoT models. They only describe the sensor concept and ignore the description of the health data source.

5.5   EHR summarization

Here, we describe a background knowledge of EHR, review, and discuss recent approaches on EHR summarization.

5.5.1   EHR definition

The EHR concept has appeared since the 1960s [68], and we note that there is no common definition of an EHR until today. Iakovidis [69] defines the EHR as digitized clinical data about a given patient in order to support health care, education, and research data analysis. The EHR-based application has to be accessible, secure, and highly usable. In Reference [70], Gunter and Terry define EHR as a set of clinical and electronic data about a given patient and a population. The U.S. National Cancer Institute defines EHR as a digitalized set of clinical data about a given patient stored on a computer. The U.S. Centers for Medicare and Medicaid Services define EHR as a digitalized version of a clinical history of a given patient including the key administrative medical data and the information related to plan care. The EHR has to be maintained by the provider over time. The WHO [71] defines EHR as medical records provided in an EHR-based system aiming at collecting data, storing and manipulating, and providing safe access.

5.5.2   EHR summarization approaches

The summarization process consists of creating a subset of data called a summary representing the most relevant information within the original content. Existing studies on EHR summarization focus on text summarization are summarized in Reference [3], the authors confirm that the EHR summarization aims at providing useful information for the general practitioner by automatically creating a compressed version of a given text. This type of summarized text depends on the clinician's needs. However, generic summaries cover as much of the medical content as included in multi-documents. The summary has to preserve the general topical organization of the original text. In this review, we focus on the approaches based on multi-document extractive summarization, which consists of producing a summary of multiple documents about the same. Summarization approaches focused on clinical variables extraction and visualization of structured and unstructured data [8], in order to provide an overview of the whole patient record. In this review, we report and discuss 38 focus papers on EHR summarization categorized into four types of EHR text summarization.

5.5.2.1   Extractive summaries

It consists of choosing a collection of sentences in the original document(s) to produce consistent summaries. Summaries are created by extracting phrases and sentences [72] from the original text. An extractive approach synthesizes the document(s) by identifying pieces of the patient's record and displaying the summary in user-friendly interfaces. In Reference [73], the authors perform an extractive summarization of specific diagnoses provided by the general practitioner. Their system is based on a supervised approach and uses the ICD codes to train a transformer-based neural model. Radiologists made some evaluations and confirm that using supervised models generates better extractive summaries than unsupervised approaches. In Reference [73], the authors provide a new model sighting at including accurate components to EHR data, such as structured data associated with the encounter, sentence level clinical aspects, and structures of the clinical records. Authors provide a clinical data processing pipeline based on an extension of the basic medical natural language processing (NLP) and on the use of concept recognition and relation detection. In Reference [9], the authors aim at customizing user views by using NLP and MedLEE NLP engine to handle modifiers [74]. The authors defined a new method able to learn and generate meaningful topic summaries from structured clinical data. It consists of learning the correspondences between structured data and the clinical note topics. To do so, the system uses existing summaries written by clinicians. Another study [75] provides a SIM (Security Information Management) card-based system based on medical devices. It consists of synthesizing clinical data and displaying them on the phone by a custom-developed "Medirec" software application [76]. It provided a new summarization approach aiming at summarizing text data in order to classify patients with and without diabetes. They evaluate their approach using two traditional classification methods such as logistic regression and Fisher linear discriminant analysis and four ML techniques such as neural networks, support vector machines, fuzzy c-mean, and random forests. This research [77] was a unique work focusing on metastases information extraction from pathology reports of metastatic lung cancer. In Reference [78], the authors propose a new approach aiming at summarizing biomedical text documents using the Bayesian summarization method. It consists of first mapping the input text to the UMLS terminology and then selecting the relevant ones to be used as classification features [7]. It proposes a new approach using various graphical presentations such as small graphs for drug dosages, timelines for medical visits and hospital stays, genograms for inherited illnesses, and textual presentation of medical notes. In Reference [8], the authors propose a new approach called UPhenome. The proposed approach is based on two steps. The first step consists of a graphical model for large-scale probabilistic phenotyping. The second step consists of modeling diseases and patients' characteristics, and generates the summarized clinical data [79]. It proposes a real-time summarization by aggregating clinical data from heterogeneous health-care systems using HL7 messages and distributed architecture.

5.5.2.2　Abstractive summaries

Abstractive summarization techniques consist of generating new text synthesizing the original text [7]. Abstractive summaries also allow providing information context to enrich the data. In References [80, 81], a first method called timeline consists of involving clinicians to code rules, while AdaptEHR consists of inferring rules automatically and relationships from ontologies and graphical models [82]. It proposes a hybrid method based on abstractive and extractive summarization of clinical variables. It aims at performing semantic, temporal, and contextual abstraction using domain-specific ontology to generate abstractions. Finally, References [13, 83], proposed a new method to graphically summarize clinical data by generating new text.

5.5.2.3　Indicative summaries

The indicative summarization approach extracts significant terms from the original text and highlights the main parts. Indicative summaries are used in conjunction with EHR, in order to integrate indirectly into the extractive summarization process. There are few approaches in the literature concerning indicative summarization [72]. It proposed a new approach to summarize and graphically visualize the EHR [72]. It proposed a task-based evaluation summarizer. In Reference [84], the authors evaluated how and when clinicians in an ambulatory setting will enter data directly into an EHR.

5.5.2.4　Informative summaries

Informative summarization approach designs summaries to be used independently of the EHR. The informative approach is used to replace the original set of raw data [80, 85]. It proposes a new method of summarizing structured clinical data, such as administrative, computerized provider order entry, and laboratory test data. Authors developed a new model to detect risks by predicting each of two severity levels of in-hospital Other studies using the visualization-based summarization approach [86–88] and Resource Description Framework: RDF-based summarization approach [89] are proposed to summarize text data. Many research groups [10, 72, 90] proposed clinical data summarization system based on the text input data. The proposed system aims to reduce data volume. Also, many frameworks are proposed for text summarization [52, 91–93] and for generating new stories and scientific articles to summarize unstructured texts [91, 94–96]. In order to overcome challenges relating to EHR summarization and to compare and discuss existing studies in clinical data summarization, all criteria defined in the previous section were used to characterize and compare clinical data summarization methods according to the challenges highlighted in the introduction section. Our analysis summarized in Table 5.4 demonstrates that most clinical summarization approaches are based on unstructured data [73, 77, 97, 98] and rely on structure [76, 99–101] and text content in order to construct the summary. Also, our comparison highlights that the evolution of the summary is still an open challenge. So, we observe that none of the existing studies consider real data in their analysis and do not consider the context of creating the summary, and few of them [100–102] rely only on the time property. Thus, existing systems are still unable to contextually interpret reason on the transferred knowledge among real data, and consequently cannot synthesize data to provide accurate desired results. All existing systems focus on one or two objectives at most, while none of them provide in the same framework various functionalities despite its importance in supporting clinicians' preferences to find the patients' data according to various needs. All objectives should be an integral part of a clinical summarization-based system. Finally, another important point is the output type of summarized clinical data. The output of most of the existing systems is a textual format. Two of them propose a graphical summarization [75, 100]. They neither propose dedicated tools that make the summary easier to be understood and interpreted by the clinician nor provide them with appropriate perceptions of their needs. An intuitive and friendly Graphical User Interface (GUI) will benefit the data summarization-based systems.

5.5.3   Discussion

In order to clearly address the challenges related to EHR summarization, we compared and discussed the existing studies based on the following criteria Table 5.5:

- Type of input Data (C1): This criterion refers to the input data which could be structured data, semi-structured data, and unstructured data.
- Data type (C2): This criterion describes the type of data incorporated (text, XML, numeric, video, and image).
- Representation standard (C3): This criterion indicates if the approach incorporates standard (i.e., information-based standard, document-based standard, or hybrid standard, e.g., Yes or No).
- Summarization technique (C4): This criterion refers to the techniques deployed to summarize EHR, which could be grouping, compression, analysis, pattern-mining, classification, and visualization.
- Summarization approach (C5): This criterion refers to the target of the summarization approach abstractive, extractive, informative, or indicative.
- Medical knowledge-based summarization (C6): This criterion describes the medical knowledge that system incorporates (e.g., Yes or No).

Table 5.4   *Summary of retrieved studies on EHR visualization*

Approach	Input data	Data type	Standard	Output	Context	User oriented	Visualization technique	Medical knowledge
Wang et al., 2021	Unstructured	Text	No	Text	No	Yes	NLP	Yes
Kwon et al., 2020	Unstructured	Not mentioned	No	Graphical	No	Yes	ML	Yes
Jin et al., 2020	Unstructured	Not mentioned	No	Graphical	Time	Yes	ESS	No
MCNaBB and Laramee 2019	Unstructured	Not mentioned	No	Map	No	No	Geospatial Visualization	No
GUO et al., 2019	Unstructured	Not mentioned	No	Pattern	No	Yes	Event Sequence Simplification	No
GlickSberg et al., 2019	Unstructured	Not mentioned	No	EHR	Time	Yes	Clustering	No
	Structured		Yes	EHR	No	Yes	ESS	Yes
Bernard et al., 2019	Unstructured	Document	No	Network	Not mentioned	Yes	Geospatial	No
Almezadeh et al., 2019	Structured	Numerical	No		No	No	NLP	No
Trivedi et al., 2018	Unstructured	Text	No	Text	No	No	Analysis Classification	
Tong et al., 2018	Structured	Geographic data	Yes	Cartogram	No	Yes	ESS	No
Guo et al., 2018	Unstructured	Numerical	Yes	Ontology	Yes	Yes	Geospatial visualization	No
Ola and Sedig 2016	Unstructured Structred	Text	No	Pattern	No	Yes	ESS	Yes
Loorak et al., 2016	Unstructured	Text	No	Temporal data	No	Yes		Yes
Kamaleswaran et al., 2016	Unstructured	Numerical	No	Temporal data	Time	No	clustering	No
Jiang et al., 2016	Unstructured	Text	Yes	Geospatial information	No	Yes	Geospatial visualization	No
Glueck et al., 2016	Unstructured	Text	No	Ontology	Yes	Yes	Comparison	yes
Bernard et al., 2014	Unstructured	Not mentioned	No	Temporal attribute	No	No	ML	Yes

(Continues)

Table 5.4 Continued

Approach	Input data	Data type	Standard	Output	Context	User oriented	Visualization technique	Medical knowledge
Malik et al., 2014	Structured	Database	No	Numerical	Time	Yes	ESS	Yes
Kamaleswaran et al., 2014	Unstructured	Stream data	No	Stream	Time	Yes	Clustering	Yes
GHOTOZ et al., 2014	Unstructured	Numerical	No	Matrix	No	Yes	ESS	Yes
Borland et al., 2014	Unstructured	Numerical	No	Curve	Time	Yes	Comparaison	Yes
Monore et al., 2013	Structured	Numerical	No	Pattern	Time	No	ESS	No
wong and Ghotz 2012	Structured	Not mentioned	No	Pattern	Time	Yes	ESS	Yes
Sopan et al., 2012	Unstructured	Not mentioned	No	Pattern	Time	Yes	ESS	Yes
Alonso et al., 2012	Unstructured	Text	No	Text	No	No	Extraction	No
Gschwandter et al., 2011	Unstructured	Not mentioned	No	Numerical	Time	Yes	ESS	Yes
Wang et al., 2009	Structured	Not mentioned	No	temporal data	Time	Yes	Clustering	Yes
BUI et al., 2007	Structured	XML	No	Document	Time	Yes	Classification	Yes
Fails et al., 2006	Unstructured	Numerical	No	Pattern	Time	Yes	ESS	Yes
Hinum et al., 2005	Unstructured	Temporal data	No	Curve, Grahics	Time	No	Classification	Yes
Goren et al., 2004	Structured	Not mentioned	No	Graphics	Time	Yes	Clustering	Yes
Bade et al., 2004	Unstructured	Not mentioned	No	Graphics	Time	NO	Abstraction	Yes
Horan et al., 2001	Unstructured	Text	No	No	Time	No	Extraction	Yes
Plaisant et al., 1998	Unstructured	Document	No	Document	No	No	Extraction	No

Table 5.5   Summary of retrievea studies on EHR and medical data summarization

Approach	Input data	Data type	Standard	Output	Context	User oriented	Summarization technique	Summarization approach
Denis Jered *et al.* 2020	Unstructured	Text	No	Text	No	No	Classification	Extractive
Liang *et al.* 2019	Unstructured	Document	No	Document	No	No	Classification	Extractive
P. Durga *et al.* 2018	Unstructured	Numerical	No	Document	Time	No	Classification	Extractive
Jen *et al.* 2018	Structured	Text	No	Text	Time	No	Classification Filtering	Extractive
Soysal *et al.* 2017	Unstructured	Text	No	Text	No	No	Visualization	Extractive
Moradi and Ghadiri, 2017	Unstructured	Text	Yes	Document	No	No	Extraction	Extractive
Razavian *et al.* 2015	Unstructured	Text	No	Text	No	No	Analysis	Extractive
Borland, 2014	Structured	Text	No	Graph	Time	No	Visualization	Extractive
Fei *et al.* 2013	Structured	Numerical	No	Document	Time	No	Analysis	Extractive
Antonelli *et al.* 2013	Structured	Numerical	No	Document	No	No	Visualization	Extractive
Tapak *et al.* 2013	Structured	Numerical	No	Document	No	No	Analysis Classification	Extractive
Klann *et al.* 2013	Unstructured	Document	No	Document	No	No	Analysis	Extractive
Roque *et al.* 2010	Unstructured	Text	No	Text	No	No	Extraction	Extractive
Rind *et al.* 2010	Unstructured	Text	No	Text	No	No	Analysis Visualization	Extraction
Krummenacher *et al.* 2010	Structured	XML	Yes	Tuple	No	No	Visualization	Extraction
were.C *et al..* 2010	Unstructured	Text	No	Text	Time	No	Extraction	Extraction
Barakat *et al.* 2010	Unstructured	Text	No	Graphic	No	No	Indicative Abstraction Informative	Abstraction Abstraction
Savova *et al.* 2010v	Unstructured	text	No	Text	No	No	Analysis	Extraction

(Continues)

Table 5.5 Continued

Approach	Input data	Data type	Standard	Output	Context	User oriented	Summarization technique	Summarization approach
Krummenacher et al. 2009	Unstructured	XML	Yes	Document	No	No	Visualization	Extractive / Abstractive
Kumar et al. 2008	Unstructured	Text	No	Text	No	No	Extraction	Extractive
Huang et al. 2007	Unstructured	Text	No	Text	No	No	Clustering	Extractive
Reeve et al. 2007	Unstructured	Text	Yes	Text	No	No	Extraction	Extractive
Afantenos, 2006	Unstructured	Text	Yes	Text	No	No	Extraction	Extractive
Ogers et al. 2006	Unstructured Structured	Text	Text	No	No	No	Aggregation	Extractive
Reeve et al. 2006	Unstructured	Text	Yes	Text	No	No	Extraction	Extractive
Bui et al. 2007	Structured	XML	Yes	Text Image	Time	No	Extraction Abstraction	Extractive Abstractive
Wilcox et al. 2005	Unstructured	Text	No	Text	No	No	Extraction	Extractive
Liu and Friedman, 2004	Structured	XML	No	Text	No	No	Extraction	Extractive
Payan, 2004	Unstructured	Text	No	Text	No	No	Extraction	Abstractive
Radevhovy and McKeown, 2002	Unstructured	Text	No	Text	No	No	Extraction	Abstractive
Plaisant et al. 1998	Unstructured	Text	No	Text	Time	No	Extraction visualization	Extractive Abstractive
Tufte, 1994	Structured Unstructured	Document	No	Document	No	No	Extraction	Extractive
Rogers, 1979	Structured	Document	No	Text	No	No	Extraction	Extractive Abstractive

- Output type (C7): This criterion concerns the type of displayed summarized data that is a combination of numerical data, textual data, document, and graph.
- Context-awareness criterion (C8): This criterion refers to the context of data or the device, and we defined: (i) Partial, used to demonstrate if an existing system uses concepts about the deployed context of the devices (e.g., time, location, and trajectory) or concepts about the static data and (ii) Total, used to determine if an existing system uses both of deployed context of devices and other static data context.
- User-oriented summarization (C9): This criterion represents that the approach-oriented user (e.g., Yes or No).

Our analysis summarized in Table 5.4 demonstrates that approaches are based on either structured data [7, 72, 103] or unstructured data [7, 10, 89, 93, 103], and none of them rely on both structured and unstructured data in order to construct the summary. Another important part of this study is the output type of summarized data. The reviewed systems are either document-based [74, 78, 102] or graph-based [88]. They neither propose dedicated tools that make the summary accessible to the user nor provide them with appropriate perceptions of their needs. Users are more and more concerned about security, confidentiality, understanding their data, and the accuracy and completeness of their data. This should be mandatory when developing a visualization method for the summary to empower them with easier means. An intuitive and friendly GUI will benefit summarization-based systems. Also, none of the studies surveyed in this chapter is user oriented and satisfy various users' needs. Our comparison highlights that the evolution of the summary is still an open challenge. So, we observe that most existing studies do not consider the context of the data in their analysis and do not consider the context of creating the summary, and they rely only on the time property except some of them consider the time in their analysis [74, 78, 88]. Thus, existing systems are still unable to contextually interpret reason on the transferred knowledge among real data, and consequently cannot synthesize data in order to provide accurate desired results. All existing systems focus on one objective, while none of them provide in the same framework various functionalities despite its importance in supporting users' preferences to find the data according to various needs. All objectives should be an integral part of a summarization-based system. Finally, we deduce that most of the studied approaches are extractive-based [72, 73]. Three of them [7, 80, 81] are abstractive-based, and four studies [10, 80, 95, 100] are extractive- and abstractive-based approaches. From this comparative study, we deduce main four limitations.

1. **The lack of access and collect data from medical devices:** Due to the heterogeneity of applications, it seems critical to synthesize health data in order to provide a relevant, comprehensive, and understanding view of the patient's history to effectively help clinical diagnostics.
2. **The lack of semantic interoperability:** Applications generate a huge amount of heterogeneous data, which make it almost difficult to synthesize the knowledge communicated between clinical applications and provide efficient results.

3. **The lack of linking data and medical devices to their contexts:** We have to describe the data and the device context toward identifying its capacity and its reliability to ensure the data consistency of the gathered data and to easily repair it when necessary.

4. **The lack of user-centered summary design:** Increased cognitive workload of clinician has consistently been linked to the text summarization. This makes it nearly impossible to provide interactive and personalized summary. Existing systems are unable to generate adaptive summaries adjusting based on clinician preference and needs.

5.6   EHR visualization

5.6.1   *EHR visualization definition*

Reference [104] has defined computer-based visualization as a visual system helping users to carry out some activities more effectively and efficiently by providing various visual representations of data sets. We distinguish two types of visualization systems: (i) information visualization focusing on data sets with nonspatial data attributes and discrete observations [105], and (ii) scientific visualization visualizes real objects in a spatial three-dimensional space [106]. In Reference [107], authors shown that the EHRs have to combine heterogeneous visualization techniques to model relevant data from both information and scientific visualization. Information visualization aims to map collected data to compact representations to generate meaningful and relevant information quickly. So, we conclude that information visualization is crucial to explore and query the heterogeneous and temporal data. On the other hand, interactive information visualization ensures analysis exploration supported by human cognition and visual abilities [108].

5.6.2   *EHR visualization approaches*

In this section, we reviewed 40 papers focusing on visualization and visual analytics of EHR data and compared them according to the same criteria used to compare EHR summarization approaches. References [100, 104, 109]provide and discuss existing studies of EHR visualization and provide a new visualization tool called LetterVis. The proposed tool supports the analysis of clinic letters using interactive visual designs and queries. The authors model a common letter and incorporate in the same interface so as to explore the related content and patterns. The text is analyzed and processed using NLP technique and explored in multiple linked interactive views. McNabb 2019 multivariate surveys work by focusing on health-care visualization and visual analytics. Reference [110] proposes a new approach based on visual interactive that trains models for prostate cancer identification. In Reference [4], the authors compare phenotype through a visual analysis tool named PhenoBlocks and defined a new hierarchy comparison algorithm. Reference [111] proposes a novel algorithm aiming at simplifying the topology by eliminating duplicates and incorporating natural language queries for searching anomalies. Reference [4] described a new toll named PhenoLines visualizing a temporal evolution of phenotypes. In Reference [112], the authors provide a novel approach by extracting heterogeneous data to a hierarchical task abstraction. Authors also proposed a new visualization tool called IDMVis to sequence temporal multidimensional events with their correlated data. Reference [113] aims at increasing the interpretability and interactivity of Recurrent Neural Network (RNNs) through visual analytic tool based on health experts, artificial intelligence scientists, and visual analytics researchers. In Reference [114], authors aim at modeling semantically meaningful care plans and their processes and identifying critical events that help adapt these plans. The proposed approach defined an unsupervised algorithm following three key steps: (i) estimating event representation, (ii) warping and alignment event sequence, and (iii) segmenting the sequences. Authors also suggest a novel visualization system illustrating the results. Reference [115] presents PatientExplore producing an interactive and dynamic interfaces to facilitate the visualization of medical data. [110], authors provided a new tool for segmenting patients' data and aggregating them using the whole history and the combination of the treatments. Finally, it visualizes the aggregated data in an interactive way. In Reference [116], authors provide a new framework to visualize the missing values by exploring, identifying, and validating their imputations. Reference [117] provides a new tool for interactive processing of clinical notes through multiple NLP models [118].

The above study shows the importance of NLP tools in analyzing and visualizing clinical text data using, especially, the pen source Gate tool supporting text mining of biomedical documents [119]. However, the authors demonstrate that it is unable to perform advanced analysis since it lacks interactive visualization features. Reference [112] proposes a new visual analytic tool named AnamneVis incorporating NLP algorithms to extract structured medical information from both the dialogue between the clinician and his patient and the textual reports. In Reference [14], the authors follow LifeLines2 approach [8] to extract structured data hidden inside clinical letters through a visual representation and using NLP method for the event system simplification technique. Reference [120] proposes a new tool named LifeFlow used to visualize interactively the event sequence data. In Reference [121], the authors provide a new tool aiming at simplifying temporal event sequence data, aggregating data, and identifying hidden trends. Reference [122] provides a new visualization tool named TimeSpan aiming at exploring the temporal aspects of a care plan process.

Reference [100] describes EventThred, a visualization system evaluating some defined patterns in event sequence data. It measures the importance of the text in the document using the Term Frequency - Inverse Document Frequency [123]. Reference [124] defined the Community Health Map, a new toll aiming at visualizing public health-care datasets. It allows clinicians to visualize heterogeneous datasets gathered from Hospitals. In Reference [123], authors propose, a new tool for infectious diseases surveillance and spatio-temporal visualization. SIMID learns existing clinical data and simulates the spread of infectious disease. Reference [101] introduces a new visualization tool. The proposed tool explores the similarity in cohorts of patients and generates new clusters.

5.6.3   Discussion

Our analysis summarized in Table 5.4 demonstrates that approaches are based on structured data [112, 120, 125, 126]. Only two approaches rely on both structured and unstructured data [44, 122]. Another important part of this study is the output type in the visualization. Most of the reviewed systems are pattern-based [44, 87, 107, 121, 127], graphical-based [86, 125, 126, 128], or text-based [120, 122, 127, 129]. They neither propose dedicated tools that make the visualization accessible to the user nor provide them with appropriate perceptions of their needs. Also, all the studies surveyed in this chapter are user oriented and satisfy various users' needs. Our comparison highlights that the evolution of the summary is still an open challenge. So, we observe that most of existing studies [87, 125, 130] do not consider the context of the data in the visualization process except some of them [80, 115, 121, 126, 130] consider the time in their analysis. From this comparative study, we deduce some major challenges faced in EHR data visualization.

1. **Providing an accessible EHR:** Providing an accessible Electronic Health Record is very challenging [131]. Many challenges have to be addressed related to relevant data acquisition and data extraction since it requires amount of time to search for. Clinical data are very sensitive and are often unstructured. It seems important to convert the data into a structured form, but it risks losing valuable insight. It also seems crucial to apply an anonymization process on EHR data taking into account the data governance group policies.
2. **Ensuring data quality:** Data can contain incomplete and erroneous values since they are entered and computed manually. For that, it seems crucial to verify data quality. On the other hand, we note that EHR contains very heterogeneous data and do not create with supporting research in mind [131]. However, amount of research about EHR is emerged and widely accepted worldwide, which improves the quality control measures for collecting clinical data [132].
3. **Improving visualization techniques:** In the literature, we found five visualization-based techniques such as ML, natural language, ESS, geospatial visualization, and clustering and comparison. First, we note the importance of incorporating ML techniques into EHR Visualization [125, 133]. We highlight that it is a new field of research but combined with EHR visualization it is not very mature yet. EHR visualization research can benefit more with the help of ML techniques by describing existing states, predicting health problems and providing guidance for the future based on domain knowledge. Many ML techniques are applied in EHR visual analytics to increase automation of processing, especially, deep learning [134], neural networks [125], support vector machines [112], and topic models [109]. Second, EHRs contain diverse and heterogeneous data requiring appropriate modifiers to capture words, phrases, and their relationships. Thus, we note that NLP techniques can be efficient in transforming unstructured text into structured data [87]. EHRs include temporal data and events, and it seems important to model and analyze these temporal elements by

improving both data-processing and visualization of EHRs. In this context, the ESS technique to reduce the visual complexity of event sequences in aggregated model [121]. LifeLines [90] and EventFlow [121] adopted such techniques. The fourth technique used in visualization process is geospatial visualization, so the most important work for this technique [123] introduces SIMID, a new spatio-temporal visualization tool aiming at surveilling infectious diseases. The proposed system uses interactive animated maps to analyze the infectious disease. Finally, another technique seems critical to provide efficient EHR analysis and to develop information visualization discipline. This shows our comparison table LABEL:tab6 where some approaches [87, 135] produce homogeneous subgroups based on similarities by the use of hierarchical clustering algorithms.

4. **Making data interoperable:** Our study confirms the lack of standard definition of an EHR. Providers often provide specific standard to support specific clinical domain and care process [136]. We highlight also that the use of terminologies such as the UMLS combined with health standards should making data more interoperable.

Many studies are proposed in order to address the above challenges such as building a freely accessibility EHR database [109] and improving data validation and interoperability [109].

5.7 Conclusion

Health Information Systems have to obey the interoperability systems in order to efficiently manage and deliver relevant clinical data and ensure better communication between individuals, processes, and technology. Being interoperable ensuring improved health-care services, the increase, and the efficiency of their quality. The summarization and the visualization processes are essential for clinicians to provide coordinated care and practice effective communication. Also, heterogeneous clinical systems are implemented in health care either in the EHR summarization or EHR visualization. In this study, we focused on interoperability challenge and the use of health standards and terminologies to ensure the interoperability specially in the summarization-based and visualization-based EHR systems. Here, we described, compared, and discussed approaches related to interoperability such as e-health standards, terminologies, and IoT ontologies. We also reviewed and discussed summarization-based and visualization-based EHR systems in order to show how interoperability issues can enhance EHR analysis to build accurate summarization-based and visualization-based EHR systems. Finally, our discussions reveal that five techniques should be adopted to enhance interoperability and the accessibility of an accruate EHR which help to improve data validation and interoperability.

References

[1]   Blaya J.A., Fraser H.S.F., Holt B. 'E-health technologies show promise in developing countries'. *Health Affairs (Project Hope)*. 2010, vol. 29(2), pp. 244–51.

[2]   Adebesin F., Kotzé P., Van Greunen D., Foster R. 'Barriers & challenges to the adoption of e-health standards in Africa'.2013.

[3]   Moher D., Liberati A., Tetzlaff J., Altman D.G., Group P. 'Preferred reporting items for systematic reviews and meta-analyses: the prisma statement'. *Annals of Internal Medicine*. 2009, vol. 151(4), pp. 264–69.

[4]   Glueck M., Naeini M.P., Doshi-Velez F, *et al*. 'PhenoLines: phenotype comparison visualizations for disease subtyping via topic models'. *IEEE Transactions on Visualization and Computer Graphics*. 2018, vol. 24(1), pp. 371–81.

[5]   Paladin L., Hirsh L., Piovesan D., Andrade-Navarro M.A., Kajava A.V., Tosatto S.C.E. 'RepeatsDB 2.0: improved annotation, classification, search and visualization of repeat protein structures'. *Nucleic Acids Research*. 2017, vol. 45(6), pp. D308–12.

[6]   Oh H., Rizo C., Enkin M., Jadad A. 'What is e-health (3): a systematic review of published definitions'. *Journal of Medical Internet Research*. 2005, vol. 7(1), e1.

[7]   Powsner S.M., Tufte E.R. 'Summarizing clinical psychiatric data'. *Psychiatric Services (Washington, D.C.)*. 1997, vol. 48(11), pp. 1458–61.

[8]   Pivovarov R., Perotte A.J., Grave E., Angiolillo J., Wiggins C.H., Elhadad N. 'Learning probabilistic phenotypes from heterogeneous EHR data'. *Journal of Biomedical Informatics*. 2015, vol. 58, pp. 156–65.

[9]   Liu J., Cao Y., Lin C.-Y., Huang Y., Zhou M. 'Low-quality product review detection in opinion summarization'. *Proceedings of the 2007 joint conference on empirical methods in natural language processing and computational natural language learning (EMNLP-CoNLL)*; 2007. pp. 334–42.

[10]   Whiting-O' Keefe Q.E., Simborg D.W., Epstein W.V. 'A controlled experiment to evaluate the use of a time-oriented summary medical record'. *Medical Care*. 1980, vol. 18(8), pp. 842–52.

[11]   Wang Q., Laramee R.S., Lacey A., Pickrell W.O. 'LetterVis: a letter-space view of clinic letters'. *The Visual Computer*. 2005, vol. 37(9–11), pp. 2643–56.

[12]   Altman D.G., Schulz K.F., Moher D, *et al*. 'The revised consort statement for reporting randomized trials: explanation and elaboration'. *Annals of Internal Medicine*. 2001, vol. 134(8), pp. 663–94.

[13]   Vandenbroucke J.P., von Elm E., Altman D.G., *et al*. 'Strengthening the reporting of observational studies in epidemiology (strobe): explanation and elaboration'. *PLoS Medicine*. 2007, vol. 4(10), e297.

[14] Berges I., Bermúdez J., Illarramendi A. 'Toward semantic interoperability of electronic health records'. *IEEE Transactions on Information Technology in Biomedicine*. 2012, vol. 16(3), pp. 424–31.

[15] Eichelberg M., Aden T., Riesmeier J., Dogac A., Laleci G.B. 'A survey and analysis of electronic healthcare record standards'. *ACM Computing Surveys*. 2005, vol. 37(4), pp. 277–315.

[16] Walker J., Pan E., Johnston D., Adler-Milstein J., Bates D.W., Middleton B. 'The value of health care information exchange and interoperability: there is a business case to be made for spending money on a fully standardized nationwide system'. *Health Affairs*. 2005, vol. 24, pp. W5–10.

[17] Denjoy N. 'European coordination Committee of the radiological, electromedical, and healthcare it industry: medical imaging equipment age, profile & density'. 2016.

[18] Whitman L.E., Panetto H. 'The missing link: culture and language barriers to interoperability'. *Annual Reviews in Control*. 2006, vol. 30(2), pp. 233–41.

[19] Veer V.D.H., Wiles A. 'Achieving technical interoperability, European Telecommunications Standards Institute'.2008.

[20] Hobbs J.R., Pan F. 'An ontology of time for the semantic web'. *ACM Transactions on Asian Language Information Processing*. 2006, vol. 3(1), pp. 66–85.

[21] Bodenreider O. 'The unified medical language system (umls): integrating biomedical terminology'. *Nucleic Acids Research*. 2004, vol. 32(Database issue), pp. D267–70.

[22] Europea C. 'ICT standards in the health sector: current situation and prospect'. *Special Study*. 2008, vol. 1.

[23] Blobel B., González C., Oemig F, *et al*. The role of architecture and ontology for interoperabilitythe role of architecture and ontology for interoperability. EFMI-STC; 2010. pp. 33–39.

[24] Hirmer P., Wieland M., Breitenbücher U., Mitschang B. 'Dynamic ontology-based sensor binding'. *East European Conference on Advances in Databases and Information Systems*; Springer, 2016. pp. 323–37.

[25] Daniele L., Hartog F.D., Roes J. 'Created in close interaction with the industry: the smart appliances reference (SAREF) ontology' in International workshop formal ontologies meet industries. Springer; 2015. pp. 100–12.

[26] Russomanno D.J., Kothari C., Thomas O. 'Sensor ontologies: from shallow to deep models'. *Proceedings of the Thirty-Seventh Southeastern Symposium on System Theory (SSST05)*; Tuskegee, AL, IEEE, 1999. pp. 107–12.

[27] Balaji B., Bhattacharya A., Fierro G, *et al*. 'Brick: towards a unified metadata schema for buildings'. *Proceedings of the 3rd ACM International Conference on Systems for Energy-Efficient Built Environments*; 2016. pp. 41–50.

[28] Haghi M., Thurow K., Stoll R. 'Wearable devices in medical internet of things: scientific research and commercially available devices'. *Healthcare Informatics Research*. 2017, vol. 23(1), pp. 4–15.

[29] Fielding R.T. Architectural styles and the design of network-based software architectures. Irvine, CA: University of California; 2000.

[30] Ouksel A.M., Sheth A. 'Semantic interoperability in global information systems'. *ACM SIGMOD Record.* 1999, vol. 28(1), pp. 5–12.

[31] ISO '*ISO I.21090 health informatics-harmonized data types for information interchange*, Bericht, ISO/CEN'..2011.

[32] ISO.I.ISO, guide 2–standardization and related activities-general vocabulary. Geneva: ISO; 2004.

[33] Kalra D., Beale T., Heard S. 'The openehr Foundation, studies in health technology and informatics 115the openehr Foundation, studies in health technology and informatics 115'. 2005. pp. 153–73.

[34] Adebesin F., Foster R., Kotzé P., Van Greunen D. 'A review of interoperability standards in e-health and imperatives for their adoption in Africa'. *South African Computer Journal.* 2013, vol. 50, pp. 55–72.

[35] Aspden P., Corrigan J.M., Wolcott J., Erickson S.M. Committee on data standards for patient safety, patient safety: achieving a new standard for care [online]. 2004. Available from http://www.iom.edu/report.asp [Accessed 3 Oct 2005].

[36] Dickinson G., Fischetti L., Heard S. 'HL7 EHR system functional model draft standard for trial use'. *Health Level.* 2004, vol. 7.

[37] Rector A.L. 'The interface between information, terminology, and inference models' in MEDINFO 2001. IOS Press; 2001. pp. 246–50.

[38] Geradi A. *IEEE standard computer dictionary: compilation of IEEE standard computer glossariesieee standard computer dictionary: compilation of IEEE standard computer glossaries.* IEEE Press; 1991.

[39] Garde S., Knaup P., Hovenga E.J., Heard S. 'Towards semantic interoperability for electronic health records'. *Methods of Information in Medicine.* 2007, vol. 46(3), pp. 332–43.

[40] Heiler S. 'Semantic interoperability, ACM computing surveys (CSUR) '.1995, vol. 27, pp. 271–73.

[41] Benson T. 'Principles of health interoperability HL7 and SNOMED' in Principles of health interoperability HL7 and SNOMED. London: Springer Science & Business Media; 2012.

[42] Association N.E.M. Digital imaging and communications in medicine (dicom) Part 1: introduction and overview. Virginia: NEMA; 2011.

[43] S. E. G*et al.* 'SDMX-statistical data and metadata exchange'.2006.

[44] Guo J., Araki K., Tanaka K, *et al.* 'The latest mml (medical markup language) version 2.3 -- xml-based standard for medical data exchange/storage'. *Journal of Medical Systems.* 2003, vol. 27(4), pp. 357–66.

[45] Kim J.-W., Jeon S.-H., Lim C.-M., Park S.-Y., Kim N.-H. 'Implementation of reporting system for continuity of care document based on web service'. *Proceedings of the IEEK Conference*; The Institute of Electronics and Information Engineers, 2009. pp. 402–04.

[46] Boone K.W. The CDA TM book. London: Springer Science & Business Media; 2011. Available from http://link.springer.com/10.1007/978-0-85729-336-7

[47] McDonald C.J., Huff S.M., Suico J.G, *et al.* 'LOINC, a universal standard for identifying laboratory observations: a 5-year update'. *Clinical Chemistry.* 2003, vol. 49(4), pp. 624–33.

[48] Tyrer P., Crawford M., Mulder R, *et al.* 'The rationale for the reclassification of personality disorder in the 11th revision of the International classification of diseases (ICD-11)'. *Personality and Mental Health.* 2011, vol. 5(4), pp. 246–59.

[49] World Health Organisation. *'International classification of primary care, -ICPC-2'.* 2009.

[50] Association A.M. 'American Medical association current procedural terminology CPT 2017'.2017.

[51] Park H.-A., Hardiker N. 'Clinical terminologies: a solution for semantic interoperability'. *Journal of Korean Society of Medical Informatics.* 1991, vol. 15(1), p. 1.

[52] Alterman R. 'Understanding and summarization'. *Artificial Intelligence Review.* 1991, vol. 5(4), pp. 239–54.

[53] Brailer D.J. 'Interoperability: the key to the future health care system: interoperability will bind together a wide network of real-time, life-critical data that not only transform but become health care'. *Health Affairs.* 2005, vol. 24, pp. W5–19.

[54] Mead C.N. 'Data interchange standards in healthcare it -- computable semantic interoperability: now possible but still difficult, do we really need a better mousetrap?'. *Journal of Healthcare Information Management.* 2006, vol. 20(1), pp. 71–78.

[55] Wager K.A., Lee F.W., Glaser J.P. Managing health care information systems: a practical approach for health care executives. John Wiley & Sons; 2005.

[56] Riazi H., Jafarpour M., Bitaraf E. 'Towards national e-health implementation -- a comparative study on WHO/ITU national e-health strategy toolkit in Iran'. *Studies in Health Technology and Informatics.* 2014, vol. 205, pp. 246–50.

[57] Bender D., Sartipi K. '2013 IEEE 26th International Symposium on computer-based medical systems (CBMS)'. Porto, Portugal, IEEE, 2013. pp. 326–31.

[58] Hussein R., Engelmann U., Schroeter A., Meinzer H.-P. 'DICOM structured reporting: part 1. overview and characteristics'. *Radiographics.* 2004, vol. 24(3), pp. 891–96.

[59] Stearns M.Q., Price C., Spackman K.A., Wang A.Y. 'SNOMED clinical terms: overview of the development process and project status'. *Proceedings of the AMIA Symposium, American Medical Informatics Association*; 2001. pp. 662.

[60] Dolin R.H., Alschuler L., Boyer S, *et al.* 'HL7 clinical document architecture, release 2'. *Journal of the American Medical Informatics Association.* 2006, vol. 13(1), pp. 30–39.

[61] Tudorache T., Nyulas C.I., Noy N.F., Musen M.A. 'Using semantic web in ICD-11: three years down the road'. *International Semantic Web Conference*; Springer, 2013. pp. 195–211.

[62] Compton M., Barnaghi P., Bermudez L, *et al.* 'The ssn ontology of the W3C semantic sensor network incubator group'. *Journal of Web Semantics*. 2012, vol. 17, pp. 25–32.

[63] Xue L., Liu Y., Zeng P., Yu H., Shi Z. 'An ontology based scheme for sensor description in context awareness system'. *IEEE International Conference on Information and Automation*; IEEE, 2015. pp. 817–20.

[64] Flury T., Privat G., Ramparany F. 'Owl-based location ontology for context-aware services'. *Proceedings of the Artificial Intelligence in Mobile Systems (AIMS 2004)*; 2004. pp. 52–57.

[65] Fikes R., Zhou Q. 'A reusable time ontology'. AAAI-2002 Workshop on Ontologies and the Semantic Web,Citeseer; 2002.

[66] Bermudez-Edo M., Elsaleh T., Barnaghi P., Taylor K. 'Iot-lite: a lightweight semantic model for the Internet of things'. *INTL IEEE Conferences on Ubiquitous Intelligence &Amp; Computing, Advanced and Trusted Computing, Scalable Computing and Communications, Cloud and Big Data Computing, Internet of People, and Smart World Congress (Uic/atc/scalcom/cbdcom/iop/smartworld)*; IEEE, 2016. pp. 90–97.

[67] Dridi A., Sassi S., Chbeir R., Faiz S. 'A flexible semantic integration framework for fully-integrated EHR based on FHIR standard'. *12th International Conference on Agents and Artificial Intelligence*; Valletta, Malta, 2020. pp. 684–91.

[68] Miotto R., Li L., Dudley J.T. 'Deep learning to predict patient future diseases from the electronic health records'. *European Conference on Information RetrievalEuropean conference on information retrieval*; Springer, 2016. pp. 768–74.

[69] Iakovidis I. 'Towards personal health record: current situation, obstacles and trends in implementation of electronic healthcare record in Europe'. *International Journal of Medical Informatics*. 1998, vol. 52(1–3), pp. 105–15.

[70] Gunter T.D., Terry N.P. 'The emergence of national electronic health record architectures in the United States and Australia: models, costs, and questions'. *Journal of Medical Internet Research*. 2005, vol. 7(1), e3.

[71] Bates D.W., Ebell M., Gotlieb E., Zapp J., Mullins H.C. 'A proposal for electronic medical records in US primary care'. *Journal of the American Medical Informatics Association*. 2003, vol. 10(1), pp. 1–10.

[72] Rogers J.L., Haring O.M., Watson R.A. 'Automating the medical record: emerging issues'. American Medical Informatics Association, 1979. pp. 255.

[73] McInerney D.J., Dabiri B., Touret A.-S., Young G., Meent J.-W., Wallace B.C. 'Query-focused EHR summarization to aid imaging diagnosis'. *Machine Learning for Healthcare Conference*; PMLR, 2020. pp. 632–59.

[74] Gong J.J., Guttag J.V. 'Learning to summarize electronic health records using cross-modality correspondences'. *Machine learning for healthcare conference, PMLR*; 2018. pp. 551–70.

[75] Abu-Faraj Z.O., Barakat S.S., Chaleby M.H., Zaklit J.D. 'A Sim card-
based ubiquitous medical record bracelet/pendant system—a pilot study'.
*4th International Conference on Biomedical Engineering and Informatics
(Bmei)*; Shanghai, China, 2011. pp. 1914–18.

[76] Tapak L., Mahjub H., Hamidi O., Poorolajal J. 'Real-data comparison of data
mining methods in prediction of diabetes in Iran'. *Healthcare Informatics
Research*. 2013, vol. 19(3), pp. 177–85.

[77] Soysal E., Warner J.L., Denny J.C., Xu H. 'Identifying metastases-related
information from pathology reports of lung cancer patients'. *AMIA Joint
Summits on Translational Science Proceedings. AMIA Joint Summits on
Translational Science*. 2017, vol. 2017, pp. 268–77.

[78] Moradi M., Ghadiri N. 'Different approaches for identifying important concepts in probabilistic biomedical text summarization'. *Artificial Intelligence
in Medicine*. 2018, vol. 84, pp. 101–16.

[79] Hirsch J.S., Tanenbaum J.S., Lipsky Gorman S, *et al.* 'Harvest, a longitudinal
patient record summarizer'. *Journal of the American Medical Informatics
Association*. 2015, vol. 22(2), pp. 263–74.

[80] Bui A.A.T., Aberle D.R., Kangarloo H. 'TimeLine: visualizing integrated patient records'. *IEEE Transactions on Information Technology in
Biomedicine*. 2007, vol. 11(4), pp. 462–73.

[81] Bashyam V., Hsu W., Watt E., Bui A.A.T., Kangarloo H., Taira R.K.
'Problem-centric organization and visualization of patient imaging and clinical data'. *Radiographics*. 2009, vol. 29(2), pp. 331–43.

[82] Shahar Y., Goren-Bar D., Boaz D., Tahan G. 'Distributed, intelligent, interactive visualization and exploration of time-oriented clinical data and
their abstractions'. *Artificial Intelligence in Medicine*. 2006, vol. 38(2), pp.
115–35.

[83] Hunter J., Freer Y., Gatt A, *et al.* 'Summarising complex ICU data in natural
language'. *Amia Annual Symposium Proceedings, volume 2008*; American
Medical Informatics Association, 2008. pp. 323.

[84] Clayton P.D., Narus S.P., Bowes W.A, *et al.* 'Physician use of electronic
medical records: issues and successes with direct data entry and physician
productivity'. *AMIA Annual Symposium Proceedings annual symposium
proceedings*; American Medical Informatics Association, 2005. pp. 141.

[85] Matheny M.E., Miller R.A., Ikizler T.A, *et al.* 'Development of inpatient
risk stratification models of acute kidney injury for use in electronic health
records'. *Medical Decision Making*. 2010, vol. 30(6), pp. 639–50.

[86] Bade R., Schlechtweg S., Miksch S. 'Connecting time-oriented data and
information to a coherent interactive visualization'. *The 2004 Conference*;
Vienna, Austria, New York, 2004. pp. 105–12. Available from http://portal.
acm.org/citation.cfm?doid=985692

[87]   Wang T.D., Plaisant C., Shneiderman B, *et al*. 'Temporal summaries: supporting temporal categorical searching, aggregation and comparison'. *IEEE Transactions on Visualization and Computer Graphics*. 2009, vol. 15(6), pp. 1049–56.

[88]   Borland D., West V.L., Hammond W.E. 'Multivariate visualization of systemwide National health service data using radial coordinates'. *Proceedings of Workshop on Visual Analytics in Healthcare*; 2014.

[89]   Carenini A., Cerri D., Krummenacher R., Simperl E. 'Enabling interoperability of patient summaries across eeurope with ttriplesspaces' in Interoperability in healthcare information systems: Standards, management, and technology, IGI globalinteroperability in healthcare information systems: Standards, management, and technology, IGI global; 2013. pp. 232–49.

[90]   Plaisant C., Mushlin R., Snyder A., Li J., Heller D., Shneiderman B. 'Lifelines: using visualization to enhance navigation and analysis of patient records' in The craft of information visualization. Elsevier; 2003. pp. 308–12.

[91]   Liu H., Friedman C. 'Cliniviewer: a tool for viewing electronic medical records based on natural language processing and xml' in MEDINFO 2004. IOS Press; 2004. pp. 639–43.

[92]   Wright A., Pang J., Feblowitz J.C, *et al*. 'A method and knowledge base for automated inference of patient problems from structured data in an electronic medical record'. *Journal of the American Medical Informatics Association*. 2011, vol. 18(6), pp. 859–67.

[93]   Radev D.R., Hovy E., McKeown K. 'Introduction to the special issue on summarization'. *Computational Linguistics*. 2002, vol. 28(4), pp. 399–408.

[94]   Aggarwal C.C., Zhai C. Mining Text Data. Boston, MA: Springer; 2002. pp. 43–76. Available from http://www.springerlink.com/index/10.1007/978-1-4614-3223-4

[95]   Lukas P.S., Krummenacher R., Biasiutti F.D., Begré S., Znoj H., von Känel R. 'Association of fatigue and psychological distress with quality of life in patients with a previous venous thromboembolic event'. *Thrombosis and Haemostasis*. 2009, vol. 102(6), pp. 1219–26.

[96]   Reeve L.H., Han H., Brooks A.D. 'The use of domain-specific concepts in biomedical text summarization'. *Information Processing & Management*. 2002, vol. 43(6), pp. 1765–76.

[97]   Liang J., Tsou C.-H., Poddar A. 'A novel system for extractive clinical note summarization using'. *Proceedings of the 2nd Clinical Natural Language Processing Workshop*; Minneapolis MN, Stroudsburg, PA, 2019. pp. 46–54. Available from http://aclweb.org/anthology/W19-19

[98]   Razavian A.S., Sullivan J., Carlsson S., Maki A. '[paper] visual instance retrieval with deep convolutional networks'. *ITE Transactions on Media Technology and Applications*. 2016, vol. 4(3), pp. 251–58.

[99]   Handelsman Y., Bloomgarden Z.T., Grunberger G, *et al*. 'American association of clinical endocrinologists and American College of

endocrinology-clinical practice guidelines for developing a diabetes mellitus comprehensive care plan-2015'. *Endocrine Practice*. 2015, vol. 21, pp. 1–87.

[100] West V.L., Borland D., Hammond W.E. 'Innovative information visualization of electronic health record data: a systematic review'. *Journal of the American Medical Informatics Association*. 2015, vol. 22(2), pp. 330–39.

[101] Gotz D., Stavropoulos H. 'DecisionFlow: visual analytics for high-dimensional temporal event sequence data'. *IEEE Transactions on Visualization and Computer Graphics*. 2014, vol. 20(12), pp. 1783–92.

[102] Xiao C., Choi E., Sun J. 'Opportunities and challenges in developing deep learning models using electronic health records data: a systematic review'. *Journal of the American Medical Informatics Association*. 2018, vol. 25(10), pp. 1419–28.

[103] Nallaperuma D., De Silva D. 'A participatory model for multi-document health information summarisation'. *Australasian Journal of Information Systems*. 2011, vol. 21.

[104] Rind A., Wang T.D., Aigner W, *et al.* 'Interactive information visualization to explore and query electronic health records'. *Foundations and Trends® in Human–Computer Interaction*. 2011, vol. 5(3), pp. 207–98.

[105] Tory M., Moller T. 'Rethinking visualization: a high-level taxonomy'. *IEEE Symposium on Information Visualization*; Austin, TX:, IEEE, 2011. pp. 151–58.

[106] Preim B., Bartz D. Visualization in medicine: theory, algorithms, and applications. Elsevier; 2007.

[107] Fails J.A., Karlson A., Shahamat L., Shneiderman B. 'A visual interface for multivariate temporal data: finding patterns of events across multiple histories'. *IEEE Symposium on Visual Analytics and Technology*; Baltimore, MD, 2006. pp. 167–74.

[108] Leinhardt G., Leinhardt S. 'Chapter 3: exploratory data analysis: new tools for the analysis of empirical data'. *Review of Research in Education*. 1980, vol. 8(1), pp. 85–157.

[109] Jiang S., Fang S., Bloomquist S., *et al.* 'Healthcare data visualization' in Geospatial and temporal integration, in *VISIGRAPP. 2:* IVAPP); 2016. pp. 214–21.

[110] Bernard J., Sessler D., Kohlhammer J., Ruddle R.A. 'Using dashboard networks to visualize multiple patient histories: a design study on post-operative prostate cancer'. *IEEE Transactions on Visualization and Computer Graphics*. 2019, vol. 25(3), pp. 1615–28.

[111] Glueck M., Gvozdik A., Chevalier F., Khan A., Brudno M., Wigdor D. 'PhenoStacks: cross-sectional cohort phenotype comparison visualizations'. *IEEE Transactions on Visualization and Computer Graphics*. 2017, vol. 23(1), pp. 191–200.

[112] Zhang Y., Chanana K., Dunne C. 'IDMVis: temporal event sequence visualization for type 1 diabetes treatment decision support'. *IEEE Transactions on Visualization and Computer Graphics*. 2018, vol. 25, pp. 512–22.

[113]   Kwon B.C., Anand V., Severson K.A, *et al.* 'DPVis: visual analytics with hidden Markov models for disease progression pathways'. *IEEE Transactions on Visualization and Computer Graphics*. 2021, vol. 27(9), pp. 3685–700.

[114]   Guo S., Jin Z., Gotz D., Du F., Zha H., Cao N. 'Visual progression analysis of event sequence data'. *IEEE Transactions on Visualization and Computer Graphics*. 2018, vol. 25, pp. 417–26.

[115]   Glicksberg B.S., Oskotsky B., Thangaraj P.M, *et al.* 'PatientExploreR: an extensible application for dynamic visualization of patient clinical history from electronic health records in the OMOP common data model'. *Bioinformatics (Oxford, England)*. 2019, vol. 35(21), pp. 4515–18.

[116]   Alemzadeh S., Niemann U., Ittermann T, *et al.* 'Visual analysis of missing values in longitudinal cohort study data'. *Computer Graphics Forum*. 2020, vol. 39(1), pp. 63–75. Available from https://onlinelibrary.wiley.com/toc/14678659/39/1

[117]   Trivedi G., Pham P., Chapman W.W., Hwa R., Wiebe J., Hochheiser H. 'NLPReViz: an interactive tool for natural language processing on clinical text'. *Journal of the American Medical Informatics Association*. 2018, vol. 25(1), pp. 81–87.

[118]   Koleck T.A., Dreisbach C., Bourne P.E., Bakken S. 'Natural language processing of symptoms documented in free-text narratives of electronic health records: a systematic review'. *Journal of the American Medical Informatics Association*. 2019, vol. 26(4), pp. 364–79.

[119]   Tablan V., Roberts I., Cunningham H., Bontcheva K. 'GATECloud.net: a platform for large-scale, open-source text processing on the cloud'. *Philosophical Transactions. Series A, Mathematical, Physical, and Engineering Sciences*. 2013, vol. 371(1983), 20120071.

[120]   Wongsuphasawat K., Gómez J.A.G., Plaisant C., Wang T.D., Taieb-Maimon M., Shneiderman B. 'Lifeflow: visualizing an overview of event sequences'. *Proceedings of the SIGCHI Conference on Human Factors in Computing Systems*; 2011. pp. 1747–56.

[121]   Monroe M., Lan R., Lee H., Plaisant C., Shneiderman B. 'Temporal event sequence simplification'. *IEEE Transactions on Visualization and Computer Graphics*. 2013, vol. 19(12), pp. 2227–36.

[122]   Loorak M.H., Perin C., Kamal N., Hill M., Carpendale S. 'TimeSpan: using visualization to explore temporal multi-dimensional data of stroke patients'. *IEEE Transactions on Visualization and Computer Graphics*. 2016, vol. 22(1), pp. 409–18.

[123]   Ramírez-Ramírez L.L., Gel Y.R., Thompson M., de Villa E., McPherson M. 'A new surveillance and spatio-temporal visualization tool SIMID: simulation of infectious diseases using random networks and GIS'. *Computer Methods and Programs in Biomedicine*. 2013, vol. 110(3), pp. 455–70.

[124]   Sopan A., Noh A.S.-I., Karol S., Rosenfeld P., Lee G., Shneiderman B. 'Community health map: a geospatial and multivariate data visualization tool for public health datasets'. *Government Information Quarterly*. 2012, vol. 29(2), pp. 223–34.

[125] Kwon B.C., Choi M.-J., Kim J.T, *et al.* 'RetainVis: visual analytics with interpretable and interactive recurrent neural networks on electronic medical records'. *IEEE Transactions on Visualization and Computer Graphics.* 2018, vol. 25, pp. 299–309.

[126] Jin Z., Cui S., Guo S., Gotz D., Sun J., Cao N. 'Carepre: an intelligent clinical decision assistance system'. *ACM Transactions on Computing for Healthcare.* 2020, vol. 1, pp. 1–20.

[127] Ola O., Sedig K. 'Beyond simple charts: design of visualizations for big health data'. [Online journal of public health informatics 8.] *Online Journal of Public Health Informatics.* 2016, vol. 8(3), e195.

[128] Horn W., Popow C., Unterasinger L. 'Support for fast comprehension of ICU data: visualization using metaphor graphics'. *Methods of Information in Medicine.* 2001, vol. 40(5), pp. 421–24.

[129] Tong C., McNabb L., Laramee R.S. 'Cartograms with topological features'. *Proceedings of the Conference on Computer Graphics & Visual Computing*; 2018. pp. 127–34.

[130] McNabb L., Laramee R.S. 'Multivariate maps—a glyph-placement algorithm to support multivariate geospatial visualization'. *Information.* 2019, vol. 10(10), p. 302.

[131] MIT Critical Data.. Secondary analysis of electronic health records. Cham: Springer Nature; 2016. Available from http://link.springer.com/10.1007/978-3-319-43742-2

[132] Kim E., Rubinstein S.M., Nead K.T., Wojcieszynski A.P., Gabriel P.E., Warner J.L. 'The evolving use of electronic health records (EHR) for research'. *Seminars in Radiation Oncology.* 2019, vol. 29(4), pp. 354–61.

[133] Bernard J., Sessler D., May T., Schlomm T., Pehrke D., Kohlhammer J. 'A visual-interactive system for prostate cancer cohort analysis'. *IEEE Computer Graphics and Applications.* 2015, vol. 35(3), pp. 44–55.

[134] Kamaleswaran R., Pugh J.E., Thommandram A., James A., McGregor C. 'Visualizing neonatal spells: temporal visual analytics of high frequency cardiorespiratory physiological event streams' in IEEE Vis 2014 workshop on visualization of electronic health records; 2014. pp. 1–4.

[135] Xu R., Wunsch D. 'Survey of clustering algorithms'. *IEEE Transactions on Neural Networks.* 2005, vol. 16(3), pp. 645–78.

[136] Cowie M.R., Blomster J.I., Curtis L.H, *et al.* 'Electronic health records to facilitate clinical research'. *Clinical Research in Cardiology.* 2017, vol. 106(1), pp. 1–9.

Chapter 6

EEG signal classification using robust energy-based least squares projection twin support vector machines

M.A. Ganaie[1] and M. Tanveer[1]

Electroencephalogram (EEG) signals have been successfully employed in the diagnosis of several neurological disorders such as epilepsy and sleep disorders. The classification of EEG signals has been done via support vector machines (SVMs) and twin support vector machines (TWSVMs). However, both SVM and TWSVM solve quadratic programming problems (QPPs) that require an external toolbox for the optimisation. To overcome this limitation, we propose a robust energy-based least squares projection TWSVM (RELSPTSVM) for the classification of EEG signals. Unlike TWSVM-based models that generate hyperplanes for each category of samples, the proposed RELSPTSVM generates a projection axis for each class in a manner that the data points of the corresponding category are proximal to its mean and data points of other categories are as farthest as possible. Unlike least squares TWSVMs (LSTSVMs) that put the samples of another category to be exactly at distance, the proposed RELSPTSVM model relaxes this constraint via energy parameters, which results in more robustness to noise and outliers. The proposed RELSPTSVM model implements the structural risk which results in avoiding the overfitting issues. Experimental results on EEG signal classification and UCI benchmark datasets demonstrate the effectiveness of the proposed RELSPTSVM model.

6.1 Introduction

One of the challenges in machine learning of significant importance is the classification of EEG signals. They are widely used for medical examinations, specifically non-invasive disorder detection techniques. EEG signals have seen application in detecting various brain disorders such as seizures, sleep disorders and epilepsy.

[1]Department of Mathematics, Indian Institute of Technology Indore, Simrol, Indore, India

A different variety of EEG signals is used for each of these applications. As they are used in many applications, several signal processing pipelines exist to process these signals. We are interested in analysing recorded EEG signals and their classification. Many feature extraction techniques are utilised to prepare the EEG signal data for classification. Wavelet transform is an extensively used method where frequency-domain features are extracted from a time-domain signal, with localisation in time. This property is significant as this distinguishes wavelet transform from Fourier transform. There are several wavelet transform families, each specialising for different signal types. Some examples of utilisation of these families are Daubechies wavelet with DB-4 [1], orthogonal decimated discrete wavelet transform [2] and Daubechies wavelet-2 [3]. Other methods used for feature extraction are the principal component analysis and independent component analysis with SVM [4, 5] as the classifier [6, 7].

SVM [4, 5] is a widely used classification algorithm due to its superior generalisation performance. SVM has been widely used for the applications of different domains [8–13]. The better generalisation performance is attributed to SVM as it implements the structural risk minimisation (SRM) principle [14]. SVM seeks a decision hyperplane in a manner that the samples of different categories are separated by the maximum margin between the two parallel supporting hyperplanes. SVM solves a single large QPP, which limits its application in practical scenarios. Hence, to resolve this issue, multiple improvements have been formulated [15–17].

SVM finds two parallel supporting hyperplanes to build the final decision hyperplane. Different from SVM, generalised eigenvalue proximal SVM (GEPSVM) generates two non-parallel hyperplanes in a manner that the samples of one class are proximal to one hyperplane and other class samples are at a maximum distance and vice versa. GEPSVM solved a generalised eigenvalue problem, which is computationally efficient than SVM. Inspired by GEPSVM, TWSVMs [18] also generated non-parallel decision planes in a manner that the samples of one category are proximal to one class and farthest from the samples of other categories. Instead of solving a generalised eigenvalue problem, TWSVM solved a pair of smaller size QPPs, which results in reduction of computation time compared to SVM. However, TWSVM may suffer from overfitting issues due to the implementation of empirical risk minimisation problems. To overcome the issues of overfitting, an improvement over TWSVM, known as twin-bounded SVM (TBSVM) [19], was proposed, which implemented the SRM principle. TSBVM showed better generalisation performance compared to the TWSVM model. Both TWSVM and TBSVM solve QPPs, which require an external toolbox to solve the optimisation problems.

LSTSVM [20] reformulated TWSVM in a manner that no external toolbox is needed to obtain the separating hyperplanes. LSTSVM uses two norm of the slack variables and replaced the inequality constraints with the equality constraints, which resulted in a pair of system of linear equations. LSTSVM may suffer from the issues of noise and outliers, as the constraints of LSTSVM require the samples of other classes to be exactly at 1 distance. To resolve these issues, the energy-based least squares TWSVM (ELSTSVM) model [21] relaxed the constraints via introduction of energy parameters. Robust energy-based least squares TWSVM (RELSTSVM) [22] introduced the regularisation term in the ELSTSVM formulation to make it robust to noise and embody the structural risk minimisation. Both ELSTSVM and RELSTSVM models are robust to noise and outliers. A recent evaluation of the TWSVM-based model for binary class problems [23] showed that RELSTSVM has a better performance compared to other TWSVM-based models. The issues of noise have also been reduced via pinball loss function. The twin parametric margin TWSVM with pinball loss [24] and general pinball loss TWSVM [25, 26] have shown improved generalisation performance in the presence of noise. However, pinball loss function results in loss of sparsity. To induce the sparsity, sparse pinball loss TWSVM [27, 28] introduced ϵ insensitive tube to preserve the sparsity of the model. TWSVM models for large-scale data [29, 30] have also been formulated. Oblique random forest via TBSVM [31] and the ensemble of random projection-based TWSVM-based models [32, 33] have improved the generalisation performance of the models in the ensemble framework.

Prior information such as universum data has also been incorporated in SVM-based models [34]. Universum data provide extra information about the data distribution, which results in improved generalisation performance. The study of evaluation of the effect of universum data [35] revealed that the universum data vary for each type of problem. To improve the computational complexity, universum TWSVM (UTSVM) [36] solved two smaller size QPPs, which resulted in reduction of the time. To further improve the computation, least squares universum TWSVM (ULSTSVM) [37] solved system of linear equations instead of solving the QPPs. ULSTSVM used two norm of error variables and replaced the inequality constraints with equality constraints. Usually, random averaging of the data samples is used as the universum data points [7, 36, 37].

The classification models suffer in class imbalance scenarios. In class imbalance scenarios, the models favour the samples of majority class. Hence, the data points of positive category are misclassified. To reduce the imbalance issues in classification problems, fuzzy weights are incorporated in SVM [38]. Boosting framework has also been incorporated in SVM [39], which results in balance of the classes. Other techniques such as oversampling [40] and undersampling [41, 42] have also been used to overcome the issues of class imbalance. Universum data have also been used to handle the class imbalance problems, which resulted in improved generalisation performance [43].

Different from TWSVM and GEPSVM, the projection-based multi-weight vector TWSVM [44] model seeks hyperplane in a manner that data points of each category are closest to its mean vector and data points of other categories are as far as possible. Recursive projection TWSVM (PTWSVM) [45] and regularised recursive projection TWSVM (RPTWSVM) [19] seek a projection axis wherein the samples of one category are clustered around its sample mean and the data points of other classes are farthest. Both PTWSVM and RPTWSVM solve QPPs to generate the optimal decision hyperplanes. As QPPs involve high computational cost; hence, least squares PTWSVM was formulated, which resulted in a system of linear equations. To reduce the computation time and the effect of outliers, fuzzy least squares projection twin for class imbalance learning [46, 47] has been proposed. Here, the samples are weighted as per their distance from the centroid of each class with the samples closer to the centroid being assigned higher fuzzy weights, while samples that are far from the centroid are assigned lower fuzzy weights. For details of the TWSVM literature, we refer the readers to [48].

Although the projection-based TWSVM and LSTSVM have been effectively used in the classification problems. However, both types of models suffer from the following drawbacks.

- Projection-based TWSVM and standard TWSVM models enforce that the data samples of other categories are at least at 1 distance and solve QPPs, which is computationally inefficient.
- Least squares projection-based TWSVM and standard LSTSVM models are computationally efficient; however, they are sensitive to noise and outliers. It enforces that the data samples of other categories are exactly at a distance of 1.

Motivated by PTSVM [45] and RELSTSVM [22], we formulate robust energy-based least squares projection TWSVM (RELSPTSVM). The advantages of the proposed RELSPTSVM model are as follows.

1. The proposed RELSPTSVM minimises the structural risk, which avoids the issues of overfitting and hence results in better generalisation performance.
2. Unlike TWSVM and RELSTSVM models that are hyperplane-based classifiers, the proposed RELSPTSVM seeks a projection axis in a manner that the data samples of each category are around its mean vector and the data samples of other categories are far as possible.
3. Unlike LSTSVM and LSPTSVM models that enforce the data samples of the opposite category to be at exactly 1 distance, the proposed RELSPTSVM model uses the energy term to make the model more robust to noise and outliers.
4. Experimental results on benchmark EEG and UCI datasets demonstrate that the performance of the proposed RELSPTSVM is superior in comparison with the existing models.

6.2   Related work

Here, we brief about the optimisation problems of TWSVM [18], LSTSVM [20] and RELSTSVM [22].

Let the samples of a positive and negative class be given by $X_1 \in \mathbb{R}^{m_1 \times n}$ and $X_2 \in \mathbb{R}^{m_2 \times n}$, respectively, for a binary classification problem. Here, $N = m_1 + m_2$ and each data point is $x_i \in \mathbb{R}^n$. We denote $\|\cdot\|$ as the two norm distance.

6.2.1   Twin support vector machines

TWSVM model generates two non-parallel hyperplanes by solving two QPPs [18]. The optimisation problems are designed in a manner such that the samples of each class are proximal to the samples of one class and the samples of other classes are at least at a distance of 1. The optimisation problems of linear TWSVM are

$$\min_{z_1, b_1} \frac{1}{2} \|X_1 z_1 + e_2 b_1\|^2 + c_1 e_1' \eta_1$$
$$s.t. \quad -(X_2 z_1 + e_1 b_1) + \eta_1 \geq e_1, \eta_1 \geq 0$$

(6.1)

and

$$\min_{z_2, b_2} \frac{1}{2} \|X_2 z_2 + e_1 b_2\|^2 + c_2 e_2' \eta_2$$
$$s.t. \quad (X_1 z_2 + e_2 b_2) + \eta_2 \geq e_2, \eta_2 \geq 0$$

(6.2)

where c_i are the positive penalty parameters and e_i is the vector of ones with appropriate dimensions and η_i are the slack variables, for $i = 1, 2$.

The first term in the optimisation problems (6.1 and 6.2) makes the plane proximal to the samples of the corresponding class and the second term minimises the error corresponding to the samples of other classes.

Assume that $A^t A$ and $B^t B$ are invertible matrices, and $A = [X_1 \ e_2]$, $B = [X_2 \ e_1]$ as the augmented matrices. The Wolfe dual of (6.1) and (6.2) are

$$\max_{\beta} \ e_1' \beta - \frac{1}{2} \beta' B (A^t A)^{-1} B' \beta$$
$$s.t. \quad 0 \leq \beta \leq c_1$$

(6.3)

and

$$\max_{\theta} \ e_2' \theta - \frac{1}{2} \theta' A (B^t B)^{-1} A' \theta$$
$$s.t. \quad 0 \leq \theta \leq c_2$$

(6.4)

where β and θ are the Lagrange multipliers.

As the matrices $A^t A$ and $B^t B$ may be ill conditioned, a small positive integer δ is added such that the matrices $(A^t A + \delta I)^{-1}$ and $(B^t B + \delta I)^{-1}$ approximate the $(A^t A)^{-1}$ and $(B^t B)^{-1}$ matrices, respectively. Here, I is the identity matrix.

Thus, the optimisation problems (6.3) and (6.4) can be written as follows:

$$\max_{\beta} \ e_1' \beta - \frac{1}{2} \beta' B (A^t A + \delta I)^{-1} B' \beta$$
$$s.t. \quad 0 \leq \beta \leq c_1$$

(6.5)

and

$$\max_{\theta} \ e_2' \theta - \frac{1}{2} \theta' A (B^t B + \delta I)^{-1} A' \theta$$
$$s.t. \quad 0 \leq \theta \leq c_2$$

(6.6)

After solving (6.5) and (6.6), the following optimal hyperplanes are given:

$$\begin{bmatrix} z_1 \\ b_1 \end{bmatrix} = -(A^t A + \delta I)^{-1} B' \beta$$

(6.7)

$$\begin{bmatrix} z_2 \\ b_2 \end{bmatrix} = (B'B + \delta I)^{-1} A' \theta \tag{6.8}$$

The test data point $x \in \mathbb{R}^n$ is given the class label as follows:

$$\text{Class} = \arg\min_{j=1,2} \frac{|x'z_j + b_j|}{\|z_j\|} \tag{6.9}$$

6.2.2   Least squares twin support vector machines

The LSTSVM model solves the system of equations to generate the optimal separating hyperplanes [20]. The LSTSVM model formulates the optimisation problem such that the samples of each class are proximal to the hyperplane of its corresponding class and the samples of other classes are at a distance of 1 from the given hyperplane. The optimisation problems of the linear LSTSVM model are as follows:

$$\min_{z_1, b_1} \frac{1}{2} \|X_1 z_1 + e_2 b_1\|^2 + \frac{c_1}{2} \|\eta_1\|^2 \tag{6.10}$$
$$s.t. \quad -(X_2 z_1 + e_1 b_1) + \eta_1 = e_1$$

and

$$\min_{z_2, b_2} \frac{1}{2} \|X_2 z_2 + e_1 b_2\|^2 + \frac{c_2}{2} \|\eta_2\|^2 \tag{6.11}$$
$$s.t. \quad (X_1 z_2 + e_2 b_2) + \eta_2 = e_2$$

For generating the proximal hyperplanes, the LSTSVM model solves a linear system of equations with order $(n+1) \times (n+1)$ for the linear case [20]. As we solve (6.10) and (6.11), the proximal hyperplanes are as follows:

$$\begin{bmatrix} z_1 \\ b_1 \end{bmatrix} = -(c_1 B'B + A'A)^{-1} c_1 B' e_1 \tag{6.12}$$

$$\begin{bmatrix} z_2 \\ b_2 \end{bmatrix} = (c_2 A'A + B'B)^{-1} c_2 A' e_2 \tag{6.13}$$

The test data point $x \in \mathbb{R}^n$ is assigned to the class by the following decision function:

$$\text{Class} = \arg\min_{j=1,2} \frac{|x'z_j + b_j|}{\|z_j\|} \tag{6.14}$$

6.2.3   Robust energy-based least squares twin support vector machines

The RELSTSVM model solves the system of linear equations for generating the optimal separating hyperplanes [22]. Since the LSTSVM model requires the samples of other classes to be at a distance of exact 1, this may not be possible in real-world scenarios. To subsidise this issue, the RELSTSVM model relaxed this condition via energy parameters, which resulted in the improvement of the generalisation performance.

Linear RELSTSVM solves the following optimisation problems:

$$\min_{z_1,b_1} \frac{1}{2} \|X_1 z_1 + e_2 b_1\|^2 + \frac{c_1}{2} \|\eta_1\|^2 + \frac{c_3}{2}(\|z_1\|^2 + b_1^2)$$

$$s.t. \quad -(X_2 z_1 + e_1 b_1) + \eta_1 = E_1 \qquad (6.15)$$

and

$$\min_{z_2,b_2} \frac{1}{2} \|X_2 z_2 + e_1 b_2\|^2 + \frac{c_2}{2} \|\eta_2\|^2 + \frac{c_4}{2}(\|z_2\|^2 + b_2^2)$$

$$s.t. \quad (X_1 z_2 + e_2 b_2) + \eta_2 = E_2, \qquad (6.16)$$

where c_j, e_i are the positive parameters and vector of ones with appropriate dimensions, for $i = 1, 2$ and $j = 1, 2, 3, 4$. E_1 and E_2 are the energy parameters and η_i are the slack variables, for $i = 1, 2$.

Similar to the LSTSVM model, the RELSTSVM model generates two proximal hyperplanes by solving a linear system of equations of the order of $(n + 1) \times (n + 1)$ for linear case [21].

Substitute the constraints into the corresponding objective function of (6.15), we have the following:

$$L_1 = \frac{1}{2} \|X_1 z_1 + e_2 b_1\|^2 + \frac{c_1}{2} \|X_2 z_1 + e_1 b_1 + E_1\|^2 + \frac{c_3}{2}(\|z_1\|^2 + b_1^2) \qquad (6.17)$$

With respect to z_1, b_1 set the gradient of (6.17) to zero, we get the solution of BAAs (6.15) and (6.16) as follows:

$$\begin{bmatrix} z_1 \\ b_1 \end{bmatrix} = -(c_1 B'B + A'A + c_3 I)^{-1} c_1 B'E_1 \qquad (6.18)$$

$$\begin{bmatrix} z_2 \\ b_2 \end{bmatrix} = (c_2 A'A + B'B + c_4 I)^{-1} c_2 A'E_2 \qquad (6.19)$$

where c_i are the positive penalty parameters, for $i = 1, 2$, $A = [X_1, e]$, $B = [X_2, e]$ and I is an identity matrix of appropriate dimensions.

The test data sample $x \in \mathbb{R}^n$ is given the class label as:

$$\text{Class} = \arg \min_{j=1,2} \frac{|x' z_j + b_j|}{\|z_j\|} \qquad (6.20)$$

6.3 Robust energy-based least squares projection twin support vector machines

The LSTSVM and RELSTSVM models have been successfully used in a wide range of applications. However, both LSTSVM and RELSTSVM models optimise the hyperplanes without caring about the structure of the data. The structure of the data like variance provides extra information that may be helpful for optimising the separating hyperplanes. To exploit the structure of the data, we propose RELSPTSVM for the classification problems. We discuss the proposed RELSPTSVM model for both linear and nonlinear cases. Also, we discuss the recursive procedure for generating the multiple projections for each class to enhance the generalisation ability of the proposed RELSPTSVM.

6.3.1 Linear RELSPTSVM

The optimisation problems of Linear RELSPTSVM are as follows:

$$\min_{z_1, \xi} \frac{1}{2} \sum_{i=1}^{m_1} \left(z_1^t x_i^{(1)} - z_1^t \frac{1}{m_1} \sum_{j=1}^{m_1} x_j^{(1)} \right)^2 + \frac{c_1}{2} \sum_{k=1}^{m_2} \xi_k^2 + \frac{c_3}{2} \|z_1\|^2$$

$$\text{s.t. } z_1^t x_k^{(2)} - z_1^t \frac{1}{m_1} \sum_{j=1}^{m_1} x_j^{(1)} + \xi_k = \tilde{E}_2 \tag{6.21}$$

and

$$\min_{z_2, \theta} \frac{1}{2} \sum_{i=1}^{m_2} \left(z_2^t x_i^{(2)} - z_2^t \frac{1}{m_2} \sum_{j=1}^{m_2} x_j^{(2)} \right)^2 + \frac{c_2}{2} \sum_{k=1}^{m_1} \theta_k^2 + \frac{c_4}{2} \|z_2\|^2$$

$$\text{s.t. } - \left(z_2^t x_k^{(1)} - z_2^t \frac{1}{m_2} \sum_{j=1}^{m_2} x_j^{(2)} \right) + \theta_k = \tilde{E}_1, \tag{6.22}$$

where c_1, c_2, c_3, c_4 are the positive parameters, $\tilde{E}_1, \tilde{E}_2 \in \mathbb{R}$ are the energy parameters, $x^{(i)}$ denotes the sample belong to class i and ξ_k, θ_k are the slack variables.

The first term in (6.21) and (6.22) minimises the variance of a class in a manner that the data points of the projected category are around its mean vector. The second term is the error minimisation term. The constraints of objective functions (6.21) and (6.22) use the energy term for better generalisation performance. Unlike the LSTSVM model wherein the hyperplane is exactly at 1 distance from the other category hyperplane, the proposed RELSPTSVM model uses the energy term to make the model more robust. The third term is the regularisation term that implements the SRM principle.

To simplify the above optimisation problems (6.21) and (6.22), we rewrite in matrix notation as follows:

$$\min_{z_1, \eta_1} \frac{1}{2} \|X_1 z_1 - e_1 \tilde{X}_1 z_1\|^2 + \frac{c_1}{2} \|\eta_1\|^2 + \frac{c_3}{2} \|z_1\|^2$$
$$\text{s.t. } X_2 z_1 - e_2 \tilde{X}_1 z_1 + \eta_1 = E_2 \tag{6.23}$$

$$\min_{z_2, \eta_2} \frac{1}{2} \|X_2 z_2 - e_2 \tilde{X}_2 z_2\|^2 + \frac{c_2}{2} \|\eta_2\|^2 + \frac{c_4}{2} \|z_2\|^2$$
$$\text{s.t. } - (X_1 z_2 - e_1 \tilde{X}_2 z_2) + \eta_2 = E_1 \tag{6.24}$$

where $\eta_1 = [\xi_1, \xi_2, \cdots, \xi_{m_2}]^t$, $\eta_2 = [\theta_1, \theta_2, \cdots, \theta_{m_1}]^t$. E_1 and E_2 represent the vectors of energy parameters and

$$\tilde{X}_1 = \frac{1}{m_1} \sum_{j=1}^{m_1} (x_j^{(1)})' \text{ and } \tilde{X}_2 = \frac{1}{m_2} \sum_{j=1}^{m_2} (x_j^{(2)})' \tag{6.25}$$

Substituting the equality constraints in the corresponding objective function of (6.23), we have

$$L = \frac{1}{2} \left\| X_1 z_1 - e_1 \tilde{X}_1 z_1 \right\|^2 + \frac{c_1}{2} \left\| X_2 z_1 - e_2 \tilde{X}_1 z_1 - E_2 \right\|^2 + \frac{c_3}{2} \left\| z_1 \right\|^2 \tag{6.26}$$

Take the gradient of (6.26) with respect to z_1 and setting it to zero, we get

$$(X_1 - e_1 \tilde{X}_1)'(X_1 - e_1 \tilde{X}_1) z_1 + c_1 (X_2 - e_2 \tilde{X}_1)'(X_2 z_1 - e_2 \tilde{X}_1 z_1 - E_2) + c_3 z_1 = 0 \tag{6.27}$$

Let $A = X_1 - e_1 \tilde{X}_1$ and $B = X_2 - e_2 \tilde{X}_1$, we get

$$z_1 = (\frac{1}{c_1} A'A + B'B + \frac{c_3}{c_1} I)^{-1}(B'E_2) \tag{6.28}$$

where I is an identity matrix with appropriate dimension.

With the similar steps given above, the solution to the optimisation problem (6.24) is

$$z_2 = -(\frac{1}{c_2} A'A + B'B + \frac{c_4}{c_2} I)^{-1}(B'E_1) \tag{6.29}$$

where $A = X_2 - e_2 \tilde{X}_2$ and $B = X_1 - e_1 \tilde{X}_2$.

The new testing data sample $x \in \mathbb{R}^n$ is given label as follows:

$$class(x) = arg \min_{i=1,2} |z_i'x - z_i' \frac{1}{m_i} \sum_{k=1}^{m_i} x_k^{(i)}| \tag{6.30}$$

where $|\cdot|$ denotes the absolute value.

6.3.2 RELSPTSVM for multiple projection directions

The aim of the proposed RELSPTSVM model is to seek projection direction instead of approximating a hyperplane; thus, multiple projection directions are generated for each class [45] to improve the performance. The recursive RELSPTSVM works as follows:

Algorithm-1: Training recursive RELSPTSVM

Step 1. Let t be the number of iterations. Initialize $t = 1$ and the training sets $T_1 = T_2 = \{x_i | i = 1, 2, \ldots, N\}$.

Step 2. Solve (6.23) and (6.24) to determine the projection directions $z_1(t)$ and $z_2(t)$ on the training sets T_1 and T_2, respectively.

Step 3. Normalize $z_1(t)$ and $z_2(t)$ to unit norm i.e. $z_1(t) = \frac{z_1(t)}{\|z_1(t)\|}$ and $z_2(t) = \frac{z_2(t)}{\|z_2(t)\|}$.

Step 4. Let $T_1(t+1) = \{x_i(t+1)|x_i(t+1) = x_i(t) - z_1^t x_i(t) z_1, i = 1, 2, \ldots, N\}$ and $T_2(t+1) = \{x_i(t+1)|x_i(t+1) = x_i(t) - z_2^t x_i(t) z_2, i = 1, 2, \ldots, N\}$.

Step 5. Stop if the criterion is met.

Step 6. Let $t = t + 1$ and goto Step-2.

6.3.3   Non-linear RELSPTSVM

Non-linear RELSPTSVM solves the following pair of optimisation problems:

$$\min_{z_1,\eta_1} \frac{1}{2}\left\|K(X_1,C^t)z_1 - e_1\tilde{X}_{1kr}z_1\right\|^2 + \frac{c_1}{2}\left\|\eta_1\right\|^2 + \frac{c_3}{2}\left\|z_1\right\|^2$$
$$s.t.\ \ K(X_2,C^t)z_1 - e_2\tilde{X}_{1kr}z_1 + \eta_1 = E_2 \tag{6.31}$$

and

$$\min_{z_2,\eta_2} \frac{1}{2}\left\|K(X_2,C^t)z_2 - e_2\tilde{X}_{2kr}z_2\right\|^2 + \frac{c_2}{2}\left\|\eta_2\right\|^2 + \frac{c_4}{2}\left\|z_1\right\|^2$$
$$s.t.\ \ -(K(X_1,C^t)z_2 - e_1\tilde{X}_2z_2) + \eta_2 = E_1, \tag{6.32}$$

where

$$\tilde{X}_{1kr} = \frac{1}{m_1}e_1^t K(X_1,C^t),\ \ \tilde{X}_{2kr} = \frac{1}{m_2}e_2^t K(X_2,C^t) \tag{6.33}$$

$C = [X_1;X_2]$ and K is the kernel function.

Substituting the equality constraints in the corresponding objective function of (6.31), we have

$$L = \frac{1}{2}\left\|K(X_1,C^t)z_1 - e_1\tilde{X}_{1kr}z_1\right\|^2 + \frac{c_1}{2}\left\|K(X_2,C^t)z_1 - e_2\tilde{X}_{1kr}z_1 - E_2\right\|^2 + \frac{c_3}{2}\left\|z_1\right\|^2$$
$$\tag{6.34}$$

Taking the gradient of (6.34) with respect to z_1 and setting it to zero, we get

$$(K(X_1,C^t) - e_1\tilde{X}_{1kr})^t(K(X_1,C^t) - e_1\tilde{X}_{1kr})z_1 + c_1(K(X_2,C^t) - e_2\tilde{X}_{1kr})^t(K(X_2,C^t)z_1$$
$$-e_2\tilde{X}_{1kr}z_1 - E_2) + c_3z_1 = 0 \tag{6.35}$$

Let $A = K(X_1,C^t) - e_1\tilde{X}_{1kr}$ and $B = K(X_2,C^t) - e_2\tilde{X}_{1kr}$, we get

$$z_1 = (\frac{1}{c_1}A^tA + B^tB + \frac{c_3}{c_1}I)^{-1}(B^tE_2) \tag{6.36}$$

With the similar steps given above, the solution to the optimisation problem (6.32) is

$$z_2 = -(\frac{1}{c_2}A^tA + B^tB + \frac{c_4}{c_2}I)^{-1}(B^tE_1), \tag{6.37}$$

where $A = K(X_2,C^t) - e_2\tilde{X}_{2kr}$ and $B = K(X_1,C^t) - e_1\tilde{X}_{2kr}$.

The new testing data sample $x \in \mathbb{R}^n$ is given label as follows:

$$class(x) = \arg\min_{i=1,2}\{d_i\} \begin{cases} d_1 \rightarrow x \in class\ 1 \\ d_2 \rightarrow x \in class\ 2 \end{cases} \tag{6.38}$$

$$d_1 = |(K(x^t,C^t) - \tilde{X}_{1kr})z_1|$$
$$d_2 = |(K(x^t,C^t) - \tilde{X}_{2kr})z_2|$$

where $|\cdot|$ denotes the absolute value.

6.4 Experimental results

The experimental pipeline for analysing the classification models is discussed in this section. All the algorithms are analysed on EEG [49] and UCI [50] datasets from domains such as biomedical, bank and fisheries [51]. The dataset is randomly partitioned into 30 : 70 ratio of testing set and training set. We performed four fold cross-validation training samples to get the best optimal hyperparameters corresponding to different classifiers. The grid search approach is used in the following range to choose the best hyperparameters: $C_i = \{10^{-7}, 10^{-6}, \cdots, 10^6, 10^7\}, \mu = \{10^{-7}, 10^{-6}, \cdots, 10^6, 10^7\}$ and $E_j = 0.5 : 0.1 : 1$, for $i = 1, 2, 3, 4$ and $j = 1, 2$. Also, Gaussian kernel is used for projecting the data into higher dimensional space, mathematically,

$$K(x_1, x_2) = exp(-\frac{\|x_1 - x_2\|^2}{\mu^2})$$ (6.39)

The performance of the models is evaluated using the accuracy metric.

6.4.1 Classification of EEG signals

Here, we analyse the classification performance of the baseline models and the proposed RELSPTSVM model for the classification of EEG signals. We used the publicly available EEG data [49]. It contains the five sets S, N, F, Z, O. Each of these sets has 100 single-channel EEG signals sampled at 173.61 Hz with a duration of 23.6 s. The EEG signals of the subjects with eyes open and closed are given in sets Z and O, respectively. The signals N and F correspond to the subjects in interictal state. The set S corresponds to the ictal state of the seizure recordings from the sites showing ictal activity. For features, we use RankFeatures() function and its various criteria of the MATLAB. The various criteria used are T-Test [52], Entropy [53], Bhattacharyya [52], ROC [52] and Wilcoxon [54]. Figure 6.1 gives the sample of the EEG signal. The performance of the classification models for EEG data is given in Table 6.1. From Table 6.1, it is clear that the proposed RELSPTSVM model achieved the highest average accuracy, i.e. 0.9123. The proposed models are followed by the RELSTSVM model with 0.8836 , TWSVM with 0.8705 and LSTSVM with 0.8352. Moreover, the average rank of the TWSVM, LSTSVM, RELSTSVM and proposed RELSPTSVM on EEG data is 3.225, 3.175, 2.45 and 1.15, respectively. One can see that the proposed RELSPTSVM model achieved the lowest average rank and, hence, better performance in comparison with the existing models.

6.4.2 Evaluation of the models with UCI datasets

The classification performance of the models with Gaussian kernel is given in Table 6.2. It is evident that the proposed RELSPTSVM model emerged as the best classifier with the highest average accuracy of 82.63%, respectively. The average

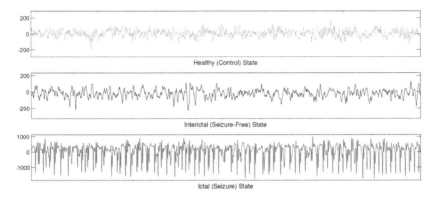

Figure 6.1   Sample of EEG signals for (a) healthy (control), (b) interictal (seizure-free) and (c) ictal (seizure) state

rank of TWSVM, LSTSVM, RELSTSVM and RELSPTSVM is 2.71, 2.43, 2.64 and 2.21, respectively. It is clear that the average rank of the proposed RELSPTSVM is the best. Hence, the generalisation ability of the proposed RELSPTSVM is superior compared to the existing models. Figure 6.2 shows the effect of parameters c_1 and c_3 on the performance of the proposed RELSPTSVM model. Thus, hyperparameters need to be chosen properly for optimal performance.

6.4.3   Statistical tests

The statistical significance of the models is evaluated in terms of the following tests.

6.4.3.1   Friedman test

As the average accuracy may be a biased measure due to outperformance in one dataset may compensate for the loss over multiple datasets. Hence, we follow the ranking approach to evaluate the efficiency approach to check the performance of the models. Here, each classifier is assigned a rank on each classifier with the high-performing model being assigned lower rank and lower performance model being assigned higher rank. Let K number of classifiers be evaluated on N datasets. The jth model rank on ith dataset is r_j^i. Then, the average rank of the model is given as $R_j = \frac{1}{N} \sum_{i=1}^{N} r_j^i$. To test the statistical significance of the models, we follow the Friedman test. Under null hypothesis, two models are performing equally, and hence their average ranks are equal. Here, in Friedman rank, the best performing is assigned lower rank and vice versa. The Friedman statistics is given as follows:

$$\chi_F^2 = \frac{12N}{K(K+1)} \left[\sum_j R_j^2 - \frac{K(K+1)^2}{4} \right]$$

(6.40)

Table 6.1   *EEG signal classification with Gaussian kernel*

Dataset name (Samples× features)	Feature selection Method	TWSVM [18] (c_1, μ)	LSTSVM [20] (c_1, μ)	RELSTSVM [22] (c_1, c_3, μ)	RELSPTSVM (c_1, c_3, μ)
Z and F 200 × 50	ROC	0.7377 $(10^{-1}, 10^6)$	0.5246 $(10^7, 10^7)$	0.7049 $(10^2, 10^{-4}, 10^6)$	0.7377 $(10^{-4}, 10^{-2}, 10^6)$
Z and F 200 × 50	Wilcoxon	0.7377 $(10^{-1}, 10^6)$	0.5246 $(10^7, 10^7)$	0.7377 $(10^3, 10^{-1}, 10^7)$	0.7705 $(10^{-4}, 10^{-2}, 10^6)$
F and S 200 × 100	Wilcoxon	0.8689 $(10^{-7}, 10^6)$	0.9016 $(10^{-1}, 10^6)$	0.8689 $(10^{-7}, 10^{-7}, 10^6)$	0.9016 $(10^5, 10^2, 10^6)$
O and N 200 × 100	Wilcoxon	0.8033 $(10^{-4}, 10^6)$	0.7541 $(10^{-1}, 10^6)$	0.8197 $(10^{-2}, 10^{-3}, 10^6)$	0.8197 $(10^{-4}, 10^{-6}, 10^6)$
Z and N 200 × 100	T Test	0.6066 $(10^2, 10^6)$	0.6557 $(10^{-1}, 10^6)$	0.6885 $(10^6, 10^3, 10^7)$	0.6885 $(10^{-5}, 10^4, 10^6)$
F and S 200 × 150	Wilcoxon	0.9016 $(10^{-6}, 10^6)$	0.7049 $(10^{-1}, 10^6)$	0.8525 $(10^{-7}, 10^{-4}, 10^6)$	0.9016 $(10^3, 10^2, 10^6)$
O and S 200 × 150	Bhattacharyya	0.9508 $(10^{-7}, 10^6)$	0.9508 $(10^{-3}, 10^7)$	0.9508 $(10^{-7}, 10^{-7}, 10^6)$	0.9836 $(10^{-7}, 10^{-7}, 10^3)$
O and S 200 × 150	Entropy	0.9508 $(10^{-7}, 10^6)$	0.9508 $(10^{-3}, 10^6)$	0.9508 $(10^{-7}, 10^{-7}, 10^6)$	0.9836 $(10^{-7}, 10^{-7}, 10^3)$
O and S 200 × 150	T Test	0.918 $(10^{-7}, 10^6)$	0.918 $(10^{-3}, 10^6)$	0.918 $(10^{-7}, 10^{-7}, 10^6)$	0.9672 $(10^{-7}, 10^{-7}, 10^3)$
Z and F 200 × 150	T Test	0.6885 $(10^5, 10^6)$	0.7213 $(10^{-1}, 10^7)$	0.7049 $(10^2, 10^{-2}, 10^6)$	0.7541 $(10^2, 10^{-3}, 10^7)$

(Continues)

Table 6.1 *Continued*

Dataset name (Samples× features)	Feature selection Method	TWSVM [18] (c_1, μ)	LSTSVM [20] (c_1, μ)	RELSTSVM [22] (c_1, c_3, μ)	RELSPTSVM (c_1, c_3, μ)
Z and S 200 × 150	T Test	$(10^{-7}, 10^6)$ 0.918	$(10^{-3}, 10^6)$ 0.9344	$(10^{-7}, 10^{-7}, 10^6)$ 0.9344	$(10^{-7}, 10^{-7}, 10^3)$ 0.9836
F and S 200 × 200	Bhattachrayya	$(10^{-7}, 10^6)$ 0.9344	$(10^{-3}, 10^6)$ 0.9344	$(10^{-7}, 10^{-7}, 10^6)$ 0.9508	$(10^{-7}, 10^{-6}, 10^3)$ 0.9836
Z and F 200 × 200	ROC	$(10^2, 10^7)$ 0.803279	$(10^0, 10^7)$ 0.803279	$(10^7, 10^{-4}, 10^7)$ 0.852459	$(10^3, 10^{-5}, 10^7)$ 0.852459
F and S 200 × 200	Entropy	$(10^{-7}, 10^6)$ 0.9344	$(10^0, 10^7)$ 0.9344	$(10^7, 10^{-4}, 10^7)$ 0.9508	$(10^3, 10^{-5}, 10^7)$ 0.9836
N and S 200 × 200	Wilcoxon	$(10^{-7}, 10^6)$ 0.918	$(10^{-3}, 10^6)$ 0.9344	$(10^{-7}, 10^{-7}, 10^6)$ 0.918	$(10^{-7}, 10^{-7}, 10^3)$ 0.9672
O and S 200 × 200	T Test	$(10^{-7}, 10^6)$ 0.9016	$(10^{-3}, 10^6)$ 0.9344	$(10^{-7}, 10^{-7}, 10^6)$ 0.9344	$(10^{-7}, 10^{-7}, 10^3)$ 0.9672
Z and S 200 × 200	Bhattachrayya	$(10^{-7}, 10^6)$ 0.9672	$(10^{-3}, 10^6)$ 0.9672	$(10^{-7}, 10^{-7}, 10^6)$ 0.9836	$(10^{-7}, 10^{-3}, 10^3)$ 1
Z and S 200 × 200	Entropy	$(10^{-7}, 10^6)$ 0.9672	$(10^{-3}, 10^6)$ 0.9672	$(10^{-7}, 10^{-7}, 10^6)$ 0.9836	$(10^{-7}, 10^{-7}, 10^3)$ 1
Z and S 200 × 200	ROC	$(10^{-7}, 10^6)$ 0.9344	$(10^{-4}, 10^7)$ 0.7213	$(10^{-7}, 10^{-7}, 10^6)$ 0.9836	$(10^{-7}, 10^{-7}, 10^3)$ 1
Z and S 200 × 200	Wilcoxon	$(10^{-7}, 10^6)$ 0.9672	$(10^{-3}, 10^6)$ 0.9672	$(10^{-7}, 10^{-7}, 10^6)$ 0.9836	$(10^{-7}, 10^{-7}, 10^3)$ 1
Average accuracy Average rank		0.8705 3.225	0.8352 3.175	0.8836 2.45	0.9123 1.15

Table 6.2   Evaluation of the classification algorithms with Gaussian kernel on UCI datasets

Dataset name	TWSVM [18]	LSTSVM [20]	RELSTSVM [22]	RELSPTSVM
(Samples × features)	(c_1, μ)	(c_1, μ)	$(c_1, c_3, E_1 = E_2, \mu)$	$(c_1, c_3, E_1 = E_2, \mu)$
Bank 4 521 × 16	0.885	0.889	0.8846	0.88
Blood 748 × 4	$(10^7, 10^{-3})$ 0.5467	$(10^3, 10^5)$ 0.72	$(1, 10^{-4}, 1, 10)$ 0.7307	$(10^{-7}, 10^{-1}, 0.8, 10^3)$ 0.6903
Breast-cancer-wisc 699 × 9	$(10^2, 10^{-1})$ 0.9231	$(10^{-1}, 10^{-1})$ 0.943	$(10^3, 10^{-2}, 0.7, 10^{-1})$ 0.9573	$(10^{-1}, 10^4, 0.5, 10^{-1})$ 0.9479
Chess-krvkp 3 196 × 36	$(10^{-7}, 10^2)$ 0.9906	$(10^{-2}, 10)$ 0.7186	$(10^{-7}, 10^{-7}, 0.5, 10^5)$ 0.9744	$(10^{-7}, 10^{-7}, 0.5, 1)$ 0.9917
Credit-approval 690 × 15	$(10, 10^2)$ 0.8468	$(10, 10^2)$ 0.8353	$(1, 10^{-3}, 0.5, 10^2)$ 0.8642	$(1, 10^{-6}, 0.7, 10^2)$ 0.799
Cylinder-bands 512 × 35	$(10^{-3}, 10^2)$ 0.7082	$(1, 10)$ 0.7004	$(10^{-6}, 10^{-7}, 0.6, 10^5)$ 0.642	$(10, 10^{-7}, 0.5, 10)$ 0.7806
Ilpd-indian-liver 583 × 9	$(10^{-3}, 10^2)$ 0.6519	$(10^2, 10^2)$ 0.7099	$(10^{-4}, 10^{-6}, 0.9, 10^3)$ 0.7099	$(10^{-2}, 10^{-7}, 0.9, 1)$ 0.7159
Mammographic 961 × 5	$(10^3, 1)$ 0.7967	$(10^3, 1)$ 0.7822	$(10^{-5}, 10^{-4}, 0.6, 10^3)$ 0.7822	$(10^{-2}, 10^{-1}, 0.9, 10)$ 0.7793
Oocytes_merluccius_nucleus_4d 1 022 × 41	$(10^{-5}, 1)$ 0.7598	$(10^2, 1)$ 0.7617	$(10^5, 1, 0.6, 10^4)$ 0.7578	$(10^{-1}, 10^{-7}, 0.9, 10^5)$ 0.763
Oocytes_trisopterus_nucleus_2f 912 × 25	$(10^7, 1)$ 0.7834 $(10^5, 10)$	$(10^2, 1)$ 0.7899 $(10^{-1}, 10^2)$	$(10^5, 10^{-6}, 0.7, 1)$ 0.6652 $(10^6, 10^4, 0.9, 10)$	$(10^{-1}, 10^{-2}, 0.9, 1)$ 0.8255 $(1, 10^{-6}, 1, 10^2)$

(Continues)

Table 6.2 Continued

Dataset name	TWSVM [18]	LSTSVM [20]	RELSTSVM [22]	RELSPTSVM
(Samples× features)	(c_1, μ)	(c_1, μ)	$(c_1, c_3, E_1 = E_2, \mu)$	$(c_1, c_3, E_1 = E_2, \mu)$
Spambase 4 601 × 57	0.7233 $(10^7, 10^3)$	0.9214 $(10^{-1}, 10^2)$	0.8827 $(10^{-3}, 10^{-7}, 0.8, 10^5)$	0.9233 $(10^{-4}, 10^{-5}, 0.6, 10^2)$
Statlog-german-credit $10^3 \times 24$	0.7246	0.7246 $(10^3, 10^3)$	0.6507 $(10^5, 10^{-3}, 0.6, 10^3)$	0.6844 $(10^{-3}, 10^6, 0.5, 10^7)$
Tic-tac-toe 958 × 9	$(10, 10^4)$ 0.9813	0.9813 $(10, 10)$	0.9813 $(10, 10^{-7}, 0.5, 10^2)$	0.9792 $(10, 10^{-7}, 0.5, 10^2)$
Vertebral-column-2clases 310 × 6	$(10^{-3}, 10)$ 0.7564 $(10^{-4}, 10)$	0.7756 $(10^4, 10)$	0.7821 $(10^{-2}, 10^{-5}, 0.6, 10^2)$	0.8085 $(10, 10^{-5}, 1, 10)$
Average accuracy	0.7915	0.8038	0.8046	0.8263
Average rank	2.7143	2.4286	2.6429	2.2143

(a) Statlog-german-credit

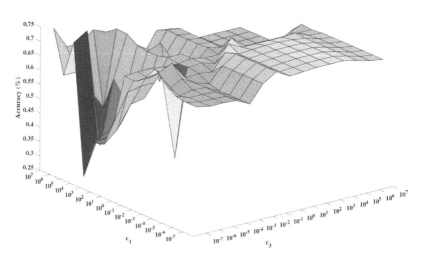

(b) Tic-tac-toe

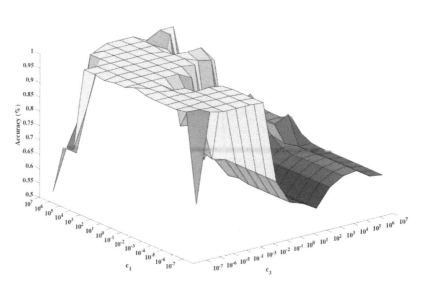

Figure 6.2   *The sensitivity analysis of the proposed RELSPTSVM model with the hyperparameters* c_1 *and* c_3

Since χ_F^2 is undesirably conservative and hence a better statistic

$$F_F = \frac{(N-1)\chi_F^2}{N(K-1) - \chi_F^2} \tag{6.41}$$

is used which follows F-distribution with $(K-1)$ and $(N-1) \times (K-1)$ degrees of freedom.

Table 6.1 gives the performance of the models on the EEG data. The average rank of TWSVM, LSTSVM, RELSTSVM and proposed RELSPTSVM is $3.23, 3.18, 2.45,$ and 1.15, respectively. After simple calculations with $N = 20, K = 4$, we get $\chi_F^2 = 34.4436$ and $F_F = 25.6072$ at 5% level of significance. From the statistical table, $F_F(3, 57) = 2.7750$. Since $25.6072 > 2.775$, the null hypothesis is rejected. Thus, a significant difference exists among the models. To get the significant difference among the models, we use Nemenyi post-hoc test. With $q_{0.05} = 2.5690$, the critical difference $CD = 1.0488$. Thus, the two models are said to be significantly different if the average ranks of the models differ at least by the CD. Table 6.3 shows that the proposed RELSPTSVM model is significantly different compared to the baseline models. Moreover, the proposed RELSPTSVM model shows better performance (lower average rank) compared to the baseline models.

With $N = 14$, $K = 4$ for the UCI datasets (Table 6.2), we get $\chi_F^2 = 0.8627$, $F_F = 0.2726$ where F_F is distributed with $F_F(3, 39)$ degrees of freedom. From the F-distribution table, $F_F(3, 39) = 2.855$. Since $0.2726 < 2.855$, the Friedman test fails to detect the significant difference among the models. However, one can see that the proposed RELSPTSVM model is better in terms of average accuracy and average rank compared to baseline models.

6.4.3.2 Win–tie–loss: sign test

The win–tie–loss sign test is used to evaluate the statistical significance of the models. In this test, under null hypothesis two models are equivalent if each of models wins on approximately $N/2$ datasets out of the N datasets. At 5% level of significance, the two models are significantly different if one of models

Table 6.3 Pairwise significant difference of the proposed RELSPTSVM model on the EEG data with Nemenyi post-hoc test

	TWSVM [18]	LSTSVM [20]	RELSTSVM [22]
Proposed RELSPTSVM	Yes	Yes	Yes

Table 6.4 Pairwise win–tie–loss analysis of the models on the EEG data

	TWSVM [18]	**LSTSVM [20]**	**RELSTSVM [22]**
LSTSVM [20]	[6, 9, 5]		
RELSTSVM [22]	[12, 6, 2]	[12, 5, 3]	
Proposed RELSPTSVM	[18, 2, 0]	[19, 1, 0]	[17, 3, 0]

wins approximately on $N/2 + 1.96\sqrt{N}/2$. Also, if there is an even number of ties between the two models, then the number of ties is evenly distributed among them; otherwise, we ignore one and distribute the rest among the given classifiers. With simple calculation, significant difference exists if $win \geq 14.3827$. Tables 6.4 and 6.5 represent the count of win–tie–loss and significant difference among the classifiers on EEG data, respectively. In Table 6.4, the entry $[x, y, z]$ denotes that the row method wins x times, loses z times and ties y times with respect to the column method. From the given tables, it is evident that the proposed RELSPTSVM model is significantly superior compared to the existing models for the classification of EEG data.

6.4.3.3 Wilcoxon signed-rank test

The nonparametric Wilcoxon signed-rank test [55] is employed to compare the performance of the given models. This test calculates d_i, i.e. the difference between the accuracy of two compared models corresponding to the ith dataset out of N datasets. The ascending order of absolute differences is ranked wherein the average ranks are given in tie cases. $R+ (R-)$ represents the sum of positive (negative) ranks, respectively. The sufficient difference between $R+$ and $R-$ demonstrates that the compared models reject the null hypothesis. The null hypothesis is rejected if the p-value for this test is smaller than 0.05. Therefore, one can see from Table 6.6 that the proposed RELSPTSVM outperforms the compared models on the EEG data.

Table 6.5 Pairwise win tie loss significance of the proposed RELSPTSVM model on the EEG data

	TWSVM [18]	**LSTSVM [20]**	**RELSTSVM [22]**
Proposed RELSPTSVM	Yes	Yes	Yes

Table 6.6   *Statistical comparison of classification models with respect to the proposed RELSPTSVM model on EEG data with Gaussian kernel via Wilcoxon signed-rank test*

	R_+	R_-	p-value	Hypoth-esis (0.05)
TWSVM [18]	171	0	0.0002	**Rejected**
LSTSVM [20]	190	0	0.00014	**Rejected**
RELSTSVM [22]	153	0	0.0003	**Rejected**

The p-value is calculated from paired Wilcoxon test.
$R_+(R_-)$ denotes the sum of positive (negative) ranks, respectively.

6.5   Conclusion

In this chapter, we proposed the RELSPTSVM model for the EEG signal classification. Unlike TWSVM, LSTSVM and RELSTSVM models that generate the hyperplanes for each category of data points, the proposed RELSPTSVM model generates a projection axis for each category in a manner that the data points of each category class are clustered around its mean vector and data points of other categories are as far as possible. Unlike the LSTSVM model wherein the data points of opposite category require to be at a distance of 1, the proposed RELSPTSVM model introduced energy parameters to relax this constraint. The formulation of TWSVM and LSTSVM assumes that matrices are positive definite and minimise the empirical risk and thus prone to overfitting. The proposed RELSPTSVM minimises the structural risk, and the matrices appearing are positive definite. The analysis of experiments demonstrates that the proposed RELSPTSVM is superior in comparison to the existing models for the classification of EEG signals. Statistical test on the EEG data reveals that the proposed RELSPTSVM model is significantly better compared to the baseline models. Moreover, the performance of the proposed RELSPTSVM model on benchmark UCI datasets is better compared to the baseline models.

Acknowledgements

The funding for this work is provided by the National Supercomputing Mission under DST and Miety, Govt. of India under Grant No. DST/NSM/ R&D_HPC_ Appl/2021/03.29, as well as the Department of Science and Technology under Interdisciplinary Cyber Physical Systems (ICPS) Scheme grant no. DST/ICPS/ CPS-Individual/2018/276. We are grateful to IIT Indore for the facilities and support being provided.

References

[1] Adeli H., Zhou Z., Dadmehr N. 'Analysis of EEG records in an epileptic patient using wavelet transform'. *Journal of Neuroscience Methods*. 2003, vol. 123(1), pp. 69–87.

[2] Rosso O.A., Hyslop W., Gerlach R., Smith R.L.L., Rostas J.A.P., Hunter M. 'Quantitative EEG analysis of the maturational changes associated with childhood absence epilepsy'. *Physica A*. 2005, vol. 356(1), pp. 184–89.

[3] Güler I., Ubeyli E.D. 'Adaptive neuro-fuzzy inference system for classification of EEG signals using wavelet coefficients'. *Journal of Neuroscience Methods*. 2005, vol. 148(2), pp. 113–21.

[4] Cortes C., Vapnik V. 'Support-vector networks'. *Machine Learning*. 2005, vol. 20(3), pp. 273–97.

[5] Burges C.J.C. 'A tutorial on support vector machines for pattern recognition'. *Data Mining and Knowledge Discovery*. 2005, vol. 2(2), pp. 121–67.

[6] Subasi A., Ismail Gursoy M. 'EEG signal classification using PCA, ICA, LDA and support vector machines'. *Expert Systems with Applications*. 2010, vol. 37(12), pp. 8659–66.

[7] Richhariya B., Tanveer M. 'EEG signal classification using universum support vector machine'. *Expert Systems with Applications*. 2010, vol. 106, pp. 169–82.

[8] Beheshti I., Ganaie M.A., Paliwal V., Rastogi A., Razzak I., Tanveer M. 'Predicting brain age using machine learning algorithms: A comprehensive evaluation'. *IEEE Journal of Biomedical and Health Informatics*. 2022, vol. 26(4), pp. 1432–40.

[9] Noble W.S. 'Support vector machine applications in computational biology'. *Kernel Methods in Computational Biology*. 2004, vol. 14, pp. 71–92.

[10] Li Y.-X., Shao Y.-H., Jing L., Deng N.-Y. 'An efficient support vector machine approach for identifying protein s-nitrosylation sites'. *Protein and Peptide Letters*. 2011, vol. 18(6), pp. 573–87.

[11] Li Y.-X., Shao Y.-H., Deng N.-Y. 'Improved prediction of palmitoylation sites using PWMS and SVM'. *Protein and Peptide Letters*. 2011, vol. 18(2), pp. 186–93.

[12] Ganaie M.A., Tanveer M., Beheshti I. 'Brain age prediction using improved twin SVR'. *Neural Computing and Applications*. 2021.

[13] Ganaie M.A., Tanveer M., Beheshti I. 'Brain age prediction with improved least squares twin SVR'. *IEEE Journal of Biomedical and Health Informatics*. 2022.

[14] Vapnik V.N. 'An overview of statistical learning theory'. *IEEE Transactions on Neural Networks*. 1999, vol. 10(5), pp. 988–99.

[15] Suykens J.A.K., Vandewalle J. 'Least squares support vector machine classifiers'. *Neural Processing Letters*. 1999, vol. 9(3), pp. 293–300.

[16] Fung G.M., Mangasarian O.L. 'Multicategory proximal support vector machine classifiers'. *Machine Learning*. 2005, vol. 59(1–2), pp. 77–97.

[17]　Qi Z., Tian Y., Shi Y. 'Successive overrelaxation for laplacian support vector machine'. *IEEE Transactions on Neural Networks and Learning Systems*. 2015, vol. 26(4), pp. 674–83.

[18]　Jayadeva.KhemchandaniR., Chandra S. 'Twin support vector machines for pattern classification'. *IEEE Transactions on Pattern Analysis and Machine Intelligence*. 2007, vol. 29(5), pp. 905–10.

[19]　Shao Y.-H., Zhang C.-H., Wang X.-B., Deng N.-Y. 'Improvements on twin support vector machines'. *IEEE Transactions on Neural Networks*. 2011, vol. 22(6), pp. 962–68.

[20]　Arun Kumar M., Gopal M. 'Least squares twin support vector machines for pattern classification'. *Expert Systems with Applications*. 2005, vol. 36(4), pp. 7535–43.

[21]　Nasiri J.A., Moghadam Charkari N., Mozafari K. 'Energy-based model of least squares twin support vector machines for human action recognition'. *Signal Processing*. 2014, vol. 104, pp. 248–57.

[22]　Tanveer M., Khan M.A., Ho S.-S. 'Robust energy-based least squares twin support vector machines'. *Applied Intelligence*. 2014, vol. 45(1), pp. 174–86.

[23]　Tanveer M., Gautam C., Suganthan P.N. 'Comprehensive evaluation of twin SVM based classifiers on UCI datasets'. *Applied Soft Computing*. 2014, vol. 83, 105617.

[24]　Xu Y., Yang Z., Pan X. 'A novel twin support-vector machine with pinball loss'. *IEEE Transactions on Neural Networks and Learning Systems*. 2017, vol. 28(2), pp. 359–70.

[25]　Tanveer M., Sharma A., Suganthan P.N. 'General twin support vector machine with pinball loss function'. *Information Sciences*. 2014, vol. 494, pp. 311–27.

[26]　Ganaie M.A., Tanveer M. 'Robust general twin support vector machine with pinball loss function' in *Machine Learning for Intelligent Multi-media Analytics*. Singapore; 2021. pp. 103–25.

[27]　Tanveer M., Tiwari A., Choudhary R., Jalan S. 'Sparse pinball twin support vector machines'. *Applied Soft Computing*. 2019, vol. 78, pp. 164–75.

[28]　Tanveer M., Rajani T., Ganaie M.A. 'Improved sparse pinball twin SVM'. *IEEE International Conference on Systems, Man and Cybernetics (SMC)* [online]; Bari, Italy, IEEE, 2019. pp. 3287–91. Available from https://ieeexplore.ieee.org/xpl/mostRecentIssue.jsp?punumber=8906183

[29]　Tanveer M., Sharma S., Muhammad K. 'Large-scale least squares twin SVMS'. *ACM Transactions on Internet Technology*. 2019, vol. 21(2), pp. 1–19.

[30]　Tanveer M., Tiwari A., Choudhary R., Jalan S. 'Sparse pinball twin support vector machines'. *Applied Soft Computing*. 2019, vol. 78, pp. 164–75.

[31]　Ganaie M.A., Tanveer M., Suganthan P.N. 'Oblique decision tree ensemble via twin bounded SVM'. *Expert Systems with Applications*. 2020, vol. 143, 113072.

[32] Ganaie M.A., Tanveer M. 'LSTSVM classifier with enhanced features from pre-trained functional link network'. *Applied Soft Computing*. 2020, vol. 93, 106305.

[33] Tanveer M., Ganaie M.A., Suganthan P.N. 'Ensemble of classification models with weighted functional link network'. *Applied Soft Computing*. 2020, vol. 107, 107322.

[34] Weston J., Collobert R., Sinz F., Bottou L., Vapnik V. 'Inference with the universum'. *The 23rd International Conference* [online]; Pittsburgh, PA, New York, NY, 2020. pp. 1009–16. Available from http://portal.acm.org/citation. cfm?doid=1143844

[35] Chapelle O., Agarwal A., Sinz F., Schölkopf B. 'An analysis of inference with the universum' in *Advances in neural information processing systems 20*. MIT; 2007.

[36] Qi Z., Tian Y., Shi Y. 'Twin support vector machine with universum data'. *Neural Networks*. 2012, vol. 36, pp. 112–19.

[37] Xu Y., Chen M., Li G. 'Least squares twin support vector machine with universum data for classification'. *International Journal of Systems Science*. 2016, vol. 47(15), pp. 3637–45.

[38] Batuwita R., Palade V. 'FSVM-CIL: fuzzy support vector machines for class imbalance learning'. *IEEE Transactions on Fuzzy Systems*. 2016, vol. 18(3), pp. 558–71.

[39] Wang B.X., Japkowicz N. 'Boosting support vector machines for imbalanced data sets'. *Knowledge and Information Systems*. 2016, vol. 25(1), pp. 1–20.

[40] Chawla N.V., Bowyer K.W., Hall L.O., Kegelmeyer W.P. 'SMOTE: synthetic minority over-sampling technique'. *Journal of Artificial Intelligence Research*. 2016, vol. 16, pp. 321–57.

[41] Liu X.-Y., Wu J., Zhou Z.-H. 'Exploratory undersampling for class-imbalance learning'. *IEEE Transactions on Systems, Man, and Cybernetics. Part B, Cybernetics*. 2009, vol. 39(2), pp. 539–50.

[42] Yu D.-J., Hu J., Tang Z.-M., Shen H.-B., Yang J., Yang J.-Y. 'Improving protein-ATP binding residues prediction by boosting svms with random under-sampling'. *Neurocomputing*. 2013, vol. 104, pp. 180–90.

[43] Richhariya B., Tanveer M. 'A reduced universum twin support vector machine for class imbalance learning'. *Pattern Recognition*. 2020, vol. 102, 107150.

[44] Ye Q., Zhao C., Ye N., Chen Y. 'Multi-weight vector projection support vector machines'. *Pattern Recognition Letters*. 2020, vol. 31(13), pp. 2006–11.

[45] Chen X., Yang J., Ye Q., Liang J. 'Recursive projection twin support vector machine via within-class variance minimization'. *Pattern Recognition*. 2020, vol. 44(10–11), pp. 2643–55.

[46] Ganaie M.A., Tanveer M. 'Fuzzy least squares projection twin support vector machines for class imbalance learning'. *Applied Soft Computing*. 2021, vol. 113, 107933.

[47] Ganaie M.A., Tanveer M., Suganthan P.N. 'Regularized robust fuzzy least squares twin support vector machine for class imbalance learning'.

International Joint Conference on Neural Networks (IJCNN) [online]; Glasgow, UK, IEEE, 2020. pp. 1–8. Available from https://ieeexplore.ieee.org/xpl/mostRecentIssue.jsp?punumber=9200848

[48] Tanveer M., Rajani T., Rastogi R., Shao Y.H., Ganaie M.A. 'Comprehensive review on twin support vector machines'. *Annals of Operations Research*. 2022.

[49] Andrzejak R.G., Lehnertz K., Mormann F., Rieke C., David P., Elger C.E. 'Indications of nonlinear deterministic and finite-dimensional structures in time series of brain electrical activity: dependence on recording region and brain state'. *Physical Review. E, Statistical, Nonlinear, and Soft Matter Physics*. 2001, vol. 64(6 Pt 1), 061907.

[50] Dua D., Graf C. *UCI machine learning repository* [online]. 2017. Available from http://archive.ics.uci.edu/ml

[51] González-Rufino E., Carrión P., Cernadas E., Fernández-Delgado M., Domínguez-Petit R. 'Exhaustive comparison of colour texture features and classification methods to discriminate cells categories in histological images of fish ovary'. *Pattern Recognition*. 2013, vol. 46(9), pp. 2391–407.

[52] Theodoridis S., Koutroumbas K. 'Feature selection' in *Pattern Recognition*. 4th Edition. Boston, MA: Academic Press; 2009. pp. 261–322.

[53] Kullback S. *Information theory and statistics*. USA: Courier Corporation; 1997.

[54] Kotz S., Johnson N.L., Wilcoxon F. 'Breakthroughs in statistics' in *Individual Comparisons by Ranking Methods*. New York, NY: Springer; 1992. pp. 196–202.

[55] Demšar J. 'Statistical comparisons of classifiers over multiple data sets'. *The Journal of Machine Learning Research*. 2006, vol. 7, pp. 1–30.

Chapter 7

Clustering-based medical image segmentation: a survey

Sanat Kumar Pandey[1], Ashish Kumar Bhandari[1], and Praveer Saxena[1]

Image segmentation is a popular phenomenon to dividing a digital image into various meaningful and disjoint segments based on certain criteria. It is used to represent the original representation of the image into a more meaningful representation which can be easily analysed. The segmentation of medical images is one of the key steps for analysis of the medical images. It has been gaining much attention due to its application in clinical diagnosis. Computer-aided image segmentation not only reduces the effort of medical practitioners but also reduces the chances of error due to the human intervention. Proper segmentation of medical images leads to accurate diagnosis of the disease which may lead to appropriate treatment. A lot of algorithms have been suggested to segment an image into its most informative form but image segmentation still remains quite a challenging problem. Out of all these segmentation algorithms the clustering-based segmentation algorithms are quite popular to segment both low- and high-dimensional medical images. These algorithms segregate the input image into a finite number of clusters each having a group of pixels based on certain criteria. In this chapter, the different clustering-based algorithms proposed for medical image segmentation have been reviewed. Concise overview of different clustering algorithms proposed for segmentation of medical images is presented along with their key benefits and limitations.

7.1 Introduction

The unbalanced lifestyle and bad environmental conditions increase the patient count day by day which creates a heavy load on the health sector of any nation, due to which the medical practitioners are also facing a heavy workload and too much stress in their day-to-day lives, so there is always a possibility for some errors even

[1]Department of Electronics and Communication Engineering, National Institute of Technology, Patna, Bihar, India

in their expertise work. In such scenarios, if technology can be added to supplement their work, it may lead to an unparalleled revolution in the medical field. Thanks to the evolution of computer-aided medical diagnosis, which can supplement the medical practitioner's work to achieve excellence.

The segmentation of medical images is one of the key steps in the analysis of medical images. It is the process of transforming digital images into various meaningful and disjoint segments based on certain criteria. In concise, image segmentation is basically the partition of an image into various nonoverlapping, pixel-wise isolated homogeneous regions on behalf of certain image parameters such as texture, color, and shape. Due to the various aspects of a particular image, the process of segmentation is not an easy phenomenon. The image complexities such as partial volume effect and intensity inhomogeneity [1, 2] can effectively change the actual pixel value due to various objects of an image. Hence, it is very difficult to provide a particular class to a single image element, so the "hard" clustering methods are not efficient for medical image segmentation because of the inability to decide a particular class for a particular pixel value. For effective segmentation, we prefer the "soft" clustering-based segmentation where a particular pixel can belong to more than one cluster. This concept is basically used in fuzzy C-means (FCM) clustering algorithms to make medical image segmentation more effective. There have been several algorithms proposed in the past for the segmentation of a digital image but there are no algorithms, which are suitable for all kinds of applications. Some algorithms perform well in certain scenarios but fail in other scenarios.

In general, segmentation algorithms can be categorized as supervised and unsupervised segmentation algorithms. To achieve decent performance supervised algorithms, we require an adequate number of labeled training data which are sometimes challenging to obtain. In contrast to supervised algorithms [3, 4], the unsupervised algorithms [5–9] do not depend on training data and their labels.

Among unsupervised algorithms, clustering has been widely used for segmentation of both color and grayscale images as it has the capability to deal with both low- and high-dimensional data.

Broadly, clustering is classified into three different categories:

1. based on graph theory [10]
2. based on decomposing a density function [11]
3. based on optimizing an objective function [12]

The fuzzy-based clustering method, which was first designed by Dunn [13], named as FCM clustering algorithm was extended and improved by Bezdek [14] and is becoming a very popular tool for the segmentation of medical images. FCM is a very effective and simple method for the segmentation of noise-free medical images due to the absence of spatial parameters [15–18], and it is not suitable for noisy images. To improve this fuzzy-based segmentation method, such as FCM, various modifications are performed in its objective function. To improve the segmentation results on noisy images, various methods are proposed to improve the objective function of the basic FCM algorithm. The decadal survey of some of those popular algorithms is presented in this chapter with reference to research scholars in this particular field. In this chapter, the medical image segmentation using FCM clustering based on minimizing an objective function is reviewed along with its various variants proposed in the recent past. This survey comprises a decadal study on various effective methods, which are suggested to segment the noisy medical images including various other artifacts.

7.2 Medical imaging modalities and challenges with segmentation

Medical imaging has been a revolution in the treatment of various diseases, as with the help of imaging one can observe the progress of the state of the disease. There are various imaging modalities that are used for the diagnosis of the diseases, e.g., magnetic resonance imaging (MRI), ultrasound, X-rays, medical radiation, computed tomography. Depending on the specific disease, the practitioner recommends different types of imaging modalities. The segmentation of medical images is quite challenging as they contain complicated boundaries and most often are affected by noise [19]. In the recent past, several improved formats of FCM have been developed, with each having its own advantages. In the next section, the various FCM algorithms used in medical image segmentation are reviewed.

7.3 FCM and its various variants

7.3.1 FCM clustering algorithm

FCM clustering is a very popular and approved clustering method, which is very useful in the analysis of data extraction from medical images. It is a soft clustering-based method in which the objective data point is associated with several clusters. Initially, the path size between the cluster center and the data point is responsible for assigning a cluster to a particular data sample.

The membership value ranges between 0 and 1. The closer the data point is to the cluster center, the higher the value of the membership. The sum of all the membership values for each data sample is equal to 1. It is an iterative method, and the result is obtained by iteratively modifying the cluster center and membership size.

Assume $X = \{x_1, x_2, x_3, ..., x_N\}$ is the data with N different data samples. The objective is to partition the data into "c" clusters with updated minimum value of cost function mentioned in (7.1).

$$J = \sum_{j=1}^{N} \sum_{i=1}^{C} u_{ij}^m \left\| x_j - v_i \right\|^2 \tag{7.1}$$

where u_{ij} = membership of data point x_j with ith cluster, v_i with ith cluster, and $\left\| x_j - v_i \right\|$ is the Euclidean distance with constant m. "m" decides the fuzziness of the partition. A constrained fuzzy partition can be local minima of the cost function J only if following conditions are satisfied:

$$v_i = \frac{\sum_{j=1}^{N} u_{ij}^m x_j}{\sum_{j=1}^{N} u_{ij}^m} \tag{7.2}$$

$$u_{ij} = \frac{1}{\sum_{k=1}^{c} \left(\frac{\|x_j - v_i\|}{\|x_j - v_k\|} \right)^{\frac{2}{m-1}}} \tag{7.3}$$

Steps in FCM clustering:

I.   Choose randomly "*c*" cluster centers.
II. Compute the fuzzy centers "v_i" using (7.2).
III. Find the fuzzy membership "u_{ij}" with (7.3).
IV. Repeat the steps 2 and 3 to find an optimum value of cost function or $\|U^{(k+1)} - U^{(k)}\| < \beta$.

For an image, the corresponding analogy between data point and pixels is that in case of an image X represents an image and x_1, x_2, x_3..., x_N are the *n* pixels of an image X. The objective is to categorize the image into C clusters.

FCM is very commonly used for the segmentation of medical images [20–22]. The conventional FCM is very sensitive to noise due to the absence of spatial information of the pixels [19].

To make FCM more effective, there are various modifications and upgradation processes performed in the recent past introducing the local spatial information in their cost function [5, 23]. The proposed method can be classified into two groups. To improve the image segmentation, the first group incorporates the neighborhood data of a center pixel using a window of fixed size [24–26]. In comparison with the first group, the second group incorporates the adaptive neighborhood data in place of window of fixed shape and size [27, 28]. Due to adaptive neighborhood data, the second group of algorithms are more robust in the case of noisy images and obtain a better segmentation effect in comparison with the first group. In this chapter, the different variants of FCM proposed from the year 2010 to 2021 have been reviewed.

7.3.2   *Fuzzy local information c-means*

Most of the algorithms [20, 24, 29] that try to use spatial information have the limitation that they are dependent on the noise density. Fuzzy local information c-means (FLICM) [25] has been proposed to overcome the drawback associated with such algorithms. FLICM possesses the following characteristics:

I.   Independency from noise type.
II. Simultaneous incorporation of both the local spatial and gray level relationship in a fuzzy way.
III. Due to the automatic determination of fuzzy local constraints, the parameter determination is not required.

IV. Automatic balance between image details and noise constraints.

To incorporate such features in the algorithm, a fuzzy factor has been inserted in the objective function of FLICM, which is shown as follows:

$$J_m = \sum_{i=1}^{N} \sum_{k=1}^{c} \left[u_{ki}^m \|x_i - v_k\|^2 + G_{ki} \right] \tag{7.4}$$

The G is defined as

$$G_{ki} = \sum_{\substack{j \in N_i \\ i \neq j}} \frac{1}{d_{ij} + 1} \left(1 - u_{kj} \right)^m \|x_j - v_k\|^2 \tag{7.5}$$

where d_{ij} is the spatial Euclidean distance and u_{kj} is the degree of membership.

FLICM is a good choice when the prior information on noise is not available. It suffers from the inability to handle intensity inhomogeneity. Due to the damping effect of neighboring pixels on Euclidean distance between central cluster pixels and observed pixels, the proposed FLICM algorithm is unable to perform well on complex images, due to this effect it is not preferred for color medical images.

7.3.3   Multidimensional FCM

Multidimensional FCM (MDFCM) [21] is also an approach to minimizing the effect of noise by utilizing spatial domain information [29]. MDFCM utilizes the various features of neighboring pixels such as standard deviation, mean, and singular value along with pixel intensity for segmentation. Because of the consideration of multiple features, it is called as MDFCM. The process diagram of the proposed method is mentioned in Figure 7.1.

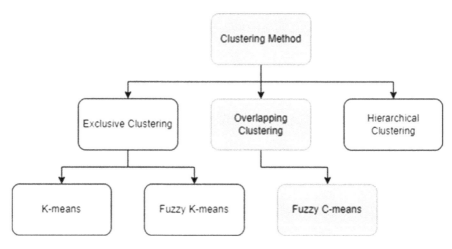

Figure 7.1   Classification of clustering-based image segmentation techniques

MRI with artifacts   Segmented Image

Figure 7.2   Process diagram of MDFCM

The first step is to extract the features. Now different combinations of these extracted features can be created. The selection of features is dependent on the requirement. To achieve high accuracy, all the characteristics give improved results but to reduce the computation complexity only a few important features such as Eigenvalue and pixel intensity are suggested. The MDFCM tends to exhibit improved results in comparison with several variations of FCM.

MDFCM tends to exhibit clear boundaries and clustering and is noise-free even in case of images corrupted by high-density noise. MDFCM suffers from the drawback of high computation requirement due to multidimensional data (Figure 7.2).

7.3.4   Weighted image patch-based FCM

Weighted image patch-based FCM (WIPFCM) [30] is again one of the approaches which utilizes the spatial information in FCM. This method is influenced by the denoising process of different image patches. In this approach, instead of considering just the pixels, image patches are considered. Because of consideration of image patches, additional information is added to the data. Different pixels in each image patch should have different weight values; due to this, all the image pixels are not equally helpful in calculation of similarity between two image patches.

Let an image be represented by $I = \{x_1, x_2, ..., x_n\}$. For each pixel x_k, the image patch is represented by a vector $P_k^I = (I_{kr}, r \in N_k)$, where N_k is a q × q neighborhood of pixel x_k.

For each pixel x_r in an image patch P_k^I, its mean squared deviation is defined as mentioned in (7.6).

$$\sigma_{kr} = \left[\frac{\sum_{r' \in N_k \backslash r} (x_{r'} - x_r)^2}{n_k - 1} \right]^{1/2} \tag{7.6}$$

The weight of the pixel x_r is calculated as

$$\xi_{kr} = \exp\left[-\left(\sigma_{kr} - \frac{\sum_{r \in N_k} \sigma_{kr}}{n_k} \right) \right] \tag{7.7}$$

The normalized weights are calculated as

$$\omega_{kr} = \frac{\xi_{kr}}{\sum_{r \in N_k} \xi_{kr}} \tag{7.8}$$

The objective function of WIPFCM is given by

$$J_{WIPFCM} = \sum_{i=1}^{c} \sum_{k=1}^{n} u_{ik}^{m} \sum_{r \in N_k} \omega_{kr} \left\| I_{kr} - v_{ri} \right\|^2 \qquad (7.9)$$

where

$V_i = (v_{ri}, r \in N^*)$ is the q × q dimensional centroid of cluster i

$U = \{u_{ik}\} \in R^{n \times c}$ is the membership matrix

$m \in (1, \infty)$ is the fuzzy parameter

The WIPFCM can also perform accurately in noisy conditions due to the consideration of spatial information in it. It also has the advantage that it does not require an external parameter to be selected. But it increases the computational load because every pixel is required to be represented by a patch and it requires an individual path to calculate their respective weights.

The proposed WIPFCM algorithms ensure high accuracy with the best robustness to noise but when the size of the images increases, the accuracy decreases and the time consumption increases.

7.3.5   Kernel weighted fuzzy local information c-means

Kernel weighted fuzzy local information c-means (KWFLICM) [26] is an approach toward overcoming the shortcomings of FLICM [25]. The FLICM has a fuzzy parameter that updates the performance of conventional FCM, which made FLICM robust to outliers. This factor utilizes the Euclidean distance and spatial distance between central pixels and neighboring pixels. Due to the presence of noisy pixels, it is not always possible to analyze the effect of each neighbor pixel. In the KWFLICM, a new trade-off weighted fuzzy factor has been introduced which adaptively controls the relationship of local neighbors. The introduced factor simultaneously depends on the spatial distance of all the surrounding pixels along with their gray level discrepancy. Because of the use of gray level and spatial constraints in the fuzzy factor, the effect of noisy pixels is decreased. If we did not have knowledge of noise in the initial stage, there is no need to set the fuzzy factor artificially, in fact, it is determined automatically. This process makes the KWFLICM more immune to outliers.

The new introduced fuzzy factor is expressed as

$$G'_{ki} = \sum_{i=1}^{N} \sum_{k=1}^{\vartheta} u_{ki}^{m} \sum_{\substack{i \neq j \\ j \in N_i}} w_{ij} \left(1 - u_{ki}\right)^{m} \left(1 - K\left(x_j, v_k\right)\right) \qquad (7.10)$$

and the objective function of KWFLICM is given by

$$J_m - \sum_{i=1}^{N} \sum_{k=1}^{c} u_{ki}^{m} \left(1 - K\left(x_i, v_k\right)\right) + G'_{ki} \qquad (7.11)$$

where

N_i = a group of pixels within the windows around pixel x_i

w_{ij} = weighted fuzzy factor

$1 - K(x_i, v_k)$ = kernel-based distance measure

$(1 - u_{ki})^m$ = penalty to make convergence faster

$\{v_k\}_{k=1}^c$ = centers of clusters

$\{u_{ki}\}$ = membership matrix

The KWFLICM algorithm takes more computational time because the fuzzy factor G'_{ki} is calculated in each iteration step, and the noise robustness behavior of this method compensates for this drawback with its very good performance as compared with all the above methods (Table 7.1).

7.3.6   Strong FCM

The data fed to FCM are translated to higher dimensional space with the help of kernels, and within that domain, the distance between data points and the center is calculated. It results in improved clustering of complex noised data [22]. Based on the above-mentioned approach, two methods have been proposed [22] along with a process to initialize the cluster center to minimize the computational complexity and also the run time.

7.3.6.1   Robust FCM-based kernel function

The proposed method transforms the real data space into a higher dimensional space with the help of some nonlinear operations. In this way, the introduced FCM tends to perform the better grouping of the complex noised data. The mathematical expression of robust FCM-based kernel function (RFCMK) is expressed as

$$J(U, V) = 2 \sum_{i=1}^{n} \sum_{k=1}^{c} u_{ik}^m \left(\beta - K\left(x_i, v_k \right) \right) \tag{7.12}$$

The kernel function is given by

$$K\left(x_i, v_k \right) = \frac{-\|x_i - v_k\|^2}{\alpha} + \beta, \beta > 0 \tag{7.13}$$

The above-mentioned method cannot differentiate similar intensity objects of different clusters. The RFCMK is very useful in removing noise but mixed two clusters into one cluster.

7.3.6.2   Tsallis entropy-based FCM

This method is basically the upgradation of RFCMK. Tsallis entropy-based FCM (TEFCM) introduces another term in the objective function of RFCMK, which is responsible to distinguish the similar intensity objects between different clusters. The objective expression of TEFCM is expressed as

$$J(U, V) = 2 \sum_{i=1}^{n} \sum_{k=1}^{c} u_{ik}^m \left(\beta - K\left(x_i, v_k \right) \right) + \frac{\alpha_i}{\gamma - 1} \left(\sum_{i=1}^{n} \sum_{k=1}^{c} u_{ik}^m - 1 \right) \tag{7.14}$$

where $\alpha_i = \frac{n}{\zeta} \left(x_i + \left((n/c) / N_R \right) \sum_{j \in N_i} x_j \right)$ is one term which includes the data from its neighborhood and ζ is one factor which controls the outcome of the neighborhood

Table 7.1   Observation for the techniques used in sections 7.3.1 to 7.3.5

Algorithm no.	Acronym	Objective function used	Strengths	Weaknesses
7.3.1	FCM	$J = \sum_{j=1}^{N} \sum_{i=1}^{c} u_{ij}^{m} \lVert x_j - v_i \rVert^2$	Efficient for medical image segmentation	Very sensitive to noise
7.3.2	FLICM	$J_m = \sum_{i=1}^{N} \sum_{k=1}^{c} \left[u_{ki}^{m} \lVert x_i - v_k \rVert^2 + G_{ki} \right]$	Introduce the spatial information in FCM Independency from noise type	Perform poor in complex images and it is not suitable for color images
7.3.3	MDFCM	$J_m(\mu, v) = \sum_{i=1}^{c} \sum_{j=1}^{n} \mu_{ij,k}^{m} d^2(x_j, v_i)$	Minimize the noise effect by utilizing the spatial information	Suffers from a drawback of high computation requirement
7.3.4	WIPFCM	$J_{WIPFCM} = \sum_{i=1}^{c} \sum_{k=1}^{n} u_{ik}^{m} \sum_{r \in N_k} \omega_{kr} \lVert I_{kr} - v_{ri} \rVert^2$	Ensure high accuracy with the best robustness to noise	The size of the images increases, the accuracy decreases, and the time consumptionincreases
7.3.5	KWFLICM	$J_m = \sum_{i=1}^{N} \sum_{k=1}^{c} u_{ki}^{m} \left(1 - K(x_i, v_k) \right) + G'_{ki}$	Noise robustness	Algorithm takes more computational time

functions. With the help of the added term, spatial information gets included in the corresponding objective function; hence, one achieves updated performance parameters. Time complexity is also reduced as the neighborhood term is calculated only one time. The proposed TEFCM algorithm has a small portion of noise in the clustered image but it maintains the edge information (Table 7.2).

7.3.7 Neighborhood-weighted FCM clustering

Neighborhood-weighted FCM (NWFCM) [31] uses local structure information and contextual data to improve the performance of FCM toward the noisy data. First, a new similarity measure model is established based on the local statistics and patches of image, where the new neighborhood-weighted distance is considered which replaces the Euclidean measure in the cost function of conventional FCM. Unlike enhanced FCM [20] and fast generalized fuzzy c-means (FGFCM) [24], which are two-stage methods in which first the denoising is performed and then the clustering. In NWFCM, denoising and clustering can be performed simultaneously due to the use of neighborhood-weighted distance. The NW distance $d_N(x_i, v)$ is defined as

$$d_N(x_i, v) = \sum_{r \in N_i} \omega_{ir} d_{x_r, v} \tag{7.15}$$

where $d_{x_r, v}$ is the distance between x_r and v. The weight ω_{ir} is the similarity measure function.

The improved form of objective function is defined by removing the Euclidean distance measure under consideration in the conventional FCM, which is upgraded by the neighborhood-weighted distance as defined in (7.14). The objective function of NWFCM can be given by

$$J_{NWFCM} = \sum_{i=1}^{n} \sum_{k=1}^{c} u_{ik}^m d_N^2 (x_i, v_k) \tag{7.16}$$

Here, the membership function can also be upgraded with the help of a Lagrange multiplier like conventional FCM. Also, considering that the updated feature vector from the neighborhood window of pixels, it can be used for segmentation of texture, the mathematical form of the objective function can be expressed as

$$J_2 = \sum_{i=1}^{n} \sum_{k=1}^{c} u_{ik}^m \left\| w_i \cdot (x_i - v_k) \right\|_1^2 \tag{7.17}$$

Due to the incorporation of spatial information as well as texture information, the NWFCM is more robust to noise and its performance is also not very sensitive to parameters as it has included local statistics.

7.3.8 Morphological pyramid with FCM clustering

In this chapter, the authors proposed a morphological pyramid-based FCM (MPFCM) clustering, which can be used for the segmentation of a multiresolution MRI brain image [32]. Here, to establish spatial context between image pixels, a wavelet multiresolution is used.

Table 7.2   *Observation for the techniques used in sections 7.3.6.1 to 7.3.6.2.*

Algorithm no.	Acronym	Objective function used	Strengths	Weaknesses
7.3.6.1	RFCMK	$J(U,V) = 2\sum_{i=1}^{n}\sum_{k=1}^{c} u_{ik}^{m}\left(\beta - K\left(x_i, v_k\right)\right)$	Very useful in removing noise	Mixed two clusters into one cluster
7.3.6.2	TEFCM	$J(U,V) = 2\sum_{i=1}^{n}\sum_{k=1}^{c} u_{ik}^{m}\left(\beta - K\left(x_i, v_k\right)\right) + \frac{\alpha_i}{\gamma - 1}\left(\sum_{i=1}^{n}\sum_{k=1}^{c} u_{ik}^{m} - 1\right)$	Time complexity is reduced	Contain a small portion of noise in the clustered image

$$C_\psi\left(b, a\right) = \int s\left(t\right)\psi\left(t\right)dt \tag{7.18}$$

where

$$\psi_{b,a}\left(t\right) = 1/\sqrt{a}\psi\left(\frac{\left(t-b\right)}{a}\right) \tag{7.19}$$

The a and b parameters are known as scaling and shifting parameters, respectively.

Next, the morphological pyramid is used to fuse the original image with the output images to enhance sharpness and to minimize the noise in the output, which is mathematically expressed as

$$J_m = \sum_{i=1}^{N}\sum_{k=1}^{c}\left[u_{ki}^m\|x_i - v_k\|^2\right] \tag{7.20}$$

Here, the main concern is to improve segmentation accuracy (SA). This novel method can be applied to reduce the noise of MRI images of the brain. In this method, the multiresolution wavelet that utilizes the spatial correlation between pixel images is fused by the proposed FCM with the morphological pyramid to determine the noise pixel. In this system, images are passed to FCM to make segmentation for each of them.

7.3.9   Malleable fuzzy local median c-means algorithm

Malleable fuzzy local median c-means method (MFLMCM) [33] is introduced to compensate for the drawback of the traditional FCM algorithm. In old FCM, high convergence time is required, and removal of the noise is difficult along with the inefficacy to contour the region of the cluster. MFLMCM indicates the desired outcome with the original biomedical images. The simulation results are analyzed with the other existing methods which give 96% accuracy.

By enhancing the qualities of fuzzification, reducing local optima, enhancing tolerance against noise, and decreasing execution time, we can make this algorithm more suitable than other existing methods. By using the term F_{mmfi}, we introduce this median-dependent FCM method.

$$F_{mmfi} = \sum_{j\in N_i}\frac{Med\left(W_{ij}\right)}{Med\left(W_{ij}\right)+1}\|D_{x_i} - C_j\|^2 \tag{7.21}$$

The F_{mmfi} is the main responsible factor that results in a more robust, optimal, and effective method. This suggested algorithm incorporates fuzzy local median methodology, which makes this efficient to cluster the information with fuzzy methodology, to reduce the problem of local optima and effective parameter selection. Achieving an accurate convergence point is the main objective that makes MFLMCM more promising in terms of results. To reduce the convergence time requirement of conventional FCM, we improve the objective function of FCM with the proposed MFLMCM technique to remove the noise.

7.3.10 Fuzzy algorithm for peak detection, spatial information, and reallocation

Peak detection, spatial information, and reallocation FCM (PDSIRFCM) is a very effective algorithm to dealing with partial volume effect but due to the unavailability of spatial information it is unable to deal with noise and other different artifacts; hence, to remove this drawback, researchers propose various modifications, such as Ahmed *et al.* proposed Fuzzy c-means (FCM) algorithms with spatial constraints (FCMS) [34], Chen and Zhang proposed FCMS1 and FCMS2 [35], and Cai *et al.* proposed FGFCM [36]. In this sequence, authors proposed a new improvement in FCM, which deals with an image artifact of high level as shown below [37],

$$F = \sum_{i=1}^{C} \sum_{j=1}^{n} u_{ij}^m d_{ij}^2 + \sum_{i=1}^{C} \sum_{1}^{n} \sum_{x_k \in N_j} R_{kj} u_{ij}^m d_{ik}^2 \tag{7.22}$$

where R_{kj} shows the pixel relevance given as

$$R_{kj} = R_{kj}^S + R_{kj}^G \tag{7.23}$$

where R_{kj}^S is the spatial relevance, and R_{kj}^G is the gray relevance.

So this proposed method is incorporated into all required artifacts of image processing, especially with noise. In the proposed algorithm, we apply two sequential phenomena to improve the conventional FCM, first by peak detection and interval analysis, which reduce the probability to find the local optimal solution. In order to find a more accurate solution, we use the concept of pixel relevance, which is very useful to improve the segmentation result.

7.3.11 Fuzzy clustering algorithm with nonlocal information

The improved fuzzy clustering algorithm with nonlocal information (NLFCM) [38] is an advancement of FLICM [39]. In the NLFCM algorithm, the image patches are responsible for pixel relevance. In this proposed method, pixel relevance is the basic parameter to govern the segmentation of an image. The validation process proves that the performance of image segmentation has been improved with this proposed NLFCM algorithm.

The FLICM algorithm is unable to deal with the images with a high level of noise. To remove this one, fuzzy factor G_{ij} was introduced, which controls the trade-off between noise insensitiveness and image detail preservation.

$$G_{ij} = \sum_{r \in N_j} \frac{1}{d_{jr} + 1} \left(1 - u_{ir}\right)^m \|x_r - v_i\|^2 \tag{7.24}$$

The mathematical expression for FLICM can be represented as

$$F = \sum_{i=1}^{C} \sum_{j=1}^{n} u_{ij}^m \left(x_j - v_j\right)^2 + G_{ij} \tag{7.25}$$

where

$$u_{ij} = \cfrac{1}{\sum_{k=1}^{C} \left(\cfrac{\|x_j - v_i\|^2 + G_{ij}}{\|x_j - v_k\|^2 + G_{kj}} \right)^{\frac{1}{(m-1)}}} \tag{7.26}$$

$$v_i = \frac{\sum_{j=1}^{n} u_{ij}^m x_j}{\sum_{i=1}^{C} u_{ij}^m} \tag{7.27}$$

After validation of this proposed NLFCM algorithm, we find that the SA of this algorithm is upgraded to its precedence one but is not suited for complex images, especially those of high-level noise.

7.3.12   Intuitionistic fuzzy sets-based credibility FCM clustering algorithm

In intuitionistic FCM (IFCM) [40], we use the hesitation parameter and fuzzy entropy to upgrade its sensitivity toward noise. To minimize the effect of outliers on the center location, we insert the term credibility. The proposed method is validated on various medical images and compared with some algorithms such as FCM and some advanced versions of it. The objective function of IFCM is actually the function of FCM with intuitionistic fuzzy entropy term shown as

$$J_{IFCM} = \sum_{i=1}^{C} \sum_{k=1}^{n} u_{ik}^m d_{ik}^2 + \sum_{i=1}^{C} \pi_i e^{1-\pi_i} \tag{7.28}$$

In (7.28), we assume the value of m is 2 and u_{ik}^* is given by

$$u_{ik}^{*m} = u_{ik} + \pi_{ik} \tag{7.29}$$

where u_{ik}^* represents the membership matrix of this proposed method IFCM and u_{ik} gives the membership matrix of FCM. To enhance the robustness of IFCM, an intuitionistic fuzzy factor is incorporated into it. The intuitionistic version of Credibilistic Fuzzy c means (CFCM) is very helpful to improve the robust characteristics of CFCM and to apply it on medical images. It is not suitable for color images.

7.3.13   Intuitionistic possibilistic FCM clustering algorithm

A novel intuitionistic possibilistic FCM (IPFCM) algorithm is an improved version of popular FCM algorithm [41]. Here, the possibilistic measure with the intuitionistic measures is introduced in conventional FCM to compensate the coincident cluster problem. The possibilistic FCM is mainly responsible to suppress the sensitivity to an outlier, which mainly reduces the noise content. By introducing intuitionistic approach in FCM, authors make this conventional FCM algorithm efficient to analyze the mammogram images to detect breast cancer. The mathematical expression for possibilistic FCM approach is given as

$$\text{PFCM} = \sum_{m=1}^{k} \sum_{l=1}^{N} u_{lm}^p d_{lm}^p + \sum_{i=1}^{C} \lambda_m \left(\sum_{l=1}^{N} 1 - u_{lm} \right) \tag{7.30}$$

The expression for membership degree function and positive number is shown in (7.31) and (7.32) as follows:

$$u_{lm} = \cfrac{1}{1 + \left(\frac{d_{lm}^p}{\lambda_m}\right)^{\frac{1}{(p-1)}}} \qquad (7.31)$$

$$\lambda_m = W \frac{\sum_{l=1}^{N} u_{lm}^p d_m^2}{\sum_{l=1}^{N} u_{lm}^p} \qquad (7.32)$$

In (7.32), W is a weight factor which is set to 1.

In this approach, authors improve the conventional FCM algorithm with the concept of possibilistic approach integrated with intuitionistic approach. This is the improved approach version of FCM, i.e., intuitionistic possibilistic fuzzy c-mean (IPFCM) to make the conventional FCM algorithm efficient and robust. It is not suitable for complex images.

7.3.14   *Internet of things-based predictive modeling for predicting lung cancer using FCM clustering (IoTPMFCM)*

The presented method Internet of Things-based Predictive Modeling FCM (IoTPMFCM) is to efficiently diagnose the prediction about lung cancer using fuzzy clustering method [42]. This effective approach is based on the concept of transition region extraction to effectively segment an image.

The proposed clustering algorithm is improved to achieve the image partitioning which has "p" fuzzy clusters in a group of features f_j.

$$J(U, M) = \sum_{i=1}^{p} \sum_{j=1}^{c} u_{i,j}^p \left(U_{i,j}\right)^m d_{i,j} \qquad (7.33)$$

where $U = (U_{i,j})$ is a fuzzy partition matrix, $U_{i,j} \in [1, \infty]$. Here, the term $M = (m_1, \dots m_p)$ represents a matrix of cluster center.

To categorize the various conventional region features from a sample set of different lung cancer images, which are already segmented with an Otsu thresholding method uses FCM clustering technique. To improve the performance of segmentation operations and identification of the actual object region in lung images, we use the concept of image region filling, and morphological thinning and cleaning are applied. The above improvements incorporated in the conventional FCM ensure the better and improved outcome of the suggested model in comparison of other existing prediction model. The proposed segmentation process is used for improving the classification accuracy.

7.3.15   *Super-pixel FCM clustering (SPFCM)*

As we know that the conventional model of FCM clustering method is best suited for segmenting image data which are free from noise, due to ignorance of spatial information, it is unable to perform with a noisy image dataset. To overcome this problem, a super-pixel-based FCM (SPOFCM) is evolved [43]. To improve the performance of SPOFCM, a crow search technique is incorporated which also improves its performance by optimizing the influential degree. The objective function of SPOFCM is given as

$$J(U, V) = \sum_{i=1}^{C} \sum_{j=1}^{N} u_{ij}^m D_{ij}^2 \tag{7.34}$$

where

$$D_{ij}^2 = d \left(1 - \alpha \frac{\sum_{k=1}^{S} u_{ik} t_{jk}^2}{\sum_{k=1}^{S} t_{jk}^2}\right) \left(1 - \beta \frac{\sum_{k=1}^{S} u_{ik} t_{jk}^2}{\sum_{k=1}^{S} r_{jk}}\right) \tag{7.35}$$

$$u_{ij} = \cfrac{1}{\sum_{i=1}^{C} \left(\cfrac{D_{ij}}{D_{kj}}\right)^{\frac{2}{m-1}}} \tag{7.36}$$

$$v_i = \frac{\sum_{j=1}^{N} u_{ij}^N F_j}{\sum_{j=1}^{N} u_{ij}^m} \tag{7.37}$$

For clinical diagnosis purpose, the performance of SPOFCM is validated with the multispectral MRIs and mammograms. This proposed SPOFCM method is also compared with some very popular segmentation methods such as k-means segmentation method, entropy thresholding segmentation technique, traditional FCM, FCMS, and kernel concept–based FCM (KFCM). The analysis of the proposed method on MRIs and mammograms ensures that this technique is best suited for organ segmentation for clinical purposes.

7.3.16   Multitask FCM clustering

The authors introduce a novel multitask FCM clustering (MT-FCM) system for finding the ordinary and specific knowledge from multitask data [44]. By using this proposed model, we can easily extract the ordinary and specified information from multitask data, which improve the segmentation process efficiently. The mathematical expression for this complete phenomenon is can be expressed as

$$(U, V, R, O) = \sum_{i=1}^{N} \sum_{j=1}^{C_k} \sum_{i=1}^{N_k} \left[u_{ij,k}^m \left\| X_{i,k} - V_{jk} \right\|^2 \right] + \lambda_a \sum_{p=1}^{N} \sum_{j=1}^{C_k} \left\| X_i - O_p \right\|^2$$
$$- \lambda_b \sum_{k=1}^{k} \sum_{p=1}^{P} \sum_{j=1}^{c_k} \left[u_{ij,k}^m \left\| V_{jk} - O_p \right\|^2 \right] s.t. u_{i,j,k} \in (0.1) \tag{7.38}$$

Although the above-mentioned MT-FCM is capable of resolving the problems associated with multitask clustering, it is efficiently able to identify the ordinary details related to complete tasks and the specified details related to individual tasks. The proposed MT-FCM also has some drawbacks mentioned as follows:

I.   Due to the large number of iterations, the processing speed of proposed MT-FCNM is slow compared with other multitask segmentation algorithms.

II.   The proposed MT-FCM can work on the known cluster only; it is unable to perform with an unknown data cluster.

Hence, the proposed model is best suited for segmentation of multiple MRI images, as the benefit of exploiting ordinary information among related tasks produces more accurate segmentation results.

7.3.17   Patch-weighted distance and fuzzy clustering-based image segmentation

In this patch-weighted distance and fuzzy clustering-based image segmentation (PWDFCM) method, the authors proposed the fuzzy clustering with a patch-weighted distance to improve the performance as compared with conventional FCM [45]. The complete performance of this proposed method is classified into two steps. The first step establishes patch-weighted distance-based pixel correlation. The next step includes removal of the influence of this neighboring information with this correlation function. This suggested model is the improved version of NLFCM, as expressed in (7.24) and (7.25).

$$F = \sum_{i=1}^{C} \sum_{j=1}^{n} u_{ij}^{m} \left(x_j - v_j \right)^2 + G_{ij} \tag{7.39}$$

$$G_{ij} = \sum_{r \in N_j} \frac{1}{d_{jr}+1} \left(1 - u_{ir} \right)^m \| x_r - v_i \|^2 \tag{7.40}$$

where

$$v_i = \frac{\sum_{j=1}^{n} u_{ij}^m x_j}{\sum_{j=1}^{n} u_{ij}^m} \tag{7.41}$$

$$u_{ij} = \frac{\left(\left(x_j - v_i \right)^2 + G_{ij} \right)^{\frac{-1}{(m-1)}}}{\sum_{i=1}^{C} \left(\left(x_j - v_k \right)^2 + G_{ij} \right)^{\frac{-1}{(m-1)}}} \tag{7.42}$$

In the proposed method of analysis, the measure of pixel correlation is an important objective. Here, it is required that the size of the search window is not so much large.

7.3.18   Fuzzy local intensity clustering model

Researchers have used fuzzy local intensity clustering model (FLICM) to perform simultaneous and automated segmentation along with the bias modification based on local clustering of intensity [46]. The k-means is repetitive in nature which can reduce the clustering criterion in the following manner:

$$F_y = \sum_{i=1}^{N} \int_{O_y} \| I(x) - m_i \|^2 u_i(x) \, dx \tag{7.43}$$

Here, $I(x)$ represents intensities in the proximity of O_y.

This is an upgradation in a fully automated method known as fast and robust FCM (FRFCM) clustering algorithm [47].

The combinational impact of FLICM and FRFCM is found in this proposed method, which can automatically segment the images without any intervention of external sources. The performance of FRFCM insures a fast and stable level for contour selection. The proposed model has various advantages, but it is not suitable for segmenting color images.

7.3.19   *Improved fuzzy clustering for image segmentation based on a low-rank prior*

The process of image segmentation is very important toward the diagnosis of a medical image. The complexity incorporated in medical images makes the segmentation process more difficult. To overcome this complexity, the improved fuzzy clustering for image segmentation based on a low-rank prior (LRPIFCM) methods are preferable to medical images due to its simplicity and high efficiency because these are also highly sensitive to noise [48]. In this improved FCM, the initialization of cluster centers based on peak detection is given as

$$G'_{ij} = \sum_{r \in W_j} S(j,r) (1 - \mu_{ir})^m \|x_r - v_i\|^2 \tag{7.44}$$

where W_j is a collection of pixels with similarity in search window and $S(j,r)$ represents correlation between pixels. Here, authors want to introduce an image segmentation scheme that improves the segmentation efficiency based on nonlocal information. The main contributions of this proposed algorithm include an optimized initialization method, effective correlation between pixels, and an optimized FLICM framework. With all these strengths, this proposed method gives poor performance for complex images.

7.3.20   *A novel kernelized total Bregman divergence-driven possibilistic fuzzy clustering with multiple information constraints for image segmentation*

To compensate the problem related to high noise sensitivity with existing robust fuzzy clustering algorithms, a novel kernelized total Bregman divergence-driven possibilistic fuzzy clustering with multiple information constraints for image segmentation (MIC-KTBD-DPFCM) model is suggested, which has the combination of two previously designed algorithms, such as total Bregman divergence-driven possibilistic fuzzy clustering and kernel metric (TSKFLICM) method [49]. First, authors establish total Bregman divergence (TBD) to eliminate the drawbacks of Bregman divergence. After this, TBD function is kernelized by the use of polynomial kernel function. Then this kernelized TBD is submerged with neighborhood information of pixels to increase its potential to suppress noise. The function of the proposed method is shown as

$$\min J(T, U, V) = \sum_{i=1}^N \sum_{k=1}^C u_{ki}^m t_{ki}^n \left[(1 - \pi_{ki}) \delta_\theta^{\phi*}(x_i, v_k) + G_{ki}^* \right] + \sum_{i=1}^c \gamma_k \sum_{i=1}^N \tag{7.45}$$
$$(1 - \pi_{ki}) u_{ki} (1 - t_{ki})^2$$

subject to $\sum_{k=1}^C u_{ki}^m = 1 \, 1 \leq i \leq n$

$$G_{ki} = \sum_{j \in N_i, i \neq j}^{N} \left(1 - \pi_{ki}\right) W_{ij} \left(1 - u_{kj}\right)^m \left(1 - t_{kj}\right)^n \delta^* \left(x_j, v_k\right)$$ (7.46)

The validation of the suggested method gives a preferable experimental outcome. The simulation outcome of suggested method against the terms, Jaccard score, SA, and peak signal-to-noise ratio, is improved by 0.0170481, 1.327%, 41.260%, 2.41611765, respectively. The proposed algorithm has better performance as compared with previously suggested methods such as WFLICM, KWFLICM, kernel weighted possibilistic fuzzy C-means clustering with local information constraints (KWPFLICM), and TSKFLICM in reference to noise robustness and suppress the SA but it has low execution accuracy (Table 7.3).

The bias-corrected format of FCM, i.e., BCFCM is proposed by Ahmed [50] by introducing the spatial parameter in the objective function of conventional FCM. Here, the weighting parameter α has a large influence on the spatial parameter. To reduce the effect of weighting parameters on objective function, Stelios and Chatzis [51] suggested a new algorithm FLICM.

The existence of damping extent in FLICM, which is highly affected by the Euclidean distance, degrades the performance of this algorithm for complex images. To improve the performance of FLICM, we introduce a weighted fuzzy factor and kernel method in the objective function which is popularly known as KWFLICM algorithm [52]. Hence, by optimization and introducing a proper weighting factor in objective function, we can also improve the various upgraded format of FCM and find particular algorithms such as NWFCM, MPFCM, MFLMCM, PDSIRFCM, IFCM, IPFCM, IoTPMFCM, SPFCM, MT-FCM, PWDFCM, FLICM, LRPIFCM, and MIC-KTBD-DPFCM for a particular objective. In the proposed survey, a decadal analysis of all these types of popular methods is considered and analyzed. Here, we review various fuzzy-based segmentation algorithms, which are improved with various modifications in objective function at one place, all these will become very helpful for research scholars toward their research topics. In all these algorithms, authors try to minimize the noise in the fuzzy-based clustering algorithms which occur due to the absence of spatial components, simultaneously it also optimizes the computational time.

7.4 Conclusion

The role of image processing in the healthcare sector has been increasing day by day. For the exact diagnosis of a patient report, image segmentation plays an important role. From various methods of medical image segmentation, we find that the clustering-based segmentation algorithms give the best results. On the basis of a large research survey on image segmentation, we understand the importance of the FCM clustering algorithm in the health sector. So, here we present a detailed survey report, especially based on medical image segmentation. In this survey report, we compile a few important and popular fuzzy-based clustering methods in a comparative study-based manner. This survey report will

Table 7.3 *Observation for the techniques used in sections 7.3.7 to 7.3.20.*

Algorithm no.	Acronym	Objective function used	Strengths	Weaknesses
7.3.7	NWFCM	$J_{NWFCM} = \sum_{i=1}^{n} \sum_{k=1}^{c} u_{ik}^{m} d_{N}^{2}(x_i, v_k)$	More robust to noise	It has included local statistics
7.3.8	MPFCM	$J_m = \sum_{i=1}^{N} \sum_{k=1}^{C} \left[u_{ki}^{m} \|x_i - v_k\|^2 \right]$	Minimize the noise in the output	Computational time is high
7.3.9	MFLMCM	$F_{mmfi} = \sum_{j \in N_1} \dfrac{Med(W_{ij})}{Med(W_{ij}) + 1} \|D_{x_i} - C_j\|^2$	Minimize the computational time	Lack of ability to remove the noise
7.3.10	PDSIRFCM	$F = \sum_{i=1}^{C} \sum_{j=1}^{n} u_{ij}^{m} d_{ij}^{2} + \sum_{i=1}^{C} \sum_{1}^{n} \sum_{x_k \in N_j} R_{kj} u_{ij}^{m} d_{ik}^{2}$	Ability to detect and reallocate the misclassified pixels	Computational time is high
7.3.11	NLFCM	$F = \sum_{i=1}^{C} \sum_{j=1}^{n} u_{ij}^{m} (x_j - v_j)^2 + G_{ij}$	SA is high	Not suited for complex images
7.3.12	IFCM	$J_{IFCM} = \sum_{i=1}^{C} \sum_{k=1}^{n} u_{ik}^{m} d_{ik}^{2} + \sum_{i=1}^{C} \pi_i e^{1-\pi_i}$	Improve the robustness	It is not suitable for color images
7.3.13	IPFCM	$PFCM = \sum_{m=1}^{k} \sum_{l=1}^{N} u_{lm}^{p} d_{lm}^{p} + \sum_{l=1}^{C} \lambda_m \left(\sum_{l=1}^{N} 1 - u_{lm} \right)$	It is efficient and robust	It is not suitable for complex images
7.3.14	IoTPMFCM	$J(U, M) = \sum_{i=1}^{p} \sum_{j=1}^{c} u_{i,j}^{p} (U_{ij})^m d_{i,j}$	Improving the classification accuracy	Computational time is high
7.3.15	SPFCM	$J(U, V) = \sum_{i=1}^{C} \sum_{j=1}^{N} u_{ij}^{m} D_{ij}^{2}$	Better performance for suspicious lesion	Computational time is high
7.3.16	MT-FCM	$(U, V, R, O) = \sum_{i=1}^{N} \sum_{r=1}^{C_k} \sum_{r=1}^{N_k} \left[u_{y,k}^{m} \|X_{i,k} - V_{jk}\|^2 \right] + \lambda_a \sum_{r=1}^{N} \sum_{r=1}^{C_k} \|X_i - O_p\|^2$ $- \lambda_b \sum_{i=1}^{K} \sum_{i=1}^{P} \sum_{r=1}^{C_k} \left[u_{y,k}^{m} \|V_{jk} - O_p\|^2 \right] s.t. u_{y,k} \epsilon(0,1)$	Produces more accurate segmentation results	Computational time is high

(Continues)

Table 7.3 Continued

Algorithm no.	Acronym	Objective function used	Strengths	Weaknesses
7.3.17	PWDFCM	$F = \sum_{i=1}^{C} \sum_{j=1}^{n} u_{ij}^{m} (x_j - v_j)^2 + G_{ij}$	The measure of pixel correlation is an important objective	The size of the search window is not so much large
7.3.18	FLICM	$F_y = \sum_{i=1}^{N} \int_{O_y} \| I(x) - m_i \|^2 \, u_i(x) \, dx$	Insures a fast and stable level for contour selection	It is not fit for segmentation of color images
7.3.19	LRPIFCM	$G_{ij}' = \sum_{r \in W_j} S(j, r) (1 - \mu_{ir})^m \| x_r - v_i \|^2$	Improves the segmentation efficiency based on nonlocal information	Not suitable for complex images
7.3.20	MIC-KTBD-DPFCM	$minJ(T, U, V) = \sum_{i=1}^{N} \sum_{k=1}^{C} u_{ki}^m k_{ki}^n$	Enhance the antinoise robustness	Computational time is high

become very helpful for researchers, especially in the field of cancer detection. In our future work, we can also modify all these above popular algorithms according to different image formats and can also optimize the different image quality parameters.

References

[1]   Ji Z.-X., Sun Q.-S., Xia D.-S. 'A modified possibilistic fuzzy C-means clustering algorithm for bias field estimation and segmentation of brain MR image'. *Computerized Medical Imaging and Graphics*. 2011, vol. 35(5), pp. 383–97.

[2]   Ji Z.-X., Sun Q.-S., Xia D.-S. 'RETRACTED: a framework with modified fast FCM for brain MR images segmentation'. *Pattern Recognition*. 2011, vol. 44(5), pp. 999–1013.

[3]   Krizhevsky B.A., Sutskever I., Hinton G.E. 'ImageNet classification with deep convolutional neural networks'. *Communications of the ACM*. 2011, vol. 60(6), pp. 84–90.

[4]   Shelhamer E., Long J., Darrell T. 'Fully convolutional networks for semantic segmentation'. *IEEE Transactions on Pattern Analysis and Machine Intelligence*. 2011, vol. 39(4), pp. 640–51.

[5]   Lei T., Jia X., Zhang Y., Liu S., Meng H., Nandi A.K. 'Superpixel-based fast fuzzy C-means clustering for color image segmentation'. *IEEE Transactions on Fuzzy Systems*. 2011, vol. 27(9), pp. 1753–66.

[6]   Zeng S., Wang X., Cui H., Zheng C., Feng D. 'A unified collaborative multikernel fuzzy clustering for multiview data'. *IEEE Transactions on Fuzzy Systems*. 2018, vol. 26(3), pp. 1671–87.

[7]   Ma J., Li S., QinH., Hao A. 'Unsupervised multi-class co-segmentation via joint-cut over L-1-manifold hyper-graph of discriminative image regions'. *IEEE Transactions on Image Processing*. 2017, vol. 26(3), pp. 1216–30.

[8]   Gong M., Li H., Zhang X., Zhao Q., Wang B. 'Nonparametric statistical active contour based on inclusion degree of fuzzy sets'. *IEEE Transactions on Fuzzy Systems*. 2015, vol. 24(5), pp. 1176–92.

[9]   Pereyra M., McLaughlin S. 'Fast unsupervised Bayesian image segmentation with adaptive spatial regularisation'. *IEEE Transactions on Image Processing*. 2017, vol. 26(6), pp. 2577–87.

[10]   Ng A., Jordan M., Weiss Y. 'On spectral clustering: analysis and an algorithm'. *Advances in Neural Information Processing Systems 14*; Vancouver, BC, 2001.

[11]   Comaniciu D., Meer P. 'Mean shift: a robust approach toward feature space analysis'. *IEEE Transactions on Pattern Analysis and Machine Intelligence*. 2002, vol. 24(5), pp. 603–19.

[12]   Pal N.R., Bezdek J.C. 'On cluster validity for the fuzzy c-means model'. *IEEE Transactions on Fuzzy Systems*. 1995, vol. 3(3), pp. 370–79.

[13] Dunn J.C. 'A fuzzy relative of the ISODATA process and its use in detecting compact well-separated clusters'. *Journal of Cybernetics*. 1973, vol. 3(3), pp. 32–57.

[14] Bezdek J.C. 'Objective function clustering' in *Pattern recognition with fuzzy objective function algorithms*. Boston, MA: Springer; 1981. pp. 43–93.

[15] Pham D. 'Robust fuzzy segmentation of magnetic resonance images'. *Proceedings of the 14th IEEE Symposium on Computer-Based Medical Systems*; 2001. pp. 127–31.

[16] Pham D.L. 'Spatial models for fuzzy clustering'. *Computer Vision and Image Understanding*. 2001, vol. 84(2), pp. 285–97.

[17] Pham D.L., Prince J.L. 'An adaptive fuzzy C-means algorithm for image segmentation in the presence of intensity inhomogeneities'. *Pattern Recognition Letters*. 2001, vol. 20(1), pp. 57–68.

[18] Roy S., Agarwal H., Carass A., Bai Y., Pham D.L., Prince J.L. 'Fuzzy C-means with variable compactness'. *Proceedings of IEEE International Symposium on Biomedical Imaging*. 2008, vol. 4541030, p. 452.

[19] Choudhry M.S., Kapoor R. 'Performance analysis of fuzzy C-means clustering methods for MRI image segmentation'. *Procedia Computer Science*. 2001, vol. 89, pp. 749–58.

[20] Szilágyi L., Benyó Z., Szilágyi S., Adam H. 'MR brain image segmentation using an enhanced fuzzy C-means algorithm'. *Annual International Conference of the IEEE Engineering in Medicine and Biology Society*. 2003, vol. 1, pp. 724–26.

[21] Ghasemi J., Ghaderi R., Mollaei M.R.K., Hojjatoleslami A. 'Separation of brain tissues in MRI based on multi-dimensional FCM and spatial information'. *Eighth International Conference on Fuzzy Systems and Knowledge Discovery*; 2011. pp. 247–51.

[22] Kannan S.R., Ramathilagam S., Devi R., Hines E. 'Strong fuzzy C-means in medical image data analysis'. *Eighth International Conference on Fuzzy Systems and Knowledge Discovery*. 2012, vol. 85(11), pp. 2425–38.

[23] Zhang Y., Bai X., Fan R., Wang Z. 'Deviation-sparse fuzzy C-means with neighbor information constraint'. *IEEE Transactions on Fuzzy Systems: A Publication of the IEEE Neural Networks Council*. 2019, vol. 27(1), pp. 185–99.

[24] Cai W., Chen S., Zhang D. 'Fast and robust fuzzy c-means clustering algorithms incorporating local information for image segmentation'. *Pattern Recognition*. 2007, vol. 40(3), pp. 825–38.

[25] Krinidis S., Chatzis V. 'A robust fuzzy local information C-means clustering algorithm'. *IEEE Transactions on Image Processing*. 2010, vol. 19(5), pp. 1328–37.

[26] Gong M., Liang Y., Shi J., Ma W., Ma J. 'Fuzzy C-means clustering with local information and kernel metric for image segmentation'. *IEEE Transactions on Image Processing*. 2013, vol. 22(2), pp. 573–84.

[27] Liu G., Zhang Y., Wang A. 'Incorporating adaptive local information into fuzzy clustering for image segmentation'. *IEEE Transactions on Image*

Processing: A Publication of the IEEE Signal Processing Society. 2015, vol. 11, pp. 3990–4000.

[28] Zhang H., Wang Q., Shi W., Hao M. 'A novel adaptive fuzzy local information C-means clustering algorithm for remotely sensed imagery classification'. *IEEE Trans Geosci Remote Sens*. 2017, vol. 9, pp. 5057–68.

[29] Chen S., Zhang D. 'Robust image segmentation using FCM with spatial constraints based on new kernel-induced distance measure'. *IEEE Transactions on Systems, Man, and Cybernetics. Part B, Cybernetics*. 2004, vol. 34(4), pp. 1907–16.

[30] Ji Z., Xia Y., Chen Q., Sun Q., Xia D., Feng D.D. 'Fuzzy c-means clustering with weighted image patch for image segmentation'. *Applied Soft Computing*. 2012, vol. 12(6), pp. 1659–67.

[31] Zaixin Z., Lizhi C., Guangquan C. 'Neighbourhood weighted fuzzy c-means clustering algorithm for image segmentation'. *IET Image Processing*. 2014, vol. 8(3), pp. 150–61.

[32] Ali H., Elmogy M., El-Daydamony E., Atwan A. 'Multi-resolution MRI brain image segmentation based on morphological pyramid and fuzzy c-mean clustering'. *Arabian Journal for Science and Engineering*. 2014, vol. 40(11), pp. 3173–85.

[33] Rajendran A., Balakrishnan N., Varatharaj M. 'Malleable fuzzy local median C means algorithm for effective biomedical image segmentation'. *Sensing and Imaging*. 2016, vol. 17(1), pp. 1–14.

[34] Ahmed M.N., Yamany S.M., Mohamed N., Farag A.A., Moriarty T. 'A modified fuzzy c-means algorithm for bias field estimation and segmentation of MRI data'. *IEEE Transactions on Medical Imaging*. 2002, vol. 21(3), pp. 193–99.

[35] Chen S., Zhang D. 'Robust image segmentation using FCM with spatial constraints based on new kernel-induced distance measure'. *IEEE Transactions on Systems, Man, and Cybernetics. Part B, Cybernetics*. 2004, vol. 34(4), pp. 1907–16.

[36] Cai W., Chen S., Zhang D. 'Fast and robust fuzzy c-means clustering algorithms incorporating local information for image segmentation'. *Pattern Recognition*. 2007, vol. 40(3), pp. 825–38.

[37] Zhang X., Wang G., Su Q., Guo Q., Zhang C., Chen B. 'An improved fuzzy algorithm for image segmentation using peak detection, spatial information and reallocation'. *Soft Computing*. 2007, vol. 21(8), pp. 2165–73.

[38] Zhang X., Sun Y., Wang G., Guo Q., Zhang C., Chen B. 'Improved fuzzy clustering algorithm with non-local information for image segmentation'. *Multimedia Tools and Applications*. 2017, vol. 76(6), pp. 7869–95.

[39] Stelios K., Vassilios C. 'A robust fuzzy local information C-means clustering algorithm'. *IEEE Transactions on Image Processing*. 2010, vol. 5, pp. 1328–37.

[40] Kaur P. 'Intuitionistic fuzzy sets based credibilistic fuzzy C-means clustering for medical image segmentation'. *International Journal of Information Technology*. 2017, vol. 9(4), pp. 345–51.

[41] Chowdhary C.L., Chiranji L.C., Debi Prasanna A. 'Segmentation of mammograms using a novel intuitionistic possibilistic fuzzy c-mean clustering algorithm' in *Nature inspired computing*. Singapore: Springer; 2018. pp. 75–82.

[42] Palani D., Venkatalakshmi K. 'An IoT based predictive modelling for predicting lung cancer using fuzzy cluster based segmentation and classification'. *Journal of Medical Systems*. 2018, vol. 43(2), pp. 1–12.

[43] Kumar S.N., Fred A.L., Varghese P.S. 'Suspicious lesion segmentation on brain, mammograms and breast MR images using new optimized spatial feature based super-pixel fuzzy c-means clustering'. *Journal of Digital Imaging*. 2019, vol. 32(2), pp. 322–35.

[44] Jiang Y., Zhao K., Xia K. 'A novel distributed multitask fuzzy clustering algorithm for automatic MR brain image segmentation'. *Journal of Medical Systems*. 2018, vol. 43(5), pp. 1–9.

[45] Zhang X., Jian M., Sun Y., Wang H., Zhang C. 'Improving image segmentation based on patch-weighted distance and fuzzy clustering'. *Multimedia Tools and Applications*. 2018, vol. 79(1–2), pp. 633–57.

[46] Khosravanian A., Rahmanimanesh M., Keshavarzi P., Mozaffari S. 'Fuzzy local intensity clustering (FLIC) model for automatic medical image segmentation'. *The Visual Computer*. 2021, vol. 37(5), pp. 1185–206.

[47] Lei T., Jia X., Zhang Y., He L., Meng H., Nandi A.K. 'Significantly fast and robust fuzzy c-means clustering algorithm based on morphological reconstruction and membership filtering'. *IEEE Transactions on Fuzzy Systems*. 2021, vol. 26(5), pp. 3027–41.

[48] Zhang X., Wang H., Zhang Y., Gao X., Wang G., Zhang C. 'Improved fuzzy clustering for image segmentation based on a low-rank prior'. *Computational Visual Media*. 2021, vol. 7(4), pp. 513–28.

[49] Wu C., Zhang X. 'A novel kernelized total Bregman divergence-driven possibilistic fuzzy clustering with multiple information constraints for image segmentation'. *IEEE Transactions on Fuzzy Systems*. 2021.

[50] Ahmed M.N., Yamany S.M., Mohamed N., Farag A.A., Moriarty T. 'A modified fuzzy c-means algorithm for bias field estimation and segmentation of MRI data'. *IEEE Transactions on Medical Imaging*. 2002, vol. 21(3), pp. 193–99.

[51] Krinidis S., Chatzis V. 'A robust fuzzy local information C-means clustering algorithm'. *IEEE Transactions on Image Processing*. 2010, vol. 19(5), pp. 1328–37.

[52] Gong M., Liang Y., Shi J., Ma W., Ma J. 'Fuzzy c-means clustering with local information and kernel metric for image segmentation'. *IEEE Transactions on Image Processing*. 2013, vol. 22(2), pp. 573–84.

Chapter 8

Artificial intelligence for genomics: a look into it

*Alessandro Bruno[1], Mingliang Gao[2], Devasis Pradhan[3],
N. Pradeep[4], and Mangesh M. Ghonge[5]*

The latest progress in genomics and artificial intelligence (AI) sees both disciplines work together to improve results in the relatively new medical area called precision medicine. This chapter aims to provide readers with a review of AI techniques ingesting genomics data to extract patterns and high-level information. Many new and sophisticated AI architectures have been introduced in the scientific community since the release of the famous Human Genome Project. The latter was delivered in 2003 and allowed sequencing and mapping of all the genes of our species (*Homo sapiens*). Genomics has paved the way for deeper insights into correlations between changes in DNA sequences and diseases. As described throughout the sections in the manuscript, deoxyribonucleic acid (DNA) sequences are big-sized. This feature makes them suitable for investigation through both machine and deep learning (DL) methods. Moreover, the disruptive advent of DL in the scientific community pushed the bar for achievable accuracy rates in many tasks. Genomics makes no exception. AI methods have been primarily employed to tackle some tasks for biomedical image analysis: detection, classification and segmentation of suspicious regions from MRI (Magnetic Resonance Imaging), PET (Positron Emission Tomography) and CT (Computer Tomography), to mention some, have been broadly addressed using machine learning (ML) and DL approaches. Over the last few years, there has been an exponential spike in the number of DL techniques for genomics. Nowadays, genomics and AI are closely twisted in the attempt to achieve ambitious objectives, such as predicting treatment outcomes to deliver patient-tailored therapies,

[1]Department of Biomedical Sciences, Humanitas University, Via Rita Levi Montalcini, 4 - Pieve Emanuele, Milan, Italy
[2]School of Electrical and Electronic Engineering, Shandong University of Technology, Zibo, China
[3]Department of Electronics and Communication Engineering Acharya Institute of Technology, Bangalore, Karnataka, India
[4]Department of Computer Science Engineering, Bapuji Institute of Engineering and Technology, Davangere, Karnataka, India
[5]Department of Computer Engineering, Sandip Institute of Technology and Research Center, Nashik, India

biomarker discoveries, radiotherapy responses and predicting drug effectiveness from cancer genomic signature. The main goal here is to check through the current state-of-the-art AI methods for genomics spanning the most challenging aspects of today's landscape.

8.1   Introduction

This section is divided into three subsections to let readers gradually delve into genomics and AI topics. Differently from other insightful reviews and survey articles, the main purpose here is to deliver a bottom-up approach by providing some basic concepts on both research fields to, then, deepen the most challenging tasks of AI for genomics. The paper content is organised as follows: section 8.1 provides an introductory pack of concepts for both genomics and AI; section 8.1.1 introduces some basic genomics concepts; section 8.1.2 presents the Human Genome Project; section 8.1.3 focuses on AI, ML and DL; section 8.2 delves into AI-based methods for genomics by focusing on genomic biomarkers, protein patterns, DNA sequences and patient drug treatment outcome prediction; and section 8.3 ends the chapter by drawing down some conclusions and discussion.

8.1.1   Insights into genomics

The first section of this chapter provides some insights into genomics, while the remainder of the manuscript will delve into AI technicalities and their applications to genomics from a computational viewpoint. DNA, to start with, is a chemical compound and consists of helices-arranged molecules. It also contains all information necessary to handle activities internal to organisms [1]. DNA bases or nucleotides, adenine (A), thymine (T), guanine (G) and cytosine (C), represent the so-called genetic alphabet. By looking at DNA from a higher perspective, one notices the order of nucleotides encoding pieces of information (see Figure 8.1). Each organism

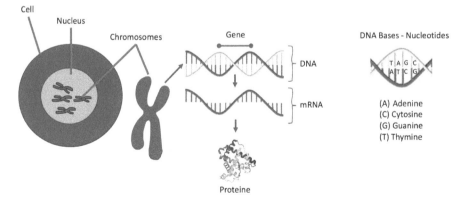

Figure 8.1   *A simple graphical description of DNA, mRNA, genes, nucleotides, chromosomes and proteins*

has a number of cells that vary depending on the organism itself. The same goes for the number of DNA molecules in cells. For instance, every cell in the human body contains around 3 billion nucleotides representing the human genome. A gene is the DNA unit necessary to build a specific or a group of proteins. Genes are housed in 23 pairs of chromosomes in the nucleus of a human cell [2]. A specific enzyme comes into play to copy the information in a gene's DNA into a messenger ribonucleic acid (mRNA) molecule. After the mRNA moves out of the nucleus and gets into the cell's cytoplasm, its content is read by a tiny particle (ribosome). The information is then used to properly combine small molecules called amino acids to build a specific protein [3] (Figure 8.1).

The preamble provides the chapter with some necessary elements to introduce the roles played by proteins and cells' DNA in organisms. The former is responsible for body structures such as organs and tissues, chemical reactions control and signals carried between cells. The latter accounts for all those effects involved in the abnormal protein generation. In simpler words, cells' DNA mutations can bring abnormal protein generation, leading to a disease such as cancer. Treating DNA sequences with increasingly sophisticated algorithms and computational processes may provide insights into segments of interest and help establish correlations between mutations and diseases. The authors care to state that what is depicted in this section is meant to cover solely introductory genomics concepts, which are also presented in a simplified manner to make them more understandable to non-experts. The next subsection gives an overall description of the Human Genome Project, which represents a milestone in scientific research.

8.1.2   Data and Human Genome Project

Back in the 1980s, scientific works [4] reported the amount of biological data doubling every 18 months. In 1982, the first nucleic acid sequence database in GenBank included 606 sequences with 680,000 nucleotide bases. In the early 2000s, Casadio *et al.* [5] updated stats, with the growth of data being characterised by a hyperbolic trend. Speaking of data and genomics, no discussion can be faced by not mentioning the Human Genome Project [6, 7]. Originally launched in 1990, it allowed the first reference human DNA sequence to be unearthed in 2003. The project brought outstanding results: the sequencing of 3 billion DNA letters in the human genome, the covers of around 99 per cent of the human genome's gene-containing regions and sequencing accuracy of 99.99 per cent. The Human Genome Project was also meant to provide the scientific community with instructions related to human genetics. Therefore, the project generated a cascade effect, involving some other tasks and disciplines such as the proposal of new techniques for the analysis of organisms' whole genomes. Due to the high volume of available data, AI comes into play to help mine data, find patterns and extract meaningful motifs by crunching sequences of DNA.

8.1.3   Artificial intelligence

Since its advent in the twentieth century, AI has been given different definitions according to the viewpoint it has analysed. Nowadays, no one would be surprised to hear that humankind has entered the AI era. Many scientific research fields and application domains are permeated by AI approaches or methods, allowing them to achieve cutting-edge solutions and high accuracy rates. A lot of water went under the bridge since one of AI godfathers defined AI as 'The science and engineering of making intelligent machines' [8]. Since then, researchers have proposed and presented several approaches on the topic. One of the main goals of AI is to infer knowledge from reality by looking into data. In greater detail, spanning several approaches throughout decades in the twentieth and twenty-first centuries, AI scientists have worked hard to have machines build up models for domain representations. For the sake of brevity, here two main aspects will be faced: how to discriminate traditional ML approaches from the newer DL ones and discerning the differences between supervised and unsupervised learning.

8.1.3.1   Machine learning

By ML, one refers to those AI methods relying on the following steps: feature extraction from data, training, validation and testing on new data (see Figure 8.2). Feature extraction plays such a critical role in the overall accuracy of the delivered model as a wrong selection of features' sets might lead to a poor representation of the application domain by the model itself. Training accounts for the model to be built with some specific functions to infer scenario-related knowledge from the extracted features. Validation is necessary to check the model's accuracy that usually means that a given dataset is split into training and validation set. The former is purely used to have the machine learn from data while the latter serves the machine as an intermediate checker of the training process. Once the model is delivered, it is necessary to run tests on previously unseen data features. Testing consists of having the model run on new data to assess the accuracy rates of the model itself on data features that

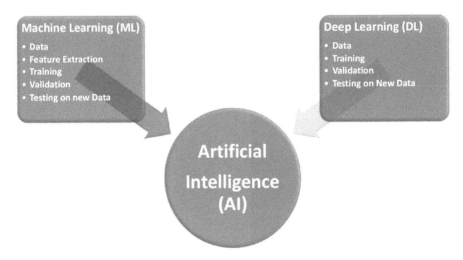

Figure 8.2   AI: ML and DL approaches

were not used during training. In this chapter, all references to ML are meant to indicate underlying methods whose pipeline consists of the steps mentioned above. An overall comparison between conventional ML and DL techniques over histological image analysis is given by Sharma *et al* [9].

8.1.3.2 Deep learning

Other than ML approaches, DL methods rely on the following steps as depicted in Figure 8.2: training, validation and testing. The three phases featuring DL approaches mainly differ from conventional ML because of the training process being conducted straight on data. As can be noticed in Figure 8.2, no feature extraction steps are involved in DL. That is possible due to the high number of layers internal to DL architectures. For instance, deep neural networks (DNNs) are characterised by functions, channels and layers responsible for extracting multilevel abstraction information straight from raw data. That was not possible with conventional ML techniques. One of the most popular DL architectures is represented by convolutional neural networks (CNNs). They are broadly employed over such heterogeneous application domains such as speech recognition, visual object recognition, object detection, drug discovery and genomics [10].

8.1.3.3 Supervised learning

Apart from the first AI methods grouping into ML and DL, it is necessary to add another AI methods' categorisation into supervised and unsupervised learning. It all refers to the way the learning process is conducted. The more traditional approaches see a set of data labelled or annotated according to classes or categories on which the model is trained. That means the learning process is supervised by the annotated data: developers and scientists know data categories ahead of time. Each data sample corresponds to a final target necessary to accomplish the so-called supervised learning. A straightforward example is to train a model to recognise dogs from cats in pictures. A supervised learning technique will train a model using images of cats and dogs and the corresponding known labels. The same goes for the biomedical scenario. Several methods have been proposed over the last few years to tackle both classification and segmentation of suspicious regions, masses, micro-calcifications, etc., from images [11].

8.1.3.4 Unsupervised

On the other side, an increasing number of AI methods and architectures is now facing a more challenging task: learning hidden properties and relations within data with no prior knowledge. That means the learning process is unsupervised. Supervised and unsupervised learning techniques for data science have been thoroughly surveyed in Reference [12]. It emerges that support vector machine (SVM), Naïve Bayes and Decision Tree algorithms are the most employed supervised learning methods, while principal component analysis, *k*-means and hierarchical clustering are the most commonly used unsupervised ML approaches.

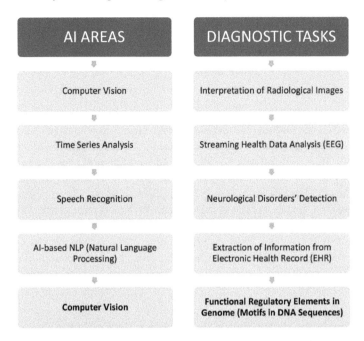

Figure 8.3   Several AI areas find their applications in clinical diagnostic tasks, as depicted above

8.2   AI for genomics

Nowadays, several diagnostics tasks are addressed by AI techniques as depicted in Figure 8.3. This section provides readers with a run-through of AI-based methods for genomics by highlighting data and technical approaches to work out clinical diagnostics address clinical diagnostics tasks (Figure 8.4). The main focus here is to highlight what genomics aspects are currently investigated through AI techniques, the main achievements, and the current trends to face the following challenges. The following observation gives a glimpse of the current challenges: increasing demand for data crunching algorithms for the biomedical community has been observed, mainly because there is a lot of crucial information hidden in the DNA that remains unknown. For instance, the human genome consists of 98.5% non-coding DNA sequences, most of which have no known function. Nevertheless, findings suggest a not negligible number of non-coding DNA variants might be correlated to diseases. Predicting the role of non-coding DNA is therefore critical.

8.2.1   AI-based applications for genomics

After checking through some fundamentals for both the disciplines, the manuscript now delves into the following AI applications for genomics topics:

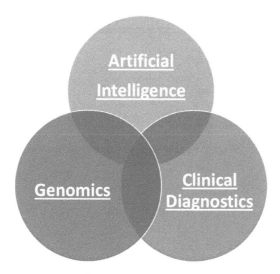

Figure 8.4   *AI, genomics and clinical diagnostics common areas correspond to scenarios, data and technical approaches to work out clinical diagnostics objectives*

- Genomic biomarkers detection
- Protein patterns detection
- Pattern recognition for DNA sequences
- Patient drug treatment outcome prediction
- Predicting the species-of-origin of a DNA sequence
- Promoter sequence detection

Since the Human Genome Project launch, human nucleic acid, protein and other biological data have been accumulated at an increasing rate. Alongside this, several new disciplines developed new methods and urged integration, which is described in the following sections. In Figure 8.5, a workflow of AI for genomics is graphically depicted. That is a common approach having the sequence of characters (input data) being ingested by a given DL architecture. As shortly mentioned before, supervised learning approaches consist of three main steps: training, validation and test. Data samples and corresponding labels, as noticeable from the pictorial representation, are necessary to run the training process. The validation step is paramount to establish whether the model is inferring knowledge correctly. Once the model is established, a testing phase enables the model to be checked on new data samples. Evaluation metrics such as precision and recall are broadly employed to check out the effectiveness of the DL architecture. Both metrics values depend on the number of true positives, false positives and false negatives.

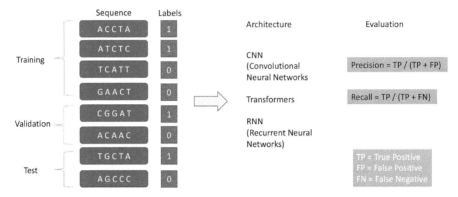

Figure 8.5   The overall workflow of DL in genomics is graphically depicted above. It consists of training, validation and test, selection of DL architecture and performance evaluation via metrics such as precision and recall.

8.2.2   Protein patterns detection

Bioinformatics, for instance, processes and analyses nucleic acid and protein sequence data and protein 3D structure data [13]. Protein sequences are analysed as a series of numbers. The development of combination models represents a way to interpret the information carried out by the sequence and the corresponding function. Extraction of patterns in protein sequences plays a key role. Paul Stothard is the author of a web tool with a plethora of biological applications [14]. Amongst many tasks, it is possible to generate short DNA and protein sequences. An example of a protein sequence is given in Figure 8.6.

Lee *et al.* [15] proposed DeepConv-drug–target interaction, a CNN-based method to detect patterns of generalised protein classes. Thanks to CNNs, their system is able to read raw protein sequences, run convolution to check out amino acid subsequences and capture local patterns of protein sequences. Their main goal was to tackle the so-called drug–target interactions prediction. Liu *et al.* [16] dealt with the analysis of protein structures and functions. In their article, they highlight the cons of the existing strategies. They worked on the proposal of a predictor, DeepSVM-fold, for protein fold recognition. The novelty introduced by Liu *et al.*'s method is represented by a new feature vector accounting for a similarity score of pairwise sequences extracted by DL networks.

Sticking around the same research field, Wang *et al.* [17] analysed the protein–protein interactions (PPIs). Detecting PPIs is not straightforward. In their article, Wang *et al.* stressed the technologies being able to see large-scale PPIs, albeit the whole PPIs identification remains a difficult task. They proposed extracting protein sequences using Zernike moments [18] from a positional matrix. The extracted features, then, feed an autoencoder [19], while a probabilistic classification vector machine classifier eventually predicts PPIs.

Random Protein Sequence results

>random sequence 1 consisting of 1000 residues.

```
RFPVHISHISSLYFADCKFLMGCVESSNHLLGNEHIRNEYDNSFMHDFRALWIWDCQGIQ
QHMVNEVVYTMWAMYQPNVSRHEIHKVEIQRICATQSNVLIDVSNYEGTYGKHQPGITYG
IFTQVNLVGYWKHVGYDETCSNTQSNVICTCHETYCADLGNHTIEYPEDQMTVYICEPMD
TFKYAWDRTQCCMIVYWMRQGKPWGKIGFYSDAFEHNFKPLDEIKMVCYENNIQLFSPWM
MWDPRQPCPRQDEQDEEMMGQSPSVGMKYFWPFLVNILYYLFAHAMWEQCDNDEVHDTNA
WFDRWFDSYKMIHQNLVKSIQYFGEMKIYKRQNRYHLVMQTNYELNENNLRPTTNQPWSL
RAWGWRQYGMGECLEMNPWHTICITHMIYVCKIMYAYKNWVFYIMHQFVSMMLPHSHRTA
VDVLAGKIKTQWRAYQCWLLMQVREVPPGVVIPWKPPYYMCMHCNEFHAYERIMFSDMPS
TMFMCKQQFISVAIYFWEGKKCEARTGCHYPNPKNPFMVWYCFIKHGCGDPCMLPAGHRW
GGRIIQFWHKSYQHFNNQTSFFWIHAVHTMDRECWSSDVRYVFIGTRLGQKNTMMRAAGM
VEMIFCHGMDRYQDMFVLLYPDIKELTRQSGKEGVAICYIAGHGDCIFNQYKMLYLWCEV
SWAHASFYRALTSKRDGHQMRTKHIHCFSNCDTIDYKGKMAVLIKEVTYLYYQYADPPDT
MHGHLMIQLYMWIEYMCSIHGEPHDMWAREDTQCWSLYTTVNKCQVVCQLSLQRLFHEPR
KQNYDTAIANARRQEYCGIPCGSAKYTQYSDKSDHTMITAETRASKPNDLVQVWPENHRC
MGCDINSITDGHNLARNQYVAQIFNYLCLKPHWKKFQHFKIHHAVIYVLNLCLKDLTLDY
MHVQQTHESLMTCEHCGWWARPTSPICMANYQMIKADIMVFSTVESERPILRMNPKQRLH
QRPVRMDVECPELCHGKEDVPCCCGGIGYGDHRMGIYNDM
```

Figure 8.6   A protein sequence sample generated by the web tool developed by Paul Stothard [14]

8.2.3   DNA sequence analysis

DNA's main role is storing information. The recent progress and the proposal of new techniques for sequencing have DNA sequence data volume increasing at a staggering rate. That prompted the scientific community to approach the DNA sequence data analysis with big data analytics. In their review article, Yang *et al.* [20] thoroughly explain how data mining and ML dramatically impact four DNA-sequence related main tasks: alignment, classification, clustering, pattern mining and matching.

Importantly, 98.5% of human genome comprises non-coding DNA sequences. There is not yet specific enough knowledge about most non-coding DNA sequence functions. Nevertheless, findings revealed associations between some diseases and non-coding DNA regions. Subsequently, research on non-coding DNA is warranted to assess the principal roles and disease-related associations. Some scientists applied the so-called deep residual learning (DRL) networks [21] to increase the detection rates of regulatory patterns and, subsequently, regulatory markers. For instance, Zhang *et al.* [22] introduced NCNet, an integrated solution combining DRL and sequence-to-sequence learning networks. In greater detail, the aim of Zhang *et al.* was oriented towards the prediction of transcription factor-binding sites. DRL networks work to increase the regulatory patterns identification rate. On the other hand, the sequence-to-sequence learning network deals with the dependency analysis between patterns. Experimental results of NCNet showed its robustness especially when compared to hybrid models.

Busia *et al.* [23] focused their efforts on predicting the species of origin of a DNA sequence using a DNN. Some researchers addressed the prediction task with the so-called string-matching techniques or with probabilistic models. Busia *et al.* ran through the effectiveness of a DL approach in predicting database-derived labels directly from query sequences. The dataset used in their work consists of short reads of 16S ribosomal DNA. The DNN was trained on 16S sequences of over 13,000 species.

Developing accurate DNA sequence alignment algorithms is challenging from a computational perspective. Zhao *et al.* [24] applied an improved ant colony algorithm to sequence alignment. Other than methods reliant on the traditional ant colony algorithms, Zhao *et al.*'s method does not get trapped into local optima. It changes the distribution of pheromones at different times to get the ability to align variable-length sequences.

In 2017, the pretty popular article by Vasawani *et al.* titled 'Attention is all you need' took the DL stage. The transformers made their appearance in 2017 [25], with Vaswani *et al.* proposing a new DL architecture based exclusively on attention mechanisms: the encoding branch ingests a sequence of symbol representations to be mapped to a sequence of continuous representations. Transformers achieved staggering performances in natural language processing (NLP).

Martinek *et al.* [26] reviewed the employment of transformers in genomics by providing benchmark datasets for the classification of genomic sequences and comparing several models. Amongst many methods, it is worth mentioning DNABERT [27] whose main goal is to decipher the language of non-coding DNA.

DNABERT consists of a pre-trained bidirectional encoder representation to catch a transferrable understanding of genomic DNA sequences. DNABERT allows visualising nucleotide-level importance and semantic relationships. Furthermore, Ji *et al.* [27] showed the transferability of pre-trained DNABERT with the human genome over other organisms.

8.2.4   Promoter sequence detection

Promoter sequence in DNA has a meaningful role, even from a pattern mining perspective as it precedes genes in DNA. Ranawana and Palade [28] dealt with the identification of *Escherichia coli* promoters to detect the corresponding gene in the DNA sequence. They addressed the task using a neural network-based approach. They encoded *E. coli* promoters and known non-promoter sequences to train four neural networks. The outputs of the neural networks were then combined using a function similar to the logarithmic opinion pool. Ranawana and Palade opted for a genetic algorithm to assign the function weights. Four encoders were employed to process a dataset containing 324 *E. coli* promoters and 429 known non-promoter sequences. Sequences, after being processed, were ingested by four neural networks to train four classification models. The four models were integrated with an aggregator based on a variation of the logarithmic opinion pool method. Ranawana and Palade opted for a genetic algorithm to assign the aggregator weights. Tests were run on a set of 159 known promoter sequences and 171 non-promoter sequences. The four neural networks showed slightly different results, albeit with the same dataset. That was due to the different architectures of the networks. Conversely, when combined through an aggregator function, performances offered better results.

8.2.5 Cancer treatment outcome prediction

Genomics and biomedical imaging provide physicians with a lot of data representing a unique resource upon which to build new knowledge. One of the main objectives in the scientific community is to employ the huge amount of available data for predicting treatment outcomes of patients diagnosed with cancer.

Mobadersany *et al.* [29] developed a method reliant on DL for predicting the overall survival rate of brain tumour-diagnosed patients. They employed both microscopic images of tissue biopsies and genomic biomarkers. In greater detail, Mobadersany *et al.* proposed survival convolutional neural networks (SCNNs) to integrate the features mentioned above into a single unified framework. SCNNs proved reliable in predicting the overall survival of patients with glioma.

As well as researchers and developers who have worked on the classification of DNA sequences, several research groups focused on the study of RNA, especially the non-coding RNA (ncRNA) as findings revealed correlations between ncRNA and the onset of malignancies [30].

The first pioneering ML method on ncRNA was proposed in Reference [31] with SVM-based classifiers, namely, coding potential calculator. Successively, other scientists worked on the same topic with alternate results.

Amin *et al.* [32] evaluated several DL architectures and presented lncFinder11, an integrated solution embedding different DL networks. lncFinder runs the algorithms on the same dataset and ranks them on accuracy rates. The one scoring higher is then used for lncRNA (long non-coding RNA) prediction.

8.2.6 Genomics biomarkers

As previously stated in the manuscript, genomics aims at identifying biomarkers in order to detect early-stage cancer. Some blood-based methods rely on the analysis of cell-free DNA (cfDNA) as an alternative to the currently adopted screenings. The main issue with cfDNA-related tasks is the low percentage of cfDNA in the early-stage of malignancies.

For instance, González *et al.* [33] confirmed cfDNA concentration and short cfDNA fragment size fraction as well as metabolic activity as markers showing the presence of tumours in patients with advanced non-small cell lung cancer .

A ML-based method was proposed by Wan *et al.* [34] to tackle the early detection of cancer. First, the extraction of whole-genome sequencing was conducted on cfDNA from blood samples. Then, reads aligning to proteins coding genes are extracted. The count of reads was normalised in the range [0,1]. IchorCNA carried out the estimation of cfDNA tumour fraction. Conventional ML models were trained using k-fold cross validation to check the generalisation capabilities of the models themselves. Results of an experimental campaign involving an early-stage colorectal cancer cohort showed the ML models proved effective against the early detection of cancer using cfDNA.

Another promising biomarker is circulating tumour DNA (ctDNA), albeit its low trace concentration level in blood samples. Li *et al.* [35] focused their efforts on enabling ctDNA as a biomarker for liquid biopsy. Due to the above-mentioned issue, automatic techniques for detecting ctDNA have been investigated over the last years.

Li *et al.* [36] recently presented CRCnet, a DL model consisting of a classifier and multi-instance learning, with the former classifying tissues and the latter setting up a survival model. The retrospective study aimed to double-check the haematoxylin and eosin image-based biomarkers' reliability in delivering treatments following surgery for Stage II/III CRC. CRCNet was trained and validated on 780 Stage II/III CRC patients from molecular and cellular oncology. Over 300 Stage II/III CRC patients' data from The Cancer Genome Atlas were used as further external validation.

Scientific findings revealed cancer genesis and harmful mutations are correlated, making the identification of cancer based on genomic information crucial to the early detection of cancer. Sun *et al.* [37] proposed a method, genome DL, to focus on genomic variations and trait relations using DNNs. In greater detail, they addressed the analysis of whole exon sequencing mutations by analysing 6,083 files from 12 cancer types and 1,991 healthy whole exon sequencing, respectively, taken from The Cancer Genome Atlas and the 1,000 Genomes project. They built up 12 specific models, each of them classify one type of cancer and healthy tissue. Each model consists of a DNN with input and output layers, as well as hidden layers. The architecture is a standard DNN employed to ingest sequences and labels, as the supervised learning paradigm suggests. Due to the huge amount of data, the system proposed achieved a pretty high accuracy rate (97.47%) in the classification of 12 cancers. On top of genome DL, a probabilistic approach allows detecting 12 cancers achieving an accuracy rate of 70.08%.

8.2.7   Drug response

Chang *et al.* [38] tackled a challenging topic such as the cancer drug response with a DL approach. They introduced the Cancer Drug Response scan (CDRscan), a DL model trained to predict anticancer drug responsiveness. Importantly, the method relies on drug screening data, including genomic and structural profiles: 787 human cancer cell lines genomic profiles and 244 drug structural profiles. Interestingly, CDRScan works out the task by employing a CNN-based architecture. Each genomic mutational fingerprint as well as drugs' molecular fingerprints, are ingested by the CNN, then merged by 'virtual docking', an *in silico* modelling of drug treatment. The experimental results showed that CDRscan proved effective in predicting drug response with high prediction accuracy rates: $R2 > 0.84$; $AUROC > 0.98$, with R2 meaning R-squared and AUROC standing for Area Under Receiving Operator Characteristics. Chang *et al.* carried out an extensive campaign over 1,487 approved drugs. One of the most interesting outcomes relates to the identification of 14 oncology and 23 non-oncology drugs having cancer-related indications.

8.3 Discussion and conclusions

Many tasks and genomic subtopics today are seen as a practicable path to accelerate some analysis processes of features that are key to the high-level information extraction from biological data. Spanning a plethora of genomics objectives, and reviewing articles published over the last few years reveal increasing employment of both machine and DL models to achieve higher accuracy rates. Genomics has followed AI trends over the last few years, gradually moving from ML to DL paradigms. Importantly, most of the ongoing projects rely on supervised DL approaches, while self-supervised and unsupervised techniques are not yet fully explored. Noticeably, some supervised DL achieve over 90% of accuracy on specific tasks such as the detection of cancer types. Nevertheless, the outstanding rates are that high as long as the models are trained to classify only one type of cancer. When classifier ensembles are in place, the accuracy drops by a not negligible factor. That might indicate the need for models with improved generalisation knowledge inference capabilities. Chances are that, as well as for other scientific disciplines, future genomics challenges might be addressed by using self-supervised DL architectures involving an unsupervised encoder branch and a supervised network branch to fine-tune the hidden properties learned in the first place. Furthermore, the latest trend sees genomics under the precision medicine umbrella along with radiogenomics, radiomics, biomedical imaging and, of course, AI. Hopefully, integrated solutions relying on multimodal data might overcome the current state-of-the-art methods' performances.

References

[1] Aguilar L. Genes, genomes, genetics and chromosomes. Waltham Abbey Essex, United Kingdom: Scientific e-Resources; 2019.

[2] Baeck T., Fogel D.B., Michalewicz Z. Evolutionary Computation 1. Boca Raton, FL: CRC Press; 2006. Available from https://www.taylorfrancis.com/books/9781482268713

[3] Alberts B., Johnson A., Lewis J., Raff M., Roberts K., Walter P. 'From DNA to RNA' in *Molecular biology of the cebiology of the cell*. New York; 2002.

[4] Bilofsky H.S., Burks C., Fickett J.W., *et al.* The GenBank genetic sequence databank. *Nucleic Acids Research*. 1986, vol. 14(1), pp. 1–4.

[5] Casadio R., Calabrese R., Capriotti E, *et al.* 'Machine learning and the prediction of protein structure: the state of the art'. *Modern Information Processing*. 2006, pp. 359–70.

[6] Collins F.S., Morgan M., Patrinos A. 'The human genome project: lessons from large-scale biology'. *Science*. 2003, vol. 300(5617), pp. 286–90.

[7] Lunshof J.E., Bobe J., Aach J, *et al.* 'Personal genomes in progress: from the human genome project to the personal genome project'. *Dialogues in Clinical Neuroscience*. 2022, vol. 12(1), pp. 47–60.

[8] McCarthy J. *What is artificial intelligence* [online]. 2004. Available from http://www-formal. stanford.edu/jmc/whatisai.html

[9]　Sharma S., Mehra R. 'Conventional machine learning and deep learning approach for multi-classification of breast cancer histopathology images-a comparative insight'. *Journal of Digital Imaging*. 2020, vol. 33(3), pp. 632–54.

[10]　Yann LeCun, Yoshua Bengio, and Geoffrey Hinton. Deep learning. nature, 521(7553):436–444, 2015.

[11]　Bruno A., Ardizzone E., Vitabile S., Midiri M. 'A novel solution based on scale invariant feature transform descriptors and deep learning for the detection of suspicious regions in mammogram images'. *Journal of Medical Signals and Sensors*. 2020, vol. 10(3), pp. 158–73.

[12]　Alloghani M., Al-Jumeily D., Mustafina J., Hussain A., Aljaaf A.J. 'A systematic review on supervised and unsupervised machine learning algorithms for data science'. *Supervised and Unsupervised Learning for Data Science*. 2020, pp. 3–21.

[13]　Zhou Q., Jiang Q., Li S., Xie X., Lin L. '*Education (ICCSE 2010)*; Hefei, China, IEEE, 2010'.

[14]　Stothard P. 'The sequence manipulation suite: javascript programs for analyzing and formatting protein and dna sequences'. *BioTechniques*. 2000, vol. 28(6), pp. 1102–04.

[15]　Lee I., Keum J., Nam H. 'DeepConv-DTI: prediction of drug-target interactions via deep learning with convolution on protein sequences'. *PLoS Computational Biology*. 2019, vol. 15(6), e1007129.

[16]　Liu B., Li C.-C., Yan K. 'DeepSVM-fold: protein fold recognition by combining support vector machines and pairwise sequence similarity scores generated by deep learning networks'. *Briefings in Bioinformatics*. 2020, vol. 21(5), pp. 1733–41.

[17]　Wang Y.-B., You Z.-H., Li X., *et al.* 'Predicting protein-protein interactions from protein sequences by a stacked sparse autoencoder deep neural network'. *Molecular BioSystems*. 2017, vol. 13(7), pp. 1336–44.

[18]　Khotanzad A., Hong Y.H. 'Invariant image recognition by Zernike moments'. *IEEE Transactions on Pattern Analysis and Machine Intelligence*. 1990, vol. 12(5), pp. 489–97.

[19]　Hinton G.E., Zemel R. 'Autoencoders, minimum description length and Helmholtz free energy'. *Advances in Neural Information Processing Systems*. 1993, vol. 6.

[20]　Yang A., Zhang W., Wang J., Yang K., Han Y., Zhang L. ' review on the application of machine learning algorithms in the sequence data mining of DNA '. *Frontiers in Bioengineering and Biotechnology*. 2020, vol. 8, p. 1032.

[21]　He K., Zhang X., Ren S., Sun J. 'deep residual learning for image recognition '. *2016 IEEE Conference on Computer Vision and Pattern Recognition (CVPR)*; Las Vegas, NV, USA, IEEE, 2016. pp. 770–78.

[22]　Zhang H., Hung C.-L., Liu M., Hu X., Lin Y.-Y. 'Ncnet: deep learning network models for predicting function of non-coding DNA'. *Frontiers in Genetics*. 2019, vol. 10, 432.

[23]　Busia A., Dahl G.E., Fannjiang C, *et al.* 'A deep learning approach to pattern recognition for short DNA sequences'. [Bioinformatics (Oxford, England)]. 2019. DOI:

[24] Zhao Y., Ma P., Lan J., Liang C., Ji G. 'An improved ant colony algorithm for DNA sequence alignment'. Presented at 2008 International Symposium on Information Science and Engineering (ISISE); Shanghai, 2008. IEEE,

[25] Vaswani A., Shazeer N., Parmar N, *et al.* 'Attention is all you need'. *Advances in Neural Information Processing Systems.* 2017, vol. 30.

[26] Martinek V., Cechak D., Gresova K., Alexiou P., Simecek P. 'Fine-tuning transformers for genomic tasks'. [Bioinformatics]. 2005. DOI:

[27] Ji Y., Zhou Z., Liu H., Davuluri R.V. 'Dnabert: pre-trained bidirectional encoder representations from transformers model for DNA-language in genome'. *Bioinformatics (Oxford, England).* 2021, vol. 37(15), pp. 2112–20.

[28] Ranawana R., Palade V. 'A neural network based multi-classifier system for gene identification in DNA sequences'. *Neural Computing and Applications.* 2005, vol. 14(2), pp. 122–31.

[29] Mobadersany P., Yousefi S., Amgad M., *et al.* 'Predicting cancer outcomes from histology and genomics using convolutional networks'. *Proceedings of the National Academy of Sciences of the United States of America.* 2018, vol. 115(13), pp. E2970–79.

[30] Grillone K., Riillo C., Scionti F., *et al.* 'Non-coding rnas in cancer: platforms and strategies for investigating the genomic "dark matter"'. *Journal of Experimental & Clinical Cancer Research.* 2020, vol. 39(1), p. 117.

[31] Kong L., Zhang Y., Ye Z.-Q., *et al.* 'CPC: assess the protein-coding potential of transcripts using sequence features and support vector machine'. *Nucleic Acids Research.* 2007, vol. 35(Web Server issue), pp. W345–9.

[32] Amin N., McGrath A., Chen Y.-P.P. 'Evaluation of deep learning in non-coding RNA classification'. *Nature Machine Intelligence.* 2019, vol. 1(5), pp. 246–56.

[33] González de Aledo-Castillo J.M., Casanueva-Eliceiry S., Soler-Perromat A, *et al.* 'Cell-free DNA concentration and fragment size fraction correlate with FDG pet/CT-derived parameters in NSCLC patients'. *European Journal of Nuclear Medicine and Molecular Imaging.* 2021, vol. 48(11), pp. 3631–42.

[34] Wan N., Weinberg D., Liu T.-Y, *et al.* 'Machine learning enables detection of early-stage colorectal cancer by whole-genome sequencing of plasma cell-free DNA'. *BMC Cancer.* 2019, vol. 19(1), pp. 1–10.

[35] Li M., Xie S., Lu C., Zhu L., Zhu L. 'Application of data science in circulating tumor DNA detection: a promising Avenue towards liquid biopsy'. *Frontiers in Oncology.* 2021, vol. 11.

[36] Li X., Jonnagaddala J., Yang S., Zhang H., Xu X.S. ' a retrospective analysis using deep-learning models for prediction of survival outcome and benefit of adjuvant chemotherapy in stage II/III colorectal cancer '. *Journal of Cancer Research and Clinical Oncology.* 2022, vol. 148, pp. 1–9.

[37] Sun Y., Zhu S., Ma K., *et al.* 'Identification of 12 cancer types through genome deep learning'. *Scientific Reports.* 2019, vol. 9(1), pp. 1–9.

[38] Chang Y., Park H., Yang H.-J, *et al.* 'Cancer drug response profile scan (CDRscan): a deep learning model that predicts drug effectiveness from cancer genomic signature'. *Scientific Reports.* 2018, vol. 8(1), pp. 1–11.

Chapter 9

Research on security of anonymous communication in wireless healthcare online system

Fengyin Li[1], Xinying Yu[1], Yanli Wang[1], and Zhongxing Liu[1]

The wireless medical sensor network is one of the emerging technologies that brought a revolution in medical image, healthcare monitoring, etc., playing a vital role in wireless healthcare online systems. However, security risks like privacy disclosure may arise since the medical sensors are connected via wireless. Secure anonymous communication is essential to protect patients' privacy. To this end, we give a seminal summary and comparison of the advanced anonymous communication technologies on wireless healthcare online systems. First, in order to solve the problem of patient privacy disclosure caused by health data disclosure, let us look at a privacy-sensitive public key infrastructure (PKI) model with advanced and advanced security that prevents disclosure of user registration keys. Next, to address the problem of spoofing users when accessing wireless sensors and to ensure that an adversary cannot modify sensor data through interception, look at key agreements and anonymous authentication protocols to address spoofing when users access wireless sensors (删掉). Furthermore, given the unreliability of wireless sensors and the hidden peril of health data transmitting in plaintext, a trust-based secure directed diffusion routing protocol is elaborated to establish a reliable routing and secure the transmission of health data. Finally, we expound on a lightweight anonymous communication model in wireless healthcare online systems, which realizes user identity authentication and the health data's confidentiality, so as to protect the privacy of patients.

9.1 Introduction

Wireless sensor networks (WSNs) consist of a number of self-configuring and resource-restricted sensor nodes used primarily in smart healthcare, environmental

[1]School of Computer Science, Qufu Normal University, Rizhao, China

monitoring, precision agriculture, and other areas [1]. Due to high privacy require-ments, information security has become a hot subject of research today. Especially in healthcare, medical sensors are initially ensconced on the patient's body to sense and collect the health data, such as pulse rate, body temperature, and heartbeat rate. Nevertheless, the disclosure of health data can encroach on the patient's privacy, and the interception has the potential to modify the sensing data. Therefore, the security of wireless medical sensors is essential to protect patients' privacy.

In security research on WSNs, identity authentication is one of the most impor-tant security technologies and is the basis for controlling access to health data [2]. Identity authentication is widely used in various areas such as the Internet of things, allowing legitimate users to securely access wireless sensors and preventing unau-thorized users from gaining sensitive information [3–6]. Anonymous authentication and key consent protocols have been proposed based on dynamic sequences and shared secrets that enable secure access to legal users' sensors. A Diffie–Hellman (D-H)-based key consent protocol has been developed to anonymously generate ses-sion keys between users and medical big data servers.

Identity verification naturally reveals PKI technology. The existing PKI is a centralized certification authority (CA)-dependent certification method. However, if the CA is damaged, the user's identity information will be leaked, until blockchain technology leads to improved identity authentication mechanisms [7]. Blockchain has created a variety of applications with decentralized accounting methods with immutability and anonymity [8–13]. You can implement a blockchain-based PKI by applying the blockchain to the identity authentication mechanism. It provides a personal information sensitive PKI model with strong transfer security such as key registration and renewal. The registration phase binds the user's real identity with the registration key and publishes it to the blockchain.

The security of wireless sensors is reflected not only in the legitimacy of the communication device identity (ID) but also in the sensitive transmission of sensi-tive data [1]. The data collected from the sensors are confidential and often associ-ated with the user's personal information. However, the sensor sends data wirelessly over public channels, and the instability and unreliability of the sensor can lead to data interception or leakage. Therefore, it is important to balance the energy con-sumption of all sensor nodes in the network and extend the lifetime of the whole net-work. Researchers at home and abroad have designed routing protocols for a variety of real-world scenarios. Among them, direct diffusion DD is a common data and query-based routing mechanism that has the potential benefits of WSN's low power consumption and high navigation values [14]. Yu *et al.* create an energy trust model using the direct trust and residual energy of the sensor node. They are also designing a secure direct forwarding routing protocol based on the energy trust model aimed at establishing reliable routing and ensuring the secure forwarding of health data.

As we all know, a large amount of personal information is stored on the Internet, and there are higher requirements for data protection. Data protection technologies protect the content of messages as well as the identities of the parties, when they are transmitted, and how they are communicated. However, existing encryption techniques are difficult to protect personal information such as identity, behavior, and network addresses. Communication participants [15, 16]. Hackers use traffic analysis attacks to obtain identities and communication relationships during the communication process, resulting in the leakage of personal information [17–19]. Therefore, it is particularly important to construct an anonymous communication model to hide the communication relationship in the communication flow.

In this chapter, a seminal summary and comparison of advanced anonymous communication techniques on wireless medical online systems are provided first. On this basis, a trust-based secure directed diffusion routing protocol is elaborated to establish reliable routing and protect the transmission of health data. The chapter also expounds on a lightweight anonymous communication model, which can provide identity authentication and data privacy transmission, thus safeguarding the user's personal information and the communication relationship in the communication flow, and realizing the user's anonymity and the confidentiality of health data.

9.2   Privacy-aware PKI model with strong forward security

Applying strong forward secure ring signatures to privacy-sensitive PKI models. Based on the Rivest–Shamir–Adleman (RSA) algorithm, we propose a privacy-sensitive PKI model with strong direct security, update the user's registration key, eliminate the hidden danger of losing the registration key, make the registration key strong, and ensure transmission security. The proposed PKI model can achieve strong forward security, which is difficult for ring signature. The model is divided into two phases: key registration and update. The registration process verifies the actual identity of the user through the blockchain structure, and the update process happens after the registration process. When the registration process is complete, the registered user will perform a key update operation to generate a new nickname and ID key. In order to disguise the real identity of registered users and gain anonymity, users use ring signatures to prove their validity. The next chapter will describe these two parts in detail.

9.2.1   Strong forward-secure ring signature based on RSA

Based on the ring signature scheme [20], this section proposes and details a new RSA-based secure ring signature technique.

1.   Key generation

According to the key generation algorithm of the RSA cryptographic algo-rithm, user $U_i\ (i = 1, \cdots, n)$ randomly selects two large prime numbers p_i, q_i and calculates $N_i = p_i \cdot q_i;\ \varphi\ (N_i) = (p_i - 1) \cdot (q_i - 1)$. Then choose two large integers e_i and y_i and share $\varphi\ (N_i)$ as the public key. Finally, U_i calculates the inverse elements d_i and x_i of the public keys according to the formula: $e_i \cdot d_i \equiv 1 mod\varphi\ (N_i), y_i \cdot x_i \equiv 1 mod\varphi\ (N_i)$ as the private keys. In this way, the public and private key pair $(d_i, e_i), (x_i, y_i)$ is obtained. In this way, a pair of public and private keys $(d_i, e_i), (x_i, y_i)$ are obtained. Then U_i chooses an anti-collision hash function $H_i: \{0, 1\}^* \to Z_{N_i}$ to issue a signature and form a private key pair:

$$SK = (d_i, x_i, p_i, q_i), PK = (e_i, y_i, N_i, H_i) \tag{9.1}$$

2. Key update

The validity period of the signing key needs to be divided into T periods (T needs to be known by all members of the system). Then, in the j $(1 \leq j \leq T)$ period, $SK_i = (d_{i,j}, x_{i,j})$ acts as the user U_i's private key. When the time goes to the jth cycle:

$$d_{i,j} = (d_{i,j-1})^2 \bmod \varphi(N_i) = d_i^{p^j} \bmod \varphi(N_i) \tag{9.2}$$

$$x_{i,j} = (x_{i,j+1})^2 \bmod \varphi(N_i) = x_i^{2^{T-j}} \bmod \varphi(N_i) \tag{9.3}$$

3. Signature

User U_k selects the public keys of some members of the ring signature to form public key set $L = \{(e_1, y_1, N_1, H_1), \cdots, (e_n, y_n, N_n, H_n)\}$. Then, in loop jth period, U_k randomly selects $r_k, r_k' \in Z_{N_k}^*$ and $c_{k+1} = H_{k+1}(L, m, r_k, r_k')$ for computation, where H is a fault-tolerant hash function $H_i: \{0, 1\}^* \to Z_{N_i}$.

For $i = k+1, k+2, \cdots, n-1, n, 1, 2, \cdots, k-1$, U_k chooses a random number $s_i, s_i' \in Z_{N_k}^*$, calculated as follows:

$$c_{i+1} = H_{i+1}\left(L, m, c_i + s_i^{(e_i)^{2^j}} \bmod N_i, c_i + s_i'^{(y_i)^{2^{T-j}}} \bmod N_i\right) \tag{9.4}$$

Notice: For $i = n$, set it to $c_{i+1} = c_1, H_{i+1} = H_1$.

Finally, the output signature $\sigma_m = \left(j, c_1, s_1, \cdots, s_n, s_1', \cdots, s_n'\right)$ needs to calculate U_k and s_k and $s_k': s_k = (r_k - c_k)^{d_{k,j}} \bmod N_k, s_k' = (r_k' - c_k)^{x_{k,j}} \bmod N_k$.

4. Verification

When a validator receives a set of signature σ_m, the message m, and the set L of public keys, it computes

$$pk_0' \tag{9.5}$$

Then the validator calculates $c_{i+1} = H_{i+1}\left(L, m, r_i, r_i'\right)$ whether it is valid and finally performs verification $c_1 = H_1\left(L, m, r_n, r_n'\right)$. If so, the signature is correct. Otherwise, the signature is invalid.

5. Correctness

According to the key update algorithm:

$$\begin{cases} d_{i,j} = (d_{i,j-1})^2 \bmod \varphi(N_i) = d_i^{p^j} \bmod \varphi(N_i) \\ x_{i,j} = (x_{i,j+1})^2 \bmod \varphi(N_i) = x_i^{2^{T-j}} \bmod \varphi(N_i) \end{cases} \tag{9.6}$$

Then:

$$r_k = c_k + s_k^{e_k^{2^j}} \bmod(N_k) \qquad\qquad r'_k = c_k + s_k^{r y_{kj}} \bmod(N_k)$$
$$= ck + ((r_k - c_k)^{d_{kj}})^{e_k^{2^j}} \bmod(N_k) \quad = c_k + ((r'_k - c_k)^{x_{kj}})^{y_{kj}} \bmod(N_k)$$
$$= c_k = ((r_k - c_k)^{d_k^{2^j}})^{e_k^{2^j}} \bmod(N_k) \quad = c_k + (r'_k - c_k^{x_k^{2^{T-j}}})^{y_k^{2^{T-j}}} \bmod(N_k)$$
$$= r_k \qquad\qquad\qquad\qquad = r'_k$$

6. .Strong forward security

Forward security is achieved by iteratively updating the user's private source key:

$$d_{i,j} = (d_{i,j-1})^2 \bmod \varphi (N_i) = d_i^{2^j} \bmod \varphi (N_i) \tag{9.7}$$

And backward security is achieved by updating the user's private key:

$$x_{i,j} = (x_{i,j+1})^2 \bmod \varphi(N_i) = x_i^{2^{T-j}} \bmod \varphi(N_i) \tag{9.8}$$

Among them, $\varphi(N_i = (p_i - 1) \cdot (q_i - 1)$ is calculated by two large primes p_i and q_i. For large composite numbers, it is difficult to take the square root, so getting the previous private key $sk_0^{k,j-1}$ from the latter private key $sk_0^{k,j}$ is not available.

9.2.2 Privacy-aware PKI model

9.2.2.1 Registration

The registration step is mainly to associate the user's actual ID with the registration key obtained through the RSA key generation algorithm and publish it on the blockchain to complete the user's ID registration. The specific registration process is shown in Figure 9.1.

In the registration phase, the user first generates a registration key and a master key according to the RSA key generation algorithm. Since the registration key is associated with the user ID, it participates as the signing key when updating the user key. The role of the core couple is to prove your identity when the other party impersonates you. The specific algorithm for generating registry keys is as follows.

1. The user randomly selects two large prime numbers p_0 and q_0 and calculates $N_0 = p_0 \cdot q_0$. Then, the user calculates $\varphi (N_0) = (p_0 - 1) (q_0 - 1)$ according to the Euler formula.
2. The user selects two large prime numbers pk_0 and pk'_0 with $\varphi (N_0)$ using the public key.
3. Next, the user calculates the inverse sk_0 and sk'_0 of the public key and the private key according to the formula $pk_0 \cdot sk_0 \equiv 1 mod \varphi (N_0)$ and $pk'_0 \cdot sk'_0 \equiv 1 mod \varphi (N_0)$ and obtains a set of registered key pairs:

$$PK_0 = \left(pk_0, pk'_0\right), SK_0 = \left(sk_0, sk'_0\right) \tag{9.9}$$

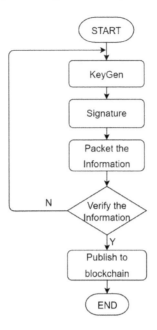

Figure 9.1   Flow chart of registration

The master key pair is also generated in the same way. First, calculate with p_m, q_m, $N_m = p_m \cdot q_m$, and $\varphi(N_m) = (p_m - 1)(q_m - 1)$. After that, the master key pair (mpk, msk) can be obtained according to the formula $mpk \cdot msk \equiv 1 mod(\varphi(N_m))$.

At this point, once the two key pairs required for user registration are created, the user must sign the identity (id) according to the RSA signature scheme to obtain σ_0, σ_0', and σ_m:

$$\sigma_0 = id^{sk_0} mod(N_0), \sigma_0' = id^{sk_0'} mod(N_0), \sigma_m = id^{msk} mod(N_m) \qquad (9.10)$$

You now have all the information you need to register. Next, the user needs to add information to get a standard format data packet $(id, register, T_0, values = (PK_0 = (pk_0, pk_0'), \sigma_0, \sigma_0', \sigma_m))$ and send it to the blockchain. In the packet, id represents the actual ID of the user; Registration represents a user registration operation; T_0 represents the current timestamp; PK_0 describes the generated public registry key; σ_0 and σ_0' describe your personal registration key to associate your registration public key with your identity; and σ_m is the secret master key that represents the ID signature. If someone impersonates the user, the user can provide a master key and signature to prove their identity. All other information currently stored, including private key $SK_0 = (sk_0, sk_0')$ and master key pairs (mpk, msk), is stored locally.

After the registration step, members of the blockchain will review the information posted by the user. First, make sure your registration ID and registration public key pk_0, pk'_0 are for the first registration. Then follow the RSA signature technique to verify the accuracy of your signature:

$$id = \sigma_0^{pk_0} \bmod(N_0) = (id^{sk_0})^{pk_0} \bmod(N_0) = id^{sk_0 \cdot pk_0} \bmod(N_0)$$
$$id = \sigma_0'^{pk'_0} \bmod(N_0) = (id^{sk'_0})^{pk'_0} \bmod(N_0) = id^{sk'_0 \cdot pk'_0} \bmod(N_0)$$

(9.11)

Once found to be signed correctly, the user in the blockchain publishes a block containing this information.

9.2.2.2 Key update

The key update step is important for the privacy PKI model, which analyzes the user's public key and hides the user's actual identity. Users who register to hide their actual identity will go through a key update process to generate new nicknames and new keys. Registered users prove their legitimacy by hiding the relationship between pseudonym and real name through ring signature technology. The specific process is shown in Figure 9.2.

Users registered during the upgrade phase will first generate a new key pair $PK_n = \left(pk_n, pk'_n\right)$, $SK_n = \left(sk_n, sk'_n\right)$ based on the RSA key generation algorithm. The user then issues a registration key $PK_0 = \left(pk_0, pk'_0\right)$, $SK_0 = \left(sk_0, sk'_0\right)$ ring signature to prove that the user is in fact a registered member.

The key update process will be described later.

1. Key iteration

The user first generates a random number $R_n \in \{0, 1\}^*$ s a pseudonym for the identity. Then it generates a new identity key pair $PK_n = \left(pk_n, pk'_n\right)$, $SK_n = \left(sk_n, sk'_n\right)$ according to the RSA key generation algorithm. Then, use the hardened secure ring signature scheme to perform ring signature operation on nickname R_n to obtain signature σ_{rn}.

(a) Key generation: Suppose the user is U_k $(1 \leq k \leq n)$. Set user U_k's registration code to $PK_{0,k} = \left(pk_{0,k}, pk'_{U,k}\right)$, $SK_{0,k} = \left(sk_{0,k}, sk'_{U,k}\right)$ and the module to be used to $N_{0,k}$.

(b) Key renewal: The validity period of the electronic user U_k registration key is divided into T periods. When the time enters the jth period, the user calculates:

$$sk_{0,k,j} = \left(sk_{0,k,j-1}\right)^2 \bmod \varphi \left(N_{0,k}\right) = sk_{0,k}^{2^j} \bmod \varphi \left(N_{0,k}\right)$$ (9.12)

$$sk'_{0,k,j} = \left(sk'_{0,k,j+1}\right)^2 \bmod \varphi \left(N_{0,k}\right) = \left(sk'_{0,k}\right)^{2^{T-j}} \bmod \varphi \left(N_{0,k}\right)$$ (9.13)

(c) Signature: The user U_k sets the public key set of the ring members as $L = \left\{\left(pk_{0,1}, pk'_{0,1}, N_{0,1}, H_1\right), \cdots, \left(pk_{0,n}, pk'_{0,n}, N_{0,n}, H_n\right)\right\}$. In the jth period, U_k

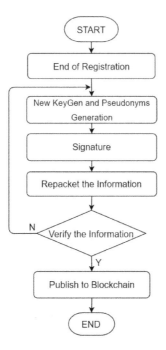

Figure 9.2   Flow chart of key update

randomly selects $r_k, r'_k \in Z^*_{N_{0,k}}$ and calculates $c_{k+1} = H_{k+1}\left(L, R_n, r_k, r'_k\right)$, where H is the anti-collision hash function $H_k: \{0, 1\}^* \to Z_{N_{0,k}}$.

For $i = k + 1, \, k + 2, \, \cdots, \, n - 1, \, n, \, 1, \, 2, \, \cdots, \, k - 1$, U_k selects the random numbers $s_i, s'_i \in Z^*_{N_{0,k}}$ and calculates

$$c_{i+1} = H_{i+1}\left(L, R_n, c_i + s_i^{\left(pk_{0,i}\right)^{2^j}} modN_{0,i}, c_i + s'_i^{\left(pk'_{0,i}\right)^{2^{T-j}}} modN_{0,i}\right) \quad (9.14)$$

where $i = n$, let $c_{i+1} = c_1$, $H_{i+1} = H_1$. Finally, U_k calculates $s_k = \left(r_k - c_k\right)^{sk_{0,k,j}} modN_{0,k}$, $s'_k = \left(r'_k - c_k\right)^{sk_{0,k,j}} modN_{0,k}$, and the signature is $\sigma_{rn} = \left(j, c_1, s_1, \cdots, s_n, s'_1, \cdots, s'_n\right)$.

2. Information collation

The user organizes and groups all relevant information into $\left(update, T_n, values = \left(PK_n = \left(pk_n, pk'_n\right), R_n, \sigma_{rn}\right)\right)$. Among them, update is the key update operation, T_n is the current timestamp, and R_n is the nickname generated this time.

3. Information verification and release

Finally, the blockchain validator verifies that the updated key was not previously stored and uses the secure ring signature verification algorithm to verify the signature and ensure the validity of the signature. After confirmation, the blockchain member sends the packet ordered in step [2] to the blockchain.

9.3 Anonymous authentication and key agreement protocols

In this section, we will review two anonymous authentication and key agreement protocols devised by different authors. Anonymous authentication and key consensus protocols based on dynamic sequences and shared secrets are mainly deployed to guarantee user access to the sensor. It then introduces a D-H-based key consensus protocol that implements two-factor authentication and key consensus in a multi-server architecture.

9.3.1 Dynamic sequence and shared secret-based anonymous identity authentication and key agreement protocol

This section first introduces the authentication model and the entire authentication process. Subsequently, five stages of the dynamic sequence and shared secret-based anonymous identity authentication and key agreement (DSAKA) protocol by Yu *et al.* have been proposed. Overview of network initialization, registration, identity pre-authentication, anonymous authentication, and key agreement and password update is provided. The performance analysis shows that the DSAKA protocol meets the more secure requirements of WSN.

9.3.1.1 Authentication model

The DSAKA protocol was proposed by Yu *et al.* There are three communication units: user, gateway, and sensor node. If the user wants to access the WSN, all three first verify the validity of the ID. The complete authentication process is divided into four steps, as shown in Figure 9.3.

Step 1 The user sends an access request to the gateway, which validates the user identity.

Step 2 If the validation passes, the gateway sends its identity credentials to the target sensor node. Similarly, the sensor node authenticates the gateway's ID.

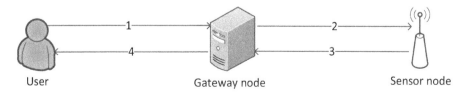

User   Gateway node   Sensor node

Figure 9.3   Authentication model

Step 3 If the validation is successful, the sensor node calculates the session key and sends the corresponding credentials to the gateway. After the gateway receives the session key, it also checks the sensor's ID.

Step 4 If the authentication is successful, the gateway sends the credentials to the user. When the user receives the session key, the gateway's ID is verified.

The session will be terminated if one party fails in the authentication. Finally, the three parties authenticate each other and receive the session key.

9.3.1.2   The DSAKA protocol

1. Network setup

Complete the following initialization steps before deploying wireless sensors, gateways, sensor nodes, and smart cards.

①Administrators store some basic operations such as hashing, XOR, join operations, and random number generators in the memory of smart card SC, gateway node GWN, and sensor node N_j. The administrator then chooses identity ID and random number R_{SC} and stores $\{ID_{SC}, R_{SC}\}$ to GWN's authentication table and SC's memory, making it a legitimate smart card. The administrator then assigns a valid smart card to the user requesting registration.

②The gateway node GWN stores the master key X in a secret, assigns an identity ID_j to the sensor node N_j, and computes the shared secret value $SV_j = h\left(ID_{N_j} \| X\right)$ shared with N_j. Before placing the sensor node N_j in the monitoring area, GWN stores $\{ID_j, SV_j\}$ in the repository table and N_j's authentication table to make it a legitimate sensor node.

2. Registration

At this point, the new user can register to the gateway node. First, the user selects a username and password to generate a registration request and send the request to the gateway. The gateway then generates the user's identity attribute and stores it in the authentication table. Finally, the user saves the ID attribute on the smart card. The specific flow of this step is shown in Figure 9.4.

3. Pre-authentication

If the user tries to access the WSN at this stage, the smart card first verifies the legitimacy of the user. That is, if the ID and password entered by the user are verified successfully, the smart card will generate a login request S_1 for the user. Then send a login request S_1 to the gateway. At this point, the smart card pre-authentication function reduces the communication and computational load between the user and the gateway. The specific flow of this step is shown in Figure 9.5.

4. Anonymous authentication and key agreement

So far, the DSAKA protocol completes anonymous authentication and key negotiation. Specifically, the DSAKA protocol performs two-way authentication and key negotiation among users, gateways, and sensors based on dynamic sequences, shared keys, and dynamic random numbers. Negotiated keys ensure the secure transmission of data over public channels in the future. The specific flow of this step will be described in detail below, as shown in Figure 9.5.

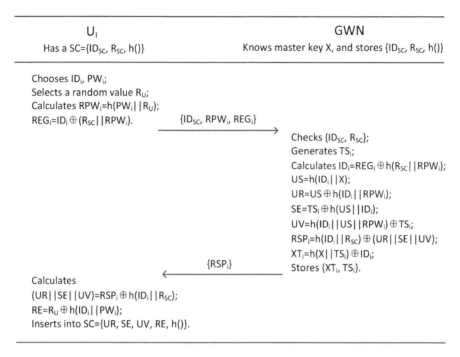

$$Figure\ 9.4\quad User\ registration\ phase$$

① After the gateway GWN receives the login request S_1, it verifies the legitimacy of the user U_i. If authentication is successful, its authentication information S_2 is computed by GWN and sent to the target sensor node N_j.

② After receiving the authentication information S_2, the target sensor node N_j verifies the GWN's legitimacy of the gateway. If the authentication is successful, its session key and authentication information S_3 are calculated by N_j. Then, N_j sends S_3 to GWN.

③ After the gateway GWN receives the authentication information S_3 from the target sensor node N_j, it calculates the session key to verify the legitimacy of the target sensor node N_j. If authentication is successful, its identity authentication information S_4 is calculated by GWN and sends it to the user U_i.

④ After the user U_i receives the authentication information S_4, the session key is calculated to authenticate the validity of the GWN gateway. After successful authentication, legitimate users U_i can log in to the WSN to obtain the required data. Session keys are used to encrypt sensitive data to ensure the confidentiality of communications.

5. Password update

The user's password belongs only to him, but there is always a risk of losing it. Therefore, users need to change their passwords frequently. The password update step is only performed on the user's terminal device and does not require communication between the user and the gateway. Therefore, this step provides the user with

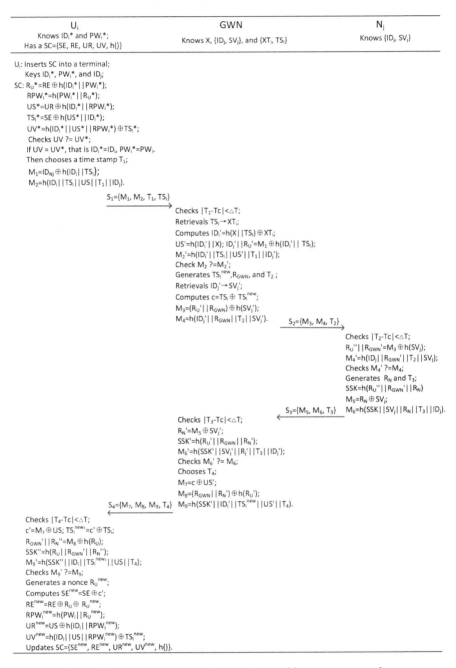

Figure 9.5　Anonymous authentication and key agreement phase

U_i
Knows ID_i* and PW_i*;
Has a SC={RE, UR, SE, UV, h()}

User: Inserts SC into a terminal;
Inputs ID_i* and PW_i*.

SC: $R_U*=RE \oplus h(ID_i*||PW_i*)$;
$RPW_i*=h(PW_i*||R_U*)$;
$US*=UR \oplus h(ID_i*||RPW_i*)$;
$TS_i*=SE \oplus h(US*||ID_i*)$;
$UV*=h(ID_i*||US*||RPW_i*) \oplus TS_i*$;
Checks $UV* ?= UV$.

User: Inputs new password PW_i^{new}.

SC: $RPW_i^{new}=h(PW_i^{new}||R_U*)$;
$UR^{new}=US \oplus h(ID_i*||RPW_i^{new})$;
$RE^{new}=R_U* \oplus h(ID_i*||PW_i^{new})$;
$UV^{new}=h(ID_i*||US||RPW_i^{new}) \oplus TS_i*$;
Repaces RE with RE^{new};
Repaces UR with UR^{new};
Repaces UV with UV^{new}.

Figure 9.6   Password update phase

a convenient password update task. The specific process will be described in detail below, as shown in Figure 9.6.

① The user U_i inserts the smart card SC into the card reader and inputs his identity ID_i and password PW_i.

② The user U_i inputs the new password PW_i^{new} if the smart card SC successfully authenticates U_i. Then, SC updates the corresponding parameters as $\{SE, RE^{new}, UR^{new}, UV^{new}, h()\}$.

9.3.1.3   Performance analysis

1. Users' anonymity and untraceability

User's anonymity means that the user's true identity is hidden from the attacker's knowledge. The DSAKA protocol uses a one-way hash function to mask the actual identity ID_i of the user in the login request $\{M_1, M_2, T_1, TS_i\}$. After the request is received, the authentication table is used for the GWN that calculates $ID_i = TS_i \oplus XT_i$ for obtaining ID_i through searching TS_i. Because the attacker does not know the primary key X of GWN, it intercepts the TS_i public channel broadcasts that the attacker cannot calculate ID_i. Therefore, in our contract, the user is anonymous.

User untraceability means that an attacker cannot track a user across different sessions through communication messages sent over a common channel. Because each user randomly accesses the gateway and new users register with the gateway, there is no connection between the dynamic sequence TS_i used in this session and TSine used in the next session. Also, since the user uses a different random number R_U for each session, the communication message $\{M_1, M_2, T_1, TS_i\}$ is different. Therefore, users cannot be traced to Yu's protocol.

2. Anonymity of sensor nodes

In the DSAKA protocol, the real ID ID_j of sensor node N_j is not explicitly present in any communication message, so an attacker cannot get sensor ID_j directly based on the communication message on the public channel. Furthermore, the opponent does not know US or the user's true identity ID_i and cannot calculate $(ID_j \| R_U) = M \oplus h(US \| ID_i \| TS_i)$. Therefore, in Yu's protocol, the sensor node is anonymous.

3. Front safety and rear safety

In the DSAKA protocol, the session key is $SSK = h(R_U \| R_{GWN} \| R_N)$. Here, R_U, R_{GWN}, and R_N are random numbers generated by U_i, GWN, and N_j, respectively. Since the session key does not depend on the GWN's X root key, disclosing this secret may be detrimental to the attacker in generating the session key and SV_j secret value shared by GWN and N_j. Even if an attacker obtains the session key of the current session, the nonce used in each session is new, so there is no way to guess the session key of the previous or next session. So Yu's protocol provides forward/reverse security.

4. Resist replay attacks

A replication attack is the point where an attacker becomes a legitimate user by sending an intercepted message to the recipient. In this protocol, after receiving a message, the user, gateway, and sensor nodes first validate the timestamp. If the timestamp is invalid, authentication is terminated. Suppose your opponent replaced T_1 in $\{M_1, M_2, T_1, TS_i\}$ with T_A, where T_A is the current timestamp. Obviously, T_A passes the freshness test, but T_1 is used to calculate $M_2 = h(ID_i \| TS_i \| US \| T_1 \| ID_j)$, so the regeneration fails. Therefore, the calculated M_2 differs from M_2 because T_A is used in the calculation of $M_2 = h(ID_i \| TS_i \| US \| T_A \| ID_j)$. For the same reason, an attacker cannot play $\{M_3, M_4, T_2\}$, $\{M_5, M_6, T_3\}$, and $\{M_7, M_8, M_9, T_4\}$ messages. Therefore, the DSAKA protocol can resist replay attacks.

5. Protect yourself from stolen smart card attacks

A smart card is a kind of anti-counterfeiting and anti-counterfeiting hardware. Legitimate smart card users are at risk of being lost or stolen. If an attacker obtains a legitimate user's smart card, they can obtain settings stored on the smart card. In the DSAKA protocol, smart cards contain $\{RE, UR, SE, UV, h()\}$, where $RE = R_U \oplus h(ID_i \| PW_i)$, $UR = US \oplus h(ID_i \| RPW_i)$, $RPW_i = h(PW_i \| R_U)$, $SE = TS_i \oplus h(US \| ID_i)$, $UV = h(ID_i \| US \| RPW_i) \oplus TS_i$, and $US = h(ID_i \| X)$. In the case of RE, the attacker cannot get the R_U because he does not know the user's ID_i and PW_i. In the case of UR, it is difficult for an attacker to calculate the RPW_i without knowing the PW_i and the R_U. Thus, the enemy cannot recover the US via $UR \oplus h(ID_i \| RPW_i)$. For SE and UV, following a one-way hash function, TS_i is exposed to the channel, but the attacker has no information of $h(US \| ID_i)$ and $h(ID_i \| US \| RPW_i)$. Also, the enemy cannot count

US because X is only secretly known by the GWN. Therefore, there are no smart card theft attacks in the DSAKA protocol.

6. Resist spoofing attacks

Spoofing attacks refer to attackers acting as legitimate users, gateways, or sensor nodes by exploiting the information contained in smart cards and intercepted communication messages over public channels. In the DSAKA protocol, US, ID_i, ID_j, and R_U are the parameters required to generate an access request $\{M_1, M_2, T_1, TS_i\}$. According to the user's anonymity, an attacker cannot obtain ID_i and US through access requests without knowing the master key X. So, the attacker calculates $\left(ID_{N_j}\|R\right) = M_1 \oplus h\left(US\|ID_i\|TS_i\right)$ without knowing R_U, ID_j, ID_i, and US. According to the protocol, even if an attacker has a legitimate user's smart card, the opponent cannot obtain ID_i and PW_i. Thus, Yu's protocol prevents an attacker from becoming a user.

The master key X of GWN and the secret value SV_j shared between GWN and N_j are the information needed to create a communication message. Because they do not know X and SV_j, attackers cannot be gateways and sensor nodes.

7. Protect yourself from offline password-guessing attacks

Offline password-guessing attacks occur when an attacker can gain access to a gateway by guessing the password of a legitimate user. An attacker could use an access request sent by a user or data stored on a smart card to guess a user's password. In Yu's protocol, access request $\{M_1, M_2, T_1, TS_i\}$ does not contain password information, so an attacker cannot guess the user's password this way. If an attacker obtains a smart card from a legitimate user U_i and guesses U_i's ID $\in \{0, 1\}^n$ and password PW $\in \{0, 1\}^n$, then the probability of ID $= ID_i$ and PW $= PW_i$ is $1/(2)^{2n}$, but negligible. Therefore, this protocol can prevent offline password guessing attacks.

8. Resistance to insider attacks

An insider attack means that an insider uses properties obtained by an insider to obtain the identity or password of a legitimate user. In the user registration phase, user U_i sends $\{ID_{SC}, RPW_i, REG_i\}$ to GWN instead of sending ID_i and PW_i directly. Because of the irreversibility of $h()$ and randomness of R_U, GWN insiders cannot get ID_i and PW_i of U_i, so the protocol is resistant to insider attacks.

9.3.2 D-H-based key-sharing protocol

In this section, a D-H-based key-sharing protocol is designed and anonymously generates session keys between users and big data servers. Only after obtaining the session key can the two communicate privately.

9.3.2.1 Network model

A two-way authentication protocol in a multi-server architecture typically has three parts [21, 22]: mobile users, big data servers, and registration servers (that is, trusted

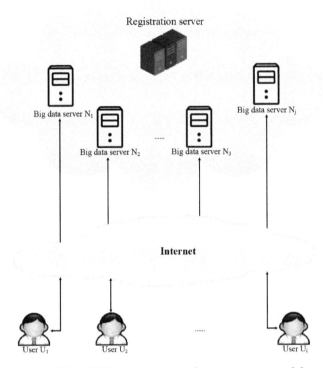

Figure 9.7   Multi-server network environment model

third parties). Generally speaking, the registration server needs to complete the initial settings of the system, be responsible for the registration of mobile users and big data servers when they enter the system and distribute secret information related to the registrant when the registration is completed [23]. When a registered mobile user wants to access the big data server in the system and obtain its network service, it needs to authenticate each other with the big data server and establish a session key between the two to ensure the security of the future network communication between the two [24]. The multi-server network environment model is shown in Figure 9.7.

The entities are divided into three parts, which are described as follows:

1. Registration server

The registration server is a trusted third party on the system and has the highest system privileges. It is responsible for generating the public key of the system and the settings of the public system and generating the private key of mobile users and big data servers.

2. User

Users acquire network services by uploading and downloading data to big data servers through their devices. Each user has a smart card to store the public parameters of the system and related authentication parameters. After the smart card and

Table 9.1   Symbols and their meanings

Symbol	Meaning
U_i	User i
N_j	Big data server j
ID_{U_i}	User U_i's identity
ID_{N_j}	Big data server N_j's identity
pw_{U_i}	User U_i's password
d_{U_i}	User U_i's private key
d_{N_j}	Big data server N_j's private key
e_{U_i}	User U_i's private key expiration time
G_1	Additive cyclic group
G_2	Multiplicative cyclic group
q	Order of group G_1, G_2
P	The identity element of group G_1 and $P \in G_1$
e	Bilinear mapping operation
g	The identity element of group G_2 and $g = e(P, P) \in G_2$
r_r, r_{U_i}, r_{N_j}	Random number and $\forall r_r, r_{U_i}, r_{N_j} \in Z_q^*$
$H_i \left(i \in \{1, 2, 3, 4\} \right)$	Hash function
P_{pub}	System public key and $P_{pub} = sP \in G_1$
b_{U_i}	User U_i's biological information (fingerprint, iris, facial information, etc.)
σ_{U_i}	User U_i's biological key
θ_{U_i}	User U_i's biometric key generation parameters

the device are successfully verified, the device controls the smart card to accumulate the user's private data. Suppose you have an I user on your system.

3. Big data server

A big data server is a cluster of servers under a multi-server architecture. We can communicate with you to provide services to you: upload of user data, download of user data, and acquisition of corresponding data. Assume you have a J user on your system.

Table 9.1 shows the symbols in the system and their meanings.

9.3.2.2   Initialization

During the system initialization phase, the registration server generates initialization parameters for subsequent registration and key negotiation phases.

The recording server runs a build function $Gen(1^n)$ that receives a security parameter $n \in Z^+$, and the output parameters and process are as follows.

1. Select a bilinear map

The registrar selects the traversal groups G^1 and G_2 of the first q, P is the generator of G_1 and $g = \hat{e}(p, p) \in G_2$, and $\hat{e} : G_1 \times G_1 \to G_2$ is the bilinear map.

2. Generate a system master key and a system public key

The log server generates a random number $s(\forall s \in Z_q^*)$ with the system primary key and computes the system public key $P_{pub} = sP \in G_1$.

3. Choose a cryptographic hash function

The registrar selects cryptographic hash functions $H_1 : \{0, 1\}^* \to Z_q^*, H_2 : G_2 \to Z_q^*$, $H_2 : \{0, 1\}^* \to G_1, H_4 : \{0, 1\}^* \to \{0, 1\}^n$,,,.

4. User registration

The registration server calculates the private key $d_{U_i} = \frac{1}{s + H_1(ID_{U_i} \| e_{U_i})}$ of the user, where $e_{U_i}(e_{U_i} \in \{o, 1\}^n)$ is the expiration date of user U_i's private key. The registrar transmits to U_i through a secure channel.

5. Big data server logs

The big data server N_j picks a random number $r_{N_j}(\forall r_{N_j} \in Z_q^*)$, computes $g_{N_j}^2 = g^{r_{N_j}}.N_j$, and sends the intermediate parameter $g_{N_j}^2$ to the registration server through a secure channel.

The registration server computes the private key $d_{N_j} = \frac{1}{s + H_1(ID_{N_j})}.P$ of the big data server N_j and sends it to N_j over a secure channel.

6. Publish parameter list to system

The recording server exposes the following system parameters: $\{G_1, G_2, q, \hat{e}, P, P_{pub}, g, H_1, H_2, H_3, H_4, g_N^2\}$.

9.3.2.3 Key agreement protocol based on D-H

In this section, the D-H-based key sharing protocol is designed to enable key sharing between users and big data servers as part of a multi-service architecture. The specific process is as follows.

1. User U_i computes session key sk_{U-N}

User U_i chooses a random number $r_{U_i}(\forall r_{U_i} \in Z_q^*)$ to calculate $sk_{U_i-N_j} = H_2\left((g_{N_j}^2)^{r_{U_i}}\right)$.

2. User U_i sends a request to big data server N_i

User U_i uses the system public key P_{pub} to compute the big data server identity ciphertext $N_j : C_{U_i-N_j} = r_{U_i}.(H_1(ID_{N_j}).P + P_{pub})$ and calculates the intermediate parameter $F_{U_i} = (ID_U \| e_U) \oplus H_2(g_U^1)$. Users use $C_{U_i-N_j}$ and F_{U_i} to send key contract requests and data servers through big data servers and public channels.

3. Big data server N_j computes session key sk_{U-N}

When the big data server N_j receives $\{C_{U_i-N_j, F_{U_i}}\}$, it calculates the equation $g_{U_i}^1 = g^{r_{U_i}} = \hat{e}(C_{U_i-N_j}, d_{N_j})$ using the secret key d_{N_j} to get $g_{U_i}^1$. Big data server N_j computes $F_{U_i} \oplus H_2(g_{U_i}^1)$ to get user's ID_{U_i}.

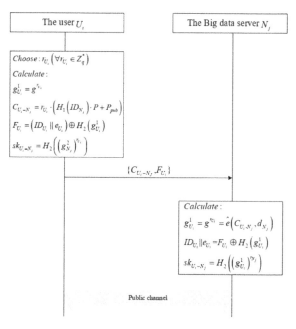

Figure 9.8   The key agreement protocol

Big data server N_j uses a random number r_{N_j} to compute a session key $sk_{U_i-N_j} = H_2((g_{U_i}^1)^{r_{N_j}})$, where r_{N_j} is created during the registration phase of the big data server.

Both parties communicating via the above process obtain a session key $sk_{U_i-N_j}$. The process of the key agreement protocol is shown in Figure 9.8.

9.4   Trust-based secure directed diffusion routing protocol

Given the unreliability of sensor nodes and the security risks of data transmission from the source node to the gateway in the original directed diffusion routing protocol, Yu *et al.* design trust-based secure direct spread routing protocol (TSDDR) to establish a trusted route and ensure secure transmission along the route.

9.4.1   Energy trust model

This represents a method to comprehensively evaluate the direct trust and residual energy of a node. Considering the direct trust and the normalized energy of the node, the energy trust is obtained by weighted summation. The TSDDR protocol selects relay nodes based on energy trust in the pass gain stage and ultimately obtains a path composed of high-energy trust nodes.

Suppose that *n* sensor nodes are deployed after network initialization. Each sensor node maintains a neighbor node list that stores the neighbor's ID, forward confidence, residual energy, normalized energy, and energy confidence. The initial forward confidence of each node in the adjacent node is set to 0.5, and the initial energy is E_0.

Definition 1: Direct trust (DT)

TSDDR protocol uses the simplified beta trust model to calculate the direct trust. In period t, it is assumed that node N_i actively communicates with node N_j for a total of $\alpha + \beta$ times, of which successful interactions are α and unsuccessful interactions are β. The direct trust from N_i to N_j is defined as:

$$\mathrm{DT}_{ij}(t) = \frac{\alpha + 1}{\alpha + \beta + 2} \left(1 - \frac{\beta}{W}\right) \left(1 - \frac{1}{\alpha + \delta}\right) \tag{9.15}$$

where $\left(1 - \beta/W\right)$ is the penalty function and W is the total number of communications between nodes N_i and N_j. $\left(1 - 1/\left(\alpha + \delta\right)\right)$ is the adjustment function. where δ is a positive constant to bring the velocity close to 1 [25].

Definition 2: Normalized energy (NE)

The normalized energy NE is the ratio of the remaining energy RE_t of the node in the current period t to the initial energy E_0. The closer $\mathrm{NE} \in [0, 1]$ and NE are to 1, the more energy is left in the node. NE will be updated with changes to direct trust DT and remaining energy RE. That is, in the current period t, node N_i computes the normalized energy of node N_j:

$$\mathrm{NE}_{ij}(t) = \frac{\mathrm{RE}_t}{E_0} \tag{9.16}$$

Definition 3: Energy trust (ET)

Energy trust takes into account the node's direct trust DT and normalized energy NE and obtains an overall trust value based on the remaining energy with a weight that reflects the overall reliability and reliability of the node. In the current time period t, the energy Trust of node N_i to node N_j is defined as:

$$\mathrm{ET}_{ij}(t) = \lambda \mathrm{DT}_{ij}(t) + \lambda_2 \mathrm{NE}_{ij}(t) \tag{9.17}$$

where λ_1 and λ_2 are weight factors and $\lambda_1 + \lambda_2 = 1$. Energy trust ET regularly updates DT and NE. Each node regularly updates its neighbor list.

9.4.2   The TSDDR protocol

TSDDR protocol includes four phases: private key distribution, propagation of interest and establishment of gradients, enhancement of paths, and propagation of data. In this section, the energy trust model is introduced into the path reinforcement phase of the TSDDR protocol by selecting the nodes with higher energy trust as the relay nodes, thereby establishing a reliable path. To realize the confidential transmission of sensitive data, Yu *et al.* propose a key distribution method based on D-H protocol and apply it to the path reinforcement phase of the TSDDR protocol to realize the key distribution between gateway and relay nodes.

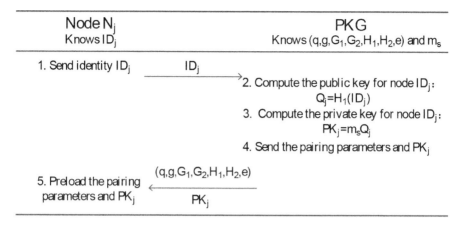

Figure 9.9   Private key distribution process

9.4.2.1   Private key distribution phase

At this point, the trusted private key generation (PKG) center uses identity-based encryption (IBE) to assign a private key to each node [27]. It is used in the data distribution phase to compute random private and shared keys of nodes.

PKG selects two cyclic groups of primary q, G_1 and G_2. Here, G_1 is an additive traversal group, and G_2 is a multiplicative traversal group generated by g. PKG determines the bilinear couple $e: G_1 \times G_1 \to G_2$ and chooses two hash functions H_1 and H_2. $H_1: \{0, 1\} \to G_1$ maps the user's ID to G_1 and $H_2: G_2 \to \{0, 1\}^n$ and the element in G_2 to plain text space $\{0, 1\}^n$. The PKG chooses a random value $m_s \in Z_q$ as the system master key. As shown in Figure 9.9, node N_j sends its ID_j to the PKG. Accordingly, the PKG calculates the public key $Q_j = H_1(ID_j)$ and the private key $PK_j = m_s Q_j$ of the node N_j and sends the system parameters $(q, g, G_1, G_2, H_1, H_2, e)$ and the private key PK_j to N_j.

9.4.2.2   Interest propagation and gradient establishment phase

After the private key distribution phase, each node is loaded with system settings and a private key. In the interest propagation phase, users diffuse their interested query tasks through the gateway. The gateway node generates the interest packet according to the user's query task and spreads to the whole network. Interest package is represented by $<$ Interest, ID, Loc $>$, where Interest denotes the interest message, ID represents the node's identity, and Loc denotes the node's current location.

Each sensor node stores an interest list locally. When a node receives an interest packet from a neighbor node, it establishes a gradient in the interest list. Interest diffusion and gradient building are carried out at the same time, and the end of interest diffusion means finding the source node. The source node then floods the detection data to the gateway based on the set gradient information.

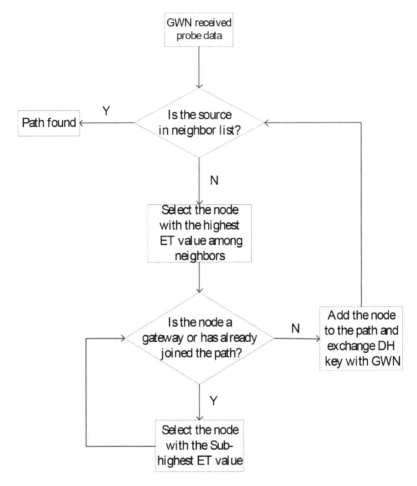

Figure 9.10   Path reinforcement process

9.4.2.3 Path reinforcement phase

In the route hardening phase, in addition to hardening route establishment, D-H key exchange is performed between the gateway and relay nodes in the route. At this point, the energy trust is used as a hardening mechanism to select the relay node. The higher the energy reliability of a node, the higher the reliability of the node. As shown in Figure 9.10, after the gateway receives sensing data from multiple paths, it begins to strengthen one of the paths based on the energy confidence value. If the path consists of a set of trusted nodes, data transfer is more reliable and reliable. As shown in Figure 9.11, whenever a new relay node joins the path, the gateway computes a D-H key using a secure key distribution method based on the D-H protocol.

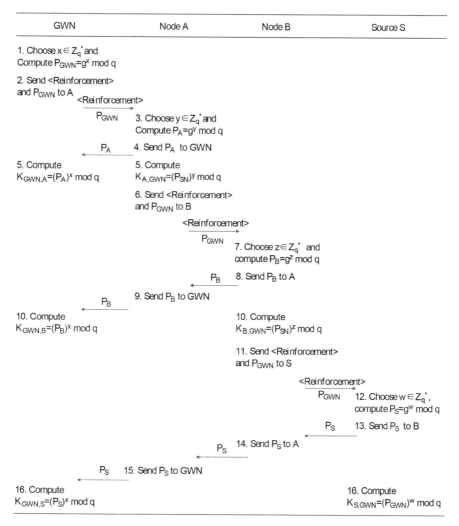

Figure 9.11   The D-H key exchange process

9.4.2.4   Data propagation phase

During the data distribution phase, encryption technology is used to encrypt and decrypt sensitive data, enabling the transmission of sensitive data over open channels and ensuring end-to-end data security. This procedure involves three encryption keys: the session key negotiated between the user and the target sensor node in the identity authentication process, the D-H key negotiated between the gateway and each relay node in route propagation, and the generated shared key. Through bilinear mapping between adjacent relay nodes. First, the source node (namely, the target sensor node) uses the session key to encrypt the original data. Every time the encrypted data passes a hop node on the path, the node uses the D-H key to

GWN	Node A	Node B	Source S
Knows Q_{GWN}, PK_{GWN}	Knows Q_A, PK_A	Knows Q_B, PK_B	Knows Q_S, PK_S

GWN	Node A	Node B	Source S
1. Compute: $SK_{GWN,A}=e(PN_A,PK_{GWN})$ $=e(n_3Q_A,m_sQ_{GWN})$ $=e(Q_A,Q_{GWN})^{n3ms}$	1. Compute $Q_{GWN}=H_1(ID_{GWN})$	1. Compute $Q_A=H_1(ID_A)$	1. Compute $Q_B=H_1(ID_B)$
2. Decrypt c_6: $c_5=H_2(SK_{GWN,A})\oplus c_6$	2. Select $n_3\in Z_q^*$, Compute $PN_A=n_3Q_A$ and $RK_A=n_3PK_A$	2. Select $n_2\in Z_q^*$, Compute $PN_B=n_2Q_B$ and $RK_B=n_2PK_B$	2. Select $n_1\in Z_q^*$; Compute $PN_S=n_1Q_S$ and $RK_S=n_1PK_S$
3. Decrypt c_5: $c_3=H_2(K_{GWN,A})\oplus c_5$	3. Compute shared key $SK_{A,GWN}=e(RK_A,Q_{GWN})$ $=e(n_3PK_A,Q_{GWN})$ $=e(n_3m_sQ_A,Q_{GWN})$ $=e(Q_A,Q_{GWN})^{n3ms}$	3. Compute shared key $SK_{B,A}=e(RK_B,Q_A)$ $=e(n_2PK_B,Q_A)$ $=e(n_2m_sQ_B,Q_A)$ $=e(Q_B,Q_A)^{n2ms}$	3. Compute shared key $SK_{S,B}=e(RK_S,Q_B)$ $=e(n_1PK_S,Q_B)$ $=e(n_1m_sQ_S,Q_B)$ $=e(Q_S,Q_B)^{n1ms}$
4. Decrypt c_3: $c_1=H_2(K_{GWN,B})\oplus c_3$	4. Compute: $SK_{A,B}=e(PN_B,PK_A)$ $=e(n_2Q_B,m_sQ_A)$ $=e(Q_B,Q_A)^{n2ms}$	4. Compute: $SK_{B,S}=e(PN_S,PK_B)$ $=e(n_1Q_S,m_sQ_B)$ $=e(Q_S,Q_B)^{n1ms}$	4. Encrypt m: $m'=SSK\oplus m$
5. Decrypt c_1: $m'=H_2(K_{GWN,S})\oplus c_1$	5. Decrypt c_4: $c_3=H_2(SK_{A,B})\oplus c_4$	5. Decrypt c_2: $c_1=H_2(SK_{B,S})\oplus c_2$	5. Encrypt m': $c_1=H_2(K_{S,GWN})\oplus m'$
	6. Encrypt c_3: $c_5=H_2(K_{A,GWN})\oplus c_3$	6. Encrypt c_1: $c_3=H_2(K_{B,SN})\oplus c_1$	6. Encrypt c_1: $c_2=H_2(SK_{S,B})\oplus c_1$
	7. Encrypt c_5: $c_6=H_2(SK_{A,GWN})\oplus c_5$	7. Encrypt c_3: $c_4=H_2(SK_{B,A})\oplus c_3$	
	$\{PN_A,c_6\}$	$\{PN_B,c_4\}$	$\{PN_S,c_2\}$

Figure 9.12   The data propagation process

encrypt the ciphertext. To prevent the man-in-the-middle (MITM) attack, the adjacent relay nodes use the shared key to encrypt the ciphertext. When the data arrive at the gateway, the gateway only obtains one layer of ciphertext after decrypting multiple layers. Finally, the gateway transmits the ciphertext to the user, who decrypts the ciphertext with the session key. To protect privacy and realize anonymous communication between adjacent nodes, relay nodes use a pseudonym to transmit data. The data propagation process is shown in Figure 9.12, it is assumed that the path propagation phase is $S \rightarrow B \rightarrow A \rightarrow GWN$.

9.4.3   Performance analysis

9.4.3.1   Anonymous communication

During data propagation, each relay node in the data path creates a new pseudonym to ensure anonymous communication. For example, to analyze a security target, relay node A on the data path uses a $PN_A = n_3Q_A = n_3H_1(ID_A)$ to generate a random alias, where $n_3 \in Z_q$ is a random integer, $H_1():\{0,1\} \rightarrow G_1$ is a one-way hash function, and G_1 is a cyclic group of prime numbers. Therefore, the alias $PN_A \in G_1$ completely hides the actual ID_A information of node A. In addition, if node A acts as a relay node for multiple paths, node A only knows the alias of the predecessor node and cannot tell exactly which one it is. This means that relay nodes on the data path only recognize the next hop and cannot identify the previous hop, further enabling anonymous communication between the nodes.

9.4.3.2   End-to-end data security

As described in the data streaming step, the source node provides end-to-end data security by encrypting the data in plaintext. First, the innermost layer of the ciphertext is encrypted by the session key negotiated in the process of identity authentication, which is owned only by the source node, gateway, and user. Therefore, only the gateway and the user can decrypt the original plaintext, and other relay nodes on the path cannot decrypt it. Second, in addition to the source node using the session key to ensure data security, each relay node on the path also uses the D-H key negotiated with the gateway to encrypt the ciphertext, which is only owned by the gateway and the corresponding relay node. Other relay nodes cannot decrypt it except the gateway, thus improving the data privacy. Finally, bilinear mapping [28] is used to calculate the shared key between adjacent nodes on the path to generate the outermost layer of the ciphertext, which is owned only by adjacent nodes. Therefore, only the immediate successor of the current node can decrypt the ciphertext, and other malicious nodes cannot decrypt it. Therefore, the TSDDR protocol can provide end-to-end data security.

9.4.3.3   No impersonation

This section analyzes spoofing attacks with examples. In this example, consider attacker Adv with ID_{Adv}, public key Q_{Adv}, and private key $PK_{Adv} = m_s Q_{Adv}$. Suppose Adv wants to pretend to be a legitimate node like relay node B on data path $S \rightarrow B \rightarrow A \rightarrow GWN$. Adv gets alias PN_S from source node S and public key Q_B from node B. If Adv decrypts the outermost ciphertext sent by S, the attacker must compute the key $SK_{B,S} = e\left(PN_S, Q_B\right)^{m_s}$ shared between B and S. However, Adv cannot get the shared secret $SK_{B,S}$ because Adv does not know m_s, which only the PKG knows. Also, if A wants to decrypt m_s from $PK_{Adv} = m_s Q_{Adv}$, it's a DL problem [26]. Therefore, no other nodes can be simulated.

9.4.3.4   Defending against MITM attack

In this section, an example is used to analyze the MITM attack. This example examines a malicious Adv node that attempts to launch an MITM attack between the gateway and any legitimate node (say node A) in the data path $S \rightarrow B \rightarrow A \rightarrow GWN$. In this case, suppose a malicious node is able to eavesdrop on the D-H public keys of node A and GWN. In addition, the malicious node computes its D-H public key P_{Adv} and sends it to GWN and A. Two D-H session keys $K_{A\leftrightarrow Adv}$ and $K_{GWN\leftrightarrow Adv}$ belonging to $(A \leftrightarrow Adv)$ and $(Adv \leftrightarrow GWN)$, respectively, can then be computed. However, the plaintext is layer-wise encrypted by each node on the data path and the outermost layer of encryption is calculated using the shared key. As shown in the previous section, the shared key is not available to the malicious node. As a result, the malicious node cannot decrypt the encrypted text and the MITM attack is effectively prevented.

9.5 Lightweight anonymous communication model

This section introduces an anonymous IBE algorithm proposed by Wang *et al*. It is applied to the encryption and decryption of messages in the anonymous communication model, and the idea of the bulletin board and group management is applied to the lightweight anonymous communication model.

9.5.1 Anonymous IBE program

The anonymous IBE program is highly scalable in terms of cipher text and does not require certificate management. In a lightweight noticeboard-based anonymous communication model, the advanced anonymous IBE scheme effectively ensures that no identifiable information about the recipient in the cipher text is compromised with ANON-IND-ID-CCA security. In this section, we review an efficient anonymous IBE scheme designed by Wang *et al*., whose scheme has shorter cipher text, reduces the use of random numbers, and improves communication costs while maintaining the same level of security. Then the proof of correctness and security is given.

9.5.1.1 Construction
Let G_1 and G_2 be multiplicative cyclic groups of prime order p and g be a generator of G_1, $e: G_1 \times G_1 \rightarrow G_2$ is the bilinear map.

> **Setup** Select a random number $\alpha \in Z_p^*$ and set $g_1 = g^\alpha$, $g_2 \in G_1$ to generate security parameters. The public parameters *params* and the secret master key *msk* are given by
>
> $$params = (g, g_1, g_2); \quad master - key = \alpha \qquad (9.18)$$

> **Key generation** Give a random number $r \in Z_p^*$, the master secret key *msk* and an identity $ID \in Z_p^*$, and the private key is:
>
> $$d_{ID} = (d_1, d_2) = \left(g_2^\alpha g_1^{ID \cdot r}, g^{-r}\right) \qquad (9.19)$$

> **Encryption** Give a message $m \in G_2$ and use public key $ID \in Z_p^*$ to encrypt the message. Give a random number $t \in Z_p^*$ and compute as follows:

$$C = (C_1, C_2, C_3) = (\hat{e}(g, g_2)^{\alpha t} \cdot m, g^t, g_1^{ID \cdot t}) \tag{9.20}$$

Decryption: Decrypt the ciphertext $C = (C_1, C_2, C_3)$ using private key $d_{ID} = (d_1, d_2)$ and output

$$m = C_1 \cdot \frac{1}{\hat{e}(C_2, d_1)\,\hat{e}(d_2, C_3)} \tag{9.21}$$

9.5.1.2 Proof of correctness

If C is a valid ciphertext with message m encrypted with the identity ID, it can be verified by the following expression:

$$\hat{e}(C_2, d_1)\hat{e}(d_2, C_3)$$
$$= \hat{e}(g^t, g_2^\alpha g_1^{ID \cdot r})\hat{e}(g^{-r}, g_1^{ID \cdot t})$$
$$= \hat{e}(g^t, g_2^\alpha)\hat{e}(g^t, g_1^{ID \cdot r})\hat{e}(g^{-r}, g_1^{ID \cdot t})$$
$$= \hat{e}(g^t, g_2^\alpha)\hat{e}(g^r, g_1^{ID \cdot t})\hat{e}(g^{-r}, g_1^{ID \cdot t})$$
$$= \hat{e}(g^t, g_2^\alpha)$$
$$= \hat{e}(g, g_2)^{\alpha t}$$

So, $m = C_1 \cdot \frac{1}{\hat{e}(C_2, d_1)\hat{e}(d_2, C_3)}$

9.5.1.3 Proof of security

Theorem 1: Assuming that the decision bilinear D-H problem is hard, the proposed anonymous IBE scheme is (t, q, ε)-ANON-IND-ID-CCA secure.

Proof: Assume A is an ANON-IND-ID-CCA adversary and B is a challenger. At the beginning of the game, B is given a tuple $(g, g^\alpha, g^b, g^c, T) \in G_1^5$ to decide whether or not $T = e(g, g)^{\alpha bc}$.

Setup: B randomly generates security parameters. Let $g_1 = g^\alpha, g_2 = g^b$, the public parameters (g, g_1, g_2) are assigned to A.

Phase 1:

Key generation query: User A assigns identity $ID \in Z_p^*$ to user B. B randomly chooses $r \in Z_p^*$ and gets

$$d = (d_1, d_2) = \left(g_1^{rID}, g^{-r} g_2^{\frac{1}{ID}} \right) \tag{9.22}$$

Let $r' = r - \frac{b}{ID}$ be a valid private key, and

$$d_1 = g_1^{rID} = g_2^\alpha g_1^{-b} g_1^{rID} = g_2^\alpha g_1^{rID-b} = g_2^\alpha g_1^{ID\left(r-\frac{b}{ID}\right)} = g_2^\alpha g_1^{r'ID} \tag{9.23}$$

$$d_2 = g^{-r}g_2^{\frac{1}{ID}} = g^{-\left(r-\frac{b}{ID}\right)} = g^{-r'} \tag{9.24}$$

Decryption query User A assigns $\langle ID, C \rangle$ to user B. B first executes the key generation query to identity ID and then decrypts C with the private key of identity ID.

Challenge: A chooses two messages m_0 and m_1 of the same length and two identities ID_0, ID_1 to B, where ID_0, ID_1, or their prefix has not appeared in any key generation query in Phase 1. B randomly selects $k', l' \in \{0, 1\}, c \in Z_p^*$ and constructs m_l as follows: $C = \left(C_1, C_2, C_3\right) = \left(TM_l, g^c, g_1^{ID_k \cdot c}\right)$. If $T=e\left(g,g\right)^{\alpha bc}$, we can obtain

$$\begin{aligned}
C &= \left(C_1, C_2, C_3\right) \\
&= \left(ZM_l, g^c, g_1^{ID_k \cdot c}\right) \\
&= \left(e\left(g,g\right)^{\alpha bc} M_l, g^c, g_1^{ID_k \cdot c}\right) \\
&= \left(e\left(g,g_2\right)^{\alpha c} M_l, g^c, g_1^{ID_k \cdot c}\right)
\end{aligned}$$

Therefore, C is a valid ciphertext.

Phase 2: A makes a key generation request and a decryption request to B as in the first phase, but the adversary must not request ID_0, ID_1 or the private keys for messages m_0, m_1.

Guess A: gives two guesses $k', l' \in \{0, 1\}$. If $k' = k, l' = l$, then B outputs 1, which means $T=e\left(g,g\right)^{\alpha bc}$; otherwise, it outputs 0 which means $T \neq e\left(g,g\right)^{\alpha bc}$.

When $T=e\left(g,g\right)^{\alpha bc}$, then A satisfies $|Pr\left(k' = k \wedge l' = l\right) - \frac{1}{4}| \geq \varepsilon$. When T is uniform, then $Pr\left(k' = k \wedge l' = l\right) = \frac{1}{4}$. Therefore, when α, b, c and T are uniform, we get

$$|Pr\left(B\left(g, g^\alpha, g^b, g^c, e\left(g,g\right)^{\alpha bc}\right) = 0\right)| - |Pr\left(B\left(g, g^\alpha, g^b, g^c, T\right) = 0\right)| \tag{9.25}$$

$$\geq |\left(\tfrac{1}{4} + \varepsilon\right) - \tfrac{1}{4}| = \varepsilon$$

This completes the proof of Theorem 1.

9.5.2 *Lightweight anonymous communication model based on IBE*

This section describes a lightweight anonymous communication model based on the anonymous IBE scheme of Wang *et al.*, which better realizes the anonymity of users and the confidentiality of health data, while saving the limited energy of wireless sensors. In the IBE scheme, the sender encrypts the message with the identity of the receiver. After encryption, the user uploads the message to a notice board, where the users download the encrypted text in groups. Only the actual recipient can decrypt and retrieve the message. Before formally introducing the anonymous communication model, translated with www.DeepL.com/Translator (free version), some symbols used in the model are explained in Table 9.2. G_1 and G_2 are multiplicative cyclic

Table 9.2   *Notations*

Notation	Meaning
α	The master key generated by PKG
ID_{ij}	User's identity
m	Message to be sent
C	Ciphertext
d_{ij}	User's private key
G_1, G_2	Multiplicative cyclic group
g	A generator of G_1
p	Prime order of G_1, G_2
g_1	$g_1 = g^{\alpha}$
g_2	Randomly selected in G_1
r, t	Randomly selected in Z_p^*

groups of prime order p, and g is a generator of G_1. e is a bilinear map satisfying $e: G_1 \times G_1 \rightarrow G_2$. $\alpha \in Z_p^*$ is PKG's the master key, $g_2 \in G_1$ is randomly selected, and $g_1 = g^{\alpha}$.

9.5.2.1   Model initialization

1. Entities

① Users. Users are very important to the system, so their privacy must be guaranteed. To meet the different needs of users, Wang *et al.* have developed two encryption methods suitable for two types of users: (1) users who want to send anonymous messages and do not want to reveal their identity to the recipient, for example, in a news story, a journalist does not want his or her identity to be revealed, and (2) users who need to reveal their identity to the recipient but do not want their identity to be revealed to other users. For example, a winning bidder needs to disclose their identity to the auctioneer for ongoing communication after the auction but should not make it known to other users of the system in order to avoid malicious competition.

② Bulletin board. The bulletin board allows users to upload and download password text. More precisely, the sender uploads the password text to the notification board and the receiver downloads the password text from the notification board. The notification board is an intermediate source of communication, with no direct interaction between users. As there is no interaction between users, the adversary cannot directly know the identity of the communicating parties.

③ PKG. In this model, the PKG is responsible for generating the system's master secret key, then generating the user's private key based on the user's identity, and also grouping the users. Furthermore, in this model, the PKG is trusted.

2. Grouping of users

① Initialization. When a user logs in, the system automatically assigns a unique, fixed *ID* $\left(ID \in Z_p^*\right)$ identity to the user.

②Grouping. The task of the PKG is to divide all users into *M* groups, each with *N* members. In order to avoid traffic analysis attacks, the number *N* must be large enough. An *ID* corresponds to a unique group number *i* and a serial number *j* within the group (*i,j* are randomly selected, and $0 \leq M, 0 \leq N$). The identity of a user is represented by an *ID*$_{ij}$, and each trusted user knows the identity and group number of all other users in the system.

The user needs to obtain their private key before communication can begin. The PKG generates the system's secret master key and the corresponding private key for each user. More specifically, the PKG generates a random number $r \in Z_p^*$, a public parameter of the system *params* $= (g, g_1, g_2)$. The private key d_{ij} corresponding to the user *ID*$_{ij}$ is as follows:

$$d_{ij} = \left(d_1, d_2\right) = \left(g_2^\alpha g_1^{ID_{ij} \cdot r}, g^{-r}\right) \tag{9.26}$$

After generating the private key, the PKG distributes the private key to the appropriate users.

3. Update the group of users

To ensure model security, updates to the private key and model group are triggered when the number of message rounds reaches a certain value. The procedure is as follows:

After the entire system has sent 1 000 message rounds, the PKG regenerates the private key for all users to increase the security of the system and prevent it from being cracked by an adversary. When the whole system has sent 100 rounds of messages, PKG groups all users to enhance the security of the system and prevent cracking by adversaries.

9.5.2.2   Anonymous communication model

In this section, we will describe how the anonymous communication model implements the communication process. During this phase, the user allocates time slots to encrypt the message, download the ciphertext, upload the ciphertext, and decrypt the ciphertext. During T_1, the sender encrypts the message to be transmitted. During T_2, all users upload the ciphertext to the noticeboard. During T_3, users download the ciphertext and decrypt it during T_4. The whole process is described below.

1. At T_1 time, the sender encrypts the message *m* using the recipient's *ID*$_{ij}$ as the public key.

All users who want to send a message to the system encrypt the message *m* using the recipient's *ID*$_{ij}$ at time T_1. Also, the sender knows the recipient's group number. To save memory, Wang *et al.* specify C_1 as the number of the recipient's group *i*. This facilitates sending the cipher text to the notice board, where the recipient can quickly filter the cipher text for retrieval.

If the sender wants the receiver to know his/her identity, he/she can encrypt the message m as follows:

$$C = (C_1, C_2, C_3, C_4) = \left(i, e\,(g, g_2)^{\alpha t} \cdot \left(m \parallel Sign_{sendID_{ij}}\right), g^t, g_1^{ID_{ij} \cdot t}\right) \quad (9.27)$$

where $t \in Z_p^*$ is randomly selected sender, ID_{ij} is the recipient's ID_{ij}, $Sign_{sendID_{ij}}$ is the sender's signature and $C_1 = i$, i is the recipient's group number.

If the identity of the sender is to be kept secret from the recipient, the following encryption is used:

$$C = (C_1, C_2, C_3, C_4) = \left(i, e\,(g, g_2)^{\alpha t} \cdot m, g^t, g_1^{ID_{ij} \cdot t}\right) \quad (9.28)$$

2. During time T_2, all users of the system must send ciphertext C to the bulletin board.

All users, whether they wish to communicate or not, must send the cipher text to the notification board and the sending process ends at time T_2. Users who wish to send a message must send the cipher text at time T_2. For security reasons, other users who do not need to communicate also stop sending pseudo-encrypted texts at time T_2.

3. During T_3, users download the corresponding cipher text C from the notice board.

After placing the cipher text on the notice board, all users evaluate whether the C_1 part of the cipher text matches their group number i to decide whether to upload the cipher text. If $C_i = i$, the recipient must download this ciphertext to avoid losing the information. The above process is completed during T_3.

4. During time T_4, the user decrypts the downloaded ciphertext C with his/her private key d_{ij}.

Each user uses his private key to decrypt the downloaded ciphertext one by one. If the decryption is successful, the real recipient can receive the message sent by the sender. The decryption process is as follows:

$$\begin{aligned} m \parallel Sign_{sendID_{ij}} &= C_2 \cdot \frac{1}{e\,(C_3, d_1)\, e\,(d_2, C_4)} \\ m &= C_2 \cdot \frac{1}{e\,(C_3, d_1)\, e\,(d_2, C_4)} \end{aligned} \quad (9.29)$$

The whole process of the lightweight anonymous communication model is shown in Figure 9.13.

9.5.3 *Experiments and results*

In this section, we analyze the performance of the model proposed by Wang *et al.* implemented in Python. All experiments were conducted on a computer with a 2.30-GHz processor and 8 GB of RAM. Table 9.3 compares the performance of the lightweight anonymous communication model with that of other anonymous communication models [27–29]. It can be seen that only the Wang model achieves full anonymity, while the other models do not.

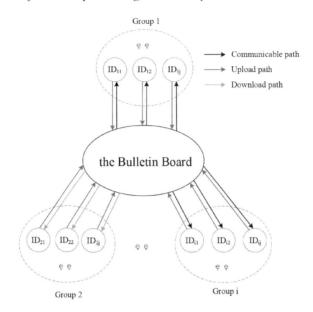

Figure 9.13   Lightweight anonymous communication model

We analyze the performance of Wang's model from the storage and communication costs. Table 9.4 shows that DCARPS has the smallest storage cost. However, it has the worst anonymity and security performance.

Assume that the communication cost of message exchange across the network is N. Add to this the additional communication cost of establishing a key pair for any two users P and the communication cost of an ACK message γ (γ is the communication cost of confirming the start of message delivery).

What is used as the public key in Wang's communication model is the user's ID, so there is no need to exchange secret key pairs. In addition, during message delivery, the sender does not need to send an acknowledgment message to the receiver

Table 9.3   Performance comparison

Anonymous communication model	Onion routing	DCARPS	Anonymous path routing	Wang's model
Sender anonymity	×	√	×	√
Receiver anonymity	√	×	×	√
Communication relationship anonymity	√	×	√	√

Table 9.4   Storage cost comparison

Model	Onion routing	DCARPS	Anonymous path routing	Wang's model
Storage cost (bits)	Two encryption and two decryption operations at lest	No extra computation cost with constant IDs	Six hashing operations at least	One hashing, one encryption, and one decryption operations

before sending the message. Therefore, the communication cost of the anonymous lightweight communication model is N. Table 9.5 shows the comparison results of communication cost.

Tables 9.3–9.5 show that Wang's model provides all three types of anonymity at low storage and computational cost.

In the lightweight anonymous communication model, the number of messages per round is unlimited. This is an important advantage over other anonymous communication models that only send one message per round. For example, a user may want to communicate with several people, or several users may want to send a single message. Other anonymous communication models limit the number of messages, so users must wait for several rounds. In Wang's model, all users can send any number of messages in a round. Figure 9.14 shows the communication costs of Wang's model and other anonymous communication models that limit the number of messages.

9.5.4   Discussion

9.5.4.1   Security analysis

1. Security of messages

The main requirement of the security model is to protect the content of messages sent by users. In Wang's model, messages uploaded to the bulletin board by users are encrypted using an anonymous encryption method. The security proof shows that the scheme cannot reveal any information about the user's identity in the encrypted text and is resistant to any CCA attacker.

Table 9.5   Communication cost comparison

Model	Onion Routing	DCARPS	Anonymous Path Routing	Wang's model
Communication cost	$P + N$	No extra communication cost with constant IDs	$N + \gamma$	N

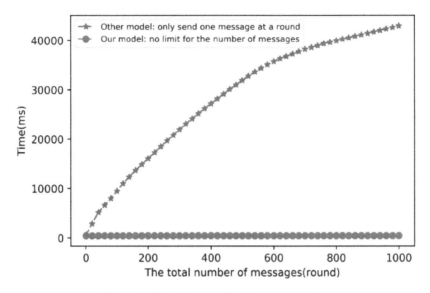

Figure 9.14   Communication consumption

2. Anonymity of messages

(a) Anonymity of the sender. Traditional public key encryption usually uses a PKI where the sender must request the receiver's public key before starting a communication. In this case, the user making the request may be the sender who wants to initiate the communication, and the receiver may have the public key to request.

In Wang's model, the sender no longer requires the receiver's public key, because the public key represents the identity of the receiver and is known to every user. All users complete the download process in a timely manner. Therefore, by analyzing the traffic, the attacker cannot determine which users are the real senders, thus ensuring the anonymity of the senders.

(b) Anonymity of the recipient. The anonymity of the recipient must ensure that no one else can determine whether a particular recipient has received the message. In addition, the model must ensure that the identity of the recipient cannot be intercepted by an adversary during the encryption process.

In Wang's model, the recipient's identity is used as the public key, and the anonymous IBE system ensures that an adversary cannot infer the recipient's identity from the cipher text. Over time, all members of the actual recipient group download the ciphertext. On the other hand, the group is relatively large and the adversary does not know which member of the group is the actual recipient, which ensures the anonymity of the recipient.

9.5.4.2   Efficiency analysis

Wang's method does not limit the number of ciphertexts sent per round. Compared to communication models that only send one message per round [31], the more messages Wang's model sends per round, the more efficient it is. Similarly, compared to the anonymous communication model designed by Jiang *et al.* [25], Wang's model allows for the management of user groups. Users must be filtered before they can download ciphertexts, which significantly reduces the number of ciphertexts that users must download and decrypt. In the case of transferring the same amount of information, Wang's solution saves not only time and storage space but also security.

9.6   Conclusion

In today's great stride of smart homes, smart medical, and precision agriculture, wireless sensors play an indispensable role, but various security issues are also prominent. This chapter provides the first comprehensive and systematic survey of state-of-art research on anonymous communication technologies in wireless healthcare online systems. We initially review the privacy-aware PKI model with strong forward security proposed by Liu *et al.* To solve the identity counterfeiting problems, we retrospect the dynamic sequence and shared secret-based anonymous identity authentication and key agreement protocol as well as the two-way authentication and key agreement protocol based on the D-H protocol. Given the limited resources in wireless sensors, a trust-based secure directed diffusion routing protocol is presented. Finally, we explore the lightweight anonymous communication model and analyze its security. In future work, we will continue to explore a trustworthy lightweight secure anonymous communication model.

References

[1]   Liu J., Lai Y., Yang S., *et al.* 'Bilateral authentication protocol for wsnwsn and certification by strand space model'. *Computing Science.* 2019, vol. 46(9), pp. 169–75.

[2]   Esposito C., Ficco M., Gupta B.B. 'Blockchain-based authentication and authorization for smart City applications'. *Information Processing & Management.* 2021, vol. 58(2), p. 102468.

[3]   Li F., Ge R., Zhou H., *et al.* 'Tesia: a trusted efficient service evaluation model in Internet of things based on improved aggregation signature'. *Concurrency and Computation: Practice and Experience.* 2020, e5739.

[4]   Wang Y., Yang G., Li T., Li F., Tian Y., Yu X. 'Belief and Fairness: a secure two-party protocol toward the view of entropy for IoTT devices'. *Journal of Network and Computer Applications.* 2021, vol. 161, p. 102641.

[5]   Tewari A., Gupta B.B. 'Security, privacy and trust of different layers in internet-of-things (IoTs) framework'. *Future Generation Computer Systems.* 2021, vol. 108, pp. 909–20.

[6]   Stergiou C.L., Psannis K.E., Gupta B.B. 'IoT-based big data secure management in the fog over a 6G wireless network'. *IEEE Internet of Things Journal.* 2021, vol. 8(7), pp. 5164–71.

[7]   Sun N., Zhang J., Rimba P., Gao S., Zhang L.Y., Xiang Y. 'Data-driven cybersecurity incident prediction: a survey'. *IEEE Communications Surveys & Tutorials.* 2018, vol. 21(2), pp. 1744–72.

[8]   Chen X., Li C., Wang D, *et al.* 'Android HIV: a study of repackaging malware for evading machine-learning detection'. *IEEE Transactions on Information Forensics and Security.* 2019, vol. 99, pp. 1–10.

[9]   Ellison C., Schneier B. 'Ten risks of PKI: what you ' re not being told about public key infrastructure '. *Computer Security Journal.* 2000, vol. 16(1), pp. 1–7.

[10]   Brands S. *Rethinking public key infrastructures and digital certificates [online].* Cambridge, MA: MIT Press; 2000. Available from https://direct.mit. edu/books/book/1912/rethinking-public-key-infrastructures-and-digital

[11]   Nakamoto S. 'Bitcoin: a peer-to-peer electronic cash system'.2009.

[12]   Meiklejohn S., Orlandi C. *'Privacy-Enhancing Overlays in Bitcoin.'* 2015, vol. 8976, pp. 127–41.

[13]   Miers I., Garman C., Green M., Rubin A.D. 'Zerocoin: anonymous distributed e-cash from bitcoin'. *IEEE Symposium on Security and Privacy (SP) Conference*; Berkeley, CA, IEEE, 2015. pp. 397–411.

[14]   Intanagonwiwat C., Govindan R., Estrin D., Heidemann J., Silva F. 'Directed diffusion for wireless sensor networking'. *IEEE/ACM Transactions on Networking.* 2015, vol. 11(1), pp. 2–16.

[15]   Ahmad A., Hawashin B. 'A secure network communication protocol based on text to barcode encryption algorithm'. *International Journal of Advanced Computer Science and Applications.* 2015, vol. 6(12), pp. 64–70.

[16]   Johnson A., Wacek C., Jansen R, *et al.* 'Users get routed: traffic correlation on TOR by realistic adversaries'. *Proceedings of the 2013 ACM SIGSAC Conference on Computer &Amp; Communications Securityconference on Computer & communications security*; ACM, 2013. pp. 337–48.

[17]   Bauer K., McCoy D., Grunwald D., Kohno T., Sicker D. 'Low-resource routing attacks against TOR' [online]'. *ACM Workshop*; Alexandria,VA, 2007. pp. 11–20. Available from http://portal.acm.org/citation.cfm?doid=1314333

[18]   Chakravarty S., Stavrou A., Keromytis A.D. 'Identifying proxy nodes in a TOR anonymization circuit'. Presented at 2008 IEEE International Conference on Signal Image Technology and Internet Based Systems (SITIS); Bali, Indonesia, 2008. IEEE,

[19]   Hopper N., Vasserman E.Y., Chan-TIN E. 'How much anonymity does network latency leak?'. *ACM Transactions on Information and System Security.* 2010, vol. 13(2), pp. 1–28.

[20]   Bao W., Wei Y. 'A forward secure ring signature scheme'. *Intelligent Information Hiding and Multimedia Signal Processing.* 2008, pp. 215–18.

[21]   Wang D., He D., Wang P., Chu C.-H. 'Anonymous two-factor authentication in distributed systems: certain goals are beyond attainment'. *IEEE Transactions on Dependable and Secure Computing.* 2014, vol. 12(4), pp. 428–42.

[22]   Cachin C., Camenisch J.L. 'Advances in cryptology-eeurocrypt 2004' in *How to generate strong keys from biometrics and other noisy generate strong keys from biometrics and other noisy.* Berlin, Heidelberg: EUROCRYPT; 2004.

[23]   Akram M.A., Ghaffar Z., Mahmood K., Kumari S., Agarwal K., Chen C.-M. 'An anonymous authenticated key-agreement scheme for multi-server

infrastructure'. *Human-Centric Computing and Information Sciences.* 2020, vol. 10(1), pp. 1–18.

[24] Barman S., Das A.K., Samanta D., Chattopadhyay S., Rodrigues J.J.P.C., Park Y. 'Provably secure multi-server authentication protocol using fuzzy commitment'. *IEEE Access.* 2020, vol. 6, pp. 38578–94.

[25] Ye Z., Wen T., Liu Z., *et al.* 'An algorithm of trust-based secure data aggregation for wireless sensor networks '. *Journal of Northeastern University.* 2019, vol. 40(6), pp. 789–94.

[26] Tian S., Li B., Wang K.. 'On the progress of elliptic curve discrete logarithm problem'. *Journal of Cryptologic Research.* 2015, vol. 002(2), pp. 177–88.

[27] Hiller J., Pennekamp J., Dahlmanns M, *et al.* 'Tailoring onion routing to the iinternet of tthings: security and privacy in untrusted environments'. Presented at 2019 IEEE 27th International Conference on Network Protocols (ICNP), IEEE; 2019.

[28] Mashal K., Mungase K. 'Secure anonymity communication protocol for wireless sensor network'. *International Journal of Science & Research.* 2016, vol. 54(17), pp. 580–85.

[29] Shirazi F., Simeonovski M., Asghar M.R., Backes M., Diaz C. 'A survey on routing in anonymous communication protocols'. *ACM Computing Surveys.* 2019, vol. 51(3), pp. 1–39.

Chapter 10

A comprehensive study on the security of medical information using encryption

Parkala Vishnu Bharadwaj Bayari[1], Gaurav Bhatnagar[1], and Chiranjoy Chattopadhyay[1]

The exponential rise in the use of the Internet and rapid progress in computer technology has revolutionised healthcare allowing medical information to be shared efficiently across networks. While these advancements make it convenient to store and share information, they also have their limitations. Medical data contain highly sensitive and confidential information about patients and can be subjected to various kinds of passive and active attacks and analyses if transferred over an insecure network. These data leakages can be catastrophic for the respective individual or organisation due to the undesirable scenarios which emanate from them. Hence, information security is a major concern and warrants developing techniques to securely transfer medical data.

This chapter discusses information security techniques and their properties in detail, reviews the research related to cryptography-based medical information security by categorising the techniques into traditional, hybrid and deep learning-based approaches and highlights their limitations. Comparative studies based on the universality of the method and metric-wise performance are also presented. We further discuss the potential challenges and prospective future directions, enabling a path forward to advance the research in this area.

10.1 Introduction

The remarkable advancements in the traditional healthcare ecosystem aided by the widespread growth in Internet and communication technologies have paved the way for smart healthcare. It has opened up many new avenues such as tclchealth/telemedicine and remote patient monitoring. The emergence of smart healthcare necessitated the need to share electronic medical records (EMRs) of patients among various

---

[1]Indian Institute of Technology Jodhpur, India

entities, such as hospitals, specialists, research institutions and healthcare centres, to provide proper treatment and diagnosis [1]. While the technological advancements made it easy to transmit data over networks, they also led to a substantial decrease in data security and privacy [2]. Sadly, there is a massive increase in breaches of medical data, including tampering, stealing and leakage resulting in regulatory sanctions, revenue loss and service disruption.

Additionally, modern medical devices, which produce enormous volumes of rich medical information, pose significant problems concerning their storage. Furthermore, the lack of standardised and interoperable medical records hinders smooth and efficient healthcare delivery due to inconsistent data [3]. The above-discussed shortcomings have mandated few medical organisations to issue guidelines and data security standards [4, 5] for the efficient storage, transmission and retrieval of medical data. Digital Imaging and Communications in Medicine (DICOM) [6, 7] is a universally adopted standard to facilitate communication and connectivity between medical imaging devices. The American College of Radiology [8, 9] standard specifies various guidelines regarding quality improvement, equipment specification, personnel qualifications, etc. The Society of Computer Applications in Radiology [10], now known as the Society for Imaging Informatics in Medicine, also highlighted the security issues in medical data and the need to address them. The whole ecosystem involving medical information has multiple stakeholders such as patients, hospitals, physicians, insurance companies, equipment vendors, pharmaceutical firms and the government. In such a complex ecosystem involving data transfer between various entities, privacy issues arise for various reasons, like stakeholders gaining access to personal data directly or indirectly to suit their vested interests [3]. The Health Insurance Portability and Accountability Act [11] and European General Data Protection Regulation [12] have mandated medical data storage, communication and protection regulations to address these concerns. Although the guidelines, as mentioned earlier, achieve interoperability by ensuring syntactic and semantic representation consistency, they still do not address data privacy concerns arising from unintended leakage or deliberate disclosure attempts.

10.1.1   Medical information

Medical information refers to any information associated with a patient's medical treatment or diagnosis. The electronic version of this information is called an EMR, which usually contains diagnosis, treatment, laboratory tests, monitoring data, insurance, prescription drugs, etc. Medical information contains sensitive information related to the patient, which should not be accessible to any unauthorised entity during storage or transmission [13]. They are also susceptible to the slightest modifications, intentional (unauthorised access by any entity) or unintentional (noise during transmission), leading to medical blunders like incorrect patient diagnoses. Medical images form a significant part of medical data when compared to other forms of data. Hence, the majority of the research concerning the security of medical information targets this particular modality. The techniques developed for medical imaging comprise magnetic resonance imaging (MRI), X-ray, computed tomography (CT),

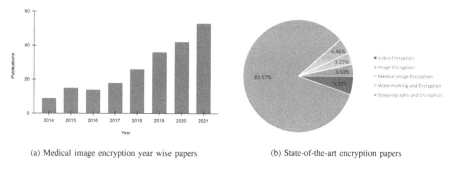

(a) Medical image encryption year wise papers (b) State-of-the-art encryption papers

Figure 10.1   Visual depiction of image encryption literature

ultrasound (US), positron emission tomography (PET), nuclear medicine imaging, optical microscopy, confocal microscopy, photoacoustic imaging, etc., which aid in the detection and diagnosis of the diseases [14, 15]. Medical image analysis entails extracting clinically relevant information from medical images for various applications [15, 16] such as image segmentation, image enhancement, image registration, image reconstruction, image-guided surgery, telemedicine, and augmented and virtual reality for surgery preparation. Considering the risk-sensitive applications involving medical information such as clinical data interventions, maintaining data integrity is paramount. So, after acquiring medical information, it is imperative to safeguard this information, which motivates creating, developing and analysing protocols for secure storage and communication. Cryptographic techniques ensure confidentiality, integrity and authenticity, making them practically viable for healthcare data delivery. This study discusses numerous cryptographic techniques based on chaotic maps, edge maps, bit-plane decomposition, elliptic curve cryptography, deoxyribonucleic acid (DNA) encryption, evolutionary algorithms, etc. The medical information to be safeguarded includes multiple data modalities such as medical images, electrocardiogram (ECG) data and electronic patient records (EPRs).

In Figure 10.1, we present a visual outline of image encryption literature. We have performed a literature search in Scopus to obtain good-quality and relevant articles on medical information encryption published for the past 7 years, i.e. 2014–2021. The visual results depicted using a bar plot in Figure 10.1a suggest a year-on-year growth in the number of articles published, conveying the concerned area's applicability and relevance. This study considers a selective number of the most prominent articles and covers a broad range of techniques. We furthermore present a pie chart analysis illustrating the various state-of-the-art encryption techniques for the same period. Based on Figure 10.1b, generic image encryption techniques are significantly higher than other techniques. As indicated in the figure, 83.57 per cent of the approaches cater to generic image encryption, with 5.20 per cent of approaches intended for video encryption. Hybrid methods comprising steganography and encryption account for 3.50 per cent, while watermarking and encryption account for 3.27 per cent of the studies. Medical image encryption schemes constitute 4.46 per cent of the total published literature. With the Covid-19 pandemic

Table 10.1   Basic terminologies

Properties	Definition
Security	Security ensures that the personal data shall be protected from unauthorised access, use during storage and transit
Privacy	Privacy ensures that an individual can limit access to his personal data

placing a massive strain on the healthcare system, remote healthcare and monitoring solutions gradually become the norm in place of traditional hospital-oriented care as they seamlessly provide optimised and personalised care. In addition to this, the phenomenal growth of the cloud computing and Internet of Things (IoT) ecosystem has prompted billions of smart devices to become ubiquitous in our daily life. The unprecedented increase in connectivity and low threshold to access has resulted in sophisticated attacks becoming more prevalent. Hence, the current scenario warrants the development of medical information encryption schemes more than ever.

10.1.2   Information security paradigms

Communication enables the passing of information between the parties involved. One of the key objectives of communication is the ability to share information selectively, which led to the vast growth of information security paradigms. In the most general terms, security means protection of assets against threats. Information security entails protecting information from unauthorised access, use, disclosure, disruption, modification and destruction. Information security paradigms are broadly classified into two approaches: 'Cryptography' and 'Information hiding'. The terms security and privacy, which constitute the core of information security, are defined in Table 10.1.

- *Cryptography:* Cryptographic techniques obfuscate the data and thereby protect the contents of the message by providing confidentiality, integrity and authentication [4, 17], which are explained in Table 10.2. The basic steps in a cryptographic technique are as follows:

Table 10.2   Properties of cryptography

Properties	Definition
Confidentiality	The information should only be accessible by the sender and the intended receiver
Integrity	To ensure that the information has not been modified or destroyed during storage or transit without detection
Authenticity	The source of information is confirmed and is as claimed

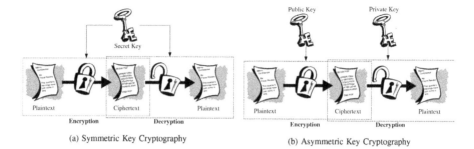

Figure 10.2   The scheme of cryptography

– Encryption: Encode the message into an incomprehensible format by changing the pixel values or information.

$$Encrypt(M, k) = M_{enc} \qquad (10.1)$$

– Decryption: The conversion of encrypted data back into its original form by intended/authorised

$$Decrypt(M_{enc}, k') = M \qquad (10.2)$$

where M is the plain message, M_{enc} is the cipher message and k and $kɟ$ are encryption and decryption keys.

A cryptographic system should ideally carry out both confusion and diffusion principles. Confusion increases ciphertext ambiguity, thereby hiding the relationship between ciphertext and key. Diffusion increases plaintext's redundancy, thereby hiding the relationship between ciphertext and plaintext. Cryptographic techniques can be classified as symmetric and asymmetric key-based encryption techniques, as shown in Figure 10.2. In symmetric key encryption, the data are encrypted as well as decrypted using a single secret key ($k = k'$), as seen in Figure 10.2a, while asymmetric key encryption performs the data encryption and decryption by the public key of the sender (k) and private key of the receiver (k'), respectively, as illustrated in Figure 10.2b. Conventional cryptography techniques such as Data Encryption Standard, Advanced Encryption Standard (AES) and International Data Encryption Algorithm are developed to secure textual data. However, medical images exhibit high redundancy, high correlation and immense volumes, making these techniques unusable and necessitating the development of encryption techniques that specifically cater to them. The ideal properties of a cryptographic system for medical image encryption are large key space, high key sensitivity, low correlation and minimal complexity.

• *Information hiding:* It is the process of concealing information within cover media [18]. Steganography is a data-hiding approach that hides data in plain

Table 10.3   Properties of steganography and watermarking

Properties	Definition
Imperceptibility	The embedding of information without degrading the cover medium
Capacity	The amount of information embedded into the cover medium
Robustness	The resistance offered by the technique and the ability to recover data under various attacks

sight by embedding them inside a non-restrictive cover. While cryptography safeguards the contents of the message, steganography hides the very existence of the message. The goal is to preserve the confidential information from the detection and ensure access control. Image watermarking involves embedding a watermark (text or image) into a restrictive cover medium. It provides authentication and ownership assertion for the owner of the data. These techniques have some properties [19], which are further elucidated in Table 10.3. While they seem similar in a broader sense, they differ in their objectives and priorities. Steganography aims to enable secret data communication without detection, whereas watermarking aims to provide authentication for cover media. Hence, imperceptibility is of prime concern for steganography, and robustness is given high priority for watermarking [20].

The general process of information hiding is depicted in Figure 10.3 and involves the following steps:

–   Embedding: The watermark/secret message is integrated within the cover medium on the sender side.

$$Embed(C, Watermark/Secret, k) + c_{emb} \qquad (10.3)$$

Figure 10.3   The process of information hiding

– Extraction: The process of getting back the watermark/secret message from the embedded image on the receiver side:

$$Extract(C_{emb}, k) = Watermark/Secret \qquad (10.4)$$

where C is the cover media, C_{emb} is the watermarked/stego media and k is the optional key used to enhance the randomness.

This study aims to present an organised and comprehensive study of techniques for medical information security via encryption. We underline the limitations of the existing approaches and furnish future research directions that will motivate researchers to address exciting and vital challenges. Although there are surveys in the literature that focus on the security of medical information, most of them deal with information hiding techniques. There are existing works that deal with medical information encryption, but they do not explore deep learning techniques in detail [1, 21, 22] or lack examining recent literature [22]. To the best of our knowledge, this is the first study of medical data encryption, incorporating deep learning-based techniques. The key contributions of this work are outlined as follows.

- We present a detailed overview of information security techniques and categorise medical information encryption techniques based on traditional, hybrid and deep learning-based models.
- We thoroughly review the advancements in security techniques for various medical data modalities. The advancements are measured in terms of the techniques' contributions to better the security and privacy of medical data by stating their methodology, advantages, limitations, applicability and metric-wise performance.
- We highlight potential issues in the existing methods and present future directions to tackle these challenges.

Section 10.2 summarises the contributions of encryption-based security techniques. Section 10.3 discusses different evaluation metrics for evaluating cryptographic techniques. It further provides comparative studies based on the universality of the method and metric-wise performance. Section 10.4 discusses the limitations of the current approaches and provides an outlook on the future research directions. Finally, in section 10.5, we put forward the concluding remarks.

10.2 State-of-the-art encryption approaches

The following section discusses several approaches for medical information security based on cryptographic techniques. We segregate the techniques into traditional, hybrid and deep learning techniques based on the class of approaches as illustrated in Figure 10.4 and discuss them elaborately. The traditional and hybrid techniques are further categorised based on their working domain, while the deep learning techniques are categorised based on the type of framework.

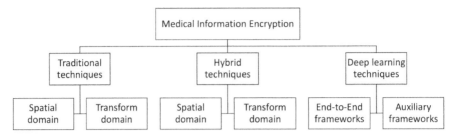

Figure 10.4   Classification of medical information encryption techniques

10.2.1   Traditional techniques

Traditional encryption techniques in the spatial domain achieve confusion, diffusion by substitution and permutation of pixel values. At the same time, transform domain techniques accomplish the same by manipulating the transform coefficients.

- *Spatial domain-based techniques*: Chaotic maps are sensitive to their initial conditions and parameter values, making them suitable for cryptographic applications. However, chaotic encryption techniques are not tamper-proof and suffer from exhaustive attacks on small key space. To overcome these limitations, Dai *et al.* [23] present a method based on chaotic encryption and bit-plane decomposition to secure medical images. The method splits the image into eight bit planes. The high four bit planes containing most information is permutated using the Arnold map. The scrambled image then undergoes diffusion using exclusive-OR (XOR) operation with sequences generated using the Henon map. The proposed method's use of the logistic map to initialise the Henon map results in a large key space. Experimental results on CT images demonstrate the satisfactory performance of the proposed method.

  Chen *et al.* [24] propose an adaptive medical image encryption technique based on the modified chaotic mapping. The image is first scrambled by the use of a logistic sine map and is divided into sub-blocks. This operation reduces the correlation among pixels. The scrambled sub-blocks are then encrypted adaptively by means of a hyper-chaotic system and pixel value diffusion. While pixel diffusion is usually performed by modifying the pixel value based on the adjacent pixel, this technique considers pixel values along the positive diagonal of the matrix. The proposed achieves good encryption, is robust to various attacks and overcomes the diffusion shortage problem in traditional single-sequence encryption schemes. The experimental results demonstrate the efficacy of the proposed system when compared to existing approaches [25, 26].

  Liu *et al.* [27] investigate the limitations of traditional chaotic cryptosystems, such as the possibility of parameter reconstruction, which results in a cryptosystem with low security. The authors have proposed a chaotic medical image encryption scheme that uses hyperbolic sine to induce non-linearity and a decorrelation operation to enhance randomness. The method first takes the average pixel value of the image as input to the chaotic system and generates a pseudo-random sequence that is decorrelated. The diffusion operation is performed by XOR operation between the image values and the pseudo-random sequence. The resultant output is permutated along the row and columns resulting in the final cipher image. The method is robust, has large key space and is resistant to various attacks. The experimental results on medical images illustrate the efficacy of the proposed method. The computation complexity can be reduced by enabling parallel execution.

An edge map consists of high contrast points representing the boundary features of objects present in an image. Cao *et al.* [16] propose a lossless image encryption (EMMIE) technique that involves three phases, namely: bit-plane decomposition, edge map generation and bit-level and pixel-level diffusion. The decomposition of a medical image into *n* bit planes is followed by an XOR operation with *n* edge maps generated utilising chaotic map thresholds. The encrypted image is formed by scrambling the XOR output, followed by bit-level and pixel-level diffusion. The algorithm is flexible concerning the type of medical image used, bit-plane decomposition technique, permutation methods and so on. Various edge detectors and thresholds can be used to generate distinct edge maps. Experimental results on medical images demonstrate significantly better results and better robustness than the state-of-the-art approaches [28–30]. Nevertheless, the method is inefficient as it encrypts unused bit planes. Chirakkarottu *et al.* [14] propose a secure medical image encryption methodology based on DNA cryptography and a two-dimensional Zaslavsky map. A chaotic map-based pseudo-random number generator is used to shuffle the image pixels, followed by diffusion employing DNA cryptography. DNA composed of a chain of nucleic acids represents pixels of images. A large DNA sequence is used for generating the key, which is added to the image DNA sequence. The resulting sequence converted back to integer form gives the final encrypted image. The decryption process involves DNA subtraction followed by image deshuffling. Experimental results on various medical image modalities show the effectiveness of the proposed method compared to prior methods [31, 32]. The approach can be improved by merely encrypting the image's extracted features.

Shankar *et al.* [33] investigate the limitations of one-dimensional chaotic systems concerning key space, such as weak security arising from improper initial conditions or inadequate control parameter range. They present an evolutionary encryption framework based on chaotic systems and adaptive grasshopper optimisation (AGO). The method first generates random numbers using chaotic maps like logistic and tent maps. The next step involves choosing optimal secret and public keys from the generated random numbers using AGO, thereby enhancing the security of the model. The method is robust to exhaustive, differential and statistical attacks but suffers from high computational complexity. Experimental results on brain, lung and iris medical images demonstrate the effective performance of the proposed method to existing methods.

Nematzadeh *et al.* [34] present a medical image encryption technique based on a modified genetic algorithm. The technique employs coupled map lattice, a chaotic function based on a logistic map to generate cipher images. These cipher images are then fed into a modified genetic algorithm, which uses a fitness function to increase entropy while reducing computational time. The method is robust against a multitude of attacks. Modifying the genetic algorithm that divides the initial population of cipher images into groups has led to faster computations because of fewer comparisons. The experimental results show that the method is more effective than other genetic algorithm-based techniques.

Kumar *et al.* [35] propose a patient-controlled encryption framework for the secure storage and transmission of patients' medical records in the cloud environment. The medical records are stored in a hierarchical representation employing ontologies. Patients have the liberty to set their preferred data hierarchy and determine which data can and must be shared with whom. Each hierarchy has a separate key. Patients own the secret keys and share data on a need basis from various hierarchies using a single compact key by using key aggregation. The blowfish method was chosen over other key-based (symmetric and asymmetric) encryption systems because it offers higher security with faster execution and lower memory requirements.

Jinyuan *et al.* [36] propose a healthcare system for patient privacy to secure electronic health records. The proposed method provides privacy and confidentiality to patients' protected health information (PHI) while ensuring access control, accountability, fail-safe and availability. The system enables efficient storage and retrieval of PHI while preserving security and privacy even with a public server. The medical records are encrypted by employing identity-based encryption, while searchable symmetric encryption (SSE) and searchable public-key encryption are used to search over encrypted data by generating trapdoors for keywords and retrieve the data. Adaptive SSE, which is more robust, can be used instead of SSE. The proposed scheme incurs high computation complexity to secure PHI information.

Dolendro *et al.* [37] present an Elgamal encryption technique to safeguard sensitive medical image data. The elliptic curve Elgamal encryption technique first encodes the image pixels onto an elliptic curve using the Koblitz encoding technique before encrypting it. Doing so results in data expansion as each pixel has to be represented as an elliptic curve coordinate. The proposed method overcomes this requirement by taking abscissa and ordinate in a way that does not produce an infinity point during encryption or decryption. This results in faster execution speed and allows multiple pixel encryption at a time, thereby solving the data expansion problem. The experimental findings confirm the validity of the proposed method, as it is resilient to numerous attacks and outperforms prior approaches.

Hua *et al.* [38] present an efficient and robust medical image encryption scheme based on scrambling and diffusion. Random values are placed into the image's surroundings in the initial phase of the process to ensure that the encryption result is unique. The next phase involves two rounds of high-speed scrambling and pixel adaptive diffusion. High-speed scrambling involves random shuffling row and column pixel positions simultaneously, reducing the correlation. Pixel adaptive diffusion performs bitwise XOR or modulo arithmetic to modify pixel values based on preceding pixel and randomly produced values. While the bitwise XOR approach is suitable for hardware applications, modulo arithmetic is superior for software applications since it is faster and more secure. The encryption scheme is ideal for any medical image. The experimental results show that the method outperforms prior methods and is robust to blurring and data loss.

Zhang *et al.* [39] propose an encryption and compression scheme for the secure storage and transmission of medical images. The proposed method has two phases. The proposed approach is divided into two phases. The medical image is compressed and encrypted simultaneously in the first phase using chaos-based compressive sensing achieved through the Bernoulli measurement matrix. The output of the first phase is permuted based on the keystream generated by the Chebyshev map in the second phase, followed by logistic map-based diffusion. Experimental results illustrate that the proposed technique effectively secures and compresses medical records. There is a tradeoff between the compression achieved and the reconstruction quality. The chosen measurement matrix should ensure lossless compression to avoid misdiagnosis of the patient due to image degradation.

- *Transform domain-based techniques*: ECG signals collected using biosensors aid in diagnosing diseases such as heart attacks, checking the heart muscle cells for blockage and damage. If the ECG data are tampered with or distorted during transmission, it may result in the misdiagnosis of the patient and lead to severe consequences. Another issue concerning ECG data is that a long monitoring period may result in massive data. To overcome these issues, Sujatha *et al.* [40] propose a novel scheme for transmitting ECG data securely in wireless body area sensor networks. The method compresses ECG data using the modified set partitioning in hierarchical trees algorithm and subsequently implements quasi-group encryption based on a genetic algorithm. Compared to RSA and standard quasi-group approaches, the experimental findings indicate that the suggested method is effective.

  Jeevitha *et al.* [41] present an encryption technique based on discrete wavelet transform (DWT) to secure medical data transmission. In this method, a medical image is transformed using DWT and then encoded into DWT planes using Fibonacci p-code or truncated Fibonacci p-code techniques. Edge maps are created from the medical image based on chaotic thresholds. The DWT planes and edge maps undergo XOR operation, and the resulting values are scrambled to form the cipher image. The method is robust, resistant to numerous attacks and flexible concerning the number of chaotic maps used, type of edge detector, thresholds, and so on. Experimental results on medical images confirm the effectiveness of the proposed method when compared to existing approaches [16, 28].

10.2.2 Hybrid techniques

Encryption techniques ensure the confidentiality of images during data transfer. However, once the data are decrypted, it is insecure and may be used for unauthorised purposes. So, a few hybrid approaches use information hiding alongside encryption to secure medical information.

- *Spatial domain-based techniques*: Abd-Eldayem *et al.* [42] present a reversible watermarking and encryption-based technique for medical images stored and transferred through hospital data management systems. A hash value is generated from the medical image based on Message Digest Five (MD5) hash function. The R-S vector is computed based on discriminating, flipping functions and further compressed using Huffman compression. The hash value, patient identity document (ID) and R-S vector are combined to form a watermark. The watermark is encrypted using AES encryption and finally embedded into a medical image. The hash value provides integrity, watermarking guarantees authentication and encryption ensures the confidentiality of patient details. The proposed technique is imperceptible and produces satisfactory results on medical data. The method does not encrypt the cover medical image, making it unsafe to transfer medical information over an insecure channel due to the possibility of data leakage or unauthorised use. Public key encryption can be used in place of AES encryption. The authors suggest that using other compression and watermarking approaches can further enhance the data embedding capacity.

  Salameh *et al.* [43] proposed a hybrid technique based on cryptography and steganography to protect private patient information during data transfer. The method first encrypts the secret medical image using a symmetric key-based block encryption method, modified Jamal encryption algorithm (MJEA). The patient information and medical image undergo XOR operation in hexadecimal representation to form a stego image. The stego image is encrypted using MJEA, followed by a scrambling algorithm to shuffle pixels between encrypted medical and steganography images and transmitted as shares. An attacker cannot recover information by intercepting one of the two images as they will have partial information. If the attacker manages to intercept both messages, the encryption algorithm still needs to be broken, which is not a trivial task. The authors recommend using a transform domain embedding technique to improve the robustness further.

- *Transform domain-based techniques:* Sharma *et al.* [44] present a dual watermarking technique in which the cover medical image is divided into a region of interest (ROI) and a non-region of interest (NROI) and undergoes transformation by making use of discrete cosine transform (DCT) and DWT. The watermark image is transformed and formatted using a modulus function to obtain the image watermark. The EPR is encrypted using the Rivest–Shamir–Adleman (RSA) technique to enhance security. The image watermark is now embedded in ROI, followed by text watermark embedding in NROI. The experimental results verify the robustness and imperceptibility of the proposed method. While the technique provides authentication by introducing dual watermarking, it does not ensure confidentiality of the medical images during transmission by not encrypting the cover medical image before sending it.

Anand *et al.* [45] propose a hybrid watermarking encryption scheme to secure medical records and thereby enhance telehealth services. The EPR is encoded using the turbo code technique, which is then embedded into DWT transformed watermark image followed by inverse DWT to generate the watermark image. After that, the watermark image is scrambled by a step space-filling curve before being encrypted with a paillier cryptosystem. The final watermarked image is generated by embedding the encrypted watermark into the encrypted cover image utilising the paillier cryptosystem's homomorphic characteristics. The proposed scheme is robust and imperceptible and performs significantly better than existing approaches. Due to the complex process involving multiple data embeddings, encryption and DWT, the computation cost of the method is extremely high.

Kannammal *et al.* [46] propose a technique based on watermarking and encryption to ensure security and the authenticity of data. A natural image is chosen as the watermark and transformed using discrete non-tensor product wavelet transform. The medical image is converted to binary format and then embedded into the LH sub-band of the watermark using the least significant bit (LSB) watermarking method. The watermarked image is formed by applying the inverse wavelet transform to the embedded image and then encrypted using the Rivest Cipher Four (RC4) algorithm. The proposed algorithm is impervious to geometric, noise and brightness attacks. Experimental results on medical images confirm the effectiveness of the technique.

Arun Kumar *et al.* [47] propose a robust block-based steganography scheme based on redundant integer wavelet transform (RIWT), singular value decomposition (SVD) and DCT. A chaotic logistic map is used to encrypt the medical image, which is then transformed using DCT. Divide the transformed medical image into four by four blocks and apply SVD. The medical image's singular values modify the transformed cover image's singular values in the LL sub-band. Inverse transform operations on the embedded cover image generate the stego image. The authors obtain significant improvements in robustness, reversibility and imperceptibility using transform operations. The chaotic map-based encryption makes the method more secure and steganalysis harder. The experimental results verify and illustrate the superior performance of the proposed scheme when compared to existing approaches [48–50]. The authors suggest embedding medical data only in selective cover image blocks based on statistical measures for enhanced performance.

Thanki *et al.* [51] present a technique for enhancing the security of medical images using encryption and watermarking. This approach embeds the patient's information into the medical image to strengthen authentication. The medical image is converted into the transform domain using the finite ridge transform (FRT) and SVD. The watermark image is transformed using SVD. To obtain the watermarked image, additive watermarking is used to embed the watermark image into the medical image, followed by inverse SVD and inverse FRT. Arnold scrambling is then used to encrypt the watermarked image (based on a chaotic map). The proposed technique is robust and imperceptible to various attacks, and the experimental results on the medical images show the scheme's effectiveness. Thakur *et al.* [52] propose a robust watermarking and encryption technique for medical image security and authentication. A combination of DWT, DCT and SVD is used to transform the cover image and watermark images. The watermark image's singular values modify the cover image's singular values. Finally, inverse transform operations on the embedded cover image yield the watermarked image. The watermarked image is encrypted using a two-dimensional logistic map to safeguard the data. The method is robust, providing both authentication and confidentiality for medical data. The experimental results on medical data establish that the proposed technique is effective as it outperforms state-of-the-art methods.

10.2.3   *Deep learning-based techniques*

Artificial intelligence encompasses all the technologies that deal with enabling machines to learn human-like intelligence. Deep learning, a subset of artificial intelligence based on neural network algorithms, has found enormous success on many challenging problems and finds applications in various fields. The recent interest at the intersection of deep learning and cryptography can be attributed to the potential research areas of confidential machine learning, adversarial neural cryptography and several auxiliary applications of deep learning frameworks in aiding encryption.

- *End-to-end frameworks*: Ding *et al.* [53] present an end-to-end cycle generative adversarial network (CycleGAN) for medical image encryption and decryption. The proposed framework achieves encryption via image-to-image transfer and performs decryption by virtue of a reconstruction network. The work also introduced an ROI mining to enable selective object extraction from encrypted images. The proposed method outperforms state-of-the-art approaches due to its ample key space and complex network structure. However, since the network parameters form the keys, storing separate keys for each image is practically challenging.
- *Auxiliary frameworks*: Ding *et al.* [54] explore a deep learning-based key generation framework. The image-to-image translation via GAN is likened to the key generation, and the transform domain images represent the keys. The image encryption is accomplished using the XOR algorithm between the original image and the generated private key. The experimental results demonstrate the efficacy of the proposed key generation and encryption methods, attributed to the large key space, high key sensitivity and resistance to various attacks.

Selvi *et al.* [55] propose a deep learning-based framework that employs a synorr certificateless signcryption at the hidden layer to perform encryption and signature generation, followed by Levenshtein entropy coding to compress the encrypted image. Decompression and decryption are performed using deep learning to obtain the original medical image at the receiver side. The proposed method performs significantly better in comparison to the existing state-of-the-art approaches. The experiments are performed only on chest X-ray images and could be extended to other modalities.

Lakshmi *et al.* [56] propose a robust adaptive encryption technique that employs a Hopfield neural network (HNN). The proposed method achieves encryption via confusion and diffusion by utilising chaotic sequences generated via HNN. An image-specific adaptive key generated using a back propagation network (BPN) seeds the HNN to further enhance security. The experimental results verify its satisfactory performance. The technique can be tested on additional datasets.

Yue *et al.* [57] present a homomorphic encryption-based convolutional long short-term memory network (HE-CLSTM) to analyse the time-series medical images. The proposed method addresses privacy concerns by analysing medical images encrypted by fully homomorphic encryption (FHE). The convolutional blocks capture the spatial features, and the long short-term memory network layers extract the temporal information. The proposed method learns better spatial and temporal representations and outperforms existing methods [58–60]. The computational complexity is significantly high due to the time taken to analyse encrypted images.

10.3   Comparative studies

10.3.1   Method universality

An information security technique should provide a well-informed assurance that the information risks and controls are balanced. One of these assurances constitutes the technique's generalisable ability and applicability to numerous data modalities. A comparative study of the applicability of the methods for multiple data modalities, i.e. the universality of the method, for the traditional, hybrid and deep learning techniques is presented in tabular forms in Tables 10.4–10.6, respectively. The techniques in References [35, 36] can secure all types of medical records, while the techniques in References [38, 42] are applicable for all modalities of medical images. Some techniques such as in References [16, 24, 27, 41, 47] can secure all medical imaging modalities as well as non-medical images, making them practically viable in a variety of scenarios. These techniques are highlighted in Tables 10.4–10.6.

Table 10.4 Comparative study for method universality of traditional techniques

Ref. no.	Working domain	Terminology used	Applicable for					Other data
			MRI	X-ray	CT	PET	US	
[23]	Spatial	Bit-plane decomposition chaotic encryption Logistic map Arnold map Henon map	–	–	✓	–	–	–
[24]	Spatial	Hyper-chaotic system pixel value diffusion Logistic-sine map Position scrambling	✓	✓	✓	✓	✓	Medical images Non-medical images
[27]	Spatial	Chaotic encryption hyberbolic sine Non-linearity	✓	✓	✓	✓	✓	Medical images Non-medical images
[16]	Spatial	Bit-plane decomposition chaotic encryption Edge map	✓	✓	✓	✓	✓	Medical images Non-medical images
[14]	Spatial	DNA cryptography chaotic encryption Zaslavsky map	✓	✓	✓	✓	✓	–

(Continues)

Table 10.4 Continued

Ref. no.	Working domain	Terminology used	Applicable for						Other data
			MRI	X-ray	CT	PET	US		
[33]	Spatial	AGO chaotic encryption Logistic map	✓	–	✓	–	–		Iris images
[34]	Spatial	Tent map Modified genetic algorithm coupled map lattices Chaotic function Logistic map	✓	✓	✓	–	–		–
[35]	Spatial	Blowfish encryption key aggregation Cloud	✓	✓	✓	✓	✓		Medical records
[36]	Spatial	Searchable public key encryption SSE Identity-based encryption	✓	✓	✓	✓	✓		Medical records
[37]	Spatial	Elliptic curve cryptography Elgamal encryption Koblitz encoding	✓	✓	✓	–	–		–
[38]	Spatial	Pixel adaptive diffusion high-speed scrambling	✓	✓	✓	✓	✓		Medical images

(Continues)

Table 10.4 Continued

Ref. no.	Working domain	Terminology used	Applicable for					
			MRI	X-ray	CT	PET	US	Other data
[39]	Spatial	Compressive sensing chaotic encryption Chebyshev map Pixel swapping	✓	✓	✓	–	–	–
[40]	Transform	Quasi-group encryption SPIHT compression Genetic algorithm WBASN	–	–	–	–	–	ECG data
[41]	Transform	Chaotic encryption DWT Deriche edge detector Edge map	✓	✓	✓	✓	✓	Medical images Non-medical images

Table 10.5   Comparative study for method universality of hybrid techniques

Ref. no.	Working Domain	Terminology used	Applicable for						Other data
			MRI	X-ray	CT	PET	US		
[42]	Spacial	Reversible watermarking AES encryption Huffman compression MD5 hash	✓	✓	✓	✓	✓		Medical images Greyscale DICOM
[43]	Spacial	Steganography MJEA Scrambling	–	✓	–	–	–		Chest images Hand images Iris images
[44]	Transform	ROI watermarking RSA encryption DWT DCT SVD	✓	–	✓	–	✓		–
[45]	Transform	Image watermarking paillier cryptosystem DWT Turbo code Homomorphic property	✓	✓	✓	✓	✓		Greyscale medical images
[46]	Transform	LSB watermarking RC4 encryption Wavelet filter bank	✓	–	✓	–	–		–
[47]	Transform	Steganography chaotic encryption RIWT SVD DWT Logistic map	✓	✓	✓	✓	✓		Medical images Non-medical images
[51]	Transform	Image watermarking FRT SVD Arnold scrambling	✓	✓	✓	–	✓		–

(Continues)

Table 10.5 Continued

| | Working | | Applicable for | | | | | |
Ref. no.	Domain	Terminology used	MRI	X-ray	CT	PET	US	Other data
[52]	Transform	Image watermarking Chaotic encryption DWT DCT SVD	✓	✓	✓	✓	✓	–

Table 10.6   Comparative study for method universality of deep learning techniques

Ref. no.	Network architecture	Terminology used	Applicable for					
			MRI	X-ray	CT	PET	US	Other data
[55]	Feedforward	Synorr certificateless signcryption Levenshtein coding Adaptive sigma filter Image compression	—	✓	—	—	—	—
[53]	CycleGAN	Internet of medical things generative adversarial network Image-to-image translation ROI mining	✓	✓	✓	—	—	—
[54]	GAN	Key generation Generative adversarial network Image-to-image translation Bit-wise XOR	✓	✓	—	—	✓	—
[56]	HNN BPN	Hopfield neural network Backpropagation network Adaptive key generation Cloud storage Chaotic sequence	—	—	✓	—	—	—
[57]	CLSTM	Computer-aided diagnosis Time-series medical images FHE Convolutional neural networks	—	—	—	—	—	Cevigram dataset BreakHis dataset

Table 10.7 *Performance comparative study*

Ref. No	NPCR (%)	UACI (%)	Entropy	Evaluation metrics			Other
				CC	SSIM	PSNR (dB)	
[23]	99.61	33.15	—	−0.005	—	—	Key sensitivity
[24]	99.59	33.42	7.9891	−0.0028	—	—	Key sensitivity
[14]	99.989–99.999	33.40–33.43	7.988–7.992	—	0.0061–0.0073	6.052–7.608	Image fidelity structural context
[16]	99.55–99.66	33.30–33.62	—	−0.0074	—	—	Encryption time
[33]	79.22–95.22	36.22–52.22	6.18–8	−0.0005 - 0.0782	—	49.45–62.22	—
[27]	99.63	33.43	7.9961	0.002	—	—	Key sensitivity
[35]	—	—	—	—	—	—	—
[36]	—	—	—	—	—	—	—
[34]	97.008–98.481	32.75–33.27	7.9981–7.9990	0.0039–0.0238	—	—	Key sensitivity
[37]	99.62	33.41	7.9993	−0.0008	0.0034–0.0066	5.955–7.863	Encryption time Decryption time
[38]	99.997–99.999	33.26–33.39	7.9981	—	—	45.2897	Encryption time Decryption time
[39]	—	—	7.9983–7.9986	−0.0131	—	33.896–36.785	Key sensitivity
[42]	—	—	—	—	—	56.20–58.13	—
[43]	—	—	7.783–7.991	−0.002 - 0.0463	—	18.52	—
[44]	—	—	—	—	—	50.867–52.743	Encryption time Decryption time
[45]	100	—	—	—	0.685–0.961	34.549–36.645	Encryption time
[46]	—	—	—	0.01–0.09	0.677	59.39–90.24	Encryption time Decryption time

(*Continues*)

Table 10.7 Continued

Ref. No	NPCR (%)	UACI (%)	Entropy	| Evaluation metrics CC	SSIM	PSNR (dB)	Other
[47]	–	–	–	–	0.985–0.995	49.26–50.18	Image fidelity
[51]	89.20–95.95	14.44–33.88	–	–	–	41.22–42.75	Encryption time Decryption time
[40]	–	–	–	–	–	34.33	Encryption time Decryption time
[41]	99.258–99.675	31.07–39.22	–	–0.03 - 0.0258	–	–	Key sensitivity
[52]	99.59–99.62	34.47–47.01	–	–	0.767–0.998	35.52	Encryption time Decryption time
[55]	–	–	–	–	–	45.20–56.08	Encryption time Compression ratio
[53]	94.21	–	7.94–7.97	–	0.01–0.02	35.34–38.03	Encryption time Decryption time
[54]	99.49–99.71	22.60–24.24	7.9985–7.9988	0.0280–0.0511	0.0012–0.0031	–	–
[56]	99.6	33.41	7.99	0.0037	–	–	–

10.3.2   Evaluation metrics

We present a brief view of evaluation metrics that measure the effectiveness of various medical encryption schemes. We further present a tabular comparison of metric-based performance of these techniques in Table 10.7.

1) *PSNR*: The peak signal-to-noise ratio (*PSNR*) quantifies the reconstruction quality for images as a ratio between the maximum possible power value and an image's corrupted value determined using mean square error (*MSE*), which is the average of the square of errors. The *PSNR* value should be low for a secure encryption scheme as the encrypted image is usually highly corrupted:

$$PSNR = 10\log\left(\frac{MAX^2}{MSE}\right) \tag{10.5}$$

$$MSE = \frac{1}{M*N}\sum_{i=1}^{N}\sum_{j=1}^{M}\left[f(i,j) - g(i,j)\right]^2 \tag{10.6}$$

where f and g are two images, M and N are dimensions of the images and MAX is the maximum supported pixel value of the image.

2) *SSIM*: The structural similarity index (*SSIM*) is a perceptual quality measure used to find the similarity between two images. The range of *SSIM* values is from negative one to positive one. The *SSIM* value between plain and cipher images should be close to zero for a perfect encryption scheme indicating no similarity. In contrast, the SSIM value between plain and watermarked/stego images should be close to one for watermarking/steganographic techniques, suggesting that both images are similar:

$$SSIM(f, g) = \frac{(2\mu_f\mu_g + C_1)(2\sigma_{fg} + C_2)}{(\mu_f^2 + \mu_g^2 + c_1)((\sigma_f^2 + \sigma_g^2 + c_2)} \tag{10.7}$$

where μ_f, μ_g and σ_f^2, σ_g^2 denote the averages, variances of the images f, g respectively. σ_{fg} denotes the covariance of f, g. C_1 and C_2 are stabilisation constants used to avoid null denominator.

3) *Correlation coefficient*: Correlation analysis denotes the relationship between adjacent pixels and helps capture the randomness in an image. The correlation coefficient (*CC*) values range from negative one to positive one. A value less than zero suggests a negative relationship, greater than zero implies a positive relationship, and zero indicates no relationship between the adjacent pixels. The correlation among adjacent pixels in an encrypted image should be ideally low to avoid information leakage. The correlation coefficient is defined as follows:

$$CC = \frac{\sum_{i=1}^{n}(x_i - \bar{x})(y_i - \bar{y})}{\sqrt{\sum_{i=1}^{n}(x_i - \bar{x})^2}\sqrt{\sum_{i=1}^{n}(y_i - \bar{y})^2}} \tag{10.8}$$

where x_i and y_i represent the grey values of adjacent pixels, $\bar{x}$ and $\bar{y}$ denote the average grey values of pixels and n denotes the number of pairs (x_i, y_i).

4) *Entropy*: Entropy, a measure of randomness, captures the information quantity present in an image. A robust encryption scheme increases the image randomness and thereby increases the entropy. Entropy is defined as follows:

$$Entropy = -\sum_{i=1}^{N} p(x_i)logp(x_i) \tag{10.9}$$

where $p(x_i)$ indicates the probability of x_i.

5) *NPCR and UACI*: Differential attacks try to estimate a plain text or key by tweaking plain text and observing the changes in cipher text. A perfect encryption scheme yields an entirely different cipher text for a slight change in plain text. The number of pixel change rates (*NPCR*) and uniform average changing intensity (*UACI*) [61] measure the total number of different pixels and the difference in pixel intensity values between two cipher images, respectively. Let K_1 and K_2 be two cipher images with slightly different plain images. Then *NPCR* and *UACI* are defined as follows:

$$NPCR(k_1, k_2) = \sum_{i=1}^{N}\sum_{j=1}^{M} \frac{Diff(i,j)}{M * N} * 100\% \tag{10.10}$$

$$UACI(k_1, k_2) = \sum_{i=1}^{N}\sum_{j=1}^{M} \frac{|K_1(i,j) - K_2(i,j)|}{M * N * (MAX - 1)} * 100\% \tag{10.11}$$

Furthermore, $Diff(i, j)$ is defined as follows:

$$Diff(i,j) = \begin{cases} 0; & K_1(i,j) = K_2(i,j) \\ 1; & K_1(i,j) \neq K_2(i,j) \end{cases} \tag{10.12}$$

where M and N are dimensions of the images and MAX is the maximum supported pixel value of the image.

10.4 Potential challenges and future scope

The security of medical information has been explored. While there are several robust techniques that achieve excellent results, there are still some limitations that we present here:

10.4.1 Potential challenges

- The majority of medical images are greyscale in nature. The proposed medical encryption techniques should not induce any degradation or modification in the image, which might result in misdiagnosis. They should also account for any distortions that might creep in deliberately (attack) or random noise (transmission).

- The most notable techniques in the existing literature based on chaotic maps, XOR operations and several transform domain techniques suffer from a plethora of attacks such as parameter reconstruction, chosen-plaintext attack and high computational time.
- The success of deep learning has also brought along its fair share of demerits. The advent of adversarial deep learning has led to several sophisticated data attacks. Non-deep learning techniques are not equipped to withstand these kinds of attacks.
- The primary focus of encryption techniques is to ensure the confidentiality and integrity of the data. However, the ever-increasing cloud and IoT scenario have entailed developing lightweight algorithms for edge and remote devices where the cost of encryption, decryption and transmission are significant factors.
- In cryptographic techniques, the existence of a message is not hidden. Most image encryption algorithms encode the secret image into a form that resembles noise or texture. As part of communication, sending these visually meaningless encrypted images leads to suspicion and various attacks and analyses.
- Cryptography does not provide robust authentication for data. Once the data are decrypted, they are insecure and may be altered or used for unauthorised purposes [62].
- Spatial domain techniques are less complex and require less computation time but are not resistant to geometric attacks. On the contrary, while transform domain techniques are robust to a multitude of attacks, they are computationally inefficient.
- In case of a denial of service attack or intruder attack, the entire system can become non-functional, disabling legitimate users from accessing data (non-availability).
- The generation and exchange of keys that form a crucial part of encryption frameworks is challenging.

10.4.2   Future scope

The more secure we want the techniques to become, the harder it is to implement them. There is always a tradeoff between computational complexity and the level of security that can be achieved. Upon examining the challenges, we believe that these are the potential future research directions.

- **Privacy-preserving deep learning**: Deep learning techniques have become the research hotspot and have achieved tremendous success in various fields. However, the evolving regulatory requirements that strictly regulate the use of sensitive data pose significant challenges for data-hungry DL applications. Moreover, the concerns involving the privacy of medical data and the black-box problem of neural networks have hindered their adoption in practical clinical applications. Deep learning as a service (DLaaS) that provides cloud-based analytics has become popular lately as they enable smooth, efficient maintenance and deployment of models at scale. Given the popularity of DLaaS that requires data to be transferred to semi-trusted cloud environments, the development of deep learning frameworks that can be run on encrypted or masked data along with the ability to explain their decisions seems to be a promising research area.

- **Neural cryptography**: Deep learning networks withstand and adapt to a wide range of attacks by virtue of transfer learning and adversarial robustness. The recent works on key generation [54] and end-to-end encryption [53] have also confirmed their successful applicability in cryptography research.
- **Hybrid approaches**: The development of computationally efficient and robust approaches by the fusion of cryptography and information hiding approaches has proven to be promising as they provide both confidentiality and authentication. But, information hiding techniques withstand detection to a certain extent as they have a minimal payload. Embedding more information within the cover medium will create a noticeable difference and leads to various attacks. Future research can focus on increasing the payload of these techniques without compromising on robustness/imperceptibility.
- **Edge computing**: Edge computing shifts the computing from the cloud to edge devices and enables the deployment of algorithms close to the data sources. A promising application in this regard is the development of lightweight cryptographic algorithms which can be run from highly resource-constrained environments like rural healthcare centres.

10.5   Conclusion

Technological advancements have propelled healthcare to become easily accessible, particularly to resource-constrained remote locations in the past few years. While this has made the digital access and sharing of medical records very easy, it also requires us to acknowledge the existing shortcomings regarding data security. In the data-centric world that we live in today, protecting the security and privacy of individuals and their information is of supreme importance. In particular, considering the risk-sensitive medical data applications, its misuse gives rise to cataclysmic consequences, which requires us to develop solutions that overcome them. In this study, we present a basic outline of information security paradigms and the need for securing medical data. We then survey various state-of-the-art medical data encryption techniques, discuss several evaluation metrics and further present comparative studies based on the applicability of methods for data modalities and metric-based performance. We emphasise the potential challenges of the existing methods and propose a way forward by discussing promising research directions.

References

[1]   Singh A.K., Anand A., Lv Z., Ko H., Mohan A. 'A survey on healthcare data: a security perspective'. *ACM Transactions on Multimedia Computing, Communications, and Applications*. 2019, vol. 17(2s), pp. 1–26.

[2] Bhatnagar G., Wu Q.J., Raman B. 'A novel image encryption framework based on Markov map and singular value decomposition'. *International Conference Image Analysis and Recognition*; Springer, 2011. pp. 286–96.

[3] Kaissis G.A., Makowski M.R., Rückert D., Braren R.F. 'Secure, privacy-preserving and federated machine learning in medical imaging'. *Nature Machine Intelligence*. 2019, vol. 2(6), pp. 305–11.

[4] Cao F., Huang H.K., Zhou X.Q. 'Medical image security in a HIPAA mandated PACS environment'. *Computerized Medical Imaging and Graphics*. 2003, vol. 27(2–3), pp. 185–96.

[5] Li M., Poovendran R., Narayanan S. 'Protecting patient privacy against unauthorized release of medical images in a group communication environment'. *Computerized Medical Imaging and Graphics*. 2005, vol. 29(5), pp. 367–83.

[6] Larobina M., Murino L. 'Medical image file formats'. *Journal of Digital Imaging*. 2014, vol. 27(2), pp. 200–06.

[7] Mildenberger P., Eichelberg M., Martin E. 'Introduction to the DICOM standard'. *European Radiology*. 2002, vol. 12(4), pp. 920–27.

[8] Berger S.B., Cepelewicz B.B. *Medical-legal issues in teleradiology*; AJR. American Journal of Roentgenology, Burnaby, BC, Canada: Berlin Heidelberg, 1996. pp. 505–10.

[9] Berlin L. 'Malpractice issues in radiology teleradiology'. *AJR. American Journal of Roentgenology*. 1998, vol. 170(6), pp. 1417–22.

[10] Huang H., Cao F., Zhang J., Liu B., Tsai M. 'Fault tolerant picture archiving and communication system and teleradiology design' in Reiner B., Siegel E.L., Dwyer S.J. (eds.). Security issues in the digital medical. Enterprise, SCAR; 2000. pp. 57–64.

[11] Annas G.J. 'HIPAA regulations – a new era of medical-record privacy?'. *The New England Journal of Medicine*. 2003, vol. 348(15), pp. 1486–90.

[12] Voigt P., von dem Bussche A. The EU General data protection regulation (GDPR). Vol. 10. 1st Ed. Cham: Springer International Publishing; 2020 Mar. p. 3152676. Available from http://link.springer.com/10.1007/978-3-319-57959-7

[13] Tuli S., Basumatary N., Gill S.S, *et al*. 'HealthFog: an ensemble deep learning based smart healthcare system for automatic diagnosis of heart diseases in integrated iot and FOG computing environments'. *Future Generation Computer Systems*. 2020, vol. 104, pp. 187–200.

[14] Chirakkarottu S., Mathew S. 'A novel encryption method for medical images using 2D zaslavski map and DNA cryptography'. *SN Applied Sciences*. 2020, vol. 2(1), pp. 1–10.

[15] Shen D., Wu G., Suk H.-I. 'Deep learning in medical image analysis'. *Annual Review of Biomedical Engineering*; Burnaby, BC, Canada: Berlin Heidelberg, 2017. pp. 221–48.

[16] Cao W., Zhou Y., Chen C.L.P., Xia L. 'Medical image encryption using edge maps'. *Signal Processing*. 2020, vol. 132, pp. 96–109.

[17] Al-Haj A., Abandah G., Hussein N. 'Crypto-based algorithms for secured medical image transmission [online]'. *IET Information Security*. 2015,

vol. 9(6), pp. 365–73. Available from https://onlinelibrary.wiley.com/toc/17518717/9/6

[18] Petitcolas F.A.P., Anderson R.J., Kuhn M.G. 'Information hiding-a survey'. *Proceedings of the IEEE*. 1999, vol. 87(7), pp. 1062–78.

[19] Byrnes O., La W., Wang H., Ma C., Xue M., Wu Q. 'Data hiding with deep learning: a survey unifying digital watermarking and steganography'. *CoRR*. 2021, vol. abs/2107, p. 09287.

[20] Kadhim I.J., Premaratne P., Vial P.J., Halloran B. *'Comprehensive survey of image steganography: techniques, evaluations, and trends in future research';* Neurocomputing, IEEE Press, 2019. pp. 299–326.

[21] Pavithra V., Jeyamala C. 'A survey on the techniques of medical image encryption'. *IEEE International Conference on Computational Intelligence and Computing Research (ICCIC)*; Madurai, India, 1999. pp. 1–8.

[22] Tan Y., Qin J., Tan L., Tang H., Xiang X. 'A survey on the new development of medical image security algorithms' in Sun X., Pan Z., Bertino E. (eds.). Cloud computing and security. Cham: Springer International Publishing; 2018. pp. 458–67.

[23] Dai Y., Wang H., Wang Y. 'Chaotic medical image encryption algorithm based on bit-plane decomposition'. *International Journal of Pattern Recognition and Artificial Intelligence*. 2016, vol. 30(4), p. 1657001.

[24] Chen X., Hu C.-J. 'Adaptive medical image encryption algorithm based on multiple chaotic mapping'. *Saudi Journal of Biological Sciences*. 2017, vol. 24(8), pp. 1821–27.

[25] Deng S., Huang G., Chen Z., Xiao X. 'Self-adaptive image encryption algorithm based on chaotic map'. *Journal of Computer Applications*. 2011, vol. 31(6), pp. 1502–04.

[26] J. Z., D. F. 'Image encryption technology applied chaotic maps index and DNA coding'. *Computer Engineering and Design*. 2015, vol. 36(3), pp. 613–18.

[27] Liu J., Ma Y., Li S., Lian J., Zhang X. 'A new simple chaotic system and its application in medical image encryption'. *Multimedia Tools and Applications*. 1999, vol. 77(17), pp. 22787–808.

[28] Zhou Y., Cao W., Philip Chen C.L. 'Image encryption using binary bitplane'. *Signal Processing*. 2014, vol. 100, pp. 197–207.

[29] Zhou Y., Panetta K., Agaian S., Chen C.L.P. '(N, K, P) -gray code for image systems'. *IEEE Transactions on Cybernetics*. 2013, vol. 43(2), pp. 515–29.

[30] Zhu Z. -l., Zhang W., Wong K. -w., Yu H. 'A chaos-based symmetric image encryption scheme using a bit-level permutation'. *Information Sciences*. 2011, vol. 181(6), pp. 1171–86.

[31] Dridi M., Bouallegue B., Mtibaa A. 'Crypto-compression of medical image based on DCT and chaotic system'. *Global Summit on Computer & Information Technology (GSCIT)*; Sousse, Tunisia, IEEE, 2016. pp. 1–6.

[32] Hanchinamani G., Kulakarni L. 'Image encryption based on 2D zaslavski chaotic map and pseudo hadmard transform'. *International Journal of Hybrid*

Information Technology. 2014, vol. 7(4), pp. 185–200. Available from http://
www.sersc.org/journals/IJHIT/vol7_no4_2014.php

[33] Shankar K., Elhoseny M., Chelvi E.D., Lakshmanaprabu S.K., Wu W.
      'An efficient optimal key based chaos function for medical image secu-
      rity'. *IEEE Access: Practical Innovations, Open Solutions.* 2021, vol. 6,
      pp. 77145–54.

[34] Nematzadeh H., Enayatifar R., Motameni H., Guimarães F.G., Coelho V.N.
      'Medical image encryption using a hybrid model of modified genetic algo-
      rithm and coupled map lattices'. *Optics and Lasers in Engineering.* 1999, vol.
      110, pp. 24–32.

[35] Vinoth B., Ramaswami M., Swathika P. 'Data security on patient monitor-
      ing for future healthcare application'. *International Journal of Computer
      Applications.* 2017, vol. 163(6), pp. 20–23.

[36] Sun J., Zhu X., Zhang C., Fang Y. 'A survey on healthcare data: a security per-
      spective'. *31st International Conference on Distributed Computing Systems
      (ICDCS)*; Minneapolis, MN, IEEE, 2011. pp. 373–82.

[37] Laiphrakpam D.S., Khumanthem M.S. 'Medical image encryption based on
      improved ElGamal encryption technique'. *Optik.* 2017, vol. 147, pp. 88–102.

[38] Hua Z., Yi S., Zhou Y. 'Medical image encryption using high-speed scram-
      bling and pixel adaptive diffusion'. *Signal Processing.* 2014, vol. 144, pp.
      134–44.

[39] Zhang L. -b., Zhu Z. -l., Yang B. -q., Liu W. -y., Zhu H. -f., Zou M. -y 'Medical
      image encryption and compression scheme using compressive sensing and
      pixel swapping based permutation approach'. *Mathematical Problems in
      Engineering.* 2014, vol. 2015, pp. 1–9.

[40] Sujatha S., Govindaraju R. 'A secure crypto based ECG data communica-
      tion using modified sphit and modified quasigroup encryption'. *International
      Journal of Computer Applications.* 2019, vol. 78(6), pp. 27–33.

[41] Jeevitha S., Amutha Prabha N. 'Novel medical image encryption using dwt
      block-based scrambling and edge maps'. *Journal of Ambient Intelligence and
      Humanized Computing.* 2014, vol. 12(3), pp. 3373–88.

[42] Abd-Eldayem M.M. 'A proposed security technique based on watermark-
      ing and encryption for digital imaging and communications in medicine'.
      Egyptian Informatics Journal. 2013, vol. 14(1), pp. 1–13.

[43] Salameh J.N.B. 'A new approach for securing medical images and patient '
      S information by using a hybrid system'. *International Journal of Computer
      Science and Network Security.* 2019, vol. 19(4), pp. 28–39.

[44] Sharma A., Singh A.K., Ghrera S.P. 'Secure hybrid robust watermarking tech-
      nique for medical images'. *Procedia Computer Science.* 2021, vol. 70, pp.
      778–84.

[45] Anand A., Singh A.K. 'Joint watermarking-encryption-ECC for patient re-
      cord security in wavelet domain'. *IEEE MultiMedia.* 2019, vol. 27(3), pp.
      66–75.

[46] Kannammal A., Subha Rani S. 'Two level security for medical images us-
      ing watermarking/encryption algorithms'. *International Journal of Imaging*

Systems and Technology. 2014, vol. 24(1), pp. 111–20. Available from http://doi.wiley.com/10.1002/ima.v24.1

[47] Arunkumar S., Subramaniyaswamy V., Vijayakumar V., Chilamkurti N., Logesh R. 'SVD-based robust image steganographic scheme using RIWT and DCT for secure transmission of medical images'. *Measurement*. 2019, vol. 139, pp. 426–37.

[48] Chang C.-C., Hsieh Y.-P., Lin C.-H. 'Sharing secrets in stego images with authentication'. *Pattern Recognition*. 2020, vol. 41(10), pp. 3130–37.

[49] Kanan H.R., Nazeri B. 'A novel image steganography scheme with high embedding capacity and tunable visual image quality based on a genetic algorithm'. *Expert Systems with Applications*. 2019, vol. 41(14), pp. 6123–30.

[50] Wu C.-C., Kao S.-J., Hwang M.-S. 'A high quality image sharing with steganography and adaptive authentication scheme'. *Journal of Systems and Software*. 2011, vol. 84(12), pp. 2196–207.

[51] Thanki R., Kothari A. 'Multi-level security of medical images based on encryption and watermarking for telemedicine applications'. *Multimedia Tools and Applications*. 2020, vol. 80(3), pp. 4307–25.

[52] Thakur S., Singh A.K., Ghrera S.P., Elhoseny M. 'Multi-layer security of medical data through watermarking and chaotic encryption for tele-health applications'. *Multimedia Tools and Applications*. 2019, vol. 78(3), pp. 3457–70.

[53] Ding Y., Wu G., Chen D. 'DeepEDN: a deep-learning-based image encryption and decryption network for Internet of medical things'. *IEEE Internet of Things Journal*. 2016, vol. 8(3), pp. 1504–18.

[54] Ding Y., Tan F., Qin Z., Cao M., Choo K.-K.R., Qin Z. 'DeepKeyGen: a deep learning-based stream cipher generator for medical image encryption and decryption'. *IEEE Transactions on Neural Networks and Learning Systems*. 2021, vol. PP, pp. 1–15.

[55] Selvi C.T., Amudha J., Sudhakar R. 'Medical image encryption and compression by adaptive sigma filterized synorr certificateless signcryptive levenshtein entropy-coding-based deep neural learning'. *Multimedia Systems*. 2021, vol. 27(6), pp. 1059–74.

[56] Lakshmi C., Thenmozhi K., Rayappan J.B.B., Rajagopalan S., Amirtharajan R., Chidambaram N. 'Neural-assisted image-dependent encryption scheme for medical image cloud storage'. *Neural Computing and Applications*. 2017, vol. 33(12), pp. 6671–84.

[57] Yue Z., Ding S., Zhao L. 'Privacy-preserving time-series medical images analysis using a hybrid deep learning framework'. *ACM Transactions on Internet Technology*. 2014, vol. 21(3), pp. 1–21.

[58] Ji S., Xu W., Yang M., Yu K. '3D convolutional neural networks for human action recognition'. *IEEE Transactions on Pattern Analysis and Machine Intelligence*. 2012, vol. 35(1), pp. 221–31.

[59] Yang H., Yuan C., Li B. 'Asymmetric 3D convolutional neural networks for action recognition'. *Pattern Recognition*. 2014, vol. 85, pp. 1–12.

[60] Zhu Y., Lan Z., Newsam S., Hauptmann A. Asian conference on computer vision. Springer; 2018. pp. 363–78.

[61] Wu Y., Noonan J.P., Agaian S, *et al*. 'NPCR and UACI randomness tests for image encryption'. *Cyber Journals: Multidisciplinary Journals in Science and Technology, Journal of Selected Areas in Telecommunications (JSAT)*. 2011, vol. 1(2), pp. 31–38.

[62] Cox I.J., Doerr G., Furon T. 'Watermarking is not cryptography' in International workshop on digital watermarking. Springer; 2006. pp. 1–15.

Chapter 11

Electrocardiogram-based dual watermarking scheme for healthcare applications

Nandita Sharma[1], Om Prakash Singh[1], Ashima Anand[2], and Amit Kumar Singh[1]

The strong need for a copy-protection scheme for healthcare data has been well recognized. Research studies show that invisibility, embedding capacity, and robustness are some of the most common watermarking features, which makes it difficult to balance the contradictions between them. Inspired by dual watermarking where multimarks are concealed inside the carrier media to offer a robust and secure model. In this chapter, we propose a watermarking scheme which embeds dual marks into a host electrocardiogram (ECG) signal using a transform-domain approach. First, we consider the redundant discrete wavelet transform (RDWT) to decompose the 2D signal into non-overlapping sub-bands, and then the selected sub-bands are decomposed by fast Walsh Hadamard transform (FWHT) followed by QR decomposition to compute the coefficient for data embedding purposes. Second, we apply the sequence of RDWT-FHWT-QR to decompose both marks in a similar manner. Third, we modify the QR coefficients of the host signal with the coefficients of both marks. The QR code of the more robust mark (patient report) is generated to ensure its security against attack. Extensive analysis shows good performance of the proposed algorithm. Our experiments on ECG signals demonstrate that the robustness of our algorithm is significantly improved up to 63.94% when compared with traditional schemes.

11.1   Introduction

With an increase in the use of the internet and multimedia communication technologies, it is convenient to transmit and collect confidential information about patients

[1]Department of Computer Science & Engineering, National Institute of Technology Patna, Patna, Bihar, India
[2]Department of CSE, Thapar Institute of Engineering and Technology, Patiala, Punjab, India

via smart devices and open communication environments for efficient monitoring and diagnosis [1]. For providing remote medical assistance to the patient in real-time, point-of-care (POC) services can be used to collect medical data such as glucose level, blood pressure, and biomedical signal using the edge level sensor [2]. However, there is a substantial authentication problem with the transmission and storage of patient data, since the data are shared with different healthcare professionals and medical centers [3]. Recently, the security of patient data has been one of the biggest challenges for medical professionals and centers during COVID-19 [4]. An ECG test is performed to monitor the activity of the human heart. ECG signals are useful to detect any abnormal functionality of the heart [5]. With the increasing probability of cardiovascular diseases among all age groups, ECG records are generated in large amount on an everyday basis [6].

To provide medical assistance in real time, the records are shared and stored on the servers of smart health centers [6]. The personal and medical records of the patient should be attached to the ECG as its characteristic varies from person to person [7]. According to the rules of the Health Insurance Portability and Accountability Act (HIPAA, 1996), providing privacy and security to the patient's private information should be the primary concern [8]. So, the ECG signal can be used as a cover to hide the private information inside for a secure transmission [9].

Authors [5, 6, 10–12] developed the latest watermarking scheme used in healthcare to resolve the authentication and ownership issues of medical data. This scheme enables us to share confidential and personal patient data from sender to receiver via smart devices and open communication environments without noticeable distortion on the host media object [1]. The primary aim of the watermarking scheme is to enhance the three features that should be maintained in a good relationship between them [9], including invisibility, capacity, and robustness. While performing the watermarking, there should not be any visible distortion of the original signal after the concealment of the hidden data [7]. Based on the embedding domain, watermarking technique can be classified into two categories, i.e., spatial domain and transform domain. The spatial domain approach to watermarking, such as correlation coefficients and least significant bit (LSB) embedding, is fast and shows minimum distortion of marked signal. Though transform domain techniques are more computationally complex and require higher computing costs, they provide better robustness and security when compared with spatial techniques. Some transform domain techniques such as discrete wavelet transform (DWT), discrete Fourier transform (DFT), and discrete cosine transform (DCT) are mostly used for embedding data within the transform coefficients [9].

In this chapter, we propose an ECG-based watermarking scheme for healthcare to resolve the authentication issue and maintain a good relationship between invisibility, capacity, and robustness. The main contributions of this research are as follows:

1. We proposed a watermarking scheme for ECG signals using the fusion of RDWT-FWHT and QR decomposition, which embeds dual marks into a host ECG signal. The RDWT is adopted to resolve the shift variance and downsampling issue

in the DWT domain [13]. Furthermore, FWHT is used due to its good energy compaction properties and low cost [14]. A QR decomposition is used to make the scheme strongly robust against well-known attacks [15].

2. In the embedding phase, both mark data are concealed within the ECG signal for the purpose of better authentication and copy protection. Here, more robust patient mark data are encoded by QR code [10] before concealing in the carrier ECG signal.

3. Experimental results show that the proposed ECG-based scheme has good invisibility and is robust in nature. Our experiments further demonstrate that the robustness of our scheme is significantly improved up to 63.94% (see Table 11.1) when compared with traditional schemes.

The remaining part of the chapter is organized in the following way: section 11.2 provides the summary of the recent works done in this field, section 11.3 describes the preliminary section, and proposed scheme , is described in section 11.4. Section 11.5 shows the derived experimental results, and section 11.6 concludes with future plans.

11.2   Related works

In this section, we introduce the most relevant work about ECG-based watermarking schemes for healthcare applications.

Since then, the authors of [10] proposed a wavelet-based ECG watermarking method for embedding secret data of patients in the form of QR images. The proposed method provides lossless data retrieval and better invisibility when compared with previous works [15, 17]. However, the storage demand could be reduced using some compression techniques. Abuadbba Khalil [2] proposed a FWHT-based 3D steganography technique to provide authenticity of secret data. Prior to embedding, secret data are encrypted using AES and then marked within the less significant coefficients of the signal. The proposed method shows less time complexity and better security when compared with previous works [18]. Kumar *et al.* [5] proposed a lossless watermarking method using an odd-even rule on ECG followed by bio-orthogonal DWT-based compression to reduce transmission overhead. The method

Table 11.1   *Performance comparison of proposed work with state-of-the-art techniques*

Methods	PSNR (dB)	PRD (%)	KL distance	NC1	NC2	BER
Natgunanathan *et al.* [6]	49.81	-	-	-	-	-
Sanivarapu *et al.* [10]	58.85	0.204	-	1.00	-	-
Mathivanan *et al.* [15]	57.43	0.246	0.0009	-	-	-
Jero *et al.* [16]	38.86	2.45	0.119	-	-	-
Proposed method	67.46	0.3530	0.0429	0.9991	0.9972	0

is invisible and has low overhead. The method gives better imperceptibility and takes lower computational time when compared with the state-of-the-art [10, 11, 13]. However, the method should be tested for real-time applications. Natgunanathan *et al.* proposed a DCT-based robust watermarking scheme for embedding the scrambled private data within the less significant region of the cover ECG signal [6]. Additionally, error buffers and synchronization bits are used to provide resistance against filter attacks. Experimental results show that the method provides better visibility than previous work [10, 19]. However, transmission volume will increase with the addition of extra synchronization bits. Kaur *et al.* proposed a blind ECG watermarking method for providing tamper detection [11]. A low-frequency chirp signal is used to conceal the secret information of the patient within the cover signal. However, encryption techniques can be used to increase the security of data further.

In Reference [12], Goyal *et al.* used a blind and reliable watermarking scheme based on a fast discrete curvelet transform to create clusters of curvelet coefficients using Euclidean distance. Furthermore, the secret data in the form of a binary image are concealed within the selected clusters. Experimental results show that the proposed method provides good imperceptibility, robustness, and embedding capacity when compared with previous work [16, 20, 21]. Mathivanan *et al.* [22] introduced a DWT-based secure ECG steganography technique, where data are encrypted in the form of a QR code to enhance the security level. The QR mark is concealed within the DWT coefficient using the additive quantization method. The method provides better invisibility when compared with previous works [16, 20, 23]. However, to validate the robustness, different external attacks can be performed.

11.3 Preliminary concepts

In this section, we introduce the concept of RDWT, FWHT, and QR decomposition in detail.

11.3.1 *Redundant discrete wavelet transform*

Although DWT has major advantages of multi-scalability, multi-resolution and space frequency localization, it suffers from the issues of shift sensitivity and poor directionality [13]. RDWT solved these issues as suffered by DWT. RDWT is shift invariant and holds all the desirable properties of DWT for robust and imperceptible watermarking [15]. As presented in Figure 11.1, the size of RDWT coefficients and original image are equal which improves the embedding capacity and helps in more precise extraction of local texture of RDWT domain [15].

11.3.2 *QR decomposition*

QR [15] is performed to decompose the image, 'C' of size $m \times m$, into two matrices such as unitary matrix, 'Q' with size of $m \times m$ and upper triangular matrix, 'R'.

$$[Q, R] \leftarrow QR(C) \tag{11.1}$$

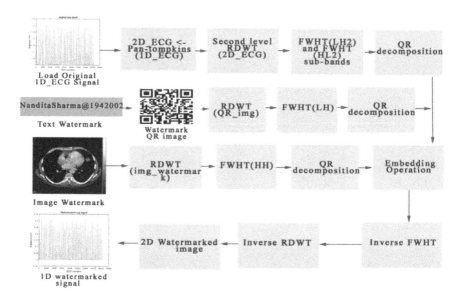

Figure 11.1   Non-blind dual watermark embedding within ECG signal

For example, pixel value of matrix '*A*' with size of 4×4 is obtained from input image is presented below.

$$A = \begin{bmatrix} 168.96 & 156.70 & 167.08 & 159.54 \\ 129.71 & 33.16 & 130.78 & 160.54 \\ 79.96 & 44.10 & 125.66 & 133.04 \\ 82.88 & 86.64 & 125.90 & 114.86 \end{bmatrix} \tag{11.2}$$

$$Q = \begin{bmatrix} -0.69 & 0.48 & 0.45 & -0.24 \\ -0.53 & -0.77 & 0.16 & 0.29 \\ -0.33 & -0.16 & -0.67 & -0.64 \\ -0.34 & 0.36 & -0.55 & 0.66 \end{bmatrix} \tag{11.3}$$

$$R = \begin{bmatrix} -242.15 & -171.32 & 271.24 & -280.56 \\ 0 & 75.86 & 6.61 & -25.35 \\ 0 & 0 & -55.26 & -52.51 \\ 0 & 0 & 0 & -1.38 \end{bmatrix} \tag{11.4}$$

11.3.3   Fast Walsh Hadamard transform

The FWHT is a special type of Fourier transforms, which has been widely used in the field of image processing, data hiding, image compression, etc. FWHT [14] contains several features, high energy compaction properties, low complexity, and

Figure 11.2   Size difference of DWT and RDWT coefficients of original image

unique sequence value. In WHT, it transforms the signal into a set of orthogonal and rectangular waveforms, which is known as Hadamard functions. The inverse WHT is used for reconstructing the original signal. The Hadamard transform is performed by a Hadamard matrix, 'H' with the size 4×4 defined in (11.5). Hadamard function contains only two values either $+1$ or -1.

$$H = \begin{bmatrix} 1 & 1 & 1 & 1 \\ 1 & -1 & 1 & -1 \\ 1 & 1 & -1 & -1 \\ 1 & -1 & -1 & 1 \end{bmatrix} \tag{11.5}$$

The FWHT is given in (11.6).

$$X_m = \frac{1}{M} \sum_{i=0}^{M-1} y_i FWHT(m, i), \quad m = 1, 2, 3 \ldots M - 1 \tag{11.6}$$

where, X_m is indicated as output coefficient, y_i is input value, and $FWHT(m, i)$ is performed transforms.

11.4   The proposed scheme

In this section, we concentrated on the embedding and extracting procedure on dual marks, which is shown in Figure 11.2. There are two major phases of our proposed algorithm, including embedding and recovery of the dual marks.

11.4.1 Pre-processing of the textual form of watermark and the ECG signal

To get the 2D ECG matrix from the 1D ECG signal, the Pan-Tompkins algorithm is used to eliminate noise in the signal, if any, and further select the R-peak-related information from QRS region of the ECG signal for embedding. Furthermore, more robust patient text data are converted into a corresponding QR image to enhance the security level.

11.4.2 Watermark embedding and extraction

To decompose the cover, the second level of RDWT is performed on the approximation (LL) sub-band of the 2D ECG matrix as it provides better imperceptibility. The received horizontal (LH2) and diagonal (HH2) sub-bands retain the R-component-related information of the signal and can provide better embedding locations and high robustness. Furthermore, to reduce the computational complexity, FWHT is performed on these LH2 and HH2 sub-bands and followed by QR decomposition, which generates the unitary matrix (Q) and lower triangular matrix (R). Similarly, the combination of RDWT-FWHT-QR decomposition has been used on the image watermark and QR image. Finally, the R matrices are used to embed the dual marks securely. Then the inverse of these techniques is performed to get the marked signal. The receiver will perform the reverse of the embedding operation to retrieve the original signal and the watermarks from the cover signal. Algorithms 1 and 2 show the complete procedure for embedding and recovery of dual marks, respectively. The description of notations used in the algorithms is given in Table 11.2.

11.5 Experimental results

In this section, we evaluate our ECG-based dual watermarking scheme in terms of multiple metrics. The proposed method uses different standard matrices for the performance evaluation. Peak signal-to-noise ratio (PSNR), percentage residual difference (PRD), and Kullback Leibler distance (KL distance) measured the visual quality of the marked signal, while normalized coefficient (NC) and bit error rate (BER) evaluated the robustness of the proposed work [3, 10, 24]. The descriptions of the used metrics are illustrated in Table 11.3. The performance of our proposed method is tested with MATLAB R2020a, where patient's personal record [25] and CT report [26] are considered as mark data whose size is of '21' characters and '128 × 128', respectively. These mark data are concealed into the cover ECG signal whose size is of '128×128'.

Table 11.2   Description of the used notations

Notations used	Description	Notations used	Description
1D_ECG	The 1D cover ECG signal	Q3, R3, Q4, R4	Unitary and right triangular matrix after using QR decomposition on Y1 and Z1 matrixes
2D_ECG	The 2D ECG image	New_X1	After embedding the lower triangular matrix R3 within decomposed Y1 matrix
LL_1, LH_1, HL_1, HH_1	After applying first-level RDWT the approximation, horizontal, vertical and diagonal sub-bands	New_U1	After embedding the lower triangular matrix R4 within decomposed Z1 matrix
LL_2, LH_2, HL_2, HH_2	After applying second-level RDWT on LL_1 sub-band	New_LH_2, New_HH_2	After performing inverse FWHT on New_X1 and New_U1
X1	2D matrix after applying FWHT on LH_2 sub-band	New_LL_1	After performing first-level inverse RDWT
U1	2D matrix after performing FWHT on HH_2 sub-band	Marked_sig	After applying second-level RDWT on watermarked New_LL_1 sub-band
Q1, R1, Q2, R2	Unitary and right triangular matrix after applying QR decomposition on X1 and U1 matrixes	Send_watsignal	The final 1D watermarked signal
text_watermark	The secret data of patient as text watermark	Sig_recv	The marked signal at receiver side
QR_img	The QR image generated from the text_watermark	[LLr1, LHr1, HLr1, HHr1]	The sub-bands after applying first-level RDWT on Sig_recv
img_watermark	The used image watermark	[LLr2, LHr2, HLr2, HHr2]	Sub-bands after using second-level RDWT on LLr1
Y1	2D matrix after applying FWHT on text_watermark	Wat_img1	Extracted QR image at receiver side
Z1	2D matrix after applying FWHT on img_watermark	Msg	The decoded text message from Wat_img1 at receiver side
A	The embedding factor used	Wat_img2	Extracted watermark image at receiver side

Table 11.3   A brief description of the used performance parameters

Performance metrics	Formula	Description
PSNR [24]	$PSNR = \log_{10} \frac{(255)^2}{MSE}$ Mean Square Error $(MSE) = \frac{1}{X \times Y} \sum_{a=1}^{X} \sum_{b=1}^{Y} (C_{ab} - W_{ab})^2$ where, C_{ab}, and W_{ab} indicated as pixel value of cover and marked image respectively of size $X \times Y$	Measure the similarity between cover signal and marked signal Acceptable value >28dB
PRD [10]	$PRD = \sqrt{\frac{\sum_{j=1}^{M}(n(j) - \hat{n}(j))^2}{\sum_{j=1}^{M} n^2(j)}} \times 100$ where $n(j)$ indicated as original signals, $\hat{n}(j)$ is the final de-noised signal, and M indicated as signal length	Measure the distortion between original and marked signal Ideally $\cong 0$
KL distance [10]	$D_{KL} = Ent[\log n(a) - \log n(a)]$ Ent is termed as entropy. $m(a)$, and $n(a)$ are indicated as actual and approximate probability distribution	Compute the difference of probability density function between cover and marked signal Ideally $\cong 0$
NC [24]	$NC = \frac{\sum_{a=1}^{X} \sum_{b=1}^{Y} (Org_{ab} \times Rec_{ab})}{\sum_{a=1}^{X} \sum_{b=1}^{Y} (Org_{ab}^2)}$ Where, Org_{ab} and Rec_{ab} indicated as the pixel value of original and recover mark image respectively, of size $X \times Y$	The similarity between extracted and original image mark Acceptable value > 0.7
BER [3]	$BER = \frac{Number\ of\ encorrect\ bits}{Total\ number\ of\ bits}$	The similarity between extracted and original text mark Ideally $\cong 0$

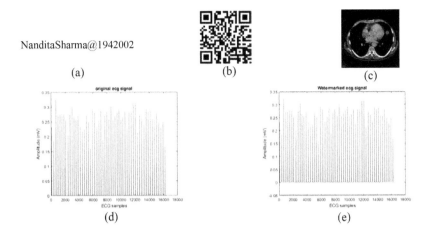

Figure 11.3   The experimental results (a) original patient personal record, (b) QR code of the record, (c) chest CT scan report, (d) original ECG signal, and (e) marked ECG signal

Table 11.4   Performance evaluation for varying embedding factor

Embedding factor	PSNR (dB)	PRD (%)	KL distance	NC1	NC2	BER
0.03	71.9017	0.2118	0.0153	0.9976	0.9948	0
0.05	67.4647	0.3530	0.0429	0.9991	0.9972	0
0.07	64.5421	0.4942	0.0846	0.9995	0.9979	0
0.1	61.4441	0.7060	0.1770	0.9997	0.9982	0
0.3	51.9017	2.1179	1.6390	0.9999	0.9985	0

Table 11.5   Performance evaluation for different length of text watermark

Character size	PSNR (dB)	PRD (%)	KL distance	NC1	NC2	BER
21	67.4647	0.3530	0.0429	0.9991	0.9972	0
40	66.5247	0.3933	0.0542	0.9990	0.9972	0
60	64.7919	0.4818	0.0766	0.9988	0.9972	0
80	63.2739	0.5719	0.1143	0.9981	0.9972	0
100	61.2515	0.7218	0.1781	0.9967	0.9972	0

Algorithm1: Algorithm for dual watermark embedding	**Algorithm2**: Algorithm for dual watermark extraction
Input: 1D_ECG, text_watermark, img_watermark, A	**Input**:Send_watsignal, A
Output:Send_watsignal	**Output**: Msg, Wat_img2
begin	**begin**
1. 1D_ECG ← Load 1D ECG signal	1. Sig_recv←reshape(Send_watsignal)
2. Get 2D_ECG ← pan_tompkins (1D_ECG)	2. [LLr1,LHr1,HLr1,HHr1] ←RDWT(Sig_recv)
3. [LL_1,LH_1,HL_1,HH_1] ← RDWT(2D_ECG)	3. [LLr2,LHr2,HLr2,HHr2] ←RDWT(LLr1)
4. [LL_2,LH_2,HL_2,HH_2] ←RDWT(LL_1)	4. A1 ←FWHT(LHr2)
5. [X1]←FWHT(LH_2)	5. B1 ←FWHT(HHr2)
6. [U1] ← FWHT (HH_2)	6. [Q5,R5] ←qr(A1)
7. [Q1,R1] ← qr(X1)	7. [Q6,R6] ←qr(B1)
8. [Q2,R2] ←qr(U1)	8. R_new1 ←(R5-R1) / A
9. QR_img←textEncode(text_watermak)	9. Wat_LH←Q3 ×R_new
10. [LLw1,LHw1,HLw1,HHw1]←RDDWT(QR_img)	10. F1 ←FWHT(Wat_LH)
11. [Y1] ←FWHT(LHw1)	11. Wat_img1
12. [LLw2,LHw2,HLw2,HHw2]←RDWT(img_watermark)	←IRDWT(LLw1,F1,HLw1,HHw1)
13. [Z1] ← FWHT(HHw2)	12. Msg←textDecode(Wat_img1)
14. [Q3,R3] ←qr(Y1)	13. R_new2 ←(R6-R2) / A
15. [Q4,R4] ←qr(Z1)	14. Wat_HH←Q4 ×R_new2
16. R11 ← R1+R3× A	15. F2 ←FWHT(Wat_HH)
17. New_X1←Q1 × R11	16. Wat_img2
18. R22 ← R2+R4×A	←IRDWT(LLw2,LHw2,HLw2,F2)
19. New_U1←Q2 × R22	**return Msg, Wat_img2**
20. New_LH_2 ← IFWHT(NEW_X1)	
21. New_HH_2 ← IFWHT(NEW_U1)	
22. New_LL_1=IRDWT	
(LL_2,New_LH_2,HL_2,New_HH_2)	
23. Marked_sig←IRDWT(New_LL_1.LH_1,HL_1,HH_1)	
24. Send_watsignal← reshape (Marked_sig)	
return Send_watsignal	

The patient personal record along with QR code, patient chest CT report, cover ECG and marked signal are shown in Figure 11.3. The performance of our scheme is tested at varying embedding strength (α), ranging between 0.03 and 0.3. If the value of 'α' is 0.03, the best scores of PSNR, PRD, and KL distance are 71.9017 dB, 0.2118, and 0.0153, respectively. If 'α' is set as 0.3, the highest NC values are obtained, i.e., 0.9999. We obtained BER as zero for the recommended range of 'α'

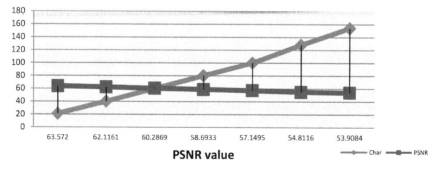

Figure 11.4   *The effect on PSNR value for chossing different length of text watermarks*

Table 11.6 Performance analysis for different ECG signals

ECG signal	PSNR (dB)	PRD (%)	KL distance	NC1	NC2	BER
100 m	63.572	0.3682	0.1519	0.999	0.9971	0
101 m	63.5466	0.4431	0.0848	0.9991	0.9977	0
102 m	62.0305	0.4626	0.062	0.9991	0.9974	0
103 m	64.3103	0.3755	0.2122	0.9994	0.9979	0
104 m	61.9161	0.5713	0.0909	0.9993	0.9979	0
105 m	63.7686	0.5352	0.389	0.9997	0.9983	0

(Continues)

Table 11.6 Continued

ECG signal	PSNR (dB)	PRD (%)	KL distance	NC1	NC2	BER
106 m	65.8010	0.3573	0.0724	0.9994	0.9979	0
121 m	67.46	0.3530	0.0429	0.9991	0.9972	0
122 m	69.25	0.1844	0.1674	0.9983	0.9965	0

Table 11.7   Performance analysis against different attacks

Attacks	Noise density	NC1	NC2
Speckle noise	0.001	0.9986	0.9978
	0.005	0.9969	0.9967
	0.01	0.9965	0.9971
Salt and pepper	0.001	0.972	0.9833
	0.005	0.8274	0.9123
	0.01	0.7564	0.8750
Gaussian	0.001	0.9708	0.9834
	0.005	0.8825	0.9438
	0.01	0.8012	0.8959
Rotation	5°	0.9975	0.9972
Median	[1, 1]	0.9993	0.9983
	[2, 2]	0.9981	0.9956
	[3, 3]	0.9989	0.9970
Crop	[20 20 110 110]	0.9996	0.9982

value. This is noticed that we can obtain a good NC score at a high value of 'α', while on the other hand, the low value of 'α' enhances the PSNR score. Furthermore, the performance of our scheme is evaluated at the varying sizes of the patient's report. A cover signal of size '128 × 128' can provide a maximum embedding capacity of 154 characters for invisible concealing. Also, Table 11.3 demonstrates the performance of our method for different ECG signal samples.

Table 11.4 demonstrates the performance of our scheme at varying embedding strengths (α). The range of 'α' is 0.03 to 0.3. If we set the value of 'α' as 0.03, the best scores of PSNR, PRD, and KL distance are 71.9017 dB, 0.2118, and 0.0153, respectively. If 'α' is set as 0.3, the highest NC values are obtained, i.e., 0.9999. We obtained BER as zero for the recommended range of 'α' value. This is demonstrated that we can obtain the good NC score at a high value of 'α', while on the other hand, the low value of 'α' enhances the PSNR score. Table 11.5 demonstrates the performance of our scheme at the varying sizes of the patient's report. Figure 11.4 shows the PSNR score for different sizes of the report.

According to Table 11.6, we get the best score of PSNR at 69.25 dB, which implies good imperceptibility. The lowest PRD and KL distance we obtain are 0.1844 and 0.0429, which indicates minimum distortion of the cover signal [11]. A lower KL value also indicates better robustness [16]. The approaching values for NC and BER show that the method also achieves strong robustness. Table 11.7 shows the robustness of the proposed scheme in the presence of common processing attacks. The results indicate that the method offers acceptable robustness (i.e., NC > 0.7) against the listed attacks. The embedded text watermark can be retrieved from the QR image without any bit loss for all cases except for Gaussian noise and salt and pepper noise with a noise density of more than 0.001.

Furthermore, the performance of the method is compared to some recent works and is summarized in Table 11.1. It gives better invisibility and robustness when compared with the state-of-the-art [6, 10, 15, 16]. The proposed technique offers promising results in terms of robustness, security, embedding capacity, and invisibility.

11.6 Conclusions

In this chapter, we developed a dual watermarking for ECG signal to resolve the issues of copy protection and ownership conflicts and offer a good relationship between invisibility, capacity, and robustness. On this basis, the proposed scheme considered the sequence of RDWT-FHWT-QR to decompose the host ECG and both mark data to obtain R-component, where R-component of the host ECG signal is modified (embedded) with the component of both marks. Here, more robust patient mark data are encoded by QR-code before being concealed in the host signal. Experimental results show that the proposed ECG-based scheme has good invisibility and is robust in nature. Our experiments further demonstrated that the robustness of our scheme is significantly improved up to 63.94% when compared with traditional schemes.

References

[1]   Singh A.K. 'Robust and distortion control dual watermarking in LWT domain using DCT and error correction code for color medical image'. *Multimedia Tools and Applications*. 2019, vol. 78(21), pp. 30523–33.

[2]   Abuadbba A., Khalil I. 'Walsh-hadamard-based 3-D steganography for protecting sensitive information in point-of-care'. *IEEE Transactions on Bio-Medical Engineering*. 2017, vol. 64(9), pp. 2186–95.

[3]   Anand A., Singh A.K. 'An improved DWT-SVD domain watermarking for medical information security'. *Computer Communications*. 2020, vol. 152, pp. 72–80.

[4]   Moccia F., Gerbino A., Lionetti V, *et al.* 'COVID-19-associated cardiovascular morbidity in older adults: a position paper from the Italian Society of cardiovascular researches'. *GeroScience*. 2020, vol. 42(4), pp. 1021–49.

[5]   Kumar A., Ranganatham R., Singh S., Komaragiri R., Kumar M. 'A robust digital ECG signal watermarking and compression using biorthogonal wavelet transform'. *Research on Biomedical Engineering*. 2021, vol. 37(1), pp. 79–85.

[6]   Natgunanathan I., Karmakar C., Rajasegarar S., Zong T., Habib A. 'Robust patient information embedding and retrieval mechanism for ECG signals'. *IEEE Access: Practical Innovations, Open Solutions*. 2020, vol. 8, pp. 181233–45.

[7]   Banerjee S., Singh G.K. 'A new approach of ECG steganography and prediction using deep learning'. *Biomedical Signal Processing and Control*. 2020, vol. 64, p. 102151.

[8]   D'Arruda K. 'HIPAA and USDHHS's final rule – first guidance from the Department of health and human services'. *AAOHN Journal*. 2001, vol. 49(12), pp. 542–44.

[9]   Singh O.P., Singh A.K., Srivastava G., Kumar N. 'Image watermarking us-
       ing soft computing techniques: a comprehensive survey [online]'. *Multimedia
       Tools and Applications*. 2021, vol. 80(20), pp. 30367–98. Available from htt-
       ps://doi.org/10.1007/s11042-020-09606-x

[10]   Sanivarapu P.V., Rajesh K.N.V.P.S., Reddy N.V.R., Reddy N.C.S. 'Patient data
       hiding into ECG signal using watermarking in transform domain'. *Physical
       and Engineering Sciences in Medicine*. 2020, vol. 43(1), pp. 213–26.

[11]   Kaur S., Singhal R., Farooq O., Ahuja B.S. 'Digital watermarking of ECG
       data for secure wireless communication'. *International Conference on Recent
       Trends in Information, Telecommunication and Computing (ITC 2010)*;
       Kochi, Kerala, 2010.

[12]   Goyal L.M., Mittal M., Kaushik R, *et al.* 'Improved ECG watermarking
       technique using curvelet transform'. *Sensors (Basel, Switzerland)*. 2020, vol.
       20(10), p. 2941.

[13]   Singh O.P., Kumar C., Singh A.K., Singh M.P., Ko H. 'Fuzzy-based secure
       exchange of digital data using watermarking in NSCT-RDWT-SVD domain'.
       Concurrency and Computation Practice and Experience. 2021, pp. 1–11.
       Available from https://doi.org/10.1002/cpe.6251

[14]   Marjuni A., Logeswaran R., Ahmad Fauzi M.F. 'An image watermarking
       scheme based on FWHT-DCT'. *International Conference on Networking and
       Information Technology (ICNIT 2010)*; Manila, Philippines, 2010.

[15]   Swaraja K., Meenakshi K., Padmavathi K. 'Hierarchical multilevel frame-
       work using RDWT-QR optimized watermarking in telemedicine'. *Biomedical
       Signal Processing and Control*. 2021, vol. 68, 102688.

[16]   Jero S.E., Ramu P. 'Curvelets-based ECG steganography for data security'.
       Electron Lett. 2016, vol. 52(4), pp. 283–85. Available from https://onlineli-
       brary.wiley.com/toc/1350911x/52/4

[17]   Candès E., Demanet L., Donoho D., Ying L. 'Fast discrete curvelet trans-
       forms'. *Multiscale Modeling & Simulation*. 2016, vol. 5(3), pp. 861–99.

[18]   Ibaida A., Khalil I. 'Wavelet-based ECG steganography for protecting pa-
       tient confidential information in point-of-care systems'. *IEEE Transactions
       on Bio-Medical Engineering*. 2013, vol. 60(12), pp. 3322–30.

[19]   Yang C.-Y., Wang W.-F. 'Effective electrocardiogram steganography based on
       coefficient alignment'. *Journal of Medical Systems*. 2016, vol. 40(3), p. 66.

[20]   Edward Jero S., Ramu P., Ramakrishnan S. 'ECG steganography using curve-
       let transform'. *Biomedical Signal Processing and Control*. 2015, vol. 22, pp.
       161–69.

[21]   Mittal M., Kaushik R., Verma A. 'Image watermarking in curvelet domain
       using edge surface blocks'. *Symmetry*. 2015, vol. 12(5), p. 822.

[22]   Mathivanan P., Edward Jero S., Ramu P., Balaji Ganesh A. 'QR code based
       patient data protection in ECG steganography'. *Australasian Physical &
       Engineering Sciences in Medicine*. 2018, vol. 41(4), pp. 1057–68.

[23]   Nambakhsh M.-S., Ahmadian A., Zaidi H. 'A contextual based double water-
       marking of PET images by patient ID and ECG signal'. *Computer Methods
       and Programs in Biomedicine*. 2011, vol. 104(3), pp. 418–25.

[24] Singh O.P., Singh A.K. 'Data hiding in encryption–compression domain [online]'. *Complex & Intelligent Systems*. 2015, pp. 1–14. Available from https://doi.org/10.1007/s40747-021-00309-w

[25] Available from https://archive.physionet.org/cgi-bin/atm/ATM

[26] Available from https://medpix.nlm.nih.gov/home

Chapter 12

Application of autoencoder in craniofacial reconstruction of forensic medicine

Shuo Wang[1], Junli Zhao[1], Zhenkuan Pan[1], Mingquan Zhou[2], and Zhihan Lv[1]

Craniofacial reconstruction is an important task of forensic medicine, which is to estimate the face from its skull. As a popular generation model in deep learning, autoencoder (AE) has attracted the attention of researchers because of their good ability to extract data features and representations. AE network can learn features from the data samples by unsupervised method on the training data. Based on the investigation of generating three-dimensional faces by AE methods, this chapter introduces in detail the methods and frameworks of traditional AE models, as well as some applications in craniofacial reconstruction and face generation after the model has been improved. We summarize the development and research status of AE models in recent years. In addition, this chapter compares and analyzes these AE models from many aspects. Furthermore, the future direction of face generation is pointed out, which will promote the technology of craniofacial reconstruction to be applied in the identification of unknown corpses in forensic medicine, medical plastic surgery and many other fields.

12.1 Introduction

Craniofacial reconstruction technology refers to a technology that uses the human skull as an object and combines anatomy, anthropology and computer technologies to reconstruct human facial appearance. Craniofacial reconstruction technology has developed rapidly and is widely used in medicine, criminal investigation and other fields. This work summarizes the autoencoder (AE) model related to craniofacial reconstruction in deep learning, which can provide new craniofacial reconstruction ideas for researchers in the forensic field to solve better the problems of low

[1]College of Computer Science and Technology, Qingdao University, Qingdao, Shandong Province, China
[2]Engineering Research Center of Virtual Reality and Applications, Ministry of Education, Beijing, China

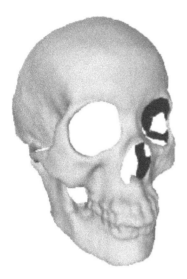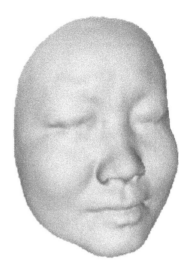

Figure 12.1   3D craniofacial data

reconstruction accuracy, poor effect and high cost, and make use of the reconstructed craniofacial information to promote the progress of related work.

Craniofacial reconstruction mainly includes two kinds of methods: manual craniofacial reconstruction and computer-assisted craniofacial reconstruction. The manual craniofacial reconstruction process takes a long time and cannot guarantee to obtain objective results. Computer-assisted craniofacial reconstruction has become an emerging technology with the development of computers in various fields. With the development of the medical field, computer technology's powerful information processing performance can be used to process the medical information of the known skull and reconstruct its appearance. Figure 12.1 shows three-dimensional (3D) craniofacial data. The related applications have attracted extensive attention.

AE [1, 2] is an important content of deep learning. It is an unsupervised learning process to make the input and output closer by designing the encoding and decoding. AE is mainly used for data dimensionality reduction or feature extraction. It can capture the main characteristics of data, perform lossy compression and reconstruction of input data and have certain anti-noise ability, strong expression ability and expansion ability. Therefore, the AE is widely used in many fields, such as craniofacial reconstruction in medical images. The craniofacial medical data processed by using the encoding process of the AE, the main information of the original data can be kept to the maximum. Then, through the decoding process, this main information is further processed so that craniofacial images or medical images can be transmitted digitally to professionals who need to obtain image information. It makes it easy for people to obtain medical information and formulate the best medical plan, which has good practical application value.

However, traditional AE also has many restrictive limitations, such as the generated images being often blurry, poor performance on complex models and so on. In order to solve the related problems, many improved AE models have emerged, e.g., variational autoencoder (VAE) [3], AE combined with generative adversarial network (GAN) [4] and so on. Each of them has improved AE model with a good performance in specific areas. However, as far as we know, there is no relevant review on the research of AE in the field of forensic craniofacial reconstruction. Therefore, we summarize the research status and application of AE in forensic craniofacial reconstruction in recent years in order to promote the relevant research in the medical field, provide a reference for relevant researchers and promote the development of craniofacial data information processing methods and the progress of relevant medical technology applications. Through this chapter, readers can understand the theory of AE and its application in the field of craniofacial reconstruction to use the powerful generation ability of AE to process craniofacial-related information and apply relevant technologies to the actual medical process.

12.2 The principle of AE

12.2.1 Traditional AE

AE is an unsupervised deep-learning method. It uses a back propagation (BP) algorithm to make the output value equal to the input value. AE has a special neural network structure, and its input and output structures are the same. It obtains the expression of low-dimensional input data through the training coding process and reconstructs these low-dimensional information expressions back to the high-dimensional data expression through the decoding process.

12.2.1.1 Model structure

The simple network structure of AE includes the data input layer, hidden layer and output layer, as shown in Figure 12.2.

There is a hidden layer h inside the AE, which can generate codes to represent the input. The network consists of two parts, an encoder

$$h = f(x) = \sigma_1 (w_1 x + b_1)$$ (12.1)

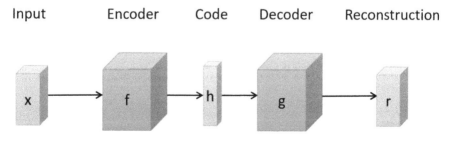

Input   Encoder   Code   Decoder   Reconstruction

Figure 12.2   Basic structure of autoencoder

and a decoder that generates reconstruction

$$r = g(h) = \sigma_2 (w_2 h + b_2) \qquad (12.2)$$

σ_1, σ_2 represent a non-linear activation function, w, b are weights and bias, respectively. Finally, the output x' is approximately equal to $g(f(x))$, which means that the output of the AE has the following relationship with the input:

$$x' \approx x \qquad (12.3)$$

The activation function of the encoder usually takes the sigmoid function or the identity function, which is :

$$s(x) = \frac{1}{1+e^{-x}} \qquad (12.4)$$

or

$$s(x) = x \qquad (12.5)$$

12.2.1.2   The principle of AE

The essence of the AE network is to compress and reconstruct the data, and it needs to learn a set of parameters, which are weights and bias terms. In order to determine the initial value of the weight matrix in the neural network, the AE needs to be pre-trained through the ordinary BP neural network so that the input value is approximately equal to the output value.

First, the weight matrix is used to encode the input. Since the AE neural network is composed of multiple neurons, the forward conduction algorithm needs to be used to find the activation value of each layer of the neural network.

After the activation function, the weight matrix is used for decoding, and the BP algorithm is used to find the 'residual error' between the final output layer and each layer of neurons. On the other hand, the weight parameters are updated by the gradient descent method to optimize the network, and finally, the output and input are approximately equal.

This process can be regarded as a compression encoding of the input data. The high-dimensional original data are represented by a low-dimensional vector. The same parameter matrix is used in the encoding and decoding processes, which can be regarded as a constraint to reduce the number of parameters and the complexity of the model.

12.2.1.3   Loss function

The selection of the loss function $L(x, y)$ depends on the type of data input by the decoder: if it is a regression problem, the loss function can use square error:

$$L(x, y) = \| x - y \|^2 \qquad (12.6)$$

If it is a classification problem, the loss function can use cross-entropy:

$$L(x, y) = -\sum_{i=1}^{n} [x_i \, log(y_i) + (1 - x_i) \, log(1 - y_i)] \qquad (12.7)$$

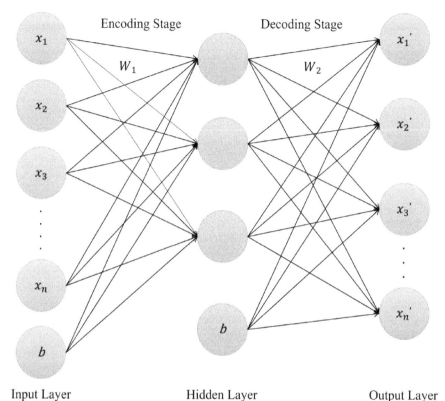

Figure 12.3 Network structure of autoencoder

In the formula, x represents the true value, y represents the predicted value and x_i, y_i represent the true label and predicted label of sample i, respectively. The network structure of the AE is shown in Figure 12.3. In this structure, x_i represents the input node, W represents the weight of the AE, b represents the bias term of the AE, x_i' represents the output node and the output is a result similar to the input. The number of neurons in the output layer is precisely equal to the number of neurons in the input layer, and the number of neurons in the hidden layer is generally less than that in the output layer.

The traditional AE has a simple structure. As a basic network model, it has been applied to various aspects of deep learning and has promoted the development of related fields.

12.3 Improved AE

As a generative model, the continuous development of AE also injects new vitality into the field of craniofacial reconstruction. At present, the improvement of AE is mainly from two aspects. One is the improvement of the AE by adding constraints,

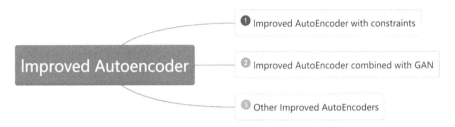

Figure 12.4   Category of the improved autoencoder

and the other is the improvement of the AE in combination with other models. In the AE, we mainly focus on the expression of the hidden layer. Therefore, many improvements to the AE are to impose some constraints on the hidden layer to force the expression of the hidden layer to be different from the input. If the model can still reconstruct the input signal well, the hidden layer expression is the effective feature learned by the model. In related aspects, the variational AE [3] is representative, which mainly improves the latent variable layer. Because the latent variable contains the main characteristics of the input data, its performance directly affects the output results, so it is necessary to improve the hidden variable. In addition, many classical methods can constrain the AE by conditions or parameters. These constraints force the model to learn valuable features of the input data. The second category is to combine the AE with other models for improvement. The most representative one is the combination of AE and GAN [4], which can play a better effect by combining their respective advantages. This chapter will introduce the AE according to the classification in Figure 12.4. In addition, Figures 12.5–12.7 show the detailed classification.

12.3.1   Improved AE with constraints

12.3.1.1   Variational AE

12.3.1.1.1   Introduction of VAE

Although the basic structure of VAE [3] is similar to that of AE [1, 2], the functional principle of VAE is entirely different from that of AE. VAE is a mixture of neural networks and Bayesian networks, and its hidden layer nodes in the VAE can be regarded as random variables. The encoder is equivalent to a variational reasoning network, and the decoder is equivalent to a generation network. The most significant difference between the structure of the VAE and the structure of the traditional AE is that the output of the encoder and decoder of the VAE is the parameters of the probability density function, rather than a specific code. Figure 12.8 shows the VAE model.

The difference in the VAE is that the regular hidden layer vector is replaced by two independent distribution vectors, which are mean value and standard deviation. So, the coding network needs to extract samples from the distribution and then input the extracted samples into the decoder, thereby training the VAE.

The loss function of the VAE is as follows:

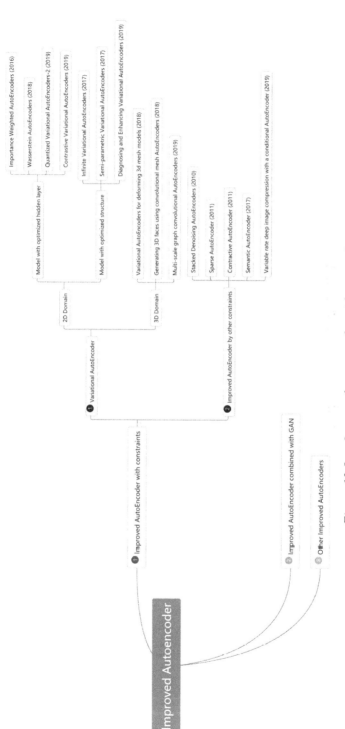

Figure 12.5   Improved autoencoder with constraints

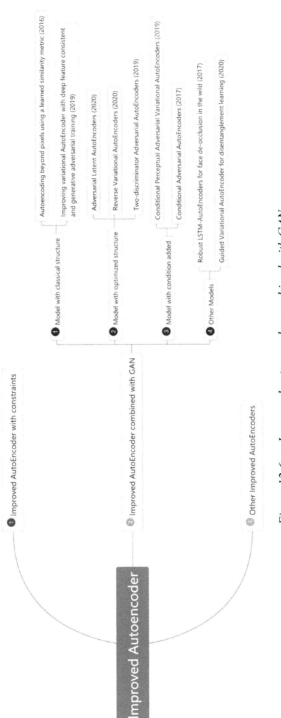

Figure 12.6   Improved autoencoder combined with GAN

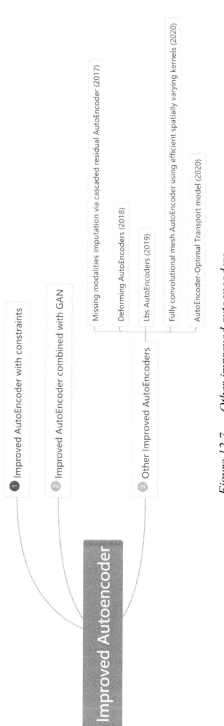

Figure 12.7   Other improved autoencoders

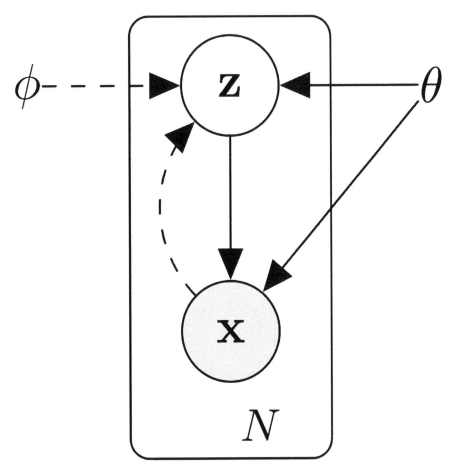

Figure 12.8   Variational autoencoder model (Kingma et al. [3])

$$l\left(\theta, \varnothing; x, z\right) = E_{q_{\varnothing(z|x)}}\left[logp_\theta\left(x|z\right)\right] - D_{KL}(q_\varnothing(z|x)\|p_\theta(z) \qquad (12.8)$$

This function consists of two parts. The former part represents the reconstruction loss, the same as that of the AE. Because we need to sample from the distribution, there is an expected value operator $E_{q_\varnothing}$. The other part of the loss function is the Kullback–Leibler (KL) divergence (D_{KL}) [5]. D_{KL} can measure the difference between two distributions p and q; $p_\theta\left(x|z\right)$ and $q_\varnothing\left(z|x\right)$ can be regarded as decoding and encoding process, respectively. $\varnothing$ and θ are the variational parameters and generative parameters, respectively. An important property is that it is always nonnegative. The KL divergence is 0 when the two distributions are precisely the same. So, the role of this part is to control the distribution to be learned not too far from the general normal distribution, and then try to make the average value of the hidden layer data mean close to 0 and the standard deviation close to 1.

12.3.1.1.2 Related methods of VAE

A large number of improved VAEs have appeared. Some scholars optimized the hidden layer of the VAE model. Burda *et al.* [6] proposed the importance-weighted autoencoder (IWAE) model, which reduces the requirements for the latent space distribution of VAE. The model assigns different weights to different potential variables in multiple layers to obtain better results. Tolstikhin *et al.* [7] designed Wasserstein autoencoder (WAE) to measure the distance between the hidden space distribution and the given distribution, thereby generating better quality images. Razavi *et al.* proposed quantized VAE-2 (VQ-VAE-2) [8] on the basis of VQ-VAE [9]. The model outputs discrete latent space coding through vector quantization, which overcomes the posterior collapse of VAE and passes multiple hierarchical organizations of scales that can generate high-quality images. Contrastive variational autoencoder (cVAE) is an improvement based on the traditional VAE algorithm, proposed by Abid *et al.* [10]. This method allows users to identify significant latent factors and generate new samples with only significant features. The samples can be denoised by removing irrelevant latent variables. The method is simple to implement, its running time is similar to that of standard VAEs and it has good robustness.

In addition, some scholars start with the model structure to improve the AE model. Ehsan Abbasnejad *et al.* [11] proposed an infinite VAE whose capacity is adapted to the input data, and it can grow to express the complexity of the input. Dai *et al.* [12] proposed a two-stage VAE. They improved the original VAE model and generated a new hidden space code through the extended ancestral process. It is proved that the hidden space of VAE may not be Gaussian distribution. Linh Tran *et al.* [13] proposed the DeepCoder model, which can well encode the target facial action by utilizing the capabilities of parametric VAE and non-parametric variational ordinal Gaussian process autoencoder (VO-GPAE) under the unified probability framework.

For the irregular mesh data, Tan *et al.* [14] proposed a mesh VAE, which uses deep neural networks to analyze deformed 3D mesh. The deformable model generated by this method has good quality. Ranjan *et al.* [15] used convolutional mesh AE to generate 3D faces. Through variational training, this method can generate 3D craniofacial faces with extreme facial expressions. In addition, Cukuan Yuan *et al.* [16] used a multiscale graph convolutional AE to represent and reconstruct human faces. The model has a lower reconstruction error and can generate higher quality 3D shapes through variational training. The above studies directly operate on the mesh, which guarantees the accuracy of the data.

Table 12.1 lists the improved VAE method while summarizing and comparing each model's strengths and weaknesses.

12.3.1.2 Improved AE by other constraints

In addition to the VAE, some AE models are constrained by conditions or parameters. Next, several related classical AE models and some recent related methods will be introduced.

Table 12.1   Features of variational autoencoder

Literature	Method	Strengths	Weakness
Yuri Burda *et al.* [6]	IWAE	Use multiple layers of latent variables and then assign different weights to different latent variables to achieve better results	Due to the difficulty of optimization, there are many inactive stochastic units
Ilya Tolstikhin *et al.* [7]	WAE	The model has good training stability and better reconstruction quality	The amount of sampling data in the experiment is limited, which may affect the actual effect
Ali Razavi *et al.* [8]	VQ-VAE-2	Overcome the posterior collapse problem of VAE	Specific visual inspection of the quality and diversity of samples is required
Abubakar Abid *et al.* [10]	cVAE	Can effectively reveal the underlying structure that is significant in a specific analysis	This method cannot completely eliminate the influence of irrelevant latent variables
M. Ehsan Abbasnejad *et al.* [11]	Infinite VAE	Can produce better predictions and use fewer parameters than a single overall model	Performance is not very good when the input is too complicated
Bin Dai *et al.* [12]	Two-stage VAE	The generation effect is significantly improved, and no additional super parameters or sensitive adjustments are required	High requirements for computing resources
Dieu Linh Tran *et al.* [13]	VAE + VO-GPAE	Able to efficiently and accurately perform AU encoding of target facial images	Data preprocessing is difficult
Qingyang Tan *et al.* [14]	mesh VAE	The framework is easy to train, requires only a few training samples and can generate high-quality results with rich details	However, this method can only handle homogeneous mesh
Anurag Ranjan *et al.* [15]	VAE + spectral convolutions	Embed the non-Euclidean structure data into the Euclidean space and simplified the mesh into a low-dimensional space structure	The scarcity of 3D face data limits the model's superiority to existing models in higher potential spatial dimensions
Cunkuan Yuan *et al.* [16]	VAE + graph convolutions	This method is based on the graph convolution algorithm of graph structure, and multiscale sampling can make the network better learn the face mesh features	The acquisition of data sets is difficult and expensive

First, three classical AE are introduced: denoising autoencoder (DAE), sparse autoencoder (SAE) and contractive autoencoder. In AE, a well-hidden layer representation is helpful to reconstruct the input signal, which requires that the hidden layer representation has good noise resistance. Therefore, Vincent *et al.* [17] proposed a DAE from the perspective of robustness. The DAE artificially adds some noise to the clean input data to make the clean data damaged and then inputs these damaged data into the traditional AE to make the model learn to remove this noise. Finally, try to reconstruct the same output as the clean input. The damaged input signal is obtained from the clean input by a random mapping. The most significant advantage of DAE is that the reconstructed signal is robust to the noise in the input, while the most significant disadvantage is that before each network training, it is necessary to artificially add noise to the clean input signal to obtain its damaged signal, which virtually increases the processing time of the model.

Under the condition of ensuring the network performance, the number of hidden layer nodes in the general AE model is few. However, when the number of hidden layer nodes is too large, the AE may have 'overfitting' or other phenomena. Therefore, Ng *et al.* [18] proposed SAE, which has a potential dimension larger than the input or output dimension. However, each time the network runs, only a small number of neurons will trigger, which means that the whole AE is essentially 'sparse', which can obtain high-dimensional and sparse expressions. These sparse expressions contain most of the main features of the input data and can be regarded as a simple representation of the input data. In this way, the dimension of the data is greatly reduced, and the performance of the model is greatly improved on the basis of ensuring the accuracy of model reconstruction.

The contractive AE was originally proposed by Rifai *et al.* [19], which is mainly to improve the robustness of the model to small disturbances around the data points of the training set. The operation process of the contractive AE is basically the same as that of the first two AE. The contractive AE adds a penalty term to the loss function, which forces the feature space to be mapped near the training data to achieve the shrinkage effect. At the same time, the method does not change the structure of the traditional AE.

In some current studies, some AEs are improved by conditional constraints. Adding semantic vectors is a relatively classic conditional constraint method. In order to realize zero-shot learning, Kodirov *et al.* [20] proposed a semantic AE. The core of the whole algorithm is that the original data are used as a constraint when encoding and decoding from the model to realize the reconstruction better. The algorithm is scalable and can be used for supervised clustering problems. This method can be used in the medical field when large-scale medical images are used as training samples. Choi *et al.* [21] proposed to train a conditional autoencoder (CAE). This method uses the Lagrange multiplier and the quantization bin size to control the rate of the model. The proposed scheme has better performance than classic image compression codecs. Using this method to compress specific medical images, data can reduce their storage/transmission requirements, improving efficiency.

Table 12.2 lists the AE improved by constraints while summarizing and comparing each model's strengths and weaknesses.

Table 12.2 *Features of autoencoder improved by other constraints*

Literature	Method	Strengths	Weaknesses
Vincent et al. [17]	DAE	The reconstructed signal is robust to the noise in the input	Before each training, it is necessary to add noise artificially, which virtually increases the processing time of the model
Ng et al. [18]	Sparse AE	Sparse representation reduces the dimension of data and greatly improves the model's performance	The robustness is poor, and the effect is poor when the test and training samples' probability distribution is quite different
Rifai et al. [19]	Contractive AE	When the input changes very little, the output result has a certain stability	The reconstruction effect of the output in general
Elyor Kodirov et al. [20]	SAE	The constraint effect on the objective function formed by the structure of the autoencoder is very obvious	In supervised cluster analysis, the model calculation costs are more expensive
Yoojin Choi et al. [21]	CAE + variable-rate compression	Lagrange multiplier and quantization bin size are introduced to adjust the rate, and a conditional network is used to solve multiple targets	Image compression requires training multiple networks at different compression rates

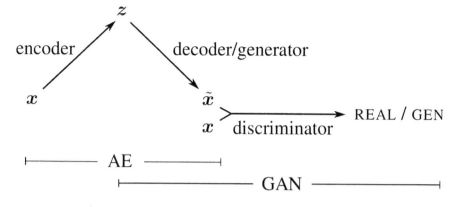

Figure 12.9   Model combining VAE and GAN [22]

12.3.2   Improved AE combined with GAN

12.3.2.1   Introduction of GAN

Nowadays, generative models based on deep learning are getting more and more attention. The deep generation model has strong generation ability and can generate high-quality content. Amongst these generation models, two kinds are very prominent: VAE [3] and GAN [4].

GAN consists of two parts: generator and discriminator. The goal of the generator is to generate as real data as possible, while the discriminator's goal is to distinguish between real data and generated data. GAN uses a neural network to automatically learn features, avoiding the tedious operation of manual feature extraction and does not require manual intervention. On the one hand, VAE can make GAN's training easier. On the other hand, GAN can make VAE generate higher quality results. As two generative models, the combination of VAE and GAN has shown great application potential in various fields.

12.3.2.2   Related methods of combining AE and GAN

The first combination is the classic VAE–GAN model. Larsen *et al.* [22] proposed an AE that uses learning representation to measure the similarity in the data space. As shown in Figure 12.9, this model combines VAE with GAN and learns the feature representation in the discriminator, which is used as the basis for the reconstruction target of the VAE. Hou *et al.* [23] proposed a method to improve the performance of the VAE model. This method realizes the principle of consistency of depth features. It combines a generative adversarial training mechanism to ensure that the output of VAE is similar to the input while ensuring the authenticity and nature of the image. These are typical methods of combining VAE and GAN.

By modifying the structure of the AE, Pidhorskyi *et al.* [24] introduced a model called the adversarial latent autoencoder (ALAE) to explore the generation capability and decoupling representation of AE compared to GAN. This model constructs two kinds of AE: one is based on the MLP encoder; the other is based on StyleGAN, which is called StyleALAE. This model constrains the similarity of the latent variable space rather than constraining the image similarity in the native AE. The 'reverse VAE' proposed by Gauerhof *et al.* [25] can perform visual attribute manipulation and anomaly detection. The model introduces a trained discriminator to distinguish the real data from the generated data and adjusts the structure of the generator network and the encoder network so that the encoder network can reconstruct the potential vector using the image data generated by the generator network. Two-discriminator adversarial autoencoder network (TAAN) is an unsupervised face image synthesis model proposed by Wu *et al.* [26]. The model can generate various styles of face images and can control the degree of perception of attributes in the generated image. This method adds a multilevel discriminator to the decoder. The decoder is very sensitive to subtle facial changes because the discriminator in the model is not used to identify the authenticity of the generated image.

Some studies control the model by adding conditions. Conditional perceptual adversarial variational autoencoder (CPAVAE) is a new GAN- and VAE-based architecture proposed by Chandaliya *et al.* [27]. This method converts facial images into latent vectors, then reconstructs faces based on age and gender tags while using sampling and perceptual loss to improve face reconstruction. In addition, Zhang *et al.* [28] also proposed a conditional adversarial autoencoder (CAAE), which can be used for face age prediction/backtracking. Drawing a face of a specified age based on the current face includes the face predicted when the age becomes older in the future (age progression), and the face predicted when the age is younger in the past (age regression). The proposed framework has great potential and can be used as a general framework for tasks related to face age.

The occlusion of human faces often occurs in the natural environment, Zhao *et al.* [29] proposed robust LSTM-autoencoders (RLA). The proposed method can reconstruct the occluded facial parts well. By using supervised and adversarial learning methods, more facial details can be preserved, and information can be identified in the reconstructed face.

In order to perform decoupling learning, Ding *et al.* [30] proposed a new representation learning method called guided variational autoencoder (GuidedVAE). The learning goal of the model is achieved by providing a signal to the potential encoding of the VAE, which does not change the main architecture, thus retaining the ideal characteristics of the VAE. GuidedVAE has transparency and the simplicity of general characterization learning tasks, which can be applied to decoupled learning.

Table 12.3 lists the improved AE combined with GAN while summarizing and comparing each model's strengths and weaknesses.

12.3.3   Other improved AE

In addition to the improved AE mentioned above, there are various AE improved by other methods, and these methods also improve the performance of the AE in various aspects.

Table 12.3   Features of the improved autoencoder combined with GAN

Literature	Method	Strengths	Weaknesses
Anders Boesen Lindbo Larsen et al. [22]	VAE + GAN	A generative model trained with learned similarity measures can produce better image samples	For unsupervised pretraining of supervised tasks, it is impossible to learn good generalizations of different object classes
Xianxu Hou et al. [23]	GAN + VAE	The output is more realistic, images with fine details and a reasonable background. Can extract effective facial features	The encoded latent vector cannot capture some subtle differences in facial attribute recognition
Stanislav Pidhorskyi et al. [24]	ALAE	The result of interpolation in the latent variable space is smoother and more separated	There is a higher computational cost
Lydia Gauerhof et al. [25]	Reverse-VAE	While generating the real image, the model successfully learned the mapping from the input image to the latent vector	In anomaly detection, the strategy based on reconstruction error is difficult to detect anomalous images with simple structure or similar appearance in other samples
Xuehui Wu et al. [26]	TAAN	The dual discriminator architecture can fully separate and fuse the expression attribute tag with the face image	There is still room for improvement in the generated image's naturalness and the conversion's accuracy
Praveen Kumar Chandaliya et al. [27]	CPAVAE	The model performs well in the aging and rejuvenation of children's faces and is robust to the changes of posture and light	Fewer female data were collected during training, which may affect the reliability of the experimental results
Zhifei Zhang et al. [28]	CAAE	There is no need for paired training samples. Given an unlabeled picture, the model can directly generate a picture of a suitable age	The age division of training data is uneven
Fang Zhao et al. [29]	RLA	More facial details can be preserved by using supervised and adversarial learning methods	Only the synthetic occlusion surface is used for training, which lacks real data

(Continues)

Table 12.3 Continued

Literature	Method	Strengths	Weaknesses
Zheng Ding et al. [30]	GuidedVAE	The learning goal is achieved by providing a signal to the potential coding of the VAE without changing the backbone architecture and retaining the ideal characteristics of the VAE	This method cannot determine its anti-noise performance

Tran *et al*. [31] proposed a new cascaded residual autoencoder (CRA) for the interpolation of missing modalities. The encoder is composed of a set of stacked residual autoencoders (RAs), which combine RAs into the cascade structure. This method can ensure the random distribution of missing values and recover damaged samples with missing patterns. It has superior performance in data interpolation and target recognition tasks of imputed data. Shu *et al*. [32] proposed deforming AE. Although the entire model is trained in an unsupervised manner using only simple image reconstruction losses, the feature decoupling and separation capabilities of the model are still very powerful. Li *et al*. [33] proposed a self-supervised autoencoding algorithm linear blending skinning-autoencoder (LBS-AE), which aligns the joint mesh model with the point cloud. The proposed algorithm can not only recover the pose but also learn the segmentation well. Zhou *et al*. [34] proposed the first template-free fully convolutional AE for registering arbitrary mesh (tetrahedral and non-manifold mesh). Dongsheng An *et al*. [35] proposed the autoencoder-optimal transport (AE-OT) model. The AE model uses the extended semi-discrete optimal transport to map the low-dimensional image manifold in the latent space into new potential codes and trains the decoder to generate a new image. This method can effectively prevent the problems of mode collapse and mode mixing.

Table 12.4 lists other improved AE methods while summarizing and comparing each model's strengths and weaknesses.

12.4 The application of AE in forensic

12.4.1 The application of AE in face reconstruction

The development of deep-learning technology provides a new idea for the research of human face reconstruction. Face reconstruction technology based on AE is also developing rapidly in deep learning. AE has the characteristics of automation and intelligence, which reduces the complexity of manual feature extraction in data processing and improves the accuracy and efficiency of human face reconstruction.

In the two-dimensional (2D) field, Huang *et al*. [36] proposed a multilayer supervised adaptive network structure based on deep AE, which considers the class label information and can extract the main features in the face image and reconstruct the corresponding face image. Zeng *et al*. [37] proposed a self-supervised hybrid model using deformable AE and GAN, which can reconstruct human faces from video and provide real results. Wang *et al*. [38] proposed a generative model, which can reconstruct a symmetrical face from a given unconstrained face image. The model adopts a three-stage training strategy from coarse to fine, avoiding the need for many symmetrical faces as training data.

In the 3D field, more and more research on face reconstruction is developing rapidly. Liu *et al*. [39] jointly learn a non-linear face model from a set of different original 3D scanning databases and can effectively establish a dense point-to-point correspondence for single-image 3D face reconstruction. Sharma *et al*. [40] used 3D voxels to reconstruct the face model, and the proposed method can also be applied to

Table 12.4 Features of other improved autoencoders

Literature	Method	Strengths	Weaknesses
Luan Tran *et al.* [31]	CRA	It can guarantee the random distribution of missing values and recover damaged samples with missing patterns	The narrow scope of application
Zhixin Shu *et al.* [32]	Deforming autoencoders	The entire architecture uses only simple image reconstruction losses for training in an unsupervised manner. This model's capability of decoupling using deep autobncoders and unsupervised learning is very powerful	The time complexity of the algorithm is not analyzed in this paper
Chun-Liang Li *et al.* [33]	LBS-AE	Introducing the LBS method into the autoencoder model can make the model use a smaller network and have better generalization ability than the unconstrained deformation depending on the deep network	The model suffers from the local optimum issues within the segmentation
Yi Zhou *et al.* [34]	Mesh AE	It has the advantage of semantically meaningful local latent code and has higher interpolation capabilities than many traditional 3D mesh generation models	The model cannot work on data sets with different topologies
Dongsheng An *et al.* [35]	AE-OT	Can effectively prevent mode collapse and mode mixing problems	The performance of the algorithm is not introduced in this study

Table 12.5   Applications of autoencoders

Application field	Classification	Application
2D face reconstruction	Face reconstruction based on 2D data [36–38]	Reconstruct corresponding similar facial images from 2D pictures or videos
3D face reconstruction	Face reconstruction based on 3D data [39–41]	Use original 3D scan, voxel, and incomplete data for face reconstruction
	Face reconstruction based on 2D data [42–50]	Reconstruct a 3D face from 2D image data, and make the reconstructed face maintain the corresponding shape and texture
3D craniofacial reconstruction	3D reconstruction of complete craniofacial data [51–53]	Use the original skull to reconstruct the corresponding face while maintaining a high reconstruction quality
	3D reconstruction of defect craniofacial data [54]	Predict the complete geometry of the defective skull and reconstruct it

face recognition. Abrevaya *et al.* [41] proposed a multilinear AE architecture, which can learn multilinear face models from incomplete training data.

In addition to directly reconstructing with 3D data, when 3D scan data are insufficient, 3D reconstruction directly from 2D data may be a better choice. Devi *et al.* [42] proposed a method called the autoencoder-based face reconstruction with simultaneous patch learning and landmark estimation method, which uses a single frontal face image for 3D face reconstruction. Cheng *et al.* [43] used a method based on graph convolution networks to reconstruct high-fidelity facial geometry. Zhou *et al.* [44] constructed a non-linear 3D morphable model (3DMM) using direct mesh convolution learning combined with texture and shape AE, which can directly reconstruct texture and shape from 2D facial images in the wild. Han *et al.* [45] reconstructed 3D human faces from 2D images and extracted 3D features. Fan *et al.* [46] performed textured 3D face reconstruction from a single unrestricted face image and achieved better surface detail performance. Tran *et al.* [47] proposed a 3DMM learning method, which can learn non-linear 3DMM face images from face images in natural scenes without using real 3D scanning. Feng *et al.* [48] proposed detailed expression capture and animation (DECA), which can obtain DECA from a single image. Model-based deep convolutional face autoencoder (MOFA) was proposed by Tewari *et al.* [49]. In MOFA, a face photo is learned through the deep-learning method to learn various parameters to reconstruct the 3D face model. In the subsequent optimization process [50], this method displays a random vertex sampling strategy in the loss function to speed up training while analyzing it through comprehensive optimization and shape coloring refinement methods to achieve high-fidelity reconstruction.

These techniques in deep learning can be applied to the forensic field to help recognize and reconstruct human faces. For example, when there are no other clues to search for missing persons or criminals, the face can be reconstructed through pictures or videos to assist in the search.

12.4.2 The application of AE in craniofacial reconstruction

Craniofacial reconstruction technology occupies a key position in the field of medicine. The reconstructed face and skull information can be used to identify pathological features and conduct medical research. This information can also be used to conduct criminal forensic investigations.

In the application of AE in craniofacial reconstruction, Hu *et al.* [51] proposed a craniofacial reconstruction method based on an end-to-end deep convolutional neural network, which can automatically predict the face of the skull, has a very low reconstruction error and can effectively achieve craniofacial reconstruction. Inspired by the structure introduced in MOFA [49, 50], Liu *et al.* [52] constructed a deep AE for facial reconstruction. The AE can perform craniofacial reconstruction and has high geometric accuracy and detail. Zhan *et al.* [53] used depth map data for 3D craniofacial reconstruction. The generator part of the model used encoder-decoder structure, combined with the designed loss function, and finally achieved high-precision craniofacial reconstruction.

Some scholars have studied incomplete craniofacial data. Kodym *et al.* [54] proposed a multiscale cascaded convolutional neural networks (CNN) architecture for the reconstruction of missing skulls. The method can learn the spatial distribution of the upper part of the normal skull and use defective skull data to predict its complete geometry.

There are many unnamed skulls in criminal cases, and these skulls are often mutilated. These reconstruction techniques can be used to reconstruct the original face of the unknown skull to determine the body source information and assist in handling cases. The development of the autoencoder makes it have broad application prospects in the field of forensic medicine. Table 12.5 lists the applications of various AE.

12.5 Summary and future work

This chapter introduces the methods and applications of AE in forensic craniofacial reconstruction. The related methods are divided into three parts: improved AE with constraints, improved AE combined with GAN and other improved AE. These methods all improve the performance of traditional AE in certain aspects.

The AE is a classic model in deep learning. The craniofacial reconstruction method based on the AE has been applied to many aspects of forensic medicine, such as criminal investigation, archaeology and forensic identification. The application in forensic medicine has promoted the advancement of craniofacial reconstruction technology, and at the same time, craniofacial reconstruction technology has also enabled the continuous development of forensic medicine.

The introduction of AE has injected strong vitality into the development of craniofacial reconstruction technology. The research on craniofacial reconstruction based on AE is only in the preliminary exploration stage. The representation of craniofacial data for neural networks, the data augmentation method and the improvement of reconstruction results are still to be studied further. In future work, with the joint efforts of researchers in various fields, the automatic encoder will make more significant contributions to craniofacial reconstruction technology to promote the development of more fields and benefit people's lives, education and culture.

Acknowledgements

This work was supported by the National Natural Science Foundation of China under Grant (Nos. 62172247, 61702293), the National Statistical Science Research Project (No.2020LY100), National Natural Science Foundation of Shandong Province (No. ZR2020QF039, ZR2019LZH002).

References

[1] Rumelhart D.E., Hinton G.E., Williams R.J. 'Learning representations by back-propagating errors'. *Nature*. 1951, vol. 323(6088), pp. 533–36.

[2] Bourlard H., Kamp Y. 'Auto-association by multilayer perceptrons and singular value decomposition'. *Biological Cybernetics*. 1988, vol. 59(4–5), pp. 291–94.

[3] Kingma D.P., Welling M. 'Auto-encoding variational bayes'. *CoRR*. 2013.

[4] Goodfellow I., Pouget-Abadie J., Mirza M, *et al.* 'Generative adversarial nets'. *Communications of the ACM*. 2020, vol. 63(11), pp. 139–44.

[5] Kullback S., Leibler R.A. 'On information and sufficiency'. *The Annals of Mathematical Statistics*. 1951, vol. 22(1), pp. 79–86.

[6] Burda Y., Grosse R., Salakhutdinov R. 'Importance weighted autoencoders'. *CoRR*. 2015.

[7] Tolstikhin I., Bousquet O., Gelly S., Schoelkopf B. 'Wasserstein auto-encoders'. *CoRR*. 2017.

[8] Razavi A., Van Den Oord O., Vinyals O. 'Generating diverse high-fidelity images with VQ-VAE-2'. *Proceedings of the 32rd International Conference on Neural Information Processing Systems (NIPS)*; Montréal, Canada, CoRR, 2019. pp. 14866–76.

[9] Van Den Oord A., Vinyals O., Kavukcuoglu K. 'Neural discrete representation learning'. *Proceedings of the 31st International Conference on Neural Information Processing Systems (NIPS)*; CA, USA, CoRR, 2017. pp. 6309–18.

[10] Abid A., Zou J. 'Contrastive variational autoencoder enhances salient features'. *CoRR*. 2019.

[11] Ehsan Abbasnejad M., Dick A., van den Hengel A. 'Infinite variational autoencoder for semi-supervised learning'. *IEEE Conference on Computer Vision and Pattern Recognition (CVPR)*; Honolulu, HI, CoRR, 2017. pp. 5888–97.

[12] Dai B., Wipf D. 'Diagnosing and enhancing VAE models'. *International Conference on Learning Representations (ICLR)*; New Orleans, CoRR, 2019. pp. 1405.

[13] Linh Tran D., Walecki R., Eleftheriadis S., Schuller B., Pantic M. 'DeepCoder: semi-parametric variational autoencoders for automatic facial action coding'. *IEEE International Conference on Computer Vision (ICCV)*; Venice, Italy, IEEE, 2017. pp. 3190–99.

[14] Tan Q., Gao L., Lai Y.-K., Xia S. 'Variational autoencoders for deforming 3D mesh models'. *IEEE Conference on Computer Vision and Pattern Recognition (CVPR)*; Salt Lake City, UT, IEEE, 2018. pp. 5841–50.

[15] Ranjan A., Bolkart T., Sanyal S., Black M.J. 'Generating 3D faces using convolutional mesh autoencoders'. *Proceedings of the European Conference on Computer Vision (ECCV)*; Munich, Germany, Springer, 2018. pp. 725–41.

[16] Yuan C., Li K., Lai Y.-K., Liu Y., Yang J. '3D face reprentation and reconstruction with multi-scale graph convolutional autoencoders'. *IEEE International*

Conference on Multimedia and Expo (ICME); Shanghai, China, IEEE, 2019. pp. 1558–63.

[17] Vincent P., Larochelle H., Lajoie I., Bengio Y., Manzagol P.-A. 'Stacked denoising autoencoders: learning useful representations in a deep network with a local denoising criterion'. *Journal of Machine Learning Research*. 2010, vol. 11(12), pp. 3371–408.

[18] Andrew N. 'Sparse autoencoder'. *CS294A Lecture Notes*. 2011, vol. 72(2011), pp. 1–19.

[19] Rifai S., Vincent P., Muller X., Glorot X., Bengio Y. 'Contractive auto-encoders: explicit invariance during feature extraction'. *Proceedings of the 28th International Conference on Machine Learning (ICML)*; Bellevue, WA, 2011. pp. 833–40.

[20] Kodirov E., Xiang T., Gong S. 'Semantic autoencoder for zero-shot learning'. *IEEE Conference on Computer Vision and Pattern Recognition (CVPR)*; Honolulu, HI, IEEE, 2017. pp. 3174–83.

[21] Choi Y., El-Khamy M., Lee J. 'Variable rate deep image compression with a conditional autoencoder'. *IEEE/CVF International Conference on Computer Vision (ICCV)*; Seoul, Korea, IEEE, 2019. pp. 3146–54.

[22] Larsen A.B.L., Sønderby S.K., Larochelle H., Winther O. 'Autoencoding beyond pixels using a learned similarity metric'. *Proceedings of The 33rd International Conference on Machine Learning (PMLR)*; New York, CoRR, 2016. pp. 1558–66.

[23] Hou X., Sun K., Shen L., Qiu G. 'Improving variational autoencoder with deep feature consistent and generative adversarial training'. *Neurocomputing*. 2019, vol. 341, pp. 183–94.

[24] Pidhorskyi S., Adjeroh D.A., Doretto G. 'Adversarial latent autoencoders'. *IEEE/CVF Conference on Computer Vision and Pattern Recognition (CVPR)*; Seattle, WA, IEEE, 2020. pp. 14104–13.

[25] Gauerhof L., Gu N. 'Reverse variational autoencoder for visual attribute manipulation and anomaly detection'. *IEEE Winter Conference on Applications of Computer Vision (WACV)*; Snowmass Village, CO, USA, IEEE, 2020. pp. 2103–12.

[26] Wu X., Shao J., Zhang D., Chen J. 'Unsupervised facial image synthesis using two-discriminator adversarial autoencoder network'. *IEEE International Conference on Multimedia and Expo (ICME)*; Shanghai, China, IEEE, 2019. pp. 1162–67.

[27] Chandaliya P.K., Nain N. 'Conditional perceptual adversarial variational autoencoder for age progression and regression on child face'. *International Conference on Biometrics (ICB)*; Crete, Greece, IEEE, 2019. pp. 1–8.

[28] Zhang Z., Song Y., Qi H. 'Age progression/regression by conditional adversarial autoencoder'. *IEEE Conference on Computer Vision and Pattern Recognition (CVPR)*; Honolulu, HI, IEEE, 2017. pp. 5810–18.

[29] Fang Z., Jiashi F., Jian Z., Wenhan Y., Shuicheng Y. 'Robust LSTM-autoencoders for face de-occlusion in the wild'. *IEEE Transactions on Image Processing*. 2018, vol. 27(2), pp. 778–90.

[30] Ding Z., Xu Y., Xu W, *et al.* 'Guided variational autoencoder for disentanglement learning'. *IEEE/CVF Conference on Computer Vision and Pattern Recognition (CVPR)*; Seattle, WA, IEEE, 2020. pp. 7920–29.

[31] Tran L., Liu X., Zhou J., Jin R. 'Missing modalities imputation via cascaded residual autoencoder'. *IEEE Conference on Computer Vision and Pattern Recognition (CVPR)*; Honolulu, HI, IEEE, 2017. pp. 1405–14.

[32] Shu Z., Sahasrabudhe M., Guler R.A., Samaras D., Paragios N., Kokkinos I. 'Deforming autoencoders: unsupervised disentangling of shape and appearance'. *Proceedings of the European Conference on Computer Vision (ECCV)*; Munich, Germany, Springer, 2018. pp. 664–80.

[33] Li C.-L., Simon T., Saragih J., Poczos B., Sheikh Y. 'LBS autoencoder: self-supervised fitting of articulated meshes to point clouds'. *IEEE/CVF Conference on Computer Vision and Pattern Recognition (CVPR)*; Long Beach, CA, IEEE, 2019. pp. 11959–68.

[34] Zhou Y., Wu C., Li Z., Cao C, *et al.* 'Fully convolutional mesh autoencoder using efficient spatially varying kernels'. *Advances in Neural Information Processing Systems.* 2020, vol. 33, pp. 9251–62.

[35] An D., Guo Y., Lei N., Luo Z., Yau S.-T., Gu X. 'AE-OT: a new generative model based on extended semi-discrete optimal transport'. *International Conference on Learning Representations (ICLR)*; Addis Ababa, Ethiopia, 2020.

[36] Huang R., Liu C., Li G., Zhou J. 'Adaptive deep supervised autoencoder based image reconstruction for face recognition'. *Math Probl Eng.* 2016, vol. 2016, pp. 1–14.

[37] Zeng X., Pan Y., Wang M., Zhang J., Liu Y. 'Realistic face reenactment via self-supervised disentangling of identity and pose'. *Proceedings of the AAAI Conference on Artificial Intelligence*; New York, NY, 2020. pp. 12757–64.

[38] Wang T., Zhang S., Dong J., Liang Y. 'A deep variational autoencoder approach for robust facial symmetrization'. *British Machine Vision Conference (BMVC)*; Newcastle, UK, 2018. pp. 318.

[39] Liu F., Tran L., Liu X. '3D face modeling from diverse raw scan data'. *Proceedings of the IEEE/CVF International Conference on Computer Vision (ICCV)*; Seoul, Korea, IEEE, 2019. pp. 9408–18.

[40] Sharma S., Kumar V. 'Voxel-based 3D face reconstruction and its application to face recognition using sequential deep learning'. *Multimedia Tools and Applications.* 2020, vol. 79(25–26), pp. 17303–30.

[41] Abrevaya V.F., Wuhrer S., Boyer E. 'Multilinear autoencoder for 3D face model learning'. *IEEE Winter Conference on Applications of Computer Vision (WACV)*; Lake Tahoe, NV, IEEE, 2018. pp. 1–9.

[42] Devi P.R., Baskaran R. 'SL2E-AFRE: personalized 3D face reconstruction using autoencoder with simultaneous subspace learning and landmark estimation'. *Applied Intelligence.* 2021, vol. 51(4), pp. 2253–68.

[43] Cheng S., Tzimiropoulos G., Shen J., Pantic M. 'Faster, better and more detailed: 3D face reconstruction with graph convolutional networks'.

Proceedings of the Asian Conference on Computer Vision (ACCV); Kyoto, Japan, 2020. pp. 188–205.

[44] Zhou Y., Deng J., Kotsia I., Zafeiriou S. 'Dense 3D face decoding over 2500fps: joint texture & shape convolutional mesh decoders'. *IEEE/CVF Conference on Computer Vision and Pattern Recognition (CVPR)*; Long Beach, CA, IEEE, 2019. pp. 1097–106.

[45] Han W., Chen F., Sun F. 'Can we extract 3D biometrics from 2D images for facial beauty analysis?'. *Proceedings of the 2020 9th International Conference on Computing and Pattern Recognition (ICCPR)*; Xiamen China, ACM, 2020. pp. 213–17.

[46] Fan Y., Liu Y., Lv G., Liu S., Li G., Huang Y. 'Full face-and-head 3D model with photorealistic texture'. *IEEE Access: Practical Innovations, Open Solutions*. 2020, vol. 8, pp. 210709–21.

[47] Tran L., Liu X. 'On learning 3D face morphable model from in-the-wild images'. *IEEE Transactions on Pattern Analysis and Machine Intelligence*. 2021, vol. 43(1), pp. 157–71.

[48] Feng Y., Feng H., Black M.J., Bolkart T. 'Learning an animatable detailed 3D face model from in-the-wild images'. *ACM Transactions on Graphics*. 2021, vol. 40(4), pp. 1–13.

[49] Tewari A., Zollhofer M., Kim H, *et al.* 'MoFA: model-based deep convolutional face autoencoder for unsupervised monocular reconstruction'. *IEEE International Conference on Computer Vision (ICCV)*; Venice, IEEE, 2017. pp. 1274–83.

[50] Tewari A., Zollhofer M., Bernard F, *et al.* 'High-fidelity monocular face reconstruction based on an unsupervised model-based face autoencoder'. *IEEE Transactions on Pattern Analysis and Machine Intelligence*. 2020, vol. 42(2), pp. 357–70.

[51] Hu Y., Wang Z., Pan Y., Xie L., Wang Z., Chen B. 'Craniofacial reconstruction via face elevation map estimation based on the deep convolution neutral network'. *Security and Communication Networks*. 2021, vol. 2021, pp. 1–9.

[52] Liu C., Li X. 'Superimposition-guided facial reconstruction from skull'. *ArXiv Preprint*. 2018.

[53] Zhang N., Zhao J., Duan F, *et al.* 'An end-to-end conditional generative adversarial network based on depth map for 3D craniofacial reconstruction'. *In Proceedings of the 30th ACM International Conference on Multimedia (MM'22)*; New York, NY, USA, ACM, 2022. pp. 759–68.

[54] Kodym O., Španěl M., Herout A. 'Skull shape reconstruction using cascaded convolutional networks'. *Computers in Biology and Medicine*. 2020, vol. 123, p. 103886.

Chapter 13

Security and Privacy in smart Internet of Things environments for well-being in the healthcare industry

Pooja Shah[1], Sharnil Pandya[2], Gautam Srivastava[3,4], and Thippa Reddy Gadekallu[5]

Privacy protection is required when communicating data in the healthcare system. The Internet of Things (IoT) in healthcare has numerous advantages, including the potential to more closely monitor patients' health and the use of data for analytics. IoT is a framework of interconnected, web-connected devices that may collect and transmit data via a wireless server without the need for human involvement. In this context, IoT-based healthcare uses many technological advances to give several services such as quick and efficient treatment, savings, and better communication. *Wireless Body Area Network* (WBAN) technology can improve the performance of data communication in smart systems. Throughout each stage of smart medical systems, machine learning (ML) can be applied. In this study, the most current research, suggested approaches, and existing smart healthcare system technologies are discussed in terms of technological advances, applications, and difficulties to provide a proper overview of what IoT signifies in the healthcare sector now and in the future.

13.1 Introduction

Smart things are progressively being used by a variety of people and in a variety of fields. It was created to keep up with the rapid advancement of technology, improve, speed up, and boost the efficiency of the work done. Due to the sensitive nature of IoT-based smart healthcare, there has always been a need to protect data, whether in print or in electronic form. IoT has improved people's lives in a variety of ways

[1]Information Technology Department, Gandhinagar Institute of Technology, Ahmedabad, India
[2]Symbiosis International University, India
[3]Math and Computer Science, Brandon University, Brandon, MB, Canada
[4]Computer Science and Mathematics, Lebanese American University, Beirut, Lebanon
[5]School of Information Technology and Engineering, Vellore Institute of Technology, India

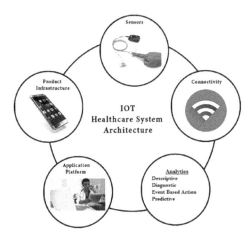

Figure 13.1   IoT healthcare system architecture

by providing useful information, increasing productivity, and reducing costs. IoT is being used in healthcare to improve patient monitoring, cut costs, and promote innovation in patient care. IoT is a new area of research, and its promising application in healthcare is still in its infancy. This Chapter describes IoT with a particular emphasis on its use in healthcare. IoT can be seen in many fields such as tourism, agriculture, smart cities, emergency responders, and urban infrastructure, in addition to addressing regular living necessities [1]. One of the key areas for artificial intelligence (AI) research implementations is healthcare [2, 3]. A number of ground-breaking projects aimed at establishing healthcare IoT (HIoT) systems have been addressed. Based on recurring patterns from past research, a generic and standardized approach for emerging end-to-end IoT healthcare systems is proposed to guide the future growth of such technologies (see Figure 13.1). There is a chance that the private data in IoT-based healthcare applications can be exposed to mischievous users and in turn be misused. Document fabrication and fraud are frequently occurring around the world, resulting in damages for individuals, organizations, and industries, as well as national security concerns. Remote monitoring of patients is one of the most essential areas of HIoT since it protects millions of people's lives while also providing additional benefits to healthcare. Patient safety, successful treatment, and patient privacy are all dependent on the security and privacy features of HIoT systems are just some examples.

The healthcare profession, on the other side, is where the largest security vulnerabilities and data privacy concerns are seen [4]. Steganography and digital security approaches such as steganography, IoT [5–7], encoding, cryptography, and identification are vital in solving the privacy protection issues [8–26]. Various methods have been developed to secure confidential material, including steganography, encryption, and watermarks [1–4, 27–33]. IoT [28–30] has increased in importance in recent years. The ability to communicate huge volumes of data has increased significantly as telecommunication technology and data transmission speeds have improved. The growing number of people suffering from chronic conditions (people with disabilities and the elderly) has required the development of a new system of healthcare [34–41]. The new model will be more customized and is less dependent on existing healthcare institutions such as healthcare centers, nursing homes, and long-term treatment centers [2, 42]. Security of the healthcare system depends on protecting the information of the users involved.

Machine Learning (ML) [43–53], blockchain [54–58], big data analytics [59–61], edge computing [62, 63], biometrics [64], and nanotechnologies are no longer linked to a specific area or application. Rather, these methods could be incorporated into a variety of IoT-related solutions.

The requirements for security and privacy such systems are as follows:

- invisibility
- payload
- capacity
- statistical attacks are not a problem because of the robustness of the code
- resistance in the presence of image modification
- unsuspicious files are documents that are suspicious regardless of their format

Encoding secret messages in text, image, audio, and video are challenging when dealing with security methods. IoT with an AI system is proposed in this research for healthcare security. Wireless sensor networks are created using IoT technologies. IoT networks bridge the gap between the physical and virtual worlds.

The budget of connectivity services via quick and reliable connections between users, clinics, and particular healthcare systems is a vital goal of any healthcare service [65]. The most recent wireless connections in health care are expected to help with serious illnesses, early treatment, actual monitoring, and crucial services [66].

Smart healthcare systems are considered pioneer solutions to the challenges faced by the healthcare industry due to technological innovations such as cognitive technologies, AI, cloud services, fog computing, edge computing, and others. Smart health services can be used to evaluate and analyze large volumes of data, as well as to link patient-generated health information with other characteristics such as age, gender, as well as the individuals' surroundings. Chronic patients' well-being can sometimes be overlooked because of their basic condition until diseases progress to the point where smart healthcare systems can give fast appropriate treatment. Using AI and ML approaches, IoT has made it very easy to forecast the beginnings of extreme distress.

Including all the benefits of smart health services, there will be several issues that must be addressed and changed for the better. In developing a better assessment of the patient's health situation, sensors and IoT devices should produce a large quantity of data.

Many articles and journals choosing to focus on the confidentiality and protection of e-health records have been authored in the last 5 years; however, no detailed analysis of the entire e-healthcare system, including e-health information, medical instruments, healthcare networks, and edge/fog/cloud computing that senses,

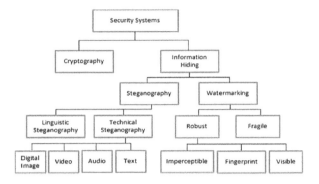

Figure 13.2   Classification of security system

communicates, stores, and procedures e-health data, has been published. Several articles can be found on the multiple aspects of e-healthcare systems, such as e-health data protection [28–31], medical equipment safety [1, 32, 33, 67, 68], and medical information security [65, 66]. Other investigations [42, 69–73] looked at various aspects of the e-healthcare system. Furthermore, all elements' security and privacy problems are yet to be investigated (see Figure 13.2).

We must first study the many characteristics and characteristics of smart healthcare to correctly identify it. The organization of the chapter is as follows. Section 13.2 reviews related work. In Section 13.3, steganography techniques and their algorithms are described. Section 13.4 illustrates the different steganography techniques. Section 13.5 describes the security challenges in health care. The conclusion is given in Section 13.6.

13.2   Related work

The adoption of IoT has altered the healthcare sector, whether through wearables or telemedicine and remote patient monitoring [1, 74–79]. Smart healthcare, as stated at the beginning of this chapter, is a service that brings together a variety of stakeholders and players, including doctors, patients, hospitals, and medical research organizations. Its introduction has resulted in a movement in the area of medicine, allowing for the particularly successful growth of society's health and allowing the battle against a range of diseases and limits that were before difficult to identify. The following are the Chapter's main contributions:

- A complete analysis of e-health information, medical equipment, healthcare networking, edges, fog, and cloud-based privacy and security issues;
- E-data, medical equipment, medical networking, and edge/fog/cloud computing security problems, objectives, and approaches;

Yaacoub *et al.* [80] investigated the Internet of Medical Things (IoMT) in the context of safety difficulties, concerns, challenges, threats, and remedies, as well as the elements of IoMT (e.g., the types of IoMT, devices, and protocols). On various levels, researchers identified 14 privacy and security objectives for the IoMT, including data, sensors, servers, and healthcare servers.

The rising number of elderly people in the world is one of the major motivations for smart healthcare implementation. As a result, ambient-assisted living attempts to create environments for the elderly that include smart healthcare service practices for excellent treatment without requiring human involvement. Many solutions, such as those suggested in References 11–13, 37, are centered on smart home technologies. Many approaches are based on smart home technologies, given that nearly 90% of geriatric patients wish to remain in their residences.

Balamurugan *et al.* established a promising cryptographic strategy to protect the Magnetic Resonance Imaging (MRI) healthcare picture into a unique container image applying integer wavelet transform [81]. Furthermore, various studies [42, 69–71] focused on e-health security problems in cloud infrastructures, mobile health systems, online medical services, and the healthcare establishment.

Chenthara *et al.* [82] explored the security and privacy in e-health platforms for cloud-based electronic health records. To recognize security and privacy challenges for e-health data, researchers studied current findings based on privacy-preserving methodologies using cryptography techniques (i.e., symmetric encryption, public-key encrypt data, and several alternative option cryptosystem primitives) and non-cryptographic methods (i.e., access control). Furthermore, Yüksel *et al.* [83] carried out a study on the security and privacy of digital health care (EHSs).

Alsubaei *et al.* [84] established a framework for web-based IoMT security evaluation. Using an ontology scenario-based methodology, their model provided security mechanisms for IoMT. It is also used to evaluate the security and complexity of IoMT techniques. The suggested approach has shown its ability to adapt to (1) innovative technologies and clients; (2) standard fulfillment; and (3) complexity. System administrators are in charge of making security-related recommendations overall. However, the conceptual framework offers opportunities for all Safety and Health Services (SHS) partners to gain more experience with cutting-edge technology in the area of IoMT protection. The system's effectiveness was demonstrated by evaluation outcomes across all assessment attributes. However, beginner users such as healthcare professionals and patients with limited security and technical understanding found the evaluation attributes used to be hard to interpret.

In [85], the authors evaluate the usability of existing IoT technologies in a system to monitor Parkinson's disease in patients. Wearable sensors that monitor movement patterns, symptoms, and overall exercise habits, according to their results, could be combined with imagination technology (i.e., cameras) throughout the home to detect Parkinson's disease progression. Furthermore, the researchers believe that ML will lead to improved treatment regimens in the future.

In [86], the authors suggested a risk-aware secured system for controlling access to medical data based on contextual data about commands. A risk evaluation unit of the architecture analyzes the data's risk, and an access control module identifies the appropriate data level of protection based on the risk. If data are requested, the limits for accessing the data are also determined by the data security requirements.

For IoMT-enabled SHS operations, Alassaf *et al.* [87] established a lightweight cryptographic method. The research looked into the characteristics of the SIMON cipher and how it could be used in IoMT-enabled SHS applications to improve efficiency. To reduce the computational burden imposed by encryption, the system advised adding an improvement via original SIMON cryptographic implementation. It also allowed for the practical combination of performance and security to be achieved. The system, however, did not generate satisfactory results.

13.3   Trending technologies in the smart healthcare system

The overall quality of smart healthcare is growing as technologies are adopted to enhance the abovementioned individual features. Each one of the emerging innovations mentioned below gives multiple improvements for various layers that can be described in terms of respective goals and the most important needs that these roles required (see Figure 13.3).

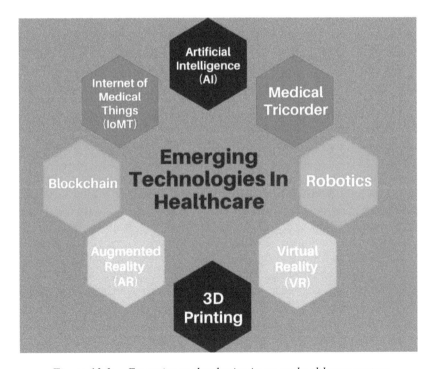

Figure 13.3   Emerging technologies in smart healthcare system

13.3.1 Wireless network technologies

For a complete understanding of smart health systems, WBANs, the most common network access kind of IoT-based smart healthcare devices, must be presented. WBANs are human-designed and constructed devices that measure and exchange constant physiological signals. In WBANs, ZigBee, WLAN, and Bluetooth are the most prevalent wireless connectivity methods.

Body sensors capture information such as the patient's heartbeats, temperatures, and circulation, as well as nerve impulses such as blood pressure. The data are then transmitted to the base stations through the wireless channel by these devices. Remotely, medical centers or the clouding system of intelligent health services collect the data transmitted.

13.3.2 Machine learning and deep learning technologies

By improving the handling of a large volumes of data and assuring low-latency and trustworthy outputs, ML and the impact of AI on smart health services is significant. The application of ML can improve the continuous detection of issues and also provide customized medical treatment, and AI has had a significant effect on the diagnosis and prognosis of challenges that require significant medical trials. ML algorithms can be used to understand the network's dynamic characteristics to propose proactive remedies to the dynamic network environment. In a short period, AI algorithms can analyze a high volume of data from many smart IoT systems and forecast the result, generating electronic medical records that are subsequently transmitted to different clinical allocations for additional research and suggestions. To provide customized health treatment, ML is used in three sectors of smart healthcare systems: investigations, supportive systems, and patient monitoring and security systems. The authors suggest a recurrent neural network method with a long-short time domain in this research [88] to deliver energy-efficient, highly accessible, and predictive medicinal therapies.

ML can assist robots and smart devices in inferring usable knowledge from data supplied by devices or humans. This is also the capability of a smartphone to modify or manage a situation or activity based on experience which is an essential element of an IoT application. In tasks including classification, regression, and density estimation, ML approaches have been applied. ML, fraud prevention, biotechnology, virus detection, identification, and voice recognition are just a few of the areas that use ML tools and approaches.

13.3.3 Blockchain technologies

One of the greatest innovations that can be applied in smart healthcare systems is blockchain technology. The confidentiality and security of patient's medical data are key issues that must be addressed given the sensitivity of the data. Thanks to the decentralization and password-protected data blocks that blockchain provides, we also note that blockchain can enhance decentralization functionality, circulated records, integration, confirmation, resiliency, and changelessness. Moreover, there exists the possibility to motivate protected and exceedingly effective affiliations between nodes such as service users, medical care suppliers, and industries on smart health systems. Due to the characteristics of blockchains, each new block is added to the blockchain, which might be ineffective considering the amount of medical information in smart healthcare systems.

BAKMP-IoMT, developed by Garg *et al.* [89], is a blockchain-based authentication key agreement mechanism for IoMT. It allowed for secure key administration across cloud servers, personal servers, and medical implants. Furthermore, the technology ensures that the right individuals have access to critical healthcare data.

13.4 Benefits of a smart healthcare system

As a result of the rising use of IoT technology in the health industry in recent years, several devices and services have been developed that are now extensively used in our everyday lives. Smart health is not widely implemented and its ecosystem even now requires effort to empower many services. Some examples include health facilities, ambulance services, primary healthcare operations, medical teams, and healthcare workers with linked smartphones and electronic technologies.

The following are some key advantages of smart healthcare:

- **Error less:** Doctors can employ smart health technology to collect located close data and apply a data-driven strategy to increase success rates.
- **Reducing time:** The patient feels that sitting in the hospital to share data with the doctor is a waste of time and money; however, today's patient wants strong communication with their doctors and less waiting time.
- **Provide specific data:** It is difficult for a person (medical practitioner) to collect all of the patient's information continuously, but smart health technology obtains data more quickly and successfully.
- **Keeping track of data over a longer period:** Smart health technology can save data for years and display it in an easy-to-understand style on dashboards.

13.5 Security challenges in the healthcare system

IoT technology has received a significant amount of interest in recent years because of its possibility to reduce the pressure on medical systems brought on by an older population and a rise in serious diseases. Smart healthcare will offer many benefits, but it will also be more vulnerable to risk. Different data problems, such as quantity, inconsistencies, and sparsity, will pose important difficulties to smart healthcare data administration and processing. In recent years, there has been a lot of discussion about the risks of HIoT. The medical profession has concluded that IoT will be a part of their future. They understand that digitization and streamlining health data sharing can help them become more effective while also saving money.

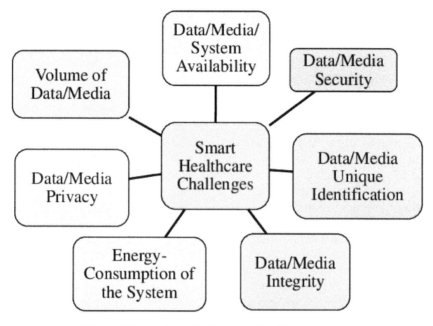

Figure 13.4   Security issues in health care system

Suppliers and producers of IoT devices can take two basic security measures: encryption and implementing a secure boot. A secure boot assures that none of a device's configurations have been modified when it is turned on [30].

Various issues must be resolved to preserve a scaled, reliable, easily accessible, and effective healthcare system, despite the existence of numerous supportive frameworks based on new technology to provide smart health care (see Figure 13.4). The integration of data from several devices is a major hurdle to smart healthcare implementation using smart devices such as smartphones. Because different sensors produce different types of data, it is necessary to translate input signals from heterogeneous sensors linked to individual patients into a form that can be used in healthcare monitoring services. Another key issue in smart technology-based health services is the safety and security of individuals' personal information. Because of the rising complexity of data and the increase in security attacks, security has been a constant challenge for wearables in IoT environments.

In the future, more confidentiality and privacy-preserving structures based on a variety of security-providing protocols, such as blockchain [10, 11, 36], will be developed to allow users to privately share data (patients, families, medical experts, and caregivers). Low power consumption and energy efficiency are critical for smart health systems built on smartphones and smart gadgets, specifically for long-term wearable sensors.

Low-power gadgets [12], long-life batteries [13], and energy harvesting approaches [37, 43] could all be utilized to address these future problems. Using the "sleep" and "wake up" functions of the sensors used to achieve the overall purposes is another technique for increasing the battery's lifetime.

Remote patient monitoring poses several practical issues, such as what to do with data that is missing or incomplete [90]. If there is a power outage, part of the data being captured may be lost. A natural disaster, such as an earthquake or a weather-related disaster, could cause data loss before it is stored on a centralized cloud server in the worst-case. This would be extremely difficult for people at home who are unwell. It becomes much more challenging when a large number of patients have significant conditions that require more attention than healthcare workers can deliver promptly. A further problem is merging ML and DL techniques with a small volume of data. Future research should focus on effective learning techniques [25], end-to-end architecture [24], and synthetic data production using generative adversarial systems [58]. However, the datasets often include some unneeded characteristics for diagnosing heart disease that is essential for the disease's occurrence, and these features commonly restrict the developed systems' efficiency. As a result, well-developed long-life sensors could be an effective way to identify and manage diabetes. Compact ML approaches [25, 41, 53] will be more suitable in embedded applications in a future study to ensure smart healthcare systems. Also, the explainability/justifiability can be incorporated in AI/ML algorithms that can enhance the trustability of them [91], [92].

13.6   Conclusion

Smart healthcare is a convenient, efficient, and easy-to-implement health monitoring system that may deliver great care at a fraction of the cost that are incurred by clinics and assisted living facilities. This Chapter examined a variety of security-related solutions for protecting the privacy of sensitive information in IoT-based areas like healthcare and the related healthcare industries. It also classified security methods that are used. This chapter examined the positive and negative aspects of various security techniques with IoT in healthcare industries. To make the security system better, encryption and decryption techniques were utilized. As a result, this chapter described new research opportunities in healthcare by presenting factors to explore for future directions. We also discussed the main challenges with recently established smart healthcare systems that are primary barriers to the development of assistive prototypes. To track and register patients accurately, healthcare professionals are looking to technological advancements. The future characteristics of the healthcare system allows for the development of mobile applications for users of all kinds. For further improvement of the quality of health service, certain possible future research areas are recommended. Although technologies will not be able to entirely substitute health services, they can help medical professionals by implementing some creative models.

References

[1] Pandya S., Sur A., Solke N. 'COVIDSAVIOR: a novel sensor-fusion and deep learning based framework for virus outbreaks'. *Frontiers in Public Health.* 2021, vol. 9, p. 797808.

[2] Jonker W., Linnartz J.-P. 'Digital rights management in consumer electronics products'. *IEEE Signal Processing Magazine.* 2004, vol. 21(2), pp. 82–91.

[3] Pandya S., Thakur A., Saxena S, *et al.* 'A study of the recent trends of immunology: key challenges, domains, applications, datasets, and future directions'. *Sensors (Basel, Switzerland).* 2021, vol. 21(23), 7786. Available from https://doi.org/10.3390/s21237786

[4] Ghayvat H., Pandya S., Bhattacharya P, *et al.* 'CP-BDHCA: blockchain-based confidentiality-privacy preserving big data scheme for healthcare clouds and applications'. *IEEE Journal of Biomedical and Health Informatics.* 2022, vol. 26(5), pp. 1937–48.

[5] Xu L., Zhou X., Li X., Jhaveri R.H., Gadekallu T.R., Ding Y. 'Mobile collaborative secrecy performance prediction for artificial iot networks'. *IEEE Transactions on Industrial Informatics.* 2021, vol. 18(8), pp. 5403–11.

[6] Reddy Maddikunta P.K., Srivastava G., Reddy Gadekallu T., Deepa N., Boopathy P. 'Predictive model for battery life in iot networks'. *IET Intelligent Transport Systems.* 2020, vol. 14(11), pp. 1388–95. Available from https://onlinelibrary.wiley.com/toc/17519578/14/11

[7] Maddikunta P.K.R., Gadekallu T.R., Kaluri R., Srivastava G., Parizi R.M., Khan M.S. 'Green communication in iot networks using a hybrid optimization algorithm'. *Computer Communications.* 2020, vol. 159, pp. 97–107.

[8] Odeh A., Elleithy K., Faezipour M., Abdelfattah E. 'Novel steganography over HTML code'. Presented at Innovations and Advances in Computing, Informatics, Systems Sciences, Networking and Engineering; Berlin/Heidelberg, Germany, 2015.

[9] Chikouche S.L., Chikouche N. 'An improved approach for LSB-based image steganography using AES algorithm'. *5th International Conference on Electrical Engineering - Boumerdes (ICEE-B)*; Boumerdes, 2015.

[10] Bhole A.T., Patel R. 'Steganography over video file using random byte hiding and LSB technique'. *IEEE International Conference on Computational Intelligence and Computing Research*; 2012.

[11] Hemalatha M., Prasanna A., Dinesh Kumar R., Vinoth Kumar D. 'Image steganography using HBC and RDH technique'. *International Journal of Computer Applications Technology and Research.* 2014, vol. 3(3), pp. 136–39.

[12] Singh A., Malik S. 'Securing data by using cryptography with steganography'. *International Journal of Advanced Research in Computer Science and Software Engineering.* 2013, vol. 3(5), pp. 404–09.

[13] Juneja M., Sandhu P.S., Assistant Professor, Uiet, Panjab University, Chandigarh, India 'Data hiding with enhanced LSB steganography and

cryptography for RGB color images'. *Indian Journal of Applied Research*. 2011, vol. 3(5), pp. 118–20. Available from http://www.theglobaljournals. com/ijar/issues.php?m=May&y=2013&id=20

[14] Thomas S.E., Philip S.T., Nazar S., Mathew A., Joseph N. 'Advanced cryptographic steganography using multimedia files'. *International Conference on Electrical Engineering and Computer Science (ICEECS)*; 2012. pp. 239–42.

[15] Rajyaguru M.H. 'Crystography-combination of cryptography and steganography with rapidly changing keys'. *International Journal of Emerging Technology and Advanced Engineering*. 2012, vol. 2, pp. 329–32.

[16] Wu N., Liu Z., Ma W., Shang P., Yang Z., Fan J. 'Research on coverless text steganography based on multi-rule language models alternation'. *4th International Conference on Mechanical, Control and Computer Engineering (ICMCCE)*; Hohhot, China, 2019. pp. 803–8033. Available from https://iee-explore.ieee.org/xpl/mostRecentIssue.jsp?punumber=8961322

[17] Yang Z., Xiang L., Zhang S., Sun X., Huang Y. 'Linguistic generative steganography with enhanced cognitive-imperceptibility'. *IEEE Signal Processing Letters*. 2021, vol. 28, pp. 409–13.

[18] Mehta P.. 'Adaptive web personalization'. *International Journal of Engineering Development and Research*. 2013.

[19] Gopalan K. Presented at Proceedings of International Conference on Multimedia and Expo. ICME '03. (cat. no.03TH8698); Baltimore, MD, 2003.

[20] Chikouche S.L., Chikouche N.. 'An improved approach for lsb-based image steganography using AES algorithm'. *5th International Conference on Electrical Engineering - Boumerdes (ICEE-B)*; Boumerdes, 2017.

[21] Chaudhary S., Dave M., Sanghi A. 'Aggrandize text security and hiding data through text steganography'. *IEEE 7th Power India International Conference (PIICON)*; Bikaner, Rajasthan, IEEE, 2021. pp. 1–5.

[22] Baawi S.S., Nasrawi D.A., Abdulameer L.T. 'Improvement of "text steganography based on unicode of characters in multilingual" by custom font with special properties'. *IOP Conference Series*. 2021, vol. 870(1), p. 012125.

[23] Datta D., Garg L., Srinivasan K, *et al.* 'An efficient sound and data steganography based secure authentication system'. *Computers, Materials & Continua*. 2021, vol. 67(1), pp. 723–51.

[24] Iwendi C., Jalil Z., Javed A.R. 'KeySplitWatermark: zero watermarking algorithm for software protection against cyber-attacks'. *IEEE Access: Practical Innovations, Open Solutions*. 2019, vol. 8, pp. 72650–60.

[25] Numan M., Subhan F., Khan W.Z. 'A systematic review on clone node detection in static wireless sensor networks'. *IEEE Access: Practical Innovations, Open Solutions*. 2019, vol. 8, pp. 65450–61.

[26] Bhole A.T., Patel R. 'Steganography over video file using random byte hiding and LSB technique'. *IEEE International Conference on Computational Intelligence and Computing Research*; 2012.

[27] Pandya S., Ghayvat H. 'Ambient acoustic event assistive framework for identification, detection, and recognition of unknown acoustic events of a residence'. *Advanced Engineering Informatics*. 2004, vol. 47, p. 101238.

[28] Davis A.G., Ambikairajah E., Wong W.T.K. 'Auditory masking and MPEG-1 audio compression'. *Electronics & Communication Engineering Journal.* 2004, vol. 9(4), pp. 165–75.

[29] Deng B., Tan J., Yang B., Li X. 'A novel steganography method based on modifying quantized spectrum values of MPEG/audio layer III'. *Proceedings of the 7th WSEAS International Conference on Applied Informatics and Communications*; 24–26 Aug, Athens, Greece: IEEE, 2007. pp. 325–30.

[30] Mehta P., Pandya S. 'A review on sentiment analysis methodologies, practices and applications'. *International Journal of Scientific & Technology Research.* 2020, vol. 9(2), pp. 601–09.

[31] Ghayvat H., Awais M., Gope P., Pandya S., Majumdar S. 'ReCognizing suspect and predicting the spread of contagion based on mobile phone location data (COUNTERACT): A system of identifying COVID-19 infectious and hazardous sites, detecting disease outbreaks based on the internet of things, edge computing, and artificial intelligence'. *Sustainable Cities and Society.* 2021, p. 102798.

[32] Mehbodniya A., Lazar A.J.P., Webber J, *et al.* 'Fetal health classification from cardiotocographic data using machine learning'. *Expert Systems.* 2022, vol. 39(6). Available from https://onlinelibrary.wiley.com/toc/14680394/39/6

[33] Mishra N., Pandya S. 'Internet of things applications, security challenges, attacks, intrusion detection, and future visions: A systematic review'. *IEEE Access: Practical Innovations, Open Solutions.* 2021, vol. 9, pp. 59353–77.

[34] Pandya, S., Patel W., Ghayvat H. *NXTGeUH: ubiquitous healthcare system for vital signs monitoring & falls detection*; IEEE International Conference, Symbiosis International University, 2018.

[35] Ghayvat, H., Pandya S. 'Wellness sensor network for modeling activity of daily livings–proposal and off-line preliminary analysis'. *in 2018 4th international conference on computing communication and automation (ICCCA)*; IEEE, 2018. pp. 1–5.

[36] Ahmed U., Lin J.C., Srivastava G. 'Deep fuzzy contrast-set deviation point representation and trajectory detection' in *IEEE transactions on fuzzy systems*; 2022 Aug 10.

[37] Pandya S., Patel W. 'An adaptive approach towards designing a smart healthcare real-time monitoring system based on iot and data mining'. *3rd IEEE International Conference on Sensing Technology and Machine Intelligence (ICST- 2016)*; Dubai, 2016.

[38] Patel W., Pandya S., Mistry V. 'I-msrtrm: developing an iot based intelligent medicare system for real-time remote health monitoring'. 8th International Conference on Computational Intelligence and Communication Networks (CICN); 23–25 Dec, Tehri, India, 2016.

[39] Patil S., Pandya S. 'Forecasting dengue hotspots associated with variation in meteorological parameters using regression and time series models'. *Frontiers in Public Health.* 2021, vol. 9, p. 798034.

[40] Wang W., Chen Q., Yin Z, *et al*. 'Blockchain and PUF-based lightweight authentication protocol for wireless medical sensor networks'. *IEEE Internet of Things Journal*. 2021, vol. 9(11), pp. 8883–91.

[41] Ke H., Chen D., Shah T, *et al*. 'Cloud-aided online eeg classification system for brain healthcare: A case study of depression evaluation with A lightweight cnn'. *Software*. 2020, vol. 50(5), pp. 596–610. Available from https://onlinelibrary.wiley.com/toc/1097024x/50/5

[42] Akhter F. 'A secured word by word graph steganography using huffman encoding'. *2016 International Conference on Computer Communication and Informatics (ICCCI)*; Coimbatore, India, IEEE, 2016. pp. 1–4.

[43] Dandvate H.S., Pandya S. 'New approach for frequent item set generation based on mirabit hashing algorithm'. *International Conference on Inventive Computation Technologies (ICICT)*; 26 August, Coimbatore, India, 2016.

[44] Pandya S., Shah J., Joshi N., Ghayvat H., Mukhopadhyay S.C., Yap M.H. 'A novel hybrid based recommendation system based on clustering and association mining'. *10th International Conference on Sensing Technology (ICST)*; IEEE, 2016. pp. 1–6.

[45] Pandya S., Vyas D., Bhatt D. 'A survey on various machine learning techniques‖, international conference on emerging trends in scientific research (ICETSR-2015)'. *International Conference on Emerging Trends in Scientific Research (ICETSR-2015)*; Trissur, India: Elsevier Procedia, 2015. pp. 978–81.

[46] Pandya S., Wandra K., Shah J. 'A hybrid based recommendation system to overcome the problem of sparcity'. *International Conference on Emerging trends in Scientific Research (ICETSR-2015)*; Trissur, India: Elsevier Procedia, 2015.

[47] Tripathi D., Sharma R.K. 'Energy systems and nanotechnology' in *Advances in sustainability science and technology*. Singapore: Springer; 2021.

[48] Rupa C., Srivastava G., Bhattacharya S., Reddy P., Gadekallu T.R. 'A machine learning driven threat intelligence system for malicious URL detection'. *ARES 2021*; Vienna, Austria, 2021. pp. 1–7. Available from https://dl.acm.org/doi/proceedings/10.1145/3465481

[49] Chiramdasu, R., Srivastava G., Bhattacharya S., Reddy P.K., Gadekallu T.R. 'Malicious URL detection using logistic regression'. *IEEE International Conference on Omni-Layer Intelligent Systems (COINS)*; IEEE, 2021. pp. 1–6.

[50] Hina, M., Ali M., Javed A.R., Srivastava G., Gadekallu T.R., Jalil Z. 'Email classification and forensics analysis using machine learning' in *IEEE smartworld, ubiquitous intelligence & computing, advanced & trusted computing, scalable computing & communications, internet of people and smart city innovation (smartworld/SCALCOM/UIC/ATC/IOP/SCI)*. IEEE; 2021 Oct. pp. 630–35.

[51] Srivastava G., Deepa N., Prabadevi B., Reddy M P.K. 'An ensemble model for intrusion detection in the internet of softwarized things'. *Adjunct Proceedings of the International Conference on Distributed Computing and Networking*;

Nara, Japan, 2021. Available from https://dl.acm.org/doi/proceedings/10. 1145/3427477

[52] Ch R., Gadekallu T.R., Abidi M.H., Al-Ahmari A. 'Computational system to classify cyber crime offenses using machine learning'. *Sustainability*. 2019, vol. 12(10), p. 4087.

[53] Punithavathi P., Geetha S., Karuppiah M., Islam S.H., Hassan M.M., Choo K.-K.R. 'A lightweight machine learning-based authentication framework for smart iot devices'. *Information Sciences*. 2019, vol. 484, pp. 255–68.

[54] Rupa C., Srivastava G., Gadekallu T.R., Maddikunta P.K.R., Bhattacharya S. 'A blockchain based cloud integrated iot architecture using A hybrid design'. *In International Conference on Collaborative Computing: Networking, Applications and Worksharing*; Cham: Springer, 2020. pp. 550–59.

[55] Kumar R., Tripathi R., Marchang N., Srivastava G., Gadekallu T.R., Xiong N.N. 'A secured distributed detection system based on IPFS and blockchain for industrial image and video data security'. *Journal of Parallel and Distributed Computing*. 2021, vol. 152, pp. 128–43.

[56] Kumar P., Kumar R., Srivastava G, *et al.* 'PPSF: a privacy-preserving and secure framework using blockchain-based machine-learning for iot-driven smart cities'. *IEEE Transactions on Network Science and Engineering*. 2021, vol. 8(3), pp. 2326–41.

[57] Kumar R., Kumar P., Tripathi R., Gupta G.P., Gadekallu T.R., Srivastava G. 'SP2F: a secured privacy-preserving framework for smart agricultural unmanned aerial vehicles'. *Computer Networks*. 2021, vol. 187, p. 107819.

[58] Ch R., Srivastava G., Reddy Gadekallu T., Maddikunta P.K.R., Bhattacharya S. 'Security and privacy of UAV data using blockchain technology'. *Journal of Information Security and Applications*. 2021, vol. 55, p. 102670.

[59] Reddy G.T., Reddy M.P.K., Lakshmanna K, *et al.* 'Analysis of dimensionality reduction techniques on big data'. *IEEE Access: Practical Innovations, Open Solutions*. 2020, vol. 8, pp. 54776–88.

[60] Deepa N., Pham Q.V., Nguyen D.C, *et al.* 'A survey on blockchain for big data: approaches, opportunities, and future directions'. *ArXiv Preprint ArXiv*. 2020, 2009.00858.

[61] Gadekallu T.R., Pham Q.V., Huynh-The T., Bhattacharya S., Maddikunta P.K.R., Liyanage M. 'Federated learning for big data: A survey on opportunities, applications, and future directions'. *ArXiv Preprint ArXiv*. 2021, 2110.04160.

[62] Prabadevi B., Deepa N., Pham Q.V *et al.* 'Toward blockchain for edge-of-things: A new paradigm, opportunities, and future directions'. *IEEE Internet of Things Magazine*. 2021.

[63] Gadekallu T.R., Pham Q.-V., Nguyen D.C, *et al.* 'Blockchain for edge of things: applications, opportunities, and challenges'. *IEEE Internet of Things Journal*. 2021, vol. 9(2), pp. 964–88.

[64] Irshad A., Usman M., Chaudhry S.A., Bashir A.K., Jolfaei A., Srivastava G. 'Fuzzy-in-the-loop-driven low-cost and secure biometric user access to server'. *IEEE Transactions on Reliability*. 2020, vol. 70(3), pp. 1014–25.

[65] Shi S., Qi Y., Huang Y. 'An approach to text steganography based on search in internet'. *2016 International Computer Symposium (ICS)*; 15 December, Chiayi, Taiwan, 2016. pp. 227–32.

[66] Liu Y., Wu J., Xin G. 'Multi-keywords carrier-free text steganography based on part of speech tagging'. *2017 13th International Conference on Natural Computation, Fuzzy Systems and Knowledge Discovery (ICNC-FSKD)*; 29–31 July, Guilin, 2017. pp. 2102–07.

[67] Mehta P., Pandya S., Kotecha K. 'Harvesting social media sentiment analysis to enhance stock market prediction using deep learning'. *Peer Journal of Computer Science*. 2021, vol. 7, e476.

[68] Ghayvat H., Awais M., Pandya S, *et al.* 'Smart aging system: uncovering the hidden wellness parameter for well-being monitoring and anomaly detection'. *Sensors*. 2019, vol. 19, p. 766.

[69] Hitesh S., Pradeep Kumar S., Kriti S. 'A survey on text based steganography'. *Proceedings of the 3rd National Conference. Bharati Vidyapeeth's Institute of Computer Applications and Management*; 2009. pp. 332–35.

[70] Ghayvat H., Pandya S., Bhattacharya P, *et al.* 'CP-BDHCA: blockchain-based confidentiality-privacy preserving big data scheme for healthcare clouds and applications'. *IEEE Journal of Biomedical and Health Informatics*. 2021, vol. 25, pp. 1–22.

[71] Baawi S.S., Mokhtar M.R., Sulaiman R. 'A comparative study on the advancement of text steganography techniques in digital media'. *ARPN Journal of Engineering and Applied Sciences*. 2018, vol. 13, pp. 1854–63.

[72] Awais M., Ghayvat H., Krishnan Pandarathodiyil A, *et al.* 'Healthcare professional in the loop (HPIL): classification of standard and oral cancer-causing anomalous regions of oral cavity using textural analysis technique in autofluorescence imaging'. *Sensors (Basel, Switzerland)*. 2020, vol. 20(20), p. 5780.

[73] Patel C.I., Labana D., Pandya S., Modi K., Ghayvat H., Awais M. 'Histogram of oriented gradient-based fusion of features for human action recognition in action video sequences'. *Sensors (Basel, Switzerland)*. 2020, vol. 20(24), p. 7299.

[74] Barot V., Kapadia V., Pandya S. 'QoS enabled iot based low cost air quality monitoring system with power consumption optimization'. *Cybernetics and Information Technologies*. 2020, vol. 20(2), pp. 122–40.

[75] Pandya S., Wakchaure M.A., Shankar R., Annam J.R. 'Analysis of NOMA-OFDM 5G wireless system using deep neural network'. *The Journal of Defense Modeling and Simulation*. 2021.

[76] Sur A., Sah R.P., Pandya S. 'Milk storage system for remote areas using solar thermal energy and adsorption cooling'. *Materials Today*. 2020, vol. 28, pp. 1764–70.

[77] Ghayvat H., Pandya S., Patel A. 'Deep learning model for acoustics signal based preventive healthcare monitoring and activity of daily living'. *2nd International Conference on Data, Engineering and Applications (IDEA)*; Bhopal, India, 2020. pp. 1–7. Available from https://ieeexplore.ieee.org/xpl/mostRecentIssue.jsp?punumber=9163074

[78] Pandya S., Shah J., Joshi N., Ghayvat H., Mukhopadhyay S.C., Yap M.H. 'A novel hybrid based recommendation system based on clustering and

association mining'. 10th International Conference on Sensing Technology (ICST); Nanjing, China, 2020.

[79] Karn A.L., Pandya S., Mehbodniya A. 'An integrated approach for sustainable development of wastewater treatment and management system using iot in smart cities'. *Soft Computing.* 2015.

[80] Yaacoub J.P.A., Noura M., Noura H.N, *et al.* 'Securing internet of medical things systems: limitations, issues and recommendations'. *Future Generation Computer Systems.* 2020, vol. 105, pp. 581–606.

[81] Balamurugan S., Shermy R.P., Shanker G.K., Kumar V.S., Prabhakaran V.M. 'An object oriented perspective of context–aware monitoring strategies for cloud based healthcare systems'. *Asian Journal of Research in Social Sciences and Humanities.* 2016, vol. 6(8), pp. 657–81.

[82] Chenthara S., Ahmed K., Wang H., Whittaker F. 'Security and privacy-preserving challenges of e-health solutions in cloud computing'. *IEEE Access: Practical Innovations, Open Solutions.* 2019, vol. 7, pp. 74361–82.

[83] Yüksel B., Küpçü A., Özkasap Ö. 'Research issues for privacy and security of electronic health services'. *Future Generation Computer Systems.* 2017, vol. 68, pp. 1–13.

[84] Alsubaei F., Abuhussein A., Shandilya V., Shiva S. 'IoMT-SAF: internet of medical things security assessment framework'. *Internet of Things.* 2019, vol. 8, p. 100123.

[85] Mantri S., Wood S., Duda J.E., Morley J.F. 'Comparing self-reported and objective monitoring of physical activity in parkinson disease'. *Parkinsonism & Related Disorders.* 2019, vol. 67, pp. 56–59.

[86] Rizwan M., Shabbir A., Javed A.R, *et al.* 'Risk monitoring strategy for confidentiality of healthcare information'. *Computers and Electrical Engineering.* 2022, vol. 100, p. 107833.

[87] Vaiyapuri T., Binbusayyis A., Varadarajan V. 'Security, privacy and trust in iomt enabled smart healthcare system: a systematic review of current and future trends'. *International Journal of Advanced Computer Science and Applications.* 2021, vol. 12(2).

[88] Shoaran M., Haghi B.A., Taghavi M., Farivar M., Emami-Neyestanak A. 'Energy-efficient classification for resource-constrained biomedical applications'. *IEEE Journal on Emerging and Selected Topics in Circuits and Systems.* 2018, vol. 8(4), pp. 693–707.

[89] Garg N., Wazid M., Das A.K., Singh D.P., Rodrigues J.J., Park Y. 'BAKMP-iomt: design of blockchain enabled authenticated key management protocol for internet of medical things deployment'. *IEEE Access: Practical Innovations, Open Solutions.* 2020, vol. 8, pp. 95956–77.

[90] Chengoden R., Victor N. 'Metaverse for healthcare: a survey on potential applications'. *Challenges and Future Directions.* 2022.

[91] Srivastava G., Jhaveri R.H., Bhattacharya S, *et al.* 'Xai for cybersecurity: state of the art, challenges'. *Open Issues and Future Directions.* 2022.

[92] Wang S., Qureshi M.A., Miralles-Pechuaán L., Gadekallu T.R., Liyanage M. 'Explainable AI for B5G/6G: technical aspects, use cases, and research challenges'.2021.

Chapter 14

A survey of medical image watermarking: state-of-the-art and research directions

Ashima Anand[1], Amit Kumar Singh[2], and Huiyu Zhou[3]

With the growth and popularity of the utilization of medical images in smart health care, the large amount of health records and related images, which needs to be transmitted, is consistently increasing. However, exchanging these medical records among hospitals, doctors, and medical team faces many challenges associated to ownership conflicts, data security, and privacy. Medical image watermarking is an effective copyright protection tool by embedding copyright/secret information/logo into the carrier image. This chapter provides a detailed overview of watermarking along with its characteristics and current applications. We then provide a comparative survey of the different state-of-the-art approaches along with their merits and limitations. We further summarized each of the state-of-the-art approaches in detail, including objectives, goals, dataset used, evaluation metrics, and weaknesses, and discussed the recent challenges and their possible solutions. We believe this chapter will provide the readers a comprehensive insight to the field of watermarking research in the health care domain.

14.1 Introduction

In recent times, the health care system is connected with advanced internet technologies, cloud environments, and smart wearable devices for easy access and transmission of electronic health record (EPR) [1]. These health care services use the Internet of Medical Things (IoMT) to collect, manage, store, and transmit medical records for various purposes at high convenience and low cost [2]. Figure 14.1 shows the framework of the IoMT-based health care system. It shows the collection of sensing devices that are responsible for data collection and forwarding the data to the cloud infrastructure using a gateway for secure connectivity, transmission,

[1]Department of CSE, Thapar Institute of Engineering and Technology, Patiala, Punjab, India
[2]Department of Computer Science and Engineering, National Institute of Technology Patna, Patna, Bihar, India
[3]School of Computing and Mathematical Sciences, University of Leicester, Leicester, UK

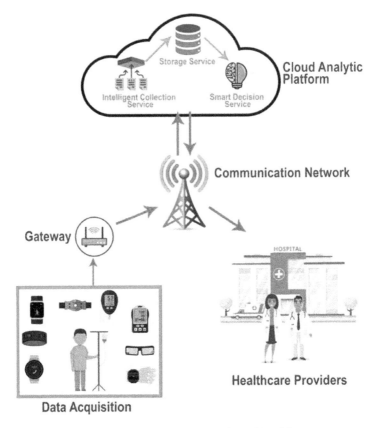

Figure 14.1   Framework of an IoMT-based health care system

and management [3]. Furthermore, during the COVID-19 pandemic, health care centers and hospitals are storing the personal information of a patient and other significant medical data on the local server [4]. This valuable information serves as a reference to make correct decisions on the patient and also provides the basis for other professionals to develop effective future plans for correct diagnosis. In accordance to the survey analysis, the size of the digital health care market is expected to rise from $96.5 billion in 2020 to $295.4 billion in 2028, with a compound annual growth rate of about 15% [5]. Moreover, a significant growth of 14.2% in the digital health care market is experienced in 2021 [5]. Although they offer convenient and potential solutions to the medical domain, these services also bring the issues of privacy leakage, identity theft, and risk of data tampering and authenticity at the same time [2]. Security and privacy of medical information are mostly presented as major issues in the telehealth services. Also, cloud-based health care applications have ensured uninterrupted clinical diagnosis with mobility support and low latency [4, 6]. Despite several advantages, the alteration and unauthorized distributions are

Figure 14.2   Applications of digital watermarking

deeply concerned and are a crucial point of research activities for several researchers since the last two decades [7, 8].

Among the different data-hiding solutions, watermarking techniques have gained massive popularity among researchers. It provides confidentiality, integrity, and identity authenticity and also maintains the privacy of the exchanged data [2]. Recently, watermarking is being used in various real-life applications. Some recent and popular applications of watermarking are listed in Figure 14.2 [2, 9–11]. A brief introduction of the major properties of watermarking methods is provided in Figure 14.3 [5, 9, 12]. Robustness, visual quality, and embedding payload are among the essential requirements of any watermarking system. Here, robustness signifies the efficient recovery of concealed mark(s) from the carrier media, which may be distorted by attacks and noise. Furthermore, the cover media should experience minimized visual distortions after embedding the mark(s), which cannot be noticeable by others. Embedding payload signifies the amount of data that can be hidden in a carrier media preserving high invisibility. As shown in Figure 14.4, there should be a balanced trade-off among these three properties to maximize the watermarking performance [3]. Spatial and transform domains are the basic approaches categorized on the basis of a software-based watermarking system [12]. Figure 14.5 summarizes the basic differences between the two approaches on the basis of embedding capacity, complexity, and other parameters. The watermarking methods in the spatial domain directly alter the pixel values of the carrier image to hide the watermark [9]. The least significant bit (LSB), spread spectrum, correlation-based techniques, and patchwork methods are commonly used strategies in this category [10]. LSB watermarking is one of the simplest methods that hide the mark by replacing the LSBs of the binary form of the cover pixels. The embedding capacity of this

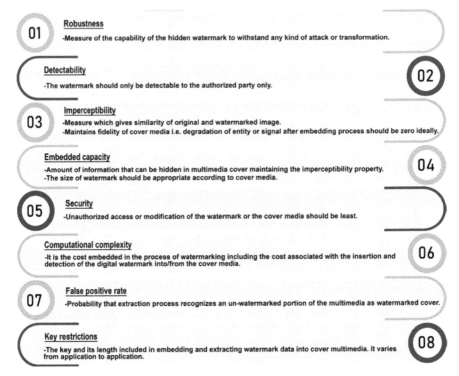

Figure 14.3   Major properties of digital watermarking techniques

method is very high. Furthermore, in patchwork-based watermarking, the position of pixels for embedding is selected in a pseudorandomly generated sequence. The spread spectrum distributes the secret mark in the frequency bin, maintaining the low energy of each bin, hence reducing the visual distortion of the carrier media [9].

On the contrary, transform domain watermarking techniques transform the cover media into suitable coefficients, which are altered by embedding the watermark into them [2]. It involves wavelet transforms, singular value decomposition (SVD), discrete Fourier transform (DFT), contourlet transform (CT), and curvelet transform [13]. The complexity of the spatial domain watermarking techniques is lower in comparison to the transform domain watermarking. However, they have less resistance to geometric attacks.

14.2   Survey of transform domain-based watermarking methods

Researchers have developed a variety of watermarking methods for medical images based on spatial and transform domains individually or in a combination of the spatial-transform domain to achieve a balanced trade-off among the watermark robustness and invisibility. In this section, our discussion focuses on watermarking

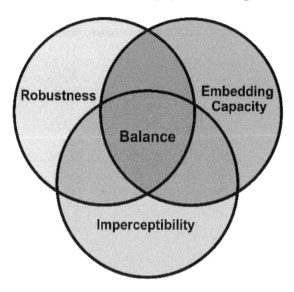

Figure 14.4   Balance between the important parameters of watermarking technique

methods in the transform domain. Furthermore, the contribution of the reviewed approaches is also summarized and compared in different technical perspectives in tabular form.

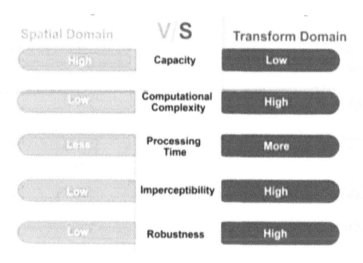

Figure 14.5   Comparison between spatial and transform domain techniques

14.2.1   Wavelet transform-based watermarking methods

The wavelet transforms perform multiresolution analysis of a matrix by decomposing it into nonoverlapping sub-bands, namely approximation (LL), horizontal (LH), vertical (HL), and diagonal (HH) [8]. It expresses the input matrix as a linear combination of the wavelet function, which offers simultaneous localization in the time-frequency domain without block artifacts. It has major advantages of multiscalability, multiresolution, and space frequency localization, which makes it highly suitable for watermarking in health care applications. Commonly used wavelet transforms include discrete wavelet transform (DWT), integer wavelet transform (IWT), randomized DWT (RDWT), lifting wavelet transform (LWT), dual tree complex wavelet transform (DTCWT), and many more. The generic 2D orthogonal wavelet can be represented as [14],

$$\varphi_{p_1 p_2 q_1 q_2}(x,y) = \frac{1}{\sqrt{p_1 p_2}} \varphi\left(\frac{x-q_1}{p_1}, \frac{y-q_2}{p_2}\right) \tag{14.1}$$

where (p_1, p_2) and (q_1, q_2) represent scale and position parameters.

Some of the wavelet-based watermarking methods proposed for the health care applications are discussed below, with a brief outline in Table 14.1.

A multiple watermarking technique for health care applications is proposed by Alshanbari [15]. This method combines robust and fragile watermarking for ownership identification and authentication. It embeds ownership information in the whole image to verify the authenticity. Furthermore, the recovery mark is generated by combining the region of interest (ROI) along with its SHA-256 hash values and compressed using an LZW compression. The principal component of the compressed recovery mark is placed inside the DWT-SVD coefficients of the region of non-interest (RONI) region of the cover image. This reversible watermarking method has a high embedding capacity and a better visual quality in comparison to References [23–26].

DWT-based blind watermarking framework for the protection of health care records is proposed by Kahlessenane *et al.* [16]. Initially, patients' details are combined with their 128-bit MD5 hash values to form the final watermark. Furthermore, DWT is applied on the cover image. The final mark is placed in the reorganized low-frequency DWT coefficients to ensure better security with high robustness. The comparative analysis of the proposed work results in better robustness in comparison to existing solutions [8, 27–30]. Rahman *et al.* [17] combined watermarking with encryption to improve the security of the medical records. This is an ROI-based watermarking, where the cover image is segmented into ROI and RONI using fuzzy technique-based segmentation. Also, for better security, the DWT coefficients of the mark image are permuted using chaotic maps. Finally, the key component of the permuted DWT coefficients is placed in the singular matrix of the cover image. Performance analysis of this work with existing work [31–38] indicated better robustness and security. Although the proposed work offers better authenticity with high security, the embedding capacity of this method is low.

Singh introduced a secure watermarking method for colored medical images in LWT and DCT domains [18]. The security is improved by encrypting the signature

Table 14.1   *Summary of wavelet transform-based watermarking methods*

Ref. No.	Objective	Techniques used	Performance parameters	Size		Dataset used	Limitations
				Cover	Watermark		
[15]	Ownership identification and tamper protection	DWT, SVD, Lempel–Ziv–Welch (LZW), and SHA-256	Peak Signal to Noise Ratio (PSNR) = 48.7738 dB and Normalized Coefficient (NC) = 0.8009	480 × 640	60 × 60, 64 bits	Ultrasound images	Not resistant to JPEG compression, sharpening mask, and average filtering
[16]	Integrity verification and copyright protection	DWT and MD5	PSNR = 74.47 dB, Net Pixel Change Rate (NPCR) = 30.42%, Structural Similarity Index Measure (SSIM) = 1, Number of pixels changed (NPC) = 81 128, and capacity = 43 690	512 × 512	43 690 bits	Medical images	The watermarked image is not secure

(Continues)

Table 14.1 Continued

Ref. No.	Objective	Techniques used	Performance parameters	Size		Dataset used	Limitations
				Cover	Watermark		
[17]	Authentication and integrity of medical images	Fuzzy-based segmentation and DWT	PSNR = 49.419 dB, NPCR = 0.9941, Unified Average Changing Intensity (UACI) = 0.3354, and NC = 0.997 at Gaussian Low Pass Filter (LPF)	512 × 512	64 × 64	Medical images	Limited embedding capacity
[18]	High robustness, confidentiality, and embedding capacity	LWT, DCT, MD5, and Bose–Chaudhuri–Hocquenghem (BCH)	PSNR = 31.02 dB, Bit Error Rate (BER) = 0, NC = 0.9800 at gain factor = 0.2, and 80 characters	512 × 512	64 × 64, 80 characters	Color medical images	Less robustness for histogram equalization, Gaussian and rotation attack
[19]	High capacity, security, and tamper detection	IWT, LSB, and chaotic encryption	PSNR = 45.41571 dB, SSIM = 0.9852, Mean Square Error (MSE) = 0.9343, Mean Absolute Error (MAE) = 0.0037, and NCC = 0.9995 using 432 538 bits	512 × 512	432 538 bits and 648 808 bits for gray scale images. 1 297 613 bits and 1 946 424 bits for color images	Color and gray scale medical and common images	Limited robustness analysis

(Continues)

Table 14.1 Continued

Ref. No.	Objective	Techniques used	Performance parameters	Size		Dataset used	Limitations
				Cover	Watermark		
[20]	High embedding capacity, authentication, and tamper detection	IWT, LSB, and Chaotic Sequence	PSNR = 74.2425 dB, BER =0, SSIM = 0.9999, NCC = 0.9999, MSE = 0.0024, and capacity = 627 648 for 1024 × 1024 cover image	512 × 512 and 1024×1024	280 bits, 164 340 bits (maximum) and 270 × 270	Medical and nonmedical images	Not robust for cropping, resizing, histogram, and Gaussian noise attacks
[21]	Authentication and integrity, and tamper detection and recovery	IWT, SHA-256, and lossless compression	Best values of PSNR = 50.47 dB, EC = 2.46 bpp, MSE = 0.5832, SSIM = 0.9977, and NCC = 0.9999	256 × 256	Logo: 50 × 50, ROI: 90 × 21, and recovery bits: 14 019	75 medical images	High time complexity
[22]	Improved robustness and security of medical images	DTCWT, DCT, Henon map, and chaotic-based encryption	NC = 1	128 × 128	-	Medical images	Analysis of computational complexity is missing

mark using MD5. Also, BCH-encoded patient details improve the resistance to channel noise. The Red-Green-Blue (RGB) color image is converted into the Y (perceived luminance), I, Q (color/luminance information) NTSC color model, and the resultant Y component is altered using the gain factor to hide the preprocessed marks. The visual quality and embedding capacity of this work are better than the traditional marking techniques.

Nazari and Maneshi developed a reversible watermarking technique for the secure transmission of digital health records [19]. The authors ensured tamper detection by transforming the cover image using IWT and hiding integrity check code and patient's details in the LSBs of the resulting IWT coefficients. Also, watermarks are encrypted using logistic sine-based chaotic encryption for better security and authentication. The proposed work offers better visual quality and an improved embedding capacity at a low computational cost when compared with the traditional schemes [39–45]. Nazari and Mehrabian [20] proposed a blind and secure watermarking scheme for medical and nonmedical images. Initially, the cover image is divided into ROI and RONI regions, which are treated as watermark and carrier images, respectively. The encrypted ROI segment, along with the patient's information, is placed in different level IWT coefficients of the RONI segment. Also, the authentication process is enhanced by hiding the doctor's signature in the third-level IWT coefficients, which provides better robustness. This technique has a high embedding capacity, better visual quality, and more resistance to attacks in comparison to the existing work [28, 46–52]. Furthermore, Ravichandran *et al.* developed an ROI-based multiple watermarking technique for medical images [21]. This method achieves a high embedding capacity by concealing multiple marks in the middle-frequency IWT coefficients of the host image. Chaotic-based embedding of patient details and hospital logo ensures authentication. Furthermore, the SHA-256 hash value of ROI and the compressed recovery bits of ROI are concealed to provide integrity verification and recovery of the tampered bits, respectively. Comparative analysis of this work with traditional methods [32, 53–57] points to better performance in terms of robustness, visual quality, and embedding capacity.

Liu *et al.* devised DTCWT-DCT and encryption-based watermarking methods supporting zero and blind extraction [22]. In the proposed work, the three marks are encrypted using a chaotic system and a Henon map ensuring better security. The encrypted marks are hidden in low-frequency DTCWT-DCT coefficients of the carrier image of size 128×128. Finally, this work has better robustness over traditional work [24, 50, 58, 59].

14.2.2   *Curvelet transform-based watermarking methods*

Although wavelet transforms offer multiresolution and spatiofrequency properties, these transforms suffer from the issues of poor directionality, shift variance, and poor capturing of the edge information [60]. In an attempt to overcome the limitation of poor directionality, ridgelet-based curvelet transform was advanced with multiscalability and strong and sparse directional information. It also allows random selection of decomposition direction, which forms a multiple-scaled pyramid with different directions and positions at each scale [61]. This transform follows the following parabolic scaling relation to present the signals using an optimally sparse representation [62],

$$\text{Width} \approx \text{Length}^2 \tag{14.2}$$

The mathematical representation of curvelet coefficients, ć (α, β, γ), is as follows,

$$ć\left(\alpha, \beta, \gamma\right) := \left\langle \chi, \omega_{\alpha, \beta, \gamma} \right\rangle \tag{14.3}$$

where $\alpha, \beta,$ and γ are the scaling, orientation, and translation parameters of the curvelet coefficients, respectively. Also, $\omega_a(\mu)$ is the waveform which is defined by its Fourier transform, $\varphi_a(\mu)$, which is defined as

$$\varphi_\alpha\left(z,\right) = 2^{\frac{-3\alpha}{4}} \left(\sigma_z \left(2^{-\alpha}z\right)\right) \left(\sigma_p \left(\frac{2\left\lfloor\frac{\alpha}{2}\right\rfloor}{2}\right)\right) \tag{14.4}$$

where, σ_z and σ_p are the radial and angular windows, respectively.

Curvelet transform offers the properties of sparse representation of the input signal with discontinuous edges and strong directional information, which is required for robust and imperceptible watermarking solutions [63]. Some of the curvelet-based watermarking for medical images are briefed below, with the summary of basic properties in Table 14.2.

Thanki *et al.* focused on delivering a blind watermarking approach for digital health care records solving the false positive problem [50]. The carrier image is decomposed into different frequency components using FDCuT, and block wise DCT is applied on high-frequency component. Furthermore, middle-frequency sub-band of DCT coefficients is altered using white Gaussian noise to hide the binary mark. The security, visual quality, and resistance of this work is better in comparison to the existing marking techniques [28, 68, 69]. Borra *et al.* [64] combined watermarking with encryption for securing the colored radiological images. This high-capacity watermarking method improves the security by applying comprehensive sensing method to encrypt the color mark. Each R, G, and B component of an encrypted mark is hidden in the respective high-FDCuT coefficient of the carrier image. The authors tested the watermarking model on multiple medical images and compared the performance with existing work. It is concluded that the proposed work has a better visual quality and embedding capacity over the techniques suggested in References [70–73].

Jero *et al.* devised a robust data-hiding method for the secure transmission of ECG signals [62]. The authors applied the Tompkins algorithm on the 1D ECG signals to find the Quasi Random Signal (QRS) region, and the curvelet transform is applied on it. Furthermore, the position of watermark pixels is calculated based on the threshold selection, and the binary mark is concealed within the selected pixels. Finally, the inverse curvelet transform is applied to obtain the marked ECG signals. However, the robustness and comparative analysis of this work are missing. Phan *et al.* [65] applied curvelet transform to develop a watermarking method, which confirms the

Table 14.2   Summary of the curvelet transform–based watermarking solutions

Ref. No.	Objective	Techniques used	Performance parameters	Size Cover	Size Watermark	Dataset used	Limitations
[50]	Security of medical image with no false positive problem	Fast Discrete Curvelet Transform (FDCuT), Discrete Cosine Transform (DCT), and white Gaussian noise	Average score of PSNR = 49.36 dB and NC = 0.9618	1024 × 1024	128 × 128	MedPix Medical Image Database	The embedding capacity is less
[64]	Integrity verification and secure transmission	FDCuT and comprehensive sensing	PSNR = 56.86 dB and SSIM = 0.9772 at α = 0.5	256 × 256	256 × 256	MedPix Medical Image Database	This method is not robust for discussed attacks
[62]	Secure transmission of Electrocardiogram (ECG) signals with high visual quality	FDCuT, and Pan Tompkins	PSNR = 43.44 dB, Root mean square distance (PRD) = 0.0132, Kullback Leibler (KL) distance = 0.1448, MSE = 2.94, and BER = 0 using 502 bits as watermark	-	83/167/251/335/418/512 bits	MIT-BIH database	Robustness analysis is missing

(Continues)

Table 14.2 Continued

Ref. No.	Objective	Techniques used	Performance parameters	Size Cover	Watermark	Dataset used	Limitations
[65]	Confidentiality and authentication of medical images	FDCuT and support vector machine (SVM)	PSNR = 15.5129 dB and SSIM = 0.9967	-	-	Medical image	Detailed robustness and cost analysis is missing
[63]	Identity verification and authentication of medical data	Fast Curvelet Transform (FCT), SVD, and Arnold transform	Average score of PSNR = 65.0162 dB, SSIM = 1, NCC = 1, BER = 0 for Fundus dataset	512 × 512	512 × 512	BIOMISA and Duke dataset	The proposed work lacks the computational cost analysis
[66]	Security and authentication of biometric data	FDCuT and SVD	PSNR = 57.41 dB and CC = 1 at gain factor = 5	256 × 256	8-bit speech at 8 kHz (256 × 256)	FVC 2002 database	Security of marked fingerprint image is not addressed
[67]	Security, authentication, and verification of medical data for accurate diagnosis	FCT, RPCA, Graph Attention Network (GAT), and SVD	Average score of PSNR = 51.9537 dB, SSIM = 0.9981, Normalized Correlation Coefficient (NCC)= 0.9963, and BER = 0.2772	512 × 512	128 × 128	Dataset from Armed Forces Institute of Ophthalmology (AFIO) of Fundus and Optical Coherence Tomography (OCT) scans	Performance can be improved with optimization and Error Correction Code (ECC)

authenticity of the transmitted medical image. This approach hides the marked image in the curvelet approximation coefficient of the carrier image. Also, SVM is implemented during extraction, which confirms high visual quality of the extracted mark. The comparative analysis with wavelet-based marking showed better imperceptibility of this method. Hassan *et al.* discussed imperceptible watermarking of OCT/Fundus scans achieving high diagnosis accuracy using marked images [63]. The red component of color image is decomposed using FCT, and SVD is applied on each 8×8 nonoverlapping blocks of resultant coefficient. Also, extra security is achieved by transforming the mark image with the Arnold transform. The transformed mark is masked within the resultant left singular matrix. Encrypting marks and embedding them in the left singular matrix helped in solving the false positive problem. The proposed work offered better robustness and diagnosis accuracy in comparison to traditional work [74–78]. Using similar hybrid of FDCuT and SVD, a fragile watermarking is developed by Thanki and Borisagar for authenticating the biometric data [66]. In the suggested nonblind method, the speech signal and fingerprint image are the mark and carrier images, respectively. The fingerprint image is transformed using curvelet transform, and the singular matrix of the high curvelet coefficient is altered with speech signal matrix and gain factors. Finally, inverse SVD and inverse curvelet transform are applied to produce the final marked image. This hybrid nonblind watermarking method offers a better score of PSNR and embedding capacity over works suggested in References 79 and 80. Furthermore, Ahmed *et al.* came up with a robust watermarking method to provide authentication and verification of medical records for computer-aided diagnosis applications [67]. The authors used GAT-based encoding of mark image for better security. A hybrid of Robust Principal Component Analysis (RPCA) and FCT is applied on the ROI of the cover image. Finally, a weight factor is used to modify the curvelet coefficient to hide the singular matrix of the encoded mark. The experimental results show high resistance of the proposed work for a variety of attacks along with acceptable visual quality. However, the comparative analysis of this approach is missing.

14.2.3   Contourlet transform-based watermarking methods

Curvelet transform offers scalability and strong directional information but lacks multiresolution properties and experiences shift sensitivity. To overcome these issues, Do and Vetterli developed CT having multiscale, multiresolution, and multidirectional properties [81]. It uses a 2D multiscale and directional filter bank (DFB), which offers better directionality and anisotropy with a dissimilar and distinct count of directions at each scale [82]. Figure 14.6 shows the framework of CT when applied on an image of size 512×512. It uses Laplacian pyramid decomposition to provide multiresolution and decompose the input image in low- and high-frequency coefficients [83]. Furthermore, DFB is applied on low-frequency coefficients to provide directional information.

In this segment, we discuss some CT-based watermarking methods which are designed for medical applications. The summary of each discussed method is presented in Table 14.3.

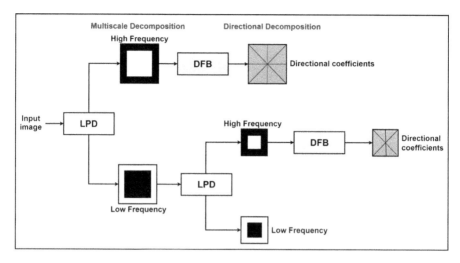

Figure 14.6   Framework of CT

With the aim to secure health care records, Wu *et al.* introduced a robust water-marking method using a combination of CT and DCT [82]. The watermark images are encrypted using logistic map-based chaotic encryption for better security. Also, the cover image is transformed into high- and low-contourlet coefficients, followed by applying DCT on the low coefficient to generate the feature vector. The embed-ding and extraction of the encrypted mark are done in the resultant DCT coefficients. The comparative evaluation results in better robustness of the proposed work over the techniques in References [89.90]. A study of adaptive DICOM image water-marking is shown by Rahimi and Rabbani in Reference [83]. Initially, the ROI and RONI regions of the carrier image are segmented. Furthermore, CT is applied on each segment, followed by the calculation of the singular matrix to implement the blind extraction of the dual marks. Marking of patient details in the ROI region achieves confidentiality and authentication. Also, the signature image is placed in RONI to authenticate the origin. This work has improved the visual quality of the marked image in comparison to the work suggested in Reference 91. Another CT-and SVD-based zero marking of medical images are presented by Seenivasagam and Velumani [84]. The method treats the patient details and QR code holding link to patient data as the two watermarks. The mark is scrambled using the Arnold trans-form for better security. The carrier image is decomposed with CT and divided into blocks. Furthermore, the Arnold transform-based block selection is done, and SVD is applied on the selected blocks. The authors used Hu invariant moments [92] to generate master share for zero marking of the scrambled mark in the singular matrix. On comparing this work with the existing techniques [93–96], better resistance to different benchmark attacks is experienced.

A robust marking using the composites of CT and DCT is proposed by the authors of Reference 85. For improved security, confidentiality, and authenticity, three marks including the encrypted patient details, doctors' unique code, and index

Table 14.3 Summary of CT-based watermarking solutions

Ref. No.	Objective	Techniques used	Performance parameters	Size Cover	Watermark	Dataset used	Limitations
[82]	To improve privacy and security of health care data	CT, DCT, and chaotic encryption	PSNR = 17.25 dB, NC1 = 1.00, and NC2 = 1.00 at Gaussian noise with 3% noise intensity	512 × 512	-	Medical images	Less resistance for cropping and rotation attacks
[83]	To authenticate and preserve privacy of medical records	CT, SVD, and segmentation	PSNR < 60 dB, SSIM <0.997, NC = 1, and BER = 0	512 × 512	230 characters, 10 × 40	DICOM images	The comparative and robustness analysis can be extended
[84]	To ensure medical data authentication and access control in cloud environment	CT and SVD	BER = 0.0001 for NC = 0.9999 for 20% cropping	512 × 512	77 × 77	Medical images	The computational cost is high
[85]	To improve privacy, authenticity, and security of medical records	CT, DCT, Advanced Encryption Standard (AES)	PSNR = 41.5157 dB, Mean SSIM (MSSIM) = 0.9747, NC = 1, and BER = 0 for brain Magnetic resonance imaging (MRI)	512 × 512	1 390 bits	Medical images	Limited comparative and robustness evaluation
[86]	To authenticate the medical data with high robustness and visual quality	CT	PSNR = 50.8 dB, NC = 1, Weighted PSNR = 62.8 dB, Contrast to noise Ratio (CNR) =1, root mean square error (RMSE) = 0.82, and SDE = 0.82	512 × 512	-	CT scan and MRI images	Not robust for median filtering and Gaussian noise

(Continues)

Table 14.3 Continued

Ref. No.	Objective	Techniques used	Performance parameters	Size		Dataset used	Limitations
				Cover	Watermark		
[87]	To secure the communication of medial data	CT and BCH encoding	PSNR = 34.5594 dB, WPSNR = 35.583 dB, MSSIM = 0.7703, and Total Perceptual Error (TPE) = 0.20	512×512	128/144 characters	Medical images	The adaptive selection of gain factor can be considered
[88]	To improve the embedding capacity and robustness with minimum distortion	CT, QIM, and SSSM	Max PSNR =43.34 dB and NC=1	512×512	Three binary marks of 64×64	Medical images	Limited performance and cost evaluation

keyword are used. The DCT coefficients of the mark are embedded in the DCT blocks of the low-pass CT sub-band of the carrier image. The PSNR score of this nonblind marking is better in comparison to the scheme by Manasrah *et al.* [97].

The effectiveness of CT-based watermarking for the health care applications is shown by the authors of Reference 86. In this work, CT is applied on the gray scale host image, and the selected contourlet coefficients are used to generate a key that holds the location of embedding the mark data using the gain factor. Furthermore, the working of CT is compared with LWT-based marking, offering better resistance for the considered attack except filtering attack. A robust watermarking solution for the secure transmission of digital medical records is shown by Das and Kundu [87]. The patient details, encrypted using AES, and ROI details of the cover image are used as mark information. Also, the cover image is transformed into low and high coefficients using CT. The lowpass coefficients are altered using the mark data and the gain factor ensuring blind extraction of marks. The subjective and objective evaluation of the proposed work confirm high performance in terms of invisibility and robustness in comparison to schemes in References 83, 97–99. Furthermore, Duong *et al.* updated the traditional quantization index modulation (QIM) and secure spread spectrum modulation (SSSM) methods using CT to generate an efficient watermarking method for medical images [88]. The binary marks are hidden in high-energy CT coefficients of the carrier image using a hybrid of QIM-SSSM and adaptive strength factor, which is dependent on CT coefficients. On comparing the major performance parameters including embedding capacity, robustness, and visual quality, this work performed better in comparison to the existing solutions [83, 100–104].

14.2.4   *NSCT-based watermarking methods*

Despite multiresolution and multidirectional properties, CT uses up- and down-sampling processes which cause the shift variant problem [60]. Based on CT, Non-Subsampled Contourlet Transform (NSCT) is capable of efficient representation of any image with better directionality, with edge and smooth contour information. It holds shift invariant property along with all the advantages of CT. The construction of NSCT includes the use of a nonsubsampled pyramid filter bank (NSPFB) and a non-subsampled DFB (NSDFB). NSPFB ensures multiscalability, and NSDFB provides better directional information. Both the filter banks eliminate the operation of up- and down-sampling, confirming the shift invariant property [60]. The procedure of NSCT decomposition of an input image is shown in Figure 14.7 [60].

The NSCT-based watermarking techniques for medical applications are briefly discussed below, with summary in Table 14.4.

Overcoming security and privacy issues, Thakur *et al.* offered a dual watermarking approach in NSCT, RDWT, and SVD domains [105]. In this approach, the singular matrices of medical images and EPR are embedded within the singular matrices of high-frequency NSCT-RDWT coefficients of the cover image. Furthermore, inverse SVD-RDWT-NSCT is applied to generate the final marked

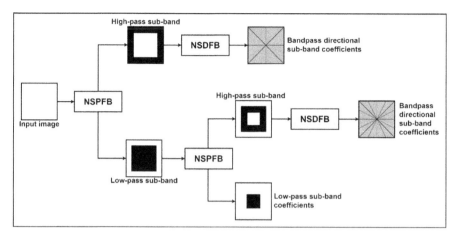

Figure 14.7   Nonsubsampled CT

image which is encrypted using lightweight encryption for better security. This work shows better robustness in comparison to the related work [111, 112].

Nouioua *et al.* offered a robust watermarking solution designed for medical applications [106]. In this work, the host image is first converted into YIQ model, and Q component is further decomposed using a combination of DTCWT and NSCT. The resulting high pass NSCT coefficients are altered to hide the binary mark. This blind watermarking method outperforms similar methods [18, 24, 113–115] in terms of time complexity and robustness. In Reference 107, Saha and Hossain introduced an NSCT-DCT-based robust watermarking scheme to secure the MRI. First, the binary mark is scrambled using Arnold's cat map, followed by scrambling and applying a tent map for better authentication and security. Furthermore, the scrambled cover image is decomposed using NSCT, and blocks of selected sub-band are transformed using DCT. The encrypted mark is hidden in the DCT coefficient using appropriate embedding factors. This scheme delivers better resistance and visual quality over the methods developed in References 98, 116 and 117.

Singh *et al.* offered nonblind watermarking by hiding the image mark in the medical cover image [108]. In this work, the host image is decomposed using NSCT, and DCT-SVD is applied on the selected sub-band. Similar series of transforms is also applied on the mark image. Finally, the singular matrix of the mark is concealed in the singular matrix of the host image using the gain factor. The comparative exploration of this work with existing methods [118–121] resulted in better robustness. In similar directions, a robust, high-capacity watermarking model is suggested by the authors of Reference 109. In this, NSCT, DCT, and MSVD are applied to hide the watermark inside the cover image. Also, the text mark is encrypted using the Arnold map for better security. Besides the high embedding capacity, the robustness of this technique is better in comparison to References [118–120, 122].

The authors of Reference 110 developed a blind watermarking framework for securing the digital medical records in the NSCT-RDWT domain. In this approach,

Table 14.4   Summary of NSCT-based watermarking approaches for medical images

Ref. No.	Objective	Techniques used	Performance parameters	Cover (Size)	Watermark (Size)	Dataset used	Limitations
[105]	To secure medical records using watermarking and lightweight encryption	NSCT, RDWT, SVD, and lightweight encryption	PSNR = 54.49 dB, NC1 = 0.9983, NC2 = 0.9626, NPCR = 0.9960, and UACI = 0.2554 for Cell	512 × 512	256 × 256 and 128 × 128	Medical images	SVD-based watermarking suffers from issues of high cost
[106]	To provide blind and imperceptible watermarking of medical images	DTCWT and NSCT	PSNR = 33.901 dB, MSE = 0.000407, SSIM = 1, NC = 1, and BER = 0	512 × 512	32 × 32	Medical and nonmedical images	Robustness against attacks can be improved
[107]	To ensure high security of medical data using chaotic maps	NSCT, DCT, Arnold's Cat Map, Logistic Map, and Tent Map	PSNR = 48.8170 dB and NC = 0.9952 for salt and pepper attack	384 × 384 × 3	-	MRI images	Limited experimental analysis
[108]	To ensure robust watermarking for medical applications	NSCT, DCT, and SVD	CC = 0.9985 and PSNR = 21.4953 dB	512 × 512	256 × 256	Medical images	Security of marked image is not confirmed
[109]	To improve embedding capacity maintaining high robustness	NSCT, DCT, MSVD, and Arnold map	NC1 = 0.9690, NC2 = 0.9953, BER = 0.0061, and PSNR = 22.6116 dB	512 × 512	256 × 256, 256 × 256, and 256 × 256	Medical images	Optimization of scaling factor can be done
[110]	Security of medical images with better robustness and visual quality	NSCT and RDWT	PSNR = 41.77 dB, NC = 0.9994, and SSIM = 1.000 for Lena image	256 × 256	8 × 8	Medical and common images	Limited embedding capacity

a sequence of random numbers is generated using a seed and noise generator, which is used for hiding the mark into the wavelet coefficients of the carrier image. A comparison of PSNR and NC scores proves better performance over the traditional work [85, 108, 123–125].

14.2.5 Other perspectives

Apart from the above-discussed transforms, there are a variety of transforms that are used by researchers to ensure efficient watermarking with high robustness at acceptable visual quality. Some of these transforms include SVD, Schur decomposition, fast Walsh Hadamard transform (FWHT), Hessenberg decomposition, and many more. SVD is highly stable, as no significant change in visual quality is observed on applying minor changes in its singular matrix, hence confirming high imperceptibility. Also, it can be applied on matrices of any size, and it has good energy compaction properties, making it a highly opted choice for watermarking techniques [126]. However, SVD suffers from the issue of high cost. Randomized SVD (RSVD) and Schur transforms help in resolving the issue of high cost. Furthermore, HD and FWHT provide high suitability for robust and imperceptible watermarking due to low cost and high energy compaction. A review of some of such watermarking methods are presented below along with their brief summary in Table 14.5.

Rai and Singh introduced a robust watermarking approach for telemedicine application [127]. In the pre-processing stage, it utilized an SVM classifier to find the RONI of the cover image. The selected part is further decomposed using DWT-SVD. The image mark is scrambled to ensure high security and concealed into the transformed coefficients of the cover image. The proposed scheme indicates better results when compared to a similar method [133]. Furthermore, the authors of Reference 24 demonstrated DWT-DCT-SVD-based watermarking techniques for health care applications. This scheme embedded three marks inside the cover image to ensure the identity authentication of medical information. Prior to the embedding process, the mark image is scrambled through Arnold transform, and text marks are encoded using arithmetic and hamming codes. During extraction, the recovered mark image is denoised using the BPNN model to enhance the robustness. The comparative analysis concludes with better robustness of the suggested work over other approaches [118, 133]. However, the computation cost of this work is very high.

In Reference 128, the author proposed an image fusion-based blind watermarking framework for radiography images. First, discrete cosine harmonic wavelet transform (DCHWT) is performed on both neutron and X-ray radiography images (NRI and XRI) to obtain a fused radiography image, which is used as a cover image. The logo mark image is concealed into fused radiography image via different schemes such as ridgelet transform, Stockwell transform, etc. Backtracking search optimization is performed to compute an optimal scaling factor, which offers better robustness along with acceptable visual quality. However, the computational cost of this scheme can be reduced. Another blind watermarking method based on Diffie-Hellman and number theoretic transform (NTT) is proposed by Soualmi *et al.* for the protection of medical records [129]. Initially, the mark is encrypted using

Table 14.5   Summary of other transforms based watermarking approaches for medical images

Ref. No.	Objective	Techniques used	Performance parameters	Size Cover	Watermark	Dataset used	Limitations
[127]	Robust and secure watermarking for medical images.	DWT, SVD, and SVM	PSNR = 52.18 dB and SSIM = 0.9872	256 × 256	128 × 128	Medical images	The computational cost of SVM classifier is high
[24]	Robust watermarking method for health care application	DCT, DWT, SVD, BPNN, and Arnold transform	PSNR = 43.88 dB, NC = 0.9888, and BER = 0	512 × 512	256 × 256	CT scan image and Lump image	High computational cost
[128]	Fusion-based robust and blind watermarking with high visual quality	DCHWT, ridgelet transform, Stockwell transform, SVD, and BSO	BCR = 0.3114, PSNR = 41.3712, entropy = 0.2705, NC = 0.9884 using Zernike Moment Method	512 × 512 or 342 × 421	32 × 32 and 73 × 78	Radiography images	Time analysis of the proposed work is missing
[129]	Blind watermarking method for protection of medical records	NTT and Diffie-Hellman	PSNR = 44.18 dB and BER = 0.197 at Noise = 0.01	256 × 256	32 bytes	DICOM medical images	The robustness to noises and attacks can be improved
[126]	Cloud-based robust and imperceptible dual watermarking method with high security	IWT, Schur, RSVD, DWT, FIS, and chaotic encryption	Average values of PSNR = 49.2554 dB, NC = 0.9961, BER = 0.0299, SSIM = 0.9847, NPCR = 0.9953, and UACI = 0.346	512 × 512	119 bits and 256 × 256	105 medical images	Cost analysis of the proposed work can be done.
[130]	Robust watermarking method for the authentication of ECG signals	QR code, QR decomposition, and DWT	PSNR = 59.969 dB, NC = 1.00, and PRD = 0.3403%	128 × 128	64 × 64	MIT-BIH database	Security of the marked signal is not ensured

(Continues)

Table 14.5 Continued

Ref. No.	Objective	Techniques used	Performance parameters	Size		Dataset used	Limitations
				Cover	Watermark		
[131]	Secure and robust watermarking for integrity protection	HT, RDWT, SVD, and 2D chaotic Arnold transform	SSIM = 0.9992, PSNR = 56.8684 dB, NPCR = 0.9999, USCI = 0.3295, and NC = 0.9998 for knee X-ray	512 × 512	512 × 512	Medical images	Limited embedding capacity
[132]	Zero watermarking scheme with high computational speed	DFT, DWT, Paillier Cryptosystem, and logistic map	PSNR = 90.21 dB and NC = 1.0 for encrypted image	128 × 128	32 × 32	Medical images	Comparative analysis of the proposed work is missing

Diffie-Hellman for better security of this scheme. In the embedding phase, the host image is transformed using NTT, and the resultant coefficients are altered to embed the encrypted mark. The performance of this scheme offers better computational complexity and visual quality when compared with methods proposed in References 134, 135. Furthermore, Anand *et al.* proposed a secure watermarking method to authenticate the digital medical content [126]. The proposed work uses wavelet domain watermarking to generate a dual watermark by hiding an encoded Media Access Control (MAC) address into the mark image. This cloud-based system uses the optimized scaling factor and a hybrid of IWT-Schur-RSVD to embed the final mark into the carrier image. The optimized scaling factor is calculated using a Fuzzy Inference System to maintain high robustness with minimum visual distortion. Finally, chaotic encryption is applied on the marked image to improve security while transmitting over the open network. Sanivarapu *et al.* [130] designed a secure QR-DWT-based ECG watermarking method. Initially, the ECG signal is converted into a 2D image using a Pan Tompkins algorithm, which is further decomposed using DWT and QR decomposition. Furthermore, the QR secret image is concealed within the vertical sub-band of the host signal using an adaptive scaling factor based on the entropy of the vertical sub-band. The scheme is significantly superior over the existing schemes [136–138] in several aspects.

To provide a solution for the integrity protection of medical images, Khare and Srivastava have proposed a secure and robust watermarking scheme [131]. Firstly, cover image is decomposed using homomorphic transform, RDWT, and SVD to obtain suitable block for the embedding purpose. Also, a series of RDWT-SVD is applied for the preprocessing of the image mark. Furthermore, 2D chaotic Arnold transform is utilized to scramble the marked image for enhanced security. The performance of this scheme offers better resistance against common attacks in comparison to the existing methods [111, 112, 118, 139, 140]. However, it does not resist against geometric attacks. Dong and Li described a zero watermarking algorithm in the encrypted domain [132]. In the preprocessing stage, host and mark images are transformed using Paillier Cryptosystem and logistic sequence, respectively. Furthermore, the encrypted mark is concealed in the host image using a hybrid of DWT and DFT in the encrypted domain. The experimental evaluation confirms strong robustness and visual quality of the marked image with high computational speed.

14.3   Conclusion

The consistent generation and transmission of digital patient records and related images are required for accurate diagnosis. However, the transmission of digital health care records has escalated the issues of illegal distribution, tampering, identity theft, and threat to copyright. This chapter presented a comprehensive survey on spatial- and transform-based watermarking schemes, especially for copyright protection and ownership control for health care applications. Along with the survey, we presented a brief introduction, background information, and the most interesting and utilized applications of watermarking. Second, the contribution of reviewed approaches is also summarized and compared in different technical perspectives. The highlights of the survey are as follows:

- Wavelet domain-based watermarking is highly popular among researchers for the development of robust and efficient watermarking methods.
- Although wavelet transforms offer multiresolution and spatiofrequency properties, these transforms suffer from the issues of poor directionality, shift variance, and poor capturing of edge information.
- To overcome the limitation of poor directionality, curvelet transform is used that offers the properties of sparse representation and strong directional information, required for robust and imperceptible watermarking solutions.
- Curvelet transform lacks multiresolution properties and experiences shift sensitivity. To overcome these issues, CT having multiscale, multiresolution, and multidirectional properties is implemented for high resistance against attacks.
- Despite multiresolution and multidirectional properties, CT causes shift variant problem. So, it is replaced with NSCT, which is capable of providing better directionality and holds shift invariant.
- However, the main disadvantage of NSCT is high time complexity which reduces the watermarking efficiency.
- NSCT can further be replaced with low complexity transforms like nonsubsampled shearlet transform to develop a low-cost highly efficient watermarking solution for securing the digital medical records.

Acknowledgements

This work is supported by research project order no. IES\R2\212111 - International Exchanges 2021 Round 2, dt. 28 February, 2022, under Royal Society, UK.

References

[1]   Thakur S., Singh A.K., Kumar B., Ghrera S.P. 'Improved DWT-SVD-based medical image watermarking through hamming code and chaotic encryption' in Dutta D., Kar H., Kumar C., Bhadauria V. (eds.). *Advances in VLSI, Communication, and Signal Processing Lecture Notes in Electrical Engineering*. Vol. 587; 2020. pp. 897–905.

[2]   Singh A.K., Kumar B., Singh G., Mohan A. *Medical Image Watermarking*. Cham: Springer International Publishing; 2020. Available from http://link.springer.com/10.1007/978-3-319-57699-2

[3]   Alam M.M., Malik H., Khan M.I., Pardy T., Kuusik A., Le Moullec Y. 'A survey on the roles of communication technologies in IoT-based personalized healthcare applications'. *IEEE Access: Practical Innovations, Open Solutions*. 2020, vol. 6, pp. 36611–31.

[4] Salehi S., Abedi A., Balakrishnan S., Gholamrezanezhad A. 'Coronavirus disease 2019 (COVID-19): a systematic review of imaging findings in 919 patients'. *American Journal of Roentgenology*. 2020, vol. 215(1), pp. 87–93.

[5] 'Digital health market size & growth report, 2021-2028'.2021.

[6] Rahman M.S., Khalil I., Mahawaga Arachchige P.C., Bouras A., Yi X. 'A novel architecture for tamper proof electronic health record management system using blockchain wrapper'. *BCI 2019 - ACM International Symposium on Blockchain and Secure Critical Infrastructure*, Co-located with Asia CCS 2019; Auckland, New Zealand, New York, NY, 2019. pp. 97–105. Available from http://dl.acm.org/citation.cfm?doid=3327960

[7] Anand A., Singh A.K. 'Watermarking techniques for medical data authentication: a survey'. *Multimedia Tools and Applications*. 2019, vol. 80(20), pp. 30165–97.

[8] Anand A., Singh A.K. 'An improved DWT-SVD domain watermarking for medical information security'. *Computer Communications*. 2019, vol. 152, pp. 72–80.

[9] Thakur S., Singh A.K., Ghrera S., Dave M. 'Watermarking techniques and its applications in tele-health: a technical survey'. *Cryptographic and Information Security*. 2019, pp. 467–508.

[10] Kumar C., Singh A.K., Kumar P. 'A recent survey on image watermarking techniques and its application in e-governance'. *Multimedia Tools and Applications*. 2019, vol. 77(3), pp. 3597–622.

[11] Mousavi S.M., Naghsh A., Abu-Bakar S.A.R. 'Watermarking techniques used in medical images: a survey'. *Journal of Digital Imaging*. 2014, vol. 27(6), pp. 714–29.

[12] Mohanty S.P., Sengupta P.G.A., Kougianos E. 'Everything you want to know about watermarking from paper marks to hardware protection'. *IEEE Consumer Electronics Magazine*. 2017, vol. 6(3), pp. 83–91.

[13] Singh Y.S., Devi B.P., Singh K.M. 'A review of different techniques on digital image watermarking scheme'. *International Journal of Engineering Research*. 2013, vol. 2(3), pp. 194–200.

[14] Zhang D. 'Wavelet transform' in *Fundamentals of image data mining*. Texts in Computer Science. Cham: Springer; 2019. pp. 35–44.

[15] Alshanbari H.S. 'Medical image watermarking for ownership & tamper detection'. *Multimedia Tools and Applications*. 2021, vol. 80(11), pp. 16549–64.

[16] Kahlessenane F., Khaldi A., Kafi R., Euschi S. 'A DWT based watermarking approach for medical image protection'. *Journal of Ambient Intelligence and Humanized Computing*. 2021, vol. 12(2), pp. 2931–38.

[17] Balasamy K., Suganyadevi S. 'A fuzzy based ROI selection for encryption and watermarking in medical image using DWT and SVD'. *Multimedia Tools and Applications*. 2021, vol. 80, pp. 7167–86.

[18] Singh A.K. 'Robust and distortion control dual watermarking in LWT domain using DCT and error correction code for color medical image'. *Multimedia Tools and Applications*. 2010, vol. 78(21), pp. 30523–33.

[19] Nazari M., Maneshi A., Irshad A. 'Chaotic reversible watermarking method based on IWT with tamper detection for transferring electronic health record'. *Security and Communication Networks*. 2010, vol. 2021, pp. 1–15.

[20] Nazari M., Mehrabian M. 'A novel chaotic IWT-LSB blind watermarking approach with flexible capacity for secure transmission of authenticated medical images'. *Multimedia Tools and Applications*. 2021, vol. 80(7), pp. 10615–55.

[21] Ravichandran D., Praveenkumar P., Rajagopalan S., Rayappan J.B.B., Amirtharajan R. 'ROI-based medical image watermarking for accurate tamper detection, localisation and recovery'. *Medical & Biological Engineering & Computing*. 2021, vol. 59(6), pp. 1355–72.

[22] Liu J., Li J., Ma J., Sadiq N., Bhatti U.A., Ai Y. 'A robust multi-watermarking algorithm for medical images based on DTCWT-DCT and Henon map'. *Applied Sciences*. 2015, vol. 9(4), p. 700.

[23] Badshah G., Liew S.C., Zain J.M., Ali M. 'Watermark compression in medical image watermarking using Lempel-Ziv-Welch (LZW) lossless compression technique'. *Journal of Digital Imaging*. 2016, vol. 29(2), pp. 216–25.

[24] Zear A., Singh A.K., Kumar P. 'A proposed secure multiple watermarking technique based on DWT, DCT and SVD for application in medicine'. *Multimedia Tools and Applications*. 2018, vol. 77(4), pp. 4863–82.

[25] Liu X.-L., Lin C.-C., Yuan S.-M. 'Blind dual watermarking for color images ' authentication and copyright protection'. *IEEE Transactions on Circuits and Systems for Video Technology*. 2021, vol. 28(5), pp. 1047–55.

[26] Ansari I.A., Pant M. 'Quality assured and optimized image watermarking using artificial bee colony'. *International Journal of System Assurance Engineering and Management*. 2018, vol. 9(1), pp. 274–86.

[27] Assini I., Badri A., Safi K., *et al.* 'A robust hybrid watermarking technique for securing medical image'. *International Journal of Intelligent Engineering and Systems*. 2017, vol. 11(3), pp. 169–76. Available from http://www.inass.org/ContentsPapers2018-3.html

[28] Thakkar F.N., Srivastava V.K. 'A blind medical image watermarking: DWT-SVD based robust and secure approach for telemedicine applications'. *Multimedia Tools and Applications*. 2017, vol. 76(3), pp. 3669–97.

[29] Sankaran K.S., Abhi Rayna H., Mangu V., Prakash V.R., Vasudevan N. 'Image water marking using DWT to encapsulate data in medical image'. *International Conference on Communication and Signal Processing (ICCSP)*; Chennai, India, 2017. pp. 568–71.

[30] Verma U., Sharma N. 'Hybrid mode of medical image watermarking to enhance robustness and imperceptibility'. *International Journal of Innovative Technology and Exploring Engineering*. 2017, vol. 9(1), pp. 351–59.

[31] Kundu M.K., Das S. 'Lossless ROI medical image watermarking technique with enhanced security and high payload embedding'. *20th International Conference on Pattern Recognition (ICPR);* Istanbul, Turkey, 2015. pp. 1457–60.

[32] Liu Y., Qu X., Xin G., Liu P. 'ROI-based reversible data hiding scheme for medical images with tamper detection'. *IEICE Transactions on Information and Systems*. 2015, vol. E98.D(4), pp. 769–74.

[33] Al-Qershi O.M., Khoo B.E. 'Authentication and data hiding using a hybrid ROI-based watermarking scheme for DICOM images'. *Journal of Digital Imaging*. 2011, vol. 24(1), pp. 114–25.

[34] Keshavarzian R., Aghagolzadeh A. 'ROI based robust and secure image watermarking using DWT and Arnold map'. *AEU - International Journal of Electronics and Communications*. 2015, vol. 70(3), pp. 278–88.

[35] Li C., Lo K.-T. 'Optimal quantitative cryptanalysis of permutation-only multimedia ciphers against plaintext attacks'. *Signal Processing*. 2015, vol. 91(4), pp. 949–54.

[36] Radwan A.G., Abd-El-Haleem S.H., Abd-El-Hafiz S.K. 'Symmetric encryption algorithms using chaotic and non-chaotic generators: A review'. *Journal of Advanced Research*. 2016, vol. 7(2), pp. 193–208.

[37] Rhouma R., Solak E., Belghith S. 'Cryptanalysis of a new substitution–diffusion based image cipher'. *Communications in Nonlinear Science and Numerical Simulation*. 2010, vol. 15(7), pp. 1887–92.

[38] Zhou Y., Panetta K., Agaian S., Chen C.L.P. '(N, K, P) -gray code for image systems'. *IEEE Transactions on Cybernetics*. 2013, vol. 43(2), pp. 515–29.

[39] Parah S.A., Ahad F., Sheikh J.A., Bhat G.M. 'Hiding clinical information in medical images: A new high capacity and reversible data hiding technique'. *Journal of Biomedical Informatics*. 2017, vol. 66, pp. 214–30.

[40] Naheed T., Usman I., Khan T.M., Dar A.H., Shafique M.F. 'Intelligent reversible watermarking technique in medical images using GA and PSO'. *Optik*. 2014, vol. 125(11), pp. 2515–25.

[41] Parah S.A., Sheikh J.A., Akhoon J.A., Loan N.A. 'Electronic health record hiding in images for smart city applications: A computationally efficient and reversible information hiding technique for secure communication'. *Future Generation Computer Systems*. 2014, vol. 108, pp. 935–49.

[42] Hu J., Li T. 'Reversible steganography using extended image interpolation technique'. *Computers & Electrical Engineering*. 2014, vol. 46, pp. 447–55.

[43] Kaw J.A., Loan N.A., Parah S.A., Muhammad K., Sheikh J.A., Bhat G.M. 'A reversible and secure patient information hiding system for iot driven e-health'. *International Journal of Information Management*. 2014, vol. 45, pp. 262–75.

[44] Lee S., Yoo C.D., Kalker T. 'Reversible image watermarking based on integer-to-integer wavelet transform'. *IEEE Transactions on Information Forensics and Security*. 2021, vol. 2(3), pp. 321–30.

[45] LixinL., ZhenyongC., MingC., XiaoZ., ZhangX. 'Reversible image watermarking using interpolation technique'. *IEEE Transactions on Information Forensics and Security*. 2010, vol. 5(1), pp. 187–93.

[46] Bhinder P., Jindal N., Singh K. 'An improved robust image-adaptive watermarking with two watermarks using statistical decoder'. *Multimedia Tools and Applications*. 2021, vol. 79(1–2), pp. 183–217.

[47]   Makbol N.M., Khoo B.E., Rassem T.H. 'Block-based discrete wavelet transform-singular value decomposition image watermarking scheme using human visual system characteristics'. *IET Image Processing*. 2016, vol. 10(1), pp. 34–52. Available from https://onlinelibrary.wiley.com/toc/17519667/10/1

[48]   Singh A.K., Dave M., Mohan A. 'Multilevel encrypted text watermarking on medical images using spread-spectrum in DWT domain'. *Wireless Personal Communications*. 2015, vol. 83(3), pp. 2133–50.

[49]   SwarajaK S., K M., Kora P. 'An optimized blind dual medical image watermarking framework for tamper localization and content authentication in secured telemedicine'. *Biomedical Signal Processing and Control*. 2015, vol. 55, 101665.

[50]   Thanki R., Borra S., Dwivedi V., Borisagar K. 'An efficient medical image watermarking scheme based on FDCuT–DCT'. *Engineering Science and Technology, an International Journal*. 2015, vol. 20(4), pp. 1366–79.

[51]   Ernawan F., Kabir M.N. 'A block-based RDWT-SVD image watermarking method using human visual system characteristics'. *The Visual Computer*. 2015, vol. 36(1), pp. 19–37.

[52]   Chauhan D.S., Singh A.K., Kumar B., Saini J.P. 'Quantization based multiple medical information watermarking for secure e-health'. *Multimedia Tools and Applications*. 2015, vol. 78(4), pp. 3911–23.

[53]   Das S., Kundu M.K. 'Effective management of medical information through ROI-lossless fragile image watermarking technique'. *Computer Methods and Programs in Biomedicine*. 2013, vol. 111(3), pp. 662–75.

[54]   Guo X., Zhuang T.-G. 'A region-based lossless watermarking scheme for enhancing security of medical data'. *Journal of Digital Imaging*. 2009, vol. 22(1), pp. 53–64.

[55]   Gao G., Wan X., Yao S., Cui Z., Zhou C., Sun X. 'Reversible data hiding with contrast enhancement and tamper localization for medical images'. *Information Sciences*. 2017, vol. 385–386, pp. 250–65.

[56]   Ustubioglu A., Ulutas G. 'A new medical image watermarking technique with finer tamper localization'. *Journal of Digital Imaging*. 2017, vol. 30(6), pp. 665–80.

[57]   Liew S.-C., Liew S.-W., Zain J.M. 'Tamper localization and lossless recovery watermarking scheme with ROI segmentation and multilevel authentication'. *Journal of Digital Imaging*. 2013, vol. 26(2), pp. 316–25.

[58]   Singh A.K., Kumar B., Dave M., Mohan A. 'Multiple watermarking on medical images using selective discrete wavelet transform coefficients'. *Journal of Medical Imaging and Health Informatics*. 2015, vol. 5(3), pp. 607–14.

[59]   Yuan X.-C., Li M. 'Local multi-watermarking method based on robust and adaptive feature extraction'. *Signal Processing*. 2015, vol. 149, pp. 103–17.

[60]   Ravi J., Narmadha R., Research Scholar, ECE, Sathyabama Institute of Science & Technology, Chennai (Tamil Nadu), India, Associate Professor, ECE, Sathyabama Institute of Science & Technology, Chennai (Tamil Nadu), India 'Image fusion based on nonsubsampled shearlet transform'.

International Journal of Engineering and Advanced Technology. 2020, vol. 9(3), pp. 4177–80. Available from https://www.ijeat.org/download/volume-9-issue-3/

[61]   Ji F., Huang D., Deng C., Zhang Y., Miao W. 'Robust curvelet-domain image watermarking based on feature matching'. *International Journal of Computer Mathematics*. 2011, vol. 88(18), pp. 3931–41.

[62]   Edward Jero S., Ramu P., Ramakrishnan S. 'ECG steganography using curvelet transform'. *Biomedical Signal Processing and Control*. 2011, vol. 22, pp. 161–69.

[63]   Hassan B., Ahmed R., Li B., Hassan O. 'An imperceptible medical image watermarking framework for automated diagnosis of retinal pathologies in an e-health arrangement'. *IEEE Access: Practical Innovations, Open Solutions*. 2011, vol. 7, pp. 69758–75.

[64]   Borra S., Thanki R., Dey N., Borisagar K. 'Secure transmission and integrity verification of color radiological images using fast discrete curvelet transform and compressive sensing'. *Smart Health*. 2019, vol. 12, pp. 35–48.

[65]   Phan T.H.D., Bui V.H., Nguyen T.A., Hoang T.M. 'A novel watermarking scheme based on the curvelet transformation method for medical images'. *7th NAFOSTED Conference on Information and Computer Science (NICS)*; Ho Chi Minh City, Vietnam, 2020. pp. 379–83. Available from https://ieeexplore.ieee.org/xpl/mostRecentIssue.jsp?punumber=9335828

[66]   Thanki R.M., Borisagar K.R. 'Securing multiple biometric data using SVD and curvelet-based watermarking'. *International Journal of Information Security and Privacy*. 2018, vol. 12(4), pp. 35–53. Available from https://services.igi-global.com/resolvedoi/resolve.aspx?doi=10.4018/IJISP.20181001

[67]   Ahmed R., Hassan B., Li B. 'Robust hybrid watermarking for security of medical images in computer-aided diagnosis based telemedicine applications'. *2018 IEEE International Symposium on Signal Processing and Information Technology (ISSPIT)*; Louisville, KY, 2018.

[68]   Dey N., Samanta S., Yang X.S., Das A., Chaudhuri S.S. 'Optimisation of scaling factors in electrocardiogram signal watermarking using cuckoo search'. *International Journal of Bio-Inspired Computation*. 2011, vol. 5(5), p. 315.

[69]   Eswaraiah R., Sreenivasa Reddy E. 'Medical image watermarking technique for accurate tamper detection in ROI and exact recovery of ROI'. *International Journal of Telemedicine and Applications*. 2014, vol. 2014, pp. 1–10.

[70]   Jia S., Zhou Q., Zhou H. 'A novel color image watermarking scheme based on DWT and QR decomposition'. *Journal of Applied Science and Engineering*. 2017, vol. 20(2), pp. 192–200.

[71]   Selvam P., Balachandran S., Pitchai Iyer S., Jayabal R. 'Hybrid transform based reversible watermarking technique for medical images in telemedicine applications'. *Optik*. 2019, vol. 145, pp. 655–71.

[72] Rahman A., Rabbi M.M.F. 'Non-blind DWT-SVD based watermarking technique for RGB image'. *Global Journal of Research In Engineering*. 2015, vol. 15, p. 4.

[73] Thabit R., Khoo B.E. 'A new robust lossless data hiding scheme and its application to color medical images'. *Digital Signal Processing*. 2019, vol. 38, pp. 77–94.

[74] Hassan B., Raja G., Hassan T., Usman Akram M. 'Structure tensor based automated detection of macular edema and central serous retinopathy using optical coherence tomography images'. *Journal of the Optical Society of America. A, Optics, Image Science, and Vision*. 2016, vol. 33(4), pp. 455–63.

[75] Hassan B., Raja G. 'Fully automated assessment of macular edema using optical coherence tomography (OCT) images'. *International Conference on Intelligent Systems Engineering (ICISE)*; Islamabad, 2016. pp. 5–9.

[76] Hassan B., Ahmed R., Li B., Hassan O., Hassan T. 'Automated retinal edema detection from fundus and optical coherence tomography scans'. *5th International Conference on Control, Automation and Robotics (ICCAR)*; Beijing, China, 2019. pp. 325–30.

[77] Wang M.S.M., Sander B., Larsen M. 'Computer aided diagnosis of idiopathic central serous chorioretinopathy'. *2nd IEEE Advanced Information Management, Communicates, Electronic and Automation Control Conference (IMCEC 2018)*; 2018. pp. 787–93.

[78] Hassan B., Ahmed R., Li B. 'Automated foveal detection in OCT scans'. *IEEE International Symposium on Signal Processing and Information Technology (ISSPIT)*; Louisville, KY, 2018. pp. 419–22.

[79] Wang D., Li J., Wen X. 'Biometric image integrity authentication based on SVD and fragile watermarking'. *'Congress on Image and Signal Processing*; Sanya, China, 2018. pp. 679–82.

[80] Joshi V.B., Ieee S.M., Raval M.S., Csi S.M. 'Multistage VQ based exact authentication for biometric images'. *Computer Society of India (CSI) Journal of Computing*. 2013, vol. 2(1–2), pp. 25–29.

[81] Do M.N., Vetterli M. 'The contourlet transform: an efficient directional multiresolution image representation'. *IEEE Transactions on Image Processing*. 2005, vol. 14(12), pp. 2091–106.

[82] Wu X., Li J., Tu R., Cheng J., Bhatti U.A., Ma J. 'Contourlet-DCT based multiple robust watermarkings for medical images'. *Multimedia Tools and Applications*. 2019, vol. 78(7), pp. 8463–80.

[83] Rahimi F., Rabbani H. 'A dual adaptive watermarking scheme in contourlet domain for DICOM images'. *Biomedical Engineering Online*. 2011, vol. 10, pp. 1–18.

[84] Seenivasagam V., Velumani R. 'A QR code based zero-watermarking scheme for authentication of medical images in teleradiology cloud'. *Computational and Mathematical Methods in Medicine*. 2013, vol. 2013, 516465.

[85] Das S., Kundu M.K. 'Hybrid contourlet-DCT based robust image watermarking technique applied to medical data management'. *Pattern Recognition*

and Machine Intelligence - 4th International Conference, PReMI; 2011. pp. 286–92.

[86] Chakrasali S., Murugesan R, *et al.* 'A contourlet transform-based versatile watermarking algorithm for medical images' in Chakravarthi V. (ed.). *Proceedings of international Conference on VLSI, communication, advanced devices, signals & systems and networking (VCASAN-2013), lecture notes in electrical engineering 258.* India, Springer; 2013.

[87] Das S., Kundu M.K. 'Effective management of medical information through a novel blind watermarking technique'. *Journal of Medical Systems.* 2012, vol. 36(5), pp. 3339–51.

[88] Duong D.M., Duong D.A. 'Robust and high capacity watermaking scheme for medical images based on contourlet transform'. *International Conference on Systems and Informatics (ICSAI)*; Yantai, China, 2010. pp. 2183–87.

[89] Liu Y., Wang J.-X., Hu H.-H., Zhu Y.-H. 'Robust blind digital watermarking scheme based on contourlet transform and QR decomposition'. *Journal of Optoelectronics Laser.* 2016, vol. 27(3), pp. 317–24.

[90] Verma V.S., Jha R.K., Ojha A. 'Significant region based robust watermarking scheme in lifting wavelet transform domain'. *Expert Systems with Applications.* 2019, vol. 42(21), pp. 8184–97.

[91] Xuan G., Chen J., Zhu J., Shi Y.Q. 'Lossless image digital watermarking based on integer wavelet and histogram adjustment'. *International Conference on Diagnostic Imaging and Analysis (ICDIA'02)*; 2002. pp. 60–65.

[92] Ming-Kuei H. 'Visual pattern recognition by moment invariants'. *IEEE Transactions on Information Theory.* 1962, vol. 8(2), pp. 179–87.

[93] Rawat S., Raman B. 'A blind watermarking algorithm based on fractional Fourier transform and visual cryptography'. *Signal Processing.* 2012, vol. 92(6), pp. 1480–91.

[94] Wang M.S., Chen W.C. 'A hybrid DWT-SVD copyright protection scheme based on k-means clustering and visual cryptography'. *Computer Standards & Interfaces.* 2012, vol. 31(4), pp. 757–62.

[95] Hou Y.-C. 'Copyright protection scheme for digital images using visual cryptography and sampling methods'. *Optical Engineering.* 2005, vol. 44(7), p. 077003.

[96] Kim J., Kim N., Lee D., Park S., Lee S. 'Watermarking two dimensional data object identifier for authenticated distribution of digital multimedia contents'. *Signal Processing.* 2005, vol. 25(8), pp. 559–76.

[97] Manasrah T., Al-Haj A. 'Management of medical images using wavelets-based multi-watermarking algorithm '. *International Conference on Innovations in Information Technology (IIT)*; Al Ain, UAE, 2005. pp. 697–701.

[98] Lee H.-K., Kim H.-J., Kwon K.-R., Lee J.-K. 'ROI medical image watermarking using DWT and bit-plane'. *Asia-Pacific Conference on Communications*; 2005. pp. 512–15.

[99] Mostafa S.A.K., El-Sheimy N., Tolba A.S., Abdelkader F.M., Elhindy H.M. 'Wavelet packets-based blind watermarking for medical image management'. *The Open Biomedical Engineering Journal.* 2010, vol. 4(1), pp. 93–98.

[100] Oueslati S., Cherif A., Solaiman B. 'Maximizing strength of digital watermarks using fuzzy logic'. *Signal & Image Processing.* 2010, vol. 1(2), pp. 112–24. Available from http://www.airccse.org/journal/sipij/currentissue. html

[101] Xueqiang L., Xinghao D., Donghui G. 'Digital watermarking based on non-sampled contourlet transform'. *International Workshop on Anti-Counterfeiting, Security and Identification*; Xizmen, China, 2007. pp. 138.

[102] Narasimhulu C.V., Prasad K.S. 'A robust watermarking technique based on nonsubsampled contourlet transform and SVD'. *International Journal of Computer Applications.* 2011, vol. 16(8), pp. 27–36.

[103] Zhenghua-Shu, Shengqian-Wang, ChengZhi-Deng, Guodong-Liu, Lin-Zhang ' Watermarking algorithm based on contourlet transform and human visual model '. *International Conference on Embedded Software and Systems*; Chengdu, Sichuan, China, 2008. pp. 348–52.

[104] Rahimi F., Rabani H. 'A visually imperceptible and robust image watermarking scheme in contourlet domain'. *10th International Conference on Signal Processing (ICSP 2010)*; Beijing, China, 2010.

[105] Thakur S., Singh A.K., Ghrera S.P. 'NSCT domain–based secure multiple-watermarking technique through lightweight encryption for medical images'. *Concurrency and Computation.* 2021, vol. 33(2), pp. 1–10. Available from https://onlinelibrary.wiley.com/toc/15320634/33/2

[106] Nouioua N., Seddiki A., Ghaz A. 'Blind digital watermarking framework based on DTCWT and NSCT for telemedicine application'. *Traitement Du Signal.* 2017, vol. 37(6), pp. 955–64. Available from http://www.iieta.org/ Journals/TS/Archive/Vol-37-No-6-2020

[107] Saha C., Hossain M.F. 'MRI watermarking technique using chaotic maps, NSCT and DCT'. *International Conference on Electrical, Computer and Communication Engineering (ECCE)*; Cox's Bazar, Bangladesh, 2018.

[108] Singh S., Singh R., Singh A.K. 'SVD-DCT based medical image watermarking in NSCT domain' in *Quantum Computing: An Environment for Intelligent Large Scale Real Application*; 2018. pp. 467–88.

[109] Singh S., Rathore V.S., Singh R. 'Hybrid NSCT domain multiple watermarking for medical images'. *Multimedia Tools and Applications.* 2017, vol. 76(3), pp. 3557–75.

[110] Thanki R., Kothari A., Borra S. 'Hybrid, blind and robust image watermarking: RDWT – NSCT based secure approach for telemedicine applications'. *Multimedia Tools and Applications.* 2017, vol. 80(18), pp. 27593–613.

[111] Singh S., Rathore V.S., Singh R., Singh M.K. 'Hybrid semi-blind image watermarking in redundant wavelet domain'. *Multimedia Tools and Applications.* 2017, vol. 76(18), pp. 19113–37.

[112] Singh A.K. 'Improved hybrid algorithm for robust and imperceptible multiple watermarking using digital images'. *Multimedia Tools and Applications*. 2017, vol. 76(6), pp. 8881–900.

[113] Kazemivash B., Moghaddam M.E. 'A robust digital image watermarking technique using lifting wavelet transform and firefly algorithm'. *Multimedia Tools and Applications*. 2017, vol. 76(20), pp. 20499–524.

[114] Ariatmanto D., Ernawan F. 'An improved robust image watermarking by using different embedding strengths'. *Multimedia Tools and Applications*. 2017, vol. 79(17–18), pp. 12041–67.

[115] Kalra G.S., Talwar R., Sadawarti H. 'Digital image watermarking in frequency domain using ECC and dual encryption technique'. *Research Journal of Applied Sciences, Engineering and Technology*. 2013, vol. 6(18), pp. 3365–71.

[116] Nedooshan A.S., Yaghmaie K., Nadooshan R.S. 'Medical image watermarking based on SVD-DWT technique'. *International Conference on Informatics, Environment, Energy and Applications*. 2012, vol. 38.

[117] Li J., Huang M., Zhang H., Dong C., Bai Y. 'The medical images watermarking using DWT and Arnold'. *IEEE International Conference on Computer Science and Automation Engineering (CSAE)*; Zhangjiajie, China, 2018. pp. 6–10.

[118] Singh A.K., Dave M., Mohan A. 'Hybrid technique for robust and imperceptible multiple watermarking using medical images'. *Multimedia Tools and Applications*. 2016, vol. 75(14), pp. 8381–401.

[119] Singh A., Tayal A. 'Choice of wavelet from wavelet families for DWT-DCT-SVD image watermarking'. *International Journal of Computer Applications*. 2016, vol. 48(17), pp. 9–14.

[120] Srivastava A., IFTM University, Moradabad, India 'DWT-DCT-SVD based semi blind image watermarking using middle frequency band'. *IOSR Journal of Computer Engineering*. 2013, vol. 12(2), pp. 63–66. Available from http://www.iosrjournals.org/iosr-jce/pages/v12i2.html

[121] Rosiyadi D., Horng S.-J., Suryana N., Masthurah N. 'A comparison between the hybrid using genetic algorithm and the pure hybrid watermarking scheme'. *International Journal of Computer Theory and Engineering*. 2016, vol. 4(3), pp. 329–31.

[122] Rosiyadi D., Horng S.-J., Fan P., Wang X., Khan M.K., Pan Y. 'Copyright protection for E-government document images'. *IEEE MultiMedia*. 2017, vol. 19(3), pp. 62–73.

[123] Kahlessenane F., Khaldi A., Kafi R., Euschi S. 'A robust blind medical image watermarking approach for telemedicine applications'. *Cluster Computing*. 2021, vol. 24(3), pp. 2069–82.

[124] Singh P., Raman B., Roy P.P. 'A multimodal biometric watermarking system for digital images in redundant discrete wavelet transform'. *Multimedia Tools and Applications*. 2017, vol. 76(3), pp. 3871–97.

[125] Roy S., Pal A.K. 'A robust blind hybrid image watermarking scheme in RDWT-DCT domain using Arnold scrambling'. *Multimedia Tools and Applications*. 2017, vol. 76(3), pp. 3577–616.

[126] Anand A., Singh A.K. 'Cloud based secure watermarking using IWT-schur-RSVD with fuzzy inference system for smart healthcare applications'. *Sustainable Cities and Society*. 2017, vol. 75(September), p. 103398.

[127] Rai A., Singh H.V. 'SVM based robust watermarking for enhanced medical image security'. *Multimedia Tools and Applications*. 2017, vol. 76(18), pp. 18605–18.

[128] El_Tokhy M.S. 'Development of optimum watermarking algorithm for radiography images'. *Computers & Electrical Engineering*. 2017, vol. 89, p. 106932.

[129] Soualmi A., Alti A., Laouamer L, *et al*. 'Medical data protection using blind watermarking technique' in Hassanien A.-E. (ed.). *Enabling AI Applications in Data Science, Studies*. Switzerland: Springer Nature; 2021. pp. 557–76.

[130] Sanivarapu P.V., Rajesh K.N.V.P.S., Reddy N.V.R., Reddy N.C.S. 'Patient data hiding into ECG signal using watermarking in transform domain'. *Physical and Engineering Sciences in Medicine*. 2020, vol. 43(1), pp. 213–26.

[131] Khare P., Srivastava V.K. 'A secured and robust medical image watermarking approach for protecting integrity of medical images'. *Transactions on Emerging Telecommunications Technologies*. 2021, vol. 32(2), pp. 1–17. Available from https://onlinelibrary.wiley.com/toc/21613915/32/2

[132] Dong J., Li J. 'A robust zero-watermarking algorithm for encrypted medical images in the DWT-DFT encrypted domain' in Chen Y.W., Tanaka S., Howlett R., Jain L. (eds.). *Innovation in medicine and healthcare 2016. inmed 2016. smart innovation, systems and technologies*. Vol. 60. Springer, Cham; 2016. pp. 197–208.

[133] Ganic E., Eskicioglu A.M. 'Robust DWT-SVD domain image watermarking: embedding data in all frequencies'. *Proc. Multimed. Secur. Work*. 2004, vol. MM Sec'04, pp. 166–74.

[134] Kannammal A., Rani S.S. 'Authentication of DICOM medical images using multiple fragile watermarking techniques in wavelet transform domain'. *International Journal of Computer Science Issues*. 2011, vol. 8(6), pp. 181–89.

[135] Singh D., Singh S.K. 'DWT-SVD and DCT based robust and blind watermarking scheme for copyright protection'. *Multimedia Tools and Applications*. 2017, vol. 76(11), pp. 13001–24.

[136] S E.J., Ramu P., Swaminathan R. 'Imperceptibility—robustness tradeoff studies for ECG steganography using continuous ant colony optimization'. *Expert Systems with Applications*. 2020, vol. 49, pp. 123–35.

[137] Mathivanan P., Edward Jero S., Ramu P., Balaji Ganesh A. 'QR code based patient data protection in ECG steganography'. *Australasian Physical & Engineering Sciences in Medicine*. 2018, vol. 41(4), pp. 1057–68.

[138] Jero S.E., Ramu P. 'Curvelets-based ECG steganography for data security'. *Electron Lett*. 2016, vol. 52(4), pp. 283–85. Available from https://onlinelibrary.wiley.com/toc/1350911x/52/4

[139] Thakur S., Singh A.K., Ghrera S.P., Elhoseny M. 'Multi-layer security of medical data through watermarking and chaotic encryption for tele-health applications'. *Multimedia Tools and Applications*. 2016, vol. 78(3), pp. 3457–70.

[140] Kumar C., Singh A.K., Kumar P. 'Improved wavelet-based image watermarking through SPIHT'. *Multimedia Tools and Applications*. 2016, vol. 79(15–16), pp. 11069–82.

Chapter 15

Secure communication and privacy preserving for medical system

Song Jingcheng[1], Chen Jingxue[2], and Liu Yining[3]

The remote medical system has been greatly developed with the help of 5G and Internet of things (IoT) technology. People, especially those living in areas lacking excellent medical resources, benefit from the remote medical system. There are a lot of data transmitted in the channel, which leads to many security and privacy anxiety. It may include: (1) the communication between users and doctors should be confident and authenticated; (2) medical equipment needs to authenticate the doctors' identity; (3) doctors and patients need a secure and private way to connect the database; and (4) patients data privacy should be protected. For solving these anxieties, a lot of security and privacy protocols, such as authentication schemes, privacy-preserving schemes, or n-sources anonymity schemes, are proposed. In this chapter, some of these security and privacy schemes are introduced, which are important and excellent. Compared with other similar protocols, the proposed protocols have advantages in terms of efficiency, safety, dynamics, etc. We believe that these security and privacy schemes can solve the above anxiety and inspire more related works.

15.1   Introduction

15.1.1   Background

The remote medical system will greatly improve people's lives, and it is generally believed that people will save billions of dollars from it. With the popularization of the Internet, the remote medical system is significantly developed nowadays, which has realized many functions such as remote monitoring, remote diagnosis, remote

[1]Guangxi Key Laboratory of Trusted Software, School of Information and Communication, Guilin University of Electronic Technology, Guilin, Guangxi, China
[2]School of Information and Software Engineering, University of Electronic Science and Technology of China, Chengdu, Sichuan, China
[3]Guangxi Key Laboratory of Trusted Software, School of Computer Science and Information Security, Guilin University of Electronic Technology, Guangxi, China

surgery, etc. In this way, the remote medical system can improve the balance of medical resources, especially in the areas with underdeveloped medical resources. Moreover, people will also benefit from the remote medical system in some special situations, such as outer space or desert. The development of the remote medical system is of great significance all over the world.

However, security and privacy greatly limit the development and use of remote medical technology:

- Security in the sense of cryptography occurs in the communication process, which ensures that two parts communicate with each other in-network just like face to face. Security can be divided into confidence, which ensures the adversary cannot get any information from the transmitted ciphertext; authentication, which can ensure that the receiver of the message is indeed the one expected by the message sender; integrity, which ensures that the message will not be added, deleted, and modified when it is transmitted.
- Privacy, which is different from security, ensures the data do not leak to the adversary outside the system and requires that the sensitive data cannot be leaked to the cooperator inside the system. For example, in machine learning, the server wants to train a model using some users' sensitive data. If the sensitive data can be transmitted to the server without any successful eavesdropping behavior, machine learning can be regarded as secure and non-private. If the sensitive data cannot be received by the server, such as FL, the scheme can be regarded as private.

The security of the system must be protected; otherwise, the remote medical system cannot operate correctly. The application of remote medical systems continues to expand around the world, especially in the United States, the United Kingdom, and Australia. Through this system, people's medical and health conditions can be tracked remotely, which is beneficial that medical advice can be given promptly and quickly to prevent the deterioration of the disease, reduce the number of hospitalized patients, and promote the results of health treatment. The widespread promotion of telemedicine systems will greatly reduce medical costs worldwide. Unfortunately, the medical and health information widely spread in the network environment is very easy to destroy the personal privacy of users.

The solution is to use an efficient authentication protocol to authenticate the identities of the parties to each other and calculate a common secret before data exchange activities start. The common secret can establish a secure channel for all parties on the public network. Using the common secret, the two communication parties can encrypt the communication content, which cannot be eavesdropped on and tampered. More details are given in Medical System Authentication Protocol Introduction.

Privacy is different from security, which is more subjective. Both doctors and patients have the right to apply to the medical system for access to relevant medical information, and the content of the access often involves the privacy of doctors and patients. Therefore, some privacy-preserving protocols have been proposed to meet various privacy-preserving requirments. The details are given in Medical System Privacy-preserving Protocol Introduction.

15.1.2   Related works

Security and privacy are very important for the remote medical system, which have attracted a lot of attention from academia. For example, Fortino *et al.* emphasized that privacy protect is very important [1]. Rahimi *et al.* [2] and Wei *et al.* [3] think that security and privacy may be the most challenging issues for medical cloud calculation. Moreover, patients' data security and personal privacy could be seriously threatened by adversary, which is exposed in Reference 4. And the traditional security and privacy techniques are not suitable for remote medical systems, since they have heavy security processing.

An important concern for the remote medical system is to guarantee the command authenticity and integrity issued by the people and medical device. The solution to these security concerns is to establish a secure communication channel [5]. The parties communicating with each other need to authenticate each other's identity. Then a common secret should be calculated by all parties. If a common secret is obtained by all parties, they can encrypt the communication channel by it. And the authentication processes and the obtainment processes of common secrets are discussed in this section.

In addition, data sharing is necessary. But it cannot be shared directly, which may lead to some security and privacy questions. Therefore, the privacy-preserving mechanisms are given, such as the generalization in Reference 6, the aggregation in References 7 and 8, and the differential privacy [9]. Data aggregation is the most widely adopted method, which can calculate the sum, median, or max/min value without decryption [10–13]. These data are very useful for medical statistics and big data training. However, at some times, more fine-grained data will be needed for calculation accuracy. N-source anonymity is given for resolving this kind of problem. For example, He *et al.* [14] adopt a trusted third party to establish an N-source anonymity data aggregation scheme. Due to the adoption of the trusted third party, the proposed scheme is weak in robustness. Guo *et al.* [15] use virtual rings to construct an n-source anonymity raw data collection scheme, but it is so dangerous since it can be broken by a collusion attack. Moreover, Shen *et al.* [16] use a shuffle method to improve the N-resource anonymity, which can improve the robustness.

15.1.3   Authentication for the communication between people and devices

In a remote medical system, the doctors often need to call various medical equipment to complete diagnosis and treatment. For example, a doctor needs to call an X-spectrometer to detect the information of a fracture patient in order to diagnose the severity of the fracture. Therefore, the medical equipment needs to authenticate the doctors' identity.

The medical devices only have limited calculation resources. Therefore, they cannot support complex cryptography protocols. Considering the limited calculation resource, a symmetrical cryptography protocol is suitable, which needs a common secret between doctors and the called devices. A common secret can be produced when the medical equipment is authenticated by the doctors.

In section 15.1.2, we introduce a secure and lightweight authentication protocol. And the **contributions** of this work are listed as follows.

1. Security: This work can resist kinds of attacks, such as eavesdropping attack and insider attack.
2. Effectiveness: This work optimizes the authentication process and integrates the authentication and key exchange process, which leads a more efficiency compared to similar solutions.
3. Low consumption: Through experimental comparison, this work has lower energy consumption.

15.1.4   Group communication authenticated protocol

In a remote medical system, many communications are worked between doctors and patients. Just like the communication between doctors and medical devices, the communications between doctors and patients also need to be protected by a lightweight authentication protocol.

Considering the limited calculation and storage resource of the patients, a secure and lightweight authentication protocol are introduced in section 15.1.3. It has the **contributions,** which are listed as follows.

1. Confidentiality: Confidentiality can ensure that the content of the communication between the two parties will not be monitored. Normally, a common secret is very important for confidentiality, which is often calculated by a communication authentication protocol.
2. Real-time authentication: For improving the response speed of the system, real-time authentication is very important.
3. Replay attack resistance: Replay attack is a very common attack method, therefore, an effective authentication scheme must be able to resist replay attacks.
4. Low consumption: The protocol needs to consume as low as possible to adapt to the limited patient calculation and storage resources.

15.1.5   Privacy protection for data query

In a remote medical system, the user's query behavior may involve the user's privacy. For example, the patients often query some data in the database. The database administrator can know what data do the patient query, so as to infer the patients' medical data. For protecting requesters' privacy, a privacy protection scheme is given in section 15.1.4.

Comparing the previous protocol, this work has **advantages**, which are listed as follows:

1. Better security: Compared with other schemes, the proposed scheme should have advantages in security.
2. Better efficiency: Considering the limited resource of the requesters, privacy protection needs to be efficient.

15.1.6 Data aggregation protocol

With the development of smart medical care, more and more people use medical sensor devices to collect their own health data. However, patients' medical data are often sensitive. Therefore, privacy protection for users' medical data is very important. Data aggregation is a useful method to protect patients' privacy by hiding single medical data in aggregation value.

Contributions

The work [17] has the following contributions:

1. The higher level of privacy: Compared with other works, this work not only meets the security requirement of resisting the known attack, such as internal attack, replay attack, and impersonation attack, but also gives a better robustness. Therefore, a higher level of privacy is achieved in this work.
2. Better decentralization: The trusted third party is not needed in this work, which takes a better decentralization.

The work [18] (DMDA) has the following contributions.

1. More efficiency: DMDA strengthens the efficiency of the processes and provides a user dynamic method. It leads that DMDA has a better efficiency, especially for the time of a user joining or a user quitting.
2. Virtual aggregation area: DMDA runs in a virtual aggregation area, which takes it can be easy to transplant to other IoT environments, such as remote medical systems.

15.1.7 Raw medical data collection and publishing protocol

For data, more accurate data are more useful; however, it is a very important challenge to collect more accurate data while protecting the privacy of data. Normally, the more accurate data can be collected privately by n-source anonymity, which realizes two goals: (1) the more accurate data can be collected, and (2) the property of unlinkability between the data and its owners can be achieved.

Contributions

The work [19] has the following contributions:

1. Better decentralization: The data can be collected anonymously without relying on any trusted third party. Therefore, this work has a better decentralization compared with other work.

2. Accurate data collection: Comparing some noise data collection schemes, this work can collect the accurate data, since noises cannot be accurate delete.

In the work [20], two contributions are achieved as follows.

1. Privacy protection: Data privacy can be protected, while the data utility is holed on.
2. More efficiency: Compared with some other schemes, this work costs less calculation and communication resources.

15.2 Secure and lightweight authentication protocol [5]

In this work, the doctor wants to call certain medical devices for diagnosis, treatment, and medical care in the remote medical system. But the medical devices cannot be called directly, considering the resource saving and the security of patients' information. The doctor must first apply to the server for permission to use the corresponding device, and then uses the permission to pass the device's identity authentication. Moreover, in order to facilitate subsequent communication, the doctor and the device need to exchange a temporary session key.

15.2.1 System model

There are three parties that will take part in the protocol: server, doctor, and devices, as shown in Figure 15.1.

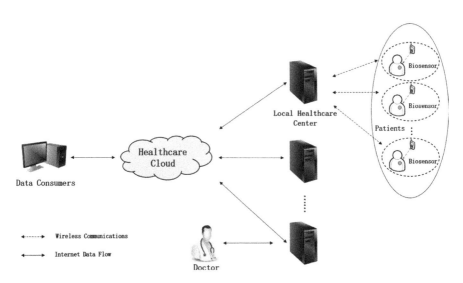

Figure 15.1   System model

Doctor: The doctor is the initiator of the agreement. He/she generates demands during his/her work and initiates the authentication. He/she will apply for permission to use the device and use the license given by the server to pass the device verification. Then he/she will exchange a key with the devices for the following communication.

Server: The server often waits for the doctors' application until a doctor initiates a device using request. Then the server needs to review the qualifications of the doctor and check the condition of the equipment. If there is no problem, grant the doctor permission to use it.

Devices: The devices often wait for the doctors' use. If a doctor applies to use a device, the called device needs to check the user permission and exchange a session key with the doctor. Then the called device will change its state to be in use, and then accepts and executes the command passed by the doctor encrypting the session key.

15.2.2   Secure and lightweight authentication protocol

First, the user and device need to be registrant in the system.

User registration

Step 1:   The doctor chooses his password PW and imprints his biometric impression B.

Step 2:   The doctor calculates $MP = h\left(PW, B\right)$ and sends $\left(Uid, MP\right)$ to the server via secure channel.

Step 3:   Server receives and stores Uid, MP.

Device registration

Before a device is equipped in the system, the server generates a random number $m_j, \left(j = 1, 2, ..., n\right)$, and injects $T_j, \left(j = 1, 2, ..., n\right)$ in a secure manner. $m_j, \left(j = 1, 2, ..., n\right)$ can be updated when necessary.

Then, the authentication protocol can be run.

Remote invoking establishment

Assume a doctor chooses to invoke t medical devices whose identities are $TID_1, TID_2, ..., TID_t$. This section includes the following three phases.

Authentication between the doctor and the server

Step 1:   The doctor wants to invoke the remote medical devices $TID_1, TID_2, ..., TID_t$, he sends the request and $\left(Uid, TID_1, TID_2, ..., TID_t\right)$ to the server.

Step 2:   Upon receiving the request, the server chooses a random number r_s and sends it to the doctor. Then, the doctor computes $A_1 = h\left(MP, r_s\right)$ and sends A_1 and a random number r_s to the server.

Step 3:   The server authenticates the doctor by checking $A_1 = h\left(MP, r_s\right)$ with the stored MP. If yes, the server computes $A_2 = h\left(MP, r_s, r_u\right)$ and sends A_2 to the doctor.

Remote invoking establishment

Step 4:
The doctor verifies if the equation $A_2 = h\left(MP, r_s, r_u\right)$ holds. If yes, the mutual authentication is achieved.

Authentication between the server and devices

Step 1:
The server forwards the invoking request to t devices by broadcasting $\left(Uid,\ TID_1, TID_2, ..., TID_t\right)$.

Step 2:
The medical device with the identity T_j sends a random number r_j^D to the server $\left(j = 1, ..., t\right)$. The server computes $AH_j = h\left(m_j, r_j^D\right),\ \left(j = 1, ..., t\right)$ and sends AH_j and a random number r_j^S to $T_j, \left(j = 1, ..., t\right)$.

Step 3:
T_j authenticates the server by checking $AH_j = h\left(m_j, r_j^D\right)$. If yes, T_j calculates $ATH_j = h\left(m_j, r_j^S, r_j^D\right)$ and sends ATH_j to the server.

Step 4:
The server authenticates the T_j by checking $ATH_j = h(m_j, r_j^S, r_j^D), (j = 1, \ldots, t)$. If true, the server believe that T_j is legal.

Session key establishment

Step 1:
The server randomly selects a session key SK and generates $f(x)$ passing through $\left(0, SK\right), \left(Uid, h\left(MP, r_u\right), \left(TID_j, h\left(m_j, r_j^D\right), \ (j = 1, ..., t)\right)\right.$. Then, the server computes additional $\left(t + 1\right)$ points $Q_1 = \left(1, f(1)\right), ..., Q_{t+1} = \left(t + 1, f(t + 1)\right)$ and broadcasts $\{Q_1, ..., Q_{t+1}\}$.

Step 2:
The doctor recovers $f(x)$ with the broadcasted messages $\{Q_1, ..., Q_{t+1}\}$ and his secret $\left(Uid, h\left(MP, r_u\right)\right.$, and T_j recovers $f(x)$ with $\{Q_1, ..., Q_{t+1}\}$ and its $\left(TID_j, h\left(m_j, r_j^D\right)\right),\ (j = 1, ..., t)$. Therefore, the session key $SK = f(0)$ is shared among them, which guarantees the secure communication.

Moreover, the multi-factor update phase.

When the doctor wants to update his password or the biometric, he sends an update request to the server. After the mutual authentication process between the doctor and the server, the doctor submits his new password PW^{new} or the new biometric B^{new} and generates the new $PW^{new} = h\left(PW^{new}, B^{new}\right)$. MP^{new} is sent to the server, and stored in the server. And the innoving notations of above-mentioned steps are listed in Figure 15.2.

15.2.3 *Experiment analysis*

Compared with other works, this work is in advantages of security, efficiency, and low consumption. The details are shown as follows

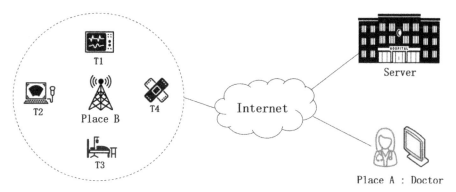

Figure 15.2   The system model

1. Security: This work can resist kinds of attacks, such as eavesdropping attack and insider attack. Moreover, the authentication of this work is proven by BAN logic. Compared with other works, this work has some advantages in security, as shown in Table 15.1.
2. Effectiveness: This work optimizes the authentication process, and integrates the authentication and key exchange process, which lead a more efficiency compared to similar solutions.
3. Low Consumption: Through experimental comparison, this work has lower energy consumption as shown in Table 15.2.

Table 15.1   Comparison of security features

	Jiang *et al.* [21]	Kumari *et al.* [22]	Park and Park [23]	The proposed scheme
E1	Yes	Yes	Yes	Yes
E2	-	Yes	No	Yes
E3	No	Yes	No	Yes
E4	Yes	Yes	No	Yes
E5	Yes	Yes	Yes	Yes
E6	Yes	Yes	Yes	Yes
E7	-	-	No	Yes

E1 Mutual authentication,
E2 Resist insider attack,
E3 User friendliness,
E4 Resist password guessing attack,
E5 Resist user impersonation attack,
E6 Resist replay attack,
E7 Resist device impersonation attack.

Table 15.2   Comparison of consumption

	User	User efficiency	Server	Server efficiency
Kumari *et al.* [22]	$5T_h + T_s$	Medium	$3T_h + T_s$	High
Jiang *et al.* [21]	$2T_h + T_s + 3T_{ch}$	Medium	$T_h + 2T_s + 3T_{ch}$	Medium
YoHan *et al.* [23]	$T_h + T_f$	High	$T_h + T_f$	High
Proposed scheme	$4T_h + T_f$	High	$4T_h + T_f$	High

15.3   Group communication authenticated protocol [24]

In addition to the authentication between people and devices, communication authentication is also required between people and people, such as doctors and patients. Normally, considering the limited computing power of the user's handheld device and the patience of the user's waiting, a lightweight authenticated communication scheme is given here. The scheme was first used to support the authentication requirements of the smart grid, which has a higher lightweight goal. And all notations are shown in Table 15.3.

The lightweight authenticated communication is often used for the security of two-way communication. Compared with other authentication communication, only the bitwise elusive-OR operations are needed for a real-time authentication. And the calculation and communication costs for authentication are also reduced.

15.3.1   System design

In this section, each participant of the protocol and the security goals of the protocol will be introduced one by one.

Users: The one with fewer resources among the two communicating parties. For example, patients use a handle phone or laptop to take part in the protocol, and the doctors can use professional equipment. Therefore, the patients can be regarded as users in remote medical systems.

Table 15.3   Notations

	Definition
ID_i	The ith patient's ID
F_p	Finite field with p-order, and p is a large enough prime
	Random number
	Running time of system
$TS_j^{ID_i}, TS_k^{NG}$	
Enc_K, Dec_k	Encryption or decryption function with secure key K

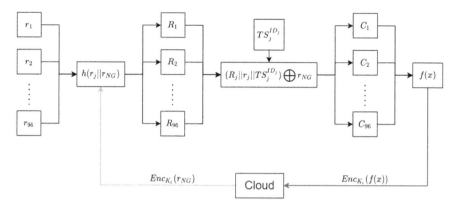

Figure 15.3   Daily initialization

Server: The one with more resources among the two communicating parties, just like the doctors in a remote medical system.

15.3.1.1   Secure goals

1. Confidentiality: Confidentiality ensures the adversary out of the system can obtain any information about the transmitted data.
2. Real-time authentication: Real-time authentication ensures the transmitted data can be authenticated as quickly as possible, which provided a high requirement of protocol efficiency.
3. Replay attack resistance: Replay attack resistance can ensure that the data that pass the authentication cannot be authenticated again. Just like that, the used ticket cannot use the second time.
4. Low calculation and communication cost: Low calculation and communication cost can ensure the protocol can run well on the users' handheld devices which only has limited resource.

15.3.2   Protocol processes

15.3.2.1   Long-term key establishment

Enc_k and Dec_k are the symmetric encryption and decryption functions with a secure key k. And $h()$ is a secure hash function.

The long-term key establishment is shown in Figure 15.3, and the details are given as follows:

Step 1: Cloud randomly selects a value r_{NG} and sends $Enc_K (r_{NG})$ to the ith user.

Step 2: The ith patient can decrypt $Enc_{K_i} (r_{NG})$ to obtain r_{NG}, and then selects 96 random numbers $r_1, r_2, ..., r_{96}$ and computes $R_j = h(r_j \| r_{NG})$,

$C_j = \left(R_j \| r_j \| TS_j^{ID_i} \right) \oplus r_{NG}, \left(j = 1, ..., 96 \right)$, where $\|$ is the concatenation operation and $TS_j^{ID_i}$ is the time such as $0:00, ..., 23:45$. Then, $r_j, R_j, C_j, \left(j = 1, ..., 96 \right)$ are stored in the i-th user.

Step 3: The i-th patient can generate $f(x)$ by $(1, C_1), (2, C_2), ..., (96, C_{96})$.

Step 4: The patient encrypts $f(x)$ and sends the ciphertext to Cloud.

15.3.2.2   Secure two-way data transmission

The secure two-way communication between the server and the users is as follows.

According to the current time $TS_j^{ID_i}, \left(j = 1, ..., 96 \right)$, the user picks the corresponding R_j and computes $S_j = D_j \oplus R_j$. Then, the user sends $ID_i \| C_j \| S_j$ to the server.

When server receives $ID_i \| C_j \| S_j$, it can authenticate these data as follows:

Step 1: The server verifies the equation $C_j = f(j)$. If not, abort. Otherwise, the server accepts this message.

Step 2: The server calculates $C_j \oplus r_{NG}$ to obtain $R_j, r_j, TS_j^{ID_i}$ and checks the time $TS_j^{ID_j}$. If not pass, abort. Otherwise, execute step 3.

Step 3: The server verifies $R_j = h\left(r_j \| r_{NG} \right)$. If it holds, the Cloud can get that r_{NG} has been used in the generation of R_j, C_j and $f(x)$. Otherwise, abort.

Step 4: The server calculates $D_j = S_j \oplus R_j$ and verifies D_j. If passed, the Cloud will accept this report. Otherwise, abort.

The server sends a control message $M_k \left(k = 1, 2, 3, 4 \right)$ to the i-th user by computing $M_k^1 = \left(M_k \| TS_k^{NG} \right) \oplus r_{NG}, M_k^2 = f\left(M_k^1 \right)$, and sending these data to the patient, where TS_k^{NG} denotes the time of the system.

When the i-th patient receives the messages M_k^1 and M_k^2 from the Cloud, he/she verifies if $M_k^2 = f\left(M_k^1 \right)$ holds or not. If hold, M_k^1 is accepted. Otherwise, abort. Then, the user calculates $M_k^1 \oplus r_{NG}$ to obtain M_k and TS_k^{NG}. If TS_k^{NG} is outdated, abort. Otherwise, M_k is accepted and executed.

15.3.3   Experiment analysis

Confidentiality: Confidentiality is an important requirement for the remote medical report. According to the security analysis of Reference 9, the proposed scheme meets the requirement of confidentiality since (1) the key shared between the Cloud and the user is secure, and (2) it is computationally infeasible if an adversary wants to calculate the usage data and the control messages from public transmitted information.

Real-time authentication: The server can authenticate the data from the patients as soon as possible. The patient can authenticate the data from the server as soon as possible.

Replay attack resistance: An adversary cannot overcome the protocol by used legal data, every legal data can pass the authentication only once. And it can be proved that replay attack is computationally infeasible.

Table 15.4   Storage cost

Time interval	AC	LAC
15 minutes	18 kB	4.5 kB
5 minutes	88 kB	13.5 kB

Table 15.5   Communication cost between the server and the users

Time interval	AC	LAC
15 minutes	13.515625 kB	4.640625 kB
5 minutes	49.515625 kB	13.640625 kB

Low storage cost: This work has advantages in storage cost. For explaining this point, the storage cost is compared in Table 15.4. Compared with other schemes, the storage cost is significantly reduced.

Low communication cost: This work also has advantages in communication cost. There is a comparison in Table 15.5. It shows that the proposed scheme has a less communication burden than normal AC.

15.4   Obvious transmission protocol in data query [25]

In the remote medical system, patients' medical data are always stored in the Cloud to save the storage and management costs. However, these data are often connected with patients' privacy, which needs to be protected [26]. In this part, a remote medical record system is proposed to protect security and privacy. However, the data retrieval behavior itself is very likely to leak the user's privacy. Liu and Wang [25] adopt the oblivious transfer to design a remote medical system. Compared with some other schemes, this work extra satisfies that the Cloud provides a query server to users without knowing which data are queried.

15.4.1   System design

This system can be divided into three phases: the initialization phase, the authentication phase, and the data request phase. In the initialization phase, the Cloud will produce some important parameters for users. In the authentication phase, the Cloud and users will verify the identity of each other to make sure that only the legal users can require data. In the data request phase, the Cloud will give some data to users, but it cannot sure what the users get. For example, the Cloud will transmit 100 data to users, but users only require 20 data. For users, they cannot decrypt the data that they have not required. For the Cloud, it cannot sure which data are obtained by users and which data are not.

15.4.2   Remote medical system design

15.4.2.1   Initialization phase

1. Cloud selects G_1 and G_2 of order r, h, H_1, and H_2.
2. The Cloud selects $s_0 \in Z_r^*$ and computes $P_{pub} = s_0 P_1$,
    $$gx = e\left(P_1, QUOTE \frac{1}{S+h(k_j)} P_1 P_1\right), \quad P_1 \in G_1.$$
3. The Cloud publishes a long-term session identity ls to users in a secure manner and stores $h(ls)$.
4. The Cloud stores $\{G_1, G_2, h, H_1, H_2, P_1, g, P_{pub}\}$.

15.4.2.2   Authentication phase

The authentication process is executed for the communication between the Cloud and the user, and the details are described as follows:

1. Using $h(ls)$ and P_{pub}, Alice calculates: $C = h(ls) P_1 + P_{pub}$. Alice sends $\{ID_{Alice}, C\}$ to Cloud.
2. With the received $\{ID_{Alice}, C\}$, the Cloud calculates $S = \frac{1}{s_0 + h(ls)} P_1$. Then, the Cloud checks $e(C, S) \overset{?}{=} g$. If yes, then Cloud sends S to Alice; otherwise, this message will be discarded.
3. Alice checks $e(C, S) \overset{?}{=} g$. If the equation holds, the authentication succeeds, and $$e(C, S) = e(h(ls)P_1 + P_{pub}, \frac{1}{s_0 + h(ls)} P_1) = e(P_1(h(ls) + s_0, \frac{1}{s_0 + h(ls)} P_1)) =$$
    $$e(P_1, P_1)^{(h(ls)+s_0)\frac{1}{s_0 + h(ls)}} = e(P_1, P_1) = g.$$

Any adversary cannot impersonate the Cloud or users since s_0 is only known by the Cloud.

15.4.2.3   Data request phase

In this part, the goal is to achieve the privacy for the data requester. In the following, for convenience, the request data are not held in the previous t records anymore.

Before a requester sends the request, the Cloud needs to calculate $X_i = m_i \oplus mask_i$, $mask_i = H_2 \left(e\left(Q_i, P_{pub}\right)^{r_i}\right)$, $Q_i = h(ID_i)$, $U_i = r_i P$, where r_i is a random number. Then, Cloud uploads $\{X_i, ID_i, U_i\}$ to the requester.

It is assumed that the requester queries the medical data m_i, the requester should first decrypt X_i and U_i, and then apply a key k_i from the Cloud, where $k_i = s_0 Q_i$. More details consist of four steps:

1. The requester selects t secrets α_i $(i = 1, 2, ..., n)$, where i sends the selected medical data, and t is the number that is needed. Then, the requester calculates $V_i = \alpha_i Q_i$ $(i = 1, 2, ..., n)$ and sends V_i $(i = 1, 2, ..., n)$ to the Cloud.

Table 15.6   Security comparison

	Reference 11	The proposed scheme
Mutual authentication	No	Yes
Non-trace ability	Yes	Yes
Resistance to man-in-the-middle attack	No	Yes
Resistance to impersonation attack	No	Yes
Requester's privacy preservation	Yes	Yes
Discontinuous data query	No	Yes

2. The Cloud computes $V_i' = s_0 V_i \oplus H_1 (ls) (i = 1, 2, \ldots, n)$ and returns $V_i' (i = 1, 2, \ldots, n)$ to the requester.
3. The requester calculates $\alpha_i^{-1} (i = 1, 2, \ldots, n)$ and recovers $k_i = s_0 Q_i$ as $k_i = \alpha_i^{-1} (V_i' \oplus H_1 (ls)) (mod\ r) (i = 1, 2, \ldots, n)$.
4. Alice deciphers t cipher as $m_i = X_i \oplus mask_i' (i = 1, 2, \ldots, n)$, where $mask_i' = H_2 (e (k_i, U_i))$.

15.4.3   Experiment analysis

Security: As a cryptography protocol, the proposed scheme has to meet the security requirements. This work has better security than other schemes. For explaining this point, the authors compare this work with Reference 11 in Table 15.6. According to the table, the proposed scheme has advantages in security.

Efficiency: Efficiency is very important since the limited calculation and communication resources. Compared with other schemes, this work is more efficient, which is shown in Table 15.7. According to the comparison, we can sure that the proposed scheme is better than the before scheme [11].

Table 15.7   Efficiency comparison

	Reference 11	The proposed scheme
Two adjacent records	$4t_p + 2t_e + 2t_h + 2t_0 + 2t_i$	$2t_e + 4t_h + 2t_0 + 2t_i$
Interval one record	$6t_p + 3t_e + 3t_h + 3t_0 + 3t_i$	$2t_e + 4t_h + 2t_0 + 2t_i$
Interval two records	$8t_p + 4t_e + 4t_h + 4t_0 + 4t_i$	$2t_e + 4t_h + 2t_0 + 2t_i$
...	...	...
Interval $n - 2$ records	$2nt_p + nt_e + nt_h + nt_0 + nt_i$	$2t_e + 2t_h + 2t_0 + 2t_i$

t_0 : The time complexity of XOR operation.
t_h : The time complexity of hash operation.
t_p : The time complexity of exponential operation.
t_i : The time complexity of inverse operation.

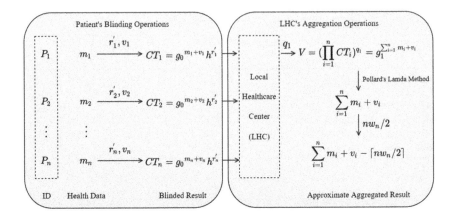

Figure 15.4   Aggregation

15.5   Data aggregation protocol in medical data publishing

In work 17, data are aggregated for privacy protection, only the sum data can be calculated without any information of single data leaking. The single data often is connected with patients' privacy, and it is protected by differential privacy [8] and the subgroup decision assumption [13].

15.5.1   System model of the protocol [17]

The system model is given in Figure 15.2, which has the following entities:

1. Patients: The patient is the owner of the data, whose privacy data will be used and protected.
2. Doctor: The doctors are data users; they will give the treatment according to the collected data.
3. Local healthcare center: Local healthcare center, which is also called data aggregation center here, can aggregate the patients' data and sends the aggregated result to the healthcare cloud.
4. Data consumers: The data consumers use the aggregated result for some work, such as regional population health statistics and the proportion of specific disease infections.
5. Healthcare Cloud: The healthcare aggregates all the data from the local healthcare center.

15.5.2   Aggregation steps of the protocol [17]

In this work, the security parameters ε, δ are given by LHC and LHC computes $wn = \lceil 3_w/2n \rceil$, where $w = 64\Delta^2 log\,(2/\delta)\,/\varepsilon^2$. Then LHC chooses three large prime number q, q_1, q_2, determines a generator g_0 and a random number $u \in G_0$ from a cyclic multiplicative group G_0 of order N, and computes $h = u^{q_2}$, $g_1 = g_0^{q_1}$. The aggregation steps are shown in Figure 15.4. And Table 15.8 is the notation for related parameters.

First, patients P_i encrypt the health data m_i, $m_i \in [0, 1, 2, \cdots \Delta]$ using homomorphic encryption and masked data $v_i \sim B\left(w_n, 1/2\right)$, and $r_i' \in Z_n$, and then send the encrypted data $CT_i = g_0^{m_i+v_i} h_i'$ to LHC.

Second, the LHC calculates the sum of all patients' ciphertext CT_i:

$$V = \left(\prod_{i=1}^{n} CT_i\right)^{q_1} = g_1^{\sum_{i=1}^{n} m_i+v_i}$$

Finally, LHC decrypts V, $\sum_{i=1}^{n} m_i + v_i - \lceil nw_n/2 \rceil$ and gets the plaintext of all patients' health data $\sum_{i=1}^{n} m_i$. Table 15.9 is the notation for related parameters.

15.5.3 Experiment analysis of the protocol [17]

This scheme is secure when it suffers well-known attacks (i.e., the external attack, the internal attack, the modification attack, and the replay attack). Then, it also meets the requirement of robustness since it needs not any trusted third party. Moreover, this scheme has a huge advantage in the terms of efficiency. The security comparison with some other works is shown in Table 15.10. The cost comparison of aggregation is shown in Table 15.11. Table 15.12 is the notation for time cost.

Table 15.8   Notation

Notation	Definition
Uid	Users' identity
$TID_1, TID_2, ..., TID_t$	Remote medical devices' identity
A_1, A_2, AH_j, ATH_j	Verifiable signature information
$h()$	Hash function

Table 15.9   Notation for related parameters

Notation	Definition
P_i	The patients in the specific area
m_i	The health data collected by P_i
CT_i	The ciphertext of P_i
$B\left(w_n, 1/2\right)$	The unbiased binomial distribution
Δ	The interval of m_i
q, q_1, q_2	three large prime numbers
V	The sum of all patients' ciphertext CT_i

Table 15.10   Security features comparison compared with related works

		The proposed scheme	Li *et al.* scheme [10]	Fan *et al.* scheme [13]	He *et al.* scheme [14]
PPR	REX	Yes	Yes	Yes	Yes
	RIN	Yes	No	Yes	Yes
	RHD	Yes	No	No	No
RIM		Yes	Yes	No	Yes
RMO		Yes	Yes	Yes	Yes
RRE		Yes	Yes	Yes	Yes
ROU		Yes	No+	No++	No++

PPR, Privacy-Preservation; REX, Resilience against External Attack; RHD, Resilience against HDA Attack; RIM, Resilience against Impersonation Attack; RIN, Resilience against Internal Attack; RMO, Resilience against Modification Attack; ROU, Robustness; RRE, Resilience against Replay Attack.
*Relying on online trusted third party
†Relying on offline trusted third party

Table 15.11   The cost comparison of aggregation

	n users (patients)	LHC (Aggregation)	Total
The proposed scheme	$2nT_e + nT_m$	$T_e + (n-1)T_m + T_{pl}$	$(2n+1)T_e + (2n-1)T_m + T_{pl}$
Li *et al.* scheme [10]	$2nT_e + nT_m$	$(n-1)T_m + T_{pc}$	$2nT_e + (2n-1)T_m + T_{pc}$
Fan *et al.* scheme [13]	$3nT_e + 2nT_m$	$3T_e + nT_m + T_{pl}$	$(3n+3)T_e + 3nT_m + T_{pl}$
He *et al.* scheme [14]	$2nT_e + nT_m$	$T_e + nT_m + T_{pl}$	$(2n+1)T_e + 2nT_m + T_{pl}$

15.5.4   System model of the protocol [18]

The dynamic users take a lot of calculation and communication costs for a data aggregation scheme. For a remote medical system on the Internet, the data

Table 15.12   Notation for time cost

Notation	Definition
T_e	Modular exponentiation computation time cost
T_m	Modular multiplication computation time cost
T_{pl}	Pollard's lambda method time cost
T_{pc}	Paillier cryptosystem decryption time cost
T_{po}	Pairing operation time cost

aggregation can be used to protect users' privacy. The principle is to let users' data cover each other and only provide the final sum result or average value. Although data aggregation can feed the questions with data processing in cipher, it has disadvantages for a virtual area, especially for a frequently changing virtual area. The remote medical system is established on the Internet, which is a frequently changing virtual area. Therefore, a lot of calculation and communication costs are wasted. In work 18, the authors adopt the homomorphic encryption and ID-based signature to deal with the dynamic membership in the virtual data aggregation area.

In this system model, there are three entities involved in this work: patients, (aggregation center) AC, and (operation center) OC.

> Patients: Patients are the owners of the data, whose data will be proposed for kinds of usages. And they may communicate with other patients to protect their privacy.
>
> Aggregation center: Aggregation center communicates with patients for collecting data. Usually, the aggregation center is assumed to be honest but curious, which will follow the protocol processes, and not launch any active attack. However, it will do its best to obtain any valuable information for analyzing users private data.
>
> Operation center: Operation center gets the aggregated ciphertext from the aggregation center and decrypts it.
>
> Adversary: Adversary is the malicious entity that is out of the remote medical system. It may launch kinds of attacks, such as monitoring the public channels, impersonating the identity of the legitimate user, stealing the information from the user's database, and so on.

Contribution

In this protocol, the operation center can calculate all data sum in cipher, so it will leak nothing about a single user's data. In the medical big data environment, the aggregated data can be used in big data analysis.

Compared with other schemes, the proposed scheme has a huge advantage in terms of efficiency, especially for a frequently changing virtual area. Therefore, this scheme is suitable for the remote medical system.

15.5.5 Aggregation steps of the protocol

In this work, the aggregation steps are as follows, users (patients) encrypt the health data m_i by adding a carefully constructed key [18]. Every user U_i selects a friend U_j to help her/him to construct the noise $sk'_i = sk_i + R_i - R_j$, where sk_i is the random number sent by OC and $\sum_{i=1}^{n} sk_i = 0$. The ciphertext is $c_i = m_i + sk'_i$. The added sk'_i is eliminable noise. Then every user sends the ciphertext to AC.

The AC calculates the sum of ciphertext c_{Sum} and then sends it to OC. OC gets rid of all the noise sk_{Sum} and gets the sum of all the plaintext m_{Sum}. The specific

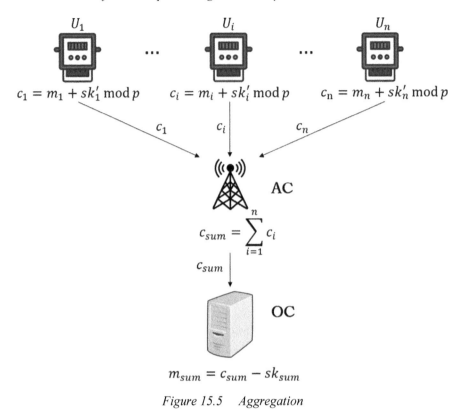

$$c_1 = m_1 + sk_1' \bmod p \qquad c_i = m_i + sk_i' \bmod p \qquad c_n = m_n + sk_n' \bmod p$$

$$c_{sum} = \sum_{i=1}^{n} c_i$$

$$m_{sum} = c_{sum} - sk_{sum}$$

Figure 15.5   Aggregation

steps are shown in Figure 15.5. And the notation for related parameters is shown in Table 15.13.

15.5.6   Experiment analysis of the protocol [18]

This work allows users to dynamically join and quit, and support forward and backward secrecies for join and exit. At the same time, confidentiality, authentication, detection of false data injection attacks, and resistant to data forgery are guaranteed. And compared with other works [10, 13, 27], this work is lightweight. The security requirements comparison and performance comparison are shown in Tables 15.14 and 15.15, respectively.

15.6   Raw medical data collection and publishing protocol

More fine-grained data are often more needed in the remote medical system, but the previous privacy-preserving data aggregation schemes only collect the sum data. Especially, some medical average value is nothing for analysis and treatment. In Reference 19, an N-resource scheme is given, which can collect data from patients

Table 15.13   Notations

Notation	Definition
U_i	The users (patients) in the specific area
m_i	The health data collected by U_i
C_i	The ciphertext of U_i
m_{Sum}	Aggregation value of all patients
sk_i'	Masked data computed by U_i
sk_i	Masked data sent by OC
c_{Sum}	The sum of all patients' ciphertext c_i

but not leak the source of data. Moreover, no trusted authority is needed in this work, which takes a better robustness.

15.6.1   System model of the protocol [19]

There are three entities: the patients (IoT devices), a series of parallel fog, and Cloud, which are listed in Figure 15.6.

1. The patients: The patients will provide their medical data by kinds of IoT devices, so the patients and IoT devices are not distinguished here. IoT devices will upload its collected data after some processes.
2. The fog: The fogs are located in some locations that are close to the patients. They will collect data from patients' IoT devices. And these data will be uploaded to the Cloud after little processing.
3. Cloud: The Cloud will be employed by the medical organization for a special data collection task. And it will collect patients' medical data following this work. Finally, the medical data from untraceable sources are delivered to the employer.

Table 15.14   Security requirements' comparison

	[27]	[28]	[29]	[30]	[9]	[31]	DMDA
Privacy	Yes	Yes	Yes	Yes	Yes	Yes	Yes
Forward and backward secrecies	Yes	No	No	Yes	Yes	No	Yes
Detection of false data injection attacks	Yes	No	No	No	No	Yes	Yes
Confidentiality	Yes	Yes	Yes	Yes	Yes	Yes	Yes
Authentication	Yes	No	No	Yes	Yes	Yes	Yes
Resistant to data forgery	Yes	No	No	No	No	Yes	Yes
Dynamic	No	No	No	No	No	No	Yes

Table 15.15   Performance comparison

Section	Cost	[27]	[10]	[13]	DMDA
Register phase	Scale multiplication	$2n$	7	5	5
	Hash operation	$3n + 3$	3	2	5
	Communication	$8n$	2	2	3
Aggregation phase	Scale multiplication	0	$2n + 7$	$8n + 12$	0
	Hash operation	$2n$	$n + 3$	$4n$	$2n$
	Communication	n	n	n	n
	Others	nothing	Pollard's lambda algorithm	n Bilinear pairing operation and Pollard's lambda algorithm	n IBS
Logout		No	No	No	Yes

15.6.2   Raw medical data collection of the protocol [19]

The health data m_i should be collected. First, every medical data is arranged in a slot by shuffle. Then, every health data is in its slot. If other slots are put to zero except the slot of m_i, it will be insecure, because adversaries have easy access to health data. Therefore, the masked data e_i^j are needed to encrypt the health data. As shown in Figure 15.7, an example is given. Assume that there are four patients, and everyone encrypts her/his health data using the masked data e_i^j. Please note that e_i^j can be eliminated by XOR, for example, in Figure 15.7, $e_1^1 \oplus e_2^1 \oplus e_3^1 \oplus e_4^1 = 0$. Hence, the raw health data are collected. The raw data are shared or released, which makes them more valuable for big data analysis.

15.6.3   Experiment analysis of the protocol [19]

This work allows the data collection party to obtain fine-grained medical data, emphasizing that the collected data cannot be traced among n patients. Compared

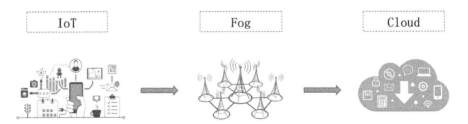

IoT   Fog   Cloud

Figure 15.6   System model

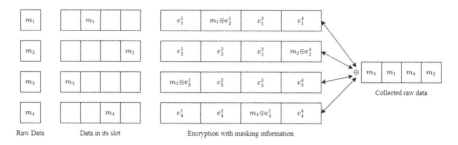

Figure 15.7   Data collection

with other solutions, this protocol can run without any trusted authority, which takes a better robustness. Moreover, this work establishes an incentive feedback mechanism, which will enhance the practicality of the work. More details of security requirements comparison and performance comparison are shown in Tables 15.16 and 15.17, respectively.

Table 15.16   Security requirements' comparison

	Reference 32	Reference 33	Reference 34	Reference 35	The proposed scheme
Raw data collection	Yes	Yes	Yes	Yes	Yes
Unlinkability	Yes	Yes	Yes	Yes	Yes
Relying on trusted authority	Yes	Yes	No	Yes	No
Neighbors' collusion attack resistance	No	Yes	Yes	No	Yes
Reward mechanism	No	Yes	No	No	Yes
Dynamic change for participants	Yes	No	No	No	Yes

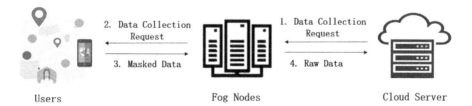

Figure 15.8   System model

Table 15.17   Communication overhead comparison

	Bits sent/received by participants	Bits sent/received by the collector
[33]	$\frac{n(n-1)}{2}S + n^2(L+Q) + n(T+Q)/$ $\frac{n(n-1)}{2}(S+2Q) + n^2L + nT$	$--/2n^2Q + n^2L + nT$
The proposed scheme	$\frac{\sum_1^n \beta_i}{2}S + n^2(L+Q) + nQ/$ $\frac{\sum_1^n \beta_i}{2}S + n^2(L+Q) - nQ$	$2n^2Q + n^2L/2n^2Q + n^2L$

Table 15.18   An example over F_p and $\mathrm{p} = 137$

	ID	Polynomial	p_1	p_2	p_3	FN
p_1	1	$f_1(x) = 5 + (80)x + (78+52)x^2 + (106)x^3$	(1.47)	(2.26)	(3.30)	(4.10)
p_2	2	$f_2(x) = 2 + (60+27)x + 69x^2 + 114x^3$	(1.135)	(2.131)	(3.126)	(4.119)
p_3	3	$f_3(x) = 1 + 30x + 16x^2 + (85+54)x^3$	(1.49)	(2.4)	(3.15)	(4.94)
MSD_i			(1.94)	(2.24)	(3.34)	(4.86)

	P_1	P_2	P_3	FN
$p_1 : f_1(x) = a_{1,0} + \lambda_{1,1}x + (a_1 + \lambda_{1,2})x^2 + \lambda_{1,3}x^3$	$(X_1, Y_{1,1})$,	$(X_2, Y_{1,2})$,	$(X_3, Y_{1,3})$,	$(X_4, Y_{1,4})$
$p_2 : f_2(x) = a_{2,0} + (a_2 + \lambda_{2,1})x + \lambda_{2,2}x^2 + \lambda_{2,3}x^3$	$(X_1, Y_{2,1})$,	$(X_2, Y_{2,2})$,	$(X_3, Y_{2,3})$,	$(X_4, Y_{2,4})$
$p_3 : f_3(x) = a_{3,0} + \lambda_{3,1}x + \lambda_{3,2}x^2 + (a_3 + \lambda_{3,3})x^3$	$(X_1, Y_{3,1})$,	$(X_2, Y_{3,2})$,	$(X_3, Y_{3,3})$,	$(X_4, Y_{3,4})$
Masked data	(X_1, Σ_1),	(X_2, Σ_2),	(X_3, Σ_3),	(X_4, Σ_4)

Figure 15.9   System model

Table 15.19   Comparison of mainstream privacy preservation techniques and the proposed scheme

| | Mainstream privacy preservation techniques | | | | | |
| | k-anonymity | Differential privacy | Data aggregation | n-source anonymity | | Our schemes |
	[36]	[37]	[38]	[32]	[19]	
Data center	Fully trusted	Fully trusted	Semihonest	Semihonest	Semihonest	Semihonest
TTP	No	No	No	Yes	No	No
Rawness	No	No	No	Yes	Yes	Yes
Unlinkability	Yes	Yes	Yes	Yes	Yes	Yes
Masked data storage	-	-	2Lbits	nLbits	nLbits	Lbits
Computational complexity of generating masked data	-	-	-	2n hashes 2nLbit XORs	nβi hashes n(βi − 1)Lbit XORs	nβi hashes secret shares generation
Computational complexity of extracting raw data	-	-	-	(n − 1)nL -bit XORs	(n − 1)nL -bit XORs	Secret recovery

-This is not considered.

15.6.4   *System model of the protocol [20]*

The execution efficiency is often the most important bottleneck for an N-resource data collection scheme. In Reference 20, the authors adopt Shamir's secret sharing and shuffling algorithm to propose a lightweight raw data collection scheme. Compared with other works, this work has some advantages in efficiency and practicality.

The system model consists of a cloud server (CS), fog node (FN), and users (patients), which is shown in Figure 15.8.

15.6.5   *Raw medical data collection of the protocol [20]*

A lightweight raw data collection scheme for publishing is proposed in this work; the raw medical data collection using Shamir's secret sharing is shown in Figure 15.9. In Figure 15.9, a_i is the raw medical data of participant P_i, every P_i randomly generates polynomial $f_i(x)$, the generates shares and sends shares to every participant and FN. $\lambda_{i,j}$ is the masked data, and $\lambda_{1j} + \lambda_{2j} + \cdots \lambda_{nj} = 0$. A specific example is given in Table 15.18.

15.6.6   *Experiment analysis of the protocol [20]*

This work has advantages in security and efficiency. For explaining this point, it is compared with some main privacy-preserving data collection techniques in Table 15.19.

15.7   Conclusion

In this part, we introduce three kinds of secure authentication schemes for the remote medical system: (1) secure and lightweight authentication for the authentication between doctors and devices; (2) a lightweight authentication communication scheme between users and doctors; and (3) an improved remote medical record system between the Cloud and users for data storage and access. These lightweight schemes can greatly improve the security, and authentication level in the medical system, users' data security, and privacy will be benefitted. Besides, two data collection methods based on data aggregation and N-source anonymity are introduced. Hence, the privacy of data collection is ensured.

Reference

[1]   Fortino G., Di Fatta G., Pathan M., Vasilakos A.V. 'Cloud-assisted body area networks: state-of-the-art and future challenges'. *Wireless Networks*. 2014, vol. 20(7), pp. 1925–38.

[2]   Rahimi M.R., Ren J., Liu C.H., Vasilakos A.V., Venkatasubramanian N. 'Mobile cloud computing: A survey, state of art and future directions'. *Mobile Networks and Applications*. 2014, vol. 19(2), pp. 133–43.

[3]   Wei L., Zhu H., Cao Z., *et al.* 'Security and privacy for storage and computation in cloud computing'. *Information Sciences*. 2014, vol. 258, pp. 371–86.

[4]   Camara C., Peris-Lopez P., Tapiador J.E. 'Security and privacy issues in implantable medical devices: A comprehensive survey'. *Journal of Biomedical Informatics*. 2015, vol. 55, pp. 272–89.

[5]   Liu Y., Zhou Y., Tian Y., Liu M., Zheng Y. 'Secure and lightweight remote medical system'. *Journal of Internet Technology*. 2019, vol. 20(1), pp. 177–85.

[6]   Fu Z., Sun X., Liu Q., Zhou L., Shu J. 'Achieving efficient cloud search services: multi-keyword ranked search over encrypted cloud data supporting parallel computing'. *IEICE Transactions on Communications*. 2015, vol. E98.B(1), pp. 190–200.

[7]   Zheng Y., Jeon B., Xu D., Wu Q.M.J., Zhang H. 'Image segmentation by generalized hierarchical fuzzy C-means algorithm'. *Journal of Intelligent & Fuzzy Systems*. 2015, vol. 28(2), pp. 961–73.

[8]   Weiwei J., Haojin Z., Zhenfu Z., Xiaolei X., Chengxin C. 'Human-factor-aware privacy-preserving aggregation in smart grid'. *IEEE Systems Journal*. 2014, vol. 8(2), pp. 598–607.

[9]   Lu R., Liang X., Li X., Lin X., Shen X. 'EPPA: an efficient and privacy-preserving aggregation scheme for secure smart grid communications'. *IEEE Transactions on Parallel and Distributed Systems*. 2012, vol. 23(9), pp. 1621–32.

[10] Li H., Lin X., Yang H., Liang X., Lu R., Shen X. 'EPPDR: an efficient privacy-preserving demand response scheme with adaptive key evolution in smart grid'. *IEEE Transactions on Parallel and Distributed Systems*. 2014, vol. 25(8), pp. 2053–64.

[11] Zhang K., Liang X., Baura M., Lu R., Shen X. 'PHDA: a priority based health data aggregation with privacy preservation for cloud assisted wbans'. *Information Sciences*. 2014, vol. 284, pp. 130–41.

[12] Badra M., Zeadally S. 'Design and performance analysis of a virtual ring architecture for smart grid privacy'. *IEEE Transactions on Information Forensics and Security*. 2014, vol. 9(2), pp. 321–29.

[13] Fan C.-I., Huang S.-Y., Lai Y.-L. 'Privacy-enhanced data aggregation scheme against internal attackers in smart grid'. *IEEE Transactions on Industrial Informatics*. 2014, vol. 10(1), pp. 666–75.

[14] He D., Kumar N., Lee J.-H. 'Privacy-preserving data aggregation scheme against internal attackers in smart grids'. *Wireless Networks*. 2016, vol. 22(2), pp. 491–502.

[15] Guo P., Wang J., Geng X., Kim C., Kin J. 'A variable threshold-value authentication architecture for wireless mesh networks'. *Journal of Internet Technology*. 2014, vol. 15(6), pp. 929–36.

[16] Shen J., Tan H., Moh S., Chung I., Liu Q., Sun X. 'Enhanced secure sensor association and key management in wireless body area networks'. *Journal of Communications and Networks*. 2015, vol. 17(5), pp. 453–62.

[17] Liu Y., Liu G., Cheng C., Shen J. 'A privacy-preserving health data aggregation scheme'. *KSII Transactions on Internet and Information Systems*. 2016, vol. 10(8), pp. 3852–64.

[18] Song J., Liu Y., Shao J., Tang C. 'A dynamic membership data aggregation (DMDA) protocol for smart grid'. *IEEE Systems Journal*. 2019, vol. 14(1), pp. 900–08.

[19] Liu Y.-N., Wang Y.-P., Wang X.-F., Xia Z., Xu J.-F. 'Privacy-preserving raw data collection without a trusted authority for IoT'. *Computer Networks*. 2019, vol. 148, pp. 340–48.

[20] Chen J., Liu G., Liu Y. 'Lightweight privacy-preserving raw data publishing scheme'. *IEEE Transactions on Emerging Topics in Computing*. 2020, vol. 9(4), pp. 2170–74.

[21] Jiang Q., Ma J., Ma Z., Li G. 'A privacy enhanced authentication scheme for telecare medical information systems'. *Journal of Medical Systems*. 2013, vol. 37(1), pp. 1–8.

[22] Kumari S., Khan M.K., Kumar R. 'Cryptanalysis and improvement of "a privacy enhanced scheme for telecare medical information systems"'. *Journal of Medical Systems*. 2013, vol. 37(4), pp. 1–11.

[23] Park Y., Park Y. 'A selective group authentication scheme for IoT-based medical information system'. *Journal of Medical Systems*. 2017, vol. 41(4), 48.

[24] Liu Y., Cheng C., Gu T., Jiang T., Li X. 'A lightweight authenticated communication scheme for smart grid'. *IEEE Sensors Journal*. 2015, vol. 16(3), pp. 836–42.

[25] Liu Y.N., Wang Y.P. 'An improved electronic medical record system (IEMRS) using oblivious transfer'. *Journal of the Chinese Institute of Engineers*. 2019, vol. 42(1), pp. 48–53.

[26] Chen S.W., Chiang D.L., Liu C.H., *et al.* 'Confidentiality protection of digital health records in cloud computing'. *Journal of Medical Systems*. 2016, vol. 40(5), p. 124.

[27] Molina-Markham A., Shenoy P., Fu K., Cecchet E., Irwin D. 'Private memoirs of a smart meter'. *Proceedings of the 2nd ACM Workshop on Embedded Sensing Systems for Energy-Efficiency in Building*; Zurich, Switzerland, Association for Computing Machinery, 2010. pp. 61–66.

[28] Badra M., Zeadally S. 'Lightweight and efficient privacy-preserving data aggregation approach for the smart grid'. *Ad Hoc Networks*. 2017, vol. 64, pp. 32–40.

[29] Garcia B.J. 'Privacy-friendly energy-metering via homomorphic encryption in proc' in *Of the International Workshop on Security and Trust Management*. Berlin, Heidelberg: Springer; 2010. pp. 226–38.

[30] Li F., Luo B., Liu P. 'Secure and privacy-preserving information aggregation for smart grids'. *International Journal of Security and Networks*. 2011, vol. 6(1), p. 28.

[31] Mármol F., Sorge C., Ugus O., Pérez G. 'Do not snoop my habits: preserving privacy in the smart grid'. *IEEE Communications Magazine*. 2012, vol. 50(5), pp. 166–72.

[32] Zhang Y., Chen Q., Zhong S. 'Privacy-preserving data aggregation in mobile phone sensing'. *IEEE Transactions on Information Forensics and Security*. 2016, vol. 11(5), pp. 980–92.

[33] Li Y., Zhao Y., Ishak S., Song H., Wang N., Yao N. 'An anonymous data reporting strategy with ensuring incentives for mobile crowd-sensing'. *Journal of Ambient Intelligence & Humanized Computing*. 2017, vol. 1-, p. 15.

[34] Yao Y., Yang L.T., Xiong N.N. 'Anonymity-based privacy-preserving data reporting for participatory sensing'. *IEEE Internet of Things Journal*. 2015, vol. 2(5), pp. 381–90.

[35] Shen W., Yin B., Cheng Y., Cao X., Li Q. 'Privacy-preserving mobile crowd sensing for big data applications'. *IEEE International Conference on Communications*; Paris, France, IEEE, 2017. pp. 1–6.

[36] Bugliesi M., Preneel B., Sassone V., Wegener I. 'Automata, languages and programming' in *The International Colloquium on Automata, Languages, and Programming*. Berlin, Heidelberg: Springer; 2006. pp. 1–12.

[37] Sweeney L. 'K-anonymity: A model for protecting privacy'. *International Journal of Uncertainty, Fuzziness and Knowledge-Based Systems*. 2002, vol. 10(5), pp. 557–70.

[38] Liu Y., Guo W., Fan C.-I., Chang L., Cheng C. 'A practical privacy-preserving data aggregation (3PDA) scheme for smart grid'. *IEEE Transactions on Industrial Informatics*. 2018, vol. 15(3), pp. 1767–74.

Chapter 16

Secure medical image encryption algorithm for e-healthcare applications

Kedar Nath Singh[1], Om Prakash Singh[1], Amit Kumar Singh[1], and Amrit Kumar Agrawal[2]

In recent years, with the constant evolution of the e-healthcare and in particular cloud services, medical images have taken a major part in data transmission. This medical data must be compressed and protected against illegal access and fraudulent usage. To ensure data confidentiality, a secure medical image encryption algorithm for e-healthcare applications is proposed in this chapter. In the first stage, precision limited logistic map (LM) and skew tent map (STM) is adopted to encrypt plain medical image, obtaining the cipher messages with a relationship to the plain image. Here, the method uses secure hash algorithm (SHA-512) to generate the initial sequences and parameters of the LM and STM. Then, Lempel–Ziv–Welch (LZW) compression scheme is utilized to compress the cipher image, which is used to reduce communication costs and storage space. According to our obtained results, the proposed encryption before compression algorithm is effective and resist to the many attacks on image and Kaggle dataset. Furthermore, extensive experimental results on real-world datasets demonstrate that the proposed algorithm outperforms the state-of-the-art approaches.

16.1 Introduction

With the proliferation of the Internet of things (IoT), the healthcare industry has experienced significant growth in recent years [1]. There is no doubt that the use of the IoT in healthcare not only improves operational efficiency for medical professionals and hospitals but also provides service convenience for supporting patients and their relatives. Especially after the COVID-19 pandemic, medical images serve

[1]Department of CSE, NIT Patna, Patna, Bihar, India
[2]Department of CSE, Galgotias College of Engineering & Technology, Greater Noida, Uttar Pradesh, India

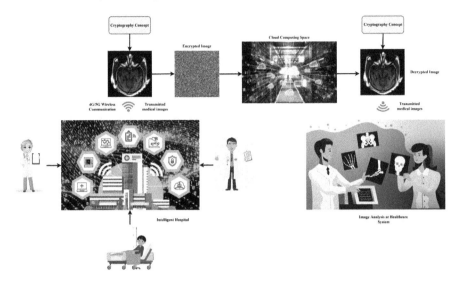

Figure 16.1   The architecture of the smart healthcare system

as the information carrier for various purposes, such as medical diagnosis, telesurgery, defence, medical education, teleconsulting, research and business analytics [2–4]. The smart healthcare system is shown in Figure 16.1. The hospital generates a large number of health data and multimedia images. These data and images are stored on the hospital's cloud in an encrypted form for security. Legitimate users (doctors, patients, medical staff, researchers, etc.) use it for specific purposes.

It is established that medical images bring convenience to communication, but it also faces serious security threats [5]. Furthermore, the issue of identity theft and copyright protection is becoming more prevalent by the day [6–8]. The integrity of data must be safeguarded against unauthorised users.

Encryption is a popular technique for protecting medical data from illegitimate access [9]. Presently, terabytes of multimedia data are generated and used by the medical professionals, staff, and research community [10]. To this end, data are compressed in order to reduce storage and communication costs.

In such context, various efficient encryption-compression-based schemes [11–13] are developed to resolve the security, high communication costs, and storage space issues related to the images. Encryption-compression system is presented in Figure 16.2. The content owner first encrypts the plain image, then applies compression to compress it. In order to reconstruct the image on the receiver side, decryption is applied after decompression.

In some cases, the content owner compresses the plain image before encrypting it to reduce the encryption cost [14]. However, image data can be exposed or destroyed if the encryption key is hacked.

In this chapter, we present an encryption before compression algorithm to resolve the security, high communication costs and storage space issues related to the medical images.

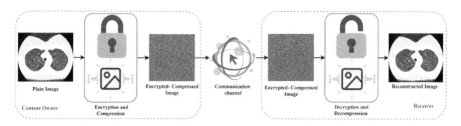

Figure 16.2   Encryption-compression system

The salient features of our proposed algorithm can be recapitulated as follows:

- Secure encryption scheme: we integrate SHA-512, precision limited LM, and STM to propose a secure and efficient encryption algorithm. SHA-512 and STM are used to generate an initial sequence of chaos. Furthermore, the encryption key is generated by the combination of precision limited LM and STM. LM and STM provide strong security and great efficiency due to unpredictability, and extreme initial state dependence. In addition, STM has a positive Lyapunov exponent, which reflects its strong chaotic nature. (Lyapunov exponent shows the randomness of the sequence of data.)
- Efficient compression in the encrypted domain: the encrypted image is compressed by the LZW lossless compression scheme [15] without knowing the encryption key. LZW is a fast and efficient coding scheme. Regardless of the likelihood of symbols, the compression and decompression cost are nearly the same for any particular image size.
- Concept of encryption before compression: it is useful to enhance the security of data in case of untrustworthy transmission channel. If data is not encrypted before transmission, the channel owner can see the private data. Compression is used for decreasing the amount of data to send by the transmission channel without having information about the encryption key to improve speed. Hence, encryption before compression is necessary steps to improve the security of data.
- Experimental analysis: the experimental results prove that the proposed algorithm is secure against chosen plaintext attacks, robust to noise attack, and reduces the bandwidth, high communication costs and storage space. Furthermore, extensive experimental results on real world datasets demonstrate that the proposed algorithm outperforms the state-of-the-art approaches.

The rest of the chapter is organized as follow: section 16.2 represents the literature review, preliminary concepts are discussed in section 16.3, proposed encryption-compression is presented in section 16.4, section 16.5 includes the simulation results and section 16.6 contains the concluding remark.

16.2   Literature review

For the past few years, different encryption/encryption-compression-based mechanisms have been proposed for healthcare scenarios. For example, Sarosh et al. [16] suggested a medical image encryption scheme for the security of e-health data. The proposed encryption scheme is based on a 3-dimensional (3D) chaotic system, piecewise linear chaotic map (PWLCM), and DNA. They used a 3D chaotic map for confusion purposes and PWLCM is for the generation of the main image, which is used for further propagation. Furthermore, to improve the security they utilized crisscross diffusion. The simulation result of the proposed scheme shows that the scheme is robust to various attacks. However, the computational cost of the proposed technique is quite high and key space analysis should be investigated. Song et al. [17] devised an encryption scheme for parallel encryption of a group of medical images. They adopt the permutation-substitution technique to encrypt the images. A certain number of medical images are selected in a group and permutations are performed on it, then substitution is implemented in cipher-block-chaining mode. Results of encryption demonstrate that the proposed technique is efficient and has good security characteristics. The permutation process of the scheme is parallel, but the substitution process is done sequentially. Rani et al. [18] proposed an encryption scheme based on a fused magic cube for both colour and greyscale images. First, the fused magic cube is generated and then the permutation and diffusion process of encryption is performed by it. Comprehensive outcome analysis shows that the proposed scheme is secure and withstands multiple attacks, although the robustness of the scheme against noise attacks needs to be verified. A chaotic map is used by Yasser et al. [19] for the encryption process in order to protect the privacy of medical images. First, a plain image is split into two parts and then each part is permuted and diffused separately by two different keys. The proposed scheme demonstrates resistance to various security attacks. Selvi et al. [20] proposed an encryption-compression system for secure and efficient communication of medical images. They utilized a deep neural network-based crypto-compression scheme. A synorr certificateless signcryption is used for encryption and then cipher images are compressed by Levenshtein entropy encoding scheme. The proposed scheme shows good compression performance and takes less time to encrypt the images. However, the security analysis of the proposed scheme needs to be verified. Zhang et al. [21] suggested a compress sensing-based crypto-compression scheme for digital images. Image encryption is performed by permutation process and negative-positive transform process. Then the efficient encoding of the encrypted image is done by 2D-compressed sensing. The proposed scheme gives a high-quality reconstructed image; however, various security features such as differential and statistical analysis are needed to be investigated to prove the security aspect of the scheme. Hu et al. [22] utilized a chaotic system and compress sensing to develop an efficient encryption-compression system. A fractional-order chaotic map is used to generate the random sequence for the encryption process. Sparse coefficients are generated by applying discrete cosine transform (DCT) on the original image and then it is compressed by measurement and Hadamard matrices, after those two times compression is employed. Finally, permutation and diffusion are applied to encrypt the image. The proposed scheme shows good security and compression performance; however, the computation time of the suggested scheme is high. Chen *et al.* [23] proposed block-based image encryption and Huffman compression to develop a data hiding scheme. First, the image is encrypted by block-based technique then the encrypted image bit-plain is compressed by Huffman coding to create the space for data hiding. The proposed scheme shows good compression performance; however, the proposed encryption scheme is weak. Wang *et al.* [24] demonstrated a deep learning-based encryption before compression scheme for digital images. Image is encrypted by modulo 256 addition and lossy compression of encrypted data is performed by uniform downsampling. Experimental findings prove the effectiveness of the proposed scheme over recent techniques.

Gupta *et al.* [25] proposed a deep neural network-based compression and encryption scheme for secure and efficient transmission of the images. They utilized a LM for confusion and substitution. Image compression is performed by a stacked autoencoder of seven layers. Then the LM is used to confuse and substitute the compressed image pixels. Results demonstrated that the proposed scheme is secure and has good compression performance.

Most of the encryption-compression systems discussed above mainly focused on the compression performance of encrypted image; however, their encryption process is weak. Furthermore, the majority of the methods have a high computational cost. Therefore, we propose highly secure encryption before compression system for medical multimedia data with low cost.

16.3 Preliminaries

16.3.1 Chaotic system

Chaotic systems are very popular in the secure design of image encryption schemes. We have utilized two chaotic systems in our proposed encryption scheme. We present limited precision equations for these maps.

a) Logistic map

The simple structure of the LM makes it popular for exploring the idea of chaos. The LM is a nonlinear system of degree 2 [26]. The map is defined by the following equation:

$$l_{n+1} = \sigma \times l_n \left(1 - l_n\right) \tag{16.1}$$

where l_{n+1} and l_n are the next and previous sequence, σ represents the map's parameter. The map shows chaotic characteristics and generates pseudo-random sequences when $\sigma \in (3.57, 4]$. A LM is very sensitive to its initial value.

In this work, we used a precision limited map of the L-bit. This is defined as

$$l_{n+1} = L\left(l_n\right) = \left[(\sigma l_n(2^L - l_n))/2^L\right] \tag{16.2}$$

where $l_n \in \left[1, 2, \ldots., 2^L - 1\right]$, map parameter $\sigma \in (3.57, 4]$, and L represents the number of precision bits whose value is 32. It generates a L-bit sequence and exhibits the same chaotic characteristics as the logistics map [27].

b) Skew tent map

STM generates pseudo random numbers with substantial dispersion [28]. STM exhibits a broad range bifurcation diagram that is distributed in the phase plane. Mathematically it is represented as

$$K_{n+1} = \begin{cases} \frac{K_n}{\lambda} & \text{if } 0 < K_n \leq \lambda \\ \frac{1-K_n}{1-\lambda} & \text{if } \lambda < K_n \leq 1 \end{cases} \quad (16.3)$$

where parameter $\lambda \in (0, 1)$, next and previous sequence generated by the map is represented as K_{n+1} and K_n, respectively. In finite precision STM is represented as

$$K_{n+1} = S\left(K_n, \lambda\right) \begin{cases} \left\lfloor \frac{(K_n \times 2^L)}{\lambda} \right\rfloor & \text{if } 0 < K_n < \lambda \\ 2^L - 1 & \text{if } K_n = \lambda \\ \left\lfloor \left(2^L \left(2^L - K_n\right)\right) / \left(2^L - \lambda\right)\right\rfloor & \text{if } \lambda < K_n \leq 2^L \end{cases} \quad (16.4)$$

where $\lfloor() \rfloor$ floor function it returns integer number less than or equal to provided number. $\lambda \in \left[1, 2^L - 1\right]$, L represents the number of precision bits whose value is 32 and K_{n+1} represents the next sequence generated by the map.

16.3.2 Lempel–Ziv–Welch compression

LZW is a very popular and efficient lossless compression technique, and it is based on the dictionary method [15]. It is employed in the removal of frequently repeating sequences. Dictionary contains the index of symbols. If the next symbol matches with the stored symbol in the dictionary, then the symbol is encoded by the index. The detailed flowchart of LZW is shown in Figure 16.3.

For example, suppose a string CDCDDCMMMD. First CD is selected, since CD is not present in dictionary, it is inserted into the dictionary and codeword 256 is assigned to it and encoded with ACSII value of prefix C (i.e. 67). Next check for DC, it is also inserted into dictionary with code word 257 and encoded as 68 (ACSII value of prefix D). CD is in present in dictionary, but CDD is not hence CDD is inserted into dictionary and code word 258 is assign and the corresponding output is 256 (ACSII value of prefix CD). Next, DC is present in dictionary. DCM is not present hence code word 259 is allotted and the corresponding encoded output is 257. Similarly remaining dictionary is created and the encoded sequence becomes (67, 68, 256, 257, 77, 260, 68). Table 16.1 shows the generation of code words and output of the LZW encoding process.

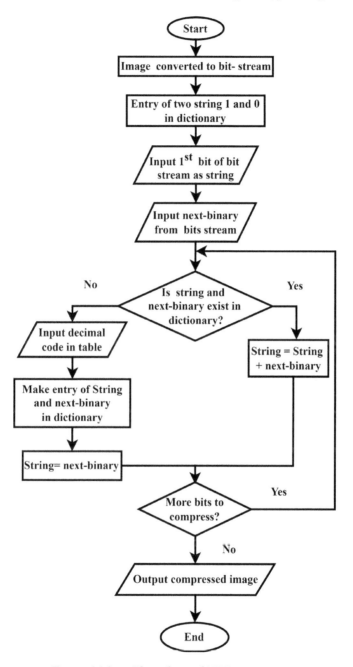

Figure 16.3   Flow chart of LZW compression

Table 16.1   Lempel–Ziv–Welch encoding

	Dictionary	
Output	Codeword	String
67	256	CD
68	257	DC
256	258	CDD
257	259	DCM
77	260	MM
260	261	MMD
68	257	

16.4   Proposed scheme

The proposed encryption-compression system has two main stages: encryption and compression. First plain image is encrypted by a chaos-based system and then efficient LZW-based encoding is performed to compress the encrypted image. The complete flow diagram of proposed system is presented in Figure 16.4. We created the key using the SHA-512 hashing algorithm of image, using this hash we created five initial values and iterate 20 times using STM map to induce chaos factor.

Result of this procedure is then taken as initial value of the three maps which are STM and LM map (precision limited), which is integrated using exclusive-OR

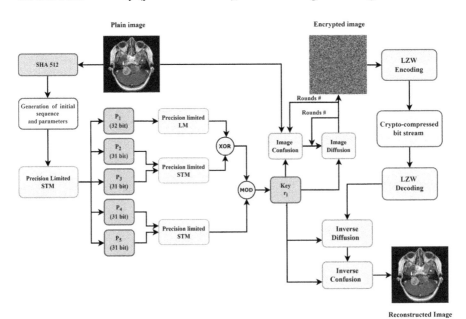

Figure 16.4   Flow diagram of proposed scheme

Table 16.2   Notations and descriptions

Notation	Explanation	Notation	Explanation
M	Plain image	r_i	The sequence of ith iteration
E	Cipher image	W, H	Height and width of the image
DK	Diffusion matrix	L_C	Length of CK
CK	Confusion matrix	L_D	Length of DK
P_1, P_2, P_3	Initial values for maps	LM()	Precision limited logistic map
P_4, P_5	Parameters	STM()	Precision limited Skew Tent map
Per$_{img}$	Confused image	C_i	ith column
$\oplus$	Exclusive OR operation	R_i	ith row

(XOR) and modulus (MOD) operation to yield encryption and decryption key. Using this key, confusion and diffusion is done on image for specific round (result of 1 and 2 round is shown in this paper). After these steps, LZW encoding is performed to encrypted image and this compressed bit stream is transmitted and decrypted using the same key on other side. Furthermore, step-by-step procedure for each algorithm (Algorithm 1 to 5) of key generation, encryption, compression, decompression and decryption is defined in detail in below subsection and the notations used in these algorithms are explained in Table 16.2.

16.4.1   Generation of chaos initial value

SHA-512 is utilized to generate the initial values and parameters of the precision limited LM and STM. First, a 512-bit image hash is generated in which the first 492 bits are selected as A and the rest are discarded. A is split into nine parts as shown in Table 16.3. B_1 to B_5 are generated by XOR operations of A_1 to A_9 as shown in Algorithm 1. The initial value generated by XOR operations is iterated 20 times using STM to generate final initial values and parameters. The detailed generation of the initial value and parameters is depicted in Algorithm 1.

16.4.2   Key generation

This process produces the key for the encryption technique. Confusion (CK) and diffusion keys (DK) are generated in this process. Length of confusion and diffusion matrix is defined as L_C and L_D, respectively, and are of size W×H. Precision limited LM and STM are used to generate the ith sequence as follows:

$$r_i = mod(((LM(P_1) \oplus STM(P_2, P_4)) + STM(P_3, P_5)), 2^{32}) \tag{16.5}$$

where P_1 is the initial sequence value of precision limited LM, P_2 and P_3 are the initial value for two precisions limited STM and P_4 and P_5 are the parameters of precision limited STM. The full description of key generation is presented in Algorithm 2.

Table 16.3   The splitting of the hash value

A (80-bits)	A (80-bits)	A (36-bits)	A (36-bits)	A (36-bits)	A (36-bits)	A (36-bits)	A (36-bits)	A (36-bits)
A_1	Null	A_2	A_3	A_4	A_5	A_6	A_7	A_8	A_9

Algorithm-1 Generation of the initial value	Algorithm-2 Key Generation
Input: original Image M	**Input:** P_1, P_2, P_3, P_4, P_5, original Image M,
Output: P_1, P_2, P_3, P_4, P_5	**Output:** *CK, DK,*

// calculate image hash using SHA512.

1. $Z \leftarrow$ SHA512(M)
2. $Z \leftarrow$ select the first 492 Bits of hash
// Leave second 80 bits

3. $A_1, A_2, A_3, A_4, A_5, A_6, A_7, A_8, A_9$ = Split Z to two 80bits, and the remaining 36 bits
4. $B1 \leftarrow$
(*First 40bits of A*1) $\oplus$ (*First 40bits of A*2)
5. $B_2 \leftarrow$ (Last 40bits of A_1) $\ominus$ (Last 40bits of A_2)
6. $B_3 \leftarrow A_3 \ominus A_4$
7. $B_4 \leftarrow A_5 \ominus A_6$
8. $B_5 \leftarrow A_7 \oplus A_8 \oplus A_9$
9. $P_1 \leftarrow (B_5 / 2^{35})$ mod 1
10. $P_2 \leftarrow (0.87 + ((B_3 \oplus (B_4)) / 2^{35})$ mod 0.13) mod 1
11. $P_3 \leftarrow ((B_3 \ominus B_5) / 2^{35})$ mod 1
12. $P_4 \leftarrow (0.87 + ((B_4 \ominus B_5) / 2^{35})$ mod 0.13) mod 1
13. $P_5 \leftarrow ((B_3 \oplus B_4 \ominus B_5)/2^{35})$ mod 1
14. $P_1, P_2, P_3, P_4, P_5 \leftarrow 2^{32} \times (P_1, P_2, P_3, P_4, P_5)$

15. N = 20
16. For i = 1: N do
17. $P_1 \leftarrow$ STM (P_1, N)
18. $P_2 \leftarrow$ STM (P_2, P_4)
19. $P_3 \leftarrow$ STM (P_3, P_5)
20. End
Return P_1, P_2, P_3, P_4, P_5

1. $[P_1, P_2, P_3, P_4, P_5] \leftarrow$ initialization(key,20)
2. [**W, H**] $\leftarrow$ size(M)
3. $R \leftarrow W \times H$
4. $L_c \leftarrow W \times H$
5. $L_D \leftarrow W \times H$
6. *for* i = 0 *to* R do
7. $r_i = ((LM(P_1) \ominus STM(P_2, P_4)) \oplus STM(P_3, P_5))$ mod 2^{32}
8.   if (i < L_C) do

9. $CK \leftarrow [i, r_i]$
10.   if (i+1) $\times 4 \leq L_D$ do
11.   Put r_i in *CK* after dividing it into four 8-bit values
12.   else
13.   Fill the *DK*, and discard the left 8- bit numbers
14. end for
15. sort *CK*
16. $CK \leftarrow$ resize (*CK*, [W×H])
17. $DK \leftarrow$ resize (*DK*, [W×H])
Return *CK, DK*

16.4.3   Encryption process

This section contains encryption of the original image by confusion and diffusion. First, the plain image is flattened to a 1D vector. 1D confusion matrix CK of size W×H is generated by utilizing (16.1) and shorted. Then the plain image vector is permuted by the shorted index of CK. Furthermore, permuted 1D vector is reshaped to W×H for the diffusion step. Next, diffusion is performed on permuted image Per$_{img}$ to final encryption of the image. Diffusion steps utilized diffusion matrix DK of size W×H. Row- and column-wise diffusion is performed in the following equation:

$$B(i) = (B(i) + B(i-1) + DK(i)) \, mod256 \qquad (16.6)$$

where $B(i)$ is the pixel value of Per$_{img}$ at the ith position, and the $i-1$th position is in a circular shift fashion. The detailed encryption process is depicted in Algorithm 3.

16.4.4   Compression and decompression of encrypted image

Efficient compression of the encrypted image is performed by LZW coding scheme. Encrypted image E is encoded as C and encrypted-compressed C and dictionary is transmitted to the receiver over the network. The receiver receives C and dictionary from the sender and performs a decoding operation to decompress C.

Decompressed-encrypted image E' then proceeds to the decryption stage. The compression-decompression algorithm is shown in Algorithm 4.

Algorithm-3 Encryption	**Algorithm-5** Decryption
Input: original Image M, CK, DK	Input: Cipher decompressed image E', CK, DK
Output: Cipher Image E	Output: Decrypted image M
//confusion	// De-diffusion
1. $[W,H] \leftarrow size(M)$	1. $[W,H] \leftarrow size(E')$
2. $Per_{img} \leftarrow flatten(M)$	2. for i=0 to 1 do
3. for i = 0 to length(CK) do	3. for C_i = W-1 to 0 do
4. $\quad$ swap($Per_{img}[i]$, $Per_{img}[CK[i]]$)	4. $\quad$ if $C_i = 0$
5. end for	5. $\quad$ $E[:, C_i] \leftarrow mod((E[:, C_i] - E[:,-1] - DK[:,C_i]),255)$
6. $Per_{img} \leftarrow reshape(Per_{img}, W \times H)$	6. $\quad$ if $C_i > 0$
//Diffusion (round =1 or 2)	7. $\quad$ $E[:, C_i] \leftarrow mod((E[:, C_i] - E[:, C_i-1] - DK[:,C_i]),$ $255)$
7. $B \leftarrow Per_{img}$	
8. for i=0 to 1 do	8. end for
9. $\quad$ for R_i=0 to H do	9. for R_i =H-1 to 0 do
10. $\quad$ if R_i=0	10. $\quad$ if R_i=0
11. $\quad$ $B[R_i, :] \leftarrow mod(DK[R_i, :] + B[-1:] + B[R_i,:]),$ $255)$	11. $\quad$ $E[R_i, :] \leftarrow mod((E[:, R_i] - E[-1, :] - DK[R_i, :]),$ $255)$
12. $\quad$ if $R_i > 0$	12. $\quad$ if $R_i > 0$
13. $\quad$ $B[R_i, :] \leftarrow mod(DK[R_i, :] + B[R_i-1,:] + B[R_i,:]),$ $255)$	13. $\quad$ $E[R_i, :] \leftarrow mod((E[:, R_i] - E[R_i-1, :] - DK[R_i, :]),$ $255)$
14. end for	14. end for
15. for C_i=0 to W do	15. end for
16. $\quad$ if C_i=0	//De-Permutation
17. $\quad$ $B[:, C_i] \leftarrow mod(DK[:, C_i] + B[:, -1] + B[:, C_i]),$ $255)$	16. $M \leftarrow flatten(E)$
	17. For i = length(CK) - 1 to 0 do
18. $\quad$ if $C_i > 0$	18. $\quad$ Swap ($M[i]$, $[M[CK[i]]$)
19. $\quad$ $B[:, C_i] \leftarrow mod(DK[:, C_i] + B[:, C_i - 1] +$ $B[:, C_i])$, $255)$	19. end for
	20. $M \leftarrow reshape(M, W \times H)$
20. end for	Return M
21. end for	
Return E	

Algorithm 4: Compression and decompression
Input: Encrypted Image E
Output: Decompressed Encrypted Image E'
1. $A \leftarrow image(E)$ // compression
2. C, *dictionary* $\leftarrow$ LZW_encode(A)   // decompression
3. $E' \leftarrow$ LZW_decode(C, *dictionary*)
Return E'

16.4.5 Decryption process

The decryption method is simply the opposite of the encryption method. The diffusion matrix DK and confusion matrix CK are generated from the key generation step, which is utilized in the decryption step. First of all, de-diffusion is performed on rows and columns by utilizing diffusion matrix DK. Then the de-diffused image is transformed into a 1D vector, and an inverse confusion is applied using a confusion matrix CK. It is converted back to its original dimension to finally get the decrypted image M. Decryption process is discussed in detail in Algorithm 5.

16.5 Experimental results

This section describes the simulation of the results of the proposed scheme. The experiment is performed on Python 3.9 with 8GB RAM and a 64-bit core i5-9300H processor. Different medical images are selected from the open-source Kaggle data set [29]. Images of different sizes (200×200, 217×232, 221×228, 220×215, 256×256, 320×420, 372×341, 438×512, 512×512, 561×569, and 1024×1024) have been selected to evaluate the effectiveness of the proposed scheme. Sample images used in the experiment are depicted in Figure 16.5.

To accommodate a variety of application circumstances, an efficient image encryption method should be able to convert a wide range of plain images into unidentifiable encrypted images and make it hard to discover anything relevant from the encrypted images. Figure 16.6 shows the result of the visual analysis test of the proposed scheme. It shows how an encrypted image differs significantly from a plain one, and one cannot find any useful information about the plain image from the encrypted image. In this section, we have also performed statistical, differential, key sensitivity, computational cost, robustness analysis, and compression ratio analysis to evaluate the security and compression performance of the proposed scheme.

16.5.1 Statistical analysis

In this section, security performance of the suggested scheme is evaluated from a statistical perspective.

a) Histogram analysis

Histogram evaluation is used to measure the effectiveness of an encryption scheme against statistical attacks. Histogram of an image represents the distribution of image pixels. In particular, a good encryption scheme provides a uniform histogram of the cipher image. The histogram analysis of the proposed scheme is presented in Figure 16.7; the histogram of plain medical images (M6, M8, M9) is centred about particular grey levels, while the histogram of the corresponding encrypted image is evenly spread. Therefore, the proposed scheme can efficiently withstand the histogram attack.

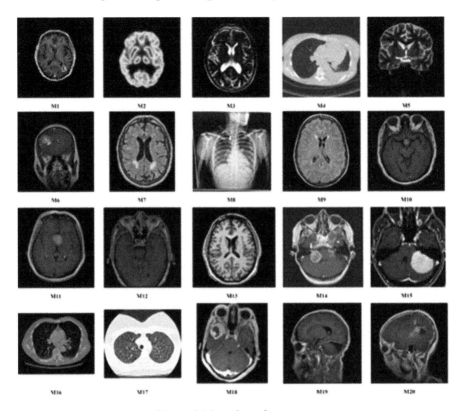

Figure 16.5   Sample images

b) Chi-square test

A Chi-square test is performed to measure the uniformity in histogram. A strong encryption scheme must have the χ^2 score less than the theoretical value, i.e., 293.2478 [30]. χ^2 test is represented as

$$\chi 2 = \sum_{n=0}^{255} \left(\frac{(A_n - B_n)^2}{B_n} \right)$$

(16.7)

where A_n: observed frequency of each intensity. B_n: expected frequency of each intensity. Table 16.4 shows the result of χ^2 test analysis for Round=1. We have performed χ^2 test on all 20 images. It can be observed that all scores are less than the theoretical score. For Round=2 all χ^2 scores also pass.

c) Correlation coefficient analysis

There is a high correlation exists among neighbouring pixels in medical images. A good encryption scheme should be able to efficiently reduce the high correlation [31]. In most cases, the correlation coefficient is used to assess the degree of correlation between neighbouring pixels in an image. Horizontal, vertical, and diagonal correlation coefficient is mathematically described as

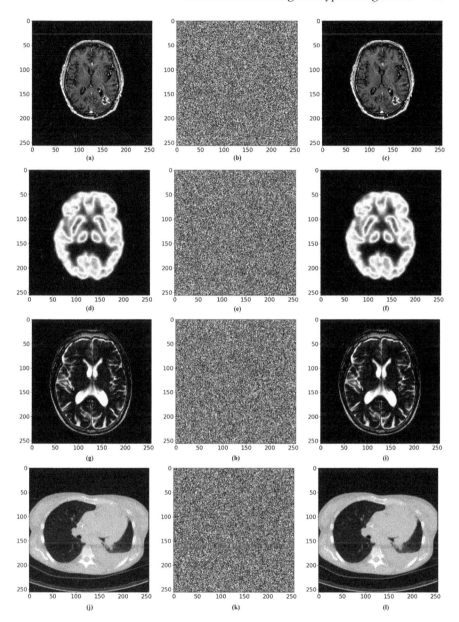

Figure 16.6   *Plain images (M1, M2, M3, M4): (a), (d), (e), (j) corresponding encrypted images: (b), (e), (h), (k) and decrypted images: (c), (f), (i), (l).*

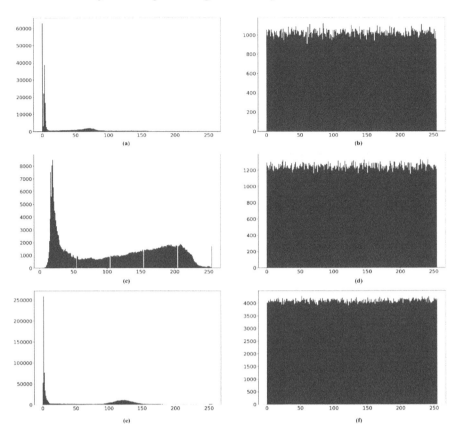

Figure 16.7   Plain image (M6, M8, M9) histogram: (a), (c), (e) and corresponding encrypted image histogram: (b), (d), (f)

Table 16.4   Chi-square test analysis

Image	χ^2_{Value}	Pass / Fail	Image	χ^2_{Value}	Pass / Fail
M1	260.2734	Pass	M11	239.0762	Pass
M2	229.1172	Pass	M12	262.1582	Pass
M3	242.4453	Pass	M13	251.4629	Pass
M4	259.9531	Pass	M14	281.6998	Pass
M5	277.7600	Pass	M15	194.4406	Pass
M6	231.5918	Pass	M16	270.6514	Pass
M7	275.2020	Pass	M17	248.8973	Pass
M8	291.4588	Pass	M18	266.1590	Pass
M9	272.3413	Pass	M19	250.2188	Pass
M10	231.8457	Pass	M20	220.7246	Pass

$$C_{a,b} = \frac{X\left[(a - X(a))\,(b - X(b))\right]}{\sqrt{Y(a)\,Y(b)}} \tag{16.8}$$

$$X(a) = \frac{1}{k} \sum_{j=1}^{k} a_j \tag{16.9}$$

$$Y(a) = \frac{1}{k} \sum_{j=1}^{k} \left(a_j - X(a)\right)^2 \tag{16.10}$$

where a and b are the pixels whose correlation $C_{a,b}$ is measured, k is the number of pixel pairs. Generally, the correlation coefficient varies from -1 to 1. Correlation score 1 indicates the high correlation between image pixels pair. A good encryption scheme should reduce the correlation score close to zero in all three directions. We have selected 5000-pixel pairs to measure the correlation coefficient in each direction. We used confusion and diffusion once (Round=1) and twice (Round=2) to investigate the security behaviour of the proposed medical image encryption technique. The correlation analysis of our proposed scheme is presented in Table 16.5. As demonstrated in this table, all correlation coefficient scores of encrypted images are very close to zero. Hence, the proposed scheme effectively reduces the correlation between neighbouring pixels. Furthermore, we also compared the results of the proposed scheme with recent encryption techniques [17, 32, 33] in this table, which shows that our scheme's result is better.

The correlation between nearby pixels is typically shown using a scatterplot. We plot the correlation of plain image M6 and M8 in the horizontal, vertical, and diagonal directions in Figure 16.8(b–d) and (j–l) and their corresponding encrypted image's correlation is shown in Figure 16.8(f–h) and (n–p), respectively. We can see from this figure that the neighbouring pixels in the plain images are strongly correlated, whereas the uniformly scattered distribution findings in Figure 16.8(f–h) and (n–p) shows that the adjacent pixels in the encrypted image have essentially no correlation. This property of the encryption scheme can withstand statistical attack which provides better security against hackers.

d) Entropy test

A strong image encryption scheme should be able to conceal the statistical information contained in plain images. Information entropy is utilized to scale the degree of randomness in an image. An entropy score of eight for a greyscale image represents the highest degree of randomness in the image. Information entropy is defined as

$$X(I) = -\sum_{k=1}^{255} \left(S(a_k) \times \log_2 S(a_k)\right) \tag{16.11}$$

where $S(a_k)$ indicates the probability of a_k.

Entropy analysis of proposed scheme is depicted in Table 16.6. We get the highest, lowest, and average entropy of 20 medical images are 7.99980, 7.99606, and 7.99811, respectively for one round encryption, and for Round=2 average entropy score is 7.99808. The simulation results show that our scheme achieves an entropy score very close to the optimal entropy value. Moreover, comparison results with References [17, 19, 33] also show the superiority of our proposed scheme. Therefore,

Table 16.5   Correlation analysis of proposed encryption scheme

Scheme	Image	Plain image			Encrypted image (Round=1)		
		H	**V**	**D**	**H**	**V**	**D**
Proposed Scheme	M1	0.884932	0.909202	0.849296	0.010585	−0.007524	0.010991
	M10	0.987216	0.986798	0.971852	−0.007105	−0.014166	−0.009961
	M11	0.986785	0.992884	0.980673	0.003613	0.009022	−0.011675
	M12	0.979965	0.983492	0.965600	−0.000017	−0.016257	0.023462
	M13	0.963881	0.971544	0.945232	0.009378	−0.003718	0.012622
	M14	0.955575	0.971543	0.940064	0.011731	−0.009357	−0.004046
	M15	0.969605	0.979357	0.952192	−0.018600	−0.001288	−0.008339
	M16	0.989650	0.982672	0.971887	−0.026277	0.010608	−0.002082
	M17	0.980101	0.972562	0.955535	0.020549	0.012620	−0.014573
	M18	0.986629	0.993406	0.981041	0.002777	−0.007167	0.014059
	M19	0.993469	0.985519	0.978578	−0.018584	−0.000904	−0.005125
	M2	0.995599	0.997075	0.991715	0.000959	−0.002243	0.006272
	M20	0.996345	0.989335	0.985374	0.009851	0.007675	0.005378
	M3	0.920273	0.921271	0.867933	−0.009452	0.005922	−0.004581
	M4	0.991148	0.979254	0.972761	0.021878	0.005787	0.008350
	M5	0.949722	0.924839	0.895583	−0.024984	0.006383	−0.026989
	M6	0.992415	0.990786	0.985890	0.000327	0.018163	−0.016665
	M7	0.962270	0.971138	0.938277	0.006328	0.018297	−0.008943
	M8	0.984293	0.987209	0.972229	−0.032602	−0.003982	−0.013000
	M9	0.993182	0.997222	0.989984	0.010763	−0.001009	−0.009364
Average correlation score of 20 medical images (Round=1)					−0.001444	0.001343	−0.002711
Average correlation score of 20 medical images (Round=2)					0.005620	−0.001003	0.001921
[17]	CT_abdomen0	0.994393	0.996926	0.992866	−0.002151	−0.002660	−0.00347
[32]	Lena				0.0053	0.0054	0.0765
[33]	Chest	0.993602	0.992463	0.987863	−0.00174	−0.00083	0.01335

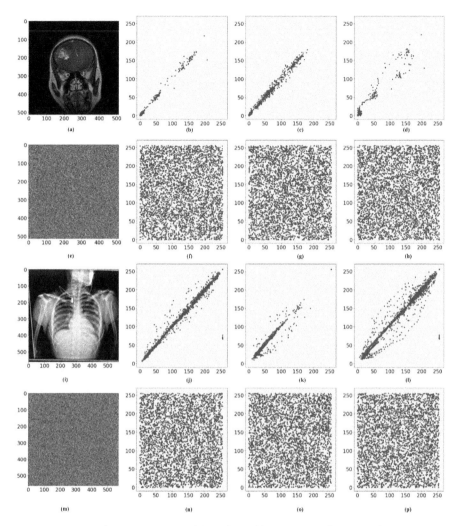

Figure 16.8   *Plain images: M6 (a) and M8 (i), corresponding correlation in horizontal, vertical, and diagonal direction: (b), (c), (d) and (j), (k), (l). Encrypted images: (e) and (m), corresponding correlation in horizontal, vertical and diagonal direction: (f), (g), (h) and (n), (o), (p).*

the proposed scheme provides the highest level of randomness in cipher images and is protected against entropy attacks.

16.5.2 *Differential analysis*

A robust encryption scheme should be highly sensitive to a very minor change in plain image. For example, if there is even a slight difference between two plain

Table 16.6   Information entropy analysis

Scheme	Image	Plain image entropy	Encrypted image entropy
Proposed	M1	2.88978	7.99710
	M2	4.10926	7.99679
	M3	4.49450	7.99731
	M4	6.20137	7.99757
	M5	5.46474	7.99606
	M6	5.23485	7.99920
	M7	6.00268	7.99653
	M8	7.58186	7.99942
	M9	5.79738	7.99980
	M10	6.34125	7.99926
	M11	5.57943	7.99917
	M12	6.15632	7.99939
	M13	5.41219	7.99661
	M14	6.47406	7.99640
	M15	6.99218	7.99680
	M16	6.11816	7.99860
	M17	6.66584	7.99901
	M18	6.69257	7.99854
	M19	6.36058	7.99924
	M20	6.41326	7.99935
	Average (Round=1)		7.99811
	Average (Round=2)		7.99808
[17]	CT_abdomen0	-	7.99130
[19]	Knee MRI	-	7.99800
[33]	Chest	6.533	7.99810

images, an ideal encryption process should produce completely different cipher images. Otherwise, a differential attack is possible on the encryption system. The differential attack is assessed by two parameters the number of pixels change rate (NPCR), and the unified average changing intensity (UACI) which are mathematically defined as

$$NPCR = \frac{1}{X \times Y} \sum_{a,b} N(a, b) \tag{16.12}$$

$$UACI = \frac{1}{X \times Y} \sum_{a,b} \frac{|E_{NC}(a,b) - (E_{NC})'(a,b)|}{255} \tag{16.13}$$

$$N(a, b) = \begin{cases} 0 & \text{if } E_{NC}(a, b) = (E_{NC})'(a, b) \\ 1 & \text{if } E_{NC}(a, b) \neq (E_{NC})'(a, b) \end{cases} \tag{16.14}$$

where $X \times Y$: size of the image, $E_{NC}(a, b)$: encrypted plain image, $(E_{NC})'(a, b)$: encrypted slightly changed plain image. A strong encryption scheme shows the ideal value of NPCR and UACI as 0.99609 and 0.33464, respectively [34]. We analysed the NPCR and UACI scores in Table 16.7 for both encryption rounds. For Round=1, the average NPCR and UACI of 20 medical images are 0.99609 and 0.33473,

Table 16.7   Differential analysis

Scheme	Image	NPCR	UACI
Proposed scheme	M1	0.99635	0.33377
	M2	0.99571	0.33407
	M3	0.99590	0.33417
	M4	0.99643	0.33507
	M5	0.99630	0.33457
	M6	0.99599	0.33573
	M7	0.99602	0.33388
	M8	0.99615	0.33458
	M9	0.99610	0.33474
	M10	0.99601	0.33456
	M11	0.99614	0.33487
	M12	0.99628	0.33395
	M13	0.99605	0.33436
	M14	0.99623	0.33451
	M15	0.99607	0.33590
	M16	0.99624	0.33565
	M17	0.99584	0.33541
	M18	0.99581	0.33491
	M19	0.99615	0.33549
	M20	0.99599	0.33439
Average of 20 images (Round=1)		**0.99609**	**0.33473**
Average of 20 images (Round=2)		**0.99619**	**0.33470**
[17]	CT_abdomen0	0.99205	0.33443
[19]	Knee MRI	0.99710	0.33640
[33]	Chest	0.996104	0.334662

respectively. The average NPCR is equal to the ideal one, and the average UACI is also very close to its ideal value. Furthermore, each image's NPCR and UACI scores are also very close to theoretical values. For Round=2, NPCR and UACI scores are also similar to Round=1. We also compare the results of our scheme with the schemes in References [17, 19, 33], which indicate that the proposed scheme provides better results to withstand the differential attack.

16.5.3   Key space analysis

Any image cryptosystem should have a large key space to resist the brute force attack. A brute force attack is trying every possible permutation of key in defined key space. An encryption scheme with a small key space can easily be cracked by an attacker. The key space must be greater than 2^{100} to efficiently withstand the brute force attack. The proposed scheme utilizes SHA-512 which generates a 512-bit hash value. Total 412-bit hash code is used to generate the encryption key; hence, the key space of our proposed scheme is 2^{412}, which is much greater than 2^{100}. Therefore, the proposed scheme is highly secure against brute force attacks.

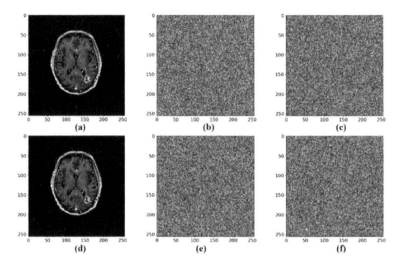

Figure 16.9　*(a) Plain image M1 (b) encrypted image with key K1, (c) encrypted image with key K2, (d) decrypted image (encryption key K1, decryption key K1), (e) decrypted image (encryption key K1, decryption key K2), (d) difference of (b) and (c)*

16.5.4　Key sensitivity analysis

A qualified cryptosystem must be very sensitive to its encryption key. That is, changing one bit in the encryption key should yield a completely different decrypted image. To measure the key sensitivity, we use two keys K1 and the other is 1-bit changed key K2 from the previous key. Figure 16.9 shows the results of the sensitivity test. Figure 16.9(a) shows the plain image M1 is encrypted by K1 and K2 (Figure 16.9(b) and (c)). Encrypted image (b) is decrypted by K1 and K2. Results are shown in Figure 16.9(d) and (e), which are completely different. Furthermore, Figure 16.9(f) shows the difference between images (d) and (e), which is about 99.67%. Therefore, the proposed encryption scheme's key sensitivity is very high.

16.5.5　Classical attack analysis

Practically, Ciphertext only (CA), known-plaintext (KPA), chosen-plaintext (CPA), and chosen-ciphertext (CCA) are the most prevalent classical attacks. CPA is one of the most powerful attacks among them. If an encryption scheme withstands CPA, it can also resist all other three attacks [35]. The proposed scheme utilized a separate key initialization step based on SHA-512, and the pseudo random number (PRN) key is dependent on the original image so the proposed scheme is eligible to effectively counter CPA attacks. Moreover, if an encryption technique effectively confuses and diffuses pure black and pure white images, it can withstand a plaintext assault [36]. Figure 16.10 shows the encryption result of pure white and pure black images. It can be seen that the histogram of encrypted black and white images ate

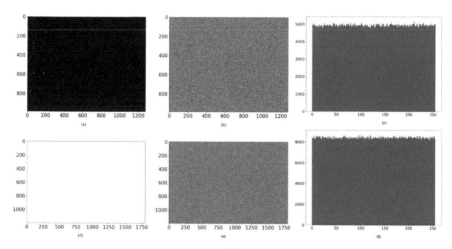

Figure 16.10   *(a) All black image (b) encrypted image of (a), (c) histogram of (b), (d) all white image, (e) encrypted image of (d), (c) histogram of (e)*

uniformly scattered, which means that our proposed encryption scheme is effective and can resist the CPA attacks.

16.5.6   Robustness analysis

During data transfer across the network, noise interference or partial data loss can corrupt the encrypted image. Therefore, a better encryption scheme must be robust against various noise and data loss. To test the robustness of proposed scheme salt and pepper noise and Gaussian noise of different strength are added into the encrypted image and we analyse the quality of decrypted image. Figure 16.11(a), (b) and (c) represents the decryption result of salt and pepper noise of strength 1%, 0.5% and 0.1%, respectively. Furthermore, Figure 16.11 (d), (e) and (f) represents the decrypted image with Gaussian noise of strength 1%, 0.5%, and 0.1%, respectively. Visual quality of decrypted image indicate that our scheme is very robust to noise. Table 16.8 represents the peak signal to noise ratio (PSNR) analysis of decrypted image. We can see that for 0.1% Gaussian noise PSNR is 33.47 db.

We also measure the effects of data loss in encrypted image. Figure 16.12(a), (b), and (c) shows the 1/16 data loss encrypted images in left corner, centre, and at right bottom corner, respectively, their corresponding decrypted images are shown in Figure 16.12 (d), (e), and (f). Furthermore, Figure 16.12(g), (h), and (i) shows the effect of 1/64 data loss in left corner, centre, and at right bottom corner, respectively, their corresponding decrypted images are shown in Figure 16.12 (j), (k), and (l). PSNR value of 1/16, 1/32, and 1/64 data loss is listed in Table 16.8, result of data loss analysis shows that proposed scheme provides good quality of decrypted image. Therefore, scheme is robust to data loss attack.

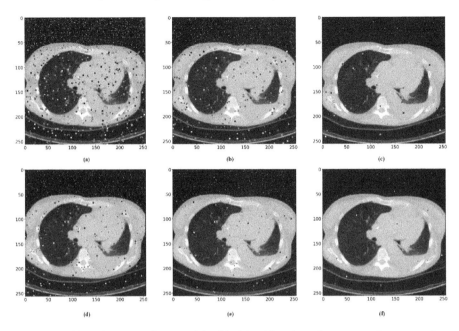

Figure 16.11   Decrypted image (a), (b), (c) with salt and pepper noise strength of 1%, 0.5%, and 0.1%. Decrypted images (d), (e), (f) with Gaussian noise strength 1%, 0.5%, 0.1%.

Table 16.8   Noise attack analysis

Noise	Noise strength	PSNR
Salt and pepper	1%	18.74
	0.50%	21.55
	0.10%	28.75
Gaussian noise	1%	22.86
	0.50%	25.85
	0.10%	33.47
Data loss (left corner)	1/16	19.67
Data loss (centre)		20.14
Data loss (right corner)		19.77
Data loss (left corner)	1/32	22.42
Data loss (left centre)		22.96
Data loss (right corner)		22.60
Data loss (left corner)	1/64	25.33
Data loss (left centre)		25.66
Data loss (right corner)		25.43

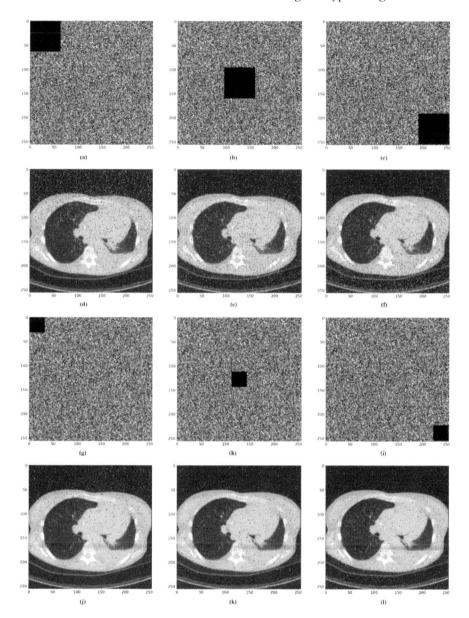

Figure 16.12   *Encrypted images (a), (b), (c) with 1/16 (left corner, centre and right corner) data loss, corresponding decrypted images (d), (e), (f). Encrypted images (g), (h), (i) with 1/64 data loss and corresponding decrypted images (j), (k), (l).*

Table 16.9   Computational cost analysis

Scheme	Image	Size	Enc_time (s)	Dec_time (s)
Proposed	M1	256×256	0.1642	0.1454
	M2	256×256	0.2103	0.1536
	M3	256×256	0.1470	0.2164
	M4	256×256	0.1575	0.1494
	M5	200×200	0.0948	0.0902
	M6	512×512	0.7500	0.7699
	M7	243×207	0.1151	0.1581
	M8	561×569	0.9078	0.9244
	M9	1024×024	3.0105	2.9908
	M10	512×512	0.6553	1.0401
	M11	512×512	0.7561	0.7396
	M12	512×512	0.6442	0.6969
	M13	217×232	0.1094	0.1235
	M14	22×228	0.1576	0.1405
	M15	220×215	0.1160	0.1182
	M16	320×420	0.3202	0.4433
	M17	438×512	0.5803	0.5950
	M18	372×341	0.3050	0.3513
	M19	512×512	0.6860	0.6278
	M20	512×512	0.6485	0.7273
Total cost of 20 images (Round=1)			**10.5357**	**11.2017**
Total cost of 20 images (Round=2)			**20.9431**	**21.1300**
[1]	Medical	256×256	3.9000	
[9]	Average of three grey image	256×256	0.2788	-
[23]	NA	256×256	0.241543	0.228897

16.5.7   Computational cost analysis

An encryption system with strong security and a short processing time is qualified for real-world applications. To measure the computational efficiency, we have calculated the encryption time (Enc_{time}) and decryption time (Dec_{time}) of proposed scheme. We have also analysed the computational cost for implementing confusion and diffusion only once and twice. Table 16.9 depicts the computational cost analysis of our scheme. From this table, it is clear that the cost of only one round of confusion and diffusion is very much less than two round of confusion and diffusion. Furthermore, encryption and decryption time is also compared with References [1, 9, 23], which clearly indicates that the computational cost of our scheme is much less. Hence, the proposed scheme is computationally efficient.

Table 16.10   Compression ratio

Image	CR	Image	CR
M1	0.299	M11	0.327
M2	0.299	M12	0.327
M3	0.2993	M13	0.291
M4	0.2993	M14	0.291
M5	0.26	M15	0.273
M6	0.327	M16	0.302
M7	0.291	M17	0.315
M8	0.354	M18	0.321
M9	0.358	M19	0.327
M10	0.327	M20	0.327

16.5.8   Compression performance

To test the compression performance of the scheme we calculated the compression ratio between the encrypted image and the compressed encrypted image. The results are shown in Table 16.10. It is clear from the result that LZW effectively compresses the encrypted image which in terms can reduce the size of image and increase the speed of transmission.

16.6   Conclusion

A secure medical image encryption algorithm for e-healthcare applications is proposed in this chapter. First, precision limited LM and STM is adopted to encrypt plain medical image, obtaining the cipher messages with a relationship to the plain image. Here, the method uses SHA-512 to generate the initial sequences and parameters of the LM and STM. After this, encrypted image is compressed by LZW lossless compression scheme, without knowing the encryption key. The experimental results prove that the proposed algorithm is secure against chosen plaintext attacks, robust to noise attack, and reduces the bandwidth, high communication costs, and storage space. Furthermore, extensive experimental results on real-world datasets demonstrate that the proposed algorithm outperforms the state-of-the-art approaches. The proposed work can be improved with efficient deep learning models in the future.

References

[1] Bhuiyan M.N., Rahman M.M., Billah M.M., Saha D. 'Internet of things (IoT): a review of its enabling technologies in healthcare applications, standards protocols, security, and market opportunities'. *IEEE Internet of Things Journal*. 2022, vol. 8(13), pp. 10474–98.

[2] Singh A.K., Anand A., Lv Z., Ko H., Mohan A. 'A survey on healthcare data: a security perspective'. *ACM Transactions on Multimedia Computing, Communications, and Applications.* 2022, vol. 17(2s), pp. 1–26.

[3] Amine K., Fares K., Redouane K.M., Salah E. 'Medical image watermarking for telemedicine application security'. *Journal of Circuits, Systems and Computers.* 2022, vol. 31(5), p. 05.

[4] Sharma N., Singh O.P., Anand A., Singh A.K. Improved method of optimization-based ECG signal watermarking. *Journal of Electronic Imaging.* 2022, vol. 31(4).

[5] Ravichandran D., Banu S A., Murthy B.K., Balasubramanian V., Fathima S., Amirtharajan R. 'An efficient medical image encryption using hybrid DNA computing and chaos in transform domain'. *Medical & Biological Engineering & Computing.* 2021, vol. 59(3), pp. 589–605.

[6] Singh O.P., Singh A.K., Agrawal A.K., Zhou H. 'SecDH: security of COVID-19 images based on data hiding with PCA'. *Computer Communications.* 2022, vol. 191, pp. 368–77.

[7] Anand A., Singh A.K. 'Hybrid nature-inspired optimization and encryption-based watermarking for E-healthcare'. *IEEE Transactions on Computational Social Systems.* 2022, pp. 1–8.

[8] Wang B., Jiawei S., Wang W., Zhao P. 'Image copyright protection based on blockchain and zero-watermark'. *IEEE Transactions on Network Science and Engineering.* 2022, vol. 9(4), pp. 2188–99.

[9] Masood F., Driss M., Boulila W. 'A lightweight chaos-based medical image encryption scheme using random shuffling and XOR operations'. *Wireless Personal Communications.* 2022, pp. 1–28.

[10] Hossain M.S., Cucchiara R., Muhammad G., Tobón D.P., Saddik A.E. 'Special section on AI-empowered multimedia data analytics for smart healthcare'. *ACM Transactions on Multimedia Computing, Communications, and Applications.* 2022, vol. 18(1s), pp. 1–2.

[11] Singh O.P., Singh A.K. 'Data hiding in encryption–compression domain'. *Complex & Intelligent Systems.* 2021, pp. 1–14.

[12] Singh K.N., Singh A.K. 'Towards integrating image encryption with compression: a survey'. *ACM Transactions on Multimedia Computing, Communications, and Applications.* 2022, vol. 18(3), pp. 1–21.

[13] Li P., Lo K.-T. 'A content-adaptive joint image compression and encryption scheme'. *IEEE Transactions on Multimedia.* 2022, vol. 20(8), pp. 1960–72.

[14] Karmakar J., Nandi D., Mandal M.K. 'A novel hyper-chaotic image encryption with sparse-representation based compression'. *Multimedia Tools and Applications.* 2022, vol. 79(37–38), pp. 28277–300.

[15] Badshah G., Liew S.-C., Zain J.M., Ali M. 'Watermark compression in medical image watermarking using Lempel-Ziv-Welch (LZW) lossless compression technique'. *Journal of Digital Imaging.* 2016, vol. 29(2), pp. 216–25.

[16] Sarosh P., Parah S.A., Bhat G.M. 'An efficient image encryption scheme for healthcare applications'. *Multimedia Tools and Applications.* 2022, vol. 81(5), pp. 7253–70.

[17] Song W., Fu C., Zheng Y., Cao L., Tie M. 'A practical medical image cryptosystem with parallel acceleration'. *Journal of Ambient Intelligence and Humanized Computing*. 2022.

[18] Rani N., Sharma S.R., Mishra V. 'Grayscale and colored image encryption model using a novel fused magic cube'. *Nonlinear Dynamics*. 2022, vol. 108(2), pp. 1773–96.

[19] Yasser I., Khalil A.T., Mohamed M.A., Samra A.S., Khalifa F. 'A robust chaos-based technique for medical image encryption'. *IEEE Access*. 2022, vol. 10, pp. 244–57.

[20] Selvi C.T., Amudha J., Sudhakar R. 'Medical image encryption and compression by adaptive sigma filterized synorr certificateless signcryptive Levenshtein entropy-coding-based deep neural learning'. *Multimedia Systems*. 2022, vol. 27(6), pp. 1059–74.

[21] Zhang B., Xiao D., Xiang Y. 'Robust coding of encrypted images via 2D compressed sensing'. *IEEE Transactions on Multimedia*. 2021, vol. 23, pp. 2656–71.

[22] Hu H., Cao Y., Xu J., Ma C., Yan H. 'An image compression and encryption algorithm based on the fractional-order simplest chaotic circuit'. *IEEE Access*. 2021, vol. 9, pp. 22141–55.

[23] Chen K.-M., Chang C.-C. 'High-capacity separable reversible data-hiding method in encrypted images based on block-level encryption and Huffman compression coding'. *Connection Science*. 2021, vol. 33(4), pp. 975–94.

[24] Wang C., Zhang T., Chen H., Huang Q., Ni J., Zhang X. 'A novel encryption-then-lossy-compression scheme of color images using customized residual dense spatial network'. *IEEE Transactions on Multimedia*. 2021, pp. 1–1.

[25] Gupta N., Vijay R. 'Hybrid image compression-encryption scheme based on multilayer stacked autoencoder and logistic map'. *China Communications*. 2021, vol. 19(1), pp. 238–52.

[26] Luo Y., Yu J., Lai W., Liu L. 'A novel chaotic image encryption algorithm based on improved baker map and logistic map'. *Multimedia Tools and Applications*. 2019, vol. 78(15), pp. 22023–43.

[27] Li H., Deng L., Gu Z. 'A robust image encryption algorithm based on a 32-bit chaotic system'. *IEEE Access*. 2020, vol. 8, pp. 30127–51.

[28] Palacios-Luengas L., Pichardo-Méndez J.L., Díaz-Méndez J.A., Rodríguez-Santos F., Vázquez-Medina R. 'PRNG based on skew tent MAP'. *Arabian Journal for Science and Engineering*. 2019, vol. 44(4), pp. 3817–30.

[29] Kaggle. *Brain MRI images for brain tumor detection*. Available from https://www.kaggle.com/datasets/navoneel/brain-mri-images-for-brain-tumor-detection

[30] Ye G., Pan C., Huang X., Mei Q. 'An efficient pixel-level chaotic image encryption algorithm'. *Nonlinear Dynamics*. 2019, vol. 94(1), pp. 745–56.

[31] Souyah A., Faraoun K.M. 'An image encryption scheme combining chaos-memory cellular automata and weighted histogram'. *Nonlinear Dynamics*. 2016, vol. 86(1), pp. 639–53.

[32]   Gupta M., Singh V.P., Gupta K.K., Shukla P.K. 'An efficient image encryption technique based on two-level security for Internet of things'. *Multimedia Tools and Applications*. 2016.

[33]   Lin H., Wang C., Cui L., Sun Y., Xu C., Yu F. 'Brain-like initial-boosted hyperchaos and application in biomedical image encryption'. *IEEE Transactions on Industrial Informatics*. 2016, pp. 1–1.

[34]   Wu Y., Noonan J.P., Agaian S. 'NPCR and UACI randomness tests for image encryption'. *Journal of Selected Areas in Telecommunications*. 2011, vol. 1(2), pp. 31–38.

[35]   Wang X., Teng L., Qin X. 'A novel colour image encryption algorithm based on chaos'. *Signal Processing*. 2016, vol. 92(4), pp. 1101–08.

[36]   Hayat U., Azam N.A. 'A novel image encryption scheme based on an elliptic curve'. *Signal Processing*. 2019, vol. 155, pp. 391–402.

Chapter 17

Conclusion and future directions

Amit Kumar Singh[1] and Huiyu Zhou[2]

With the development of Internet technologies, large volumes of multimedia and more generally, multimodal data, can easily be shared in digital forms among different users or entities for the purpose of diagnosis, analysis and prediction in healthcare. To address these challenges, this book presented some important medical information processing and security studies and approaches for smart healthcare applications. Beginning with the introduction of the detailed concepts of medical information processing and security, Chapter 1 presented background information on the Internet of Medical Things (IoMT), interesting and utilized applications, and security requirement of smart healthcare. This is followed by a detailed overview of important medical information processing and security techniques along with their merits and limitations. In Chapter 2, the author used the American College of Surgeons National Surgical Quality Improvement Program database to compare the performance of logistic regression to that of other machine learning algorithms for predicting complications during spine surgery. The database included 177 681 patients who underwent spine surgery. The occurrence of intraoperative morbidity was relatively low (9.4%) in comparison to the total number of the dataset population, and hence, the dataset under study was considered imbalanced. To thoroughly evaluate and compare the proposed machine learning algorithms, the dataset was balanced and the algorithms were applied to both the balanced and imbalanced datasets. The results indicated that, in general, no significant difference was found between the performance of Logistic Regression and Random Forest, Boosted Tree and Decision Tree. Chapter 3 briefly discussed the recent development and challenges and also highlighted the future possibilities in histopathological image analysis. The chapter further summarized different publicly available datasets and emphasized the key challenges along with the limitations of emerging deep learning techniques for Computer-Aided Diagnosis (CAD) of cancer. Furthermore, insights for future research in this area have been provided. One of the greatest biomedical potentials of terahertz imaging is the use of molecular spectroscopy for diagnostics,

[1]Department of Computer Science & Engineering, National Institute of Technology Patna, Patna, Bihar, India
[2]School of Computing and Mathematical Sciences, University of Leicester, United Kingdom

which is exponentially advanced and moved closer towards. Terahertz imaging systems can help in detecting early cancer before it is visible or sensitive to any other identification resources. In this direction, Chapter 4 presented the research status and prospects of several terahertz medical imaging systems and their applications for medical imaging in biological tissues. Additionally, this chapter summarized the obstacles in the applications of terahertz biomedical imaging in clinical research. Chapter 5 focused on the interoperability challenge and the use of health standards and terminologies to ensure interoperability, especially in the summarization- and visualization-based Electronic Health Record (EHR) systems. The chapter described, compared and discussed approaches related to interoperability such as e-health standards, terminologies and internet of things (IoT) ontologies. Furthermore, the author reviewed and discussed summarization- and visualization-based EHR systems in order to show how interoperability issues can enhance EHR analysis to build accurate summarization- and visualization-based EHR systems. Finally, our discussions reveal that five techniques should be adopted to enhance interoperability and so build free accessibility and accurate EHR and improve data validation and interoperability. Chapter 6 suggested a robust energy-based least squares projection twin support vector machines (RELSPTSVM) model for the Electroencephalogram (EEG) signal classification. The proposed RELSPTSVM minimizes the structural risk, and the matrices appearing are positive and definite. Analysis of experiments demonstrates that the proposed RELSPTSVM is superior to the existing models for the classification of EEG signals. A statistical test on the EEG data reveals that the proposed RELSPTSVM model is significantly better compared to the baseline models. Moreover, the performance of the proposed RELSPTSVM model on the benchmark UC Irvine (UCI) datasets is better than the baseline models. Due to the importance of fuzzy-based c-means clustering algorithm in the health sector, Chapter 7 presented a detailed survey especially based on medical image segmentation. In this survey, the authors have compiled a few important and popular fuzzy-based clustering methods in a comparative study-based manner. Recent state-of-the-art artificial intelligence methods for genomics on different prospects and scenarios have been presented in Chapter 8.

A comprehensive and systematic survey of state-of-the-art research on anonymous communication technologies in wireless healthcare systems is provided in Chapter 9. Furthermore, a trust-based secure directed diffusion routing protocol has been presented. Finally, the lightweight anonymous communication model and its security were explored and analysed in detail. A basic outline of information security paradigms and the need for securing medical data were presented in Chapter 10. Furthermore, the authors have reviewed various state-of-the-art medical data encryption techniques, discussed several evaluation metrics, and further presented comparative studies based on the applicability of the methods for data modalities and metric-based performance. Lastly, the potential challenges of the existing methods and a way forward by discussing promising research directions are presented. In Chapter 11, the authors have proposed an ECG-based watermarking scheme for healthcare to resolve the authentication issues and maintain a good relationship between invisibility, capacity and robustness. The proposed method considered a sequence of Redundant Discrete Wavelet Transform-Fast Walsh Hadamard Transform-QR Decomposition to decompose the host ECG and both mark data to obtain the R-component, where the R-component of the host ECG signal is modified (embedded) with the component of both marks. Here, more robust patient mark data are encoded by QR-code before it is concealed into the host signal. Experimental results show that the proposed ECG-based scheme is invisible and robust in nature. Chapter 12 has introduced the methods and applications of AutoEncoders in forensic craniofacial reconstruction. The related methods are divided into three parts: Improved AutoEncoder with constraints, Improved AutoEncoder combined with Generative Adversarial Network (GAN) and Other Improved AutoEncoders. These methods all improve the performance of traditional AutoEncoders in certain aspects. The positive and negative aspects of various security techniques with IoT in healthcare industries are examined in Chapter 13. To make the system more secure, encryption and decryption techniques were utilized. As a result, this chapter describes new research opportunities in healthcare by presenting factors to explore for future directions. Finally, the main challenges with recently established smart healthcare systems that are primary barriers to the development of assistive prototypes are discussed. Chapter 14 presented a comprehensive survey on spatial and transform-based watermarking schemes, especially for copyright protection and ownership control for healthcare applications. Along with the survey, the author presented a brief introduction, background information, and the most interesting and utilized applications of watermarking. In addition, the contribution of the reviewed approaches is also summarized and compared from different technical perspectives. In Chapter 15, the authors have introduced different kinds of secure authentication schemes for remote medical systems. Compared with other similar protocols, the proposed protocols have advantages in terms of efficiency, safety, dynamics, etc. A secure medical image encryption algorithm for e-healthcare applications is proposed in Chapter 16. First, precision limited logistic map (LM) and skew tent map (STM) were adopted to encrypt plain medical images, obtaining the cipher messages with a relationship to the plain image. Here, the method uses Secure Hash Algorithm (SHA-512) to generate the initial sequences and parameters of the LM and STM. After this, the encrypted image is compressed by an Lempel–Ziv–Welch (LZW) lossless compression scheme, without knowing the encryption key. The experimental results prove that the proposed algorithm is secure against the chosen plaintext attacks, robust to noise attacks, and reduces the bandwidth, high communication costs and storage space. Moreover, extensive experimental results on real-world datasets demonstrate that the proposed algorithm outperforms the other state-of-the-art approaches.

In summary, processing of this medical data involves computer processing and understanding of perceptual inputs from speech, text and images and reacting to it is much more complex and involves research from engineering, computer science and cognitive science. This is the newest area of research that has seen an upsurge over the last few years. Presently, soft computing, deep learning and artificial intelligence are emerging fields that have gained attention for medical data processing. Furthermore, due to their strong learning, cognitive ability and good tolerance of uncertainty and imprecision, these techniques have found wide applications in healthcare and ensure a higher level of accuracy in the early diagnosis and detection of diseases. The management and analysis of large volumes of medical data require machine support and intelligent data analysis. Hence, researchers should develop a scalable technique using deep learning and media processing which can provide more reconcilable solutions and effective decision-making strategies in emerging IoMT. Nowadays, medical data security is gaining engrossment and has become a proactive area of research. Therefore, it is urgent to provide strong algorithms and techniques that can resolve the discussed threats to medical data. At the same time, relevant regulatory authorities should strengthen supervision and introduce more detailed laws and regulations. Healthcare practitioners also need to raise their awareness of cybersecurity. Future research work will be driven to handle challenges such as (1) real-time alerting to the large volume of medical data collected from daily practice, (2) reducing fraud and enhancing privacy in different set-ups and environments and (3) making predictive analytics self-explainable and self-contained that allows the authorized parties to examine the process for fairness and protection.

Index